Lecture Notes in Artificial Intell

Edited by J. G. Carbonell and J. Siekmann

Subseries of Lecture Notes in Computer Science

Balázs Kégl   Guy Lapalme (Eds.)

Advances in Artificial Intelligence

18th Conference of the Canadian Society
for Computational Studies of Intelligence, Canadian AI 2005
Victoria, Canada, May 9-11, 2005
Proceedings

 Springer

Series Editors

Jaime G. Carbonell, Carnegie Mellon University, Pittsburgh, PA, USA
Jörg Siekmann, University of Saarland, Saarbrücken, Germany

Volume Editors

Balázs Kégl
Guy Lapalme
Université de Montréal
Département d'informatique et de recherche opérationelle
CP 6128 succ. Centre-Ville, Montréal, Canada H3C 3J7
E-mail: {kegl;lapalme}@iro.umontreal.ca

Library of Congress Control Number: 2005925178

CR Subject Classification (1998): I.2

ISSN   0302-9743
ISBN-10   3-540-25864-7 Springer Berlin Heidelberg New York
ISBN-13   978-3-540-25864-3 Springer Berlin Heidelberg New York

Springer is a part of Springer Science+Business Media

springeronline.com

© Springer-Verlag Berlin Heidelberg 2005
Printed in Germany

Typesetting: Camera-ready by author, data conversion by Scientific Publishing Services, Chennai, India
Printed on acid-free paper   SPIN: 11424918   06/3142   5 4 3 2 1 0

Preface

The 18th conference of the Canadian Society for the Computational Study of Intelligence (CSCSI) continued the success of its predecessors. This set of papers reflects the diversity of the Canadian AI community and its international partners.

AI 2005 attracted 135 high-quality submissions: 64 from Canada and 71 from around the world. Of these, eight were written in French. All submitted papers were thoroughly reviewed by at least three members of the Program Committee. A total of 30 contributions, accepted as long papers, and 19 as short papers are included in this volume.

We invited three distinguished researchers to give talks about their current research interests: Eric Brill from Microsoft Research, Craig Boutilier from the University of Toronto, and Henry Krautz from the University of Washington.

The organization of such a successful conference benefited from the collaboration of many individuals. Foremost, we would like to express our appreciation to the Program Committee members and external referees, who provided timely and significant reviews. To manage the submission and reviewing process we used the Paperdyne system, which was developed by Dirk Peters. We owe special thanks to Kellogg Booth and Tricia d'Entremont for handling the local arrangements and registration. We also thank Bruce Spencer and members of the CSCSI executive for all their efforts in making AI 2005 a successful conference.

May 2005   Balázs Kégl and Guy Lapalme

Préface

La dix-huitième édition de la conférence de la Société canadienne pour l'étude de l'intelligence par ordinateur (SCEIO) poursuit la longue tradition de succès des ses prédécesseurs. Cet ensemble d'articles est un témoignage à la diversité des intérêts des chercheurs canadiens et internationaux.

AI 2005 a suscité 135 soumissions de haute qualité: 64 du Canada et 71 d'ailleurs dans le monde. 8 de ces articles ont été soumis en français. Tous les articles ont été relus et annotés par au moins trois membres du comité de programme. 30 contributions, acceptés comme articles longs, et 19 comme articles courts sont inclus dans ce livre.

Nous avons invité trois chercheurs réputés à venir présenter leurs intérêts de recherche actuels: Eric Brill de Microsoft Research, Craig Boutilier de l'Université de Toronto et Henry Krautz de l'Université de Washington.

L'organisation de cette conférence a profité de la collaboration de plusieurs personnes. Tout d'abord, nous remercions le comité de programme et les arbitres externes qui ont retourné des commentaires motivés et étoffés à l'intérieur de délais très courts. Pour la gestion des contributions et des commentaires, nous avons utilisé le système Paperdyne développé par Dirk Peters. Nous remercions spécialement Kellogg Booth and Tricia d'Entremont pour la gestion locale de la conférence et de l'enregistrement. Nous remercions également Bruce Spencer et les autres membres de l'exécutif de la SCIAEIO pour leurs efforts et leur collaboration pour le succès de AI 2005.

Mai 2005   Balázs Kégl et Guy Lapalme

Organization

AI 2005 was organized by the Canadian Society for the Computational Studies of Intelligence (Société Canadienne pour l'Étude de l'Intelligence par Ordinateur).

Executive Committee

Program Co-chairs: Balázs Kégl and Guy Lapalme (Université de Montréal)

Local Organizers: Kellogg Booth and Tricia d'Entremont (University of British Columbia)

Program Committee

Esma Aïmeur (U. de Montréal)
Caroline Barrière (NRC)
Sabine Bergler (Concordia U.)
Michael Buro (U. of Alberta)
Cory Butz (U. of Regina)
Laurence Capus (U. Laval)
Brahim Chaib-draa (U. Laval)
Yllias Chali (U. of Lethbridge)
David Chiu (U. of Guelph)
Robin Cohen (U. of Waterloo)
Cristina Conati (U. of BC)
Lyne Da Sylva (U. de Montréal)
Douglas D. Dankel (U. of Florida)
Jim Delgrande (Simon Fraser U.)
Jörg Denzinger (U. of Calgary)
Chrysanne DiMarco (U. of Waterloo)
Douglas Eck (U. de Montréal)
George Foster (NRC)
Richard Frost (U. of Windsor)
Scott Goodwin (U. of Windsor)
Jim Greer (U. of Saskatchewan)
Howard Hamilton (U. of Regina)
Bill Havens (Simon Fraser U.)
Graeme Hirst (U. of Toronto)
Diana Inkpen (U. d'Ottawa)
Nathalie Japkowicz (U. d'Ottawa)

Froduald Kabanza (U. de Sherbrooke)
Greg Kondrak (U. of Alberta)
Leila Kosseim (Concordia U.)
Stefan C. Kremer (U. of Guelph)
Luc Lamontagne (U. Laval)
Philippe Langlais (U. de Montréal)
Bernard Lefebvre (UQàM)
Omid Madani (U. of Alberta)
Choh Man Teng (U. of West Florida)
Stan Matwin (U. of Ottawa)
Gord McCalla (U. of Saskatchewan)
Bob Mercer (U. of Western Ontario)
Evangelos Milios (Dalhousie U.)
Guy Mineau (U. Laval)
Martin Müller (U. of Alberta)
Eric Neufeld (U. of Saskatchewan)
Alioune Ngom (U. of Windsor)
Jian-Yun Nie (U. de Montréal)
Roger Nkambou (UQàM)
Simon Parsons (MIT)
Gerald Penn (U. of Toronto)
Petra Perner (Ibai Leipzig)
Fred Popowich (Simon Fraser U.)
Robert Reynolds (Wayne State U.)
Luis Rueda (U. of Windsor)
Anoop Sarkar (Simon Fraser U.)

Abdul Sattar (Griffth U.)
Weiming Shen (NRC)
Bruce Spencer (NRC and UNB)
Stan Szpakowicz (U. of Ottawa)
Ahmed Tawfik (U. of Windsor)
Nicole Tourigny (U. Laval)
Andre Trudel (Acadia U.)
Peter van Beek (U. of Waterloo)
Julita Vassileva (U. of Saskatchewan)
Herna Viktor (U. d'Ottawa)

Shaojun Wang (U. of Alberta)
Kay Wiese (Simon Fraser U.)
Michael Wong (U. of Regina)
Dan Wu (U. of Windsor)
Yang Xiang (U. of Guelph)
Yiyu Yao (U. of Regina)
Jia You (U. of Alberta)
Hong Zhang (U. of Alberta)
Nur Zincir-Heywood (Dalhousie U.)

Additional Reviewers

Mohamed Aoun-allah
Philippe Besnard
David Billington
Narjes Boufaden
Li Cheng
Michael Cheng
Bistra Dilkina
Lei Duan
Al Fedoruk
Joel Fenwick
Jie Gao

Yongshen Gao
Liqiang Geng
Edward Glen
Baohua Gu
Jasmine Hamdan
Qi Hao
Malcolm Heywood
Zina Ibrahim
Kamran Karimi
Sehl Mellouli
Andrei Missine

Milan Mosny
Jagdeep Poonian
Stuart Seyman
Tarek Sherif
Zhongmin Shi
Pascal Soucy
Herbert Tsang
Wendy Wang
Haiyi Zhang
Lingzhong Zhou

Sponsoring Institutions

Canadian Society for the Computational Studies of Intelligence
Société Canadienne pour l'Étude de l'Intelligence par Ordinateur

Table of Contents

Agents

Constraint Satisfaction and Search

Data Mining

Knowledge Representation and Reasoning

Machine Learning

Natural Language

Reinforcement Learning

Dynamic Maps in Monte Carlo Localization

Adam Milstein

School of Computer Science, University of Waterloo,
200 University Ave W., Waterloo, ON, N2L 3G1
ahpmilst@cs.uwaterloo.ca

Abstract. Mobile robot localization is the problem of tracking a moving robot through an environment given inaccurate sensor data and knowledge of the robot's motion. Monte Carlo Localization (MCL) is a popular probabilistic method of solving the localization problem. By using a Bayesian formulation of the problem, the robot's belief is represented by a set of weighted samples and updated according to motion and sensor information. One problem with MCL is that it requires a static map of the environment. While it is robust to errors in the map, they necessarily make the results less accurate. This article presents a method for updating the map dynamically during the process of localization, without requiring a severe increase in running time. Ordinarily, if the environment changes, the map must be recreated with user input. With the approach described here, it is possible for the robot to dynamically update the map without requiring user intervention or a significant amount of processing.

1 Introduction

In order for a mobile robot to accomplish anything in the world, it must know its own location and be able to determine the results of its motion. Localization is the name given to the problem of tracking a mobile robot given a map of the environment and the robot's sensor readings. If the robot's sensors worked perfectly, localization would be an easy task, since the odometers would give the exact location. The problem is that no sensor is perfect and the errors in odometer readings may be large. Another common sensor for a robot to have is some kind of range sensor. Sonars and laser rangefinders are two popular devices for localization. These sensors report the distance to the nearest wall but, like the odometers, they are prone to errors. Localization is the problem of compensating for the errors in odometry and sensor data in order to accurately determine the robot's location.

One solution to localization uses particle filters to represent the robot's location. The particle filter approach is known as Monte Carlo Localization (MCL) [3]. One problem with MCL is that it requires a static map of the environment. Sensor readings are compared with the expected values from the map and the comparison generates the probability of the robot's location. Errors in the map are partially compensated for by increasing the error that is assumed for the sensors. Another way to compensate for map errors is that the number of correct sensor readings will probably overrule incorrect ones. However, because MCL combines sensor error and map error, as map error

B. Kégl and G. Lapalme (Eds.): AI 2005, LNAI 3501, pp. 1–12, 2005.

increases, the allowable sensor error decreases until finally the algorithm fails and the map must be rescanned. Each error in the map is usually a minor matter for a localized robot; it is the combination of minor errors that can cause problems.

A localized robot rarely becomes mislocalized due to map errors, but this is not true of global localization, where the robot's initial location is unknown. Especially in symmetric environments, global localization can easily fail due to minor map errors that would be ignored by a localized robot.

The approach described in this article is based on the idea that if a robot is localized it may reasonably expect its sensor data to reflect the environment. If that is the case, then it should be possible to update the map according to the sensor data. If a known error in the map is fixed, then the robot will have a greater ability to deal with any subsequent errors. Since global localization may depend heavily on minor features, having an updated map can be a great benefit.

2   Background

2.1   Recursive Bayes Filter

Monte Carlo Localization is an implementation of a recursive Bayes filter. It estimates the posterior distribution of robot poses as conditioned by the sensor data. The key assumption is the Markovian assumption that, given the present, past and future are independent. In terms of localization, it means that if the current location of the robot is known, its future location does not depend on where it has been. Although this may not be completely true, it is a reasonable assumption to make.

Bayes filtering estimates the belief, which is the probability over the state space as conditioned by the data. This posterior is represented as:

$$Bel(x_t) = p(x_t \mid z_t, z_{t-1}..., z_0, u_t, u_{t-1},..., u_0) \qquad (1)$$

x_t is the location at time t, z_t is the sensor data at time t and u_t is the motion data at time t. Sensor data is usually some form of range data, such as laser rangefinder data, while motion data is the robot's odometry readings from time t − 1 until time t.

Given the definition in (1), MCL uses a recursive Bayes filter to determine $Bel(x_t)$. In order to determine something recursively we need a recursive formula. Let $a^t = a_t,...,a_0$, then equation (1) is converted using Bayes rule, the Markovian assumption, and integration into:

$$Bel(x_t) = \eta p(z_t \mid x_t) \int p(x_t \mid x_{t-1}, u_t) p(x_{t-1} \mid z^{t-1}, u^{t-1}) \qquad (2)$$

where h is a normalizer constant.

Obviously, $p(x_{t-1} \mid u^{t-1}, z^{t-1})$ is $Bel(x_{t-1})$, the prior belief of the robot's location, so we have our recursive equation. $p(x_t \mid u_t, x_{t-1})$ is the motion model. It represents the probability of moving to a specific location given the prior location and the motion reported by the odometers. Finally, $p(z_t \mid x_t)$ is the sensor model, representing the probability of receiving a specific sensor reading given the robot's position in the environment. These two models are determined by the hardware of the robot and an approximation must be created experimentally.

2.2   Particle Approximation

Although equation (2) allows us to calculate $Bel(x_t)$, it is not as straightforward as it appears. The difficulty is that in the localization problem, the state space is continuous. Therefore the integral in equation (2) is over a continuous space and so there is no simple way to calculate it. In MCL the continuous state space is approximated by a set of weighted particles. $Bel(x_t) \approx \{x_t^{[i]}, w_t^{[i]}\}_{i=1,...,N}$. Each $x_t^{[i]}$ is a sample of the random variable while the $w_t^{[i]}$ values are the importance factor, or weight, of the sample. As N approaches infinity the approximation becomes $Bel(x_t)$. Let X_t be a set of particles representing the state at time t. MCL creates X_t from X_{t-1} by choosing random members of X_{t-1} and moving them according to $p(x_t| x_{t-1}^{[i]}, u_t)$. A new weight is calculated for each particle and then the whole set is resampled by randomly drawing particles, with replacement, according to their weight. Resampling replaces the weight with the number of particles at a particular location. The higher the weight of a particle, the more times it will occur in X_t. The number of particles representing likely locations for the robot will increase and then in the motion step, the robot will not be lost. More detail on MCL can be found in [6].

One problem with the particle approximation is that, as an approximation, it introduces error. In particular, because there are not an infinite number of particles, some locations of low probability die out and are no longer considered in the algorithm. If the robot is really at one of these locations it can never be found.

2.3   Raytracing

Calculation of $p(z_t| x_t)$ involves determining the probability of receiving a particular sensor reading given the location in the environment. For a laser rangefinder the readings are distance measurements. A common map implementation for MCL is an occupancy grid map with each cell holding the probability that it is occupied. Given a robot's possible location in the map, the expected distance to the wall is usually determined by raytracing from the robot to the nearest wall. The sensors determine the actual distance to the wall and, once the two values are known, the probability can be calculated either mathematically or by a table lookup.

3   Dynamic Maps

In order to alter the map, it needs to be added to the MCL formula. Consider each cell of the map to be an independent object, which can be either present or absent. Although independence is usually not entirely valid, it is an assumption that is often made. Consider $y_t = \{y_{1,t},...,y_{K,t}\}$ the set of individual cells in the map. Since we are considering these cells to be independent, if the location is known, then $p(y_t |x_t,z_t) = \prod p(y_{k,t}| x_t,z_t)$.

With this background, the new state equation is $p(y_t,x_t|z_t,u_t)$. Unfortunately, it turns out that this equation cannot be factored, since the map state is not fully determined with only the current location. However, notice that each sample in MCL represents not only a current location, but also the history of locations that lead to that location.

Since each particle is only moved according to the motion model, they may be considered as x^t instead of x_t with no change to the algorithm. If we use the equation $p(y_t, x^t | z^t, u^t)$, then it is possible to factor it and we can also use the MCL algorithm without significant changes. The factorization used is similar to the one in [2], which was used to add the state of doors into the MCL algorithm.

3.1 Factoring

The size of the state space of (y_t, x^t) is exponential in the size of y_t, so we need some way of factoring the posterior in order to reduce the state space.

First, Bayes rule and the Markovian property give us:

$$p(y_t, x^t | z^t, u^t) = \eta p(z_t | y_t, x_t) p(y_t | x^t, z^{t-1}, u^t) p(x^t | z^{t-1}, u^t) \qquad (3)$$

Now, consider the 3 parts of equation (3).

Without any data we assume that all states are equally likely, and also that the probability of a random sensor scan is a constant. Therefore:

$$p(z_t | x_t, y_t) = \frac{p(x_t, y_t | z_t) p(z_t)}{p(y_t, x_t)} = \eta' p(x_t | z_t) \prod_k p(y_{k,t} | x_t, z_t) \qquad (4)$$

Remembering that cells in the map change status independently in the model, and again using the Markovian assumption, we get:

$$p(y_t | x^t, z^{t-1}, u^t) = \prod_k \sum_{y_{k,t-1}} p(y_{k,t} | y_{k,t-1}) p(y_{k,t-1} | x^{t-1}, z^{t-1}, u^{t-1}) \qquad (5)$$

Finally:

$$p(x^t | z^{t-1}, u^t) = p(x_t | x_{t-1}, u_t) p(x^{t-1} | z^{t-1}, u^{t-1}) \qquad (6)$$

Recombining these three equations and simplifying we get the factorization:

$$p(y_t, x^t | z^t, u^t) = p(x^t | z^t, u^t) \prod_k p(y_{k,t} | x^t, z^t, u^t) \qquad (7)$$

which contains the original MCL posterior and a new probability for the cells in the map. See [2] for more details about the factorization.

3.2 Binary Object Bayes Filtering

Since the method for calculating $p(x^t | z^t, u^t)$ is already known in the MCL algorithm, the only new method needed is to calculate the probability of each cell in the map. These cells are binary objects since they are either present or absent. Each $y_{k,t}$ can be either 0 or 1 with the probability of each summing to 1. Thus the method for calculating the probabilities is the same as in [2]. Let $\pi_{k,t} = p(y_{k,t} = 1 | x^t, z^t, u^t)$. Then

$$\pi_{k,t} = \frac{p(y_{k,t}=1|x_t, z_t) p(z_t | x^t)}{p(y_{k,t}=1) p(z_t | x^t, z^{t-1}, u^t)} \pi^+_{k,t} \qquad (8)$$

Where

$$\pi_{k,t}^{+} = p(y_{k,t} = 1 \mid y_{k,t-1} = 1)\pi_{k,t-1} + p(y_{k,t} = 1 \mid y_{k,t-1} = 0)(1 - \pi_{k,t-1}) \qquad (9)$$

In equation (8) the only unknown probability is $p(z_t|x^t,z^{t-1},u^t)$ in the denominator. Rather than trying to calculate it, we exploit the fact that $y_{k,t}$ is binary so $(1 - \pi_{k,t})$ can be calculated in the same way as $\pi_{k,t}$ using $y_{k,t} = 0$ instead of $y_{k,t} = 1$. The two equations are then divided to cancel the unknown quantities.

$$\frac{\pi_{k,t}}{(1 - \pi_{k,t})} = \frac{p(y_{k,t}=1|x_t,z_t)}{1 - p(y_{k,t}=1|x_t,z_t)} \frac{1 - p(y_{k,t}=1)}{p(y_{k,t}=1)} \frac{\pi_{k,t}^{+}}{\pi_{k,t}^{-}} \qquad (10)$$

The result, equation (10), consists entirely of known quantities. $p(y_{k,t}=1)$ is the prior probability that a cell is occupied. The various $p(y_{k,t}|y_{k,t-1})$ values are the transition probabilities for a cell, $\pi_{k,t-1}$ are, of course, the prior occupancy probabilities and finally, $p(y_{k,t=1}|x_t,z_t)$ is the probability of occupancy given robot location and sensor data. To get a useful value from the odds ratio, we use the equality $\pi_{k,t} = 1 - (1 + \pi_{k,t}/(1 - \pi_{k,t}))^{-1}$.

The representation of $\pi_{k,t}$ is actually in closed form, so it requires only a constant time operation to calculate. Since $p(y_{k,t}=1|x_t,z_t)$ involves sensor values and raytraces which are already used for MCL, little additional processing should be required. It is possible to modify the importance factor, as in [2], to take into account the new map data, where each cell is not merely present or absent but has a probability of presence. Using this data results in a runtime increase at least logarithmic in the number of binary objects. The probability of a location becomes the sum of the probabilities of that location for both states of all visible objects, multiplied by the probability of the object states. While that is acceptable if there are only a small number of objects, such as doors, if the objects are the cells of a map, the number becomes unmanageable. However, most map data used for MCL is actually represented as probabilities in an occupancy grid map, but is thresholded to be either present or absent. I decided to use the same simplification for my algorithm and consider each cell as either present or absent depending on a threshold value on its probability. The processing time therefore remains unchanged, since the importance factor is calculated in the same way.

3.3 Cell Correlations

In order to perform the factorization, it is necessary to assume that map cells change independently of each other. However, this assumption is not entirely accurate. In fact, groups of adjacent cells that represent the same objects are likely to be completely dependent. To some extent, ordinary MCL also assumes cells are independent, but it only becomes relevant when the cell probabilities are changed in dynamic MCL. It is easy to model correlations by annotating the map with correlation probabilities between adjacent cells, however, using this information is more difficult. Methods such as loopy belief propagation or variational methods [11] can propagate belief through a connected graph, but they are time consuming and sometimes do not converge. Since dynamic MCL must run in real time without being much slower than ordinary MCL, these techniques are not sufficient. However, it should be noticed that the cell correlations in a map are of restricted types. Small groups of adjacent cells are highly correlated, while being uncorrelated with their neighbors. Because of the limited correlation, it is possible to use a modified variational technique in order to implement cell correlations. When a cell is updated, the update is propagated to adjacent cells along the links, but the propagation is not permitted to flow back to a cell that has already been modified. Also, the flow stops when the accumulated correlation probability falls below a threshold. In practice, only a few steps occur, but these achieve a significant improvement in the results.

The key to using cell correlations is to perform operations using two different and conflicting sets of assumptions. Each set of assumptions reduces one part of the problem to a solvable operation, but makes the other part intractable. We have already seen that, by assuming cells to be independent, we can factor the belief as:

$$p(y_t, x^t \mid z^t, u^t) = p(x^t \mid z^t, u^t) \prod_k p(y_{k,t} \mid x^t, z^t, u^t) \qquad (11)$$

This factorization is used to update the individual cells according to the robot's sensors. However, once the update is performed, we discard both the assumption and the resulting factorization. Instead, we assume that each cell depends on its neighbors and is independent of the robot's sensors and position. According to this set of assumptions:

$$p(y_t, x^t \mid z^t, u^t) = p(x^t \mid z^t, u^t) p(y_{k,t} \mid x^t, z^t, u^t) \qquad (12)$$

$$= p(x^t \mid z^t, u^t) p(y_t)$$

$$= p(x^t \mid z^t, u^t) \prod_k p(y_{k,t} \mid y_{k-up,t}, y_{k-down,t} y_{k-left,t} y_{k-right,t})$$

The determination of the robot's position is unchanged, but the map cells now depend on their neighbors and not on the robot. By making this assumption, any changes made to the map can be propagated to the adjacent cells and the weight of the cell correlations adjusted. Separating the algorithm into two phases with different assumptions allows the algorithm to consider additional dependencies without having to deal with the intractable problems caused by the interaction of the new dependencies with the old. In effect, during the first phase of the algorithm, as represented by equation (11), we assume that cells are influenced only by the robot, with additional effects coming from some unknown source. During the second phase, shown by equation (12), we assume that cells are only affected by their neighbors, with other changes caused by external, unconsidered forces. Of course, two sets of contradictory assumptions cannot possibly be a reflection of reality, however, each assumption is a reasonable simplification and using both sets iteratively results in less simplification than either set exclusively.

In dynamic MCL, it is necessary to modify the cell correlation probabilities dynamically on each cycle. However, given the nature of the sensors used, it is unlikely that adjacent map cells will be observed on a single scan. The solution to the problem is to cache observed changes to each cell until an adjacent cell has also been observed. At that point, the difference in the changes of the cells can be used to adjust the correlation between them.

Adding cell correlations significantly improves the dynamic MCL algorithm, since a correlated group of cells can change together whenever any member of the group is observed. The result is that, although the update of individual cells must be slow to allow localization to work, if a group of cells change, they will update very quickly, since each observation will correlate them, and as they become more correlated, every observation of a member of the group will update the entire group. Thus, an object can appear or vanish more quickly than any single cell.

4 Algorithm

The preceding formulae can be used to augment an implementation of MCL in order to modify the map dynamically during processing. The MCL algorithm must raytrace along all sensor paths to calculate the probability of a particle. However, if the robot's position is known with high probability, then any differences between the sensor reading and the raytrace are more likely to be errors in the map than in the sensors. In that case, the logical action is to correct the map.

The method I used is to consider each cell of the map to be present with probability $\pi_{k,t}$. On each step of the MCL algorithm, an augmented raytracer is used for the robot's most likely location. The augmented raytracer follows a ray normally, passing through each map cell along the ray. However, at each cell along the path, the probability of that cell is altered according to equation (10). Although the augmented raytracer could be run on all samples, it is more productive to determine the most likely location and use the augmented raytracer only on it. When the robot's location is not known, the new raytracer is not used.

For calculating the sensor probability of each cell, the simplifying assumption that either that cell or the existing wall is correct is used. The assumption is necessary because the normalizer for the sensor probabilities is not known, so some method must be used to normalize the values. In practice, when a new cell becomes occupied, it exceeds the threshold before any other cell, and then the assumption becomes valid again. The short period during which it is invalid for some cells does not affect the operation of the algorithm.

In order to find the robot's most likely location, the sample with the highest importance factor is used. Other locations are possible, including the weighted average of all samples. The algorithm cannot run if the robot's location is unknown.

These implementation details do not change the fundamental algorithm, which is an implementation of MCL together with the binary object formulae as described above. The only simplification to equation (10) is in the calculation of $p(y_{k,t} = 1 | x_t, z_t)$, a value which is at best a numerical approximation to the error in a physical sensor device.

The following pseudocode summarizes the algorithm for dynamic MCL.

```
Repeat N times
   Draw a random particle
   Move particle according to the motion model
   Annotate particle with a weight from the sensor model
Resample a new set of particles from the annotated set
Find the most probable location (mean of particles)
For each sensor reading
```

```
Raytrace to the nearest occupied cell
For each cell on the path
    Alter the occupancy probability of the cell
    Alter the occupancy probability of neighboring
        cells according to influence
    Mark cell as observed
    If neighboring cell marked observed
        Adjust influence between cells
        Unmark cells as observed
```

5 Results

The dynamic map algorithm was implemented and tested using real data collected in our building. The data was created using a Pioneer 2Dxe robot equipped with a laser rangefinder. The objective of the tests was to show that the map could be updated correctly without introducing errors or causing localization to fail. Since the algorithm has an almost constant runtime there is no tradeoff necessary between the time required to update the map and the benefit obtained by doing so.

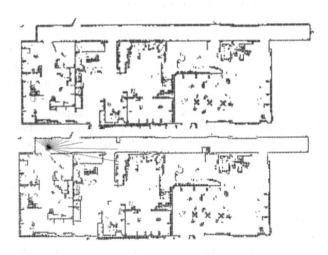

Fig. 1. Before and after two passes through the environment

Figure 1 shows the map of the environment used to generate the test data. Changes were made to the environment after the map was scanned by opening and closing doors and by placing boxes in the corridors. After one pass through the changed environment the robot has mostly added the new features to the map and has correlated the changed objects, allowing them to be completed very quickly.

After two passes, all changes have been completely added to the map. The rate of update is slower than in [2] because each cell must be observed several times, instead of each object. However, without correlations it takes at least five passes to completely adapt the map. Allowing cells to become correlated permits much faster updating without compromising localization. In [2] the dynamic objects can be updated in a single pass because they are manually defined ahead of time and are known to be completely correlated. Since dynamic MCL has no predefined objects or correlations, it is necessarily slower, but because it can discover the correlations it can still update very quickly.

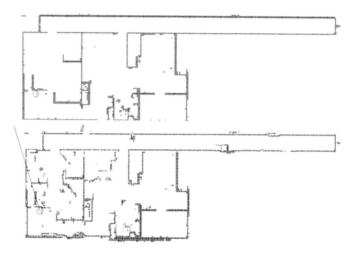

Fig. 2. Before and after five passes through the environment using a schematic map

Another test, shown in figure 2, was to use the same data but starting with a map consisting of the minimum possible information. From a schematic map consisting of only the walls and partitions, the algorithm was able to adapt it with all the features that were missing. Those portions of the map that were observed were corrected properly. The benefit of being able to start with a limited map is that it may not be necessary to scan a map manually with a robot. Instead, the map could be entered using blueprints of the environment and, as the robot passed through, it could correct the map until it was accurate. Usually, MCL uses the most accurate map possible, since it will lose accuracy over time, but with a dynamic map the accuracy of the map increases as the robot traverses the environment. Of course, portions of the environment that were insufficiently observed were not completely added to the map, so the result is not identical to the environment. However, observed areas have become more accurate and the map will only become a better reflection of the environment as the robot traverses it over time.

Another feature noticeable in figure 2 is that some of the objects in the corridor are somewhat more diffuse than they appeared in figure 1. Since the map is less accurate to begin with, localization is necessarily less accurate. As the map is corrected and localization becomes better, the location of the objects becomes clearer. After five passes, the objects are almost completely defined in the map, but some of them obviously require several more passes to full correct them. The benefit of dynamic MCL is that the robot can operate independently of this process. As it performs its task, the map becomes more accurate. All other data files tested exhibited similar behaviour, with the observed portions of objects being added to the map and no new errors introduced.

6 Related Work

Related work in dynamic mapping for MCL involves identifying binary objects, such as doors, and tracking their status using similar probabilistic methods [2]. There are several benefits of having explicit objects. Since an object consists of multiple cells that have the same probability, each scan provides more information about the object, allowing its state to be altered more quickly. Also, since most of the map is not dynamic, the probability of objects can be changed much more rapidly, since changes in the objects probably will not be able to change the map to make an invalid location match the sensors. However, explicit objects need to be manually defined before execution, adding to the work of defining maps. Since objects are binary, either present or absent, a moving object must be represented explicitly by creating a binary object at each possible location. With the dynamic maps described here, an object can appear anywhere without user interference. Finally, the method in [2] involves a different importance factor, which increases the runtime logarithmically in the number of objects.

Members of a set of algorithms for simultaneous localization and mapping (SLAM) have the ability to localize the robot and generate the map simultaneously in real time [5]. These algorithms are meant to dynamically alter the map in the same way as my dynamic map MCL. Many of these methods use an algorithm which is guaranteed to converge to a correct solution. However, they suffer from the data association problem. On every sensor scan it must be possible to uniquely identify which feature of the map is responsible for each sensor reading. If this is impossible, then the guarantee of correctness does not hold. SLAM does not discover and use cell correlations, so the rate of update is slower if the map changes, since each cell must be considered independently. Further, SLAM involves significantly more processing than MCL, using up computing power that may not be necessary, especially after the map is generated. Dynamic map MCL was created specifically to provide an accurately changing map without incurring any significant overhead. Since it is a constant time addition to MCL, the map can be updated without requiring any more computing power than ordinary localization. Of course, the map cannot be generated from nothing as it can with SLAM, but once the map exists it can be kept up to date almost without cost. SLAM also, in common with ordinary MCL, makes the assumption that the map is static. Over time, the algorithm becomes more certain of the map and any changes will take longer to appear. Dynamic MCL explicitly makes the assumption that the map will change.

Algorithms that consider dynamic environments typically assume a static map with dynamic elements, such as people, which must be eliminated from consideration. In effect, these algorithms assume a static map but allow an additional form of sensor noise in the form of moving people. [13] describes a method for creating a map, using standard EM SLAM techniques, which can discover the static map of the environment despite dynamic elements. Similarly, [12] gives an algorithm for using MCL in an environment with many moving objects. Although both these papers give a method for handling a dynamic environment, they both assume an underlying static map. The benefit of dynamic MCL is that the static map assumption is no longer necessary. As the algorithm runs, it changes the map to correspond to the environment. Since dynamic MCL is implemented as an augmentation to ordinary

MCL, there is no reason that other augmentations could not be used if warranted by the problem. For example, the algorithm described in [12] to discard readings relating to dynamic objects during MCL can coexist with my algorithm for modifying the map in accordance with changes in the environment. Dynamic MCL allows fundamental changes to be accounted for, as opposed to merely ephemeral objects that are only observed once.

7 Conclusions and Future Work

This paper describes an augmentation to MCL which allows the map to be updated according to the sensor measurements of a localized robot without a serious increase in running time. By considering each cell of the map to be an independent binary object and by making some simplifying assumptions, the static map required by MCL can be modified dynamically without requiring any user intervention. Instead of becoming less accurate over time, the map becomes more accurate as the robot traverses the environment. Experiments with real datasets show that the map can be updated properly without introducing errors. A change in the environment can be reflected in the map after very few passes by the robot. Since the map is not updated incorrectly and the running time is minimal, there is no drawback to using dynamic map techniques as an addition to ordinary MCL. However, the result of the algorithm, having an accurate map, will always benefit the accuracy of MCL.

Future work will involve calculating the rate of change of various cells so that more rapid updating of changing objects in the map is possible. It might be possible to generate a graph of important locations in the map marked with transitions between them. Then, when the map was updated, the graph could be modified as well, providing a high level abstraction that could be used for planning under uncertainty.

References

1. A. Milstein, J. Sanchez, and E.Williamson. Robust global localization using clustered particle filtering. In AAAI-02.
2. D. Avots, E. Lim, R. Thibaux, and S. Thrun. A probabilistic technique for simultaneous localization and door state estimation with mobile robots in dynamic environments. In IROS-2002.
3. Thrun, S. 2000. Probabilistic Algorithms in Robotics. School of Computer Science, Carnegie Mellon University. Pittsburgh, PA.
4. Thrun, S.; Montemerlo, M.; and Whittaker, W. 2002. Conditional Particle filters for Simultaneous Mobile Robot Localization and People-Tracking. Forthcoming.
5. M. Montemerlo, S. Thrun, D. Koller, and B. Wegbreit. FastSLAM: A factored solution to the simultaneous localization and mapping problem. In AAAI-02.
6. Thrun, S.; Fox, D.; Burgard, W.; and Dellaert, F. 2001. Robust Monte Carlo Localization for Mobile Robots. Artificial Intelligence Magazine.
7. J.Liu and R. Chen. 1998. Sequential monte carlo methods for dynamic systems. Journal of the American Statistical Association 93:1032-1044.
8. Borenstein, J.; Everett, B.; and Feng, L. 1996. Navigating Mobile Robots: Systems and Techniques. A.K. Peters, Ltd. Wellesley, MA.

9. Thrun, S.; Fox, D.; and Burgard, W.   2000.   Monte Carlo Localization with Mixture Proposal Distribution. In Proceedings of the AAAI National Conference on Artificial Intelligence, Austin, TX.

10. Thrun, S.; Particle Filters in Robotics. In Proceedings of Uncertainty in AI 2002.

11. M. I. Jordan, Z. Ghahramani, T. S. Jaakkola, and L. K. Saul. In M. I. Jordan (Ed.); An introduction to variational methods for graphical models. Learning in Graphical Models, Cambridge: MIT Press, 1999.

12. Fox, D.; Burgard, W. and Thrun, S.; Markov Localization for Mobile Robots in Dynamic Environments. In Journal of Artificial Intelligence Research, 1999.

13. Hähnel, D.; Triebel, R.; Burgard, W. and Thrun, S.; Map building with mobile robots in dynamic environments. In ICRA, 2003.

Handling Over-Constrained Problems in Distributed Multi-agent Systems

Lingzhong Zhou[1], Abdul Sattar[1], and Scott Goodwin[2]

[1] Institute for Integrated and Intelligent Systems,
Griffith University, Brisbane, Australia
{l.zhou, a.sattar}@griffith.edu.au
[2] School of Computer Science, University of Windsor, Canada
sgoodwin@uwindsor.ca

Abstract. The distributed constraint satisfaction problem is a general framework used to represent problems in distributed multi-agent systems. In this paper, we describe a detailed investigation of handling over-constrained satisfaction problems in a dynamic and multi-agent environment. We introduce a new algorithm, *Over-constrained Dynamic Agent Ordering*, that treats under and over-constrained problems uniformly. While the existing approaches generally only consider a single variable per agent, the proposed algorithm can handle multiple variables per agent. In this approach, we use the *degree of unsatisfiability* as a measure for relaxing constraints, and hence as a way to guide the search towards the best possible solution(s). Through an experimental study, we demonstrate that our algorithm performs better than the one based on asynchronous weak commitment search.

1 Introduction

A constraint satisfaction problem (CSP) consists of a finite number of variables, each having a finite and discrete set of possible values, and a set of constraints over the variables. A solution to a CSP is an instantiation of all variables for which all the constraints are satisfied. When the variables and constraints of a CSP are distributed among a set of autonomous and communicating agents, this can be formulated as a distributed constraint satisfaction problem (DCSP). A DCSP framework can naturally represent problems in distributed multi-agent systems. A solution to a DCSP is an instantiation of variables that satisfies all constraints among the agents in the problem.

Often, many real world problems lead to CSPs that cannot be solved, because there is no consistent instantiation of variables that satisfies all constraints. These problems are known as over-constrained satisfaction problems [1]. In a distributed multi-agent environment, we refer to such problems as distributed over-constrained satisfaction problems (DOCSPs). In recent years, there have been a few attempts to address DOCSPs, namely, distributed partial constraint satisfaction problem framework (DPCSPs) and distributed maximal constraint

B. Kégl and G. Lapalme (Eds.): AI 2005, LNAI 3501, pp. 13–24, 2005.

satisfaction problem framework (DMCSP) by [2]; the distributed hierarchical constraint satisfaction problem framework (DHCSPs) by [3]; distributed constraint optimization problems (DCOPs) [8]; asynchronous distributed optimization (Adopt) [6]; and optimal asynchronous partial overlay (OptAPO) [4]. All of these approaches are based on an assumption that each agent has a single variable. While it can be argued that multiple variable problems can be reduced to single variables with tupled domains, in many realistic problems this results in an impractical blow-out in domain size.

In this paper, we describe an algorithm that can handle multiple variables per agent and efficiently find partial solution(s) to the given over-constrained problem. This study extends our earlier work on dynamic agent ordering for under-constrained distributed problems [10] that was an improvement over the state-of-the-art method, asynchronous weak commitment search [9]. We refer to the new algorithm as the over-constrained dynamic agent ordering algorithm (ODAO). Here, we use the degree of constraint unsatisfaction (*degreeUnsat*) as a measure of relaxation in the weakened problem. This value not only reflects how unsatisfied the constraints are in the current instantiation, but also guides the search by dynamically determining the order in which agents are allowed to change their particular variable instantiations. This measure can be used to calculate the degree of relaxation of the global solution. An empirical analysis demonstrates that the proposed algorithm performs better than the one based on asynchronous weak commitment search.

In the rest of the paper, we define a DCSP and a DOCSP and examine the shortcomings of existing approaches to DOCSPs. We then introduce a new method for finding an optimal solution to a DOCSP using the *degree of unsatisfaction*. We then report an experimental study of the proposed algorithm, and analyse its performance in comparison with asynchronous weak commitment search [9] suitably adapted to handle over-constrained problems. Finally, we conclude the paper.

2   Distributed Constraint Satisfaction Problems

2.1   Definition

In a distributed constraint satisfaction problem:

1. There exists an agent set A:

$$A = \{A_1, A_2, ..., A_n\}, \ n \in Z^+;$$

2. Each agent has a variable set X_i and domain set D_i,

$$X_i = \{X_{i1}, X_{i2}, ..., X_{ip_i}\};$$
$$D_i = \{D_{i1}, D_{i2}, ..., D_{ip_i}\}, \forall i \in [1, n], \ p_i \in Z^+;$$

3. There are two kinds of constraints over the variables among agents: *Intra-agent constraints*, which are between variables of the same agent. *Inter-agent constraints*, which are between variables of different agents.

4. A solution S, is an instantiation for all variables that satisfies all intra-agent and inter-agent constraints.

A DCSP with no solution is referred to as a DOCSP. Many real world situations make DCSPs unsolvable, i.e., there is no instantiation that can satisfy all constraints. We can only hope for an optimal solution (partial solution) for the problem at hand. Clearly, the quality of these partial solutions depends on the heuristic (rationalization) we use for selecting constraints for relaxation.

2.2 Difficulties with Current Approaches

In this section we examine the existing methods to highlight any difficulties they may have, particularly in relation to handling multiple variables per agent problems.

Asynchronous Backtracking [7] was proposed to deal with DOCSPs. When an empty nogood is found, a new related threshold is generated, and the search is restarted. By iteratively applying this procedure, an optimal solution will eventually be found. However, this is not a very efficient approach, as an agent with a lower priority has to perform an exhaustive search to determine if there are no solutions for the current threshold. When the number of local variables increases to more than one per agent, this approach becomes increasingly impractical.

A DOCSP can be formalised as a distributed partial CSP (DPCSP), a distributed maximal CSP (DMCSP) or a distributed hierarchical CSP (DHCSP). The DMCSP is actually a subclass of the DPCSP. The difference is that, for a DPCSP, agents search for variable values that minimize the total number of constraints relaxed; and, for a DMCSP, agents search for variable values that minimize the maximum number of violated constraints in each agent. Both methods use *global distance* to measure the degree of the relaxation. In a DPCSP, this value is the total number of constraints relaxed, $G = \sum_{i=1}^{n} d_i$[1]; and, in a DMCSP, it is the maximal number of constraints relaxed over the agents, $G = max(d_i)$.

If we were to adapt these methods to handle multiple variables per agent, then relaxing an intra-agent constraint would present little difficulty, i.e., it would cause the agent in charge of that constraint to increase the distance measure by one. However, if an inter-agent constraint is relaxed, the two related agents would both add one to their respective distances. Hence, although only one constraint was relaxed it would be counted twice. This double-counting does not matter in the single variable problem as all constraints are, by definition, inter-agent constraints. The addition of intra-agent constraints complicates this situation and requires a more sophisticated distance measure to be defined.

In a DHCSP, each constraint is labelled with a positive integer called the *importance value*. The larger the value, the more important the constraint. Agents search for variable values that minimize the maximum importance value of violated constraints over all agents. Processing can either start at the top of the

---

[1] Where G is the global distance; n is the number of agents in the problem; d_i is the local distance for each agent, and the value of d_i is the number of constraints relaxed.

hierarchy (top-down), in which case agents try and satisfy the constraints with the greatest importance value first. Then the next level down is attempted, and so on. Alternatively, agents may start by trying to satisfy all levels of constraints (bottom-up). If this is not possible then the lowest level constraints are relaxed. If this relaxed problem cannot be satisfied then the next least important layer is relaxed, and so on. In bottom-up processing, if one agent cannot find a solution at certain level, all agents have to relax their constraints on that level, even if other agents' constraints can be satisfied at that level. Hence, an optimal solution for a DHCSP would not necessarily be optimal according to the DPCSP or DMCSP global distance measure. In addition, the efficiency of a DHCSP is poor. The worst case is that the optimal solution level is far away from the starting point. For some problems a bottom-up approach is preferable, whereas for others a top-down would be more efficient. Unfortunately, we cannot tell which starting point should have been used until the problem has been solved.

The distributed constraint optimization problem framework was developed in [8]. The aim of solving this kind of problem is to find a minimal or maximal cost over all constraints. It has been commonly used for distributed over-constrained satisfaction problems. A cost function relates each pair of variables, whose different instantiation combinations result in different values of the cost function. Agents cooperatively select values, in order to optimize the cost function.

Multiple variables per agent are common in real-life DCSPs and its variants. When solving these problems, it is generally necessary to considering inter- and intra-agent constraints. This is not the case for DCSPs where one variable per agent is assumed. All variables in one agent can be considered as one virtual variable. All local solutions can be considered as possible values for the virtual variable. However, this is impractical in DCOPs, especially when cost functions are taken into account. When cost functions are involved, it is impossible to view each agent as having just has one virtual variable. A cost function is directly applied to each pair of variables—not local solutions. So multiple variables can not be represented by one virtual variable in distributed constraint optimization problems. Earlier mentioned approaches (Adopt, OptAPO, etc.) can only deal with DCOPs with a single variable per agent. When the number of variables is more than one in per agent, these algorithms can not to be used any more. In addition, the cost functions have to be pre-processed. The results of each pair of variables' instantiations have to be fully listed before problem solving. This requires large memory storage and extra computations.

The above methods do not describe how problems with multiple variables per agent could be handled. Some of them even do not have the ability to solve this kind of problem because of the mechanisms of the methods. Such problems would cause considerable difficulty, since relaxing an intra-agent constraint and relaxing an inter-agent constraint can be mistakenly considered as being equal. Relaxing different kinds of constraints will result in a weakened problem that has different hardness and structure.

We propose a new approach for measuring and solving distributed over-constrained satisfaction problems with multiple variables per agent. First of all, the concept of distributed *constraint density* (related to both intra-agent and inter-agent constraints) will be introduced as part of a new distance measure for constraint relaxation.

3 Constraint Density in Distributed Over-Constrained Satisfaction Problems

Constraint density in DCSPs has been introduced and defined in [10]. By looking at two problem features, intra- and inter-agent constraint densities were fairly measured. In addition, the dynamic constraint density much more reveals the current state of each agent during a search. *degreeUnsat* as the ratio of the static constraint density to the dynamic constraint density is used to measure the degree of unsatisfaction in each agent. The *degreeUnsat* ranges from a value of zero, if all constraints are satisfied, to one, if all constraints are unsatisfied. Solving a DCSP is actually a process of minimizing the value of *degreeUnsat* for each agent. When all agents' *degreeUnsat* = 0, all constraints are satisfied and the problem is solved. We developed a dynamic agent ordering (DAO) algorithm by using this technique [10], where Agents autonomously order themselves to re-instantiate their variables. This improves the search efficiency and requires less memory usage than other state-of-the-art approaches. We now extend this technique to measure the degree of relaxation of a DOCSP. The benefit of this approach is that it combines both intra- and inter-agent constraint relaxations into a single measure.

Relaxing constraints in DOCSPs is different from relaxing constraints in an ordinary (non-distributed) over-constrained problem. We should consider not only the relaxation of constraints, but also the communication cost and the effects on agents' relations. For example, we generally treat inter-agent constraints as more important than intra-agent constraints, because they have a greater impact on the overall problem (i.e. they affect more than one agent). Hence, we would normally prefer to relax an intra- rather than an inter-agent constraint.

However, inter-agent constraint relaxation should be considered as well. Relaxing an inter-agent constraint will loosen the associated intra-agent constraint problems, providing more opportunities for agents to solve subproblems locally, and so reduce future communication costs. Relaxing an intra-agent constraint is easier than relaxing an inter-agent constraint, since only one agent involved. Relaxing an inter-agent constraint is more efficient than relaxing an intra-agent constraint, as both agents will directly benefit from it. Hence there is a trade-off between these two types of relaxation.

From the perspective of the processing cost and the outcome, we may consider that relaxing one inter-agent constraint is equal to relaxing a number of intra-agent constraints. This kind of equality does not mean that the process of relaxation is equivalent, but it does mean that the consequences may be the same.

In this context, we use *degreeUnsat* to guide the search and measure (as a threshold) the satisfiability of the relaxed DOCSP. Next, we propose a method for finding an optimal solution to a DOCSP using thresholds:

Threshold Repair Method: We can use the *degreeUnsat* as a threshold to define the degree of constraint relaxation required for each agent in the problem. If *degreeUnsat* = 1, then no constraint need be satisfied, and if *degreeUnsat* = 0 then all constraints must be satisfied. For values between 0 and 1, the number of unsatisfied constraints depends on the structure of the problem, remembering that the *degreeUnsat* takes into account the *difficulty* of satisfying individual constraints. If an empty nogood is discovered, (i.e., the threshold is not achievable) the threshold value is increased by an amount that depends on the related constraints. By iteratively applying this method the optimal *degreeUnsat* solution will eventually be found.

If we are uncertain as to whether a problem is over-constrained, setting the initial threshold to zero will guarantee finding the optimal solution. Otherwise, setting the threshold at a reasonable lower bound on the optimal solution threshold will reduce the amount of processing required. It should be noted that existing approaches require that the over-constrained status of a problem is known in advance, whereas our method can solve both under- and over-constrained problems without modification. It should also be noted that the *threshold* has a different meaning in the different formalisations we have discussed. In DPC-SPs, the threshold is the number of constraints that can be relaxed in the entire problem, in DMCSPs, it is the maximal number of constraints that can be relaxed for each agent in the optimal solution, and, in DHCSPs, it is the minimal importance value on the constraints that can be reached. In our algorithm, it reflects the degree of the relaxation or *degreeUnsat* of the optimal solution.

For a DOCSP, an optimal solution is found when minimal values are reached for all *degreeUnsat* of each agent. The global measure of unsatisfiability can be represented as

$$G_{degreeUnsat} = \frac{\sum_{i=1}^{n} degreeUnsat_i}{n}$$

where n is the number of agents in the problem. The *global degreeUnsat* ($G_{degreeUnsat}$) shows the degree of relaxation for the entire problem. Using our approach, each agent may have a different threshold, whereas the other approaches we have discussed require a global threshold that is imposed uniformly on each agent.

4   Algorithm

In this section, we introduce the Over-constrained Dynamic Agent Ordering (ODAO) algorithm, which uses the threshold repair method to solve DOCSPs, as follows:

1. A threshold (a value of *degreeUnsat*) is decided before the search started. All variables in each agent are alphabetically ordered and assigned a priority of 0;
2. In the initial state, each agent concurrently instantiates their variables to construct a local solution, while checking consistency to guarantee the local

degreeUnsat $\leq$ *threshold*. Each agent then sends its local solution to its neighbouring agents (i.e., those with which it shares at least one inter-agent constraint);

3. Each agent then starts to construct a local solution which attempts to satisfy both intra-agent constraints with higher priority variables and inter-agent constraints with higher priority agents (i.e., agents with lower *degreeUnsat*). Each agent attempts to satisfy as many constraints as possible for each variable such that its *degreeUnsat* is minimised. If an agent is unable to instantiate a variable with any value in its domain, a nogood is discovered. If this nogood is not a repeat and is not empty, it will be recorded and the priority of the variable will be increased by one. For each constraint involved in the nogood, the *degreeUnsat* resulting from relaxing that constraint is calculated. The minimum value of these *degreeUnsat* calculations is then stored as well. If the nogood is empty, this implies the threshold is still too tight, and threshold repair will be carried out, i.e., the new threshold is the minimal *degreeUnsat*, T_{min} recorded for the agent, such that T_{min} is greater than the current threshold.

4. The agent calculates the value of *degreeUnsat*. If *degreeUnsat* $\leq$ *threshold*, the agent sends messages to neighbouring agents. Each message contains the *degreeUnsat* value and the local instantiation of the agent. Otherwise, we go back to 3;

5. The search will stop when each agent i detects that its *degreeUnsat*$_i$ $\leq$ *threshold*$_i$.

In effect, ODAO is using the change in *degreeUnsat* as a distance measure, and so is implicitly placing an importance value on each constraint. This importance value is the amount by which the *degreeUnsat* will change for an agent, when a particular constraint is relaxed, i.e., when a relaxation needs to occur, the constraint that causes the smallest change in *degreeUnsat* is selected. Put simply, an agent will relax the constraint it calculates as easiest to satisfy. This distance measure has two features that distinguish it from the approaches discussed earlier: firstly, it is *local* to the agent, and secondly it is *dynamic*, i.e., it will change according to which constraints are currently unsatisfied. Also note that no constraint is *permanently* flagged as relaxed. Each agent has a *degreeUnsat* threshold it is trying to attain, and is free to relax any constraint to attain that threshold, each time it gets a turn.

Example: To further clarify the details of the algorithm, we use a distributed 3-colouring problem shown in Figure 1. The goal of the problem is to assign colours to each node so that nodes connected by the same arc have different colours[2]. In Figure 1 (a), Agent 1 has two intra-agent constraints and Agent 2 has three intra-agent constraints, and they both have four inter-agent constraints. The static constraint densities for Agent 1 and 2 are $\frac{17}{3}$ and 7 respectively. Before a search is started, we assume that the threshold is 0, which means the problem is solvable.

---

[2] B = blue, R= red, W = white.

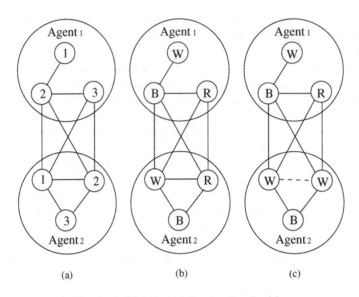

Fig. 1. A Distributed 3-colouring Problem

In Figure 1 (b), two agents assign colours to their variables, such that their intra-agent constraints are satisfied, and then send messages to each other. As Agent 1 has higher priority than Agent 2 ($degreeUnsat_{A_1} < degreeUnsat_{A_2}$), it will do nothing and just await. In Agent 2, variable 1 has the highest priority and its value satisfies all constraints. Variable 2 has higher priority, but its value violates the constraint between Agent 1's variable 3 and itself. Although Agent 2 tries to assign a new value to variable 2, it cannot find any colours that satisfy all constraints. Hence, a nogood is produced, and is recorded as $\{A_2, v_2, \{A_1, v_2, \text{'B'}\}, \{A_1, v_3, \text{'R'}\}, \{A_2, v_1, \text{'W'}\}\}$, where Agent 2's ($A_2$) variable v_2 cannot be instantiated with any colour because A_1's variable v_2 is instantiated with 'B', A_1's variable v_3 is instantiated with 'R' and A_2's variable v_1 is instantiated with 'W'. The nogood is also sent to A_1 to avoid the same assignment in the future. A_2 assigns a colour 'W' to variable v_2 to minimize the number of unsatisfied constraints, and the priority of variable v_2 is increased by 1 as well. Next, variable v_1 detects another nogood $\{A_2, v_1, \{A_1, v_2, \text{'B'}\}, \{A_1, v_3, \text{'R'}\}, \{A_2, v_2, \text{'W'}\}\}$. Later, Agent A_1 will discover another two nogoods for variable v_2 and v_3, containing A_2's variable v_1 and variable v_2. Finally, an empty nogood will be produced. It reveals the problem is over-constrained and has no solution. The agent generating the empty nogood then checks its nogood history, and relaxes the constraint that causes the minimal *degreeUnsat*. In this case, Agent A_2 selects the constraint between variable v_1 and v_2 to relax. The threshold for the Agent A_2 is $\frac{1}{21} \approx 0.04762$. Then an optimal solution found in Figure 1 (c).

The pseudo code of the algorithm is detailed Over-constrained Dynamic Agent Ordering. Note that all variables from a neighbouring agent have higher priority than any local variable *iff* $degreeUnsat < local\_degreeUnsat$.

Algorithm *Over-constrained Dynamic Agent Ordering*
1.   **while** received($Sender\_id$, $variable\_values$, $degreeUnsat$) do
2.   calculate $local\_degreeUnsat$;
3.   **if** $local\_degreeUnsat \leq threshold$ and all other agents' $degreeUnsat \leq threshold$
4.   **then** the search is terminated;
5.   **else** add ($Sender\_id$, $variable\_value$, $degreeUnsat$) to $agent\_view$;
6.   **if** $local\_degreeUnsat > degreeUnsat$
7.   **then** Assign_Local_Variables;

Algorithm *Assign_ Local_ Variables*
1.   calculate $local\_degreeUnsat$;
2.   **if** $local\_degreeUnsat \leq threshold$ and $degreeUnsat < local\_degreeUnsat$
3.   **then** send($Sender\_id$, $variable\_values$, $local\_degreeUnsat$) to neighbouring agents;
4.   **else** select an inconsistent variable v with the highest priority and assign a value from its
             domain;
5.   **if** no value for this variable
6.   **then if** nogood is empty
7.   **then** *Threshold Repair*;
8.   **else** **if** nogood is new
9.   **then** nogood is recorded;
10.   the priority of the variable is increased by one;
11.   **else** assign a value with minimal violations to the variables with lower priorities;
12.   *Assign_ Local_ Variables*;

Algorithm *Threshold Repair*
1. $T_{min} = 1$;
2. $temp\_degreeUnsat = degreeUnsat$ from first nogood in the nogood set;
3.   **while** not the end of nogood set do
4.   **if** $temp\_degreeUnsat > threshold$ and
5. $temp\_degreeUnsat < T_{min}$
6.   **then** $T_{min} = temp\_degreeUnsat$;
7. $temp\_degreeUnsat = degreeUnsat$ from next nogood;
8. $threshold = T_{min}$;

In a realistic problem, different agents may arrive at different values for their
$local\_degreeUnsat$, meaning that different levels of optimization can be reached
by different agents. Finally, the *global degreeUnsat* can be used to measure the
degree of relaxation for the entire problem.

5   Experimental Results

We evaluated our algorithm on a benchmark set of 3-colouring problems, using
the problem generator described in [5]. We then added a number of constraints
to make the problem over-constrained. Each agent was also constrained to have
at least one inter-agent constraint. Then, we randomly distributed n constraints
to groups of four nodes from the same or different agents, where each group is
required to be fully connected (each node has three constraints connecting to
the other three nodes). As a result, the problem is over-constrained.

We also implemented our own variant of the AWC algorithm [9], Asynchronous Over-constrained Weak-commitment search (AOWC) to deal with distributed over-constrained satisfaction problems. This was necessary as there was
no available complete search algorithm that could handle DOCSPs with multiple
variables per agent. We chose AWC as a starting point because it was the only
available algorithm that can handle multiple variables per agent in a distributed
under-constrained environment.

Table 1. Results for Distributed 3-colouring Over-constrained Problems

A	V	C	Method	Constraints Relaxed	Final Threshold	Checks	Nogoods	Local Solutions	Time (s)
3	15	43	AOWC	1.65		1198	179	162	0.143091
			ODAO		0.0043	611	81	66	0.096632
4	20	58	AOWC	3.71		3145	1021	579	0.471683
			ODAO		0.0055	1218	337	192	0.291953
5	25	72	AOWC	4.14		10726	1779	741	2.392564
			ODAO		0.0038	6642	853	369	1.210876
6	30	87	AOWC	5.37		42170	5472	2011	10.686257
			ODAO		0.0023	17134	1862	758	4.568762
7	35	101	AOWC	5.82		99374	8653	2437	23.561248
			ODAO		0.0030	52836	3893	1095	9.498762
8	40	116	AOWC	7.21		473291	31059	3624	94.398217
			ODAO		0.0034	116174	9187	1952	21.079638
9	45	130	AOWC	7.96		1087532	417206	8167	171.896542
			ODAO		0.0020	459961	13624	2751	76.504976
10	50	145	AOWC	7.49		3963721	119394	18364	564.749568
			ODAO		0.0016	1217286	35397	4858	144.126825

AOWC operates in the following way: when an empty nogood is discovered, it randomly relaxes one of the constraints from the nogood at the bottom of the nogood stack (i.e., the last non-empty nogood that was discovered). It then restarts the search on this relaxed problem. If the problem cannot be solved, i.e., it results in a further empty nogood, then another constraint from the original nogood is relaxed. If all constraints in the first nogood are relaxed, then this nogood is removed from the bottom of nogood stack, and the next nogood is selected for relaxation. Since AOWC cannot recognize an optimal solution, we allow it to repeat this process until a solution is found that equals the optimal solution from our own approach (in terms of a count of the number of constraints relaxed).

Table 1 shows the experimental results comparing AOWC with our new approach, where A is the number of agents, V is the total number of variables and C is the total number of constraints in a problem. All data points are averaged over 100 trials. We set up the initial ODAO threshold to be 0.1% (0.001), with the final threshold (*global degreeUnsat*) shown in the table. It should be noted that the values of *Threshold* are not the ratios of the number of unsatisfied constraints to the number of the total constraints, rather they are the averaged values of the *degreeUnsat*, when the optimal solutions are found.

From these results it is clear that our algorithm (ODAO) is considerably more efficient than AOWC in terms of communication cost and execution time. The number of nogoods and local solutions for AOWC are approximately 2 to 5 times more than for ODAO. As a result, the communication load is much heavier. In addition, more checks are needed during search. AOWC also spends a significant amount of time on producing intermediate non-optimal solutions during a search. This means that AOWC takes much longer than ODAO to find an optimal solution. Conversely, ODAO can find an optimal solution in a reasonable time, and it also allows each agent to find a precise threshold when an optimal solution is found.

6   Conclusion

This study has addressed the important issue of over-constrainedness in DC-SPs. We proposed an algorithm that can directly address DOCSPs. In contrast, existing approaches rely on formalising a DOCSP into a DPCSP, a DMCSP, a DHCSP, or DCOPs then using the relevant algorithms to solve it. Our approach also can handle DOCSPs in which an agent may have multiple variables, while existing approaches allow only one variable per agent. We further conclude that intra- and inter-agent constraint relaxation cannot be treated identically. When searching for an optimal solution for a DOCSP, it is easier to relax an intra- rather than an inter-agent constraint. This is because intra-agent constraints only have local effects. However, an inter-agent constraint relaxation can make it easier to satisfy the intra-agent constraints of the agents to which it is connected, i.e., it can make the overall problem easier. Another effect of relaxing an inter-agent constraint is that it will reduce the communication and external computation costs for the two agents it connects. Conversely, when relaxing an intra-agent constraint, only one agent gets the benefit. Hence the question of the relative importance of inter- and intra-agent constraints is not clear-cut. In our approach, we allow the autonomous agents to make decisions about relaxing intra- versus inter-agent constraints, based on the current *degreeUnsat* measure, rather than mandating a fixed trade-off. At the same time, this approach acts as an efficient mechanism to guide the search. Finally, an ODAO agent has the ability to dynamically adjust the threshold at which it will accept a solution. This means our algorithm can deal with DCSPs without knowing whether a problem is under- and over-constrained.

References

1. Eugene C. Freuder and Richard J. Wallace. Partial constraint satisfaction. *Artificial Intelligence*, 58(1-3):21–70, 1992.
2. Katsutoshi Hirayama and Makoto Yokoo. Distributed partial constraint satisfaction problem. In *Proceedings of the Third International Conference on Principles and Practice of Constraint Programming (CP-97)*, pages 222–236, 1997.
3. Katsutoshi Hirayama and Makoto Yokoo. An approach to over-constrained distributed constraint satisfaction problems: Distributed hierarchical constraint satisfact. In *Proceedings of the Fourth International Conference on MultiAgent Systems (ICMAS-2000)*, 2000.
4. Roger Mailler and Victor Lesser. Solving Distributed Constraint Optimization Problems Using Cooperative Mediation. In *Proceedings of Third International Joint Conference on Autonomous Agents and Multiagent Systems (AAMAS 2004)*, pages 438–445. IEEE Computer Society, 2004.

5. S. Minton, M. D. Johnston, A. B. Philips, and P. Laird. Minimizing conflicts: a heuristic repair method for constraint satisfaction and scheduling problems. *Artificial Intelligence*, pages 161–205, 1992.
6. Pragnesh Jay Modi, Wei-Min Shen, Milind Tambe, and Makoto Yokoo. An asynchronous complete method for distributed constraint optimization. In *Proceedings of the second international joint conference on Autonomous agents and multiagent systems*, pages 161–168. ACM Press, 2003.
7. Makoto Yokoo. Constraint relaxation in distributed constraint satisfaction problem. In *Proceedings of 5th International Conference on Tools with Artificial Intelligence*, pages 56–63, 1993.
8. Makoto Yokoo and Edmund H. Durfee. Distributed constraint optimization as a formal model of partially adversarial cooperation. Technical Report CSE-TR-101-91, Ann Arbor, MI 48109, 1991.
9. Makoto Yokoo and Katsutoshi Hirayama. Distributed constraint satisfaction algorithm for complex local problems. In *Proceedings of the Third International Conference on Multiagent Systems (ICMAS-98)*, pages 372–379, 1998.
10. Lingzhong Zhou, John Thornton, and Abdul Sattar. Dynamic agent ordering in distributed constraint satisfaction problems. In *Proceedings of the 16th Australian Joint Conference on Artificial Intelligence, AI-2003, Perth*, 2003.

Performance Evaluation of an Agent Based Distributed Data Mining System

Sung Baik[1], Ju Cho[1], and Jerzy Bala[2]

[1] Sejong University, Seoul 143-747, Korea
sbaik@sejong.ac.kr
[2] Datamat Systems Research, Inc.,
1600 International Drive, McLean, VA 22102, USA
jbala@dsri.com

Abstract. This paper presents a distributed approach to build decision trees in a lock step manner with each node proposing an attribute on which to split. A central mediator chooses the attribute, among the candidates, with the highest information gain. The chosen split is then effectively communicated to the other agents to partition their data. The distributed decision tree approach is performed on the agent based architecture dealing with distributed databases. This paper mainly focuses on the evaluation of the system performance in distributed data mining. Even though there are several trials suggesting algorithms of distributed data mining, few efforts have made on the definition of the system performance. It is very important to define the performance for the further development of distributed data mining.

1 Introduction

Computational efficiency and scalability is a very critical issue in data mining [1] since the amount of data is rapidly increasing in the real world. Also, it is very important in data mining to deal with huge amounts of data located at different sites since these data are naturally located at geographically distributed sites, and some of them are relevant to each other. In such a distributed environment, a basic approach for data mining is to move all of the data to a central data repository and then to analyze them with a single data mining system. However, even though it guarantees accurate results of data analysis, the approach requires overly expensive computation and communication costs. It also has a critical security problem in that it reveals private information data, although privacy preserving issues [2-7] are major concerns in inter-enterprise data mining when dealing with private databases located at different sites. An alternative approach is high level learning with in-place strategies in which all the data can be locally analyzed, and the local results at their local sites are combined at the central site to obtain the final result (global data model). This approach is less expensive but may produce ambiguous and incorrect global results. To make up for such a weakness, many researchers have spent great efforts looking for more advanced approaches of combining local models built at different sites. Most of these approaches are agent-based high level learning such as meta-learning [8], knowledge probing [9],

B. Kégl and G. Lapalme (Eds.): AI 2005, LNAI 3501, pp. 25–32, 2005.
© Springer-Verlag Berlin Heidelberg 2005

and mixture of experts [10], Bayesian model averaging [11], and stacked generalization [12]. However, these approaches still only have the ability to estimate a global
data model through the aggregation of the local results, rather than generating an exact correct global model. In particular, they have the critical weakness of not dealing
with heterogeneous databases located at different sites.

2   System Architecture and Distributed Learning Algorithm

This paper presents an agent based distributed data mining approach, in which the
modified decision tree algorithm on an agent based framework can deal with heterogeneous data sets in the distributed environment [13,14] and produce accurate global
results. The data mining based the algorithm takes full advantage of all the available
data through a mechanism for integrating data from a wide variety of data sources and
is able to handle data characterized by geographic (or logical) distribution, complexity
and multi feature representations, and vertical partitioning/distribution of feature sets.

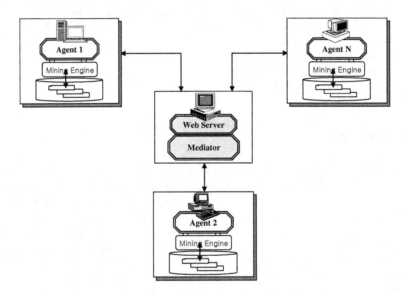

Fig. 1. System architecture of an agent based distributed data mining

Fig. 1 shows the architecture of an agent based system, which consists of a web
server, a mediator, and agents. The web server supports users with a web based interface through which they can access databases located at different sites and manipulate
data mining facilities. The mediator coordinates the communication between several
agents with security concerns such as authentication. Each agent is located at each
heterogeneous data site to achieve coordinated learning through the cooperation of local learning and communication with the other agents. The mining engine and the
communication interface within the agent are implemented in C and Java, respectively (See Fig. 2).

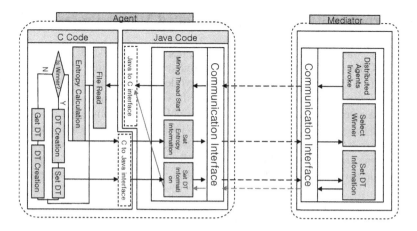

Fig. 2. The communication structure between mediator and agents

The Distributed Data Mining (DDM) component includes a number of Data Mining Agents whose efforts are coordinated through a facilitator. One of the major functions of the facilitator is to collect information from various DM Agents and to broadcast the collected information to other Agents involved in the mining process. To this end, there is a certain amount of cost associated with the distributed mining process, namely that of the communication bandwidth. For very large datasets, the high cost of transferring information from one agent to another can become a major hindrance in the data mining process.

The distributed learning algorithm of a decision tree in an agent-mediator communication mechanism is as follows:

1. [Mediator] Start the local data mining processes associated with local agents.
2. [Agent] Find the attribute and its associated value that can best split the data into the various training classes during local mining.
3. [Agent] Send the best local attribute and its associated value to the mediator.
4. [Mediator] Select the best attribute from the best local attributes of all the agents.
5. [Mediator] Notify each agent of its role for the next action (splitting or waiting).
6. [Agent] Split the data, according to the best global attribute and its associated split value, in the formation of two separate clusters of data in the selected agent.
7. [Agent] Distribute the structural information in each cluster and the best attribute to the other agents through the mediator.
8. [Agent] Construct the partial decision trees according to the structural information in other agents.
9. [Agent] Generate decision rules at each agent and notify the mediator for termination if there is no more splitting. Otherwise, go to step 2.
10. [Mediator&Agent] Terminate.

3 Performance Evaluation of Distributed Mining Process

This section evaluates the performance of the presented agent-based decision tree algorithm (DDM) with a comparison of a centralized decision tree algorithm (SDM) such as C5.0 of Quinlan [15]. In the centralized decision tree algorithm, the entropy calculation is very critical in processing huge data. So, the time to find the best entropy from a given table of the database can be defined as a computation cost. In the distributed data mining, there are generally two extra main costs such as communication costs and knowledge integration costs. However, we do not need to compute the knowledge integration costs, which is too complicated to define since our approach is distributed data mining through the exchange of information during the decision making process.

The presented distributed mining process is evaluated by comparing the response times of DDM (RT_{ddm}) and SDM (RT_{sdm}) for the construction of the simple decision tree with two branches under the following assumptions:

T_{ddm} : Time of decision tree construction by each agent from its own local database.
T_{com} : Time of the communication between each agent and the mediator.
p : The number of records selected for analysis from database.
k : The number of fields selected for analysis from database.
n : The number of agents participated in mining process.
t_{tr} : Transmission Time (sec/bit)
r_c : Compressed rate for transmitted data.
t_{cpu} : CPU processing time for a component.

The entropy computation time of SDM is as follows:

$$RT_{sdm} = T_{sdm} = k \cdot p^2 \cdot t_{cpu} \tag{1}$$

On the other hand, since the given table is vertically partitioned into the same number of agents, the entropy computation time of DDM is as follows:

$$T_{ddm} = \frac{k \cdot p^2 \cdot t_{cpu}}{n} \tag{2}$$

When considering the communication time (T_{com}), the transmission data amount becomes $p \cdot r_c$ bits for the communication between each agent and the mediator. Therefore, the communication time is as follows:

$$T_{com} = p \cdot r_c \cdot t_{tr} \tag{3}$$

Through Equations of (2) and (3), the distributed processing time of DDM is as follows:

$$RT_{ddm} = \frac{k \cdot p^2 \cdot t_{cpu}}{n} + p \cdot r_c \cdot t_{tr} \tag{4}$$

Here, we get to a point ($RT_{sdm} - RT_{ddm} \geq 0$) where the performance of DDM becomes better than that of SDM.

Suppose that $RT_{sdm} - RT_{ddm}$ is ΔT , we can get Eq. 5 according to Eq. 1 and 4.

$$\Delta T(kp) = k \cdot p^2 \cdot t_{cpu} - \left(\frac{k \cdot p^2 \cdot t_{cpu}}{n} + p \cdot r_c \cdot t_{tr} \right) \tag{5}$$

To obtain the table size ($k * p$) when $\Delta T(kp) > 0$, we try to find the solution in Eq. 6.

$$k \cdot p^2 \cdot t_{cpu} - \left(\frac{k \cdot p^2 \cdot t_{cpu}}{n} + p \cdot r_c \cdot t_{tr} \right) \geq 0 \tag{6}$$

Eq. 6 is equivalent to 7,

$$p \left(\frac{(n-1)}{n} \cdot t_{cpu} \cdot kp - r_c \cdot t_{tr} \right) \geq 0 \tag{7}$$

Since $p > 0$, Eq. 7 is equivalent to 8,

$$\frac{(n-1)}{n} \cdot t_{cpu} \cdot kp - r_c \cdot t_{tr} \geq 0 \tag{8}$$

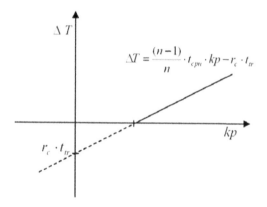

Fig. 3. The graph of response time (ΔT) in terms of kp

Fig. 3 represents a graph of Eq. 8 and shows that the performance of DDM becomes better at a certain size of data (kp) than that of SDM. We can say there are full benefits on the distributed processing if there are huge amounts of data.

4 Experimentation

Experimental data sets are synthetic data created by a random value generator specially developed for the purpose of the construction of decision trees. The software can generate any data set with different depths of decision trees and different numbers of records and fields in the databases. We vertically partitioned the generated data set into several subsets which correspond on agents located at different sites. With such data sets, we evaluate the performance of the proposed distributed data mining method under 10 experiments conducted by increasing the number of records in its local database, step by step, whereas the number of fields is fixed. Each experiment compares the performance, of the proposed system, altered with a different number of agents. Table 1 summarizes the performance of the system with a flexible number of agents throughout all experimentation.

The decision rule set generated in each experiment is exactly the same to that of a centralized data mining system, since the proposed algorithm for distributed data mining uses all the available data located at different sites, without moving them to each other. These decision rules are revealed simply because geographical data, easily discriminated on aerial images, are used in the experiments. In conclusion, the experimental results show that the distributed version with more agents outperforms the version with fewer agents when the rule generation from a large database is not complicated with low communication overhead between agents and the mediator.

Table 1. Experimental results

Experiment S tep	# of Recor ds	Processing Time (seconds)			
		None	2 agents	3 agents	4 agents
Exp 1.	0.3×10^5	11.7	6.3	3.2	2.1
Exp 2.	0.6×10^5	23.1	15.8	10.1	4.9
Exp 3.	0.1×10^6	35.2	23.2	15.4	10.7
Exp 4.	0.2×10^6	50.5	32.8	23.0	15.8
Exp 5.	0.3×10^6	62.8	38.8	31.4	21.8
Exp 6.	0.4×10^6	73.8	44.5	37.2	24.1
Exp 7.	0.5×10^6	89.6	55.7	42.2	33.8
Exp 8.	0.6×10^6	101.5	62.5	50.1	37.9
Exp 9.	0.7×10^6	121.8	71.6	53.8	44.9
Exp 10.	0.8×10^6	148.2	82.7	61.0	49.8

5   Conclusion and Future Work

Even though the concept of distributed data mining is very helpful in data analysis, there is a limitation for use in the real world due to its low performance. This paper presented a new paradigm of distributed data mining and its performance evaluation so that this technique can be applied to a specific situation. As hardware techniques are improving, this approach will be more useful for data analysis considering information security. As a future work, we plan to build a consortium of several agent based systems with a mediator-agents communication mechanism for more efficient data analysis in a distributed way. An example of the consortium system is presented in Fig 4.

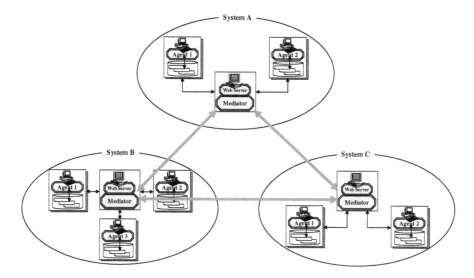

Fig. 4. Consortium of several agent based (distributed data mining) systems with a mediator-agents communication mechanism

References

1. Kamber, M., Winstone, L., Wan, G., Shan, S. and Jiawei, H.: Generalization and Decision Tree Induction: Efficient Classification in Data Mining, Proceedings of the Seventh International Workshop on Research Issues in Data Engineering, pp.111-120, 1997

2. Agrawal, S., Krishnan, V. and Haritsa, R. J.: On Addressing Efficiency Concerns in Privacy Preserving Mining, Lecture Notes in Computer Science, Vol. 2973, pp.113-124, 2004

3. Malvestuto, M. F. and Mezzini, M.: Privacy Preserving and Data Mining in an On-Line Statistical Database of Additive Type, Lecture Notes in Computer Science, Vol. 3050, pp. 353-365, 2004

4. Lindell, Y. and Pinkas, B.: Privacy Preserving Data Mining, Lecture Notes in Computer Science, Vol. 1880, 2000

5. Krishnaswamy, S., Zaslavsky, A. and Loke, S. W.: Techniques for Estimating the Computation and Communication Costs of Distributed Data Mining, Lecture Notes in Computer Science, Vol. 2329, pp. 603-612, 2002

6. Aggarwal, C. C. and Yu, P. S.: A Condensation Approach to Privacy Preserving Data Mining, Lecture Notes in Computer Science, Vol. 2992, pp. 183-199, 2004

7. Kargupta, H., Datta, S., Wang, Q. and Sivakumar, K.: On the privacy preserving properties of random data perturbation techniques, Proceedings of the Third IEEE International Conference on Data Mining, pp. 99-106, 2003

8. Stolfo, S., Prodromidis, A. L., Tselepis, S. and Lee, W.: JAM: Java Agents for Meta-Learning over Distributed Databases, Proceedings of the International Conference on Knowledge Discovery and Data Mining, pp. 74-81, 1997

9. Guo, Y. and Sutiwaraphun, J.: Knowledge probing in distributed data mining, In Advances in Distributed and Parallel Knowledge Discovery, 1999

10. Xu, L. and Jordan, M. I.: Em learning on a generalized finite mixture model for combining multiple classifiers, In Proceedings of World Congress on Neural Networks, 1993
11. Raftery, A. E., Madigan, D. and Hoeting, J. A.: Bayesian model averaging for linear regression models, Journal of the American Statistical Association, Vol. 92, pp. 179-191, 1996
12. Wolpert, D.: Stacked generalization, Neural Networks, Vol. 5, pp. 241-259, 1992
13. Caragea, D., Silvescu, A., and Honavar, V.: Decision Tree Induction from Distributed, Heterogeneous, Autonomous Data Sources, Proceedings of the Conference on Intelligent Systems Design and Applications (ISDA 03), 2003
14. Giannella, C., Liu, K., Olsen, T. and Kargupta, H.: Communication Efficient Construction of Decision Trees Over Heterogeneously Distributed Data, Proceedings of the Fourth IEEE International Conference on Data Mining(ICDM 04), pp. 67-74, 2004
15. Quinlan, J. R.: Induction of Decision Trees, Machine Learning, Vol. 1, pp. 81-106, 1986

Adjusting the Autonomy of Collections of Agents in Multiagent Systems

Michael Y.K. Cheng, Chris Micacchi, and Robin Cohen

School of Computer Science, University of Waterloo
(mycheng, cdmicacc, rcohen)@cs.uwaterloo.ca

1   Introduction

A topic of recent interest to researchers is designing multiagent systems that allow agents to reason about adjusting their autonomy, determining when and to whom control of decision making should be transferred (e.g. [2, 6]). What is lacking, however, is a method for integrating these individual adjustable autonomy algorithms into a cohesive solution for the delegation of tasks for the society. In this paper, we first discuss one approach that employs a central coordinating agent in order to not only adjust the levels of autonomy, but also ensure that there is coordination of this adjustment across all agents in the system. Fully autonomous agents elect to have their autonomy adjusted when faced with unexpected events that they are unable to resolve. The coordinating agent revokes the autonomy of other agents in the system, temporarily, in order to address these events. We discuss how this strategy for the adjustment of autonomy of agents is well suited for multiagent systems operating in soft real-time environments. We then present a model for agent-initiated adjustable autonomy that reasons not only about decision-making delegation, but also about interaction in order to make more informed decisions. Coordination of decision-making delegation amongst agents is addressed by a locking mechanism, while the provision for interaction allows run-time monitoring of the degree of bother of a potential resource/entity, resulting in possible refinements to the selection of entities to which decision making is delegated.

2   Coordinator-Based Adjustable Autonomy

The goal of this research [4] is to allow certain agents in soft real-time multiagent systems to continue to operate autonomously as much as possible, thereby reducing the amount of negotiation and communication required to address new tasks in the environment. We consider a scenario where an overall mission is first assigned to the multiagent system by a human user and each agent develops a well defined plan in order to address this mission, for the collective. The autonomy of the worker agents in the society needs to be adjusted, however, in cases where the worker encounters unexpected events that cannot simply be ignored, and that the agent cannot address by itself. In these cases, assistance is solicited from a coordinator agent, who may then revoke the autonomy of other agents, to address these new events.

In this research, we classify the possible kinds of unexpected events that may be encountered and include a definitive strategy for addressing each of these kinds of events

B. Kégl and G. Lapalme (Eds.): AI 2005, LNAI 3501, pp. 33–37, 2005.
© Springer-Verlag Berlin Heidelberg 2005

(some suggesting that agents simply continue to operate autonomously and others requiring that the agents defer to a more authoritative coordinating agent). The events include: opportunities (conditions that are not detrimental but may lead to new goals and plans being adopted; the worker can inform the coordinator of its new goal or defer decisions of what to do, to the coordinator); barriers (conditions that may prevent the worker from progressing with its goals; the worker can inform the coordinator of its new goal or defer to the coordinator to resolve the barrier); potential causes of failure (conditions, which, if not corrected, will cause failure in the future; the worker can generate a plan to handle the problem and inform the coordinator, or send the problem to the coordinator to handle).

The worker's control thread iterates quickly to allow fast response to problems. It must respond to *revoke autonomy* messages sent to it by the coordinator, must send *notification* messages to the coordinator if it adopts a new goal to address unexpected events, or send a *panic* message to the coordinator if it is unable to resolve a barrier or PCF. Workers also send *heartbeat* messages to the coordinator, at regular intervals, to register their current activities. The coordinator continuously merges state information from workers into a global state representation. It revokes the autonomy of agents selected to respond to *panics* sent by workers requiring assistance and provides new tasks to these agents. When agents sent to assist with new problems have completed their tasks, their autonomy is restored.

Overall then, the adjustable autonomy algorithm is one where an agent that cannot find a solution to a problem will give up its autonomy by asking the coordinator for assistance; it does not regain autonomy until the tasks assigned to it by the coordinator are completed. Likewise, an agent selected by the coordinator to assist with a task will have its autonomy revoked until that task is completed. This centralized method is particularly effective when agents have limited resources and it is best to offload decision making to a coordinating agent.

3   Coordinating Reasoning About Decision Transfers

In this section, we discuss a decentralized approach to adjustable autonomy, based on the Electric Elves (E-Elves) project [6], where agents compute a *transfer-of-control strategy*, specifying a sequence of decision-making control transfers to other entities (agents or humans), and how long the agent should wait for a response before giving up, and transferring control to another entity.

In our approach [1], we allow an agent to possibly query a user for information, but still retain decision-making authority. In addition, as in [2], we incorporate a bother cost factor into the model, to account for the user's annoyance at being interrupted by agents. Our agents will follow an *interaction strategy* that specifies what query to ask whom, for how long, and depending on the response, what to do next (e.g., ask another query, or make a decision). Visually, one can imagine a strategy as a tree, with two types of nodes, *query/internal nodes*, and *decision/leaf nodes*. A query node will have several branches corresponding to the various possible responses, with each branch leading to a strategy subtree. There are many possible paths of execution through a strategy tree.

The basic idea to determine an optimal strategy is for the agent to use a branch and bound search to generate all possible strategies containing up to a fixed number of queries K, evaluate the generated strategies, and then simply choose the best one.

The optimal strategy s^* is simply the generated strategy that is evaluated to have the highest expected utility (EU). The expected utility of a strategy s is calculated as follows:

$$EU(s) = \sum_{LN}[P(LN) \times (EQ(LN) - W(T_{LN}) - BC_{LN})]$$

where LN refers to a decision/leaf node, $EQ(LN)$ and $W(T_{LN})$ are adapted from E-Elves[6] and refer to the expected quality of the agent's decision at that particular leaf node, and the costs of waiting until the time of the leaf node to finish the interaction, respectively, and BC_{LN} is the cumulative bother cost incurred by all users queried along the path to the leaf node LN.

The expected utility of the overall strategy is a sum of the utility of each of the individual paths in it, factoring in the probability that the particular path will be taken. We denote this term as $P(LN)$, defined as follows: $P(LN) = \prod_{r_{j,k}} P_{Q_j}^{U_i}(resp = r_{j,k})$ where we iterate $r_{j,k}$ over all the response branches that lead to the leaf node LN, and $P_{Q_j}^{U_i}(resp = r_{j,k})$ refers to the probability of user U_i responding with $r_{j,k}$ to the question Q_j.

One of the main criteria for querying one user over another is the user's $PUK_{Q_j}^{U_i}$ value, denoting the probability that user U_i knows the answer to question Q_j (as in [2]). Another criterion is the user's $PR_{Q_j}^{U_i}(t)$ value, denoting the probability distribution over time that U_i responds to Q_j at time point t (as in [6]). The three possible cases for how to compute the value of $P_{Q_j}^{U_i}(resp = r_{j,k})$, are as follows:

[No response]: $P_{Q_j}^{U_i}(resp = r_{j,\neg resp}) = 1 - \int_{T_s}^{T_e} PR_{Q_j}^{U_i}(t)dt$

["I don't know"]: $P_{Q_j}^{U_i}(resp = r_{j,?}) = \int_{T_s}^{T_e} PR_{Q_j}^{U_i}(t)dt \times (1 - PUK_{Q_j}^{U_i})$

[Answer response]: $P_{Q_j}^{U_i}(resp = r_{j,a}) = \int_{T_s}^{T_e} PR_{Q_j}^{U_i}(t)dt \times PUK_{Q_j}^{U_i} \times PA(r_{j,a})$

where T_s is the time point at which the question was asked, and T_e is the time point that the agent will wait until for a response, and $PA(r_{j,a})$ denotes the probability that the answer to question Q_j is $r_{j,a}$. Note that $\int_{T_s}^{T_e} PR_{Q_j}^{U_i}(t)dt$ gives the probability of U_i responding to Q_j during time frame $[T_s, T_e]$.

In the more general case, an agent will be reasoning not only about interactions with other entities (termed "partial" transfers of control or PTOCs, since decision-making control will still rest with the agent who initiates the interaction), but also about transferring decision making control entirely to another entity (termed "full" transfer of control or FTOC). This results in what we refer to as a "hybrid" transfer-of-control strategy for the agent, with each agent selecting the strategy that will maximize the expected utility.

In a multiagent system, we encounter the problem that locally planned optimal strategies may not be globally optimal. In particular, a major problem is that many agents may transfer control to the same user for the same time period, leading to excessive user bother and lower user response rate. We now consider a possible mechanism for coordinating agent strategies as follows. We first of all assume that each user in the system will have a corresponding proxy agent, and that requests to query a user will go through the proxy. Now assume that in response to a request from an agent, the proxy can impose a lock for a given time period $[t_a, t_b]$, for its user and can ensure that no new locks will be provided to other requesting agents within the specified timeframe, until the lock is released. In addition, for any agent that requires a lock before t_a, the proxy will refuse to grant a lock[1]. Any agent requiring a lock after t_b, will be allowed to, but with a warning that there may be additional bother generated from earlier interactions with that user by the first agent.

One challenge is that the agent that locks up the user for a given timeframe may in fact not make use of that resource at all, if it is successful in a full control transfer to another entity earlier in its transfer of control strategy. So, other agents that are requesting locks on the user for later timeframes will not know for sure whether the user will have incurred some bother from previous interactions or not.

The locking mechanism for agent strategy coordination then works as follows: (i) *Agent* computes an optimal strategy s^* (ii) *Agent* tries to acquire from the various proxies all the locks that may be used in strategy s^*. So, for each transfer node in s^*, *Agent* will request a lock on the user and timeframe indicated by that transfer node. As part of the lock request, *Agent* will inform the *Proxy* of the probability that *Agent* will reach/use that lock. (iii.a) *Agent* receives all requested locks with no warnings. Then, *Agent* can just start executing strategy s^*. (iii.b) *Agent* receives all requested locks but is given warnings by one or more of the proxies. Each warning informs the *Agent* that there is an earlier lock that may be used with a certain probability. Then, *Agent* may need to adjust the strategy s^* so that *Agent* will first check with the proxy on whether or not the user really has been bothered earlier, before transferring control to the user, or to some other entity. (iii.c) *Agent* does not receive all the requested locks, due to conflicts with existing locks. Then, *Agent* goes back to step [i] and recomputes the next best strategy that does not involve the conflicts.

With the use of locks and the facility for interaction, it is now possible for an agent to avoid simply transferring control to another entity that is ill-disposed to reply to its request. Instead, when an agent plans to transfer control to a user, it will first obtain a lock on that user, to ensure that the user will be free to respond during the required timeframe. In addition, an agent can decide to forgo trying to transfer control to a user, by being sensitive to accumulating bother costs: if the agent is warned by the proxy that there is an earlier lock that might have been exercised (hence increasing bother cost) and the agent reasons that the extra bother cost makes it worthwhile for it to change its strategy (e.g., transferring control to someone else). What this enables, therefore, is a much more accurate estimate of the expected utility of a transfer-of-control strategy than is possible in a framework such as E-Elves ([6]). Each agent's adjustable autonomy algorithm now considers how other agents may be affecting the resources (i.e., users) it is competing for; factors such as the bother cost to the user may be monitored to determine if it is better to transfer to others.

Consider the following scenario: $Agent_A$ reasons a strategy s_A involving transferring to John at time [3,10]. $Agent_A$ requests a lock on John during time [3,10] from

---

[1] This is to ensure that this second agent does not generate bother for the user that the first agent cannot anticipate. Less stringent locks are possible; details are omitted here.

John's proxy agent (denoted as $Proxy$). There are currently no conflicting locks on John, so $Proxy$ grants the lock to $Agent_A$. This guarantees to $Agent_A$ that John will be free at time [3,10] and moreover, that John will have the expected bother cost (ie: John will not have been bothered earlier than time point 3). Now suppose $Agent_B$ reasons a strategy s_B involving transferring to John at time point [15,20]. $Agent_B$ requests a lock on John from $Proxy$. $Proxy$ grants the lock, but warns $Agent_B$ that John may or may not have been bothered earlier with a certain probability (the probability that $Agent_A$ uses the lock). $Agent_B$ may then reason that it is good to do a PTOC at time point around 15 (assuming that proxy agents respond very quickly) and check with $Proxy$ first before transferring control to John, in case John was already bothered. If John was bothered already, then it decides to transfer to others. Note: we say $Agent_B$ *may* reason to alter its strategy, because depending on the example scenario, the best strategy for $Agent_B$ may still be to transfer control to John anyway, even with the higher bother cost (in which case, there's no need for a PTOC).

4   Discussion

Our coordinator-based approach relates well to that of Scerri et al. [5], that employs proxies to help to allocate new tasks. Our approach of relying on communication to detect when tasks are completed and to prevent conflicting commands through centralization is encouraged by the crew proxy approach of Schreckenghost et al. [7]. Our model for coordinating transfer-of-control strategies to be sensitive to possible bother to users is motivated by the work of Fleming [2] on modeling bother. Its locking strategy contrasts with that of Martin et al. [3], proposed as a user-driven method for coordinating agent actions. In short, our research aims to advance the state of research in the design of adjustable autonomy agents, to consider collectives of agents.

References

1. M. Cheng and R. Cohen. Reasoning about Interaction in a Multi-User System. In *Proceedings of the Tenth International Conference on User Modeling*, July 24-29 2005.
2. M. Fleming and R. Cohen. A Decision Procedure for Autonomous Agents to Reason About Interaction With Humans. In *The AAAI 2004 Spring Symposium on Interaction between Humans and Autonomous Systems over Extended Operation*, pages 81–86, 2004.
3. C. Martin, D. Schreckenghost, and R. Bonasso. Augmenting Automated Control Software to Interact with Multiple Humans. In *Proceeedings of AAAI04 Spring Symposium on Interaction Between Humans*, 2004.
4. C. Micacchi. An Architecture for Multi-Agent Systems Operating in Soft Real-Time Environments With Unexpected Events. Master's thesis, University of Waterloo, Waterloo, Canada, 2004.
5. P. Scerri, L. Johnson, D. Pynadath, P. Rosenbloom, M. Si, N. Schurr, and M. Tambe. A prototype infrastructure for distributed robot-agent-person teams. In *AAMAS-03*, 2003.
6. P. Scerri, D. Pynadath, and M. Tambe. Adjustable Autonomy for the Real World. In *Agent Autonomy*. Kluwer Publishers, 2004.
7. D. Schreckenghost, C. Martin, P. Bonasso, D. Kortenkamp, T. Miliam, and C. Thronesbery. Supporting Group Interaction Among Humans and Autonomous Agents. In *Proceedings of the AAAI2002 Workshop on Autonomy, Delegation, and Control: From Inter-agent to Groups*, pages 72–77, Menlo Park, CA, 2002. AAAI Press.

ARES 2: A Tool for Evaluating Cooperative and Competitive Multi-agent Systems

Jörg Denzinger and Jordan Kidney

Dep. of Computer Science, University of Calgary
{denzinge, kidney}@cpsc.ucalgary.ca

Abstract. The Agent Rescue Emergency Simulator (ARES) system provides a simplified rescue scenario similar to Robocup Rescue for use in the educational or research fields when evaluating multi-agent systems. The environment within ARES abstracts ideas down to key features while still allowing for a wide range of scenarios requiring different skills to be presented to the agents. This is achieved by combining different features together and changing the configuration of the environmental rules incorporated in ARES. With the simplified environment ARES can be used for quick evaluations of concepts based upon the results from a range of different configurations of the system. The results from these tests can be used as a basis for further experiments when transitioning the work from a theoretical level to more real world scenarios, where the requirement for a more complex system is needed. Our newest version of ARES, ARES 2, allows for scenarios that range from cooperation between all agents to strong competitiveness of agents or even agent teams.

1 Introduction

The Agent Rescue Emergency Simulator (ARES) system (see [4, 2]) provides a simplified rescue scenario similar to Robocup Rescue (see [5, 6]). The Robocup initiatives helped to expand the field of multi-agent systems, bringing many different areas together in a single competition. From this initiative, a set of simulators was produced for the competitions, allowing the agents to interact without robotic bodies. These simulators also provided a consistent environment for evaluating teams entered in the competition. Slowly these simulators have started to find their way into the research and educational fields (see [1, 3]), but several problems have surfaced. One such problem is the fact that the simulators were created for a very specific application, mainly the environment needed for the competition. As a result, the range of concepts that can be demonstrated is limited to what the competition required. What is needed now is to extend upon the success of the simulators from the Robocup initiatives, but with the main goal of providing a flexible testbed for the research and educational communities, allowing for the quick evaluation of new concepts in multi-agent systems. Our solution to this problem is the ARES system, which follows the same ideas as Robocup rescue, but focuses on providing a very flexible environment that can be tailored to particular research or educational needs.

The basic ideas realized in ARES 2 are as follows. The environment simulated within ARES 2 is a city after an earthquake has struck (similar to Robocup rescue).

B. Kégl and G. Lapalme (Eds.): AI 2005, LNAI 3501, pp. 38–42, 2005.

The components of the environment have been simplified down to what we consider to be the basic features relevant for multi-agent systems. As such we do not concentrate upon providing an environment to simulate real world scenarios, but one that concentrates on providing an area for demonstrating a range of different concepts. This allows us to break some real world rules with the main goal of allowing a range of concepts that can be demonstrated through the use of the system.

Next for the agents there are two basic tasks, finding survivors and rescuing them, that emphasize the need for independent exploration, coordination, and cooperation between agents. Agents have a rather limited set of actions, including the ability to communicate and they act within a world that is more or less known to them. The agents acting in a scenario in ARES 2 might be one team or they can be in several teams, thus allowing various combinations of cooperation aspects and competition aspects.

A key concept in ARES 2 are the so-called world rules that result in configuring key features of the ARES 2 world scenarios. Selecting a set of world rules essentially creates basic requirements on the agents and the scenarios using this set of rules. And if we assume that we want to develop agents and their interactions in such a way as to optimize their task performance, then different sets of world rules create different agent goals and different requirements on what is a good behavior. This achieves a high flexibility for the use of ARES 2 to evaluate teams of agents, since we can target particular aspects of multi-agent systems by choosing the right set of world rules. Features that are influenced by world rules include competitiveness between agent teams, cost of communication, precision of world information and observability of the world, or fulfilling the basic survival needs of agents.

So far, ARES and ARES 2 have been mostly used in educational settings, although several researchers have expressed an interest in them for evaluating agent teams using particular concepts. In the educational setting, the possibility of changing world rules has proved very useful, since plagiarism essentially is eliminated. With the addition of world rules influencing the competitiveness and interaction possibilities of several agent teams acting in the same scenario in ARES 2, concepts like trust and communication outside of the own team can now also be evaluated with ARES simulations.

2   ARES 2: Basic Ideas

For a more technical explanation of the ARES System, please refer to [4, 2].

2.1   The Environment

The environment simulated within ARES 2 is based upon a city that has been hit by an earthquake. This is very similar to Robocup Rescue, but the objects within the world and the actions that can been taken have been simplified down to what we consider to be the basic features relevant for multi-agent systems. Now depending upon the configuration of the system the agents will either have the ability to work with all the agents currently connected to the system or only with agents that have been declared as part of their group. This allows for the creation of environmental rules that can push the interaction between teams of agents from a cooperative scenario to a more competitive environment. Agents within the system interact within a two dimensional grid environment built up of squares. Each square in the grid represents a single point where an agent can influence the environment directly. The agents "jump" from square to square as they move throughout the world. Each square in the world has the following properties:

1. It can be of one of the following types: (1) Normal - agents can safely move onto the square. (2) Fire - the entire square is on fire. (3) Killer - represents a zone where agents will die (like holes, etc ...) and finally (4) Charging - a zone that can be used to regain lost energy
2. It consists of a stack of layers (build up of material), where each layer holds only a single object. Currently there are only three types of objects in the ARES system: (1) Rubble - represents material that has to be removed by the agents. Each rubble object has as associated value the number of agents that are needed to remove this object. This forces agents to coordinate and come together upon the same square in the world at the same time to remove the object. (2)Survivor - a single person that can be saved in the world. When they are saved, the survivors are simply "beamed" to safety. (3) Survivor Group - this is the same as a survivor, it just allows for multiple survivors to be located in a single layer on the stack.
3. Each square also has an associated move cost value; this value indicates the cost in energy for moving onto the square from any direction

In general, the interaction of an agent with ARES 2 consists of the agent sending messages indicating its actions (including any communication actions to other agents) to ARES 2 when they are informed that it is their turn to run. Once ARES 2 has given all agents a chance to run and send an action it then applies all the actions to the current state of the environment. Next each agent is informed about the results of their actions (if a reply is expected). This process is repeated until the specified number of simulation steps has been met. For the agents in the environment, each action that they take has a corresponding consequence based upon the type of action that is being taken. In the ARES 2 system, agent actions fall into two groups: (1) Actions that influence the environment directly. These actions include things such as moving around, removing rubble, etc. With the execution of these actions the agents lose energy, as a result the agents must manage their energy usage and when they must recharge. (2) Communication/Observational actions. Actions such as communication and observing squares in other areas of the world fall into this group. With the execution of these actions the agents have to deal with things such as communication delays and distortion of information.

2.2   World Rules, Environment Features, and Their Connection to Multi-agent Systems

As already stated, a major goal in the development of ARES and ARES 2 was to provide a lot of possibilities of how to configure the environment to allow for different foci on the general problems of multi-agent systems. ARES 2 achieves this by implementing different so-called world rules that describe how effects in the environment can be or have to be achieved by the agents. This is possible in ARES 2, because of the rather simplified worlds that agents are acting in within ARES 2.

By combining the selected world rules for different world features, the resulting environment will require rather different strategies by the agents to be successful. And these strategies will focus on different aspects of the agents, of their implementation, and of how the agents interact. The world features new in ARES 2 (compared to ARES) are how to deal with different agent teams interacting in the same simulation run. For example, by allowing multiple distinct teams to participate in the simulation the agents are presented with a competitive environment to work in. By changing the way scoring is done for saving survivors the ways that agents from different teams work together will change. By giving the point to all who participate it gives the opportunity for all agents to work together and gain a mutual benefit. If we just change the scoring to give the point to the team who had the most participants in the save action then the environment becomes a little bit more hostile for agents from different teams to work together and always gain a mutual benefit. The main world features influenced by world rules in ARES 2 are as follows:

1. Score for saving survivors - changes to this feature effect the competitiveness of the environment.
2. Single or multiple teams in the simulation - cooperative vs competitive environment.
3. Maximum number of agents required to remove rubble - causes the agents to deal with resource allocation issues by having to get other agents to help in the removal of the rubble object.
4. Energy Control - agents need to deal with monitoring their energy level and regaining energy back as it is needed. In some configurations of the system this becomes a resource allocation issue as the agents may have to move onto a specific square in the world to regain energy.
5. Communication - changes in how the agents communicate effect everything from agent models and cooperation concepts to resource allocation. For example, by limiting the amount of communication an agent can do in one step, the number of steps needed to get help for a rubble removal can become higher and the general task more difficult.

It should be noted that individual features can be influenced by several world rules, which allows us to provide a large variety of feature instantiations.

3   Experimental Evaluation

So far, our experiences with ARES and ARES 2 have been in the educational field. The ARES system has been used for the past three years at the graduate level –once at the undergraduate level– for courses on multi agent systems at the University of Calgary. Feedback from the students has shown a positive image of the ARES system. The system has provided a consistent way to compare the agents produced by different teams in the class. Each time the class has been taught different configurations of the world rules have been used to present the students with a different challenge while still working in the common rescue environment. Another reason for the change in the world rules has been to prevent the "reuse" issue of students using everything from agents produced in previous versions of the class. The thought behind these variations is to make an environment where agents that in one year would not work properly in the newly changed environment. This would mean that they would be slower at finishing tasks, or would be at a greatly elevated risk of dieing off faster. The students could look at old designs but would have to develop their own ideas and implementation to deal with the new environment. Each time the multi-agent course has been taught there has been a noticeable improvement in the quality of the agents produced by the students. Students in the latest version of the class were able to take into account faults and observed problems of the teams from previous years and could improve upon the concepts successful in previous years in their own way. Overall many positive results have come from using the ARES and ARES 2 system in the course and not only were the students rather enthusiastic about applying what they have learned in the lectures to a scenario where even the instructor did not know exactly what the best concepts would be, concepts have been developed that have the potential to be used in more realistic testbeds or scenarios.

4   Conclusion

We presented the ARES 2 system, a testbed for evaluating multi-agent systems that was motivated by the Robocup initiatives, but aims at providing much more flexibility in the environments it offers to the agents. ARES 2 in particular introduced the ability of having scenarios with several competing teams interacting at the same time and allowing for some cooperation between these teams. While this is rather common in the real world, the known testbeds for multi-agent systems, including the Robocup testbeds do not offer this possibility. Our use of ARES and ARES 2 as testbed for systems build as assignments for multi-agent courses showed that the simplified worlds of ARES make it rather easy to build agents for ARES. In the future, we want to make ARES even more flexible by adding more world rules, respectively more instantiations of the current ones. We also hope to attract other researchers to use ARES not only in educational settings, but also to evaluate their research results at a higher level.

References

1. Paul Buhler, José M. Vidal. Biter: A platform for the teaching and research of multiagent systems' design using robocup, Proceedings of the Robocup International Symposium, 2001.
2. Jörg Denzinger, Jordan Kidney, Melissa Bergen. Teaching Cooperation in Multi-Agent Systems with the help of the ARES System, Proc. WCCCE-03, Courtenay, 2003.
3. F. Heintz, J. Kummeneje. Simulated robocup in university undergraduate education, technical report., Department of Computer and Information Science, Linkoping University, 2000.
4. Jordan Kidney. ARES Website http://www.cpsc.ucalgary.ca/kidney/ARES (as viewed on March 8, 2004).
5. RoboCup Rescue. http://jelly.cs.kobe-u.ac.jp/robocup-rescue/ (as viewed on Nov 24, 2003).
6. RoboCup. http://www.robocup.org/ (as viewed on Nov 24, 2003).

Multiagent Systems Viewed as Distributed Scheduling Systems: Methodology and Experiments

Sébastien Paquet, Nicolas Bernier, and Brahim Chaib-draa

DAMAS Laboratory, Department of Computer Science,
and Software Engineering, Laval University, Canada
{spaquet, bernier, chaib}@damas.ift.ulaval.ca

Abstract. In this article, we present a design technique that facilitates the work of extracting and defining the tasks scheduling problem for a multiagent system. We also compare a centralized scheduling approach to a decentralized scheduling approach to see the difference in the efficiency of the schedules and the amount of information transmitted between the agents. Our experimental results show that the decentralized approach needs less messages, while being as efficient as the centralized approach.

1 Introduction

In this short paper, we present how a multiagent problem can be modelled as a task scheduling problem and how this formulation can help to find good scheduling algorithms. We define scheduling as the problem of assigning limited resources to tasks over time to optimize one or more objectives [1]. Furthermore, in multiagent systems, the scheduling can be done in a centralized or decentralized way [2] and in this article we study the impact on the agents' efficiency and on the amount of information transmitted when using these two approaches.

2 Modelling of the Tasks Scheduling System

In a tasks scheduling system, we use a set of resources to accomplish a set of tasks in an order maximizing an optimization criterion [3]. For example, we could want to accomplish the set of tasks as fast as possible or we could want to accomplish as many tasks as possible in a given time. This article focuses on multiagent systems in which the work of some agents can be described as a tasks scheduling system. So, agents are considered as resources that can complete tasks. Evidently, not all multiagent systems can be modelled as a task scheduling system. However, it can be possible in several cases, because in many multiagent systems, agents have to accomplish tasks and the order of these tasks influences the efficiency of the system. To structure the modeling process, we present a methodology with three steps: (1) scheduling problem definition, (2) scheduler type definition and (3) scheduling algorithm definition.

B. Kégl and G. Lapalme (Eds.): AI 2005, LNAI 3501, pp. 43–47, 2005.
© Springer-Verlag Berlin Heidelberg 2005

2.1   First Step: Scheduling Problem Definition

Firstly, we have to identify the characteristics of the scheduling problem which consists of defining the set of tasks to execute, the tasks' parameters (execution cost, deadline, etc.) and the optimization criterion. When the scheduling problem has been carefully analyzed, we can formalize it using the following notation [4]. A scheduling problem, with the goal of managing a set of tasks T, is described with three fields separated with the character "|", as in: $\alpha \mid \beta \mid \gamma$.

- α : the machines' environment. This field tells how many machines are present and what their characteristics are.
  - 1 :   Mono-machine environment.
  - P_m :   Multi-machines environment with m machines.
- β : the constraints and the characteristics. This field tells for example, if the tasks have deadlines or if there is a cost to change from one task to another.
  - p_j :   The execution cost of the task j.
  - d_j :   The deadline of the task j.
  - s_{jk} : The cost to change from task j to task k.
- γ : the optimization criterion. This field defines what the scheduler is supposed to optimize.
  - $\sum C_j$: The sum of completion times of all tasks.
  - $\sum U_j$: The sum of unit penalty of all tasks where:

$$U_j = \begin{cases} 1 & \text{if } C_j > d_j \\ 0 & \text{if not} \end{cases}$$

2.2   Second Step: Scheduler Type Definition

The scheduler, in a scheduling system, represents the abstraction level where the tasks ordering is decided in order to maximize the optimization criterion. We can create two main categories of scheduler: centralized and decentralized.

In the centralized approach, the tasks ordering is done by only one agent. This agent has to schedule and distribute the tasks for all the agents. To do that, it needs a global knowledge of the environment that it can acquire by exploration or by inter-agent communication.

In the distributed approach, the tasks ordering is not the responsibility of one agent, but many agents. All agents schedule their own tasks according to what they know about the environment. However, to stay coordinated, they need to synchronize themselves using inter-agent communication.

2.3   Third Step: Scheduling Algorithm Definition

In this third step, we have to choose the task scheduling algorithm to solve the problem defined in the first step. Many optimal and approximation algorithms already exist in the literature to solve different types of scheduling problems [5]. This shows the advantage of formalizing a multiagent problem in a scheduling formalism because, by doing so, we can search in the scheduling theory literature to find good algorithms for our problem.

3   Application to a Multiagent Problem

In this section, we show how to use our methodology in a multiagent system (the RoboCupRescue simulation) by explaining all the steps and specially focus on the scheduler part. This simulation environment consists of a simulation of an earthquake happening in a city [6]. The goal of the agents (representing firefighters, policemen and ambulance teams) is to minimize the damages caused by a big earthquake, such as civilians buried, buildings on fire and roads blocked.

In this article, we focus only on the work of the ambulance team agents. In the simulation there can be between 0 to 8 ambulance team agents that are in charge of rescuing civilians. The civilians are wounded when they are buried in collapsed buildings and they can die if they are not rescued fast enough. Rescuing a civilian is considered as a task and since the health state of a civilian is uncertain, the parameters of the tasks could change in time. Also, there are important constraints on the communications, thus it becomes critical to manage them efficiently.

3.1   Step 1: Scheduling Problem Definition

To rescue as many civilians as possible, ambulance team agents have to make a choice about in which order they will try to rescue the civilians. In this context, the task's duration is the time needed to save a civilian and the deadline of a task is the civilian's estimated death time.

Formally, our problem can be expressed as: $P_m|s_{jk}|\sum U_j$. The problem as it is defined has been proven to be NP-Hard [7]. Thus, we have to relax some constraints and make some changes to the original problem so that it can become solvable in polynomial time. First, we have relaxed the s_{jk} constraint by giving a value of 0 for each s_{jk} and by adding a constant travel time to the rescuing time. We also modified the scheduling problem definition by setting $m = 1$. In other words, it means that we consider that we have only one agent. Since this is not true, in practice it will result in all agents working on the same civilian because, for the scheduler, the group of agents is only seen as one indivisible resource.

Formally, our new problem can now be defined as: $1||\sum U_j$, which means that we consider a centralized execution in which all agents are considered to be one big resource working on one task at a time and trying to maximize the number of tasks accomplished in the time allowed.

3.2   Step 2: Scheduler Type Definition

In this step, we must choose between centralized and distributed scheduling. For this article, we compare both approaches in order to schedule the tasks of the ambulance team agents in the RoboCupRescue simulation.

In this article, we propose an implementation for each one of the two approaches and we compare their performance on the efficiency of the schedule and on the required amount of communication. Both approaches use the same scheduling algorithm, i.e. EDD (Earliest Due Date) [8]; we will justify this choice in section 3.3. This greedy algorithm orders a set of tasks by sorting them in increasing order of their deadline. An interesting property of this algorithm is that it is possible to have a distributed version that does not lose any efficiency.

With a centralized scheduler, there is one agent taking alone the decision about the ordering of the tasks. In brief, the steps of the scheduling process are:

1. All agents send their perceptions about possible tasks to the scheduler agent.
2. The scheduler agent combines all the information received.
3. The scheduler agent applies the EDD algorithm to schedule the tasks.
4. The scheduler agent sends the best global task to all agents.

As we can see, at step 1 all the agents send the information they know about all possible tasks. These messages can be quite long. Afterwards, at step 4, the scheduler agent sends the best global task to all agents, which then accomplish it.

In the decentralized approach, the scheduler is an entity composed of many agents. In brief, the steps of the scheduling process are:

1. All agents build their own list of possible tasks.
2. All agents apply the EDD algorithm to find the best local task to accomplish.
3. All agents broadcast their best local task to all other ambulance team agents.
4. All agents build a list with all the best local tasks received.
5. All agents apply EDD to find the best global task to accomplish.

As we can see, agents send messages only at step 3 and those messages are quite small because they contain only the information about one task.

3.3   Step 3: Scheduling Algorithm Definition

In the preceding step, we have already identified the scheduling algorithm, which is EDD. This algorithm can be executed in time $O(nlog_n)$ [9]. This type of greedy algorithm is well adapted to a problem of decentralized decision making because it is never necessary to reconsider a decision previously made. This enables us in practice to find the next task to accomplish in time $O(n)$. This algorithm is interesting because it is optimal if there is no overload, i.e. it is possible to accomplish all the tasks in the given time. Although some overload could happen in our environment, the performances of this algorithm stay good and its simplicity enables us to demonstrate how we can distribute the decision making in a scheduling system.

4   Results

The goal of these tests is to compare the performances and the communication burden of the decentralized scheduling approach compared to the centralized approach. For our experiments, we have created six different simulation scenarios.

Figure 1 presents the comparison between the performances of each approach. The centralized approach is slightly better in five scenarios out of six. However, this difference is really subtle and if we consider the 95% confidence interval, the two approaches can be considered equal.

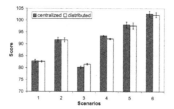

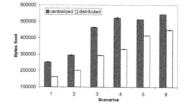

Fig. 1. Performances   **Fig. 2.** Number of bytes sent

However, the diminution of the communication burden is really at the advantage of the decentralized approach. Figure 2 presents the comparison of the number of bytes sent by the agents. On average, there is a 30% reduction of the quantity of information sent. This is mainly because the agents do not have to send all the information they know, but only the most interesting task.

5   Conclusion

In short, we have presented a methodology that can take advantage of algorithms developed in scheduling theory and to apply them in multiagent settings. Conversely, we have shown how we can use some multiagent ideas to decentralized a scheduling algorithm and gain on the amount of information transmitted.

We have demonstrated the efficiency of the decentralized approach in a complex environment (partially observable, uncertain and real-time). In brief, the decentralized approach is able to obtain the same performance with 30% less information sent. Future work could be to also distribute the execution and thus enabling the agents to be split on more than one problem at a time.

References

1. Mali, A.D., Kambhampati, S.: Distributed Planning. In: The Encyclopaedia of Distributed Computing. Kluwer Academic Publishers (1999)
2. Durfee, E.H.: Distributed Problem Solving and Planning. In Weiss, G., ed.: Multiagent Systems: A Modern Approach to Distributed Artificial Intelligence. The MIT Press, Cambridge, MA (1999) 121–164
3. French, S.: Sequencing and Scheduling. Wiley (1982)
4. Lawer, E., Lenstra, J., Kan, A.R.: Recent developments in deterministic sequencing scheduling : A servey. Deterministic and Stochastic Scheduling (1982) 35–74
5. Blazewick, J.: Scheduling computer and manufacturing processes. Springer (2001)
6. Kitano, H.: Robocup rescue: A grand challenge for multi-agent systems. In: Proceedings of ICMAS 2000, Boston, MA (2000)
7. Pinedo, M.: Scheduling: Theory, Algorithms and Systems. Prentice Hall (1995)
8. Jackson, J.R.: Scheduling a production line to minimize maximum tardiness. Research Report 43, Management Science, University of California (1955)
9. Brucker, P.: Scheduling Algorithms. Springer (2001)

Planning for a Mobile Robot to Attend a Conference

Eric Beaudry, Froduald Kabanza, and Francois Michaud

Université de Sherbrooke, Sherbrooke, Canada
{eric.beaudry, froduald.kabanza, francois.michaud}@usherbrooke.ca

Abstract. The AAAI Mobile Robot Challenge requires robots to start from the entrance of the conference site, find their own way to the registration desk, socially interact with people and perform volunteer duties as required, then report at a prescribed time in a conference hall to give a talk and answer questions. These specifications convey some interesting planning problems that appear to be too complex for some of the most efficient AI planning systems that we analyzed. Based on this analysis, we present a new planning approach that we are developing to meet the challenge. Preliminary results show that our approach performs much better on robot conference planning problems than any of the other AI planning systems we tested.

1   Introduction

The AAAI Mobile Robot Challenge, introduced in 1999, is to have a robot start at the entrance of the conference site, find the registration desk, register, perform volunteer duties and give a presentation [6]. The long-term objective is to have robots receive no more information than usually given to human participants attending the conference. These specifications imply that robots must be able to plan tasks, such as registering, navigating to the presentation room and making a presentation, while at the same time interacting with people, ensuring its energetic autonomy and accepting duties.

We plan to participate in the 2005 AAAI Challenge. For this endeavour, we have been developing a planning system to be integrated with the basic robot behavior-producing modules to recommend tasks the robot should be working on at a given point of execution. Planning problems we are dealing with involve metric time constraints (e.g., the robot has to be on time for it presentation), resource constraints (e.g., complex robot processes such as navigation, map registration and planning consume more battery power), safety goals generated reactively at unpredicted times (e.g., charging the battery whenever it becomes low), preferences among goals (e.g., it is more critical to charge the battery than doing anything else; or presenting the paper on time has priority over helping other attendees) and uncertainty in plan execution (e.g., the time it takes to navigate from one point to another depends on the accuracy of the robot's navigation behaviour).

The decisions about which features are to be handled using an automated planning system and which ones are to be managed by the robot behavior-producing modules are ultimately a matter of design choice, depending on the capabilities of the planning system being used. We may choose to ignore uncertainty during the planning phase, and handle it at the level of the robot architecture, by generating deterministic plans

B. Kégl and G. Lapalme (Eds.): AI 2005, LNAI 3501, pp. 48–52, 2005.

that are sequences of actions, and monitoring failures to re-invoke the planner whenever necessary, as is done with Xavier [4]. It is also conceivable not to involve any automated planning at all and still manage to make the robot accomplish complex tasks, as did many teams participating in previous AAAI Challenges [8].

In our case, we have decided to include some form of planning to increase modularity by having automatically behaviors. This should facilitate reconfigurations of the robot onsite as well as adaptation of the robot to new applications that are similar to existing ones. Experimenting with existing probabilistic and nondeterministic planners such as SGP [12] and MBP [1] to handle some degree of uncertainty, we observed that they do not scale up to the complexity of problems in the AAAI Challenge. Using deterministic planners (SAPA [2], Metric-FF [5] and SHOP2 [9], which are among today's most efficient planning systems) and assuming an interleaving of execution monitoring and re-planning for failure situations, the performance observed revealed also to be insufficient.

A planning problem is in general both an action selection problem (i.e., selecting actions relevant to the goal) and a scheduling problem (i.e., assigning resources to actions, include time resource) [11]. The problem of planning to attend a conference is more biased towards scheduling then towards action selection, whereas the planners we tested are biased towards action selection or task decomposition. Based on these observations we designed a planner that has a task scheduling bias (i.e., it more often tries to assign tasks to time windows than examining alternate task decomposition methods). It combines HTN decomposition from SHOP2 [9], with plan post-processing ideas from SAPA [2], to obtain plans with time window execution flexibilities. Preliminary results show that our algorithm performs much better than the others, with a sufficient level of performance that will complement other decision modules embedded in the robot's decison-making architecture.

2   Robot Platform

The robot platform we intend to use is the U2S robot (see Figure 1a), developed at Université de Sherbrooke. It will be equipped with autonomous navigation capabilities using a laser SICK range finder, visual recognition of badges, faces and people, audio sound source localization and separation capabilities, and a graphical tactile interface. The decision-making architecture is based on EMIB [7] (see Figure 1b). EMIB's behavior-producing modules (BPM) are essentially processes that produce commands that directly control the robot's actuators. Primitive tasks are conceptually similar to abstract primitive tasks [9] or actions [2] in AI planning, with the key difference that in EMIB they are not directly executable by the robot. Rather, they are interpreted as recommendations in determining what BPM are desirable and which ones are not, and these recommendations compete with recommendations from other recommendation modules, using an emotion/intentional arbitration metaphor, to produce the actual robot commands.

From a planning application point of view, many robot architectures have already integrated task planning and robot execution, including the Procedural Reasoning System (PRS) [3] and Xavier [4]. Our approach differs with these approaches by having

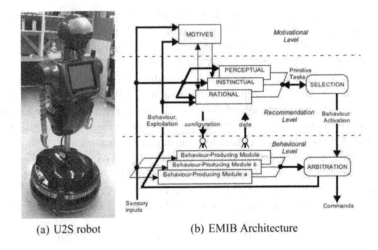

(a) U2S robot   (b) EMIB Architecture

Fig. 1. Our robotics platform and decision mechanism

the planner more tightly coupled with the underlying behaviour-based architecture. Our planner competes with the other robot components that recommend its basic actions, hence preserving the design principles of behaviour-based robot programming. This in line with the proposal in [10], but our approach is more general in that EMIB decouples behavior activation conditions from the corresponding actuators. Therefore, the planner is not a central component of the architecture, of which all the decisions will be based. This limitation of the scope of intervention of the planner allows us to use other mechanisms more suitable to handle unpredictable events. Integrating a planner into EMIB is one issue, and designing the planner itself is another. So far, efforts in the development have been on implementing the planner. We tested it using a simplified simulator in which EMIB's primitive behaviors are directly implemented without going through the emotion/intentional arbitration.

3   Reactive Planning Process

To deal with uncertainty, a deterministic planning algorithm is invoked in a reactive loop that combines a plan monitor that monitors the execution of a plan, to update the current plan by removing completed tasks, inserting new tasks, removing existing tasks in order to accommodate tasks with a higher priority, (e.g., it changes its mission or the task turns out to be infeasible), or repairing its plan when failure occurs (e.g., by inserting new tasks to re-enable a failed task precondition, taking into account its time execution window). Tasks priorities are handled essentially via plan merging by accommodating first tasks with a higher priority. For instance, once the robot has its plan for the mandatory tasks, it should accept volunteer duties depending on time availability. This is done by first trying to merge the duties with existing tasks using heuristics. If unsuccessful, a systematic merger is attempted by planning for a conjunction of mandatory and volunteer tasks. If still unsuccessful, the volunteer duties are refused.

Plans are generated with safety constraints such as maintaining a minimum battery level. However, at execution time, a plan may violate them if something unexpectedly goes wrong (e.g., going to the conference room may take longer than expected, overusing the battery in the process). This situation can be detected by the plan monitoring process, causing the introduction of battery-recharge task at an appropriate time.

4   Conference Planner

Our planner (ConfPlan) is a HTN planner but includes a plan post-processing procedure and a built-in time variable in the state representation of which the planner can take advantage. Methods that decompose tasks into smaller tasks can add metric time constraints. With these new constraints, some partial orders of tasks may be discovered. Since our domain is biased towards scheduling, these partial orders help to reduce the search space. Like SHOP2, when primitive tasks are introduced in the resulting plan, we apply effects on the current state. The current-time variable is increased as in SAPA. Once a valid plan is generated, it is passed to the post-processing phase. This procedure takes as input a total ordered plan and generates a partial ordered plan for more flexibility at execution time.

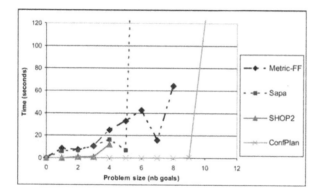

Fig. 2. Performance comparaison

Figure 2 compares ConfPlan to SAPA [2], Metric-FF [5] and SHOP2 [9], on planning problems of different complexities in the conference domain. The results show that ConfPlan solves more problems in the set than any of the three other planners. These problems involve goals of registering at the registration desk, making (or assisting to) one or more presentations at specified periods, presenting posters and taking picture of interesting posters. SAPA has timed initial literals of which we took advantage. For Metric-FF and SHOP2, whi ch do not support them, we introduced a metric time variable. Because we need a fast reactive planning engine, plan solutions taking more than two minutes were rejected.

5 Conclusion

From a general AI planning perspective, our planner improves SHOP2 algorithm by adding time constraints and integrating SAPA like post-processing to obtain flexibility. This flexibility will be crucial when repairing a plan or merging in new tasks. As mentioned before, the development of ConfPlan is primarily motivated by the need of a planning system into the EMIB robot architecture with the aim of participating at the next 2005 AAAI Challenge. We have just iniitiated the integration work. It remains interesting to see how the planner will behave on problems different to the conference domain: we are currently in the process of assessing this.

Acknowledgment

This research is supported by the Natural Sciences and Engineering Research Council of Canada and the Canada Research Chair program. We would also like to thank anonymous reviewers, Sylvain Clavette and Ian Bailey for helpful comments.

References

1. A. Cimatti, M. Pistore, M. Roveri, and P. Traverso. Weak, strong, and strong cyclic planning via symbolic model checking. *Artificial Intelligence*, 147(1-2):35–84, 2003.
2. M.B. Do and S. Kambhampati. Sapa: A scalable multi-objective metric temporal planner. *Journal of Artificial Intelligence Research*, 20:155–194, 2003.
3. Ingrand F, F and O. Despouys. Extending procedural reasoning toward robot actions planning. In *ICRA*, pages 9–14, 2001.
4. K.Z. Haigh and M. Veloso. Interleaving planning and robot execution for asynchronous user requests. *Autonomous Robots*, March 1998.
5. J. Hoffmann. The Metric-FF planning system: Translating "ignoring delete lists" to numeric state variables. *Journal of Artificial Intelligence*, 20:291–341, 2003.
6. B.A. Maxwell, W. Smart, A. Jacoff, J. Casper, B. Weiss, J. Scholtz, H. Yanco, M. Micire, A. Stroupe, D. Stormont, and T. Lauwers. 2003 AAAI robot competition and exhibition. *AI Magazine*, 25(2):68–80, Summer 2004.
7. F. Michaud. EMIB - computational architecture based on emotion and motivation for intentional selection and configuration of behaviour-producing modules. *Cognitive Science Quarterly*, pages 340–361, 2002.
8. F. Michaud, J. Audet, D. Létourneau, L. Lussier, C. Théberge-Turmel, and S. Caron. Experiences with an autonomous robot attending the AAAI conference. *IEEE Intelligent Systems*, 16(5):23–29, 2001.
9. D.S. Nau, T.C. Au, O. Ilghami, U. Kuter, J.W. Murdock, D. Wu, and F. Yaman. SHOP2: An HTN planning system. *Journal of Artificial Intelligence Research*, 20:379–404, 2003.
10. M. Nicolescu and M. J. Mataric. Deriving and using abstract representation in behavior-based systems. In *National Conference on Artificial Intelligence '00*, page 1087, 2000.
11. D.E. Smith, J. Frank, and A.R. Jonsson. Bridging the gap between planning and scheduling. *Knowledge Engineering Review*, 15(1), 2000.
12. D.S. Weld, C.R. Anderson, and D.E. Smith. Extending graphplan to handle uncertainty & sensing actions. In *National Conference on Artificial Intelligence '98*, pages 897–904, 1998.

A Decision Theoretic Meta-reasoner for Constraint Optimization

Jingfang Zheng and Michael C. Horsch

Department of Computer Science,
University of Saskatchewan,
Saskatoon, Saskatchewan, Canada

Abstract. Solving constraint optimization problems is hard because it is not enough to find the best solution; an algorithm does not know a candidate is the best solution until it has proven that there are no better solutions. The proof can be long, compared to the time spent to find a good solution. In the cases where there are resource bounds, the proof of optimality may not be achievable and a tradeoff needs to be made between the solution quality and the cost due to the time delay. We propose a decision theoretic meta-reasoning-guided COP solver to address this issue. By choosing the action with the estimated maximal expected utility, the meta-reasoner finds a stopping point with a good tradeoff between the solution quality and the time cost.

1 Introduction

Constraint optimization problems (COPs) can be very much harder than solving constraint satisfaction problems (CSPs), because CSP solving algorithms can stop once a solution is obtained; but for COP solving, unless the optimal cost is known before hand, an algorithm that optimizes COPs cannot stop until it has proven that a solution is optimal. Even problems of modest size can be costly in terms of time. For some applications, the time cost may be as important as the solution quality.

A simple approach to this tradeoff is to spend as much time as is allowed by the application. In effect, this approach amounts to spending the user's entire budget for computation. When time is cheap, this approach may be effective, but when time is costly, a user may prefer a good solution sooner than a better solution later. Another approach is to search for a solution whose quality is no less than a given quality. This approach may result in solutions whose quality could be improved with a little more computation, or as before, solutions whose quality is not justified by the expense of the computation. By explicitly considering the costs and benefits of computation, a system may be able to optimize the comprehensive value of a solution, namely the quality net of computational costs.

In this paper we present the design of a practical COP solver that uses decision theoretic meta-reasoning to control computation. In this approach, computational actions are associated with utilities [Horvitz 1989, Russell & Wefald 1991]. The value of the computational action is the solution quality that results, and the cost is associated with resources used in the solving (e.g., time). We apply this approach by

B. Kégl and G. Lapalme (Eds.): AI 2005, LNAI 3501, pp. 53–65, 2005.

monitoring the status of the solver and deciding to halt when the solver seems trapped in a proof of optimality. Since different users have different requirements for time and solution quality, we allow for different user preference models. Our results show that the meta-reasoning solver obtains a good trade-off when resource costs are high.

Our work differs from that of Horvitz et al. [2001], in that the decision problem is different. For a satisfiability problem, every solution is equally valuable, and the decision problem faced by a stochastic local search method is to choose whether to restart the search, or carry on from the current location. In a COP, solutions vary in quality, and the tradeoff is more flexible since the value of the solution is part of the decision.

Many of the issues addressed in the domain of planning under uncertainty (eg, [Boddy and Dean, 1994] and [Dean et al., 1995]) arise in constraint optimization and soft constraint propagation. The main difference lies in the information available during deliberation, and the extent to which the representation provides structure to the meta-reasoner. Our approach does not exploit the structure of the COP as much as is done in the planning domain.

To evaluate our approach, we focus on the problem of finding an assignment that violates the fewest number of constraints, i.e., Max-CSP, when all constraints are binary. However, our approach generalizes to any COP that can be expressed as a Valued-CSP (VCSP), or equivalently, a Semiring-based CSP (SCSP) [Bistarelli et al. 1996]. The details of these representations are not important for the purposes of this paper. However, we refer the reader to [Zheng and Horsch 2003] for details concerning the COP solver used in this study.

1.1 Decision Theoretic Meta-reasoning

In problems like CSPs and COPs, there is always uncertainty in the solving process. Horvitz [1988] summarizes the sources of uncertainty during computation: the value of alternative computed results in a particular situation, the difficulty of generating results from a problem instance, and the costs and availability of resources (such as time) required for reasoning. Meta-reasoning refers to the deliberation concerning possible changes to the computational state of an agent [Russell & Welfald 1991]. More concisely, it is the reasoning *about* computation.

The uncertain trade-off between the costs and benefits of a computation can be modeled with decision theory. A decision theoretic meta-reasoner tries to determine the object-level computation that maximizes the agent's expected utility, considering the trade-off explicitly. The comprehensive utility uc refers to the net value associated with the commitment to a computation. Comprehensive utility can be decomposed into two components: the object-level utility uo and the inference-related utility ui. The object level utility uo of a strategy is the utility of the outcome, omitting the costs associated with computation. The inference-related utility ui includes the costs that are be involved in the computation, such as time cost, memory cost and network cost, etc. The relation between these 3 utilities can be represented by: $uc = f(uo, ui)$. In many cases, f can be treated as additively separable: $f(uo,ui) = g(uo) + h(ui)$ for some functions g and h. We assume that f is separable in this way.

We make the further simplification of assuming that the on-line cost of meta-reasoning is negligible, by designing our meta-reasoning to have negligible costs, compared to the object-level algorithm. In our approach, there are non-negligible costs off-line in compilation and analysis, which we assume can be amortized over the use of a meta-reasoning system, but we ensure that on-line costs are negligible.

A simple approach to meta-reasoning is due to [Russell & Wefald, 1991]. Suppose the system maintains a "current best answer" a, which will be returned if it is interrupted during inference. The work of the future computation is to refine a for a higher utility. The algorithm is given as follows:

Step 1. Keep performing the object-level computation with highest expected net value (uc), until none has positive expected net value.

Step 2. Return answer a that is preferred according to Step 1.

More assumptions can be made to simplify the estimated computations [Russell & Wefald, 1991]. Meta-greedy algorithms consider only single computational steps, estimate their ultimate effect, and then choose the step that appears to have the highest benefit. The single-step assumption assumes the value of a partial computation as a complete computation, as if the system only had time for one more complete computation step. This assumption can cause underestimation of the value of some computations. The expensive alternative is to search for an optimal sequence of steps.

2   A Meta-reasoning COP Solver

The task of computing the expected utility uc for each action is hard because of the uncertainty in the results of computation. A meta-reasoning agent should select its current best action by making explicit numerical estimates of the utilities of action outcomes. Statistical knowledge of the probability distributions over the results of computation can be used for future utility estimates of actions. Thus, our meta-reasoning system consists of

- branch-and-bound search combined with consistency propagation in VCSPs
- a statistical model for the outcome of a computational step
- a user preference model of the costs of computation, and the value of a solution

2.1   The Branch-and-Bound Search Method

Recent research has been devoted to building COP frameworks extended from constraint satisfaction problem (CSP) frameworks, including valued-CSPs (VCSPs) [Schiex et al. 1995] and Semiring-based CSPs (SCSPs) [Bistarelli et al. 1996]. Early approaches to COP solving use partial consistency propagation, combined with branch and bound search, such as Russian Doll Search [Verfaillie et al. 1996] and partial consistency propagation [Schiex et al. 1995]. More recently, Schiex [2000] proposed a definition of node and arc consistency in a VCSP framework.

The constraint propagation we use is based on Larrosa's variation [2002] of Schiex's approach, as implemented in [Zheng and Horsch 2003]. It consists of the systematic repetition of *projections* of constraint costs from the (binary) constraints in C to unary constraints over variables involved in the constraint, and then to a special 0-ary constraint for the entire COP instance. This method achieves node and arc consistency in a VCSP framework, and can also prune the inconsistent values from variables' domains. The 0-ary constraint gathers the projected costs from the binary constraints and the unary constraints, and becomes a good lower bound (*lb*) for use in branch-and-bound search. The upper bound in the search is the valuation of the current best solution. Furthermore, the unary constraints on each variable provide a value-ordering heuristic, which has been shown to be effective [Zheng & Horsch 2003]. This combination of soft arc consistency, with branch-and-bound search, using the value ordering heuristic (BB-SRFL-H) is the object-level solver.

The solving algorithm is parameterized by a time bound that acts as a hard deadline: once the time bound is reached, the solving will stop, reporting the current best solution. The solving algorithm can also be interrupted by the meta-reasoner, which can halt the solver, and report the current best solution, even if the total time is not reached. The solver reports data to the meta-reasoner at regular intervals, as well as when the current best solution is updated. This data is outlined below.

2.2 The Meta-reasoning Problem

The objective of meta-reasoning, as mentioned above, is to maximize the expected comprehensive utility *uc*, which is a combination of object-level utility *uo* and inference related utility *ui*. In this system, the object-level utility *uo* is defined as the value of the solution quality, and the inference-related utility *ui* is the cost of achieving *uo*, mainly the required time. With the assumption that these two utilities can be separated additively, the relation is simply $uc = g(uo) + h(ui)$. This equation can be expressed in terms of cost. Suppose *cc*, *co* and *ci* are respectively the cost for *uc*, *uo* and *ui* ($cc = -uc$, $co = -uo$ and $ci = -ui$). The objective of maximizing *uc* is the objective of minimizing *cc*.

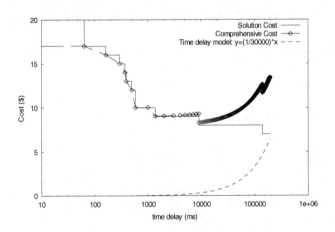

Fig. 1. An example graph of the combined cost *cc* from solution cost *co* and time cost *ci*. The optimal *cc* occurs just before the 10 second point

To compute *cc*, we have to choose functions *g* and *h*. Here we use "dollar ($)" units to describe the costs, just for convenience. For the object-level cost *co*, (the solution cost), we suppose the violation of any constraint costs $1. The cost function for *ci* will depend on the user. For example, every 30 seconds of time delay costs the user $1. These are arbitrary choices that do not affect the design of the meta-reasoner, and a later section will give a detailed discussion on user preference models.

The task for the meta-reasoner is to analyze data at short intervals, to predict or observe the point when the minimal cc (maximal uc) is achieved, at which point it should make the decision to halt computation. Figure 1 shows the graph of cc based on a solved problem. Initially, the solution improves quickly and the increase of the time cost was insignificant, so the combined cost cc decreases with the update of solutions. As time goes on, cc will increase if there is no update. But a new update would still reduce cc. The figure shows the ideal stopping point at the place of the minimal cc: the point after an update and before a long "no-update" period was about to start. This long interval would accumulate a high time cost, and even a new update to the solution does not pay off.

This ideal analysis was obtained in retrospect using a solved problem. However, for most problems, the solver cannot be certain if there will be another quick update after the update that it just found. The task of our meta-reasoner is to predict the stop point that achieves the expected maximal comprehensive utility uc. The meta-greedy assumption is used to simplify the situation: the system will consider only one step at every meta-reasoning point. Thus, our system takes the estimation of maximizing the next step's utility instead of directly maximizing the final decision's utility. At every short interval, say 1 second, the solver will pause and the meta-reasoner will consider, as we outline below, whether or not to let the object level solver continue.

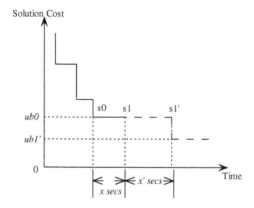

Fig. 2. A visualization for the notation that will be used throughout the method

The following notation is used to derive the meta-reasoning process:

- $s0$: the previous state at which the solution was updated most recently;
- $ub0$: the cost of the best solution (upper bound) at $s0$;
- $s1$: the current meta-reasoning state; we assume that there is no update from $s0$ (from the definition of $s0$), and the solution cost for $s1$ is still $ub0$.
- x: the number of meta-reasoning decision intervals passed from $s0$ to $s1$. If meta-reasoning is performed every second, the time between $s0$ and $s1$ is x seconds.
- $s1'$: the state that the meta-reasoner predicts to have the next update after $s1$.

- $ub1'$: the next update of solution cost, or the solution cost at $s1'$;
- x': the time from the current meta-reasoning state s1 to the next update state $s1'$
- Uc: the utility function for uc
- Uo: the utility function for uo
- Ui: the utility function for ui

With the knowledge of how much the update will cost the user (from $ub0$ to the predicted $ub1'$), the task for the meta-reasoner is to decide whether to continue from $s1$ to $s1'$, based on the knowledge that it already has, and its prediction of how long $s1$ to $s1'$ will take, and whether it will be less than the cost the user is willing to accept.

The meta-reasoner will say "continue" if it believes in an increase of uc, and on the contrary "halt". The change of uc brought by the action of "continue" can be expressed in Equation 2 (from $s0$ to $s1'$).

$$U_c(continue) = U_c(s1') \tag{1}$$

$$U_c(halt) = U_c(s0)$$

$$\Delta U_c(continue) = U_c(s1') - U_c(s0)$$

Since state $s1'$ is unknown, its real utility is uncertain, which we will model in Equation 3 by the expected utility $EUc(s1')$.

$$\Delta EU_c(continue) = EU_c(s1') - U_c(s0) \tag{2}$$

With the knowledge of state $s1$, we can rewrite this as follows:

$$\Delta EU_c(continue) = (EU_c(s1') - U_c(s1)) + (U_c(s1) - U_c(s0)) \tag{3}$$

Equation 4 estimates the utility change in two periods: from $s0$ to $s1$ and from $s1$ to $s1'$. Using the additive separation assumption, Uc can be replaced by Uo and Ui. Since there is no update from $s0$ to $s1$, the change of object-level utility $U_o(s1) - U_o(s0)$ is 0; the change of the inference-related utility is the function of the time spent for this period (x seconds as known), which can be expressed as $U_i(x)$. From $s1$ to $s1'$, the computation is based on prediction. The expected solution cost is $ub1'$ as mentioned, and the expected time from $s1$ to $s1'$ is x'. Thus the change of utility can be expressed as $EU_o(|ub1'-ub0|) + EU_i(x')$.

$$\Delta EU_c(continue) = EU_o(|ub1'-ub0|) + EU_i(x') + 0 + U_i(x) \tag{4}$$

Equation 5 can be expressed using probabilities and utilities:

$$\Delta EU_c(continue) = \sum_{ub1'} P(ub1') \times U_o(|ub1'-ub0|) + \sum_{x'} P(x') \times U_i(x') + U_i(x) \tag{5}$$

Equation 6 is the equation used in the meta-reasoner. If the estimated expected change in computing one more step is positive, solving will continue. We assume that the user preference model for costs due to time produces a single, global optimal uc. Otherwise, the meta-reasoner may halt the system when it detects a local maximum. Notice that ui only included the cost of solving; recall we require that the meta-reasoning costs be negligible. If the probabilities P(ub') and P(x'), and the utilities Uo

are available cheaply during on-line computation, the meta-reasoning costs will be negligible. The probabilities will come from a simple statistical model (Section 2.3), and the utility functions will be based on different user models (Section 2.4).

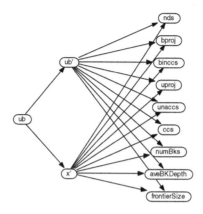

Fig. 3. The statistical model for predicting *ub0*' and *x*'

2.3   A Statistical Model for Predicting Outcomes of Computation

To obtain probabilities for *ub1*' and *x*' in Equation 6, we used a simple model based on a naïve Bayes classifier, extending it to 3 layers. The variables *ub1*' and *x*' are considered the classifications, and we used the following features which are easily available during the runtime of the solving mechanism:

1. *ub0* : the cost of the current best solution.
2. *nds* : the number of nodes in the search tree visited since last solution update.
3. *bproj* : the number of binary projections from last solution update.
4. *binccs* : the number of binary constraint checks since last solution update.
5. *uproj* : the number of unary projections since last solution update.
6. *unaccs* : the number of unary constraint checks since last solution update.
7. *ccs* : the number of checks since last solution update. This is a second level feature, which is the sum of features 3 to 6.
8. *numBks* : the number of backtracks since last solution update.
9. *aveBKDepth* : the average depth of search.
10. *frontierSize* : the length of the current unvisited node list for the search.

According to the naïve Bayes model, the features are assumed to be conditionally independent given the classifications. Our modified model puts *ub0*, the value of the current best assignment, as a parent to the classifications, acting as a kind of switch. For example, if the input of current solution cost *ub0* equals to 5, the probability of *nextub* being larger than 5 will be 0, because they can only be better than the current best solution. The model is shown in Figure 3.

To generate the training data, we solved randomly generated training problem instances using the same object level algorithm (BB-SRFL-H), reporting data at every point where an obvious change is observed. We tried three different strategies for reporting runtime data. One alternative was to report at the point where a search node was visited; the second reported data when a backtrack occurred. Experiments showed that both of these two options produced too trivial information and very large data files, so we used a third option: whenever the solving algorithm found a solution which was better than the current best one, it reported the new solution cost, the time spent, the number of nodes, checks and all the input features mentioned in above.

The data are distributed over a wide range, and therefore were "discretized" into abstract states by visual inspection of the distribution of the data for each variable. This has two consequences. First, the summations in Equation 6 are feasible with discretized values, and second, the computed change in expected value is an approximation of the actual change.

The statistical model was constructed using the maximum a posterior hypothesis (MAP) learning rule, as is common in naïve Bayes models. Problem sets of 2, 5, 10, 20, 50, 100, 200, 400 and 800 COPs were used to generate training data and smaller numbers of testing data were used to test the models. Five statistical models were constructed from training data collected by solving COP instances. The average error rate for each set of 5 models was measured by counting correct predictions of ub' on a test set, as well as by computing the predicted error in the expectation of ub' for the test set. The error rates converged for trials greater than 200 COP instances. Specifically, the average prediction accuracy for the 200 instance models was 72% (standard deviation: 0.02), and the relative accuracy in the predicted $ub1'$ for these models was 86% (st. dev. 0.004). Therefore, we used one of the five models constructed using 200 COP instances as the model to be used in our system.

2.4 User Preference Models

We have assumed that time is the main resource cost in this system. Future work can include other costs such as the memory cost. Focusing on the time cost, we introduce different user preference models in this section. Several classes of utility functions of ui (time) have been examined, including urgency, deadline, and urgent-deadline situations [Horvitz 1988]. Section 2.2 demonstrated meta-reasoning with a simple time model wherein 30 seconds costs $1. However, different users may have different requirements about urgency and deadlines. To measure how the time delay affects the solving and the decisions, utility functions are associated with time delay.

We focus on urgency models, rather than deadlines. Where there are pure deadlines, the utility function Ui has two stages: before the deadline, $Ui=0$, and after the deadline $Ui=-\infty$. Thus, meta-reasoning is not even useful for pure deadlines.

An urgency model is a general class of utility functions in which the cost increases monotonically as the time delay increases. We focus on the urgency model to convert time to utilities for the computation of expected value (see Equation 6). If the system is trapped in a long proof without any solution improvement, the cost will increase significantly. Our urgency models are linear with time as examples only; our approach is not limited to linear models.

3 Experimental Results

This section reports on the experiments of testing our solver for several different user models. The performance of our meta-reasoner solver is compared with the results from the original non-meta-reasoning solver.

For complete generality, a meta-reasoning system would be able to solve many different kinds of COP instances. However, in this system we focus on a very specific class of COP instance: randomly generated Max-CSPs with 17 variables, 8 values, a constraint density of 0.5, and an average constraint tightness of 0.5. Our implementation is limited to problems from this class, but our design can be extended to any class; we are pursuing the open research issue of developing an approach that can be used for many classes of COP problems. Our experiments use very small COP instances, because of the need to solve them completely to analyze the results. The details of our experimentation follow.

3.1 Testing the Meta-reasoning Solver

We tested the meta-reasoner on 50 random problems from the same class as above, using the user model from Section 2.3: each 30 seconds delay costs the user $1. Figures 4, 5 and 6 are the graphs showing the comparison between using the meta-reasoning solver and the same solver without the meta-reasoning. The graphs show the result for each of the problems in terms of the solution costs and the time spent.

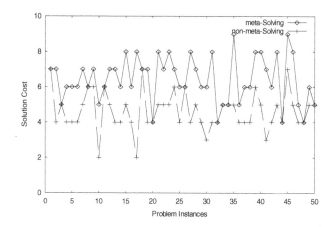

Fig. 4. Comparison on solution costs on 50 COPs. The average difference is 1.84 and the standard deviation is 1.40, in favour of the non-metareasoning solving

In Figure 4, the x-axis shows the independent problem instances and the y-axis shows the solution costs from the two solvers. The solution cost for non-meta-solving is the cost of the solution at the end of the complete solving, and the solution cost for meta-solving is the cost of the current best solution at the point where the solver decided to stop. From Figure 4, we can see that using the meta-solver results in solutions that are about 2 constraint violations worse on average.

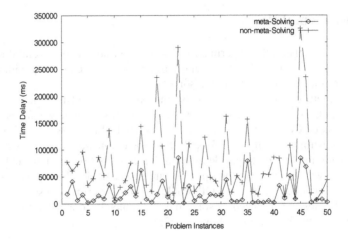

Fig. 5. Comparison on used time, on 50 problem instances as above. The average time difference is 53 seconds and the standard deviation is 55 seconds

Figure 5 shows the comparison of the run time of the two methods. Here, the y-axis shows the amount of time used. The meta-solver almost always stops before the non-meta-solver does, and on average, about 53 seconds sooner. In a few cases, the two solvers require nearly exactly the same time.

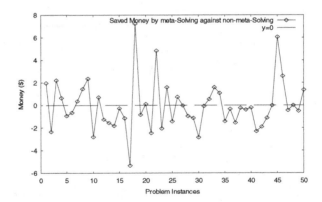

Fig. 6. Difference in comprehensive utility between the two solvers. The average difference in "dollars" is -0.05 and the standard deviation is 2.17, in favour of the non-metareasoning solver

Figure 6 compares the comprehensive utility of the two solvers, using $1 per violation, and $1 per 30 seconds. The average *uc* is –$0.05, which is close to zero as one would expect, given that two violations equals one minute's computation.

3.2 Testing Different User Preference Models

To see how our meta-reasoning solver provides different results for different user models, 7 user models were tested with 50 COPs. These 7 models were just examples that show the time cost from expensive to cheap: M1 (1s = $1), M2 (5s = $1), M3 (10s = $1), M4 (20s = $1), M5 (30s = $1), M6 (60s = $1), and M7 (120s = $1).

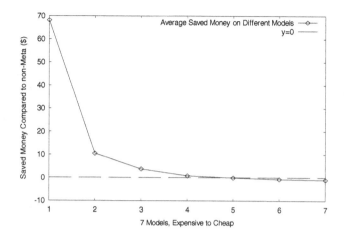

Fig. 7. Average difference in comprehensive utility using the metareasoning solving on 7 user preference models

Figure 7 shows the average of the saving on these 7 models. The x-axis is the 7 models, from expensive to cheap, and the y-axis is the average saving for these 50 COP instances using these 7 models. This figure shows that our meta-reasoner pays off when time is expensive, but is comparable to the complete solver if time is cheap.

4 Summary and Future Work

We designed and implemented a decision theoretic meta-reasoning COP. The system is able to make run-time trade-offs based on a model of expected comprehensive utility. A traditional machine learning method was used to build a model of the way a COP solver improves solutions. Different user models were used to test the system's adaptability and its advantages or disadvantages according to different time urgency. Experiments suggest that this system is useful on expensive time models, but on average did not perform badly in cases when time was cheap.

Currently the meta-reasoner only provides the solver with the decision to halt or to continue, providing no other help during the solving. We are developing a meta-reasoner to predict the next *ub* value. This could be used as an expected upper bound, which could be used to limit search. This is similar to the binary choice meta-reasoner of Carlsson et al [1996]; however, we expect the *ub* from the meta-reasoner will be more accurate than the binary choice algorithm, and thus we should have fewer wrong predictions and fewer backtracks.

The design of the system is not limited to any specific variety of VCSP. However, the implementation that was tested is specific to a class of very small VCSP. This limitation was imposed by the need to test the solver on problems for which the best objective solution (ignoring computational costs) is feasible to compute. We are currently working on testing the design on larger problems. To extend the approach to a wider class of problem, the features used to estimate expectations and probabilities need to be made independent of the problem class. We do not claim that the features presented in our model are optimal in any sense. A different set of relationships or features may improve the accuracy of the predictions.

The Bayesian model was designed so that inference in the model would be easy, but because it is based on the "naïve Bayes" assumption, the manual construction of the network leaves significant space for improvement. Learning a model structure from the data may improve the predictive power of the meta-reasoner, but the choice of model has to take on-line meta-reasoning costs into account.

Acknowledgements

The second author acknowledges support by NSERC through RGPIN2387870-01.

References

Boddy, M. and Dean, T. 1994. Decision-Theoretic Deliberation Scheduling for Problem Solving in Time-Constrained Environments. Artificial Intelligence, Volume 67, Number 2, pp 245-286, 1994.

Bistarelli, S.; Fargier, H.; Montanari, U.; Rossi, F.; Schiex, T.; and Verfaille, G. 1996. Semiring-based CSPs and valued CSPs: Basic properties. In M. Jampel, E. C. Freuder, and M. Maher, editors, *Over-Constrained Systems*, Volume 1106 of Lecture Notes in Computer Science, pp111-150. Springer, Berlin, 1996.

Carlsson, M.; Ottosson, G. 1996. Anytime Frequency Allocation with Soft Constraints. CP96 Pre-Conference Workshop on Applications. 1996

Dean, T.; Kaelbling, L.; Kirman, J.; Nicholson, A. 1995. Planning Under Time Constraints in Stochastic Domains. Artificial Intelligence, Volume 76, Number 1-2, Pages 35-74, 1995.

Horvitz, E. J. 1988. Reasoning under Varying and Uncertain Resource Constraints. In Proceedings of the National Conference on AI (AAAI-88), pp 111-116. 1988.

Horvitz, E. J. 1989. Reasoning about Beliefs and Actions under Computational Resource Constraints. In Uncertainty in Artificial Intelligence 3. Elsevier Science Publishers, 1989.

Horvitz, E. J.; Ruan, Y.; Gomes, C.; Kautz, H.; Selman, B. and Chickering, D. M. 2001. A Bayesian Approach to Tackling Hard Computational Problems. Proceedings of the Seventeenth Conference on Uncertainty in Artificial Intelligence, pp235-244, 2001.

Larrosa, J. 2002. Node and Arc Consistency in Weighted CSP. In Proceedings of the 18th National Conference on Artificial Intelligence (AAAI-2002), pp48-53 2002 .

Russell, S.; Wefald, E. 1991. The principles of meta-reasoning. 1st International Conference on Knowledge Representation and Reasoning, pp406-411. Morgan Kaufmann. 1991

Schiex, T. 2000. Arc consistency for soft constraints. In CP-2000, pp411-424, 2000.

Schiex, T.; Fargier, H.; and Verfaillie, G. 1995. Valued Constraint Satisfaction Problems: Hard and Easy Problems. In Proc. of the 14th International Joint Conference on Artificial Intelligence (IJCAI-95), pp 631--637. 1995.

Verfaillie, G.; Lemâitre, M.; and Schiex, T. 1996. Russian doll search. In AAAI-96, pp181–187, 1996.

Zheng, J. and Horsch, M. C. 2003. A Comparison of Consistency Propagation Algorithms in Constraint Optimization. In Proceedings of the Sixteenth Canadian Conference on Artificial Intelligence, pp160-174, 2003.

Heuristic Search Applied to Abstract Combat Games

Alexander Kovarsky[1] and Michael Buro[2]

University of Alberta, Edmonton, Alberta, Canada
{kovarsky[1], mburo[2]}@cs.ualberta.ca

Abstract. Creating strong AI forces in military war simulations or RTS video games poses many challenges including partially observable states, a possibly large number of agents and actions, and simultaneous concurrent move execution. In this paper we consider a tactical sub–problem that needs to be addressed on the way to strong computer generated forces: abstract combat games in which a small number of inhomogeneous units battle with each other in simultaneous move rounds until all members of one group are eliminated. We present and test several adversarial heuristic search algorithms that are able to compute reasonable actions in those scenarios using short time controls. Tournament results indicate that a new algorithm for simultaneous move games which we call "randomized alpha–beta search" (RAB) can be used effectively in the abstract combat application we consider. In this application it outperforms the other algorithms we implemented. We also show that RAB's performance is correlated with the degree of simultaneous move interdependence present in the game.

1 Introduction

Abstract combat games — also known as combat attrition scenarios in military literature — have long been a focus of military research [5]. In the area of computer generated forces these models can be used to predict the outcome of simulated battles and to compute actions that would for instance maximize the inflicted damage or unit survival probability. In order to simplify the problem, states are usually abstracted. For instance, terrain is often represented as collection of convex cells — typically squares or hexagons — and objects as vectors that describe attack values, health or so–called hit–points, position, size, maximum and current speed, heading, and sight–range, etc.

The purpose of this research is to design and study fast heuristic decision procedures for abstract combat games that belong to the class of two–player simultaneous move games with otherwise perfect information. Such algorithms have applications in popular real–time strategy (RTS) video games — such as Warcraft (http://www.blizzard.com) — which essentially are real–time battle simulations. For instance, incorporating abstract combat algorithms in graphical user interfaces relieves human players from laborious unit micro–management and lets them focus on more strategic decisions. In extreme cases where hundreds of fighting units have to be managed or several separate battles are fought, issuing fire commands to units manually in timely fashion may not even be possible. When delegating local fights to AI modules the tactical performance could even improve because programs may select targets and concentrate fire faster and more accurate than any human. Increasing the playing strength of

B. Kégl and G. Lapalme (Eds.): AI 2005, LNAI 3501, pp. 66–78, 2005.

allied or opponent computer players in RTS games to make game playing more challenging is another immediate application from which military combat simulators can benefit, too.

The central idea of this research is to go beyond established analytical methods — that model warfare globally with differential equations [11] — by studying adversarial heuristic search techniques in this domain. In general terms, such algorithms conduct look–ahead searches in (abstract) two–player state spaces by repeatedly generating successor states, deciding where to proceed, evaluating states, and propagating those values in the constructed search graph. Minimax–search and its enhancements, for example, fall into this category. Often, deep search can compensate for less than perfect domain knowledge. A good example is chess, where PC programs now have reached World-champion–level performance by combining deep search with relatively simple (fast) evaluation functions. Using the chess example again, it is a non–trivial task to write an evaluation function that can statically detect and assess capture sequences. On the other hand, look–ahead search that makes use of simple material features can find and evaluate capture sequences quickly. Here, too, the hope is that look–ahead search can overcome the need for accurate evaluation models — which in general are hard to find — and that search even under real–time constraints produces high–quality actions.

Video games have been the focus of several AI research projects in recent years. E.g. in [4] evolutionary algorithms are used to enable AI characters to develop novel behaviours in an RTS–like combat situations. In [8] complex artificial characters for a custom designed adventure game are developed based on the Unreal Tournament game engine and the SOAR AI architecture. Stochastic search has been studied in this area, too (e.g. [9]). However, to our knowledge, no previous research has applied randomized heuristic search to two player games with simultaneous moves.

The remainder of the paper is organized as follows: first we define the class of combat games we consider. Next, a number of search algorithms are presented for these games ranging from an optimal solution based on solving linear programs to a Monte Carlo algorithm. We then describe a new algorithm for simultaneous move games. Finally, we present and discuss experimental results and conclude the paper with suggestions for future research.

2   Abstract Combat Games

In abstract combat games two players are in control of teams of units which attack each other in simultaneous move rounds. In each turn, both players give orders to their units which then are executed simultaneously. Games start with two groups of units and end after a sequence of rounds when one group is eliminated. We make the following simplifying assumptions:

- there are no hidden state variables
- all units have the ability to attack any opponent unit at any time
- units are static objects, they cannot move

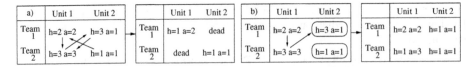

Fig. 1. State transitions in abstract combat games. Arrows indicate attacks, boxes indicate defensive stance. a) non–defensive scenario. b) defensive scenario. When a unit defends, its attack value is temporarily added to its hitpoints. This decreases the damage the unit receives in case it is attacked. If a defending unit is not attacked, its hitpoint value remains unchanged

In the games we consider here units have the following numerical properties:

h : Hitpoints   — the defensive strength of a given unit
a : Attack value (const.)   — the amount of damage a unit can inflict
c : Cool–down period (const.) — how long to wait before next attack

Each unit has one weapon with a specific attack value and cool–down period. If the weapon has cooled down, i.e. the weapon was last fired at least $c + 1$ rounds ago, it can fire again. Before attacking, units have to select their target. In the next turn they can shoot only at that target. If a unit wants to attack another target it needs to aim. Aiming costs one time step. When a unit gets attacked its hitpoint value is decreased by the attackers attack value. If a unit's hitpoint value drops below 1, it is considered destroyed and removed from the game. A typical state transition is shown in Fig. 1a).

In the basic set–up despite actions being executed simultaneously we theorize that the success of a player's action does not strongly depend on what the opponent chooses to do. I.e., announcing a move hardly hurts. This is because damage is inflicted regardless. To study the performance of the heuristic search algorithms we implemented in more Rock–Paper–Scissor–like scenarios, where announcing moves is foolish, we add a defensive action and call games with this additional move option "defensive". The defensive action enables the unit to use its attack value for defending rather than for attacking. Specifically, if a unit decides to defend instead of attacking, a certain proportion (possibly > 1) of its attack value is temporarily added to its hitpoints. When this unit is attacked the attacker will only cause damage to the unit if its attack value is bigger than the unit's proportion of attack value used for defence. If a defending unit is not attacked its hitpoints remain unchanged (i.e. not increased). In addition, a defending unit can also cause damage to the attacker. There is a certain benefit to take a defensive stance. But there is also a degree of risk because a unit taking a defensive action might not be attacked and is therefore risking to waste its turn. A defensive game scenario is shown in Fig. 1b).

3   Heuristic Search in Abstract Combat Games

The major challenges in the abstract combat games we just described are large branching factors, limited decision time, and simultaneous move execution. In the simplest case — simultaneous move zero–sum — games consist of one start state and $n \times m$ successor states which are reached after executing single simultaneous action pairs.

Here, player A has n actions to choose from and player B has m. The values of the terminal states are given in form of a $n \times m$ payoff matrix. Optimal (mixed) strategies for these games always exist [12] and can be computed by solving a pair of associated linear programs. Abstract combat games can be viewed as multi–step matrix games and as such can be solved by dynamic programming [3]. Unfortunately, this technique has no practical relevance because state spaces — even for small scenarios — are huge.

An alternative approach is to trade solution quality for speed by considering heuristic search algorithms. In the remainder of this section we first present the evaluation function used in all heuristic algorithms we implemented. Then we will describe all algorithms in turn.

Evaluation Functions for Abstract Combat Games. The heuristic algorithms we describe below rely on an evaluation function that measures the goodness of a state in view of player 1 or 2. The following function estimates the differential of the total lifetime damage two groups of units can inflict:

$$\sum_{i=1}^{n_1} \frac{h_i^{(1)} \times a_i^{(1)}}{c_i^{(1)} + 1} - \sum_{i=1}^{n_2} \frac{h_i^{(2)} \times a_i^{(2)}}{c_i^{(2)} + 1}, \tag{1}$$

where unit attribute superscripts indicate the unit owner and n_1, n_2 denote the number of units for player 1 and 2, respectively. Here, hitpoints are used as estimator of the life expectancy of a unit, while attack value over cool–down plus 1 represents the average damage a unit will deal during one time step. Evaluation function (1) is monotone in the h and a values, takes cool–down into account, and can be computed quickly. We used it for a while in our experiments before a serious weakness became apparent: its inability to differentiate between hitpoint distributions. In general, it is more beneficial for a player to have units with a uniform hitpoint distribution than having some units with low hitpoint values and others with high hitpoint values. This is because units with low hitpoints values are much closer to elimination. For a fixed average attack value, evaluation function (1) only considers the sum of hitpoints. Thus, values for widely varying hitpoint distributions — everything else being equal — could be the same. The following function fixes this problem at the expense of introducing non–linearity and departing from modeling the lifetime damage:

$$\sum_{i=1}^{n_1} \frac{\sqrt{h_i^{(1)}} \times a_i^{(1)}}{c_i^{(1)} + 1} - \sum_{i=1}^{n_2} \frac{\sqrt{h_i^{(2)}} \times a_i^{(2)}}{c_i^{(2)} + 1} \tag{2}$$

By applying the square root to hitpoints the evaluation function implicitly prefers more uniform hitpoint distributions. Function (2) was used in the experiments reported in section 5 after initial tournaments indicated that it performs better than function (1). We have not tried to optimize the evaluation function further — for instance by introducing parameters and optimizing them, because the focus of this work is search rather than evaluation function construction, which is a research topic by itself.

Linear Programming (LP). We have seen that solving abstract combat games by means of dynamic programming and linear programs is impractical. One idea to compute approximate move distributions in this setting is to stop at a certain search depth and to apply a heuristic evaluation function to the end states reached at that depth. Our LP player searches at depth 1. I.e. it generates all moves for both players, considers all possible move pairs, evaluates the reached states using the evaluation function (2), creates a payoff matrix from these values, and solves the linear program associated with the player to move (see e.g. [3]). It then draws a move with respect to the computed optimal move distribution. We limit the search depth to one because depth 2 computations take too much time in our RTS game setting. This figure may change in future experiments when using better linear program solvers or faster hardware.

Alpha–Beta Search (AB). Minimax search and its enhancements have been proven effective in perfect information games where two players alternate turns under moderate real–time constraints (e.g. chess). The minimax search procedure traverses a search DAG in depth–first order until a certain depth is reached. It then evaluates the resulting position and propagates values to the parent node according to the minimax rule, i.e. maximizing scores in MAX nodes and minimizing scores in MIN nodes. The search continues until the value of the root node has been established, in which case the move leading to the best result is chosen. Alpha–beta pruning [7] is an enhancement of the the minimax algorithm which can reduce the search time exponentially in the depth while still computing the correct minimax values and moves. It is therefore tempting to apply alpha–beta search to abstract combat games, even though the algorithm originally was designed for alternating move games. The way we approximate simultaneous moves is by postponing the execution of the first player's action until the second player has chosen a move. This implicitly gives away the first player's choice, but there is hope that this approximation can still lead to strong performance because of deeper searches compares with other methods. There are many ways to improve the performance of alpha–beta search. For this application we implemented iterative deepening and sorting moves based on their 1–ply evaluations.

Monte Carlo Sampling (MC). Monte Carlo methods solve problems by executing a large number of possibly biased random actions and examining the numerical results such actions generate. The method is used for finding solutions to problems that are too complex to solve analytically. In game AI research, Monte Carlo approaches have been successfully applied to Bridge and recently to the game of Go [2]. In our approach we play out a game until one player is eliminated. For each of the main player's (i.e. the player who performs the simulation) moves at the root, a series of simulations is performed given the available resources. After the runs, the average scores and standard deviations for each move at the top are computed. The move with the "best" average score and standard deviation combination is selected by the player to be executed. Score calculation details are presented in Section 5. In each turn the MC player randomly selects one of the the available actions and then executes it. The run continues in this fashion with both players executing their randomly selected moves, until one of the players is eliminated. A score is calculated for the position, propagated to the top node, and then recorded as one of the values for the selected move.

Move Selection. One way to combat large branching factors in search is to forward–prune subtrees. In some games (e.g. backgammon [6]), limited–depth searches can produce a subsets of moves that likely contain the best moves available. We use move selection for all our search–based methods (i.e. AB, MC, and RAB (described in the next section). Before the start of each of the proposed methods at each level in the tree we perform a complete depth one search for each of the successors. After that, the top N successors are sorted in decreasing order of their scores. Then the search will concentrate only on those top N successors. Because of the decreased branching factor the search can go much deeper. For such a move sorting scheme to be successful, it is important to have an accurate state evaluation function.

Delayed Move Execution. Delayed move execution is required when using algorithms for alternating move games, such as alpha–beta, in simultaneous move games. In alternating move games, the first player will change the game state by executing a move. After that the second player will change the state by executing his move. Such a sequence of events does not represent the situation accurately, because the state of the game should have remained the same when the second player decides on its move. Therefore, in our search algorithms we delay move executions until both players have committed to an action.

4   Randomized Alpha–Beta Search (RAB)

Our goal when designing the RAB algorithm was to overcome the major disadvantage of the basic alpha–beta algorithm of not addressing possible move dependencies in simultaneous move games. Alpha–beta is a search algorithm for alternating move perfect information games in which all actions are observable. Therefore, players have the advantage of seeing the previous opponent action, which when alpha–beta search is applied to simultaneous move games results in over– or underestimating the value of positions. To soften the effect of advance knowledge of opponent's moves we propose an algorithm based on alpha–beta search which randomizes the color to move in certain nodes. Thus, in some nodes in the tree player one will have the advantage of knowing player two's move, while in other nodes the situation will be reversed.

The algorithm is quite simple: at even depths the color to move is randomized and at odd depths the color to move is changed. The only exception occurs at the root of the tree where the first move always belongs to the player performing the search and its moves are always followed by opponent moves. A sample RAB tree is shown in Fig. 2.

Our hope is that with RAB the advantage of the second player to move will be reduced, because in the whole search tree both players will have equal chances of knowing the opponent's moves. In RTS games, however, algorithms need to perform under tight

Fig. 2. Sample RAB tree. Black moves first at the root, followed by White. At the next level, the player to move is randomly selected. This player's move is followed by a move of the opponent

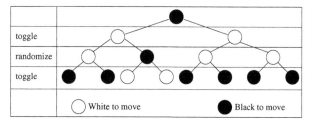

time constraints. RAB, as opposed to AB is non–deterministic, because every run of the algorithm is likely to produce different results. Being a sampling–based approach, it requires multiple runs to be performed for every move that is available to the player executing the search at the root. For every such move, the best scores will be recorded for every run. Then, for each move the average score and the standard deviation are calculated. Multiple runs are required for drawing valid conclusions about the quality of moves. The move that is chosen for execution is determined by taking into account the average scores and standard deviations for each considered move. The move with the best combination of average score and standard deviation is then executed. Section 5 gives details on score calculation. We think that the score average combined with the standard deviation for each move simulates the effect of simultaneous move execution better than a single regular alpha–beta run. However, the main concern with RAB is the number of runs that it will require to find a good move. Also, if there is very little advantage of knowing the opponent's moves in a given game, it is possible that alpha–beta search can find a good move or possibly the best move in just a single run. It is also possible that it is more worthwhile to invest the extra resources into deeper searches than on repeated searches. Fig. 3 shows pseudo–code of the RAB search algorithm.

```
// compute scores for all moves
void TopLevelRAB(State state, vector<double> &moveScores, int
depth) {
  vector<Move> moves;
  moveScores.clear();
  GenerateMoves(state, moves);
  for i = 1..moves.size() {          // evaluate all generated moves once
    newState = makeMove(state, moves[i]);
    score = RAB(newState, -infinity, infinity, depth, 0);
    moveScores.append(score);
  }
}

// recursive randomized tree search; uses the negamax variant of alpha-beta
void RAB(State state, int alpha, int beta, int depth, int
randGenerate) {
  if (terminalNode(state) || depth == 0) return evaluate(state);
  if (randGenerate) toMove = random() & 1;    // pick 0 or 1 randomly
  else              toMove = opponent(state); // toggle color to move
  randGenerate = 1 - randGenerate;            // toggle flag
  if (parentPlayerToMove(state) == currentPlayerToMove(state)) {
    alpha = -beta; beta = -alpha;
  }
  SetToMove(state, toMove);
  maxScore = -infinity;
  GenerateMoves(state, moves);
  for i = 1..moves.size() {
    newState = MakeMove(state, moves[i]);
    // nega-scout alpha-beta variant
    value = - RAB(newState, -beta, -alpha, depth-1, randGenerate);
    if (value > maxSscore) maxSscore = value;
    if (maxSscore > alpha) alpha = maxSscore;
    if (maxSscore >= beta) break;
  }
  if (parentPlayerToMove(state) == currentPlayerToMove(state)) return -score;
  else return score;
}
```

Fig. 3. RAB Pseudo–code

RAB Implementation and Score Calculation Details. The RAB algorithm is implemented using iterative deepening [10] which is often utilized in environments with real–time constraints. It performs multiple searches starting with the lowest depth and increases the search depth at every successive iteration. The rationale behind the technique is that lower depth searches take only a fraction of the time the next higher depth search will take and thus not much time will be wasted. The main benefit is that at any time a reasonable solution is available which makes the search algorithm fit for real–time applications. At each search depth RAB needs to complete several iterations in order to gather meaningful statistics. The higher the search depth the more iterations RAB needs to complete at that depth, because the deeper the search the higher the variability or standard deviation of the results.

5   Experiments

A tournament environment was set up for performing the experiments and for gathering statistics on the results. A tournament game is a match between two players who battle with each other until one player is eliminated. At each state both players implement their respective algorithms to find their best move. Then both moves are executed simultaneously, the state of the game is updated, and the game continues until one or both players are eliminated (refer to Section 3 for an example). Given two players A and B, a win for A(B) occurs when A(B) has unit(s) remaining while B(A) does not. A draw occurs when both players have no units remaining. Each experiment consists of 200 games. To make the summary of experiments easier to understand and analyze, the experimental results are presented in terms of the *win ratio*:

$$(\#\text{wins} + 0.5 \cdot \#\text{draws}) / (\#\text{wins} + \#\text{losses} + \#\text{draws})$$

The number of wins, losses, draws, as well as the average scores achieved in each run is recorded. To minimize the variance, symmetric starting positions are chosen. The units in each team are generated randomly within predefined boundaries. There are three types of units: tanks, marines, and artillery. Each type has the ranges of hitpoints, attack values and cool–down periods as shown in Table 1.

The node count limits that are used in the experiments were selected in order to produce acceptable real–time performance on the machines used for the experiments. Specifically, the experiments are run on Athlon MP/XP 2400+ to 2500+ processors with 512–1024 MBs of memory. For non–defensive experiments the node limit for one move in a game for each player when set at 200k nodes results in average game durations of ≈4.5 seconds, consisting of ≈5-6 moves for each player. For defensive experiments, when the node limit is set at 300k nodes, each game lasts on average 9 seconds, consisting of ≈6-7 moves for each player.

To calculate the score in both RAB and MC the setting of (average score − 1 × standard deviation) is used. This setting was determined in a preliminary set of experiments and will be used in all of our experiments. For all experiments the square root evaluation function (2) is used as it performed best in a preliminary experiment. The empirically values for N — the number of considered moves in the move selection function — were determined in a series of experiments as well. We chose $N = 10$ for 3

Table 1. Hitpoint, attack value, and cool–down period ranges used in the experiments

Attribute	Tank	Marine	Artillery
Hitpoints	60..90	30..40	20..30
Attack value	30..45	15..25	40..60
Cool–down period	1	0	2

Table 2. Cumulative win ratios for each algorithm obtained by a round–robin tournament for non–defensive and defensive 3 vs. 3 scenarios

Algorithm	Cumulative Win % non–defensive	Cumulative Win % defensive
RAB	73%	75%
AB	68%	68%
MC	64%	53%
LP	43%	53%
RAND	2%	2%

Table 3. Round–robin tournament results. Reported are win percentages in view of the player named in the left–hand column for the non–defensive and defensive 3 vs. 3 scenarios

Players	RAB	AB	MC	LP	RAND
RAB	—	52%,60%	56%,72%	84%,67%	99%,99%
AB	48%,40%	—	53%,67%	75%,66%	97%,99%
MC	44%,28%	47%,33%	—	64%,52%	99%,98%
LP	16%,33%	25%,34%	36%,48%	—	96%,97%
RAND	1%,1%	3%,1%	1%,2%	4%,3%	—

vs. 3 non–defensive and $N = 20$ for defensive scenarios. In 4 vs. 4 non–defensive and defensive scenarios N is set to 40 and 60, respectively.

The two types of starting positions examined in all experiments are the 3 versus 3 units and 4 versus 4 units. In the 3 vs. 3 case teams consist of two marines and one tank. In the 4 vs. 4 case, teams consist of one artillery unit, two marines, and one tank.

Performance of all Methods. The results of the 3 vs. 3 experiments shown in Table 2 and Table 3 suggest that the RAB and AB players are the best performers in two typical scenarios, with MC coming third. The LP player's performance is not very close to that of the best methods, because of its limited search depth. In defensive scenarios LP's performance improves significantly, but still is not on par with that of either RAB or AB. Therefore, the remaining experiments will concentrate only on RAB and AB.

Varying RAB Nodes vs. Constant AB. This experiment, shown in Fig. 4(A,B), is designed to determine how providing RAB more resources changes its performance. RAB is playing against the AB algorithm whose maximal node count is held constant, while the number of nodes assigned to RAB is varied. For 3 vs. 3 defensive and non–defensive scenarios AB is assigned 50k and 100k nodes, respectively. For both 4 vs. 4 defensive and non–defensive scenarios AB is assigned 200k. The general trend is that as the number of RAB's node budget increases, the quality of RAB's moves increases. The increase is more gradual in the case of defensive scenarios, as compared to the non–defensive ones. In non–defensive scenarios there is less interdependence than in the defensive scenarios, therefore reaching higher depths has more effect on the quality of the resultant solution.

Strict Constraints Experiment. The results in Fig. 4(C,D) for both defensive and non–defensive scenarios show that RAB performs better than AB across most of the settings. The most surprising finding is that given a very limited number of nodes for both defensive and non–defensive scenarios RAB outperforms AB. This shows that even though AB can reach greater depth than RAB given the same node limit, investing into randomization and extra runs rather than into deeper searches pays off very early for the RAB algorithm. Another general trend observed is the gradual reduction of RAB's improvement over AB. The results show that as the number of nodes increased for both algorithms, RAB reaches a ceiling in its winning percentage over AB.

Degree of Move Interdependence. The independent variable in the experiment shown in Fig. 4(E,F) is the degree of dependence of a given scenario. This variable can be eas-

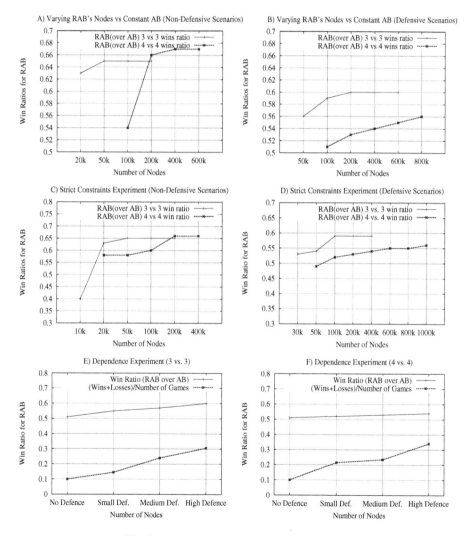

Fig. 4. Tournament Results: (A,B), (C,D), (E,F)

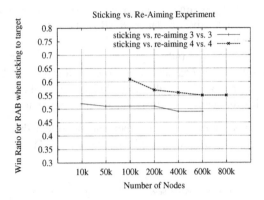

Fig. 5. Sticking to target vs. re–aiming results

ily adjusted in our domain starting with a setting with no defensive actions, and finishing with the setting where there is a very high potential reward for selecting defensive actions. Specifically, in a scenario with no reward for the defensive actions units are not motivated to execute such actions since the defensive actions do not benefit them. The exact settings for labels in Fig. 4(E,F) are as follows: "no defence": no defensive action used; "small defence": 0.5 × attack value is used for defence and 0.1 to hit back at the attacker; "medium Defence: 1.0 × attack value for defence and 0.2 to hit back at the attacker; "high Defence": 1.3 × attack value for defence and 0.3 to hit back. The results for both 3 vs. 3 and 4 vs. 4 situations show that as the reward for a defensive action increases so do the win ratios for RAB over AB. This result underpins our initial hypothesis that in highly interdependent scenarios the RAB will perform better. Another correlation that can be observed in both graphs is between the win ratio of RAB and the number of wins and losses as a percentage of the number of simulations. This is not surprising, since as the move interdependence increases the success of actions increasingly depends on what the opponent will choose to do. Therefore, in a highly defensive scenario there is no single move that guarantees at least a draw for a player. The opponent can counteract most moves taken by the player leading to a higher standard deviation of the results.

Sticking to Target Improvement. One of the constraints that can significantly reduce the branching factor is not allowing re–aiming. It means that if a unit has picked a target it should keep shooting (stick) at that target. That is, from the time the unit has picked a target until the target elimination, that unit has only one action available to it. We would like to see whether not allowing units to re-aim could lead to a better real–time performance. The results in Fig. 5 show a small advantage when units implement the sticking to the target policy. Because of the reduced branching factor when no re-aiming is allowed it is more advantageous to stick to the target when the number of nodes is small. As the node budget increases, the performance of the method that does not stick to its target slowly increases to over 50% in the 3 vs. 3 case. We can conclude that sticking to a target is especially useful when there are strict real–time constraints, however when the node limit is increased the performance of the no-sticking algorithm improves.

6   Conclusion and Future Work

One of the goals of our research was to examine whether search–based methods can be used effectively in real–time domains with simultaneous move execution. We have shown that heuristic adversarial search can be successful in small–scale abstract combat games with real–time constraints. Moreover, experimental evidence suggests that non–deterministic search methods perform better than traditional minimax algorithms in games with higher simultaneous move dependence. This result shows that search depth is not a crucial feature when designing algorithms for simultaneous move games, as opposed to alternating move perfect information games, where search depth strongly correlates with the quality of the found solution.

The best overall performer in the field of algorithms we have considered was a naive implementation of RAB which is based on the idea of combining deep alpha–beta searches with sampling to robustly compute actions in case of simultaneous move dependencies. This result is very promising and encourages us to look at RAB improvements that make better use of gathered sample data and would allow the algorithm to return better estimates of the current state value. Scalability to larger problem instances should also be addressed in order to make RAB truly suitable for handling close–combat scenarios in RTS games. Another interesting line of future research could address more theoretical aspects of generalized abstract combat games such as their computational complexity and how to define the degree of simultaneous move interdependence rigorously. Our next step will be to incorporate our methods into an ORTS [1] client, either as part of a stand–alone RTS game AI or as a helper module in the graphical user interface to alleviate the burden of manually micro–managing units in RTS game combat.

Acknowledgments

Financial support was provided by the Natural Sciences and Engineering Research Council of Canada (NSERC).

References

1. ORTS — a free software RTS game engine: http://www.cs.ualberta.ca/~mburo/orts.
2. B. Bouzy. Associating domain–dependent knowledge and Monte Carlo approaches within a go program. In *Proc. of the Joint Conf. on Information Sciences*, pages 505–508, Cary, 2003.
3. M. Buro. Solving the Oshi–Zumo game. In *Proceedings of the 10. Advances in Computer Games Conference*, pages 361–366, Graz, 2003.
4. B. Fogel, T. Hays, and D. Johnson. A platform for evolving characters in competitive games. In *Proceedings of CEC2004*, pages 1420–1426, 2004.
5. R. Gozel. Firepower score attrition algorithms in highly aggregated combat models. *RAND*, pages 47–60, 2000.
6. T. Hauk, M. Buro, and J. Schaeffer. *–minimax performance in backgammon. In *Proceedings of the Computers and Games Conference*, 2004.
7. D. Knuth and R. Moore. An analysis of alphabeta pruning. *Artif. Intell.*, 6(4):293–326, 1975.
8. J. E. Laird and et al. A test bed for developing intelligent synthetic characters. In *Proceedings of Spring Symposium on Artificial Intelligence and Interactive Entertainment, AAAI*, 2002.

9. W. Ruml. Incomplet tree search using adaptive probing. In *Proceedings of the International Joint Conference on AI*, pages 235–241, 2001.

10. D. Slate and L. Atkin. Chess 4.5. *Springer-Verlag*, 1977.

11. J. Taylor. Lanchester models of warfare. In *Operations Res. Soc. Vol 1+2*, Arlington, 1983.

12. J. von Neumann. Zur Theorie der Gesellschaftsspiele. *Math.Ann.100*, pages 295–320, 1928.

Modelling an Academic Curriculum Plan as a Mixed-Initiative Constraint Satisfaction Problem

Kun Wu and William S. Havens

Simon Fraser University,
Vancouver, BC
{Karen, havens}@cs.sfu.ca

Abstract. This paper describes a mixed-initiative constraint satisfaction system for planning the academic schedules of university students. Our model is distinguished from traditional planning systems by applying mixed-initiative constraint reasoning algorithms which provide flexibility in satisfying individual student preferences and needs. The graphical interface emphasizes visualization and direct manipulation capabilities to provide an efficient interactive environment for easy communication between the system and the end user. The planning process is split into two phases. The first phase builds an initial plan using a systematic search method based on a variant of dynamic backtracking. The second phase involves a semi-systematic local search algorithm which supports mixed-initiative user interaction and control of the search process. Generated curriculum schedules satisfy both academic program constraints and user constraints and preferences. Part of the challenge in curriculum scheduling is handling multiple possible schedules which are equivalent under symmetry. We show to overcome these symmetries in the search process. Experiments with actual course planning data show that our mixed-initiative systems generates effective curriculum plans efficiently.

1 Introduction

The curriculum planning problem is defined as constructing a set of courses for each semester - over a sequence of semesters - in order to satisfy the academic requirements for an undergraduate university degree. There are many academic constraints including course availability, prerequisites, breadth requirements, eligibility rules, and so forth. In addition, there are student imposed constraints and preferences regarding which major to pursue and which courses to take in a particular semester and which electives to choose. Thus curriculum planning is a mixed-initiative (MI) constraint satisfaction problem (CSP) with preferences. Traditional constructive algorithms for solving CSPs do not support MI reasoning well. In this paper, we explore a two phase approach. An initial schedule is constructed using constructive backtrack search, which satisfies all the academic constraints. Then a second semi-systematic local search algorithm is applied to

B. Kégl and G. Lapalme (Eds.): AI 2005, LNAI 3501, pp. 79–90, 2005.

the initial solution. This algorithm supports MI interaction by allowing the user to modify the current course plan directly through the GUI while maintaining consistency of the academic constraints.

Figure 1 illustrates a plan produced by the system with semesters as rows and courses as columns. Each cell of the plan can be seen as a variable, whose domain is the set of all available courses. The number of columns in the table is the number of semesters required to fulfill an academic degree. The maximum number of rows is the maximum number of courses that a student may take in each semester. When an initial plan is constructed and posted to the user (Figure 1), the user can directly modify the plan by changing the content of cells in the table. For example, if the user plans to be on-leave for a term, he or she simply changes the course load to zero and then clicks the "Make a New Plan" button. The system will produce a new plan with zero courses assigned in that term and then wait for the user to perform further verification and modification. Plan construction, revision, and improvement proceed iteratively within a *decide and commit* cycle until the user is satisfied with the result.

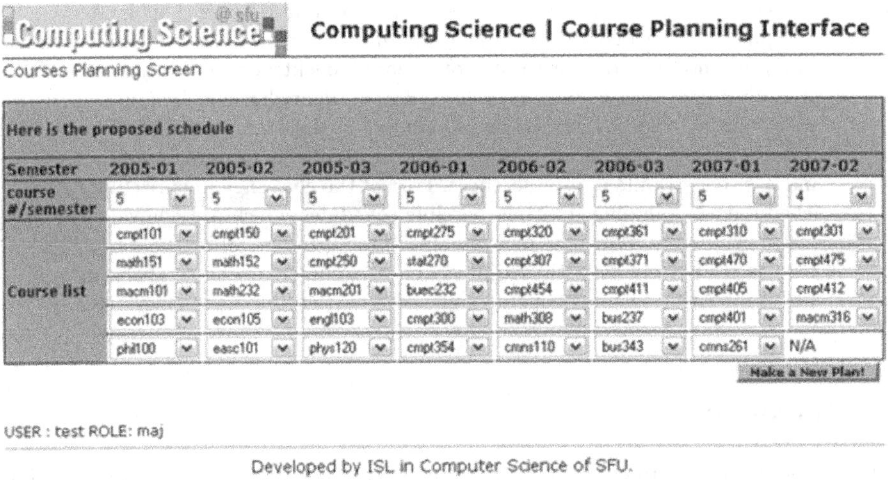

Computing Science | Course Planning Interface

Courses Planning Screen

Here is the proposed schedule								
Semester	2005-01	2005-02	2005-03	2006-01	2006-02	2006-03	2007-01	2007-02
course #/semester	5	5	5	5	5	5	5	4
Course list	cmpt101	cmpt150	cmpt201	cmpt275	cmpt320	cmpt361	cmpt310	cmpt301
	math151	math152	cmpt250	stat270	cmpt307	cmpt371	cmpt470	cmpt475
	macm101	math232	macm201	buec232	cmpt454	cmpt411	cmpt405	cmpt412
	econ103	econ105	engl103	cmpt300	math308	bus237	cmpt401	macm316
	phil100	easc101	phys120	cmpt354	cmns110	bus343	cmns261	N/A

Make a New Plan!

USER : test ROLE: maj

Developed by ISL in Computer Science of SFU.

Fig. 1. Curriculum Planning System User Interface

Academic regulations used to construct system constraints handled in our model are listed as follows. They forms the system constraints.

- All-different constraint: students should not take the same course twice.
- Prerequisite constraint: some courses must have other courses or a number of credits as prerequisites. For example, in Figure 1, 'cmpt300' can not be planned for a semester unless 'cmpt201' and 'macm201' have been planned in previous semesters.
- Mandatory-requirement constraint: some courses must be taken in order to obtain an academic degree, *e.g.*, 'cmpt300' and 'cmpt354' must be taken in order to obtain a bachelor's degree in computer science.

- Equivalent-course constraint: a course is equivalent to another course and, thus, students can not take both courses for credits. For example, 'ensc250' is equivalent to 'cmpt250'. Therefore, only one of these should be included in a feasible plan.
- Breadth constraint: courses offered in a department are divided into different academic levels and different areas. The school usually requires students to take a number of courses in certain levels from several academic areas to ensure students breadth knowledge coverage. For example, undergraduate courses in computer science are numbered from 100 level up to 400 level. Courses numbered 300 or higher are divided into six areas such as AI, networks, and so on. Students have to take five 300-level courses from five areas among the six.
- Depth constraint: a number of courses in a higher academic level from the same subject chosen to satisfy breadth requirements have to be taken, so that students can gain a deeper knowledge in these subjects.
- Maximum-load constraint: a student's course load can not exceed the maximum course load stated in the student handbook.

Symmetry occurs in many scheduling, assignment, and routing problems [12] and in the curriculum planning problem as well. Courses in a semester are indistinguishable and can be freely permuted in a semester. In order to break this symmetry and prune the search tree more efficiently, we add a partial-order constraint to the model, which prevents to search equivalent schedules.

The rest of the paper is organized as follows: Section 2 discusses works in related areas. Section 3 defines the system and system constraints; Section 4 describes scheduling techniques used in the system; In section 5, we present the experimental results of using different techniques; We conclude the paper in section 6.

2 Background

The curriculum planning problem is not a timetabling problem. The timetabling problem is to fix a sequence of meetings between teachers and students in a pre-fixed period of time with a set of constraints satisfied[1]. The curriculum planning problem discussed in this paper is about producing curriculum plans for university students to fulfill their academic career. Few works have studied curriculum planning. Most university students still perform their planning manually, which is error prone. *Castro et al.* [2] proposed a CSP model on solving curriculum problems, which only handles prerequisite and maximum load constraints. Compared with their model, our model manages higher number of general constraints in the curriculum planning and also it integrates mixed-initiative reasoning into the system.

A mixed-initiative (MI) system is one in which both the system and the user have an active role to play in a dialogue or problem-solving process[5]. The earliest investigations into the design of mixed-initiative dialogue systems were presented in the paper of Whittaker and Walker [3] in 1990. At the early stage of MI research, researchers usually designed MI systems with a concrete model of initiative [3, 4, 5]. They believed that initiative should be equated with the control over the flow of conversation so that the metaphor of conversation is important in designing MI systems. Recently, Miller and Traum [6] questioned - whether it is necessary to model initiative in order to design an MI system. They ultimately argued that a MI system can be designed effectively without a concrete model of initiative. Our model supports their view. It shows that when the application domain is in a task-oriented collaborative planning environment, it is not important for participants to realize who has the initiative. Thus, it is not necessary to model initiative explicitly, but view it narrowly as controlling how a problem is being solved.

Constraint programming techniques are widely used to model and solve planning and scheduling problems. Various efficient algorithms have been proposed during the past few decades. They usually fall into three main categories: systematic algorithms, local search algorithms, and hybrid search algorithms. Systematic searching algorithms are built upon various backtracking mechanisms [7]. They are complete and guaranteed to find a solution if one exists [7]. Local search algorithms (e.g., min-conflict, tabu search) perform an incomplete exploration of the search space by repairing infeasible complete assignments and, thus, they are incomplete and cannot guarantee a solution. Cooperation between local and systematic search algorithms has been studied [9, 10, 11]. These hybrid methods have led to good results on large scale problems. In this paper, we take a systematic approach and take a hybrid approach in the second phase. Indeed, our goal was to show that modelling the curriculum planning problem in different ways at different processing stages using different methods is a good strategy to produce high quality solutions.

3   Modelling

In this section, we describe the structure of the system first, and then give the formal definitions of the system and system constraints.

3.1   The Curriculum Planning System

The model contains two components: a system agent and a user agent. The system agent is responsible for maintaining system constraints and a current set of feasible solutions, propagating the consequences of decisions, and constructing the final solution incrementally. The role of the user agent is to make choices among alternative plans and retract requests that have proved unsatisfactory. The system agent has higher priority than user agents. System constraints derived from academic regulations are registered with the system agent but not shared with the user agent. Requests from a user are transformed into user constraints, which are registered with the user agent and shared with the system agent. User constraints are unary and retractable as well.

The system uses a two-phase approach to solve the problem. It models the first phase as a search problem and uses a modified DBT method with value ordering heuristics to find an initial solution and then posts it to the user. In the second phase, a user specifies requirements by directly changing the content of cells in the plan (Figure 1). These assignments will be registered as user constraints with the user agent. These newly added user requests may make the problem over constrained. For example, because of not being familiar with course regulations, a user requests to take two courses that are equivalent. In this case, no solution can be found to satisfy all system constraints and the user requests simultaneously. Thus, the system models the phase two into an optimization problem based on the requests from the user, which includes creating new variables and posting new constraints if necessary. A systematic local search method that combines min-conflicts local search with conflict-directed backjumping [10] is applied. The system returns an optimal solution found in a given time frame and takes the initiative to ask the user for further assistance.

3.2 Definitions of the System and Its Constraints

The problem is solved using constraint programming techniques. A Constraint Satisfactory Problem (CSP) is a triple of (V, D, C), where V is a set of ordered variables, domain D is a set of possible values associated with a variable v, *where* $v \in V$, and C is a set of constraints that restrict value assignments of variables. In our model, every cell in the table contains a variable. V is organized as a matrix of variables with p columns and r rows (Figure 1). Here, p is the number of possible semesters that the user may take to finish an academic degree, and r is the maximum course load per semester. The collection of available courses is the domain D. We use m to represent the size of D. An assignment pair (v_{ij}, d_j) *for* $\forall v_{ij} \in V$ indicates that the value d_j is assigned to the variable v_{ij}. A solution is denoted as the matrix of variable assignment pairs that satisfy the set of constraints. System constraints managed in the system are defined below.

Here we give formal definitions of the system constraints described informally in Section 1 as follows:

All-different constraint: For any two variables v_{ij}, v_{st}, where $1 \le i \le r$, $1 \le s \le r$, $1 \le j \le p$ *and* $1 \le t \le p$, if $v_{ij} \ne v_{st}$, and then for the corresponding variable assignment pairs of $(v_{ij}, d), (v_{st}, d_2), d$ *and* $d_2 \in D$ in the solution, it is always true that $d \ne d_2$.

Prerequisite constraint: Case 1: $D' : \{d_r, \dots, d_s\} \in D$ and a value $d \in D$ but $d \notin D'$, where $1 \le r \le m$ and $1 \le s \le m$. Consider variables at column i, $V' : \{v_{1i}, \dots, v_{ri}\}$, where $1 < i \le p$, for a variable $v \in V_i$ may have a variable assignment pair of (v, d), if and only if, it is true for $\forall d_k \in D'$ where $r \le k \le s$ that $\exists v_{xy} \in V_j$, *where* $V_j : \{(v_{11}, \dots, v_{r1}), \dots, (v_{1y} \dots, v_{ry})\}$ with $1 \le y < i \le p$, there exists a variable assignment pair (v_{xy}, d_k) in the solution; Case 2: For a value $d \in D$, related to a threshold ϵ, whenever ϵ is reached after a variable assignment (v_{ij}, d_i), the value d can be assigned to a variable $v_{xy} \in V$ *where* $y > j$.

Mandatory-requirement constraint: A subset of values $D' : \{d_1, \dots, d_j\} \in D$ *with* $j < m$, *for* $\forall d_k \in D'$, $\exists v \in V$, such that a variable assignment pair (v, d_k) exists in the solution.

Equivalent-course constraint: In a subset of values $D' : \{d_1, \ldots, d_j\} \in D$, if $\exists d, \ d \in D'$, such that there exists a variable assignment $(v, d), v \in V$ and then for every other variable $x \in V$ *and* $x \neq v$, the variable assignment (x, d_x) with $d_x \notin D'$.

Breadth/Depth constraint: A subset of domain values D' is divided into k groups, s.t. $D' = \{D'_1, D'_2, \ldots, D'_k\}$. For $\forall D'_i \in D', \exists d \in D'_i$, s.t. there is a variable assignment $(v, d), v \in V$ in the solution.

Maximum-load constraint: Let $c_1, \ldots, c_i$ represent the number of credits for $d_1, \ldots, d_i$, respectively. Let Max represent the constant defined in the system, it is always true that

$$\sum_{r=1}^{i} c_r \leq Max$$

4   Planning Techniques

In this section, we first present the two algorithms and then discuss other techniques used to speed up the performance of the model.

4.1   Searching Methods

Due to the characteristics of the problem, a systematic search method is used in the first phase. A university freshman always starts with an empty academic record. The record will be filled out semester by semester after the student starts to take courses. Hence, it is proper to choose a search method that generates a curriculum plan in the way of mimicking the procedure of a student's taking courses gradually. Many students in a department graduate with different academic records, which indicates that there are many feasible solutions. Hence, a systematic searching method, which starts from a zero variable assignment, fills out the plan chronologically and guarantees a solution, is used to solve the problem in this phase.

The method is based on Ginsberg's DBT [8] with two changes. One change is not to perform variable reordering when a backtrack occurs during the search and the other one is to add forward checking. Modifications are made because of the characteristics of the partial-order prerequisite constraints. These constraints propagate in one direction from earlier semesters to later ones. Thus, when all cells in previous semesters have been assigned, the prerequisite constraint posed on variables in the current semester can propagate properly. It cannot propagate backwards to prune the domain of variables in previous columns. Thus, it is desired to assign variables in a lexicographical order and not change the ordering, hence, we remove the step of reordering variable when backtracking occurs. However, adding forward checking [7] is to take advantage of the one-way propagation of prerequisite constraints and reduce the number of backtracks.

The algorithm is listed in Figure 2. It starts from an empty variable assignment with each variable having the full domain D (Line 1) as the live domain. The loop starting at line 2 is repeated until all variables have been assigned

v_i : represents a variable $\in V$ at position i according to the variable ordering.
A : the set stores all variables that have been assigned a consistent value.
U : the set stores all variables that have **not** been assigned a value.
C_i: the set of constraints on variable v_i.
D : the live domain of variables. D_i represents the live domain for variable v_i.
R : the set of elimination explanations. $\forall R_i \in R$, R_i is associated with v_i. R_i remembers all reasons for eliminating certain values from the live domain D_i for v_i. Each reason is represented as a pair composed of a value and a list of variables $d, (v_x, \ldots, v_y)$, where $d \in D$, $v_x \in V$, and $v_y \in V$. The intended meaning is that v_i can not take the value d because of the current assignments of variables $v_x, \ldots, v_y$.

```
1.    Set A = φ, U = V, and then set Rₓ = φ, and Dₓ = D for ∀vₓ ∈ V
2.    Begin loop
3.        if U = φ, return A.
4.    else
5.        Select a variable vᵢ ∈ U according to the variable ordering,
6.        Set Rᵢ based on Cᵢ and A and update live domain Dᵢ of i based on Rᵢ.
7.        if Dᵢ ≠ φ
8.            if ∃d ∈ Dᵢ s.t. Dₓ ≠ φ for ∀vₓ ∈ U, then
9.                Update live domain Dₓ for ∀vₓ ∈ U and vₓ ≠ vᵢ.
10.               Add (vᵢ, d) to A,
11.               Remove vᵢ from U, go back to Line 3.
12.       else
13.           if R = φ, return no solution.
14.           else
15.               find (vⱼ, dⱼ) be the last entry in A, s.t. vⱼ ∈ Rᵢ.
16.               Remove (vⱼ, dⱼ) from A and add vⱼ to U
17.               Update Rⱼ, and Rₓ for every variable vₓ assigned after vⱼ.
18.               Set i = j, go back to Line 6.
19.   End loop
```

Fig. 2. Modified dynamic backtracking algorithm

and U becomes empty and then a solution is returned (line 3). While U is not empty, a variable v_i is chosen from U based on the variable ordering rule (line 5); Update the live domain D_i of v_i, and remember the eliminating explanations R_i for v_i (line 6). R_i remembers reasons of pruning values out of the live domain D_i for v_i (See the definition of R_i in Figure 2). If the live domain D_i is not empty, forward checking is performed on the future variables, which are those unassigned variables in U. Forward checking is performed at line 8 by trying to instantiate v_i repeatedly until a trail instantiation is found, which ensures no annihilation of the live domain of every future variable. With a successful instantiation of v_i, v_i is removed from U, the assignment of v_i is added into A (line 10 and 11). If a domain-wipe-out occurs when pruning live domain D_i of v_i or when performing forward checking on the future variables, then backtracking from v_i to v_j is performed, where v_j is the last assigned variable that occurs in R_i (line 16). If backtracking is needed while the set of eliminating explanations becomes empty then the algorithm returns a failure (line 13).

In the second phase, Optimization is needed. Therefore, we use a systematic local search algorithm (see Figure 3), which is based on the search method described in [10]. The algorithm extends the problem from a CSP to an optimization problem. It looks for maximal solutions. A solution is maximal if all variables are chosen maximal assignments. A variable v has a maximal assignment d if the defined evaluation function f, not $\exists a \in D, s.t. f(d) \leq f(a)$. D is the live domain of v. Every time the algorithm reaches a maximal solution, it checks if the solution satisfies all constraints. If so, it returns the solution. Otherwise, it keeps looking for the next maximal solution. It remembers the one with the best quality. Because the system is an interactive system, the response time is crucial. Once the predefined search time is up, the current best solution is returned.

---

uc: the set of user constraints that currently registered with the user agent.
R : a collection of noGood.
A: the list of variable assignment pairs, initialized with the assignments from the GUI.
B: the best inconsistent solution that has found so far, initially $B = A$.

1.   initialize A, and set $B=A$
2.   loop
3.   pick v from V;
4.   assign a value d to v;
5.   if an empty noGood is derived or predefined searching time is exceeded, return B
6.   end loop when (A is *a maximal solution*)
7.   if A is consistent with all C and uc, return A
8.   else
9.   let B to be the better one between A and B, set A as a noGood , add it to R;
10.   go back to line 3

Fig. 3. Systematic Local Search Algorithm

The algorithm operates as follows. It initializes the current solution A and the best solution B with variable assignments obtained from the GUI. The loop starting at line 2 is repeated until A is a maximal solution. Then it checks to verify if A is consistent (line 7), if so, it returns A, otherwise it remembers the better one between A and B, fails A as a noGood (line 8). Then it goes back to line 3 to look for the next maximal solution (line 9). While A is not maximal, a variable v is chosen based on the variable ordering rule (line 3). Then v is assigned based on the value ordering heuristics and the maximal assignment rule (line 4). Whenever an empty noGood[1] is derived or the predefined search time is exceeded, the current best solution is returned (line 5).

---

[1] noGood is a list of variable assignments, whose partial assignment of variables is precluded from any global solution.

4.2   Symmetry Breaking

The curriculum planning problem, like many scheduling problems, encounters the symmetry problem as well. We handle the problem with a partial-order constraint. Courses are grouped into classes according to their subjects. Each class has an associated value, which determines if it has a higher order than another one. For example, all mathematics courses belong to the class of 'math.' All computer science courses belong to the class of 'cmpt.' The system defines that the 'cmpt' class has a higher order than the 'math' class. The symmetry-breaking constraint that enforces the partial ordering on variables in a column evaluates the ordering on variables by class values rather than domain values. This is because the later case is too strict and may hinder the search by causing unnecessary backtracks in the second search phase.

For example, suppose that the symmetry-breaking constraint directly uses domain values to evaluate the ordering on those variables. There are three variables in the column i (v_{1i}, v_{2i}, v_{3i}), four domain values with $d_1 < d_2 < d_3 < d_4$, and three classes $A_1 < A_2 < A_3$, where $d_1 \in A_1$, $d_2 \in A_2$, and $d_3, d_4 \in A_3$. The three variables have the assignment pairs of $\{(v_{1i}, d_1), (v_{2i}, d_2), (v_{3i}, d_3), \ldots\}$ for a column i, where $1 \leq i \leq p$. When the user changes the assignment of the variable v_{2i} from one course d_2 to d_4, provided no system constraints are violated by the change, the partial order on the three variables evaluated by domain values ($d_1 \leq d_4 > d_3$) is broken. Thus, the constraint is violated after the change, and then backtracking has to be performed. However, the ordering among class values still exists ($A_1 \leq A_3 \leq A_3$), and this backtracking can be avoided if class values are used to evaluate the partial ordering on variables. Hence, symmetry-breaking constraints check the ordering on variables in a column using class values, by which the efficiency of pruning the search space is ensured. Meanwhile, unnecessary backtracks are avoided.

4.3   Variable and Value Ordering

It is known that, when using symmetry-breaking constraints, the variable and value ordering are very important[13]. In particular, if variable ordering moves from a direction that increasing conflicts with the symmetry-breaking constraint, we can expect to gain from both the lower complexity and increased pruning [13]. Hence, variables are grouped by semesters, ordered from top to bottom within a semester, and chronologically among semesters.

As for value ordering, courses loaded into the system are divided into different classes. If two courses are in a same class, two courses are ordered by the value of their integer representations; otherwise, a course that has a lower class level is less than the one having a higher class level. Values in a live domain are chosen based on value ordering heuristics. Value ordering heuristics simulates what a human advisor would suggest. When students make their plans manually, they usually choose courses under the guidance of an academic advisor. These rules are transformed into value ordering heuristics stored in the system to guide the search. Through the experimental results given below, we found that it can speed up the search efficiently.

5   Experimental Results

We implement the proposed model on top of a Java-based Constraint Programming (CP) framework called ConstraintWorks [14]. The experimental data are from the computing science department at Simon Fraser University, BC, Canada. The number of available courses are from 60, 80 to 120 courses. Experimental results presented in Table 1 are based on the configuration of 39 variables and 40 system constraints. We compare the performance of different search methods as the domain size changing from 60, 80, up to 120 in the first stage. We use the number of backtracks and the number of iterations, which is the iteration number that the loop has repeated during the search, to evaluate the performance of the method. Table 1 shows that as domain size increases, the number of backtracks and the number of iterations of both the local search method and the systematic search method with no heuristics increase dramatically. In contrast, the systematic search with heuristics can find a solution without backtracking in all 3 cases. It maintains good performance as the domain size increases. Hence, the results confirm that a systematic search method needs good heuristics to have good performance, especially when the size of the domain becomes large.

Table 1. Performance comparison with 39 variables and 40 system constraints

Search method	size of domain	number of backtracks	number of Iterations
Systematic search with no heuristic	60	7189	4435
	80	32991	8997
	106	99760	31216
Local search	60	740	10
	80	6740	983
	120	11811	5585
Systematic search with heuristics	60	0	39
	80	0	39
	120	0	39

For the second stage, we study the performance when the user's requests break numbers of constraints at different positions in the schedule. We define the position in a plan as follows: for a plan with p number of columns, a slot S is at column c with $c/p < 30\%$, then we say S is at an early position of the plan; if $30\% < c/p < 70\%$, then S is at a middle position, otherwise it is posted at a late stage of the schedule. In order to compare the performance of the systematic local search method, we also ran the second phase using the systematic search algorithm. In this case the systematic method solves the second phase as a CSP. It returns a solution satisfying all constraints including newly added user constraints if indeed a solution exists. Otherwise, it returns the old solution and discards all newly added user constraints.

Table 2. Performance comparison between the systematical Local search and the modified DBT search

# of breaking constraints	Position in the plan	Systematic Local Search		Modified DBT search	
		# of iterations	time used (seconds)	# of iterations	time used (seconds)
1	Early	222	39	1222	171
	Middle	31	44	910	79
	Late	10	16	62	10
2	early	1838	151	1638	193
	Middle	40	13	379	64
	Late	194	25	70	11
3	early	13	9	93	29
	Middle	2024	180	8324	6478
	Late	3	2	3	4

Table 2 shows the performance of local search and systematic search at the second stage when the posted user requests break one, two, or three system constraints respectively at different places in the schedule. The number of courses is 120. Maximum course load is 12 credit hours and the number of total constraints is 40. The search time limit is three minutes. We test a special case: the user requests posted in the middle and breaking 3 system constraints are taking two equivalent courses. In this case, the systematic method takes a very long time and returns a failure. The local search method halts with one user constraint satisfied when the predefined search time is up. The results show that the systematic local search method usually is able to solve the problem within a minute and overall has better performance with respect to the response time. The local search method can return a better solution in the given time frame.

6   Conclusion

We have presented a mixed-initiative curriculum planning model. Due to the diversity in the characteristics and the needs of different users, we have integrated mixed-initiative into the planning system, which provides a direct-manipulation environment for the efficient communication between a user and the system. Through a cycle of plan construction, revision, and improvement, the system serves various users effectively. The solving process is split into two phases. A backtrack-based systematic search method is used in the first phase to produce an initial solution. A systematic local search method is employed to construct the final plan gradually under the interactive guidance from the user. Partial-order constraints are added in order to break the symmetry arising in the model. Value ordering heuristics are used as well to speed up the search. Experimental results shows that the system generates effective curriculum plans efficiently.

References

1. A. Schaerf. A survey of automated timetabling. Artificial Intelligence Review, Vol. 13(2) (1999) pp. 87-127.
2. C. Castro and S. Manzano. Variable and Value Ordering: When Solving Balanced Academic Curriculum Problems. In *Proceedings of 6th Workshop of the ERCIM WG on Constraints*, Prague. June, 2001.
3. M. Walker. and S. Whittaker. Mixed-initiative in dialogue: an investiation into discourse segmentation. In *Proceedings of ACL90*, (Pittsburgh, PA, 1990) pp. 70-76.
4. C. Guinn. Mechanisms for mixed-initiative human-computer collaborative discourse. In *Proceedings of ACL96*, (Santa Cruz, CA, 1996) pp. 27-205.
5. J. Allen. Mixed-initiative planning: position paper. Presented at ARPA/Rome Labs Planning Initiative Workshop, 1994.
6. B. Miller. Is explicit representation of initiative desirable? Working Notes of AAAI97 Spring Symposium on Mixed Initiative Interaction. Stanford, CA, 1997.
7. P.Prosser. Hybrid algorithms for the constraint satisfaction problem. Computational Intelligence, Vol. 9(3) (1993) pp. 268-299.
8. M. L. Ginsberg. Dynamic backtracking. Journal of Artificial Intelligence Research, Vol. 1 (1993) pp. 25-46.
9. P. Shaw, Using constraint programming and local search methods to solve vehicle routing problems. In *Proceedings of fourth Conference on Principles and practice of Constraint Programming*, (Pisa, 1998) pp. 417-431.
10. W. S. Havens, Bistra N. Dilkina. A Hybrid Schema for Systematic Local Search. In *Proceedings of Canadian Conference on AI 2004*, (London, ON, Canada, 2004) pp. 248-260.
11. N. Jussien, and O. Lhomme. Local search with constraint propagation and conflict-based heuristics. Journal of Artificial Intelligence, Vol. 139 (2002) pp. 21-45.
12. P. Flener, A. Frisch et. al. Breaking row and column symmetries in matrix models. In *Proceedings of CP'2002*, (Springer, 2002) pp. 94-107.
13. A. Frisch, B. Hnich et. al. Global Constraints for Lexicographic Orderings. Constraint Programming 2002. pp.93-108, 2002.
14. Actenum Corporation, ConstraintWorks, Vancouver, British Columbia, Canada, www.actenum.com.

SWAMI: Searching the Web Using Agents with Mobility and Intelligence

Mark Kilfoil and Ali Ghorbani

Intelligent and Adaptive Systems (IAS) Research Group,
Faculty of Computer Science,
University of New Brunswick,
Fredericton, NB, Canada
{mark.kilfoil, ghorbani}@unb.ca

Abstract. The rapid growth of the World Wide Web has complicated the process of web browsing by providing an overwhelming wealth of choices for the end user. To alleviate this burden, intelligent tools can do much of the drudge-work. This paper describes the SWAMI system. It combines multiple aspects of adaptive web technologies into a framework for an intelligent web browsing system. It uses a multi-agent system to represent the interests of the user dynamically and takes advantage of the active nature of agents to provide a platform for parallel look-ahead evaluation, page searching, and cooperative link recommendation swapping. The collection of agents reflects the user's interests by self-organizing into a hierarchicy according to the evidence of apparent interest demonstrated by the user. Example results of the functioning prototype are presented, demonstrating its ability to infer and react to a user's interests.

1 Introduction

The continual growth and complexity of the World Wide Web has impacted its effectiveness in a negative way. An individual user must sift through a vast number of pages that are of little or no interest to them to discover pages that address his or her interests. Tools have been developed to assist in this process, one of the most successful being the keyword-based search engine, such as Google [1]. However, keyword-based search engines require a user to carefully craft his or her query to be an accurate statement of information desires, which is often difficult to perform.

Another approach is to build web sites that are *adaptive*. Adaptive web sites allow users to describe themselves (specifically including information desires and form factors) and use this information to modify their responses to suit each user (or group of similar users) individually.

This paper introduces SWAMI, a client-side, multi-agent-based approach to personalizing the user experience of web browsing. Section 2 describes the domain of the problem, as well as describing other approaches, including other agent solutions. Section 3 briefly describes the architecture of the SWAMI

B. Kégl and G. Lapalme (Eds.): AI 2005, LNAI 3501, pp. 91–102, 2005.

system. In Section 4, preliminary results gathered from experimental data are included. Finally, Section 5 presents a summary of the benefits and drawbacks of the SWAMI approach, and discusses future directions for research.

2   Background and Related Work

The web is a relatively new phenomenon, and has elevated certain problems to a critical level. In this section, the two most prominent problems of web navigation and web personalization are discussed, and a short summary of current solutions is presented.

2.1   Navigation

Because of the large size, dynamic nature and inconsistent structure, the web is difficult to navigate. "Traditional", direct navigation approaches depend on an evaluation of the relevance of the currently viewed page as the best indicator of the value of pages pointed to by it. This approach relies upon the benevolence of the creator of the link [2], and the hope that by following a series of related links the user will end up at another cluster of useful pages.

The traditional strategy closely resembles a depth-first graph search, where leaf nodes are represented by pages of interest. Effectively, however, the user must go "one page too far" in such a scheme, and travel deeper and deeper distances from the original page they were browsing into possibly uninteresting areas. This, intuitively, is the opposite of the desired result as pages directly connected to the current page are most likely to be the most relevant pages to it [3].

An alternative approach is to use a search engine, which, in effect, reconstructs the graph of the Web, reconnecting all the distant pages together into a single layer. In this way, more relevant pages become more likely at an earlier stage of browsing. In the case of Yahoo [4], this rearrangement is done explicitly through a hierarchical, soft categorization of web site links. In contrast, Google [1] builds a response page (effectively the top-level of a tree or entrance to a graph) dynamically around a set of initial keywords in a query.

Once the user has selected a link from a search engine, however, they are out of the arena of that technology and browsing returns to the traditional strategy. Thus, this technology produces only a one-shot or one-level navigational benefit, not ongoing navigational support.

An additional criticism of search engine approaches is that the criteria for the evaluation of results is very specific: the keywords of the request are the only measure of relevance to the user that the system can use, although there are additional measures of the relative importance of a page (some partially dependant of the particular request made) [2].

Adaptive web sites take a highly personalized approach, using knowledge about the specific user to modify both the presentation [5] of individual pages and/or the navigation from one page to another [6]. In this way, they can be seen to either add additional links between pages of relevance to the user or do a similar rearranging of the graph to the search engine, although beyond just a single level of rearrangement and navigational support. Prominent examples of adaptive web systems include WebWatcher [7], AHAM [3] and AVANTI [8]. Each of these systems provides server-side adaptive navigation or presentation based on perceived user characteristics.

Server-side adaptive web solutions are generally limited to a single web site or set of close web sites operated by the same people, something to which the search engine approach is not limited. Client-side personalized approaches, on the other hand, can work across all websites, but do not have the benefit of an internal view of the website (to allow adaptations based on non-disclosed information) or collaborative recommendations (because there is no common place for all users). Client-side solutions include Letizia [3] and Personal WebWatcher [9], and to a certain degree the proxy-based system PVA [10].

SWAMI is primarily a client-side solution, but it allows interaction with peers and with internal sections of web sites by allowing parts of its representation to be mobile, and move to a location to interact with the mobile parts of other users' SWAMI, or with representatives of an SWAMI-aware website.

2.2   Personalization and User Representation

Personalization on the Web means to modify the contents in or navigation on a web page to reflect the particular user who is viewing it. It is adaptive to the user's characteristics or behaviour, responding in a way to enhance the user's experience.

SWAMI models the user's apparent interests in order to make forward evaluations, user-centric web searches and navigation suggestions about pages to visit. Interests are roughly characterized into three kinds: **long-term interests**, which are stable and rarely changing, although at a particular instant may be unexpressed; **short-term interests**, which are sudden and strong, but vanish quickly, never to return; and **periodic interests**, which have the qualities of both long- and short-term interests, in that they are strong for short periods of time and relatively unimportant for the rest of the time.

Because specifying interests is difficult (perhaps even impossible) for a user to express, the approach in SWAMI is to infer interests from the browsing behaviour of the user. This has proven to be effective in other cases [11, 12, 13]. By having the system continually learning about interests from the user's ongoing browsing behaviour, the problem of following interest changes is also addressed.

A similar approach to [14] has been taken in SWAMI for interest modelling, but with a significant difference: where in [14] an externally organized hierarchy was used and the user's apparent interests mapped over it with pages placed into nodes in that hierarchy, in SWAMI the hierarchy is developed entirely from scratch, allowing it to be a customized size to reflect the user's interests.

3   The SWAMI Architecture

SWAMI consists of a front-end interface, a user representation, and components which perform page searching. It is implemented using a (custom) multi-agent

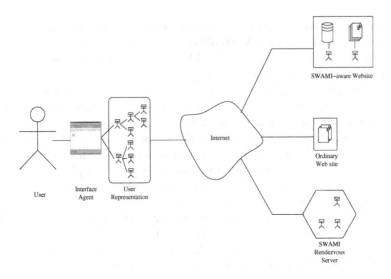

Fig. 1. A high level view of SWAMI

system (see Figure 1. This section describes each of these three components in more detail.

3.1   The Interface

The user interacts with the system using the SWAMI interface agent. The interface agent is currently integrated into a simple browser, allowing the agent to observe user activity easily and report the search and evaluation results of the user representation to the user. The browser also allows the user to display the agents currently representing them.

3.2   The User Representation

The user is represented by a hierarchically-arranged collection of agents. Each representation agent represents a cluster of pages the user has viewed, with the hierarchies representing the relationships between clusters.

The hierarchies of agents are created using an online, dynamic clustering technique. An agent collects pages as they are viewed by the user that are similar to the pages it has already gathered. The agent continually checks the tightness of its cluster, and if it is too loose (beyond a threshold), it will attempt to split the collection of pages up into tighter subgroups. If it is successful, it creates (or "hires") new agents to represent the subgroups. These agents are positioned below the original agent, so that incoming pages are first examined by the original agent, and then may be passed down to the more specialized sub-agents, and so on, until the best match has been made.

Initially, the interface agent collects all pages until a distinct group is discovered, forming the first representation agent. If no current agent is representative of a given page, the interface agent holds on to it until a new group manifests itself. Each of these top level groups is referred to as a "corporation", and represents a major interest of the user.

Each agent has a measurement of "wealth", which reflects the importance and relevance to the user of the cluster the agent represents. The wealth combines the agent's size, the success the agent has had in finding new pages for the user, the success the agent has had in having found pages accepted by the user and a history momentum which allows an agent to rest on its laurels briefly.

When an agent's wealth falls below a threshold, the agent is removed from the hierarchy and moved into a holding area. In this way, agents which are not useful are pruned from the hierarchy. However, to represent periodic interests, these agents are not immediately deleted, but rather they remain in the holding area, continuing to decay until one of three conditions is satisfied: either they are the best representative for a new page the user views, they represent a newly discovered subcluster better than a blank agent or they decay to a point where they are considered truly unimportant and are removed. In the first case, they become the head of a new corporation; in the second case they are simply added into the hierarchy at the appropriate point. This also allows subclusters to migrate to the most appropriate place; for example, a "Mexican cooking" agent might be retired from beneath the general "cooking" agent, but later be rehired under a "Mexican culture" agent. (Note that agents are not labelled in this way; this is merely for illustrative purposes.)

3.3   The Search Components

When a representation agent reaches a sufficient level of wealth and experience, it may create search agents to work for it. Search agents take criteria from the representation agent (the set of word features the representation agent has used to form its cluster, for example) and attempt to find and evaluate pages on its behalf.

Four types of search agents have been considered for the system: link-following search agents, search-engine based search agents, topic expert consulting search agents and colloborative search agents.

The **link-following search agent** follows links from pages the user has already viewed and evaluates them based on its criteria. The agent acts similarly to a user in its browsing pattern, but has more capacity to remember pages closer to the original page and backtrack immediately to any page it has previously viewed (rather than following a linear retreat strategy like a user.)

The **search-engine based search agent** can submit different combinations of word features to a search engine and evaluate the results. It can take advantage of the massive database of knowledge available to a search engine but provide the personalization that the search engine lacks.

The **topic expert consulting search agents** are mobile agents which can travel to SWAMI-aware web sites and interact with topic expert agents representing the web page owner. These topic expert agents may have access to information that cannot be gathered from simply browsing the pages, and may be in a better position to provide recommendations. For example, the topic expert agents may know about arbitrary groupings of pages that do not have labels on the pages themselves.

The **collaborative search agent** seeks to take advantage of the browsing behaviour of people with similar interests. It travels to a host (referred to as the "rendezvous server") where it can interact with agents representing other people. There, they can swap recommendations based on how similar the agents are to each other. Agents of another type, rendezvous hosts, remain in the rendezvous server at all times, interacting with all the visiting search agents and collecting all recommendations that they have. The rendezvous host becomes a "memory" for the rendezvous server, so that not all interactions between agents need be synchronized.

3.4   Implementation

SWAMI was implemented from scratch in approximately 18000 lines of pure Java code. The implemented system included a specialized agent implementation, page representation and comparison techniques, and a simple, integrated browsing environment (see Figure 2) . The interface allowed traditional user navigation (jump to URL, back button, follow a link) as well as providing a list of recommendations provided by the system that the user could follow. The interface also allows the user to inspect what agents have been created on their behalf, what pages those agent have taken ownership of, and what features those agents have extracted from the given pages.

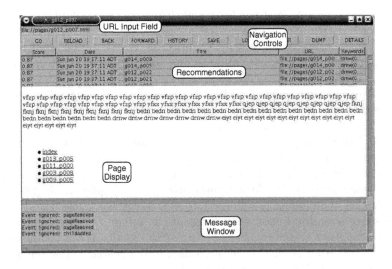

Fig. 2. A snapshot of the SWAMI interface

4   Evaluation

The evaluation of the SWAMI system consists of verifying that it can detect the growth and shift of user interests, provide a usable model of the user, and act upon that model on behalf of the user.

To perform this evaluation, test data was generated that represents a web of pages that are interconnected and that have localized coherence. From this test data, numerous trial runs were conducted in order to demonstrate that all of the key events expected of the system were observed, and that the system was behaving as expected. Two illustrative example runs are highlighted here in detail.

Because the test data was generated offline and never made available to a search engine, no examination of the search-engine-based search method could be attempted, without implementing a specialized search engine, which was beyond the scope of this initial research.

4.1   Results

The following sections describe the results from two particular trial runs in detail. These trial runs were chosen to clearly illustrate the performance of the system, but are otherwise typical.

To describe the life-cycle of an agent, a chart showing the agents' wealth over time is used. This chart is calibrated in absolute terms, meaning that while an individual's age is calculated relative to when they were born, it has been adjusted to the appropriate real outside age relative to the age of the Interface Agent. The age also describes the number of unique pages viewed. Where a line begins on the graph indicates when an agent was born; if the line ends prematurely, that agent was removed from the system.

The lower threshold for an active agent's wealth before being retired is 0.2; only the Interface Agent cannot be retired. If their wealth continues to drop, an agent will be removed when it falls below 0.15.

Pages within a particular group are known to be similar to each other, and thus represent a topic. This is used both to train the system and to interpret its results. Also, as the agents search, they discover pages in other page groups that are relevant to the topic, thus forming a virtual topic group based on the user's demonstrated interests.

4.2   Example 1: Interest Shifts

This example demonstrates SWAMI's ability to follow a user's changing interests and react accordingly. The page groups that the user visited can be seen in Figure 3. On the weight track in Figure 4, five agents (in addition to the Interface Agent) are shown.

Each agent was created when the system detected a cluster of similar pages. The set of pages initially chosen all came from pre-generated group 40, followed by a number of pages selected from group 38. Charlie_0 was created

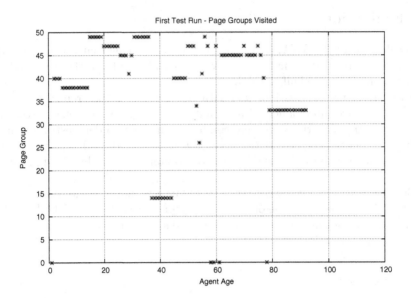

Fig. 3. The page groups visited by the user on the first example test run

when the subset of pages from group 40 were detected as distinct, at age 4. At age 11, a second agent (Charlie_1) was created to take control of the second subcluster discovered (for group 38). Note that while the pages were chosen from the pre-generated group, the system itself has no knowledge of these groups.

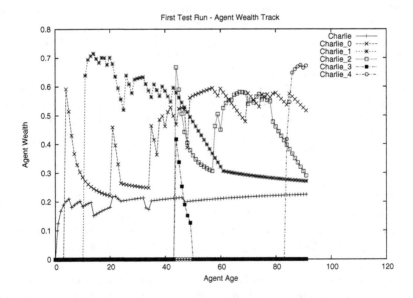

Fig. 4. Agent activity from the first example test run

Between ages 14-36, links were followed semi-randomly from existing pages, but not corresponding to any previous page. These pages were similar enough to existing agents that Charlie_0 rose in wealth during this time period, and Charlie_1 maintained a high wealth. Concentration by the user on a single pre-generated page group again from age 36-43 resulted in the creation of a new agent, Charlie_2, to handle a newly-discovered cluster formed out of those pages. Another agent, Charlie_3 was created at the same time, as the new pages highlighted some previous cluster in the previous pages.

Between ages 53 and 77, recommendations made by Charlie_0 were followed, resulting in that agent's consistent wealth, while other agents diminished. At age 77, a new topic was focused on, and a new agent, Charlie_4 was created in response.

Note that when the user concentrated on a particular topic, the system responded by creating a new agent to handle this new topic when it detected it. As the user drifted away from that topic (by not visiting again), the agents that had been responsible for it waned in wealth.

The longevity of both Charlie_0 and Charlie_1 indicate long-term interests. Charlie_0, in particular, has received a lot of attention from having suggestions followed.

Charlie_2 and Charlie_3 accurately map to short-term interests. In the case of Charlie_3, no recommended pages from that agent were viewed, leading it to degrade in wealth very quickly and disappear within about 5 page views. Charlie_2 was a short-term interest which the user paid a little attention to.

Finally, Charlie_4 is a new interest to which the user is paying attention and good recommendations have been found. The system responds quickly to the newly discovered cluster, and it becomes the most influential among them.

This example has shown that the system creates new agents to handle new user interests, and the wealth of those agents reflects the ongoing interest in the topic they represent.

4.3   Example 2: Interest Specialization

In stark contrast to the previous example, this example demonstrates the creation of specialized agents for sub-topics discovered within the context of a larger topic. While the page group activity shown in Figure 5 seems to be chaotic (particularly after age 57), the corresponding location on Figure 6 shows relatively stable behaviour.

Charlie_0 represents a long-term interest (page group 42) which was concentrated on for a considerable period of time. Two sub-topics were detected from within this one, represented by Charlie_0_0 and Charlie_0_1. The second of these was pursued momentary, but was forgotten for a period of time. Note that Charlie_0_1 was retired but brought back instantaneously when the user returned to that topic. At that point, it actually triggered a split, creating the very short term topic represented by Charlie_0_1_0.

At approximately age 45, the system has detected that the user has decided to view another topic intensely for which good suggestions could be found. This is represented by Charlie_1, whose continued strength is due to its suggestions being

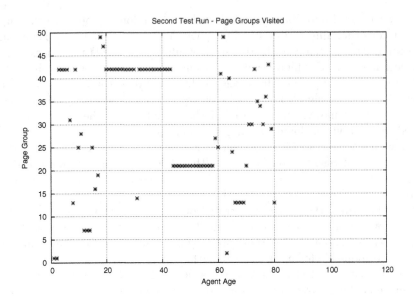

Fig. 5. The page groups visited by the user on the second example test run

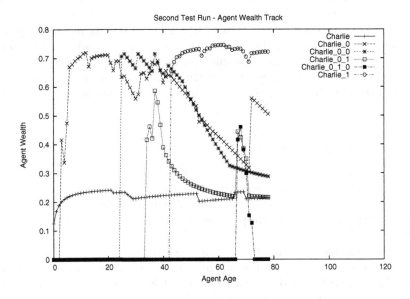

Fig. 6. Results from the second example test run

followed. The return of a peak in Charlie_0 at approximately age 72 was due to following a link on a page suggested by Charlie_1 which led off to an older topic.

The relative stability of the wealth track of Charlie_1 after age 45 despite the apparent randomness of the page group activity for the same time period is due to the agent having found pages within multiple groups which are similar to the topic at hand. In this way, it has created a virtual group of pages centred around the user's interests.

5   Discussion and Conclusions

This paper describes a framework for a multi-agent system for providing personalized web page recommendations to users. The SWAMI framework features a sophisticated user model using a social multi-agent system with a cost-driven and time-variable interaction model organized into hierarchies of related topics. Agents representing particular topical interests in this system can search for recommendations for the user with one of multiple strategies. Among those search strategies is the ability of the search agents to become mobile. Mobile search agents can travel to particular, SWAMI-aware web sites and interact with local topic experts, or they can travel to SWAMI "rendezvous servers", where they can interact with user-independent collaborative recommendation agents and with other search agents representing users.

Key features of this framework include local representation of a user's interests (allowing the system to "learn once, apply everywhere"), the integration of local, site-based and collaborative recommendations, and an active user profile representation which takes into account short-term, long-term and recurring interests, as well as the specialization of interests.

This holistic approach to web search represents a more realistic solution to the problem of web search than site-specific or user-agnostic approaches.

Several trial runs were performed, from which typical examples were chosen to examine in detail. These trial runs demonstrate that the agents do grow to mirror the user activities and change over time to reflect changes in the user intentions. Short-term, long-term and recurring interests have been detected by the system, as well as specialization to accommodate a particularly important interest. Recommendations could be gathered successfully by using a link-search algorithm, by consulting with site experts or through interacting with a community. Recommendations in the community were successfully distributed between members of that community.

This work has demonstrated that a system of organized agents can represent a user's multiple, changing interests. Future studies will examine automatic parameter setting, alternative approaches to agent hierarchy reorganization, more sophisticated page models and page comparison mechanism, "lazy" cluster updates, standardized local expert and rendezvous interfaces and different search mechanisms that can be integrated into the system.

Acknowledgments

This work was funded by the Atlantic Canada Opportunity Agency (ACOA) through the Atlantic Innovation Fund (AIF) to Dr. Ali A. Ghorbani.

References

1. Google: Google search engine (2004) `http://www.google.com`.
2. Kleinberg, J.M.: Authoritative sources in a hyperlinked environment. Journal of the ACM **46** (1999) 604–632
3. Lieberman, H.: Letizia: An agent that assists web browsing. In: Proceedings of the Fourteenth International Joint Conference on Artificial Intelligence, San Mateo, CA, USA, Morgan Kaufmann Publishers Inc (1995) 924–929
4. YAHOO!: Yahoo! search engine (2004) `http://www.yahoo.com`.
5. Kobsa, A., Koenemann, J., Pohl, W.: Personalized hypermedia presentation techniques for improving online customer relationships. The Knowledge Engineering Review **16** (2001) 111–155
6. Brusilovsky, P.: Methods and techniques of adaptive hypermedia. User Modelling and User-Adapted Interaction **6** (1996) 87–129
7. Joachims, T., Freitag, D., Mitchell, T.: WebWatcher: A tour guide for the World Wide Web. In: Proceedings of the Fifteenth International Joint Conference on Artificial Intelligence, Morgan Kaufmann (1997) 770–775
8. Fink, J., Kobsa, A., Nill, A.: Adaptable and adaptive information access for all users, including the disabled and the elderly. In Jameson, A., Paris, C., Tasso, C., eds.: User Modeling: Proceedings of the Sixth International conference, UM97, Vienna, New York, Springer Wien New York (1997) 171–173
9. Mladenic, D.: Personal WebWatcher: design and implementation. Technical report, Department of Intelligent Systems, J. Stefan Institute, Slovenia (1996)
10. Chen, C.C., Chen, M.C.: PVA: A self-adaptive personal view agent. Journal of Intelligent Information Systems **18** (2002) 173–194
11. Pazzani, M.J., Billsus, D.: Learning and revising user profiles: The identification of interesting web sites. Machine Learning **27** (1997) 313–331
12. Chan, P.: Constructing web user profiles: A non-invasive learning approach. In: KDD-99 Workshop on Web Usage Analysis and User Profiling, San Diego, CA, USA (1999) 7–12
13. Schwab, I., Pohl, W., Koychev, I.: Learning to recommend from positive evidence. In: Proceedings of the 2000 International Conference on Intelligent User Interfaces, New Orleans, LA, USA (2000) 241–248
14. Godoy, D., Amandi, A.: A user profiling architecture for textual-based agents. In: Proceedings of the 4th Argentine Symposium on Artificial Intelligence (ASAI 2002) in the 31st International Conference on Computer Science and Operational Research (JAIIO 2002), Santa Fe, Argentina (2002)

Queuing Local Solutions in Distributed Constraint Satisfaction Systems

Ronnie Mueller and William S. Havens

Intelligent Systems Laboratory,
School of Computing Science,
Simon Fraser University,
Burnaby, B.C., Canada V5A 1S6
{rmueller, havens}@cs.sfu.ca

Abstract. When solving Distributed Constraint Satisfaction Problems (DCSP), it is desirable that the search exploits asynchronism as much as possible so that the employed agents can perform much of the work in parallel. This allows to utilize the processing power available in a distributed environment. However, in many of todays DCSP algorithms, only a few agents are working at any given time and the others are idling. This is caused by the fact that once an agent is consistent with its neighbors, it becomes idling until it is forced by other agents to choose a different assignment for its local variables.

In this paper we propose a method that utilizes the idling time of the agents to increase the efficiency of a distributed backtracking algorithm where agents have complex local problems and share variables among them. An agent computes solutions to its local problem in advance while it is waiting for incoming messages. This means that when an agent finds a solution to the local problem that is consistent with higher order agents, it not only informs lower order agents but continuous to search for further solutions which then are stored in a queue. When the current local solution becomes invalid due to a nogood received from a lower order agent, the agent does not have to search for a new local solution but can retrieve a precomputed one from the queue. This approach increases the amount of work the agents can perform in parallel since higher order agents search ahead for local solutions while lower order agents are trying to expand the current partial solution.

Our experiments show that some increase in performance can be gained by queuing local solutions in distributed backtracking.

1 Introduction

A Constraint Satisfaction Problem (CSP) is defined as a set of variables $X = \{x_1, x_2, ..., x_n\}$ and a set of constraints $C = \{c_1, c_2, ..., c_m\}$. The variables take their values out of finite, discrete domains D_1, D_2, ..., D_n, respectively. Each constraint c involves a set of variables $X_c = \{x_{c1}, ..x_{ck}\}$. A relation R_c specifies the allowed tuples for c over the Cartesian product $D_{c1}, .., D_{ck}$. A constraint c is satisfied if the values assigned to the variables in X_c are allowed by R_c. A

B. Kégl and G. Lapalme (Eds.): AI 2005, LNAI 3501, pp. 103–107, 2005.

solution to the CSP is found when all variables are assigned a value and all constraints are satisfied. A CSP is binary if each constraint involves exactly two variables. From here on, we will consider only binary CSPs.

A distributed constraint satisfaction problem (DCSP) is a CSP where the variables and constraints are distributed among a finite set $A = \{a_1, a_2, .., a_m\}$ of autonomous processes called agents. The agents have to coordinate their search by message passing to find a solution to the DCSP that is globally consistent. In a DCSP the constraints are partitioned into two categories, the ones involving two agents are called inter-agent constraints and the ones within one agent are called intra-agent constraints. In the simple case, each agent has exactly one variable and all constraints are inter-agent constraints. A DCSP where the agents have more than one variable is called a DCSP with a complex local problem. In a DCSP with a complex local problem each agent a_i has a local CSP which is defined by the variables belonging to a_i and its intra-agent constraints. In this paper we call solution to the local CSP which is consistent with higher order agents a local solution.

Some research has been done on how to solve DCSPs. Yokoo et al. [1, 2] present Asynchronous Backtracking (ABT), a backtracking algorithm that allows the agents to work concurrently and make decisions asynchronously. Distributed Dynamic Backtracking [3] avoids adding permanent links between unrelated agents as ABT does. The distributed backtracking algorithm [4] uses the given constraint structure for its backtracking. In all of the mentioned algorithms so far, the agents have a static order among them. Armstrong and Durfee [5], Yokoo and Hirayama [2], and Yokoo [6] have proposed algorithms that reorder the agents dynamically to avoid bad assignments of higher order agents. In most of the algorithms an agent only has one local variable, Armstrong and Durfee [5], Silaghi and colleagues [7] and Yokoo and Hirayama [2] address the case where agents have to deal with complex local problems.

In most of the algorithms mentioned above, only a few agents are working at any given time while the others are idling. This is caused by the fact that agents only change the values of their variables when they are forced to by other agents. For constructive algorithms this means, that once an agent finds an assignment that is consistent with higher order agents, it becomes idling and waits for the higher order agents to change or a nogood to be reported by a lower order agent. When a agent receives a nogood message , it tries to find a different local solution that satisfies the nogood and is compatible with the same values of variables shared with higher order agents that were used to compute the previous local solution. This gives us the opportunity to compute local solutions in advance, so an agent can respond quickly once a nogood message is received.

In this empirical study we propose the novel idea for queuing local solutions to increase the performance of a distributed backtracking algorithm. The basic idea is that once an agents finds a local solutions, it continues to search for additional local solutions and stores them in a solution queue, so that they are available quickly in case a nogood message is received and the agent has to backtrack.

2 Queuing Local Solutions in Distributed Backtracking

We developed a backtracking algorithm based on Asynchronous Backtracking (ABT) [1] but extended it so it can handle DCSPs with complex local problems. Instead of choosing a value for its single variable as in ABT, the agents have to search for a solution to their local CSP that is consistent with values of variables shared with higher neighbors.

A queuing mechanism can easily be added to the backtracking algorithm described above. Each agent employs a local solver which continuously searches for solutions to the local CSP that are compatible with variables shared with higher agents. The agent maintains a solution queue where the additional local solutions are stored. All the local solutions kept in the solution queue are compatible with variables shared with higher agents.

The agents start their local solver and react to incoming messages and events from their solver. There are four events that are handled by the following procedures.

ok_message. This procedure is called whenever an ok? message is received. The agent signals the new values of the shared variables to the local solver. The agent clears the solution queue since the ok? message changes the agent_view, which makes the local solution in the solution queue invalid.

nogood_message. The agent tries to dequeue the next local solution from the solution queue and informs the lower neighbors. If the solution queue is empty and the local solver has not reached bottom then no action is taken since the local solver is still searching and will respond with a solution_found or a bottom_reached event eventually. If the solution queue is empty and the solver has already reached bottom then there are no local solutions left and a nogood is created and sent to the culprit agent.

solution_found. When the local solver reports a new local solution, it is appended to the solution queue. If there is space left in the solution queue, the local solver is forced to search for further local solutions.

bottom_reached. When the local solver reaches bottom, a nogood is sent to higher order neighbors if the solution queue is empty. Otherwise the local solver is stopped and the sending of the nogood is delayed until the solution queue becomes empty.

3 Experimental Results

To study the effects of queuing local solutions we randomly generated graph 3-coloring. Our DCSP generator takes the four parameters (n,k,x,y) where n is the number of agents, k the number of variables per agent, x the total number of inter-agent links (shared variables) and y the total number of intra-agent constraints.

We compare the performance by counting the number of total backtracks needed by all agents to arrive at a global solution without counting work which is done in parallel by multiple agents multiple times. Further, we do not count the

number of backtracks an agent uses to search ahead to find local solutions that
are stored in the solution queue during its idling time. We call these backtracks
blocking backtracks.

In our experiments each agent is running on a separate computer. We tested
several problem classes with a various number of agents and inter-agent links. We
generated 100 DCSP instances of each problem class and compared the number
of blocking backtracks for maximum solution queue sizes of 0, 1 ,5, 10, 20 and 100.

Figure 1 shows the relative amount of blocking backtracks in relation to the
maximum solution queue size. For each problem instance we recorded the number
of blocking backtracks used to find the first solution to the DCSP for different
solution queue sizes. Then we calculated the ratio of the number of blocking
backtracks used with a particular queue size limit to the number of blocking
backtracks used without a solution queue (queue size limit 0) for each instance.
Every data point in the diagram shows the median of 100 problem instances. We
kept the number of agents, variables and intra-agent constraints constant and
show multiple graphs for various numbers of inter-agent links x.

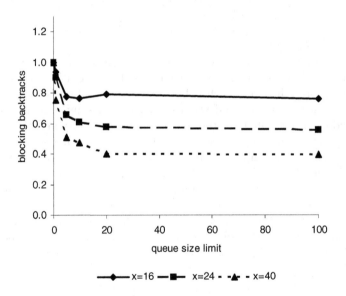

Fig. 1. Blocking backtracks (5 agents, 10 variables each, 40 intra-agent constraints)

We can see that queuing local solutions can help to increase the performance
of distributed backtracking. In some cases a reduction in blocking backtracks
can be achieved by more than 50%.

The increase of the performance is related to the maximum size of the solution
queue. When a small limit on the solution queue size is used, the chance that a
valid solution can be retrieved from the queue when a nogood message arrives
is smaller then when a larger limit is used.

Increasing the maximum solution queue size beyond a certain size (for our problems around 20) does not reduce the number of blocking backtracks any further. We think that this is caused by the limited time an agent has available to search for additional local solutions before a lower order agent sends a nogood message.

When only a small number of variables are shared among agents, the increase in performance is generally smaller then when more variables are shared.

4   Conclusion

We presented the new idea of queuing local solutions to increase the performance of a distributed backtracking algorithm. Our approach uses the time an agent waits for incoming messages to search ahead for additional local solutions which are stored in a solution queue and retrieved when a nogood message is retrieved.

The results from our experiments are promising, they show that queuing local solutions increases the performance of distributed backtracking. We found that the performance gain depends on the structure of the DCSP. Queuing local solutions performs well for tightly coupled agents, but is less effective when agents only share few variables among them.

References

1. Yokoo, M., Durfee, E.H., Ishida, T., Kuwabara, K.: Distributed constraint satisfaction for formalizing distributed problem solving. In: International Conference on Distributed Computing Systems. (1992) 614–621
2. Yokoo, M., Durfee, E.H., Ishida, T., Kuwabara, K.: The distributed constraint satisfaction problem: Formalization and algorithms. Knowledge and Data Engineering **10** (1998) 673–685
3. Bessire, C., Maestre, A., Meseguer, P.: Distributed dynamic backtracking. In Proceedings of the IJCAI'01 workshop on Distributed Constraint Reasoning (2001) 9–16
4. Hamadi, Y., Bessire, C., Quinqueton, J.: Backtracking in distributed constraint networks. In Proceedings ECAI'98 (1998) 219–223
5. Armstrong, A., Durfee, E.H.: Dynamic prioritization of complex agents in distributed constraint satisfaction problems. In AAAI97 Workshop on Constraints and Agents (1997) 8–13
6. Yokoo, M.: Asynchronous weak-commitment search for solving distributed constraint satisfaction problems. In Proceedings of the First International Conference on Principles and Practice of Constraint Programming (CP-95) **976** (1995) 88–102
7. Silaghi, M.C., Sam-Haroud, D., Faltings, B.: Asynchronous search with aggregations. In: AAAI/IAAI. (2000) 917–922

A Bayesian Model to Smooth Telepointer Jitter

Jeff Long and Michael C. Horsch

Department of Computer Science,
University of Saskatchewan,
Saskatoon, SK, Canada S7N 5A9
jrl909@mail.usask.ca
horsch@cs.usask.ca

Abstract. Cursor prediction is the problem of predicting the future location of a user's mouse cursor in a distributed environment where network lag is present. In general, cursor prediction is desirable in order to combat network jitter and provide smooth, aesthetically pleasing extrapolation. Gestures can also be difficult to interpret if network jitter becomes too severe.

This paper proposes a Bayesian network model for addressing the problem of cursor prediction. The model is capable of predicting the future path of the cursor while drawing a gesture, in this case an alphabetic character. The technique makes use of Bayesian learning techniques in order to obtain realistic parameters for the proposed solution. The model is then implemented and tested, yielding substantial improvements over previous methods. In particular, the model is at least twice as accurate as a simple linear dead reckoning algorithm run on the same dataset. Furthermore, a by-product of the model is its ability to correctly recognize the alphabetic character being drawn 84% of the time.

1   Introduction

Cursor prediction is an interesting problem that has received some amount of recent attention ([7, 6]). In general, cursor prediction is desirable in order to combat network jitter and provide smooth, aesthetically pleasing extrapolation. This problem primarily arises in the domain of networked groupware, and gesture interpretation. However, the challenges in thus far finding a suitably accurate prediction method have been daunting.

This paper proposes a Bayesian network model for addressing the problem of cursor prediction. The model is capable of predicting the future path of the cursor while drawing a gesture, in this case an alphabetic character. The technique makes use of Bayesian learning techniques in order to obtain realistic parameters for the proposed solution. The model is then implemented and tested, yielding substantial improvements over previous methods [7]. In particular, the model is at least twice as accurate as a simple linear dead reckoning algorithm run on the same dataset. The model is also able to correctly recognize the alphabetic character being drawn 84% of the time.

B. Kégl and G. Lapalme (Eds.): AI 2005, LNAI 3501, pp. 108–119, 2005.

Section 2 provides an outline of the problem of predicting cursor movement, and some previous work in this area. Section 3 presents a brief introduction to Bayesian networks, as well as techniques used for learning Bayesian networks. Section 4 describes the proposed Bayesian model for smoothing telepointer jitter, while Section 5 describes the results of this model. Section 6 discusses future work to be done in this area, and Section 7 concludes the paper.

2   Cursor Prediction

The problem of cursor prediction primarily arises in distributed groupware environments. In such applications, participants are typically represented by some form of cursor, which they may move around the screen and, depending on the application, may use to draw symbols and characters which can be viewed by other participants in the networked environment.

Interpretation problems of these movements and gestures can arise, however, when there is jitter present in the network. Jitter is defined as variable network latency. Sometimes, due to external factors such as heavy network traffic, cursor update packets from remote participants can be delayed or even lost in the network. As a result, the local side of the application may have to wait up to several hundred milliseconds for an update, only then to receive all of the delayed packets in a single 'burst.' The visual artefacts of jitter will be a 'freezing' of the cursor for some amount of time, before it 'skips' to the new location in a very jerky and unnatural manner. The longer the jitter period, the worse this effect is. In general, this effect is aesthetically displeasing to users [7]. Furthermore, accurate gesture interpretation begins to become more difficult once jitter periods reach 200ms [6]. Ideally, a smooth and accurate gesture-prediction technique would help to address both of these issues.

Gutwin, Dyck and Burkitt [7] investigated solving this problem using a very simple linear dead-reckoning algorithm. The gestures being predicted were all reasonably complex, for the most part consisting of alphanumeric characters. Jitter of varying lengths was introduced into the system to 'delay' the receipt of cursor update messages. In the event of missing data at a cursor-update timestep (generally, every 20 ms), the cursor's next position would be extrapolated using the equation:

$$x_{i+1} = x_i + V_{x_i} + A_{x_i} \qquad (1)$$

V_{x_i} represents the cursor's velocity in the x-direction at time i, while A_{x_i} represents the cursor's average acceleration in the x direction. The equation is similar for the y-coordinate. This equation is presented here exactly as it appears in Gutwin, Dyck and Burkitt [7].

The problem with the dead reckoning algorithm, according to Gutwin, Dyck and Burkitt [7], is that its error rate seems to grow faster than the visual discontinuities caused by network jitter that make interpretation difficult. They also found that omitting the acceleration term from the dead reckoning model in fact increased the predictive performance. Although the authors do not discuss this finding, it likely arises because over a long jitter period, adding a constant acceleration to the cursor's velocity will cause it to reach highly unrealistic speeds that would never result from a real user. They also set a bound on the accuracy a prediction algorithm would have to achieve in order to significantly improve gesture interpretation. For a jitter period of 320ms, this bound is a Maximum Mean Error (i.e. the largest error per jitter period) of 40 pixels for their particular data set. The error of dead reckoning is over four times this, at 188 pixels, on this same data [7].

Clearly, what is required is a prediction algorithm that can maintain its accuracy for a much longer interval than dead reckoning. In search of such a model, we present the following section as an overview of Bayesian networks and Bayesian learning as background for the solution that is proposed.

3   Bayesian Networks

In this section, we briefly review our terminology used to discuss Bayesian networks. A Bayesian network (sometimes also called a Bayes net) is a Directed Acyclic Graph (DAG), consisting of a set of nodes, which represents random variables, and a set of arcs which represent conditional dependence between variables. Associated with each node is a Conditional Probability Table (CPT), which lists the probabilities that the node will take on a given value, given the possible states of its parents in the graph. Taken together, the CPTs are sufficient to specify the full joint probability distribution (JPD) of the network. Probabilities of interest are calculated by summing over unobserved values and multiplying the CPTs of the network together.

The major strength of Bayesian networks is their ability to compactly represent conditional independence. Unless the graph is very dense, this can result in an exponential savings in space requirements over the pure JPD.

Working directly from such a JPD, probabilistic inference is also exponential. It has been shown that in the general case, inference in a Bayesian network is also NP-hard. However, quite often this inference can in fact be very efficient, depending on the network structure. Again, this is because the graph takes explicit advantage of conditional independence which is present, but not always obvious, in the full JPD. In Section 3.2, we will examine restricted classes of Bayesian networks for which inference is known to be tractable.

3.1   Learning Bayesian Networks

There are several ways in which Bayesian networks can be constructed. Often, the structure of the network is constructed manually by domain experts. The parameters of the network, namely the CPTs, can be assigned manually, or learned from data. In the case of complete data, this task is trivial and involves little more than book-keeping. When data is incomplete, approximation algorithms such as Gibbs' sampling [8] and Expectation-Maximization [4] must be used to average over the missing data. Such approximations usually suffer from the limitations that they require an exponential amount of run-time for accurate results, or run the risk of being fooled by local maxima.

The above algorithms for parameter learning assume that the structure of the network is known. Automatically learning the structure of the network from data is a considerably more difficult proposition. This difficulty arises from the fact that the number of possible network structures will be worse than exponential in the number of nodes. This problem is discussed in the literature ([8, 9]), but in this paper, we chose instead to focus on tractable, restricted network models in order to circumvent this problem. It is these models that are presented in the following section.

3.2   Restricted Classes of Bayesian Networks

A simple but surprisingly effective restricted network is the so-called Naive Bayesian Classifier. This is a Bayes net for which the variables are divided between Attribute nodes and a single Class node. The only arcs allowed in the network extend from the class node to each of the attribute nodes. This means that all of the attributes are assumed to be conditionally independent, given the class. Of course, this assumption may not be very realistic, and hence the "naivete" of the model. As their name implies, Bayesian classifiers are typically used for classifying objects of interest into distinct categories or classes. In this regard, the CPTs of the of the attribute nodes represent the probability that a particular attribute will be present, or take a certain value, for each possible class.

Most often in such networks, we are trying to infer the class variable given an observation of the attributes, or perhaps a subset of them. It is a simple matter to show that this calculation is always polynomial in the number of attributes and classes. Let C be our class variable, c a possible value of the class variable, and $a_1, \ldots, a_n$ our attributes. By Bayes' Rule we have:

$$p(C = c|a_1, \ldots, a_n) = \frac{p(a_1, \ldots, a_n|C = c)p(C = c)}{p(a_1, \ldots, a_n)} \qquad (2)$$

$p(a_1, \ldots, a_n)$ is simply the normalization constant. By the structural restrictions placed on Bayesian classifiers, we also know that the attributes $a_1, \ldots, a_n$ are conditionally independent given the class, C. Therefore, the above can be simplified as follows:

$$p(C = c|a_1, \ldots, a_n) = \alpha p(C = c) \prod p(a_i|C = c) \qquad (3)$$

All of the probabilities on the right-hand side of this equation can be read directly from the network. Thus, calculating the desired probability requires only the multiplication of n terms from the network. This calculation must be repeated once for each possible class (both to determine the most probable class and to obtain the normalizing constant), assuming m classes, then the time complexity of this operation is $O(nm)$.

Friedman, Geiger and Goldszmidt [5] propose a Bayesian network model that partially eliminates the strong assumption of conditional independence between attributes of Naive Bayes, while maintaing polynomial computation properties. This model is termed Tree-Augmented Naive Bayes (or TAN). TANs are similar to Naive Bayes except that a limited number of interactions are permitted between the attribute nodes. Specifically, leaving aside the class variable, the attribute nodes must form a tree. A directed acyclic graph, such as a Bayes net, is a tree if and only if each node has exactly one parent in the graph, with a single exception that has zero parents which we refer to as the root node. In the context of a TAN, we temporarily omit the class node, and construct a tree from all the attributes. Once this is done, we simply add the class variable to the network, and designate it as a parent of every other node. Thus, every attribute node will have as parents the class node and at most one other attribute node.

Intuitively, it does seem that the increased expressive power of TANs should result in better prediction accuracy than Naive Bayes. Friedman, Geiger and Goldszmidt [5] show this is indeed the case with some empirical results. Other results which compare TAN with Naive Bayes confirm this [1, 2]. Furthermore, not only is inference polynomial in a TAN, but they maintain the highly desirable property of Naive Bayes that they can be induced from data in polynomial time, the reason being that the in-degree of each node is bounded. The method to do so is based on a much older result by Chow and Liu for constructing Bayesian network tree structures [3]. Friedman et al. [5] show the details of how to use this result to achieve the polynomial-time learning algorithm.

4   A Bayesian Network for Cursor Prediction

As mentioned in Section 2, it seems that what is required for the problem of gesture prediction is a model with higher long-term accuracy. In particular, the model must be able to capture the long-term direction and velocity changes of the cursor, which dead reckoning fails to do. Tree Augmented Naive Bayes seems to provide the framework we need in the following manner.

As in the study by Gutwin, Dyck and Burkitt [7], we will restrict our attention to gestures consisting of a discrete set of characters. In particular, these characters will be the lower-case letters of the English alphabet. For each such character, we have a set of data consisting of cursor positions at regular intervals (roughly every 20 ms). This data all stems from a single user, and thus represents the manner in which this single user habitually draws these characters (ramifications of this will be discussed later). We use this data to build a Tree Augmented Bayesian network that can predict the general shape of these characters.

Several model structures were considered in the design of this network. The principal problem is in determining exactly what the attribute nodes of the network will represent. Absolute position has far too many values, and is not independent of where the character is being drawn on the screen. One possible model we considered assumed each attribute node x_i to be the cardinal direction of the cursor's travel at time i. Actual velocities were calculated using a simple modified version of dead-reckoning, with provisions to account for change in cardinal direction as predicted by the model. This model was later modified to include the prediction of both direction and velocity in a single Bayesian network.

The final proposed structure of the network is as follows. The attributes nodes of the network represent cursor velocities at each time-step. There will be one set of such nodes for velocity along the x-axis, and another for velocity along the y-axis. If node X_i represents the cursor's x-velocity at some time t, then node X_{i+1} represents the cursor's x-velocity at time t+20 (in milliseconds). Each node X_i has an arc in the direction of node X_{i+1}. Thus, each such node will have exactly one parent except for node X_0, fulfilling the structure requirements for Tree Augmented Bayes. The set of nodes representing y-velocity follow an identical structure to that just described. The classnode of the network is the character being drawn, and thus has 26 possible values.

It is worth noting than in this model, the X_i nodes are conditionally independent of the Y_i nodes, given the class. We considered the model in which node $X_i + 1$ depends on both X_i and Y_i (and similarly for $Y_i + 1$), but decided against it in order to maintain the guaranteed computational advantages of the TAN structure.

This representation still poses some challenges, however. The first is devising a scheme to reduce the number of values that the velocity nodes may take. In order to keep the CPTs to a manageable size and to keep the network as general as possible, it was decided to use discretized velocity categories as the values for the velocity nodes. The velocity nodes in the network, then, only represent the cursor's velocity at the given time-step. Each node may take up to 11 values; each such value is a discretized velocity range, measured in pixels per timestep. The granularity of the discretization is 10 pixels per timestep. Thus, the 11 value categories range from less than -50 pixels/timestep to greater than +50 pixels/timestep. This keeps the number of rows in each conditional probability table to a 'mere' 286. Note that there is no claim of this discretization being optimal; the discretized ranges were determined based solely on manual examination of the general range of the data. Optimizing this process could lead to improved performance of the resulting network.

Another issue is the question of how many velocity nodes to include in the network. The problem arises from the fact that different characters take different amounts of time to draw. One potential solution would be to build a different network for every different character. Such multinets are discussed briefly in Friedman et al. [5]. However, even for individual characters, the time will vary from case to case, and thus it was decided to simply build a single network with a number of nodes sufficient to handle the character with the longest average draw time. Characters that took fewer time-steps to draw would simply have 'missing' data values for the later velocity nodes.

With these questions resolved, we have finalized the TAN structure of the proposed network. All that remains is to learn the probabilities for each of the nodes from the data. Figure 1 is a diagram of the structure of the completed network.

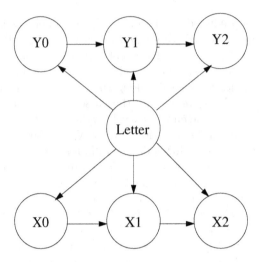

Fig. 1. The structure of our Bayesian network for cursor prediction. The class node, denoted 'letter,' represents the character that the user is drawing. The attribute nodes represent velocity along the x and y axis respectively

5   Results

The proposed Bayesian network was implemented, using a dataset of 21 of the 26 letters of the English alphabet, with approximately 25 samples for each character, all obtained from a single user. Characters that required more than one mouse-stroke to be drawn on the screen were omitted from the data for reasons of simplicity. This is in fact only a very small amount of data for a Bayesian network of this size, and it is possible that better results could be obtained with a larger dataset.

The data was then randomly split into 80% training data and 20% testing data, which was then used to compare the proposed Bayes' net approach against dead reckoning and linear extrapolation. The process was then repeated several times to obtain different random splits of the data.

The conditional probabilities for the model were learned from data using the maximum a posteriori (MAP) learning rule (as implemented in Norsys Netica [10]). Netica was also used to perform the experimental inference in the model. Given that inference in Bayesian networks can often incur severe computational costs, a major concern was the feasibility of an 161 node network with 236 row entries at each node. However, the proposed TAN structure seems to have resulted in a practically efficient network structure. Even on a simple desktop PC with an AMD-K63 450Mhz processor and 512MB of RAM running Windows XP, inference in the network took no noticeable amount of time. Learning the required probability tables also took no more than 2 seconds for this small data set. In our case, there was no need to learn network structure.

The principal error metric used to measure the results of the proposed model was Mean Maximum Error, which is the same metric used by Gutwin, Dyck and

Table 1. Results of the three different model approaches as applied to our dataset. All values are given in units of number of pixels

	MME	MSD
Dead Reckoning	572	754
Linear Extrapolation	300	329
TAN	197	145

Burkitt [7] in their earlier study. This metric is defined as the average of the maximum distance between a predicted point and the temporally corresponding real point in each jitter period. A simple dead reckoning prediction algorithm run on our data set resulted in a Mean Maximum Error of 572 pixels. Gutwin, Dyck and Burkitt [7] postulate that simple linear extrapolation (i.e. leaving out the acceleration term from the dead reckoning algorithm) can lead to better results, and we found this to be the case here, yielding an MME of 300 pixels. The Bayes net representation significantly outperforms both, achieving an MME of 197 pixels. Gutwint, Dyck and Burkitt [7] report a Mean Maximum Error of 188 pixels for dead reckoning in their earlier study; however, this study was done using a different data set than what was used in this paper. With an absolute scale such as a pixel count, different size and timing of the gestures used could quite possibly account for this discrepancy. For instance, the gesture displayed by Gutwin, Dyck and Burkitt [7] in their study took at least 1440ms to draw, whereas the very same character in our dataset took no more than 800ms. One would expect that gestures drawn more quickly would be more difficult to predict - this could be a potential area for future investigation.

However, the Bayesian model displays even better results when we consider a different metric which we will term Maximum Spatial Displacement (MSD). We define this metric to be the maximum distance in pixels between each predicted cursor point and the spatially closest point on the cursor's true path. This is in contrast to the Mean Maximum Error, which measures the distance between a predicted cursor location and the cursor's corresponding true temporal location. In our opinion, the MSD is an important metric to consider, since it is a better indicator than the MME of whether or not the actual shape of a gesture is correctly predicted. Although the speed at which a gesture is drawn may vary from the prediction to the actual data, it seems reasonable that gesture interpretation, one of the major concerns of Gutwin, Dyck and Burkitt [7] would improve if the predicted cursor position stayed within some boundary of the actual gesture. This is a factor that MME does not take into account. It is quite conceivable that a given prediction may have a poor MME score, even though when visually plotted it looks extremely similar to the actual gesture being predicted. In our experiments, the MSD for dead reckoning is 754 pixels, which is even worse than its MME. Linear extrapolation does better, with an MSD of 329 pixels. However, for the Bayesian model, the MSD is only 145 pixels, substantially less than its MME. This result would seem to indicate that the Bayesian model does very well at predicting the true path of the gesture, but is less successful in predicting the

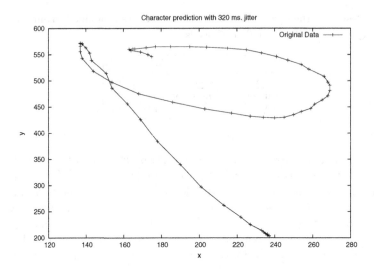

Fig. 2. Original data of a hand-written lower-case e. Each point represents the cursor's x-y coordinates at 20 ms. intervals

speed at which it will be drawn. However, we must be careful when considering this metric, as it tends to reward 'conservative' prediction algorithms - that is to say, algorithms that do not in fact move the cursor very far in between updates and thus do not stray far from the true path of the character.

Key to the Bayesian network approach is the model's ability to predict which character is currently being drawn. It does this implicitly every time inference is performed to predict the next position, but it can of course also be queried explicitly. After 8 positional updates (with each such update corresponding to roughly 20 ms of real time), the model predicts the correct character 52% of the time. After 24 updates, the correct prediction ratio rises to 74%, and after all updates (which varies from about 30 to 80 updates depending on the character) reaches 84%. Since dead reckoning makes no attempt at such prediction, it is impossible to compare the two methods in this regard.

The following images depict the output of the prediction algorithm, as compared with a dead reckoning approach very similar to that used by Gutwin, Dyck and Burkitt [7]. For these images, we assumed a jitter period of 320 ms. Each plotted point indicates a pixel coordinate, and the time interval between each point is 20 ms. In the two predicted figures an expected velocity is calculated (using dead reckoning in figure 3 and the Bayesian model in figure 4) to predict the position of the next point. When an update is received, we immediately plot the true location and begin the prediction process again. In these examples, it seems visually clear that the Bayesian model provides more accurate long-term prediction than simple dead-reckoning, in accordance with the analytical results above.

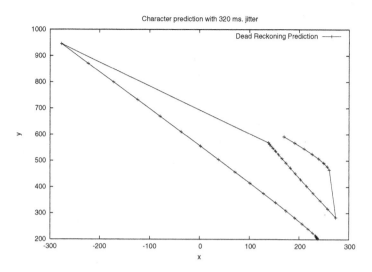

Fig. 3. Dead reckoning prediction with jitter period of 320 ms. Each point represents the predicted x-y coordinates of the cursor at 20 ms. intervals. Every 320 ms., the cursor's position is instantly corrected to the true location

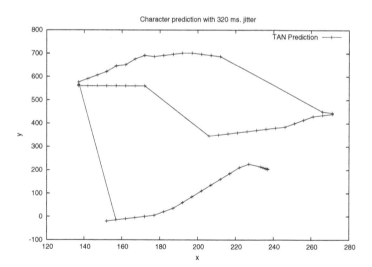

Fig. 4. Bayesian network prediction with jitter period of 320 ms. Each point represents the predicted x-y coodinates of the cursor at 20 ms. intervals, as determined by our TAN model. Every 320 ms., the cursor's position is instantly corrected to the true location

6   Future Work

One shortcoming of the discussion above is the metric used to measure error in the prediction. In this paper, a Mean Maximum Error measured in absolute pixels was used so as to be consistent with the previous work in this field; however, it seems very likely that such a method is highly sensitive to differences in scale and cursor speed of the data. In this paper we propose another error metric, Maximum Spatial Displacement, to be used in conjunction with MME, but it suffers from the same problem of being measured in absolute pixels. It would be preferable to devise a metric that takes into account both the average velocity at which the gesture is being drawn, and possibly the size of the gesture itself. Both of these factors would affect the error measurements of any algorithm, when measured in absolute pixels. Devising a more general error metric would make comparisons between different methods much simpler and more meaningful.

In this paper, we compare our Bayesian method against dead reckoning, which was used in the previous work but may not be the most suitable baseline. Other general curve-fitting methods may provide a more realistic bottom line for the effectiveness of our algorithm. Furthermore, a hybrid approach in which dead reckoning or some other simple means is used when the Bayesian model is unable to recognize the character with sufficient confidence may yield better results in a realistic setting.

Another issue arises in dealing with characters that consist of more than a single stroke, which as previously mentioned were omitted from the dataset used in this paper. Accurate prediction was difficult for these characters, since the model breaks down when the cursor can effectively 'teleport' from one place to another. Furthermore, there is no easy way to identify when a new stroke by the user indicates the beginning of a new character, or the continuation of an old one. The study by Gutwin, Dyck and Burkitt [7] uses only continuous characters as gestures, and does not consider this problem. In the future, optical character recognition (OCR) techniques may be examined address this shortcoming.

It was previously mentioned that the data used to build this network all came from a single user. In general, for a gesture prediction program, it seems that it would be the required procedure to have an individual and personalized model for a given user. This is because cursor gestures, like hand-writing, are likely to be highly individualized. As an example, consider the simple character of lower-case 'c.' The user in this paper always draws their c's counter-clockwise, starting from the upper horn. However, there is no reason to assume that another user might not start from the bottom horn and draw clockwise. This matter may well be worth further investigation, but it seems likely that a model that averaged data from both users would result in less predictive accuracy for either user individually.

A final issue to consider is how well this TAN-based method can be generalized. Can we go from predicting alphabetic characters to predicting general cursor movement in a distributed groupware application? What other techniques may be necessary in order to make this move? The question certainly does not seem to be an easy one, but Bayesian methods provide a promising framework for future investigation in this area.

7   Conclusion

We provide a Bayesian network model to solve the problem of cursor prediction. This method uses real data in order to learn accurate parameters of the model, resulting in twice the accuracy of previously used methods in this field, such as dead reckoning. The model is also capable of predicting alphabetic gestures being drawn by the user in 84% of cases. We also propose a new error metric, Maximum Spatial Displacement, to be used in conjunction with the Mean Maximum Error metric, in order to more accurately compare solutions in this field.

Acknowledgements

The authors would like to sincerely thank Dr. Carl Gutwin for providing the data used both to train and evaluate our proposed model. Both authors would like to thank NSERC for support of this research.

References

1. J. Cheng and R. Greiner. Comparing bayesian network classifiers. *UAI-99 - Proceedings of 15th Conference on Uncertainty in Artificial Intelligence*, 1999.
2. J. Cheng and R. Greiner. Learning bayesian belief network classifiers: Algorithms and system. *Lectures Notes in Computer Science*, 2001.
3. C. K. Chow and C. N. Liu. Approximating discrete probability distributions with dependence trees. *IEEE Transactions on Information Theory*, 1968.
4. N. Dempster, A. Laird and D. Rubin. Maximum likelihood from incomplete data via the em algorithm. *Journal of the Royal Statistical Society*, 1977.
5. D. Friedman, N. Geiger and M Goldszmidt. Bayesian network classifiers. *Machine Learning*, 1997.
6. C. Gutwin and R. Penner. Improving interpretation of remote gestures with telepointer traces. *Proceedings of ACM CSCW*, 2002.
7. J. Gutwin, C. Dyck and J. Burkitt. Using cursor prediction to smooth telepointer jitter. *To appear, the 2003 ACM Conference on Group Work*, 2003.
8. D. Heckerman. A tutorial on learning with bayesian networks. *Technical Report MSR-TR-95-06. Microsoft Corporation, Redmon, USA*, 1996b.
9. P. Krause. Learning probabilistic networks. *http://www.auai.org/bayesUS krause.ps.gz*, 1998.
10. Norsys Netica. *http://www.norsys.com.*

A Comparative Study of Two Density-Based Spatial Clustering Algorithms for Very Large Datasets

Xin Wang and Howard J. Hamilton

Department of Computer Science,
University of Regina,
Regina, SK, Canada S4S 0A2
{wangx, hamilton}@cs.uregina.ca

Abstract. Spatial clustering is an active research area in spatial data mining with various methods reported. In this paper, we compare two density-based methods, DBSCAN and DBRS. First, we briefly describe the methods and then compare them from a theoretical view. Finally, we give an empirical comparison of the algorithms.

1 Introduction

A *spatial database system* is a database system for the management of spatial data. Rapid growth is occurring in the number and the size of spatial databases for applications such as geo-marketing, traffic control, and environmental studies [3]. *Spatial data mining*, or *knowledge discovery in spatial databases*, refers to the extraction from spatial databases of implicit knowledge, spatial relations, or other patterns that are not explicitly stored [9].

Finding clusters in spatial data is an active research area, with recent results reported on the effectiveness and scalability of algorithms [4][10][12][13]. Based on the techniques adopted to define clusters, clustering algorithms can be categorized into four broad categories [11], hierarchical, partitional, density-based, and grid-based.

Hierarchical clustering methods can be either agglomerative or divisive. An *agglomerative method* starts with each point as a separate cluster, and successively performs merging until a stopping criterion is met. A *divisive method* begins with all points in a single cluster and performs splitting until a stopping criterion is met. The result of a hierarchical clustering method is a tree of clusters called a *dendogram*.

Partitional clustering methods determine a partition of the points into clusters, such that the points in a cluster are more similar to each other than to points in different clusters. They start with some arbitrary initial clusters and iteratively reallocate points to clusters until a stopping criterion is met. They tend to find clusters with hyperspherical shapes.

Density-based clustering methods try to find clusters based on the density of points in regions. Dense regions that are reachable from each other are merged to formed clusters. Density-based clustering methods excel at finding clusters of arbitrary shapes.

B. Kégl and G. Lapalme (Eds.): AI 2005, LNAI 3501, pp. 120–132, 2005.

Grid-based clustering methods quantize the clustering space into a finite number of cells and then perform the required operations on the quantized space. Cells containing more than a certain number of points are considered to be dense. Contiguous dense cells are connected to form clusters.

Spatial clustering aims to group similar objects into the same group based on considering both spatial and non-spatial attributes of the object and a regular clustering algorithm can be modified to account for the special nature of spatial data to give a spatial clustering algorithm [11].

In this paper, we compare two spatial clustering algorithms, DBSCAN and DBRS, theoretically and empirically. Both are density-based spatial clustering algorithms, but they each perform best on particular types of datasets.

The paper is organized as follows. In Section 2, we briefly discuss the two algorithms. In Section 3, we compare DBSCAN and DBRS from a theoretical viewpoint. Section 4 presents an empirical evaluation of the effectiveness of DBSCAN and DBRS. Section 5 presents our conclusions.

2 Algorithms

2.1 DBSCAN

DBSCAN was the first density-based spatial clustering method proposed [4]. To define a new cluster or to extend an existing cluster, a neighborhood around a point of a given radius (*Eps*) must contain at least a minimum number of points (*MinPts*), the minimum density for the neighborhood.

Figure 1 gives the DBSCAN algorithm. DBSCAN starts from an arbitrary point q. It begins by performing a ***region query***, which finds the neighborhood of point q. If the neighborhood is sparsely populated, i.e., it contains fewer than *MinPts* points, then point q is labeled as noise. Otherwise, a cluster is created and all points in q's neighborhood are placed in this cluster. Then the neighborhood of each of q's neighbors is examined to see if it can be added to the cluster. If so, the process is repeated for every point in this neighborhood, and so on. If a cluster cannot be expanded further, DBSCAN chooses another arbitrary unlabelled point and repeats the process. This procedure is iterated until all points in the dataset have been placed in clusters or labeled as noise. For a dataset containing n points, n region queries are required.

Given a dataset D, a distance function *dist*, and parameters *Eps* and *MinPts*, the following definitions (adapted from [4]) are used to specify DBSCAN.

Definition 1. The ***Eps-neighborhood*** (or ***neighborhood***) of a point p, denoted by $N_{Eps}(p)$, is defined by $N_{Eps}(p) = \{q \in D \mid dist(p,q) \leq Eps\}$.

Definition 2. A point p is ***directly density-reachable*** from a point q if (1) $p \in N_{Eps}(q)$ and (2) $|N_{Eps}(q)| \geq MinPts$.

Definition 3. A point p is ***density-reachable*** from a point q if there is a chain of points $p_1,...,p_n$, $p_1=q$, $p_n=p$ such that p_{i+1} is directly density-reachable from p_i for $1 \leq i \leq n\text{-}1$.

Definition 4. A point *p* is ***density-connected*** to a point *q* if there is a point *o* such that both *p* and *q* are density-reachable from *o*.

Definition 5. A ***density-based cluster*** *C* is a non-empty subset of *D* satisfying the following conditions: (1) $\forall p, q$: if $p \in C$ and *q* is density-reachable from *p*, then $q \in C$; (2) $\forall p, q \in C$: *p* is density-connected to *q*.

```
Algorithm DBSCAN (SetOfPoints, Eps, MinPts)
ClusterId = nextId(NOISE);
For i = 1 to SetOfPoints.size
  { Point = SetOfPoints.get[i];
    If (Point.ClId == Unclassified)
       If ExpandCluster(SetOfPoints, Point, ClusterId, Eps, MinPts)
              ClusterId = nextId(ClusterId);
  }

ExpandCluster(SetOfPoints, Point, ClId, Eps, MinPts) : Boolean
Seeds = SetOfPoints.regionQuery(Point, Eps);
If (Seeds.size < MinPts)
  SetOfPoint.changeClId(Point, NOISE);
  Return False;
Else
  { SetOfPoints.changeClIds(Seeds, ClId);
     Seeds.delete(Point);
     While (Seeds != Empty)
       { CurrentP = Seeds.first();
          result = SetOfPoints.regionQuery( currentP, Eps);
          If (result.size >= MinPts)
            { For i = 1 to result.size
                 { resultP = result.get[i];
                    If resultP.ClId  In {UNCLASSIFIED, NOISE}
                        { If (resultP.clId == UNCLASSIFIED)
                             Seeds.append (resultP);
                             SetOfPoints.changeClId(resultP, ClId);
                        }
                 }
            }
          Seeds.delete(currentP);
       }
     Return True;
  }
```

Fig. 1. DBSCAN Algorithm (Adapted from [4])

2.2 DBRS

DBRS is a density-based spatial clustering algorithm [13]. Given a dataset *D*, a symmetric distance function *dist*, parameters *Eps* and *MinPts*, and a property *prop* defined with respect to a non-spatial attribute, the following definitions are used to specify DBRS. (Extension to multiple non-spatial attributes is straightforward.)

Definition 6. The ***matching neighborhood*** of a point p, denoted by $N'_{Eps}(p)$, is defined as $N'_{Eps}(p) = \{q \in D \mid dist(p,q) \le Eps \text{ and } p.prop = q.prop\}$.

DBRS handles non-spatial attributes in the neighbor finding function and uses a minimum purity threshold, called *MinPur*, to control the purity (or consistency) of the neighborhood. A ***core point*** is a point whose matching neighborhood is dense enough, i.e., it has at least *MinPts* points and over *MinPur* percent of its neighbors are matching neighbors. A ***border point*** is a neighbor of a core point that is not a core point itself. Points other than core and border points are ***noise***.

Definition 7. A point p and a point q are ***directly purity-density-reachable*** from each other if (1) $p \in N'_{Eps}(q)$, $|N'_{Eps}(q)| \geq MinPts$ and $|N'_{Eps}(q)| / |N_{Eps}(q)| \geq MinPur$ or (2) $q \in N'_{Eps}(p)$, $|N'_{Eps}(p)| \geq MinPts$ and $|N'_{Eps}(p)| / |N_{Eps}(p)| \geq MinPur$.

Directly purity-density-reachable is a reflexive relation. It is symmetric for two core points as well as for one core point and one border point, but it is not symmetric for two border points. Directly density-reachable used in DBSCAN is only symmetric for two core points, but not symmetric for one core point and one border point, or two border points.

Definition 8. A point p and a point q are ***purity-density-reachable (PD-reachable)*** from each other, denoted by $PD(p, q)$, if there is a chain of points $p_1,...,p_n$, $p_1=q$, $p_n=p$ such that p_{i+1} is directly purity-density-reachable from p_i for $1 \leq i \leq n-1$.

```
Algorithm DBRS(D, Eps, MinPts, MinPur)
ClusterList = Empty;
while (!D.isClassified( ))
        { Select one unclassified point q from D;
          qseeds = D.matchingNeighbors(q, Eps);
          if ((|qseeds| < MinPts) or (qseeds.pur < MinPur))
             q.clusterID = -1; /*q is noise or a border point */
          else
             {  isFirstMerge = True;
                Cᵢ = ClusterList.firstCluster;
                   /* compare qseeds to all existing clusters */
                while (Cᵢ != Empty)
                        { if ( hasIntersection(qseeds, Cᵢ) )
                             if (isFirstMerge)
                                { newCᵢ = Cᵢ.merge(qseeds);
                                  isFirstMerge = False; }
                             else
                                { newCᵢ = newCᵢ.merge(Cᵢ);
                                  ClusterList.deleteCluster(C);}
                          Cᵢ = ClusterList.nextCluster;
                        } // while != Empty
                /*No intersection with any existing cluster */
                if (isFirstMerge)
                   { Create a new cluster Cⱼ from qseeds;
                     ClusterList = ClusterList.addCluster(Cⱼ);
                   } //if isFirstMerge
             } //else
        } // while !D.isClassified
```

Fig. 2. DBRS Algorithm (Adapted from [13])

Definition 9. A ***purity-density-based cluster*** C is a non-empty subset of D satisfying the following condition: $\forall p, q \in D$: if $p \in C$ and $PD(p, q)$ holds, then $q \in C$.

The intuition behind DBRS is that a cluster can be viewed as a minimal number of core points (called *skeletal points*) and their neighborhoods. In a dense cluster, a neighborhood may have far more than *MinPts* points, but examining the neighborhoods of these points in detail is not worthwhile, because we already know that these points are part of a cluster. If an unclassified point in a neighbor's neighborhood should be part of this cluster, we are very likely to discover this later when we select it or one of its other unclassified neighbors.

To find a cluster, it is sufficient to perform region queries on the skeletal points. However, identifying skeletal points is NP-complete (see Section 3.2). Instead, we can randomly select sample points, find their neighborhoods, and merge their neighborhoods if they intersect. If enough samples are taken, we can find a close approximation to the cluster without checking every point. The sample points may not be the skeletal points, but the number of region queries can be significantly fewer than for DBSCAN for datasets with widely varying densities.

Figure 2 represents the DBRS algorithm.

3   Theoretical Comparison of DBRS and DBSCAN

In this section, we compare DBRS and DBSCAN from two theoretical viewpoints, including the neighborhood graphs they construct and the heuristics they provide for the skeletal points decision problem. To simplify the discussion, we assume all points have the same property.

3.1   Comparison from the Viewpoint of Neighborhood Graphs

First, three definitions are introduced. Then we describe the neighborhood graphs relevant to DBSCAN and DBRS.

Definition 10. The **neighborhood graph** for a spatial relation *neighbor* is a graph $G = (V, E)$ with a set of vertices V and a set of edges E such that each vertex corresponds to a point and two vertices v_1 and v_2 are connected iff *neighbor*(v_1, v_2) holds [3]. Depending on the *neighbor* relation, a neighborhood graph can be directed or undirected.

Definition 11. A neighborhood (sub-)graph is **connected** iff for any pair of vertices in the (sub-) graph there is an undirected path joining the vertices.

Definition 12. A directed neighborhood (sub-)graph is **strongly connected** iff for any two nodes p, q with *neighbor*(p, q) holding, there is a directed path from p to q.

Lemma 1. A density-based cluster corresponds to a connected neighborhood subgraph with density-reachable used as the *neighbor* relation.

From Lemma 1, given n points, the clustering process of DBSCAN can be viewed abstractly as constructing neighborhood graphs. Each time a core point is found, the algorithm finds the directly density-reachable relation between the core point and each of its neighbors. The directly density-reachable relation holding for the two points can be viewed as the directed edge between the two corresponding vertices in the neighborhood graph. Each cluster in the dataset is constructed as a connected neighborhood sub-graph. Without considering noise, if a dataset has k clusters, then its corresponding neighborhood graph will have k connected sub-graphs.

For example, suppose the nine points in Figure 3(a) are in one cluster. We assume *MinPts* is 3. DBSCAN is applied with Point 1 arbitrarily selected as the initial point. The region query for Point 1 finds that Points 2, 3, 4, 5 and 6 are Point 1's neighbors. These points are shown inside the circle centered on Point 1 in Figure 3(a). So edges from 1 to its neighbors are inserted in the neighborhood graph. Points 2, 3, 4, 5 and 6 are organized in a list and checked for neighbors one by one, and so on for their neighbors. When DBSCAN terminates, the neighborhood graph is connected, as shown in Figure 3(b).

Lemma 2. If the density-reachable relation is the *neighbor* relation, DBSCAN's clustering process corresponds to constructing the strongly connected neighborhood graph.

In Figure 3(b), for any two points if one point is density-reachable from the other, then a directed path connects them. So, Figure 3(b) shows a strongly connected neighborhood graph.

Lemma 3. A purity-density-based cluster correspond to a connected neighborhood graph with PD-reachable used as the *neighbor* relation.

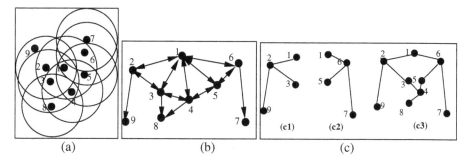

Fig. 3. (a) Example Cluster; (b) Strongly Connected Neighborhood Graph; (c) Connected Neighborhood Graph

Since PD-reachable is a symmetric relation, the neighborhood graph corresponding to DBRS is an undirected graph. Suppose we apply DBRS to the points in Figure 3(a), with Point 2 arbitrarily picked as the initial point. After calling the matchingNeighbors function, DBRS finds that Points 1, 3, and 9 are Point 2's neighbors and generates the neighborhood sub-graph shown in Figure 3(c1). 1-2-3-9 becomes the first sub-cluster. Then DBRS randomly picks Point 6 and generates the neighborhood sub-graph shown in Figure 3(c2) for sub-cluster 1-5-6-7. This subcluster intersects existing sub-cluster 1-2-3-9 at Point 1. After merging, the sub-cluster includes 1-2-3-5-6-7-9. Next, suppose DBRS picks Point 4. 1-3-4-5-8 is generated and merged into the existing cluster. The final neighborhood graph is a connected neighborhood graph, as shown in Figure 3(c3).

In the worst case, i.e., all points are noise points, the costs of constructing the two types of neighborhood graphs are the same, because no directed or undirected edges are generated. Otherwise, constructing a strongly connected neighborhood graph (as DBSCAN does) is more expensive than constructing a connected neighborhood graph (as DBRS does). In the simplest case, two core points are directly density-reachable from each other. In a strongly connected neighborhood graph with directly density-reachable as the neighbor relation, we need to check both nodes to find two directed edges to connect them. In the other words, with DBSCAN, for any two directly density-reachable core points, two directed edges are required to connect them. In the connected neighborhood graph generated with PD-reachable as the neighbor relation, if the two core nodes are directly PD-reachable from each other, we only need to check one of them because after checking one, the undirected edge connecting them is generated. In a strongly connected neighborhood graph, the number of directed edges required is greater than or equal to the number of undirected edges required in the corresponding connected neighborhood graph. Thus, constructing a strongly connected neighborhood graph requires making region queries for more points than constructing a connected neighborhood graph.

For the clustering process, regardless of whether the connectivity is directed or undirected, all connected points should belong to the same cluster. It is irrelevant whether two points are density reachable via a directed neighborhood path or via an undirected path. So, in most of the cases, DBRS can obtain the clusters more cheaply than DBSCAN.

3.2 Comparison from the Viewpoint of Skeletal Points

Definition 13. Given a cluster C, a set of $S \subseteq C$ is a set of *skeletal points* S for C if and only if

$$(1) \quad S = \{x \mid \bigcup_{x \in S} N'_{Eps}(x) = C \text{ and } |N'_{Eps}(x)| \geq MinPts\} \text{ and}$$

(2) there is no other set of points $S' \subseteq C$ that satisfies condition (1) but $|S'| < |S|$.

Informally, the skeletal points are a minimal set of core points, whose neighborhoods cover the cluster. Every point in a cluster is a skeletal point or a neighbor of a skeletal point. Therefore, to find a cluster, it is sufficient to perform region queries on the skeletal points. Although skeletal points are defined for a cluster, the skeletal points for a dataset can be viewed as a union of the skeletal points for each cluster in the dataset.

The skeletal points can also be used to represent a clustering result, which saves space. Additionally, when a new point is added to a cluster, we can avoid running the cluster algorithm again if the new point belongs to the neighborhood of a skeletal point.

A relevant question to address concerns whether it is possible to identify the skeletal points for a cluster in polynomial time.

Definition 14. Given a cluster C, the *skeletal points decision problem* is to determine whether there is a set of skeleton points S for C of size J or less.

Theorem. The Skeletal Points Decision Problem is NP-complete.

Proof Sketch. Proof of the theorem is based on transforming the skeletal points decision problem for a cluster to the minimal cover decision problem for its corresponding neighborhood graph. The detailed proof is shown in [14].

First, given a neighborhood graph, we can simply guess a cover with size J or less for the neighborhood graph and check in polynomial time whether the cover and the neighborhoods of every point in the cover include all nodes of the neighborhood graph. So the problem belongs to NP.

Then, we reduce a known NP-complete problem, the dominating set decision problem [5], to the minimal cover decision problem. The dominating set decision problem is defined for a general graph, but the minimum cover decision problem is defined for a neighborhood graph. We transform any general graph to a neighborhood graph with *MinPts* = 3, that is, where one vertex of every edge has a degree of at least 3. Vertices with degrees of 1 or 2 in the general graph are added to the neighborhood graph along with dummy vertices sufficient to ensure *MinPts* = 3. All other vertices and edges are transferred directly to the neighborhood graph. This transformation can be done in polynomial time.

Since the skeletal point belongs to NP and one subproblem (when *MinPts* $\geq$ 3) can be reduced from a known NP-complete problem, the skeletal point decision problem is NP-complete. ♦

From the above theorem, we can conclude that no algorithm is known that obtains skeletal points in polynomial time. The next question is whether a heuristic method can find an approximate solution for the skeletal points decision problem in polynomial time. As explained below, DBSCAN and DBRS can be viewed as two kinds of heuristic methods for the skeletal points decision problem, where given the points of a single cluster, we need to select the skeletal points.

DBSCAN can be viewed as a heuristic method that uses a depth-first local spanning search. It randomly selects the first point, saying p, finds its neighborhood, and checks whether p and its neighbors cover the whole cluster. If not, it picks a neighbor of p, called it q, adds it to the set, and checks its neighbors. If q is a border point, the next selected point is another neighbor of p. If q is a core point, the next point will be one of q's neighbors. The process continues until the whole cluster has been covered. The selected points may not be skeletal points, but together they form a cover for the corresponding neighborhood graph.

DBRS can be viewed as a heuristic method that uses a random search. The algorithm randomly selects one point, finds its neighborhood, and checks whether the selected point and its neighbors cover the whole cluster. If not, another point is randomly selected and added to the set. After checking for overlap and merging as necessary, the algorithm checks whether the two points and their neighbors cover the whole cluster. If not, the process is repeated until the whole cluster has been covered. As with DBSCAN, the selected points may not be skeletal points, but together they form a cover for the corresponding neighborhood graph.

4   Performance Evaluation

In this section, we give a series of results from applying the two clustering methods to cluster both synthetic and real datasets. Each synthetic dataset includes x, y coordinates and one non-spatial property for the attributes and 2-10 clusters. The clusters in the datasets have different shapes and densities. Each result reported in a table or graph in this section represents the average of 10 runs. All experiments were run on a 500MHz PC with 256M memory.

Since the original DBSCAN implementation, which is based on R*-trees, cannot handle duplicate points in datasets and also mistakenly removes some points from large datasets, we re-implemented DBSCAN using SR-trees, and called the result DBSCAN*. DBRS is implemented using SR-trees.

4.1 Scalability

Figure 4 shows the scalability of DBSCAN* and DBRS on synthetic datasets when the *Eps* is 5, *MinPts* is 10 and *MinPur* is 0.98 for DBRS.

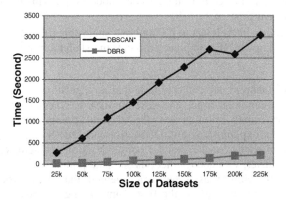

(a) Running Time in Seconds

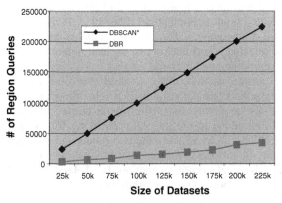

(b) Number of Region Queries

Fig. 4. Scalability of DBSCAN* and DBRS

Figure 4 (a) shows that the running time for DBSCAN* ranges from 268 seconds for 25 000 points to 3038 seconds for 225 000 points. In Figure 4 (b), the number of region queries of DBSCAN* is almost equal to the size of the dataset, ranging from 24348 queries for 25 000 points to 224870 queries for 225 000 points. The running time for DBRS increases with the size of the datasets in an almost linear fashion, going from 17 seconds in the case of 25 000 points to 209 seconds for a dataset with 225 000 points. The numbers of region queries for different datasets increases from 3167 times for a 25000 point dataset to 33919 for a 225 000 point dataset.

4.2 Scalability with Respect to the Number of Noise Points

The most time-consuming part of density-based algorithms is the region query operation. Since CLARANS is a partitional clustering algorithm, it does not have the region query operation. In Sections 4.3 and 4.4, we will study the region query operation for the two density-based algorithms, DBSCAN and DBRS. First we show the number of region queries with respect to the percentage of noise points.

Figure 5 shows the number of region queries for various percentages of noise for dataset sizes ranging from 10 000 to 100 000 points for the two algorithms. For DBSCAN, it makes the region query for every point in the dataset. The number of region queries only depends on the size of the dataset. Thus, the number of region queries is equal to the number of points in the datasets, which is same as the number of region queries of DBRS with 100% of noise. For DBRS, as the percentage of noise increases, the number of region queries needed for DBRS increases. For example, for 100 000 points, when a dataset has 0% noise, it takes approximately 3000 region queries to finish the clustering, but when the percentage of noise reaches 100%, it takes exactly 100 000 region queries. For every dataset, when the percentage of noise reaches 100%, DBRS requires the same number of region queries as DBSCAN*. In every case, this number is equal to the number of points in the dataset.

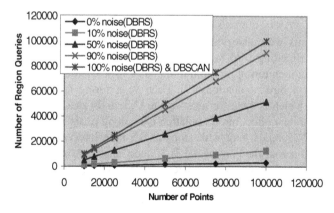

Fig. 5. The Number of Region Queries for Datasets with Various Percentages of Noise Vs. Data Sizes

4.3 *Eps* and Number of Region Queries

The second factor affecting the number of region queries for the two density-based methods is the value selected for the *Eps* parameter. Figure 6 shows the number of region queries required for a dataset of 10 000 points with clusters of varying densities. With DBSCAN, the number of region queries does not change as *Eps* increases, while with DBRS, it decreases. For our data, increasing *Eps* is equivalent to reducing the density of the overall cluster. Thus, for higher-density clusters, DBRS can achieve better performance than DBSCAN because for DBRS denser clusters take fewer region queries to find than for DBSCAN.

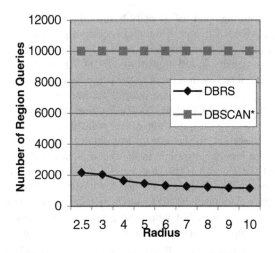

Fig. 6. *Eps* Vs. Number of Region Queries (10k Dataset)

4.4 Real Dataset

The two algorithms were also tested on the real datasets. The dataset is from the North American Breeding Bird Survey (BBS). The BBS is a long-term, large-scale, international avian monitoring program initiated in 1966 to track the status and trends of North American bird populations [7]. Each year during the height of the avian breeding season, which is June for most of the U.S. and Canada, participants skilled in avian identification collect bird population data along roadside survey routes. Each survey route is 24.5 miles long with stops at 0.5-mile intervals. Over 4100 survey routes are located across the continental U.S. and Canada. Among the BBS data, we picked data for the Canada goose to test DBRS. There are 2091 survey routes reporting Canada goose populations. We set *Eps* to 1 and *MinPts* to 10 for the two density-based methods. Figure 7 shows the clustering result of DBRS. DBSCAN* made 2066 region queries, had a running time of 12 seconds, and found 5 clusters. DBRS made 892 region queries, had a running time of 3 seconds, and found 6 clusters. The biggest cluster is in eastern North American.

Fig. 7. Canada Goose Data (in DBRS) (in color)

The reason that DBRS has more clusters is because it missed joining certain clusters. For example, for the points shown in Figure 8, all points are close together and should be placed in the same cluster. However, if the algorithm picks Point 1 and then Point 5, all points will be clustered, and no unclustered point will remain that can be picked to merge the two sub-graphs.

5   Conclusion

Clustering spatial data has been extensively studied in the knowledge discovery literature. In this paper, we compare two spatial clustering methods. DBSCAN gives extremely good results and is efficient in many datasets. However, if a dataset has clusters of widely varying densities, DBSCAN is not able to handle it efficiently. If non-spatial attributes play a role in determining the desired clustering result, DBSCAN is not appropriate, because it does not consider non-spatial attributes in the dataset.

DBRS aims to reduce the running time for datasets with varying densities. It scales well on high-density clusters. As well, DBRS can deal with a property related to non-spatial attribute(s), by means of a purity threshold, when finding the matching neighborhood. One limitation of the algorithm is that it sometimes may fail to combine some small clusters.

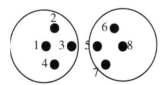

Fig. 8. A Difficult Case

References

[1]   Beckmann, N., Kriegel, H-P., Schneider, R., and Seeger, B.: The R*-Tree: An Efficient and Robust Access Method for Points and Rectangles. SIGMOD Record, 19(2) (1990) 322-331

[2]   Cai, Y., Cercone, N., and Han, J.: Learning In Relational Databases: An Attribute-Oriented Approach. Computational Intelligence 7(1991) 119-132

[3]   Ester, M., Kriegel, H-P., and Sander, J.: Spatial Data Mining: A Database Approach. In: Proc. 5th Int'l Symp. on Large Spatial Databases, Berlin (1997) 48-66

[4]   Ester, M., Kriegel, H., Sander, J., and Xu, X.: A Density-Based Algorithm for Discovering Clusters in Large Spatial Databases with Noise. In: Proc. of 2nd KDD, Portland (1996) 226-231

[5]   Garey, M.R. and Johnson, D.S.: Computers and Intractability: A Guide to the Theory of NP-Completeness. W. H. Freeman (1979)

[6]   http://www.dmtispatial.com/geocoding_software.html

[7]   http://www.mp2-pwrc.usgs.gov/bbs/about/

[8]   Katayama, N. and Satoh, S.: The SR-tree: An Index Structure for High-Dimensional Nearest Neighbor Queries. SIGMOD Record 26(2) (1997) 369-380

[9]   Koperski, K., and Han, J.: Discovery of Spatial Association Rules in Geographic Information Databases. In: Proc. 4th Int'l Symp. on Large Spatial Databases, Portland, Maine (1995) 47-66

[10] Ng, R. and Han, J.: Efficient and Effective Clustering Method for Spatial Data Mining. In: Proc. of Int'l Conf. on Very Large Data Bases, Santiago, Chile (1994) 144-155

[11] Shekhar, S. and Chawla, S.: Spatial Databases: A Tour, Prentice Hall (2003)

[12] Tao, Y., Zhang, J., Papadias, D., Mamoulis, N.: An Efficient Cost Model for Optimization of Nearest Neighbor Search in Low and Medium Dimensional Spaces. IEEE Transactions on Knowledge and Data Engineering, 16(10) (2004) 1169-1184

[13] Wang X. and Hamilton, H. J.: DBRS: A Density-Based Spatial Clustering Method with Random Sampling. In: Proc. of the 7th PAKDD, Seoul, Korea (2003) 563 – 575

[14] Wang, X., and Hamilton, H.: DBRS: A Density-Based Spatial Clustering Method with Random Sampling. Technical Report, University of Regina (2003)

A Markov Model for Inventory Level Optimization in Supply-Chain Management

Scott Buffett

Institute for Information Technology – e-Business,
National Research Council Canada
46 Dineen Drive, Fredericton, New Brunswick, Canada E3B 9W4
Scott.Buffett@nrc.gc.ca

Abstract. We propose a technique for use in supply-chain management that assists the decision-making process for purchases of direct goods. Based on projections for future prices and demand, requests-for-quotes are constructed and quotes are accepted that optimize the level of inventory each day, while minimizing total cost. The problem is modeled as a Markov decision process (MDP), which allows for the computation of the utility of actions to be based on the utilities of consequential future states. Dynamic programming is then used to determine the optimal quote requests and accepts at each state in the MDP. The model is then used to formalize the subproblem of determining optimal request quantities, yielding a technique that is shown experimentally to outperform a standard technique from the literature. The implementation of our entry in the Trading Agent Competition-Supply Chain Management game is also discussed.

Keywords: supply-chain management, Markov decision process, dynamic programming, purchasing.

1 Introduction

With the dramatic increase in the use of the Internet for supply chain-related activities, there is a growing need for services that can analyze current and future purchase possibilities, as well as current and future demand levels, and determine efficient and economical strategies for the procurement of direct goods. Such solutions must take into account the current quotes offered by suppliers, likely future prices, projected demand and storage costs in order to make effective decisions on when and from whom to make purchases. Based on demand trends and projections, there is typically a target inventory level that a business hopes to maintain. This level is high enough to be able to meet fluctuations in demand, yet low enough that unnecessary storage costs are minimized (see Shapiro [13] for example). The focus of this paper is to provide an algorithm for purchase decision-making that strives to keep inventory close to its optimal level, while minimizing total cost.

B. Kégl and G. Lapalme (Eds.): AI 2005, LNAI 3501, pp. 133–144, 2005.
© Springer-Verlag Berlin Heidelberg 2005

In a perfect world, the best strategy for keeping inventory as close to the optimal level as possible would be to delay ordering to the last moment. That is, if demand trends indicate that a new shipment will be needed on some particular day, it would be best to delay ordering as long as possible so that the quantity needed can be assessed with the most certainty. An accurate estimate of the optimal quantity is critical since an inventory shortage may result in lost sales, while excessive inventory could result in unnecessary storage costs. Because of the variance in demand, the quantity needed a few days from now can usually be more accurately assessed than the quantity needed several days from now. Thus by delaying ordering the expected utility of future demand levels is increased. On the other hand, one may want to order earlier if current prices are low, if there will be more selection (i.e. many quotes from which to choose), or simply to ensure timely delivery. Thus there can be incentive to bid both early and late.

In this paper, we propose a decision-theoretic algorithm that advises the buyer when and from whom to buy by looking at possible future decisions. The buyer is advised to take an action if and only if there is no present or future alternative that would yield greater overall expected utility. We consider the request-for-quote (RFQ) model where the buyer requests quotes from suppliers by specifying the quantity needed and the desired delivery date, receives quotes a short time after which specify the price and quantity that can be delivered by the specified date (if not the entire order), and has a fixed period of time to decide whether or not to accept each quote. Factors that are of concern include the projected demand for each day (or whatever time period granularity is desired), current and projected sale prices each day for each supplier, storage costs, and RFQ costs. While there might not be direct costs associated with requesting quotes, indirect costs such as the time taken to compute optimal RFQs, as well as the possibility of being neglected by suppliers if we repeatedly fail to respond to their quotes, must be considered. To compute optimal decisions, we model the problem as a Markov decision process (MDP) [12] and use dynamic programming [3, 9] to determine the optimal action at each decision point. Actions include submitting RFQs to the various suppliers and accepting/rejecting quotes. With this model, the value (i.e. expected utility) of future consequential decisions can be taken into account when determining the value of choices at current decisions. Based on this model, the subproblem of determining optimal quantities to request in an RFQ is formalized and results are presented.

The new Trading Agent Competition-Supply Chain Management game (TAC-SCM) [1, 2] now provides a vehicle for testing various techniques related to supply-chain management in a competitive environment. While the theory in this paper deals with supply chain management in general, we briefly discuss how the techniques can be implemented for our entry in the competition, NaRC.

The paper is organized as follows. In section 2 we give a formal description of the problem. In section 3, we formulate the problem as an MDP and define the dynamic programming model. The subproblem of determining optimal request quantities is presented in section 4, and results of a few experiments are given. In section 5 we discuss the TAC-SCM game and describe how the research discussed in this paper fits. Finally, in section 6 we offer a few conclusions and outline plans for future work.

2   Problem Formalization

We consider the model where the buyer wants to purchase multiple units of a single good for resale (perhaps first being assembled with other items). Let $SUP = \{sup_1, \ldots, sup_m\}$ be the set of suppliers from whom the good can be obtained. Let $d = 0, 1, \ldots n$ denote the days over the procurement period (e.g. the next fiscal year, etc.). These could instead be hours, weeks, etc., depending on the desired granularity of time. Also, let $k \in Z$ be an integer denoting the inventory on a particular day d, and let h be the holding cost per unit per day. That is, if k' units are left over at the end of the day, they are held at a cost of hk'. Also, let $uk(k, d)$ be the utility of holding k units at the start of day d. This is a function of the expected income for d, taking into consideration the expected demand on d and the expected cost of holding the leftover inventory at the end of the day. This function will be maximized with higher k during high-demand periods and lower k over low-demand periods.

Our research is placed in the context of the request-for-quote (RFQ) procurement model. At any time, the buyer can send an RFQ to various suppliers. A subset of those suppliers will then respond to the request by offering a quote which specifies the terms of the offer. Let each RFQ be a tuple $\langle sup_i, q, d_{del} \rangle$ specifying the supplier sup_i, the quantity q needed and the day d_{del} on which to deliver. Let each quote be a tuple $\langle sup_i, p, q_{del}, d_{del}, d_r \rangle$ specifying the supplier sup_i, the price p of the order, the quantity q_{del} that can be delivered on d_{del} (in case the entire order cannot be filled by that day), and the day d_r on which the quoted price will be rescinded if the buyer has not yet responded. Let c be the small cost associated with each RFQ. Payment for the order is assumed to be made when the quote is accepted.

Also, for the purposes of projecting future outcomes, assume we have three probability distribution functions that are used to predict future outcomes: the demand distribution function, the supply distribution function and the price distribution function. The demand distribution function $df(d, q)$ takes a day d and a quantity q and returns the probability of selling q units on d. The supply distribution function $sf(sup, d, d', q)$ takes a supplier sup, days d and d' and a quantity q and returns the probability that sup can (and will agree to) to deliver q units on day d' if they were ordered on day d. We assume that if the supplier does agree to this delivery, then all q units will arrive on d' with certainty. The model could, however, be extended to allow for late deliveries by using a probability measure over all possible d'. Finally, the price distribution function $pf(sup, d, d', q, p)$ takes a supplier sup, days d and d', a quantity q and a monetary amount p and returns the probability that sup will quote a price of p for q units ordered on d to be delivered on day d'. Each of these functions can be constructed by examining market history, supplier history, or by using statistical projection techniques.

The problem is to decide each day 1) which quotes that have already been obtained to accept, and 2) whether to request new quotes, and if so, how the RFQ's should be formulated. That is, we must decide on which days we will likely need new shipments, and also what the optimal quantity is. The goal is to make decisions that maximize the overall inventory utility (i.e. keep the inventory close to optimal each day), while minimizing the total amount spent on orders over the duration of the purchase period.

3   Modeling the Problem as a Markov Decision Process

In this paper we capitalize on the idea of examining exactly what information will be known at future choice points when determining the optimal actions. For example, consider two suppliers sup_1 and sup_2. If we choose to request a quote for k units from each of them on some future day d, at the time we receive the quotes we will know the exact price being offered by each supplier. Based on this knowledge, plus the knowledge of the expected utility of not ordering at all, we can choose either to accept the cheaper quote or pass altogether. While the expected utility of any course of action on day d may not be as high as the expected utility of any action at the current decision point (i.e. current quotes), it is possible that the overall expected utility of waiting until day d to take action is higher. This is due to the fact that more information will be known on d than is known now, which will allow the decision-maker to make a more informed decision, thus increasing expected utility.

To determine the optimal quotes to accept and RFQs to submit, the problem is modeled as a Markov decision process (MDP) [12]. An MDP is a mathematical tool used to aid decision-making in complex systems. In an MDP, the possible *states* S that the decision-making agent can occupy are defined, as well as the set of *actions* A that the agent can take in each state. If action a is deterministic in state s, then the transition function maps (s, a) to a new state s'. Otherwise the action is stochastic, and the transition function maps (s, a) to states according to a probability function Pr, where $Pr(s'|s, a)$ is the probability of occupying s' given that a is performed in s. Also, some or all of the states may have an associated *reward*. The purpose of modeling a problem as an MDP is to determine a *policy* function $\pi : S \to A$, which takes any state and specifies the action such that the expected sum of the sequence of rewards is maximized. Dynamic programming is used to determine the optimal action in each state.

3.1   States

Each state s in the MDP for our problem is a tuple $\langle I, Q, C, d, k \rangle$ where

- I is the set of incoming orders. That is, I contains the orders known to be coming in on the day specified in s or on some future day. Each $i \in I$ is a tuple $\langle q, d \rangle$ where d is the day of the shipment and q is the quantity.
- Q is the set of currently open quotes.
- C is the total amount spent on purchases thus far.
- d is the day.
- k is the current inventory.

3.2   Actions

Actions consist of accepting quotes and sending RFQs. Since quote rescind times are always known (i.e. quotes are not pulled without warning), we assume that decisions on whether or not to accept a quote are delayed to the last possible moment, to allow decisions to be as informed as possible. Thus quotes are only accepted the day before they are to be rescinded. We also assume that at most one RFQ is sent to each supplier each day. This assumption is put in place merely to reduce the number of possible actions at each state, and could easily be lifted if desired. Let $req(rfq)$ represent the act of submitting a request-for-quote rfq, and let $acc(qu)$ represent the act of accepting quote qu. For a state s with quotes Q_s and day d_s, let $\{req(\langle sup, q, d_{del}\rangle) \mid sup \in SUP, q_{min} \leq q \leq q_{max}, d_s < d_{del} \leq d_n\}$ be the set possible quote requests, where q_{min} and q_{max} are the minimum and maximum quantities that can be ordered, respectively, and d_n is the final day of the procurement period. Also let the set $\{acc(\langle s, p, q, d_{del}, d_r\rangle) \mid \langle s, p, q, d_{del}, d_r\rangle \in Q_s, d_r = d_s + 1\}$ be the set of possible quote acceptances. The set A of actions is then the union of these two sets. Any subset A' of the actions in A for a state s can be performed with the restriction that at most one RFQ is submitted to each supplier. Let the set of these valid subsets for a state s be denoted by A_s.

3.3   Rewards

The value of a state in an MDP is equal to the reward for that state plus the expected rewards of future states. The optimal action at each state is then the one defined to yield the highest expected value. Our technique aims to optimize the utility of the inventory held each day, and minimize the total cost over the entire purchase period. Thus there are two types of rewards given in the MDP. To assess the reward to be assigned to each state, two utility functions are used: the inventory utility function uk and the cost utility function uc.

The inventory utility function $uk : Z \times Z \to \Re$ takes an inventory level k and a day d and returns the utility of holding k units on d. This utility is determined by measuring the ability of meeting the expected demand for day d with k units against the expected costs associated with holding the leftover units. For example, if k' is the optimal number of units to hold on d (thus maximizing uk for d), then for $k < k'$ inventory may not be high enough to meet the demand so money may be lost, and for $k > k'$ inventory may be too high and too costly to be worth holding.

As an example, let the demand function be such that either 1 or 2 units will be sold, each with 0.5 probability, on day d. Also let the sale price of each unit be 10, and the inventory holding cost be $h = 1/\text{unit}/\text{day}$. The expected net income (revenue - minus inventory cost) $E(x, d)$ for x units on day d is 0 if $x = 0$ (since no units are sold and no units are held), 10 if $x = 1$ (the one item will be sold with certainty, since the demand function says that 1 or 2 units will be sold today), and $16.5 - x$ if $x \geq 2$ (taking into account losses incurred by possible leftover inventory). The utility function uk is then a function of $E(x, d)$ (perhaps concave to indicate aversion to risk).

The cost utility function $uc : Z \to \Re$ is a monotonically decreasing function that takes a cost c and returns the utility of spending c. It is typically a concave function reflecting the risk-averseness of the decision-maker.

For each state s, the *inventory reward* is given. That is, if k is the inventory for s and d is the day, then the inventory reward for s is $uk(k, d)$. For each terminal state a *cost reward* is given, which is the utility $uc(C)$ of spending a total of C over the duration of the procurement period.

The value of each state is then a function of the expected cost reward and the expected inventory rewards for the remainder of the procurement period, given that the state is reached.

3.4   The Transition Function

The transition function specifies which states can follow from an action in a given state in the MDP. Let $T(s, a)$ be this function which takes a state $s \in S$ and action $a \in A_s$, and returns the set of states that can be occupied as a result of performing a in s. Let $Pr(s'|s, a)$ be the transition probability function, which specifies the probability of occupying state $s' \in T(s, a)$ directly after a is performed in s. These two functions are computed as follows.

Let $s = \langle I, Q, C, d, k \rangle$ be a state and $a \in A_s$ an action where a is a valid subset of requests and acceptances that can be performed in s. Then $s' = \langle I', Q', C', d', k' \rangle \in T(s, a)$ if

- I' contains the incoming orders from I, minus those offers that arrived on day d, plus new incoming orders that result from the quotes accepted in a. More formally, let $I_{old} = \{\langle q, d_{del} \rangle \mid \langle q, d_{del} \rangle \in I, d_{del} = d\}$ be the orders that came in on d, and let $I_{new} = \{\langle q, d_{del} \rangle \mid acc(\langle sup, p, q, d_{del}, d \rangle) \in a\}$ be the new incoming orders that arise as a result of accepting quotes. Then $I' = I \setminus I_{old} \cup I_{new}$.

- Q' contains the quotes from Q, minus those that were rescinded on day d, plus those that are received as a result of the requests in a. Let $Q_{old} = \{\langle sup, p, q, d_{del}, d_r \rangle \mid \langle sup, p, q, d_{del}, d_r \rangle \in Q, d_r = d'\}$ be the orders that are rescinded on d', and let $Q_{new} = \{\langle sup, p, q, d_{del}, d+1+ql \rangle \mid req(\langle sup, q, d_{del} \rangle) \in a\}$ be the quotes received in response to the requests in a, where ql is the quote length (i.e. the number of days for which the quote is valid). This could be assumed to be constant over all suppliers. Thus $Q' = Q \setminus Q_{old} \cup Q_{new}$. Note that there may be several possible values for the price p and the deliverable quantity q in the quotes in Q_{new}. The transition probability function will consider the probability of each outcome in determining the probability of the state as a whole.

- C' is the amount spent C by day d, plus the amount spent on accepted quotes in a, plus the RFQ costs. Thus $C' = C + \sum p + c_{req}$ over all $acc(\langle sup, p, q, d_{del}, d + 1 \rangle) \in a$, where c_{req} is the cost of requests in a.

- k' is the starting inventory k for day d, minus the units sold t_d on d, plus those received via incoming orders in I_{new}. Thus $k' = k - t_d + \sum q$ for all $\langle q, d_{del} \rangle \in I_{new}$. Note that there may be several possible values for t_d, each with some probability of occurring. The probability of any t_d greater than $k + \sum q$ is 0.

- $d' = d + 1$.

Let s be a state and let $T(s, a)$ contain the states that can follow from performing a in s. Then for each state $s' \in T(s, a)$, the probability $P(s'|s, a)$ of occupying s' after a is performed in s is the probability of receiving the new quotes in s' given the requests in a, multiplied by the probability of the sales realized in the transition from s to s'. Let d be the day specified in s, let Q_{new} be the set of new quotes received on day $d + 1$ (i.e. the quotes that are in s' but not in s), and let t_d be the number of units sold on day d, which is the inventory in s' minus the sum of the inventory in s and the units received (i.e. in I_{new}). Let the demand distribution function df, supply distribution function sf and price distribution function pf be as defined in section 2. Then the probability of getting the quotes in Q_{new} is

$$Prob(Q_{new}) = \prod_{qu_i \in Q_{new}} sf(sup_i, d+1, d_{del_i}, q_i) \cdot pf(sup_i, d+1, d_{del_i}, q_i, p_i)$$

(1)

where $qu_i = \langle sup_i, p_i, q_i, d_{del_i}, d_{r_i} \rangle$. Note that there must be a qu_i for every request in a. Unanswered or rejected requests should have a corresponding quote $qu_i = \langle sup_i, 0, 0, d_{del_i}, d_{r_i} \rangle$ in Q_{new}. Since the probability of selling t_d units on d is $df(d, t_d)$, the probability of s' occurring given that a is performed in s is

$$P(s'|s, a) = Prob(Q_{new}) \cdot df(d, t_d)$$

(2)

3.5   The Dynamic Programming Model

The value iteration method of dynamic programming is used to determine the optimal action at each state. Let $v : S \to \Re$ be the value function that assigns to each state its value (i.e. utility), let $\pi : S \to Q$ be the optimal policy and let $s = \langle I, Q, C, d, k \rangle$ be a state. Then

$$v(s) = \begin{cases} f_d(uk(k, d), uc(C)) & \text{if } d = d_n \\ \max_{a \in A_s} \sum_{s' \in T(s,a)} f_d(uk(k, d), v(s')) \cdot P(s'|s, a) & \text{otherwise} \end{cases}$$

$$\pi(s) = \begin{cases} null & \text{if } d = d_n \\ \arg\max_{a \in A_s} \sum_{s' \in T(s,a)} f_d(uk(k, d), v(s')) \cdot P(s'|s, a) & \text{otherwise} \end{cases}$$

(3)

where f_d is the function for computing the value of the state in terms of the inventory reward of the current state and the expected value of the following states, and arg is the operator that returns the maximizing a. This function may be constant or variable and can be constructed to factor in the decision maker's relative importance for optimizing either cost or inventory level.

4   Using the Model to Determine RFQ Quantities

4.1   Modeling the Subproblem

While the Markov model presented in the previous section laid a framework for all decision-making involved in optimizing target inventories, in several situations the model may be too complex to solve in a reasonable length of time. In this section we show how the model can be used to solve a more manageable piece of the puzzle, and formalize the subproblem of determining the optimal quantity to request in a given RFQ.

In this case, elements such as quoted costs are not considered, and thus decision-making does not depend on the onerous task of enumerating all outcomes for price. Instead, an *acceptance rate* is used, which is a static measurement of the likelihood any quote will be accepted based on its price. For example, if it is found that the quotes are accepted 55% of the time (or in the case when multiple quotes are solicited simultaneously for purpose of comparison, that *some* quote is accepted), then the acceptance rate is 55%. While demand typically changes each day, we assume that the acceptance rate is the average taken over the procurement period. The only dynamic factor under consideration here is the current inventory. The question is then, based on the current inventory, how many units should be requested?

The problem is stated more formally as follows: Given a current inventory level k, shipping time st (in days), daily inventory utility function $uk(k, d)$, daily demand function $df(d, k)$ indicating the probability that k units are sold on day d, and acceptance rate α, if an RFQ were to be submitted, how many units should be ordered? The MDP for this problem is then a portion of the MDP for the general problem. Each state s is a tuple $\langle I, d, k \rangle$ where

- I is the set of incoming orders
- d is the day.
- k is the current inventory.

An action is an RFQ $rfq = \langle q, d + st \rangle$ for a particular quantity q to arrive on day $d + st$. Every state has an associated reward equal to $uk(k, d)$ where k is the starting inventory on day d. The optimal action $\pi(s)$ then specifies the optimal RFQ given state s.

4.2   Testing the Performance

To assess the potential performance of using this model, the method was tested against a method from the literature that uses a Monte Carlo algorithm [13]. With this method, a reorder point r and a quantity q are randomly chosen from some distribution. Market behaviour is then simulated within the specified parameters, where an order for q units is placed each time the inventory falls below r. This process continues for several (r, q) pairs, and the optimal result is noted.

Tests were run over a 150 day procurement period, with an inventory utility function $uk(k, d) = \max\{0, 15 - |15 - k|\}$ (utility maximized at $k = 15$, minimized

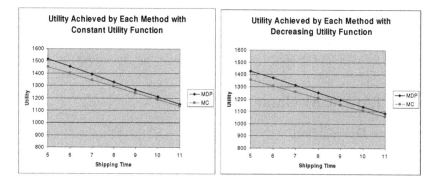

Fig. 1. (a) Utility achieved using our method (MDP) and Monte Carlo (MC) using a constant utility function over all 150 days in the procurement period, (b) Utility achieved using our method (MDP) and Monte Carlo (MC) using a decreasing utility function where 0 inventory is desired on day 150

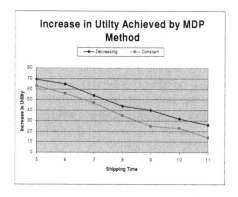

Fig. 2. The increase in utility achieved by our method over Monte Carlo for a constant and decreasing utility function

at $k = 0$, $k \geq 30$) for all d, and a quote acceptance rate of $\alpha = 50\%$. Shipping time was varied throughout the tests. A summary of the results is demonstrated in Figure 1(a).

The Monte Carlo method is quite rigid, since at any given time either q or 0 is ordered. Even though the optimal quantity and the optimal times at which to order are utilized, it still does not perform as well as our method, which adapts to the situation and determines the appropriate amount. Notice that both methods perform worse as the shipping time is lengthened because of increased uncertainty. To further demonstrate the advantages of our technique, Figure 1(b) shows results of tests where the utility function is not constant. In particular, this test utilized a decreasing utility function over time. This models the situation where no inventory is desired at the end of the procurement period.

Our method performs even better, since order quantities can be adjusted to accommodate a changing utility function, where the Monte Carlo method uses a static q and r values. Figure 2 demonstrates the overall increase realized by our method for each of the constant and dynamic utility functions.

5   The TAC-SCM Game

5.1   Game Description

The Trading Agent Competition has occurred annually since 2000. The competition was designed to encourage research in trading agent problems, and it provides a method for direct comparison of different approaches, albeit in an artificial environment. The original competition focused on acquiring a package of items in set of auctions, but in 2003 the "Supply Chain Management" (SCM) [1, 2] game was introduced. The TAC-SCM game charges the competing agent with the task of successfully managing a computer dealership: acquiring components from suppliers, assembling these components into complete PCs, and selling these PCs to a group of customers. Starting with an initial bank balance of 0 and unlimited borrowing capabilities, the agents' goal in the competition is to make the most profit. To compete successfully, agents must be quite complex and able handle different purchasing models. To win contracts with customers, agents must win a first-price sealed-bid auction. To acquire goods successfully from suppliers, agents must be able to effectively judge pricing trends. At the same time, they must also consider that supply is limited, and thus rejecting an offer could result in inability to acquire goods. Several other stochastic factors such as customer demand, customer reserve values and delivery delays must also be handled for the agent to be successful.

The procurement model of the TAC-SCM game loosely reduces to our MDP model. Each day, an agent receives quotes from suppliers based on the previous day's requests, as well as quote requests from customers. From the procurement point of view, the goal is to determine which quotes from suppliers to accept and what new quotes to request, to optimize inventory and cost. Quotes and RFQs take the same form as those described in this paper. Based on the bidding strategy used in response to customer requests (we do not focus on bidding in this paper, only procurement), the agent can judge the demand function by assessing how likely it is to sell certain quantities each day. Based on previous dealings with the various suppliers, the agent can also model the supply and price distribution functions, and build the MDP. Dynamic programming is then used to determine the optimal accepts and requests.

5.2   Our "NaRC" Agent

NaRC [7] competed in the 2004 TAC-SCM competition in New York. While we qualified for the tournament (top 24 teams out of about 35), we were eliminated in the quarter-final round (the first of three days of competition). Aspects of NaRC utilized the MDP model described in this paper. In particular, the purchase decision-making engine modeled the sequence of subsequent purchase decisions as an MDP in order to determine the value of current quotes. While thus far untested in the TAC-SCM competition, the technique of using an MDP to compute optimal RFQs has been shown above to be quite promising. We plan to implement the method in our agent for future installments of the competition.

6   Conclusions and Future Work

In this paper we present a mathematical model for determining when to request quotes from suppliers, how to construct the RFQs, and which of the resulting quotes to accept. Decisions are made in such a way as to optimize the level of inventory each day, while lowering total cost. The problem is modeled as a Markov decision process (MDP), which allows for the computation of the utility of actions to be based on the utilities of consequential future states. Each action is considered to be a set containing quote requests and accepts. Dynamic programming is then used to determine the optimal action at each state in the MDP. The model is then used to formalize the subproblem of determining optimal request quantities, and experiments show that the technique performs better than a standard technique from the literature. The TAC-SCM game is also discussed, and the implementation details for own agent, NaRC, are briefly described.

The idea of modeling problems similar to this as an MDP has been done before. Boutilier *et al.* [4, 5], Byde [8], and Buffett and Grant [6] have previously used MDPs for auction decision-making. However our model differs from these works in two ways: 1) we consider the request-for-quote model rather than the auction model, and 2) we buy items for resale with the extra aim of maintaining a certain level of inventory, in addition to cost minimization. Other techniques have been presented by Priest *et al.* [10, 11] for purchasing items for resale; however, these works do not attempt to measure the value of current choices based on the value of consequential future decisions.

For future work, we intend to test the technique against other strategies to determine under what conditions and situations the technique performs well and not so well. Such strategies range from the more naïve where quotes are requested simply when inventories reach certain levels and the cheapest quote is immediately accepted, to the more sophisticated where massive amounts of inventories are built up (regardless of overhead costs) and intelligent selling methods are employed to maximize profit. We believe that the latter type of strategy, which was employed by several agents in the TAC-SCM game in 2003, might not yield as much profit per unit as our technique, but could surpass our technique in total profit because of the higher volume of transactions. As far the potential success of using our technique in the actual TAC-SCM game, we believe that while these high-volume agents may monopolize supply early in the game, in the long run our agent will perform better, especially in low-demand games. Only after experimentation with real-world examples as well as the TAC-SCM will these questions be answered.

References

1. R. Arunachalam, J. Eriksson, N. Finne, S. Janson, and N. Sadeh. The supply chain management game for the trading agent competition 2004. http://www.sics.se/tac/tacscm_04spec.pdf. Date accessed: Apr 8, 2004, 2004.
2. Raghu Arunachalam and Norman Sadeh. The 2003 supply chain management trading agent competition. In *Proc. International Conference on Electronic Commerce (ICEC2004)*, pages 113–120, Delft, The Netherlands, 2004.
3. R. Bellman. *Dynamic Programming.* Princeton University Press, Princeton, NJ, 1957.
4. C. Boutilier, M. Goldszmidt, and B. Sabata. Continuous value function approximation for sequential bidding policies. In *the Fifteenth Annual Conference on Uncertainty in Artificial Intelligence (UAI-99)*, pages 81–90, Stockholm, 1999.
5. C. Boutilier, M. Goldszmidt, and B. Sabata. Sequential auctions for the allocation of resources with complementaries. In *the Sixteenth International Joint Conference on Artificial Intelligence (IJCAI-99)*, pages 527–534, Stockholm, 1999.
6. S. Buffett and A. Grant. A decision-theoretic algorithm for bundle purchasing in multiple open ascending price auctions. In *the Seventeenth Canadian Conference on Artificial Intelligence (AI'2004)*, pages 429–433, London, ON, Canada, 2004.
7. S. Buffett and N. Scott. An algorithm for procurement in supply chain management. In *Proc. of the Trading Agent Design and Analysis Workshop (TADA'04)*, pages 9–14, New York, NY, 2004.
8. A. Byde. A dynamic programming model for algorithm design in simultaneous auctions. In *WELCOM'01*, Heidelburg, Germany, 2001.
9. R.A. Howard. *Dynamic Programming and Markov Processes.* M.I.T. Press, Cambridge, Mass., 1960.
10. C. Preist, C. Bartolini, and A. Byde. Agent-based service composition through simultaneous negotiation in forward and reverse auctions. In *Proceedings of the 4th ACM Conference on Electronic Commerce*, pages 55–63, San Diego, California, USA, 2003.
11. C. Priest, A. Byde, C. Bartolini, and G. Piccinelli. Towards agent-based service composition through negotiation in multiple auctions. In *AISB'01 Symp. on Inf. Agents for Electronic Commerce*, 2001.
12. M.L. Puterman. *Markov Decision Processes.* Wiley, 1994.
13. J. F. Shapiro. *Modeling the Supply Chain.* Duxbury, Pacific Grove, CA, 2001.

Analysis and Classification of Strategies in Electronic Negotiations

Marina Sokolova and Stan Szpakowicz

School of Information Technology and Engineering,
University of Ottawa, Ottawa, Canada
{sokolova, szpak}@site.uottawa.ca

Abstract. The intensive use of the Web, email and instant messaging for inter- and intra-business communications has resulted in rapid increase of electronic business communication, including negotiations. Simulated electronic negotiations have become an important tool in the study of "real world" electronic negotiations. We explore negotiation strategies by applying Statistical Natural Language Processing and Machine Learning methods to the text data of simulated electronic negotiations. We derive conclusions about strategies in successful and unsuccessful negotiations. We support our claims by extracting information about strategies and representing data through this information. We classify data and analyze classification results with respect to learning abilities of the classifiers and the data representation.

1 Electronic Negotiations

The intensive use of the Web, email and instant messaging for inter- and intra-business communications [8] has resulted in commonly practised electronic business communication, including negotiations. Electronic negotiations present new tasks for text classification, information extraction, statistical and symbolic natural language processing (NLP) and machine learning (ML) methods. This paper presents results obtained on one of such tasks - classification of the negotiation outcomes based on the text representation of negotiators' strategies.

Electronic negotiations, e.g., negotiations conducted through electronic means, are more dynamic than traditional face-to-face negotiations. Electronic means allow participation in several negotiations simultaneously, simplify direct links between businesses, and connect people globally regardless of their cultural and social differences [4, 25]. On the negative side, e-negotiations have time, prediction, judgement and competition biases [26]. The biases make the positive outcome more difficult to achieve than in face-to-face negotiations.

Currently electronic means enable either quantitative automated negotiations, where the system makes decisions, or non-automated negotiation support, where decisions are made by negotiators [21]. The former — electronic auctions and intelligent software agents — are outside the scope of our research. The latter comprise *process-oriented* communication systems and negotiation support systems. Figure 1 shows the relations among e-negotiation means.

B. Kégl and G. Lapalme (Eds.): AI 2005, LNAI 3501, pp. 145–157, 2005.
© Springer-Verlag Berlin Heidelberg 2005

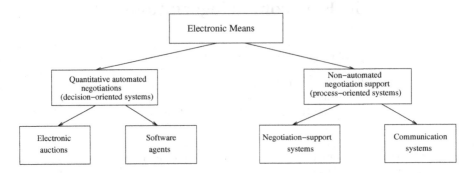

Fig. 1. Types of electronic means in e-negotiations

The data obtained through e-negotiations depend on the features of the electronic means that support negotiations. The electronic means can have only communication functions that allow the exchange of unstructured, free-form written messages, or structured information – negotiation offers and messages. Another type of electronic means are negotiation-support systems (NSS) with communication and decision-support functions. If an NSS supports the pre-negotiation, negotiation and post-negotiation stages, the resulting data are a combination of the corresponding three types of data.

This study continues the work on e-negotiation data presented in [22, 24, 23] where ML and NLP methods analyzed how the language of negotiators affects the outcome of negotiations. We aim to devise methods that would work on any data gathered through negotiation, regardless of the specific conditions of negotiations such as the means, environment or goals [7]. That is why we analyze the characteristics common to (almost) all negotiations. We combine textual and non-textual data to discover how the language reflects the negotiation strategies. We propose two ways of extracting the strategy-related information.

Our empirical approach is based on a bootstrapping procedure of information extraction from corpora, our analytical approach – on combining the negotiation theory and linguistic properties. We compare the results in both cases, perform feature selection by comparing classification results for different data representation, and analyze the classification results with respect to the learning ability of the classifiers and the data representation. The obtained empirical results are useful in the design of knowledge-based negotiation systems, to be able to warn negotiators that their language use suggests failure.

Section 2 of the paper reviews previous research relevant to our studies. Section 3 introduces the procedure of learning strategies from corpora and reports on the results of learning. Section 4 explains how the negotiation strategies and the influence strategies are reflected in language. Section 5 reports on the use of strategies to represent data for classification of negotiation outcomes and the analysis of classification results. Section 6 lists conclusions and directions for future work.

2   Electronic Business Negotiations

The strategic approach to negotiations states that the outcome of negotiations is the result of the negotiators' strategic choices. In language, these strategies are exhibited in the exchange of offers, agreement, refusal, questioning, answering [18]. During negotiation, participants employ influence strategies intended to make the counterpart concede. Such strategies can be direct or indirect, expressed by various types of appeal [2]. The direct influence strategies are used when the participant says what she wants the other party to do. In the indirect influence strategies, such requests are implied and often masked by asking for sympathy. The influence strategies are exhibited in such negotiation moves as **argumentation, persuasion, threats** and **substantiation**, and in general behaviour such as questions, reactions, offers, exchange of information [2, 7].

A negotiator uses influence strategies to express personal power. The absence of face-to-face situations, e.g., in phone or electronic negotiation, results in lower use of pressure tactics, less impasse, and achievement of higher joint profit. This corresponds to showing less personal power [25]. The sources of power used in negotiations are: resource control, information power, personal power (attractiveness, emotion, integrity, persistence and tenacity).

The general assumption for highly transparent markets, including electronic markets, is that both parties always have the same level of information, so none can benefit from excessive information power. The sources of personal power are not present in an electronic exchange, except for texts of messages. Ströbel [25] claims that the avoidance of threats, positional statements and other messages related to personal power promotes integrative solutions. Cellich and Jain [4] draw the opposite conclusion: competitive behaviour prevails in electronic negotiations. They also emphasize that personal power increases due to the reduced risk of personality conflicts and the absence of face-to-face discussions.

In order to reach a goal, negotiators apply negotiation strategies and influence strategies. The effect of the strategies depends on the style of their delivery [7]. We will show how the delivery of the strategies is related to and reflected in the language of negotiators. We concentrate our studies on the analysis of parts of speech (POS). We look for POS whose employment corresponds to agreement, refusal, exchange of information, argumentation, persuasion, and substantiation. We seek to find out how the negotiator's indirect and direct influences on the counterpart are implemented in the language. Threats can be real (to end negotiations) or imaginary (to find another supplier if only one is possible).

A word of caution: although we investigate strategies that negotiators implement, we do not support the assumption that all participants in interpersonal communications are rational agents, that is, always choose actions that will satisfy their goals. This assumption has been relaxed in current studies on negotiations [1, 6].

3   Learning Strategies from Corpora

The textual e-negotiation data bear all the structural and style characteristics of the computer-mediated communication data; for a detailed overview see [22]. The following characteristics are important for this study: short and dense sentences, simplified grammar, and restricted lexicon.[1] We use those characteristics to establish the basic parameters of a learning procedure.

In the first hypothesis we suggest that the strategies employed in successfully completed (henceforth, *successful*) negotiations differ from the strategies used in incomplete (henceforth, *unsuccessful*) negotiations. Our second hypothesis is that we can learn differences in strategies by comparing corpora of texts that accompany successful negotiations with those for unsuccessful negotiations.

To support the hypotheses, we perform empirical studies on the data of simulated electronic negotiations supplied by NSS Inspire. Inspire is a research and training tool with the largest available collection of e-negotiation data [11, 22]. We have worked with transcripts of 2557 negotiations conducted in English. The number of the data contributors is over 5000, 72% of them non-native English speakers. The data contains 1,514,623 word tokens and 27,055 word types. The Inspire system identifies the outcomes of 1427 negotiations as *an agreement* (successful) and the outcomes of the remaining 1130 negotiations as *no agreement* (unsuccessful). We build corpora of texts that accompany successful negotiations, concatenating all messages, and the same for unsuccessful negotiations.

Obviously, there are many ways of comparing corpora. We chose to use N-grams ranks where N-grams are ranked by their occurrences in corpora. The reliability of word frequencies makes the statistical results a trustworthy measure [12]. For each corpus we rank N-grams according to their frequencies; the lowest rank indicates the highest frequency. We look for N-grams that show the negotiators' goal (win by any means, reach a compromise, do away with the assignment), their attitude to partners (friendliness, aggressiveness, indifference), and behaviour in the negotiation process (flexibility, stubbornness). The same N-grams must be noticeably present in either successful or unsuccessful negotiations. Two major elements that affect N-gram selection are the words it contains and its rank. The idea behind finding N-grams representative of each corpus is quite simple. It is a bootstrapping procedure [10] with the seeds corresponding to the basic negotiation moves, such as agreement, refusal, negotiating issues.

It is a bootstrapping procedure [10] which learns from a small number of words corresponding to the basic negotiation moves, such as agreement, refusal, negotiating issues. These words are called seeds. The procedure allows us to learn differences in corpora of successful and unsuccessful negotiations.

---

[1] This is also supported by the unusually low type-token ratio of the data.

A bootstrapping procedure of building the lists of representative N-grams for successful and unsuccessful negotiations

Input: text data of all negotiations, text data of successful negotiations, text data of unsuccessful negotiations, seeds.

1. Build the list L of unigrams for all negotiations
2. Build the lists of N-grams ($N = 1, 2, 3$) for successful negotiations (NS).
3. Build the lists of N-grams ($N = 1, 2, 3$) for unsuccessful negotiations (NU).
4. In L find unigrams of seeds among k most frequent unigrams (k is a predefined cut-off point). Build the list W of such seeds.
5. For each $w \in W$:
   - Find its rank r_s^1 in the list of the unigrams of NS.
   - Find its rank r_u^1 in the list of the unigrams of NU.
   - Calculate $d_w^1 = r_s^1 - r_u^1$.
6. Delete from W all w such that $d_w^1 < d$ (d is a predefined distance).
7. For each $w \in W$:
   - Find its bigrams among m most frequent bigrams on the list of bigrams of NS (m is a predefined cut-off point).
   - Find its bigrams among m most frequent bigrams on the list of bigrams of NU.
   - • Find the rank r_s^2 of the $i - th$ bigram on the list of the bigrams of NS.
     • Find the rank r_u^2 of the $i - th$ bigram on the list of the bigrams of NU.
     • Calculate $d_i^2 = r_s^2 - r_u^2$.
   - Calculate $d_w^2 = \sum_{i=1}^{m} d_i^2$
8. Delete from W all w such that $d_w^2 < d$.
9. Find most frequent trigrams containing unigrams from W: repeat steps 7-8 for trigrams instead of bigrams.
10. Build the list L_R of trigrams, containing $w \in W$, with their ranks.

Output: L_R.

Although it is possible to investigate N-grams with $N > 3$, the procedure stops at trigrams because of the data characteristics listed earlier: simplified grammar, dense and short sentences, restricted lexicon. The only adjustable parameters are the distance d and the cut-off points k, m. In order not to overload the procedure, we do not use weights to tune distances between N-grams, though it seems a natural thing to do. We have tested the procedure with $d = min(100, 2 * rank_s)$, $k = 100$, $m = 700$. To find k, m we have chosen the values that guarantee that the procedure works with N-grams covering the same percentage of texts in both successful and unsuccessful negotiations and eliminate low-frequency N-grams, thus keeping representative N-grams in negotiation data. Needless to say, the choice of distance depends on the cut-off points. For our cut-off points, the distance ensures that the ranks used to calculate it correspond to different N-gram frequencies. Examples from the resulting list appear in Table 1.

Table 1. Examples of Representative Trigrams

word	N	trigram	rank$_s$	trigram	rank$_u$
have	3	we have to	66	that you have	75
	4	that you have	92	that we have	92
accept	2	to accept your	55	to accept your	103
	3	you can accept	90	you will accept	132
agree	2	agree with your	395	you will agree	533
	3	I agree with	426	agree with you	565
will	3	I will be	69	you will find	44
	4	that we will	83	I will be	52

We notice that in the trigrams from unsuccessful negotiations there is a trace of aggressive behaviour (**you will accept, you will agree**), which is absent from the corresponding trigrams in successful negotiations (**you can accept, agree with your**). Examining the trigrams with "you", we found that in successful negotiations they correspond to politeness, in unsuccessful negotiations – to aggressiveness. Expectedly, trigrams with the positive "accept" are more frequent in successful than in unsuccessful negotiations. Among other findings we note that trigrams indicating negotiation moves (sending or receiving an offer) are more frequent in successful than in unsuccessful negotiations. The last result corresponds to the results reported in [11].

4   Negotiation Strategies and Language

In the absence of external sources to validate our conclusions from corpus analysis, we take another approach to the problem. We study how the negotiation and influence strategies are connected with the language used in e-negotiations. We take into account the non-standard characteristics of the data listed at the beginning of section 3. Grammar simplification, density and shortness mean that the language implementation of strategies is straightforward and concentrates on the expression of the main goal of a strategy. Hence, we have looked for the parts of speech (POS) that express logical necessity, appeal, intention with respect to the subject of discussion, intention with respect to continuation of negotiations. The resulting correspondence between the strategies and the POS is the following:

- logical necessity - modals, e.g., *can, will, have, may, should, would, could,* and not-negations, e.g., *cannot, haven't, shouldn't, couldn't, wouldn't*;
- appeal - personal pronouns, e.g., *I, we, you, my, your*, no-negations, e.g., *never, neither, no, none, nor, nothing, nowhere*, not-negations *not, don't, aren't*, and superlative adjectives *latest, best*;
- intention with respect to the subject of discussion - positive volition verbs, e.g., *hope, want, wish, like, prefer, agree, accept, promise, ask, afford, aim, choose, decide, intend, look, plan, propose, make, made, manage, move, pro-*

ceed, try, and negative volition verbs, e.g., *decline, refuse, reject, disagree, delay, hesitate*;
- intention with respect to continuation of negotiations - mental verbs, e.g., *know, think, understand, consider* and adjectives, e.g., *new, last, latest.*

The modal auxiliary verbs (modals) have both logical and pragmatic meaning. They express permission, possibility and necessity as the representatives of logic; primary modals *can, will, have, may* are more direct and less hypothetical than secondary modals *should, would, could* [13]. One of the indicators of argumentation is an openness to feedback from the counterpart. The mental verbs used in the positive statements *I/we think/know/consider* aim to get feedback from the counterpart [17]. Such statements suggest careful deliberation and reflective weighing. Verbs expressing volition of a speaker are divided into positive volition and negative volition verbs with respect to the speaker's intentions about the subject of discussion and communications with the counterpart [20]. The viewpoints of the negotiating sides are represented through personal pronouns [3]. We consider that the viewpoint of a negotiator can be expressed in positive and negative ways. The negative viewpoint can be expressed explicitly, through not-negations, which are negations of the primary verbs *be, have, do* and the modal *can* [10], and implicitly, through no-negations, e.g., *no, nowhere, neither*, and fuzzy negations *any, few* [27].

We compared the use of the POS in the data of successful and unsuccessful negotiations. Positive volition verbs, mental verbs, and no-negations are used more often in successful negotiations. Negative volition verbs, not-negations and primary modals are used more often in unsuccessful negotiations. We have run two-tailed/non-directional *t*-test on the relative frequencies of these POS in the data. The null hypothesis is the assumption that the difference between two samples is due to chance. The null hypothesis was rejected with 5 per cent confidence level for not-negations of the verb *be* and with 20 per cent confidence level for primary modals and collocations *PersPronoun PrimModal*. Table 2 presents the *t*-test results. Statistically significant difference between the data from "suc-

Table 2. Statistical difference between samples

Sample	Degrees of freedom	*t* value	Significance level
Primary Modals	10	**1.435**	0.2
Secondary Modals	6	0.180	insignificant
You PrimModal	10	**1.7328**	0.2
I/we PrimModal	10	**1.738**	0.2
Positive Volition Verbs	40	0.051	insignificant
Negative Volition Verbs	12	0.452	insignificant
Mental Verbs	10	0.021	insignificant
Negations	8	0.150	insignificant
Be Not	7	**2.524**	0.05
PersPronoun do/have/can not	12	0.602	insignificant
the latest & is the best	7	0.716	insignificant

cessful" and "unsuccessful" corpus is shown in bold, followed by the confidence level with which the null hypothesis was rejected. *Be not, do/have/can not* correspond to negations of all inflections of the verbs *be, do, have, can* and their spelling versions found in the data, e.g., "can not".

Looking into the context of the use of POS, we conclude that there is a difference in the strategies employed by different negotiator classes, labelled according to the negotiation outcomes. We have found that:

1. participants in successful negotiations show different attitude towards continuing negotiation than participants in unsuccessful negotiations: the former signal to continue negotiation, the latter signal to stop;
2. participants in unsuccessful negotiations are more demanding than participants in successful negotiations;
3. negation varies among four data classes; it is more implicit in successful negotiations than in unsuccessful negotiations.

5   Classification of the Negotiation Outcomes and Discussion

We want to support experimentally our claim that the language implementation of strategies differs in successful and unsuccessful negotiations. We represent the data through the words corresponding to the strategies ("strategic" words) and run classification experiments.

We have a total of 2557 examples in our data set, of which 1427 are positive (successful negotiation) and 1130 negative (unsuccessful negotiation).[2]

The data are represented by bags of "strategic" words, and a bag corresponds to one negotiation. In a bag, attributes have numerical values equal to the number of occurrences of a "strategic" word in negotiation, and an additional attribute whose value is equal to the number of other words in the negotiation.

We compare the performance of kernel, decision-based and probabilistic classifiers on negotiation data. The first class is represented by Support Vector Machines (SVM) [5], the second by decision trees (C5.0) [19] and the third one by probabilistic Naive Bayes (NB) [28]. We use tenfold cross-validation to estimate the accuracy. To make a fair comparison of all classifiers we do not perform any additional data preprocessing such as scaling. Therefore, we use the sequential minimal optimization (SMO) implementation of SVM in Weka 3 [28], not the widely used SVM^{light} [9]. Note that the SMO's drawback is a slow convergence to a solution on noisy data [28].

We use C5.0 [19], a decision tree learner that classifies entries by separating them into classes according to information gain $G(a, y)$ of the attributes [14]. The main reason for applying the decision-based classifiers is that their outputs are

---

[2] The class labels are noisy, partially due to the Inspire system's flaws. Analysis of the data has shown that 3-5 % of the negotiations that the system records as unsuccessful ended with the participants agreeing verbally to accept an offer.

easy to understand. We also justify the use of decision-based classifiers by high accuracy - up to 75% - on the e-negotiation data [11], although those results had been obtained on the non-textual data, and on the domain-specific data representation [22].

In spite of the characteristics of decision-based classifiers, we do not want to restrict ourselves to only one type of classifiers. Kernel methods, especially SVM, have been successfully used for text classification. In general, SVM builds a hyperplane that separates training examples of one class from examples in another, with the largest possible separation. The search for the hyperplane is done by solving a constrained optimization problem. This explanation applies to SMO as well. The accuracy and running time of SMO highly depend on the polynomial degree and upper bound on polynomial coefficients. We performed the exhaustive accuracy search for both parameters in SMO. The best accuracy was achieved on the linear version with the upper bound equal to 1.

We apply the Naive Bayes classifier (NB) because of its high accuracy in topic and sentiment categorization [16]. The simplifying assumption states that the feature values are conditionally independent given the class label. In the experiments, we have modeled numeric values by the normal distribution and by the kernel density estimators.

To estimate how the classification algorithms work, we calculate the accuracy (Acc) on the test data. We want to know how the classifiers work on different data classes, thus we employ the standard text classification metrics: precision (P), recall (R) and F-measure (F) [10]. F is calculated with P and R given equal weights. Note that P, depending on true positives and false positives, and R, depending on true positives and false negatives, are antagonistic [10, 14] and F tends toward results with more true positives.

In order to verify our claim that the data representation using the "strategic" words is necessary and sufficient, we compare the results with the results of two sets of experiments. In the first set we represent the data using personal pronouns, modal verbs, the verbs do and be, and their negative versions. That is, we form bags of words for each negotiation using the number of occurrences of the words in the negotiation. In the second set of experiments the data are represented by top 500 unigrams including function words [22].

To justify adding the number of other words in negotiation when bags of words are built with word frequencies, we evaluate the attributes using the "Select attributes" option in Weka. For each of the reported data representations we evaluate the attributes with the Best First, Forward Selection, and Genetic Search methods. The additional attribute was selected in all cases.

In Tables 3 and 4 we list the classification results, obtained for the equal costs of misclassification and equal weights of precision and recall. We report the results of NB with kernel density estimation because it classified negotiations more accurately than NB with normal distribution.

Table 3. Classification accuracy, equal costs

Features	#	NB	SMO	C5.0
"strategic" words	100	65.25	71.26	74.5
pers pronouns + modals + negations	26	63.57	67.4	71.4
top 500 unigrams	501	63.4	71.7	74.3

Table 4. Classification of negotiations, equal costs

Features	#	NB			SMO			C5.0		
		P	R	F	P	R	F	P	R	F
"strategic" words	100	58.3	74	65.2	73.2	74.8	74	72.5	87.6	79.25
pers pronouns + modals + negations	26	54.9	73.2	62.7	66.5	72.7	69.5	69.2	87.91	77.45
top 500 unigrams	501	46.4	71.2	55.83	76.8	70.6	73.6	73.17	85.19	78.54

We report the average multi-fold cross-validation results[3] for all the experiments. These results were obtained over the set of parameters for each classifier that yielded the highest classification accuracy. The baseline *Acc* equals 55.8%, when all negotiations are classified as positives. Corresponding P, R, and F are equal to 55.8, 100, 71.6 per cent respectively. # denotes the number of features in the representations, or the number of attributes in bags of words.

High values of P and R, and expectedly high value of F, mean that the overall good performance of C5.0 is due to the high accuracy of classification of the positive examples which dominate in the data. C5.0 performs poorly on the negative examples, which makes its application to the "real world" negotiation data questionable. With P and R values closer than those in the C5.0 experiments, SMO has shown more balanced performance. It classifies the positive examples slightly worse than C5.0, and the negative examples considerably better.

For NB the low precision and moderate recall lead to expectedly low F-measure. With the number of negative examples lower than the number of positive examples, this shows that NB classifies negative examples better than positive examples. This characteristics of NB will be very important when we gain access to the data of the real world negotiations. Analyzing the learning rules and performance results of NB we conclude that the assumption of conditional independence is not met in successful negotiations and is met in unsuccessful negotiations. The words are correlated more in successful negotiations and less in unsuccessful negotiations. The fact that the kernel density estimators perform better than normal distribution shows that the normality assumption does not hold for e-negotiation data. The latter is consistent with conclusions [14] on natural language texts.

Now we consider three data representations discussed earlier. Performance is the weakest when negotiations are represented only through personal pronouns,

---

[3] All results on 500 unigrams, except for SVM, were produced with tenfold cross-validation; the SVM results – with fivefold cross-validation.

modals and negations. Although there is a statistically significant difference in their use in successful and unsuccessful negotiations, they do not provide enough information to separate the two classes.

The addition of mental and volition verbs to personal pronouns, modals and negations reduces the difference between the precision and recall values and improves the classification accuracy and F-measure for all three classifiers. However, the representation through 500 most frequent unigrams worsens recall and F-measure for NB if compared with the representation by "strategic" words. This means that positive examples are classified more accurately and negative examples less accurately, when represented by all the most frequently used words. We attribute this to the fact that words not related to negotiation strategies, such as greetings, closure, casual words, are similarly correlated in both successful and unsuccessful negotiations.

We conclude that a reliable classification of negotiations is possible if the representation includes elements of logical reasoning (personal pronouns, modals, negations) and the attitude toward the issues (volition verbs in our case) and the intention on continuity of negotiation (mental verbs in our case). Representation only via logical reasoning is insufficient to produce reliable classification results.

6   Conclusions and Future Work

We have presented the results of research on strategies in electronic negotiations. We worked on the data supplied by a negotiation support system. The size of data and a large number of data suppliers provide enough grounds for the generality of the results. We have suggested two different procedures of studying the implementation of strategies in language, one based on applying the bootstrapping procedure to corpora of e-negotiation texts and another based on an analytical exploration of negotiation strategies and language of e-negotiations. The results on negotiation strategies produced by both methods correspond. The results show that different strategies are employed in successful and unsuccessful negotiations.

In this work we have used the data representation that does not bear the characteristics of the specific negotiation domain. Thus the approach is rather general and applicable to data gathered through other negotiation sources. We have used the parts of speech corresponding to strategies to represent the data of e-negotiations for classification purposes. We discussed the learning abilities of the C5.0, SMO and Naive Bayes classifiers. We showed that, although C5.0 achieves higher accuracy than other classifiers, the performance of Naive Bayes is more reliable if applied to the data from real-world negotiations.

We want to emphasize that although sentiment and emotion analysis is a well-developed area of DM, ML and NLP research, as well as the planning dialogues with the application of dialogue act technique, we could not find any other related research on the strategies in negotiations.

In our future work we want to consider representation of negotiations through both textual and non-textual data, e.g., numerical values used in negotiation offers. This will give us more insight into the strategies of negotiators and the correspondence of words and actions.

Acknowledgment

This work is supported by SSHRC through a major grant and by NSERC through a doctoral scholarship. The authors want to thank Mohak Shah for the thorough comments on the Machine Learning part of the paper.

References

1. M. H. Bazerman, J. R. Curhan, D. A. Moore, K. L. Valley, Negotiation, *Annual Review of Psychology*, http://arjournals.annualreviews.org/doi/pdf/10.1146/annurev.psych.51.1.279
2. J. M. Brett. *Negotiating Globally*, Jossey-Bass, San Francisco, 2001.
3. W. R. Cantrall. *Viewpoint, Reflexives, and the Nature of Noun Phrases*, Mouton, The Hague, 1974.
4. C. Cellich, S. C. Jain. *Global Business Negotiations : A Practical Guide*, Thomson, South-Western, 2004.
5. N. Cristianini, J. Shawe-Taylor. *An Introduction to Support Vector Machines and other kernel-based learning methods*, Cambridge University Press, 2000.
6. L. E. Drake. "The Culture-Negotiation Link", *Human Communication Research*, 27(3), 317-349, 2001.
7. O. Hargie, D. Dickson. *Skilled Interpersonal Communication: Research, Theory and Practice*, Routledge, 2004.
8. J. Hu. "Message in the bottleneck", *News.Com*, 2003, http://news.com.com/2009-1033-992348.html
9. T. Joachims." Making large-Scale SVM Learning Practical", *Advances in Kernel Methods - Support Vector Learning*, B. Schlkopf and C. Burges and A. Smola (ed.), 169-185, MIT-Press, 1999.
10. D. Jurafsky, J. H. Martin. *Speech and Language Processing*, Prentice Hall, 2000.
11. G. E. Kersten, G. Zhang. "Mining Inspire Data for the Determinants of Successful Internet Negotiations", *Central European J. of Operational Research*, 11(3), 297-316, 2003.
12. A. Kilgarriff. Comparing Corpora, *International Journal of Corpus Linguistics*, 6(1), 97-133, 2001.
13. G. N. Leech. *Meaning and the English Verb*, Longman, 1987.
14. C. D. Manning, H. Schütze. *Foundations of Statistical Natural Language Processing*, The MIT Press, 1999.
15. M. P. Oakes. *Statistics for Corpus Linguistics*. Edinburg University Press, 1998.
16. B. Pang, L. Lee, S. Vaithyanathan. "Thumbs up? Sentiment Classification using Machine Learning Techniques ", *Proc EMNLP'2002*, 79-86, 2002.
17. M. R. Perkins. *Modal Expressions in English*, Ablex Publishing Corporation, 1983.
18. R. M. Perloff. *The Dynamics of Persuasion*, Lawrence Erlbaum Associates, 2003.
19. J. R. Quinlan. *C4.5: Programs for Machine Learning*, Morgan Kaufmann Publishers, San Mateo, California, 1993.

20. J. Rudanko. *Complementation and Case Grammar*, State University of New York Press, 1989.
21. M. Schoop. A Language-Action Approach to Electronic Negotiations, *Proc (LAP 2003)*, 143-160, 2003.
22. M. Shah, M. Sokolova, S. Szpakowicz. "The Role of Domain-Specific Knowledge in Classifying the Language of E-negotiations",*Proc ICON 2004*, 99-108,Hyderabad, India.
23. M. Sokolova, S. Szpakowicz, V. Nastase. "Using language to Determine Success in Negotiations: A Preliminary Study", *Proc Canadian AI 2004*, 449-453, 2004.
24. M. Sokolova, V. Nastase, S. Szpakowicz. "Language in Electronic Negotiations: Patterns in Completed and Uncompleted Negotiations", *Proc ICON 2004*, 142-151, Hyderabad, India.
25. M. Ströbel. Effects of Electronic Markets on Negotiation Processes, *Proc ECIS 2000*, 445-452, 2000.
26. L. Thompson, J. Nadler. "Negotiating Via Information Technology: Theory and Application", *Journal of Social Issues*, 58(1), 109-124, 2002.
27. G. Tottie. *Negation in English Speech and Writing*, Academic Press Inc., 1991.
28. I. Witten, E. Frank. *Data Mining*, Morgan Kaufmann, 2000. http://www.cs.waikato.ac.nz/ml/weka/

Fast Protein Superfamily Classification Using Principal Component Null Space Analysis

Leon French, Alioune Ngom, and Luis Rueda

School of Computer Science, University of Windsor,
401 Sunset Avenue, Windsor ON, N9B 3P4, Canada
{french1, angom, lrueda}@uwindsor.ca

Abstract. The protein family classification problem, which consists of determining the family memberships of given unknown protein sequences, is very important for a biologist for many practical reasons, such as drug discovery, prediction of molecular functions and medical diagnosis. Neural networks and bayesian methods have performed well on the protein classification problem, achieving accuracy ranging from 90% to 98% while running relatively slowly in the learning stage. In this paper, we present a principal component null space analysis (PCNSA) linear classifier to the problem and report excellent results compared to those of neural networks and support vector machines. The two main parameters of PCNSA are linked to the high dimensionality of the dataset used, and were optimized in an exhaustive manner to maximize accuracy.

1 Introduction

Recently the human, rat, and mouse genomes have been sequenced and many more are in progress[1]. For example, Craig Venter is leading the Sorcerer II Expedition on a global quest to discover millions of new genes. His most recent results provided 1.2 million new genes [1]. It is important to organize and annotate this massive amount of sequence data to maximize its usefulness. In this regard, *DNA sequences* can be translated into *protein sequences* by using standard bioinformatics tools. A protein sequence encodes a protein, which are the primary machines, tools, materials, and messengers of any organism. An important tool for the sequential analysis of this process is protein sequence classification which consists of determining the type or group of proteins to which an unknown protein sequence belongs.

Protein sequence classification is an important problem in the area of bioinformatics. Protein sequence classification is used to organize the large amount of data produced by the genome sequencing projects. Once a protein is classified it becomes much more useful to the general research community. Molecular evolution studies, protein function and structure prediction are examples in which superfamily classification is important. This organization aids in the finding of specific proteins for certain tasks, a researcher would be able to search for a certain type of protein to solve a very specific problem.

---

[1] National Human Genome Research Institute, http://www.genome.gov.

B. Kégl and G. Lapalme (Eds.): AI 2005, LNAI 3501, pp. 158–169, 2005.

Stated more formally, protein sequence classification consists of determining a superfamily (or class) of an unknown sequence S given a known set of c superfamilies $\{\omega_1, \omega_2, \ldots, \omega_c\}$. A superfamily is defined as a set of sequences with similar global sequence similarity and having the same domain architecture [2]. Normally, a sequence can belong to more than one superfamily, but the datasets tested in this paper contain only disjoint superfamily sets.

Many methods that deal with the protein classification problem have been proposed. Approaches used sequence alignment [3] and hidden Markov modelling [4]. Sequence alignment is fast for two sequences but becomes very slow when aligning a sequence to an entire superfamily. Hidden Markov model approaches are tied to the quality of a time consuming task of multiple sequence alignment. Artificial neural networks have also been applied to the problem [5, 6]. Wang describes a classifier that combines the three aforementioned methods, and gives a good benchmark of the three methods [6]. Recently SVMs making use of customized string kernels have been applied [7]. These past results have produced accuracies reaching the 99% range. In this paper, we present a novel approach for protein classification based on principal component null space analysis (PCNSA) [8], a recently developed linear classifier. Our results show very high accuracy, in some cases misclassifying only seven samples of 2,500.

2   A Principal Component Null Space Analysis Based Approach

The classification approach that we provide is based on PCNSA [8]. The latter involves first reducing noise and dimensionality by performing *principal component analysis* (PCA) on the entire training dataset. The second step then finds a *null space* for each class. The null space is extracted by taking the dimensions with the *least* variance of each class using eigenvalue decomposition. The null space is a subspace of the feature space in which a given class has very little variance. The classification metric used to classify a sample is the euclidian distance at unclassified sample to the mean of each class inside the class null space. The classification rule is based on *Bayes*'; i.e. the unknown sample is assigned to the class that minimizes this distance. Both the PCA and the null space creation steps reduce the dimensionality of the dataset, or at least keep it the same. This dimension reduction allows for classification of samples with many features, such as protein sequences. Previous classifiers do not cope well with datasets of such dimensionality (also known as the "The Curse of Dimensionality"). The main disadvantages are a slow learning phase and overfitting when the entire feature space is used.

PCNSA has previously been only applied to image and video classification [9]. In this area, PCNSA has proven itself on datasets that have quite different within-class covariance matrices, such as object recognition and abnormal activity detection [9]. Datasets of this type are referred to as "Apples vs. Oranges" problems, or stated in a different way: unequal and non-white noise covariance matrices. Datasets with similar matrices are referred to as "Apples vs. Apples". In this case, the resulting null spaces are very similar and should result in poor results.

The approach that we propose is based directly on the PCNSA algorithm [8]; r and s are the two input parameters to our algorithm and specify the dimensionality of the PCA space and null space, respectively. Consider a dataset $D = \{x_1, \ldots, x_n\}$ where

$x_i = [x_i^{(1)}, \ldots, x_i^{(d)}]^t$ is a d-dimensional feature vector that represents a protein sequence. Our modified PCNSA algorithm proceeds as follows:

1. Normalize every data sample on a feature basis. For each feature/dimension and data sample, x_i, perform:

$$z_i^{(j)} = \frac{x_i^{(j)} - \min\limits_{1 \le q \le n} \{x_q^{(j)}\}}{\max\limits_{1 \le q \le n} \{x_q^{(j)}\} - \min\limits_{1 \le q \le n} \{x_q^{(j)}\}}. \tag{1}$$

2. For the full dataset, compute the sample mean vector and covariance matrix as follows:

$$\hat{\mu} = \frac{1}{n} \sum_{i=1}^{n} z_i, \text{ and} \tag{2}$$

$$\hat{\Sigma} = \frac{1}{n} \sum_{i=1}^{n} (z_i - \hat{\mu})(z_i - \hat{\mu})^t. \tag{3}$$

3. Obtain the PCA projection matrix (an orthogonal matrix that is used in step 4), W, by taking the eigenvectors corresponding to the r largest eigenvalues of $\hat{\Sigma}$.
4. Project the training samples of each class into the PCA space as below:

$$y_i = W^t(z_i - \hat{\mu}), \tag{4}$$

obtaining a new dataset $D_y = \{y_1, \ldots, y_n\}$.
5. For each class, ω_k, compute the estimates for the class mean, $\hat{\mu}_k$, and the class covariance, $\hat{\Sigma}_k$ in the PCA space, using (2) and (3), and a data subset that contains the samples which just belong to ω_k.
6. Obtain the approximate null space $(N_k)_{r \times s}$ for each class ω_k as the s trailing eigenvectors of $\hat{\Sigma}_k$. The PCNSA classification matrix for class ω_k, W_k, is formed from these trailing eigenvectors.
7. Classify an unknown sample x, by projecting x into the PCA space as follows:

$$y = W^t(x - \hat{\mu}) \tag{5}$$

Then, assign x to class ω_k as per the following rule:

$$k = \min\limits_{1 \le i \le c} \{||W_i^t(y - \hat{\mu}_i)||\}. \tag{6}$$

There are various differences between our algorithm and the versions given by Vaswani and Chellappa [8, 10]: two filters on the null space eigen vectors are not used, and the data is normalized. Although it is understood that both of these changes significantly undermine the assumptions and theoretical basis of PCNSA, the following reasons support our modifications.

Normalization was originally performed to aid in accurate tracking of feature weights. This normalization led to the null space failing to check for Σ_i having a high condition number or a large range of eigenvalues when computing the null space. Thus, the filter (eigenvalues $\lambda \le 10^{-4}\lambda_{max}$) on the null space vectors was removed. We experimentally found that higher accuracy resulted from this change. A second check on the null space was also removed and a parameter was instead used to limit the number of null space dimensions, s, as seen in the original PCNSA paper [8]. These changes result in another variable(s) and removes a variable that was involved in the null space filtering. These changes made for a simpler, faster and more accurate classifier for the protein sequence dataset.

3   The Protein Sequence Dataset

The dataset that we used in our experiments was created from the protein sequence database (PSD) release 79.05 at the protein information resource (PIR) databank [2]. PSD provides fully annotated protein data in XML format for over 280,000 sequences. For this application, only the sequence, sequence type and superfamily of the entries were used. Some entries in the databank only have the sequence of a protein fragment, or are ambiguous in describing the sequence (e.g. GLS(D.G.E)WXQL). All complete non-ambiguous sequences of the four selected superfamily classes were processed.

The four classes collected and their size are ras transforming proteins (455), kinase-related transforming proteins (517), globin proteins (672) and ribitol dehydrogenase proteins (868). Although the PIR-PSD database entries contain one or more superfamily classifications, none of the selected data subsets intersect. Two datasets were created: a two-class dataset containing kinase and ras transforming proteins (972), and a second multiclass dataset that includes all four classes mentioned above (2,512).

The string sequence data of each protein was processed to create an array of 465 numeric features plus the class label. At a high level, the features of a vector x that represents a sample are:

$$x^{(1)} = \text{length of sequence}$$
$$x^{(2)} = \text{isoelectric point (pI)}$$
$$x^{(3)} = \text{mass}$$
$$x^{(4)}, x^{(5)}, \ldots, x^{(23)} = \text{amino acid distribution (20)}$$
$$x^{(24)}, x^{(25)}, \ldots, x^{(423)} = \text{two-grams (400)}$$
$$x^{(424)}, x^{(425)}, \ldots, x^{(429)} = \text{exchange group distribution (6)}$$
$$x^{(430)}, x^{(431)}, \ldots, x^{(465)} = \text{exchange group two-grams (36)}$$

All of these features were generated directly from the sequence string. The pI and mass features are estimates based on the polypeptide encoded by the sequence. Originally, the dataset contained only two-grams and exchange two-grams. As the research progressed, more data was added with the resulting accuracies increasing.

The two-gram features account for the majority of the attributes. They represent the frequencies of every consecutive "two-letter" sequence in the protein sequence. Two grams have the advantages of being length invariant, insertion/deletion invariant, not requiring motif finding and allowing classification based on local similarity [11].

Exchange grams are similar but are based on a many-to-one translation of the amino acid alphabet into a six letter alphabet that represents six groups of amino acids, which represent high evolutionary similarity. Exchange groups used for this dataset are: $e_1=\{H, R, K\}$, $e_2=\{D, E, N, Q\}$, $e_3=\{C\}$, $e_4=\{S, T, P, A, G\}$, $e_5=\{M, I, L, V\}$ and

e_6={F, Y, W}. The exchange groups are based on information from the point accepted mutations (PAM) matrix [12], which statistically describes the probability of one amino acid replacing another over time.

Given an example sequence "GLALLA" the non-zero two-grams are GL=1, LA=2, AL=1 and LL=1. Translating "GLALLA" to an exchange group sequence results in "$e_4e_5e_4e_5e_5e_4$", with the resulting exchange two-grams of e_4e_5=2, e_5e_4=2, and e_5e_5=1. The frequency of the amino acids and exchange groups are also added to the dataset entry, and result in G=1, L=3, A=2, e_4=3, and e_5=3. Next, the two-gram counts are converted to *probability estimates* by dividing by the total number of one-grams or two-grams of the sequence. For "GLALLA" the frequencies estimates are: G=$\frac{1}{6}$, L=$\frac{1}{2}$, A=$\frac{1}{3}$, e_4=$\frac{1}{2}$, and e_5=$\frac{1}{2}$, and the two-gram counts become: GL=$\frac{1}{5}$, LA=$\frac{2}{5}$, AL=$\frac{1}{5}$, LL=$\frac{1}{5}$, e_4e_5=$\frac{2}{5}$, e_5e_4=$\frac{2}{5}$, and e_5e_5=$\frac{1}{5}$.

The full two-gram encodings result in a very sparse dataset[2], with some features having a zero frequency value for over 85% of the instances. With the example there are $(20^2 - 4) + (6^2 - 3) = 429$ zero-valued two-grams. The shortest protein sequence in the dataset is 63 amino acids in length, which results in at most 62 non-zero two-grams out of 400, further demonstrating the sparseness of the dataset. Past work has reduced the two-grams given to the classifier in order to decrease training time. In this paper all of the described features are given as input to the PCNSA algorithm.

4   Implementation

The dataset processing was implemented in Java 1.4, using the BioJava bioinformatics toolkit[3]. The worst-case time complexity of the dataset creation is $O(nl)$ where n is the number of sequences matching the selection criteria and l is the length of the longest sequence. The selection criteria is: complete, non-ambiguous sequences that are classified as a selected superfamily class. The PCNSA algorithm was also implemented in Java using the colt high performance scientific and technical computing package for fast matrix operations [13]. In addition to the core PCNSA algorithm, a feature was added to produce the attribute weights for the hyperplane used in classification. The worst-case time complexity of our PCNSA algorithm is $O(nd^2 + d^3)$ where d is the dimension of the feature space and n is the number of samples in the training set. Classification is $O(d^2)$ per test. These time complexities can be lowered depending on algorithms used for matrix multiplication and eigen value decomposition. Computation of the best scoring PCNSA parameter pair (320,297) takes approximately 8.5 minutes for a ten fold cross validation on a 2.0Ghz, 32bit AMD processor.

5   Experiments and Results

All experiments were performed using ten fold cross validation, at least once and some data is computed using 5 runs or 10 runs of ten fold cross validation. The accuracy

---

[2] The term "sparse" refers to a matrix with a large percentage of zero valued entries.

[3] Available at http://www.biojava.org.

is computed as the number of correctly classified divided by total number of samples tested, averaged across the ten folds. When more than one run is performed, the accuracy is averaged across all runs and folds, plus or minus the unbiased standard deviation of the run accuracies.

5.1 Two-Class Scenario

For the two-class case, Figure 1 shows the accuracy of PCNSA by varying the value of r. The accuracy displayed is an average of all possible values of s for that r value, where $465 \geq r \geq s \geq 1$. Again, ten fold cross validation was used for each test.

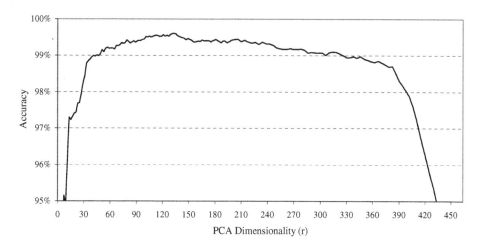

Fig. 1. Effect of PCA space dimension, r, on two-class accuracy averaged across all s values, using ten fold cross validation for each (r, s) pair

Table 1. Comparison of a SVM to PCNSA, ten runs of ten fold cross validation

Method	Options	Ras	Kinase	Average
PCNSA	$r=80, s=30$	$99.52\% \pm 0.20$	$99.96\% \pm 0.08$	$99.75\% \pm 0.11$
PCNSA	$r=133, s=97$	$99.98\% \pm 0.07$	$99.98\% \pm 0.06$	$99.98\% \pm 0.04$
PCNSA	$r=330, s=280$	$99.87\% \pm 0.15$	$99.94\% \pm 0.09$	$99.91\% \pm 0.10$
SVMLight	Linear Kernel	$99.49\% \pm 0.15$	$100\% \pm 0$	$99.76\% \pm 0.07$
SVMLight	Polynomial Kernel degree 2	$99.60\% \pm 0.09$	$100\% \pm 0$	$99.81\% \pm 0.04$
SVMLight	Polynomial Kernel degree 3	$99.60\% \pm 0.14$	$100\% \pm 0$	$99.81\% \pm 0.07$
SVMLight	Polynomial Kernel degree 4	$99.41\% \pm 0.15$	$100\% \pm 0$	$99.72\% \pm 0.07$

A high scoring r value of 133 was obtained from results in the Figure 1. Figure 2 expands on that value by showing the effect of s on the accuracy. Additionally charted are the results of PCNSA given the dataset as two-grams plus exchange grams only, and unnormalized data. The "standard" line is the normal dataset setup, as described in the previous section. The unnormalized line skips the first step in the PCNSA algorithm.

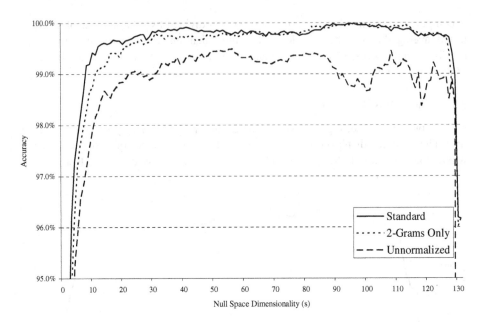

Fig. 2. Effect of null space size and dataset type on two-class accuracy when r=133, based on 5 runs of ten fold cross validation

Five runs were performed and averaged for each value of s. This graph supports earlier claims that normalizing the data reduces accuracy.

A SVM classifier was setup for comparison purposes. This was performed using SVM-Light support vector machine version 6.01 [14]. The exact same datasets and folds were given to SVM-Light and PCNSA. Three top scoring parameter choices for PCNSA and four for SVM-Light are given. The only options provided to SVM-Light was the kernel function, all others were left as default. Radial basis function and Sigmoid kernels did not provide good results using the default kernel parameters. Table 1 shows the resulting accuracies across 5 runs of ten fold cross validation.

5.2   Four-Class Scenario

The four class problem contained proteins from the ras transforming protein (ras), kinase-related transforming protein(kinase), globin and ribitol dehydrogenase (ribitol) superfamilies. Figure 4 demonstrates the accuracy across all values of s, where r = 233. The value of 233 was chosen from an exhaustive search of all possible parameter choices. Again, we can see the results of unnormalized and the two-gram plus exchange gram datasets for 5 runs of ten folds. In this case, the difference between these datasets is less clear and the two-gram plus exchange grams dataset actually has the highest scoring result of 99.61%±.05 accuracy. This lessens the hypothesis that the added attributes of mass, length, pI, amino acid and exchange gram frequencies increase accuracy. Additionally, it is seen that the unnormalized performs best for low null space size.

The exhaustive search results was used to find three high scoring parameter combinations which were then further evaluated for ten runs to provide an accurate estimate

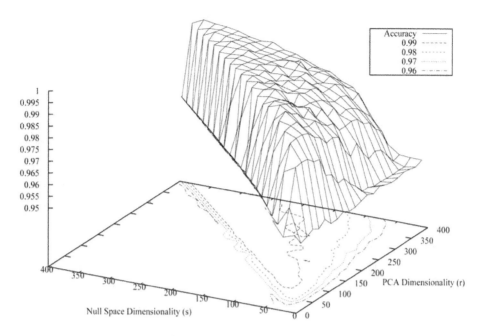

Fig. 3. Effect of null space size and dataset type on four-class accuracy when r=233, based on 5 runs of ten fold cross validation

Table 2. Four class accuracies on three of the top r and s combinations, ten runs of ten fold cross validation

r	s	Ras	Kinase	Globin	Ribitol	Accuracy
185	150	97.95% ± 0.45	99.48% ± 0.23	100% ± 0	99.75% ± 0.09	99.43% ± 0.10
233	209	98.50% ± 0.17	99.42% ± 0.18	100% ± 0	99.77% ± 0.06	99.53% ± 0.06
320	297	98.54% ± 0.26	99.44% ± 0.14	100% ± 0	99.85% ± 0.10	99.57% ± 0.08

of accuracy. The results of this test are provided in Table 2. Accuracy on a per class basis is also provided, it is important to note that the globin samples were classified perfectly on all ten runs and all three parameter pairs.

In Table 3 it is possible to see how the algorithm accurately classifies data. This table gives the seven highest weighted attributes for each class, from a single run for r=320 and s=297. They are calculated using the PCA projection (W) and class null space projection (W_{class}) matrices. These are approximate weights as certain variables, such as class means, are not involved in the computations. Normalization of each attribute – step 1 of the algorithm, makes these weights more accurate. Every two-gram seen in the table occurs only once, demonstrating the uniqueness of the null spaces.

Table 4 provides a good comparison to other methods. All of the past work was tested by the original authors on the PIR–PSD dataset but the class sizes and PSD

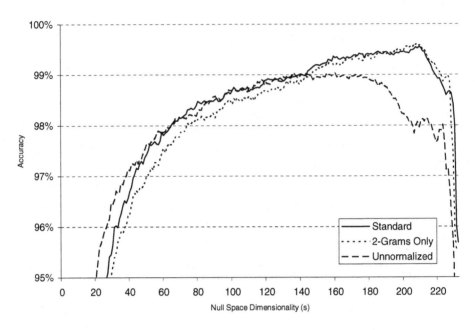

Fig. 4. Effect of null space size and dataset type on four-class accuracy when $r=233$, based on 5 runs of ten fold cross validation

Table 3. Approximate highest weighted attributes, generated from a single ten fold cross validation using $r=320$ and $s=297$. Every entry is an amino acid two-gram

Ras	Kinase	Globin	Ribitol
VA -7.36	RT -9.24	SR -8.42	PT -10.07
AI +7.13	IE +9.24	TE +7.80	WV +7.85
MV -6.96	DQ +7.77	QK +7.72	FN -7.74
ED -6.91	RE -7.43	NF +7.21	KA +7.46
GE -6.90	WD +7.16	HP +7.09	RP -7.28
FM +6.76	CM -6.93	EG -7.02	RL +6.95
VT +6.50	MF +6.71	YY -6.79	WL -6.78

version varied. All two-class cases used kinase versus ras, and the three class case added the globin superfamily.

The Combiner method by Wang [6] provides the highest accuracy but there are several differences in the experimental setup involved. Primarily, the problem definition used stated that a protein sequence can be classified into one or more superfamilies. This effected the dataset used, it contained 5 data subsets. The four sets corresponded to kinase, ras, globin, ribotol and a fifth set of 1650 negative sequences that did not contain any samples from the previous four sets. The classification took place in four binary experiments – a superfamily set (positive) versus the 1650 negative sequences. This suggests an easier-to-classify dataset than the one used in PCNSA experiments. Accuracy shown

Table 4. Comparison table of past and proposed classifiers on the PIR–PSD database

Method	Author(s)	PIR–PSD Release	Classes	Dataset Size	Accuracy
Fisher's	Rueda, Ngom[15]	62	2	731	96.54
PCNSA 2-Class	French et al.	62	2	731	98.00
SVMLight default	Joachims[14]	79.05	2	972	99.81
PCNSA 2-Class	French et al.	79.05	2	972	99.98
Multiclass NN	Xi Zhang[16]	N/A	3	3137	94.10
Bayesian NN[4]	Wang et al.[6]	62	4	1886	98.08 [5]
Combiner [4]	Wang et al.[6]	62	4	1886	99.64 [5]
PCNSA 4-Class	French et al.	79.05	4	2512	99.57±0.08

for Combiner and the Bayesian NN was computed from the average accuracy of the four binary classification experiments, weighted by number of test sequences.

It is important to note the complexity of the Combiner method. Combiner is based on the results of four classifiers: primarily, the Bayesian neural network, and then the results of classifiers based upon BLAST[3], SAM and SAM-T99 [17]. When compared to previous methods PCNSA is much simpler, faster and almost equal in accuracy.

Most of these competing methods used smaller training datasets and different experimental setups. Two of them provide the same experimental conditions under the 2-class case. First is the SVM using the above-described dataset and experimental setup. Second is Fisher's classifier, where a smaller training set was tested, as described in Rueda and Ngom [15]. This second experimental setup had a 60/40 train and test split with only 50 features. To assess PCNSA under similar conditions, we tested it using the *same* 60/40 training and testing datasets leading to 98% classification accuracy, and hence demonstrating its superiority over Fisher's classifier.

6   Conclusion and Future Work

In this paper, we present an approach to the protein classification problem. Our method is based on the PCNSA linear classifier, which is slightly modified from its original version by introducing feature based normalization and removing two null space filters.

We have tested our method on four superfamilies for the PSD–PIR databank, and compared our results to previous methods. The empirical analysis presented shows that our method is superior to any previous results on the two-class problem, achieving an accuracy of 99.98%, with a standard deviation of 0.04. In the four-class case, our method performs at par to Combiner with 99.57%±0.08 accuracy, while possessing the advantage of higher speed and lowered complexity.

Future work will involve testing this method on a larger dataset with sequences from SCOP [18] or PROSITE [19]. The protein classification problem definition could

---

[4] Binary classification performed for each of the superfamilies which is a very different experimental setup from this paper.

[5] Computed from the average of four binary classification experiments, weighted by number of test sequences.

be modified so that a protein sequence can be classified into zero or more superfamilies, which is a more biologically accurate model for the problem.

Bioinformatics has a large amount of pattern classification problems. Microarray datasets are very very large in dimension and are often not fully analyzed. Microarray datasets are a promising match for PCNSA because of their propensity to very high noise and intuitively fits the description of an "Apples vs. Oranges" problem. Furthermore, the weight tracking module developed for PCNSA would allow output of the most heavily weighted genes or features in the microarray datasets.

Another avenue of research involves an interesting algorithm, similar to PCNSA named Multispace KL[6] for pattern representation and classification [20]. Since it is similar to PCNSA, it may perform well on the protein classification problem.

Acknowledgements: This research has been partially supported by NSERC, the Natural Sciences and Engineering Research Council of Canada.

References

1. Venter, J.C., Remington, K., Heidelberg, J.F., Halpern, A.L., Rusch, D., Eisen, J.A., Wu, D., Paulsen, I., Nelson, K.E., Nelson, W., Fouts, D.E., Levy, S., Knap, A.H., Lomas, M.W., Nealson, K., White, O., Peterson, J., Hoffman, J., Parsons, R., Baden-Tillson, H., Pfannkoch, C., Rogers, Y.H., Smith, H.O.: Environmental Genome Shotgun Sequencing of the Sargasso Sea. Science **304** (2004) 66–74
2. Wu, C.H., Yeh, L.S., Huang, H., Arminski, L., Castro-Alvear, J., Chen, Y., Hu, Z., Kourtesis, P., Ledley, R.S., Suzek, B.E., Vinayaka, C.R., Zhang, J., Barker, W.C.: The Protein Information Resource. Nucleic Acids Res **31** (2003) 345–7
3. Altschul, S.F., Madden, T.L., Schaffer, A.A., Zhang, J., Zhang, Z., Miller, W., Lipman, D.J.: Gapped BLAST and PSI-BLAST: a new generation of protein database search programs. Nucleic Acids Res **25** (1997) 389–402
4. Madera, M., Gough, J.: A comparison of profile hidden Markov model procedures for remote homology detection. Nucleic Acids Res **30** (2002) 4321–8 1362-4962 Journal Article.
5. Wu, C.H., Berry, M., Fung, Y., McLarty, J.: Neural Networks for Full-Scale Protein Sequence Classification: Sequence Encoding with Singular Value Decomposition. Machine Learning **21** (1995) 177–193
6. Wang, J., Ma, Q., Shasha, D., Wu, C.: New techniques for extracting features from protein sequences. IBM Systems Journal **40** (2001)
7. Leslie, C., Eskin, E., Noble, W.S.: The spectrum kernel: a string kernel for SVM protein classification. Pac Symp Biocomput (2002) 564–75
8. Vaswani, N.: A Linear Classifier for Gaussian Class Conditional Distributions with Unequal Covariance Matrices. In: Intl. Conference on Pattern Recognition (ICPR). Volume I. (2002) 240
9. Vaswani, N., Chellappa, R.: Principal Component Null Space Analysis for Image/Video Classification. submitted to IEEE Transactions on Image Processing (2004)
10. Vaswani, N., Chellappa, R.: Classification Probability Analysis of Principal Component Null Space Analysis. Intl. Conference on Pattern Recognition (ICPR) (2004)

---

[6] KL or the Karhunen-Loeve transform is also known as Principal Component Analysis (PCA).

11. Wu, C., Whitson, G., McLarty, J., Ermongkonchai, A., Chang, T.C.: Protein classification artificial neural system. Protein Sci **1** (1992) 667–77
12. Dayhoff, M., Schwartz, R., Orcutt, B.: A Model of Evolutionary Change in Proteins. Atlas of Protein Sequence and Structure **15** (1978) 345–358
13. Hoschek, W.: Uniform, Versatile and Efficient Dense and Sparse Multi-Dimensional Arrays. (2000)
14. Joachims, T., Schlkopf, B., Burges, C.: Making large-Scale SVM Learning Practical. Advances in Kernel Methods - Support Vector Learning. MIT-Press (1999)
15. Rueda, L., Ngom, A.: An Empirical Evaluation of the Classification Error of Two Thresholding Methods for Fisher's Classifier. In Arabnia, H.R., ed.: International Conference on Artifical Intelligence and International Conference on Machine Learning; Models, Technologies and Applications. Volume II., Las Vegas, Nevada, USA, CSREA Press (2004) 837–842
16. Zhang, X.: Protein Family Classification Using Multiple-Class Neural Networks. Master's thesis, University of Windsor (2004)
17. Karplus, K., Barrett, C., Hughey, R.: Hidden Markov models for detecting remote protein homologies. Bioinformatics **14** (1998) 846–56
18. Murzin, A.G., Brenner, S.E., Hubbard, T., Chothia, C.: SCOP: a structural classification of proteins database for the investigation of sequences and structures. J Mol Biol **247** (1995) 536–40
19. Bairoch, A., Bucher, P.: PROSITE: recent developments. Nucleic Acids Res **22** (1994) 3583–9
20. Cappelli, R., Maio, D., Maltoni, D.: Multispace KL for Pattern Representation and Classification. IEEE Transactions on Pattern Analysis and Machine Intelligence **23** (2001) 977–996

First Steps Towards Incremental Diagnosis of Discrete-Event Systems

Alban Grastien[1], Marie-Odile Cordier[1], and Christine Largouët[2]

[1] Irisa, University of Rennes 1, Campus de Beaulieu,
35042 Rennes Cedex, France
{agrastie, cordier}@irisa.fr
[2] University of New Caledonia, BP. 4477, 98847 Nouméa Cedex,
New Caledonia
largouet@univ-nc.nc

Abstract. This paper deals with the incremental off-line computation of diagnosis of discrete-event systems. Traditionally, the diagnosis is computed from the global automaton describing the observations emitted by the system on a whole time period. The idea of this paper is to slice this global automaton according to temporal windows and to compute local diagnoses for each of these windows. It is shown that, under some conditions, the global diagnosis can be computed from the local diagnosis. This paper presents the formalization used to compute an incremental diagnosis, relying on the new concept of *automata chain*. It is then shown that it is possible to take into account the diagnosis obtained for the previous temporal windows to incrementally compute the current diagnosis more efficiently. This work is a first and necessary step before considering the on-line diagnosis computation. The main difficulty is then to ensure the correct slicing of the observation automaton and to determine the appropriate temporal windows.

1 Introduction

It is well-established in the Model-Based Diagnosis community that a diagnosis is defined as the set of trajectories consistent with the observations. Different terminologies can be used as *histories* [1], *scenarios* [2], *narratives* [3], *consistent paths* [4] or *trajectories* [5]. A diagnosis is then formally defined as the synchronized product of the automaton modelling the system and the automaton modelling the observations emitted by the system on the considered time period. In an off-line context, this observation automaton can be huge (especially when taking into account uncertainties on delays) and its size depends directly on the length of the time period. This is for instance the case for the computation of an *a posteriori* diagnosis from observations collected on a few days, as for alarm logs in telecommunication networks. In this paper, we present the idea of slicing the observation automaton according to appropriate temporal windows in order to compute incrementally the diagnosis rather than globally considering the computation of diagnosis.

B. Kégl and G. Lapalme (Eds.): AI 2005, LNAI 3501, pp. 170–181, 2005.

To reach this objective, we propose the concept of automata chain to represent observations and diagnoses by slices. We then show that it is possible to compute the global diagnosis from this modular representation of observations. For each temporal window, a local diagnosis is computed and the global one can be correctly represented by the automata chain of these local diagnoses. A first formalization of diagnosis by slices is given. The problem that appears is the huge size of these local diagnoses when computed in parallel. A second formalization is then proposed to compute incrementally the current diagnosis from the previous one, elaborated on a past temporal window. This work is a first and necessary step motivated by the ambitious problem of on-line incremental diagnosis.

The formalism used to represent the system model, the observations and the diagnosis is given in Section 2. Section 3 defines the automata chain concept and shows how the automata chain can be used to compute the global diagnosis. Two approaches for the incremental computation of the diagnosis are detailed and discussed in Section 4.

2   Automata and Global Diagnosis

This section deals with the problem of computing a global diagnosis without considering the problem of incrementality. These definitions are necessary for the incremental computing of diagnosis discussed in the following sections.

2.1   Automata and Trajectories

The system considered evolves with the occurrence of *events* and an event can cause, by propagation, other events (case of reactive systems, see for example [6]). Consequently, events can occur simultaneously. We denote E the set of events.

The behaviours of the system are represented as classic automata:

Definition 1 (Automaton).
An automaton *is a tuple* $A = (Q, E, T, I, F)$ *where:*

- Q *is a set of states,*
- E *is a set of events,*
- $T \subseteq (Q \times 2^E \times Q)$ *is a set of transitions* $t = (q, l, q')$ *where* t *connects the source state* q *to the target state* q' *on a label* l *which is a non-empty set of events* $(l \subseteq E)$,
- $I \subseteq Q$ *is the set of initial states and*
- $F \subseteq Q$ *is the set of final states.*

We consider that the transition labels are non-empty sets of events. However, $\forall q \in Q$, $(q, \emptyset, q)$ is an implicit transition of T.

Definition 2 (Trajectory).
A trajectory, *denoted traj on an automaton* $A = (Q, E, T, I, F)$ *is the couple of a finite* state sequence $(q_0, \ldots, q_n)$ *and of a* label sequence $(l_1, \ldots, l_n)$ *such that:*

- $\forall i \in \{0, \ldots, n\}$, $q_i \in Q$,
- $\forall i \in \{1, \ldots, n\}$, $t_i = (q_{i-1}, l_i, q_i) \in T$,
- $q_0 \in I$ and
- $q_n \in F$.

A trajectory is defined as a sequence of states (such that the first state is an initial state and the last state a final state) and a sequence of labels over the transitions between each state of the trajectory.

A trajectory can contain implicit transitions of the automaton. We consider that a trajectory is equal to the trajectory from which implicit transitions have been removed. Let $traj = ((q_0, \ldots, q_i, q_{i+1}, \ldots, q_n), (l_1, \ldots, l_i, l_{i+1}, \ldots, l_n))$ and $traj' = ((q_0, \ldots, q_i, q_i, q_{i+1} \cdots, q_n), (l_0, \ldots, l_i, \emptyset, l_{i+1}, \ldots, l_n))$. Then $traj = traj'$.

Two automata A and A' are identical if their set of trajectories are identical. We call *simplified automaton of A* the automaton $A' = A$ where all the states and transitions that do not appear in at least one trajectory have been removed. In the following, when computing new automata, only simplified ones are considered.

2.2   Synchronized Automata

Definition 3 (Synchronization of labels).
Let l_1 be a label on E_1 and l_2 be a label on E_2. We say that l_1 and l_2 are synchronized iff $l_1 \cap (E_1 \cap E_2) = l_2 \cap (E_1 \cap E_2)$. Their synchronization, denoted $\Theta(l_1, l_2)$ is the label $l_1 \cup l_2$ on the set of events $E_1 \cup E_2$.

Two labels are synchronized if the synchronization events $(E_1 \cap E_2)$ present in one label are present in the other label.

Definition 4 (Synchronization).
Let $A_1 = (Q_1, E_1, T_1, I_1, F_1)$ and $A_2 = (Q_2, E_2, T_2, I_2, F_2)$ be two automata. The synchronized automaton of A_1 and A_2, denoted $A_1 \otimes A_2$, is the automaton $A = (Q, E, T, I, F)$ defined by:

- $Q = Q_1 \times Q_2$,
- $E = E_1 \cup E_2$,
- $T = \{((q_1, q_2), l, (q'_1, q'_2)) \mid \exists l_1, l_2,$
    - $(q_1 = q'_1 \wedge l_1 = \emptyset) \vee (q_1, l_1, q'_1) \in T_1$
    - $(q_2 = q'_2 \wedge l_2 = \emptyset) \vee (q_2, l_2, q'_2) \in T_2$
    - $l = \Theta(l_1, l_2)$
  $\}$,
- $I = I_1 \times I_2$ and
- $F = F_1 \times F_2$.

Each transition of the synchronized automaton A corresponds to a pair of transitions on automata A_1 and A_2 such that the labels of the transitions are synchronized.

It can be easily proved that $(A_1 \otimes A_2) \otimes A_3 = A_1 \otimes (A_2 \otimes A_3)$ with the following state renaming: $((q_1, q_2), q_3) \rightarrow (q_1, (q_2, q_3))$. In the following, and to simplify, we denote: $A = A_1 \otimes \ldots \otimes A_n = A_1 \otimes (\ldots \otimes A_n) = (A_1 \otimes \ldots) \otimes A_n = (Q, E, T, I, F)$ with $Q = Q_1 \times \ldots \times Q_n$. Moreover, we consider that $A_1 \otimes A_2 = A_2 \otimes A_1$. In a more general way we consider that $((q_1, q_2), q_3) = (q_1, q_2, q_3)$.

2.3   Diagnosis

Definition 5 (System model).
We denote by $MOD = (Q^{MOD}, E^{MOD}, T^{MOD}, I^{MOD}, F^{MOD})$ the system model. I^{MOD} is the set of possible states at the time t_0. The final state may be any of the states: $F^{MOD} = Q^{MOD}$. The set of observable events is $E_{OBS}^{MOD} \subseteq E^{MOD}$.

Let us now consider the observations and diagnosis definitions. Usually, due to uncertainties on the observations, we do not know the total order of the observations emitted by the system. Consequently the observations are represented by an automaton, each trajectory of which representing a possible order on the emitted observations during the period $[t_0, t_n]$.

Definition 6 (Observations).
The observations, denoted OBS, are represented by an automaton describing the observable events emitted by the system during the period $[t_0, t_n]$.

Definition 7 (Diagnosis).
The global diagnosis, denoted Δ_n is an automaton describing the possible trajectories on the system model compatible with the observations emitted by the system during the period $[t_0, t_n]$.

The global diagnosis of the system can be computed in the following way (see for instance [7, 8]):

$$\Delta_n = OBS_n \otimes MOD \tag{1}$$

3   Automata Chain and Global Diagnosis

3.1   Objectives

At the end of the previous section we have presented a way to compute the global diagnosis of the system on the period $[t_0, t_n]$. Our goal is now to compute a diagnosis on the period $[t_0, t_i]$ $(i < n)$ and, given this diagnosis as well as the observations on the period $[t_i, t_{i+1}]$, to *incrementally* compute the diagnosis $[t_0, t_{i+1}]$. In order to achieve this goal we introduce the concept of *automata chain* and first apply it to the case of global diagnosis. We then extend the principle to the problem of incremental computation detailled Section 4.

Figure 1 illustrates the principle of slicing an automaton into an automata chain and conversely (called the reconstruction). The use of automata chain for the diagnosis is also presented in this figure. Given the observation automaton OBS_n and the model of the system MOD, it is possible to compute the global diagnosis by synchronization, as presented Section 2. The idea is to *slice* the observations automaton into a sequence of automata OBS^i called *automata chain*, so that the original observation automaton can be rebuilt from the automata chain by a *reconstruction*. Each automaton OBS^i is *local to a temporal window* $\mathcal{W}^i$. The local diagnosis of the temporal window $\mathcal{W}^i$ is computed using OBS^i. Finally, the global diagnosis is obtained by reconstruction of the local diagnoses.

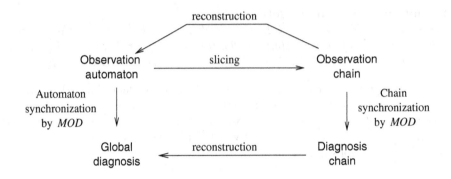

Fig. 1. Principle of the use of an automata chain

We define below the automata chain and give the properties that enable us to compute the diagnosis with the automata chain as illustrated on Figure 1.

3.2 Υ-Transition

We define a special class of events called Υ-events (denoted Υ_i for $i \in \mathbf{N}$). An Υ-event corresponds to a clock tick associated with the date t_i. It does not correspond to an event of the system.

We assume that an Υ-event and a system event $e \in E$ cannot occur simultaneously: if l is such that $\exists k, \Upsilon_k \in l$ then $l = \{\Upsilon_k\}$. In the following of this paper, we note $l = \Upsilon_k$ for $l = \{\Upsilon_k\}$. We call Υ-transition a transition labeled by Υ_k.

We change the definition of synchronization by adding the following property to the definition 3. To be synchronized, two labels l_1 and l_2 should satisfy this condition: if $(\exists i \in \{1, 2\}, j \in \{1, 2\}, j \neq i), l_i = \Upsilon_k$, then either $l_j = l_i$ or $l_j = \emptyset$. Given this new definition, we ensure that the property on the Υ-event is satisfied by the synchronization of two labels.

A temporal window $\mathcal{W}^i$ is defined as the period between two ticks represented by Υ_{i-1} and Υ_i. The period $\mathcal{W}^i$ is the period coming after Υ_1 and the period $\mathcal{W}^n$ is the period coming after the last tick Υ_{n-1}.

3.3 Automata Chain

Definition 8 (Automata chain).
A sequence of automata $(A^1, \ldots, A^n)$ with $A^i = (Q^i, E^i, T^i, I^i, F^i)$ is called an automata chain and denoted $\mathcal{E}_A$ if $\forall i \in \{1, \ldots, n\}, \forall k \in \mathbf{N}, \Upsilon_k \notin E^i$.

The meaning of an *automata chain* is the following: from a state q_1 from I^1, it is possible to reach by the transitions of A^1 a state q of $F^1 \cap I^2$; and then, it is possible to visit A^2 from q, etc. The automaton A^i is associated to the temporal window $\mathcal{W}^i$. An automata chain $(A^1, \ldots, A^n)$ can also be represented $((A^1, \ldots, A^{n-1}), A^n)$.

The length of the chain is the number of automata in the chain. A 3-long automata chain is presented on Figure 2. To simplify the representation the labels over the transitions are not represented.

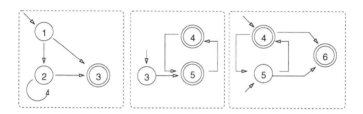

Fig. 2. Chain of three automata

Definition 9 (Chain concatenation).
Let $\mathcal{E}_A = (A^1, \ldots, A^n)$ be an automata chain with $A^i = (Q^i, E^i, T^i, I^i, F^i)$. The chain concatenation of $\mathcal{E}_A$, denoted $\oplus \mathcal{E}_A$ is an automaton $A' = (Q', E', T', I', F')$ defined by:

$$- \ Q' = (Q^1 \cup \ldots \cup Q^n) \times \{\mathcal{W}^1, \ldots, \mathcal{W}^n\},$$
$$- \ E' = (E^1 \cup \ldots \cup E^n) \cup \{\Upsilon_1, \ldots, \Upsilon_{n-1}\},$$
$$- \ T' = \{((q, \mathcal{W}^i), l, (q', \mathcal{W}^i)) \mid (q, l, q') \in T^i\} \ \cup$$
$$\{((q, \mathcal{W}^i), \Upsilon_i, (q, \mathcal{W}^{i+1})) \mid q \in F^i \wedge q \in I^{i+1}\},$$
$$- \ I' = I^1 \times \{\mathcal{W}^1\} \ and$$
$$- \ F' = F^n \times \{\mathcal{W}^n\}.$$

Since different automata of an automata chain can have states in common, the knowledge of a state q is not necessary related to a single temporal window. Consequently, the states q of the automata chain are said *relative* while the states $(q, \mathcal{W}^i)$ from the chain concatenation are said *absolute*. The concatenation

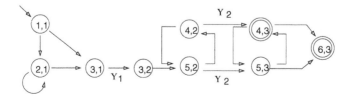

Fig. 3. Concatenation of the chain of Figure 2

transforms relative states into absolute states. The automaton obtained by a concatenation is called an *absolute automaton*.

The concatenation of the automata chain presented Figure 2 is shown Figure 3. To simplify, the states $(q, \mathcal{W}^i)$ are noted (q, i).

Generally, we note: $\oplus \mathcal{E}_A = A^1 \oplus \ldots \oplus A^n = (A^1 \oplus \ldots \oplus A^{n-1}) \oplus A^n$.

We introduce now the representation of an automaton by an automata chain. In order to achieve this goal, we first give some definitions about trajectories.

Definition 10 (Trajectory abstraction).
Let $traj' = ((q'_0, \ldots, q'_n), (l'_1, \ldots, l'_n))$ be a trajectory on absolute states. Then, the abstraction of $traj'$ is the trajectory defined by $traj = ((q_0, \ldots, q_n), (l_1, \ldots, l_n))$ so that:

- *$\forall i \in \{0, \ldots, n\}, \exists k, q'_i = (q_i, \mathcal{W}^k)$ and*
- *$\forall i \in \{1, \ldots, n\}, (\exists k, l'_i = \Upsilon_k \Rightarrow l_i = \emptyset) \wedge (\nexists k, l'_i = \Upsilon_k \Rightarrow l_i = l'_i).$*

Definition 11 (Automaton abstraction).
Let $A' = (Q', E', T', I', F')$ be an automaton on absolute states and let $A = (Q, E, T, I, F)$ be an automaton on relative states. A is an abstraction of A', denoted $A \simeq_{abs} A'$, iff;

- *for any trajectory $traj$ of A, there exists $traj'$ from A' and a trajectory $traj_2$ from A so that $traj_2 = traj$ and $traj_2$ is the abstraction of $traj'$ and*
- *for any trajectory $traj'$ from A', there exists a trajectory $traj$ from A so that $traj$ is the abstraction of $traj'$.*

Definition 12 (Reconstruction).
Let $\mathcal{E}_A$ be an automata chain. Let $A = (Q, E, T, I, F)$ an automaton so that $\forall k, \Upsilon_k \notin E$. A is the reconstruction of $\mathcal{E}_A$ (denoted $A \simeq_{rec} \mathcal{E}_A$) iff A is an abstraction of $\oplus \mathcal{E}_A$.

Definition 13 (Slicing).
Let A be an automaton and $\mathcal{E}_A$ be an automata chain. $\mathcal{E}_A$ is a slicing of A iff A is a reconstruction of $\mathcal{E}_A$.

The links between the automaton, the automata chain and the absolute automaton are presented on Figure 4.

The automaton presented Figure 5 is the abstraction of the automaton shown Figure 3. Thus, the automata chain given Figure 2 is a slicing of this abstract automaton (cf. Figure 5).

Property 1. *Let A be an automaton. Let $\mathcal{E}_A$ be a slicing of A. Let $A_2 = (Q_2, E_2, T_2, I_2, F_2)$ be an automaton so that $\forall k, \Upsilon_k \notin E_2$. Then $A \otimes A_2 \simeq_{abs} (\oplus \mathcal{E}_A) \otimes A_2$.*

3.4   Synchronization of Automata Chain

Definition 14 (Prefix-closed automaton).
Let $A = (Q, E, T, I, F)$ be an automaton. The prefix-closed automaton of A, denoted A^+, is equal to the automaton A in which all states are final ($F^+ = Q$).

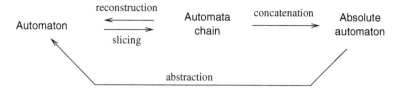

Fig. 4. Links between the automaton, the automata chain and the absolute automaton

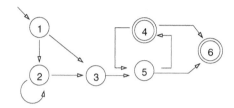

Fig. 5. Abstraction of the automaton of Figure 3

Definition 15 (Suffix-closed automaton).

Let $A = (Q, E, T, I, F)$ be an automaton. The suffix-closed automaton of A, denoted A^-, is equal to the automaton A in which all states are initial $(I^- = Q)$.

We denote $A^\#$ the automaton prefix-closed suffix-closed $(A^\# = (A^+)^- = (A^-)^+)$.

Definition 16 (Synchronization of a chain by an automaton).

Let $\mathcal{E}_A = (A^1, \dots, A^n)$ be an automata chain. Let A_2 be an automaton. The synchronization of $\mathcal{E}_A$ by A_2 is the automata chain, denoted $\mathcal{E}_A \otimes A_2$, defined by: $\mathcal{E}_A \otimes A_2 = (A^1 \otimes A_2^+, A^2 \otimes A_2^\#, \dots, A^{n-1} \otimes A_2^\#, A^n \otimes A_2^-)$.

The synchronisation of a chain automata with an automaton A_2 consists in synchronizing each automaton of the chain with the automaton A_2. In the synchronization of an automata chain $\mathcal{E}_A = (A^1, \dots, A^n)$ with an automaton $A_2 = (Q_2, E_2, T_2, I_2, F_2)$, all the states of A_2 are considered to be initial, during the synchronization with A^i $(i \neq 1)$, since the state q_2 of A_2 current during Υ_{i-1} is not necessary initial. Thus, we have used the suffix-closed automaton of A_2. A similar reasoning has been applied for the final state and then the prefix-closed automaton is also used.

Property 2.

Let $\mathcal{E}_A$ be an automata chain and let $A_2 = (Q_2, E_2, T_2, I_2, F_2)$ be an automaton so that $\Upsilon \notin E_2$. Then, $\oplus(\mathcal{E}_A \otimes A_2) = (\oplus\mathcal{E}_A) \otimes A_2$.

Proof. This property can be checked by proving that the set of trajectories of $\oplus(\mathcal{E}_A \otimes A_2)$ and the set of trajectories of $(\oplus\mathcal{E}_A) \otimes A_2$ are equal.

Corollary 1.
*Let A be an automaton. Let $\mathcal{E}_A$ be a slicing of A. Let $A_2 = (Q_2, E_2, T_2, I_2, F_2)$
be an automaton so that $\Upsilon \notin E_2$. Then, $\mathcal{E}_A \oplus A_2$ is a slicing of $A \otimes A_2$.*

3.5   Diagnosis

Let $MOD = (Q^{MOD}, E^{MOD}, T^{MOD}, I^{MOD}, F^{MOD})$ be the model of the system
as presented in Section 2. Let us remark that MOD does not give any information
on the final states of the system ($F^{MOD} = Q^{MOD}$). Thus, we have the following
properties: $MOD^+ = MOD$ and $MOD^{\#} = MOD^-$.

Let OBS_n be the automaton representing the observations emitted by the
system and $\mathcal{E}_A$ be a slicing of OBS_n.

We have:

$$\Delta_n \simeq_{rec} \mathcal{E}_{OBS_n} \otimes MOD \tag{2}$$

4   Incremental Diagnosis

In this section, we consider the incremental computation of the diagnosis. Our
goal is to compute the diagnosis on the temporal window $\mathcal{W}_{i+1} = [t_0, t_{i+1}]$ from
the diagnosis on the window $\mathcal{W}_i$ and the observations on the window $\mathcal{W}^{i+1}$.

In the following, the diagnosis is formalized as a diagnosis chain. We first
present the interest of using diagnosis chain rather than the complete diagnosis
automata as described previously. We first propose a parallelized computing to
elaborate the diagnosis from the results obtained in the previous section. Finally,
we show that it is possible to take into account the diagnosis obtained for the
previous temporal windows to incrementally compute the current diagnosis in a
more efficient way.

4.1   Diagnosis Chain

As presented Section 2, the diagnosis is defined as a set of trajectories on the
system model and then can be easily formalized by an automata chain.

Definition 17 (Trajectories concatenation).
*Let $traj^k = ((q_0^k, \ldots, q_{nk}^k), (l_1, \ldots, l_{nk}))$ be i trajectories so that $\forall k \in \{1, \ldots, i -
1\}$, $q_{nk}^k = q_0^{k+1}$. Then, the concatenation of the i trajectories $traj^k$ is defined by:*
$traj = ((q_0^1, \ldots, q_{n1}^1, q_1^2, \ldots, q_1^i, \ldots, q_{ni}^i), (l_1^1, \ldots, l_{n1}^1, \ldots, l_1^i, \ldots, l_{ni}^i))$.

Property 3.
Let A be an automaton and let $\mathcal{E}_A = (A^1, \ldots, A^i)$ be a slicing of A.

- *Let $\forall k \in \{1, \ldots, i\}$, $traj^k = ((q_0^k, \ldots, q_{n(k)}^k), (l_1, \ldots, l_{n(k)}))$, i trajectories on
  the automata A^k so that $traj$, the concatenation of the i trajectories, exists.
  Then, $traj$ is a trajectory of A.*

- Let $traj$ be a trajectory of A. Then, there exists i trajectories $traj^k$ on the automata A^k so that the concatenation of the i trajectories is $traj$.

This property is a logical extension of the previous properties. It shows that an automata chain *represents* the set of trajectories of the automaton that is obtained by reconstructing the chain.

4.2   Parallelized Computation

Let $\mathcal{E}_{\Delta i} = (\Delta^1, \ldots, \Delta^i)$ be the diagnosis of the period $\mathcal{W}_i$ incrementally computed. Let $\mathcal{E}_{\Delta(i+1)}$ be the diagnosis of the system during the window $\mathcal{W}_{i+1}$. Then, we have:

$$\mathcal{E}_{\Delta i+1} = (\Delta^1, \ldots, \Delta^i, \Delta^{i+1}) \quad \text{with } \Delta^{i+1} = OBS^{i+1} \otimes MOD^- \qquad (3)$$

This result comes from the fact that $MOD^{\#} = MOD^-$.

The advantage of this approach is that the local diagnoses can be computed in parallel. However, if the set of states Q^{MOD} is huge, then MOD^- has a huge number of initial states, and also Δ^{i+1}. The computation of Δ^{i+1} can then be very expensive. It is thus necessary to limit as much as possible the set of initial states in the diagnosis on a temporal window $\mathcal{W}^i$. This is the goal of the second approach uses the *incremental synchronization*.

4.3   Incremental Synchronization

Definition 18 (Restriction).
Let $A = (Q, E, T, I, F)$ be an automaton. The restriction of the automaton A by the set I', denoted $A[I']$, is the automaton $A' = (Q, E, T, I \cap I', F)$.

Definition 19 (Incremental synchronization).
Let $\mathcal{E}_A = (A^1, \ldots, A^n)$ be an automata chain. Let A_2 be an automaton. The incremental synchronization of the automata chain $\mathcal{E}_A$ and A_2 is the automata chain $\mathcal{E}_B$, denoted $\mathcal{E}_A \odot A_2$ and defined by $\mathcal{E}_B = (A_B^1, \ldots, A_B^n)$ with $\forall i \in \{1, \ldots, n\}$ so that:

- $A_B^1 = A^1 \otimes A_2^+$,
- $\forall i \in \{2, \ldots, n-1\}$, $A_B^i = (A^i \otimes A_2^{\#})[F_B^{i-1}]$ and
- $A_B^n = (A^n \otimes A_2^-)[F_B^{n-1}]$.

The incremental synchronization restricts the automaton A_B^i by the set of final states of the previous automaton A_B^{i-1}.

Property 4.
Let $\mathcal{E}_A$ be an automata chain and $A_2 = (Q_2, E_2, T_2, I_2, F_2)$ so that $\Upsilon \notin E_2$. Then, $\oplus(\mathcal{E}_A \odot A_2) = \oplus(\mathcal{E}_A \otimes A_2)$.

We note $\Delta^i = (Q_\Delta^i, E_\Delta^i, T_\Delta^i, I_\Delta^i, F_\Delta^i)$. Let $\mathcal{E}_{\Delta_i} = (\Delta^1, \ldots, \Delta^i)$ be the diagnosis of the system during the temporal window $\mathcal{W}_i$. It is possible to incrementally compute the diagnosis Δ^{i+1} on the temporal window $\mathcal{W}_{i+1}$:

$$\mathcal{E}_{\Delta i+1} = (\Delta^1, \ldots, \Delta^i, \Delta^{i+1}) \quad \text{with } \Delta^{i+1} = (OBS^{i+1} \otimes MOD^-)[F_\Delta^i] \qquad (4)$$

This method enables us to limit the number of initial states of the local diagnoses.

5   Conclusion

In this paper, we have shown that an automaton can be sliced and represented by an automata chain. We explain the relations between these two representations and define the synchronization operation for each of them. Diagnosis is usually formally defined as resulting from synchronization between the system automaton and the observation automaton. We propose to replace the observation automaton by an automata chain, each automaton representing the observation emitted during the corresponding temporal window. It is then possible to compute the diagnosis as an automata chain, each automaton representing a local diagnosis for a given temporal window. We show that it is equivalent to compute the global diagnosis for the global observation automaton. Moreover, we show that this computation can be performed in an incremental way, and thus more efficiently by taking profit of the already computed diagnoses to improve the computation of the current one.

This work concerns the off-line case. The next step is to study the on-line case. The incremental approach means computing a diagnosis for a given time, and then extending it by taking into account the next temporal window. It requires to be able to build, on-line and incrementally, the observation automata chain. The main difficulties are to determine the adequate temporal windows and to ensure that the slicing is correct whenever the future observations are unknown.

References

1. Baroni, P., Lamperti, G., Pogliano, P., Zanella, M.: Diagnosis of large active systems. Artificial Intelligence **110** (1999) 135–183
2. Cordier, M.O., Thiébaux, S.: Event-based diagnosis for evolutive systems. In: 5th International Workshop on Principles of Diagnosis (DX-94). (1994) 64–69
3. Barral, C., McIlraith, S., Son, T.: Formulating diagnostic problem solving using an action language with narratives and sensing. In: International Conference on Knowledge Representation and Reasoning (KR'2000). (2000) 311–322
4. Console, L., Picardi, C., Ribaudo, M.: Diagnosis and diagnosability analysis using PEPA. In: 14th European Conference on Artificial Intelligence (ECAI-00), Berlin, Allemagne (2000) 131–135
5. Cordier, M.O., Largouët, C.: Using model-checking techniques for diagnosing discrete-event systems. In: 12th International Workshop on Principles of Diagnosis (DX-2001). (2001) 39–46

6. Lamperti, G., Zanella, M.: Diagnosis of Active Systems. Kluwer Academic Publishers (2003)
7. Sampath, M., Sengupta, R., Lafortune, S., Sinnamohideen, K., Teneketzis, D.: Failure diagnosis using discrete-event models. In: IEEE Transactions on Control Systems Technology (CST-96). (1996) 105–124
8. Rozé, L., Cordier, M.O.: Diagnosing discrete-event systems : extending the "diagnoser approach" to deal with telecommunication networks. Journal on Discrete-Event Dynamic Systems: Theory and Applications (JDEDS) **12** **(1)** (2002) 43–81 errata **14** **(1)** (2004) 131.

Integrating Web Content Clustering into Web Log Association Rule Mining*

Jiayun Guo, Vlado Kešelj, and Qigang Gao

Faculty of Computer Science, Dalhousie University,
6050 University Avenue, Halifax, NS, Canada B3H 1W5
{jguo, vlado, qggao}@cs.dal.ca,
http://www.cs.dal.ca/~{jguo,vlado,qggao}

Abstract. One of the effects of the general Internet growth is an immense number of user accesses to WWW resources. These accesses are recorded in the web server log files, which are a rich data resource for finding useful patterns and rules of user browsing behavior, and they caused the rise of technologies for Web usage mining. Current Web usage mining applications rely exclusively on the web server log files. The main hypothesis discussed in this paper is that Web content analysis can be used to improve Web usage mining results. We propose a system that integrates Web page clustering into log file association mining and uses the cluster labels as Web page content indicators. It is demonstrated that novel and interesting association rules can be mined from the combined data source. The rules can be used further in various applications, including Web user profiling and Web site construction. We experiment with several approaches to content clustering, relying on keyword and character n-gram based clustering with different distance measures and parameter settings. Evaluation shows that character n-gram based clustering performs better than word-based clustering in terms of an internal quality measure (about 3 times better). On the other hand, word-based cluster profiles are easier to manually summarize. Furthermore, it is demonstrated that high-quality rules are extracted from the combined dataset.

1 Introduction

Web Mining is an important application of data mining in the web environment. The problems in this research area became very important due to the immense size of the web resources and intensive user activity. The general area of Web Mining is typically divided into the sub-areas of:

- Web Content Mining, which is concerned with the content of Web pages,
- Web Stucture Mining, concerned with the link structure of the Web, and
- Web Usage Mining, concerned with the patterns of user behaviour when using the Web.

---

* This work is supported by NSERC.

B. Kégl and G. Lapalme (Eds.): AI 2005, LNAI 3501, pp. 182–193, 2005.

Table 1. Different Approaches to Web Site Organization

	Organized by	Server location	Examples
(1)	Product	www.microsoft.com	/windows, /games, /sql...
(2)	Location	www.ibm.com	/us, /ca/en, /cn, /jp...
(3)	Person	www.cs.dal.ca	/~prof01, /~stydent03
(4)	Other	forums.devshed.com	/showthread.php?p-2119#post211...

The data source for Web Usage Mining are typically web server log files. For each user access, a log file includes information such as the user IP number, time of access, file path, user browsing agent, returned status, and the size of transferred data. Data mining on this data set can discover frequent patterns in user access, but they are mostly content oblivious. The file path may be a content indicator, but it may not be reliable. Although many Web sites are constructed according to their content, there are also many others that are not. As shown in Table 1,[1] the directory structure of a web site may be organized in different ways.

Web site organization can be based on content such as product information ((1) in Table 1), business locations (2), user space (3), and many other conceptual hierarchies. If a Web site is organized according to user space, different directories may contain similar content; e.g., same products or services provided at different places, professors teaching the same class or sharing similar research interests. Also, with the development of Web design techniques, more and more CGI programs are used instead of the traditional static HTML files. In this case ((4) in Table 1), Web pages are generated according to a set of input parameters. Typical examples would be BBS/forum systems. In this case, it may be hard to make any inference about page content based on the URL path.

In this paper we propose and evaluate an approach to integrate the content of Web pages into mining of the Web server log files. We experiment with two different clustering approaches to conceptually organize web pages, and then use cluster labels in association rule mining from the Web log file. The cluster labels represent content information, which is merged with the log file, giving an integrated log file.

2   Related Work

Web Mining is categorized into three categories according to what part of the web is mined [1, 2]: Web Content Mining [3], which focuses on the discovery of useful information from the Web contents; Web Structure Mining [4], which attempts to discover the model underlying the link structure of the Web; and Web Usage Mining [5], which attempts to discover knowledge from the data generated by the

---

[1] For privacy reasons, the user information from the www.cs.dal.ca data is anonymized.

Web surfer's activity. Web site servers generate a large volume of data from user accesses, which is used to mine knowledge about user browsing behaviour.

Web usage mining is still relatively isolated area from other two areas of Web mining, even though it seems obvious that it is intrinsically related to the page content. For example, the knowledge about user profiles is considered to be a part of Web usage mining [3] and it is hard to learn something useful about user profiles without consulting the content of the visited pages. In analyzing user interaction and profile data, Web usage mining uses only the URL links in the log file, for instance, as indication of the Web page contents. Some ideas of integrating Web content information into Web usage mining have been expressed in some papers like [6, 7, 8]. However, most of these attempts still do not use much of information from really looking at the Web pages contents. They either assume that the URLs strongly indicate the Web page contents [7], or use information from log files, like user click streams, to build Web page models or clusters [8]. There are also other attempts to improve the Web server log file mining by integrating some semantic concepts [9, 10], which requires awareness of the content of Web pages beforehand.

3   System Design

Figure 1 illustrates the overall design of our system.

3.1   Preprocessing

In the preprocessing step, there are two major tasks: re-formatting the log file and retrieving Web pages to a local disk-space. Log file re-formatting involves revising the log file to a suitable format for further steps. Each field in the log access log file is revised in order to reduce the cardinality of the corresponding domain set. E.g., the IP numbers are generalized to their sub-net mask consisting of the first two numbers, the access time is discretized into a 4-valued set {morning, afternoon, evening, night}, the dates are grouped into the seven days of week bins, and the numerosity of file paths is reduced by using only their prefix sub-paths. Web page retrieving involves reading the URL address parts of the log file, retrieving the associated Web pages, and storing them to the local space. Only hypertext and plain text files are considered in this phase.

3.2   Document Clustering

Before document clustering, several steps are performed including eliminating HTML/XML tags, eliminating stop words and word stemming for word-based clustering, and translating all letters into their lowercase version for character n-gram-based clustering.

Document clustering requires vector representation of the documents. For vector components, we use the standard TF-IDF measure, defined in the following way [11]:

$$TFIDF(i, j) = tf(i, j) \cdot \left(1 + \log \frac{N}{df(j)}\right)$$

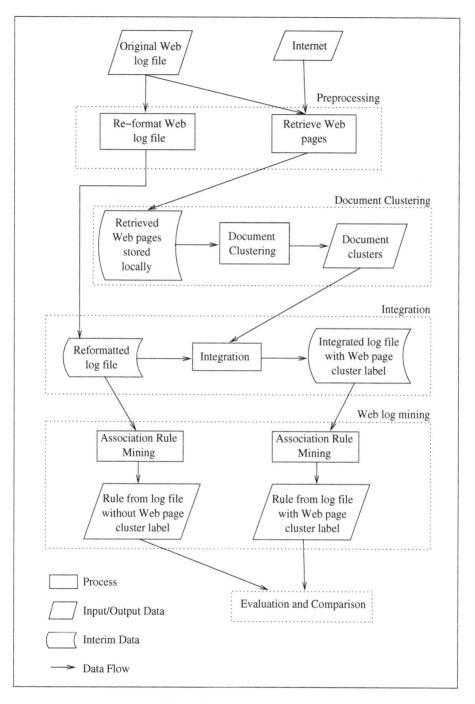

Fig. 1. System Architecture

where $tf(i,j)$ is the frequency of feature (term) t_j in document d_i, N is the number of documents in the collection, and $df(j)$ is document frequency, i.e., the number of documents in the collection containing the term t_j.

In the vector space model, one of the most common measures for similarity between documents is the cosine measure, defined by [12]

$$\cos(d_1, d_2) = \frac{d_1 \cdot d_2}{||d_1|| \cdot ||d_2||}$$

where d_1 and d_2 are two document vectors. The measure returns values close to 0 for very dissimilar documents, and high values close to 1 for very similar documents. The k-means clustering algorithm requires a distance measure which produces distance close to 0 for very similar documents and higher values for dissimilar documents, we use the sinus distance measure [12]:

$$\sin(d_1, d_2) = \sqrt{1 - \cos(d_1, d_2)^2}$$

Another obvious option would be simply to use $1 - \cos(d_1, d_2)$, but a more detailed analysis shows that the sinus measure is more appropriate since the k-means algorithm relies on centroid calculation, which is a linear transformation, and since $\sin(x)/x \to 1$ when $x \to 0$.[2]

The well-known K-means algorithm is used for document clustering and its pseudo code is given in Algorithm 1. A centroid is calculated as the arithmetic mean and mass-center of all points in a cluster. There are typically three options for a stopping criterion: We may stop when clusters settle. Since clusters may oscillate instead of settling at a fixed point, there is a limit on the maximal number of iterations. The third option is to observe a clustering quality measure and stop when this measure reaches a local maximum. We use the fixed point criterion with a limit on the number of iterations.

Algorithm 1 K-means

Partition object into k non-empty subsets randomly
repeat
    Compute the centroids of the clusters
    Assign each object to the cluster with the nearest centroid
until some stop criterion is met

The clustering quality is evaluated using either *external* quality measures, which rely on some external knowledge such as a gold clustering standard of a data set, or *internal* quality measures, which do not rely on any external knowledge. Since our set of web pages is not labeled, we first use an internal evaluation function to evaluate clustering. After using clustering results in the web log association rule mining, we evaluate the final results manually, and this is

---

[2] Another way of presenting the argument is to depict document clustering as clustering of points at the surface of a unit n-dimensional sphere.

an external evaluation. However, unlike the internal evaluation, it is a qualitative rather than quantitative evaluation.

For the internal evaluation, we use the internal evaluation function proposed in [13] and defined as

$$EI = \frac{1}{mN} \sum_{j=1}^{N} E(t_j) \sum_{i=1}^{m} E_i(t_j) \tag{1}$$

where $E(t_j)$ and $E_i(t_j)$ are defined in the following way:

$$E(t_j) = 1 - \frac{m_j - 1}{m - 1} \log_m \sum_{i=1}^{m} E_i(t_j)$$

$$E_i(t_j) = \frac{n_{ij} - 1}{n_i - 1} \log_{f_{i\,max}+1} (\overline{f_j} + 1)$$

In the equations above, N is the number of documents, m is the number of clusters, $E(t_j)$ is called inter-cluster entropy, $E_i(t_j)$ is called intra-cluster entropy, n_{ij} is the number of documents including feature t_j in cluster C_i, $f_{i\,max}$ is the maximum frequency of feature t_j in cluster C_i, $\overline{f_j}$ is the average frequency of feature t_j in cluster C_i, and m_j is the number of clusters in which feature t_j appears.

3.3   Integration

The integration step involves integration of the Web document cluster information into log files. Two data sets are obtained for further mining: one is *log_origin* with only the information obtained from the web log file, and the other is named *log_integ* and it includes information from the web log file, integrated with the cluster labels. In order to be able to interpret the results of the association rule mining, the clusters are manually summarized and described by brief descriptive paragraphs in plain language.

3.4   Association Rule Mining

In this last step, the Apriori association rule mining algorithm [14] is applied to the two data sets obtained from the above steps.

The number of unique values of each field in the re-formatted log file is limited, and all the values can be displayed as strings. They are then used as *items* in the standard association rule mining terminology. Each different value either is present or not, so it is treated as a Boolean value. Since the domain sets of different fields are disjoint, we do not need to present field (attribute) names when presenting the association rules. The purpose of this association mining step is to discover the rules of co-occurrence and the implications underlying the large amount of access records.

After applying association rule mining on the two datasets *log_origin* and *log_integ*, two sets of rules were obtained from the datasets respectively. These two sets of rules are compared. The rules obtained from the dataset *log_origin* are a subset of the rules obtained from the dataset *log_integ*, so we explore the rules obtained from *log_integ* but not from *log_origin* to see whether they provide any useful and novel information.

4   Results and Evaluation

We used an Apache log access file from the graduate Web server of the Faculty of Computer Science at Dalhousie University, for a one-month period in October 2003. In this period, there were 161,499 access records producing a 230MB log file. Using a widely used data set in the experiment would be beneficial for comparative reasons with other published results, however we were not able to locate such dataset that would involve both web pages and the web log data. In other published work, this scenario is often seen, were the experiments are based on a local departmental web server.

All the experiments are executed on a Sun Solaris server at the CS Faculty of Dalhousie University. The server type is SunOS sparc SUNW, Sun-Fire-880. The system was implemented using Perl (preprocessing, document clustering, and integration) and C++ (Association Rule Mining).

4.1   Cluster Summarization

In the document clustering step, after the K-means algorithm is performed, the frequencies of features in each cluster are obtained. From these, the most frequent key features of each cluster are extracted and used to manually summarize the major topic of each cluster. In the manual summarization, beside the set of the most frequent features, some sample Web pages from a cluster are examined in order to produce a reliable cluster summary. Even though we could not successfully use any existing summarization tool, a part of future work is to make a further attempt to use this option.

The analysis of these summaries produced to following observations:

(1) When the number of clusters k is relatively large (k=12 for k-means) with word representation, some different partitions share same or similar topics.

(2) When k is relatively small (k=8 for k-means) with word representation, some of important clusters, which appear when k is larger, were not partitioned from the others.

(3) The optimal clustering summaries are obtained for $k = 10$ with the word representation.

(4) When the character n-gram representation is used, it is very difficult to summarize clusters manually.

4.2   Internal Cluster Evaluation

The results of the internal cluster evaluation using equation 1 are shown in Table 2. We can see that k=10 produced the best results for both word and n-gram representation, which is an interesting result since it coincides with our analysis based on cluster summaries. Character n-gram representation produced

Table 2. Comparison of Document Clustering

	Word-rep	Ngram-rep
K=8	0.00953	0.03478
K=10	0.01183	0.036515
K=12	0.01077	0.03556
K=14	0.01032	0.03427

significantly better results (3 times) than word representation. However, since it is much harder to summarize character n-gram based clusters than word-based clusters, so we chose to proceed with the word clusters to the association rule mining step. An important open question is how to summarize clusters based on their character n-gram profiles. If this problem could be successfully solved our hope is that we would obtain even better association rules.

4.3   Association Rule Mining Evaluation

In the association rule mining step, after applying Apriori on both datasets of *log_origin* and *log_integ*, we got two lists of association rules. Table 3 shows the number of association rules obtained from the two datasets.

Table 3. Number of rules obtained

[support, confidence]	Log_origin	Log_integ
[2%, 30%]	64	203
[2%, 50%]	20	81
[1%, 50%]	37	187
[1%, 60%]	9	58

The integrated log file produce three to four times more rules than the original log file. As all the attributes in *log_origin* are also included in *log_integ*, it is obvious that the rules from the latter are also included in those from the former. Since the number of access records is very large, we mine rule with a support threshold of only 1 or 2%, however the confidence threshold is kept at higher levels of 30, 50, and 60%.

Table 4 and Table 5 list some rules obtained from the two datasets, *log_origin* and *log_integ* respectively. The left side columns display the rules obtained from program, while the right side columns display the same rules interpreted in the plain language. Since all the rules obtained from *log_origin* are also included in the rules obtained from *log_integ*, in Table 5 we show only the rules that are not obtained from *log_origin*.

We can make interesting observations about the web site usage based on the extracted rules. According to Table 5, the rules indicate when and from where the access queries occurred, who visited, and what kind of information was requested. These rules provide information which can be used in various applications, including web site organization, Web content distribution, and analysis of user access behavior. For example, from the rule "/~prof33 ⇒ ERROR", we would conclude that *prof33* had changed a lot of his web pages, and we may suggest an update or creation of redirection Web pages under his domain. The rules like "cluster5 ⇒ /~prof11", "cluster6 ⇒ /~prof07", provided information about the user domains that provide the content of a certain category or certain topic. The rules such as "24.222 ⇒ cluster7" and "156.34 ⇒ cluster7" tell us about the topics of interest of visitors from certain internet domains. These rules are related to the document cluster labels, i.e., the web contents, and were not included in the results from the conventional data provided in the web log file (*log_origin*).

Table 4. Association Rules from *log_origin*

K=10 with Word Representation Support=1% Confidence=50%	
Association Rules	Rules in plain language
/~prof12 ⇒ 129.173 [10, 53]	A majority of accesses to user *prof12*'s web pages are from the CS building log-ons
129.173 ⇒ afternoon [20, 51]	Over half of the accesses from CS building were in the afternoon;
/~prof12 ∧ Tue ⇒ afternoon [2, 56] /~prof12 ∧ Wed ⇒ afternoon [2, 52]	Accesses on Tue and Wed to user *prof12*'s web pages occurred mainly in the afternoon;

From the original dataset, we obtained the rules that typically describe certain visitor groups that are interested in certain professors' web pages. However, one single professor's web site may contain different topics. From the integrated dataset, we obtained the rules that contain information about visitor groups that are interested in certain kinds of topics. Pages with similar topics may exist in different professors' directories, and these rules are not found from the original dataset.

Therefore, we can conclude that we demonstrated that some useful rules are obtained from integrating web document clusters and web log files. These rules are related to the content of web pages, and provide information that can be further used for user profiling and web site evaluation and improvement.

5   Conclusion and Future Work

In this paper, a novel approach to Web log file mining combined with the information from automatic Web page clustering is presented. The methods for

Table 5. Association Rules from *log_integ*

K=10 with Word Representation Support=1% Confidence=50%	
Association Rules	Rules in plain language
cluster5 ⇒ /~prof11 [3, 51]	A majority of Java programming pages are from user *prof11*.
/~prof11 ⇒ cluster7 [6, 54]	A majority of user *prof11*'s web pages are personal or course information pages.
cluster6 ⇒ /~prof07 [3, 86] /~prof07 ⇒ cluster 7 [10, 59]	User *prof07* provides over eighty percent of administration pages, however more than half of user *prof07*'s web pages are personal or course information pages.
/~prof33 ⇒ ERROR [4,81]	User *prof33* has deleted or modified many of his web pages since Oct. 2003.
/~prof13 ⇒ cluster1 [5,78] cluster1 ⇒ /~prof13 [5,67]	User *prof13* has many empty pages.
129.173 ⇒ cluster7 [21,51] 142.177 ⇒ cluster7 [3,52] 156.34 ⇒ cluster7 [2,55] 24.138 ⇒ cluster7 [1,56] 24.215 ⇒ cluster7 [1,54] 24.222 ⇒ cluster7 [7,55] 24.224 ⇒ cluster7 [3,53]	Over 50% of accesses from outside CS building are for general information.
/~prof10 ∧ afternoon ⇒ cluster7 [1,53]	A majority of accesses to user *prof10*'s web pages in afternoon are for general information.
/~prof12 ∧ cluster0 ⇒ 129.173 [1,60] /~prof12 ∧ 24.222 ⇒ cluster7 [1,62]	

document clustering are used: word-based and character n-gram based. The K-means algorithm was used in web page clustering. After manually summarizing clusters obtained form the web log file, and from the integrated data file, the Apriori association rule mining algorithm is applied. Several evaluation results are produced: an "optimal" number of clusters is found based on manual summarization and cluster analysis, and it was confirmed that this number of clusters is locally optimal in terms of the internal quality measure. Furthermore, it was demonstrated that some interesting content-related rules can be discovered from the integrated web log data, while they could not be discovered using only the standard web log data. These rules provide useful information related to the web usage mining, and can be useful in tasks of the web site organization, web content distribution, customer behaviour profile, and similar.

The designed system is a proof-of-a-concept prototype of the idea of combining the web content mining and web usage mining, and there are many obvious aspects in which it can be improved:

- The algorithm should be improved to handle larger data sets.
- More types of files should be analyzed, beside HTML and plain text only.
- Automatic summarization technique should be applied.
- Generating summaries for n-gram based clusters would open the doors of using better clustering results in rule mining.
- The use of concept hierarchies could improve quality or association rule mining.
- The data mining functionalities other than association rule mining could be used in web log analysis.

Acknowledgments

We would like to thank Haibin Liu and anonymous reviewers for providing useful comments. The authors gratefully acknowledge the financial support from the Natural Sciences and Engineering Research Council of Canada (NSERC).

References

1. Madria, S., Bhowmick, S., Ng, W., Lim, E.: Research issues in web data mining. In: Proceedings of Data Warehousing and Knowledge Discovery, First International conference, DaWaK'99. (1999) 303–312
2. Borges, J., Levene, M.: Data mining of user navigation patterns. In: Proc. of WEBKDD'99 ws. on Web Usage Analysis and User Profiling. (1999) 92–111
3. R.Kosala, H.Blockeel: Web mining research: A survey. ACM SIGKDD **2** (2000) 1–15
4. Chakrabarti, S., Dom, B., Gibson, D., Kleinberg, J., Kumar, S., Raghavan, P., Rajagopalan, S., Tomkins, A.: Mining the link structure of the World Wide Webx. IEEE Computer **32** (1999) 60–67
5. Cooley, R., Mobasher, B., Srivastava, J.: Web mining: Information and pattern discovery on the world wide web. In: Proc. of the 9th IEEE International Conference on Tools with Artificial Intelligence (ICTAI'97). (1997) 558–567
6. Mobasher, B., Dai, H., Luo, T., Sun, Y., J.Zhu: Integrating web usage and content mining for more effective personalization. In: Proc. of the Intl. Conf. on Ecommerce and Web Technologies (ECWeb). (2000) 165–176
7. Kato, H., Nakayama, T., Yamane, Y.: Navigation analysis tool based on the correlation between contents distribution and access patterns. In: Proc. of the Web Mining Workshop KDD00. (2000) 95–104
8. Ypma, A., Heskes, T.: Categorization of web pages and user clustering with mixtures of hidden markov models. In: Workshop on Web Knowledge Discovery and Data mining (WEBKDD 2002). (2002) 31–43
9. Jin, X., Zhou, Y., Mobasher, B.: A unified approach to personalization based on probabilistic latent semantic models of web usage and content. In: Proc. of the AAAI 2004 Workshop SWP'04. (2004) pp. 26–34

10. Eirinaki, M., Lampos, C., Paulakis, S., Vazirgiannis, M.: Web personalization integrating content, semantics and navigational patterns. In: ACM Web Information and Data Management Workshop. (2004) 72–79
11. Aslton, G., Buckley, C.: Term-weighting approaches in automatic text retrieval. Information Processing and Management **24** (1988) 513–523
12. Miao, Y., Keselj, V., Milios, E.: Comparing document clustering using n-grams, terms and words (2004)
13. Jo, T.: Evaluation function of document clustering based on term entropy. In: Proc. of 2nd International Symposium on Advanced Intelligent System. (2001) 95–100
14. Han, J., Kamber, M.: Data Mining: Concepts and Techniques. Morgan Kaufmann Publishers (2001)
15. M.Steinbach, G.Karypis, V.Kumar: A comparison of document clustering techniques. In: Proc. of the Text Mining Workshop, KDD00. (2000)
16. Pandey, A., Srivastava, J., Shekhar, S.: A web proxy server with an intelligent prefetcher for dynamic pages using association rules. Technical Report TR-01-004, Department of Computer Science, University of Minnesota (2001)
17. Porter, M.: An algorithm for suffix stripping. Program **14** (1980) 130–137
18. Etzioni, O.: The World Wide Web: Quagmire or gold mine. Communications of the ACM **39** (1996) 65–68
19. Saltonandand, G., Wong, A., Yang, C.: A vector space model for automatic indexing. Communications of the ACM **18** (1975) 613–620
20. Punin, J., Krishnamoorthy, M., M.J.Zaki: Mining web log data across all customers touch points. In: Web Usage Mining—Languages and Algorithms, WEBKDD01 Workshop. (2001) 88–112

Privacy Compliance Enforcement in Email

Quintin Armour, William Elazmeh, Nour El-Kadri,
Nathalie Japkowicz, and Stan Matwin⋆

School of Information Technology and Engineering, University of Ottawa, Canada
{qarmour, welazmeh, nelkadri, nat, stan}@site.uottawa.ca

Abstract. Privacy is one of the main societal concerns raised by critics of the uncontrolled growth and spread of information technology in developed societies. The purpose of this paper is to propose a privacy compliance engine that takes email messages as input and filters those that violate the privacy rules of the organization in which it is deployed. Our system includes two main parts: an information extraction module that extracts the names of the sender and recipients as well as sensitive information contained in the message; and an inference engine that matches the email information against a knowledge base owned by the organization. This engine then applies compliance rules to the information obtained from the extraction and database matching steps of the process. This prototype is currently being developed for a university setting. In this setting, it was shown to obtain a precision score of 77%. The next step of our research will be to adapt our system to the context of a health organization, where privacy rules are more complex and more sensitive.

1 Introduction

Privacy is one of the main societal concerns raised by critics of the uncontrolled growth and spread of information technology in developed societies. On the one hand, the complexity of the modern information systems maintaining our personal data is constantly growing. On the other hand, these systems are often accessed by personnel who are not sufficiently sensitive to the issue of personal data privacy. The fact that private information is in the hands of other people introduces the possibility of human error. To bring order to this complex privacy landscape, most countries have introduced, in the last several years, data privacy laws. In Canada, the main law is the Privacy Information Protection in Electronic Documents Act of 2000. Recently, Ontario has introduced Bill 31 to regulate the issues of privacy and information access in the healthcare sector. This legal framework is normative, and as such, it addresses privacy violations after they have been committed. We believe that IT, in general, and AI in particular, can assist in the development of tools that will detect privacy violations as they happen. Here, we focus on email exchanges initiated from an organization and worry about information breaches with respect to the privacy rules of that organization. Several factors contribute

---

⋆ Stan Matwin is also affiliated with the Institute of Computer Science, Polish Academy of Sciences, Warsaw, Poland.

B. Kégl and G. Lapalme (Eds.): AI 2005, LNAI 3501, pp. 194–204, 2005.
© Springer-Verlag Berlin Heidelberg 2005

to the fact that information breaches are very likely. The quick pace of information exchanges is the first such factor: lots of information is being exchanged, and emails are often sent in a hurry. People put less thought into the content of their messages or in the nature of attachments than they do in the slower, manual correspondence process. Another factor relates to the complexity of the matter: privacy rules can be numerous, unobvious (legal vs. lay language) and very specific, and thus hard to interpret for the variety of staff handling personal information, as is found in a hospital. To illustrate this point, consider that Ontario's Bill 31 is 116 pages long.

There is a lot of interest in offering such capabilities, but most solutions do not seem to go beyond the lexical level for detecting and matching data against encoded privacy rules. Despite the clear potential, little has been done to employ knowledge-based techniques in developing privacy-aware solutions. For instance, Vericept (vericept.com) detects the presence of social security numbers, credit card numbers, and other specific identifiers in messages, yet it is clear that detection of privacy violations often requires inference. Privacy rules must be connected with the knowledge about the people and the types of information involved. It is this added degree of complexity which has motivated our work.

In this paper we describe the research and development of a compliance engine that would, once installed in an organization, warn employees of the potential privacy breaches their email messages may cause. The idea is to flag the various violations and hold the message until the violations are inspected (and potentially corrected) by a human operator. We give an overview of the various components required for such a system and discuss some of the technical details related to their interaction. The current prototype targets the academic environment, where emails are exchanged between students, professors, and administrators, each having different access rights to private information. The final goal of our work is to port this research to the healthcare environment. We are collaborating with The Ottawa Hospital (TOH) on this application of the research.

2   The Envisioned Engine

As mentioned, the compliance engine described in this paper is conceived for a university setting. In such an organization, different people are allowed access to different pieces of information about other people according to the role they play in the organization. These access rules are not always clearly set which can result in frequent privacy violations. For this reason, languages for the internal privacy practices of enterprises and for technical privacy enforcement must offer possibilities for the fine-grained distinction of users, purposes, data categories, purposes and conditions as well as clear semantics. Our engine offers a solution which is consistent with that of the standard EPAL language [1] that addresses all of the aforementioned elements. For illustration purposes, we show that all the elements of the rules addressed in this engine can be represented with EPAL syntax and can take advantage of the XML representation.

Our system considers some of the rules taken from the University of Guelph Privacy Policy on the release of student information [2]. The subset of rules implemented in our system is presented in Section 2 along with an EPAL representation.

The following is an example of an email that violates a student's (Student B) privacy in the context of the set rules. The email sender (Professor A), the program's advisor who is entitled to know the student's personal information such as his home address and phone number, has cc'ed this information to a professor (Professor C) who will only be teaching the student a course and is not entitled to view such information.

```
From: A@uoguelph.ca
To: B@uoguelph.ca
CC: C@uoguelph.ca
Subject: Please Confirm Correct Information

Dear Student name(nameB),
  This message is to confirm your enrollment in CIS 2520,
  your instructor will be professor name(nameC). Also,
  for our records, could you please confirm your current
  contact information below:

  home_address(address)
  home_phone(phoneNum).

  Thank you kindly,
    program_adviser_name(nameA)
```

Our system blocks A's message to C, but it can be sent to B since B owns the personal information in the message. Furthermore, the system informs A of the fact that his message was not sent to C and indicates which rules of the policy were violated.

Building such a compliance engine presents a number of challenges. First, the language used in the drafting of legal documents is often obtuse and difficult to understand. It needs to be interpreted with a certain amount of skill, and then translated into a logical language appropriate for computer processing. Second, the database has to be organized in a way that allows for efficient access to and processing of data and rules. As well, the database should be modular enough so that new rules as well as new facts can be added and removed easily. Finally, the information extraction engine is difficult to implement given the fact that emails are expressed in free-form text and do not follow the types of schemas usually relied upon in typical information extraction tasks [3]. Though some information such as student and phone numbers will be easy to extract, other information pertaining to the context in which these simpler types of information occur will be extremely difficult to assess.

In the final version of the prototype we will incorporate the lessons learned from earlier work on AI and Legal reasoning [4], as well as Information Extraction [5]. Also, as we include other information types for extraction, the methods described in [6] and [7] will become useful.

3   Our Prototype

3.1   Overall Design

The main objective of the prototype is to develop the building blocks necessary to perform privacy compliance enforcement in email. The first element to consider is how this system, or compliance engine, will interface with its environment. As shown in Fig. 1, for a given enterprise, the system has three elements as inputs: 1) the email, 2) the privacy policy and 3) the database. The only output of the system is whether or not the email conforms to the policy restrictions.

The email is a well-known input type. It is obtained by diverting the flow of emails handled by a mail server. These emails are segmented into the two major parts: header and body. Within each email, the headers of quoted reply chains can be used to establish context and help resolve pronouns.

The privacy policy is the starting point for the compliance engine. The policy can either be expressed in plain English or using IBM's XML-based language EPAL. The benefit to using EPAL is that the privacy policy would be more directly expressed in terms of rules and therefore more easily interpreted. Once the policy has been expressed as a set of rules, the component terms can be extracted from a document and violations detected.

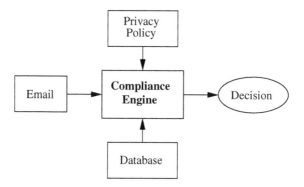

Fig. 1. An overview of the proposed system. The compliance engine is the element of interest

The database is the place where all the domain information is stored. For all types of domains, a database of items such as employees and customers is usually present. For the academic domain, this includes information about professors, students, administrators, courses, etc. This database is used to help in the identification of the entities extracted by the entity extraction module discussed below.

The core of the compliance engine is composed of two major components. The first is the entity extraction module and the second is the privacy verification module. Each will now be discussed in turn.

The entity extraction module is needed to pull the elements required by the privacy verification module from the email. These elements are delivered to the verification module in the form of two lists. The first list is composed of the recipients and sender and the second contains all of the potentially private information in the email.

The privacy verification module uses the entities extracted by the entity extraction module and verifies their consistency with the database. First, the recipients and sender are identified. Once they have been identified, the types of information that each has access to is considered. If there are any elements for which one of the parties involved does not have access, it constitutes a violation of the privacy rules. If a violation is detected then the email is flagged and the compliance engine makes the decision of whether to bounce, copy, divert or drop the email.

3.2 Detailed Description of the Prototype

In this section we describe the design and scope of the prototype outlined in the previous section. The focus is primarily on the privacy verification module because it is in this module where the reasoning (to decide whether an email is in violation of the privacy policy) is performed. The entity extraction module is essentially a tool which enables its operation. At this stage in the development, the extracted elements are relatively simple and will become more interesting as the rules become more abstract. The details of the extraction module are first presented, followed by those of the verification module.

At present, the system is only concerned with protecting the privacy of the elements in the database. As such, the task of the entity extraction module is to identify those items of interest in the source email documents. We are currently working to extend the system to consider the privacy of more abstract concepts. Although it complicates the information extraction module, the process is modular allowing more sophisticated methods to be incorporated as needed. In its current form, the system knows what it is looking for, and the challenge comes from the fact that the elements can present themselves in many different forms. The first task it performs is to take from the email header, the email addresses (and names if available) of the sender and the recipients. Since this module resides on the same level as the mail server it has access to all email header information, including bcc. The next step is to extract the information available from the body of the email. In the academic domain, the types of information found in the body of the email are for example, names, phone numbers, social insurance numbers, student numbers, dates of birth, addresses, etc. In order to extract these elements from the body of the email, we work backwards from the database, identifying different possible formats for each type of entity. This extraction can be performed using finite state automata with high accuracy. In later versions, the data will not necessarily be available in the database and more evolved information extraction techniques will be employed. The final step performed generates a series of queries which are then delivered to the privacy verification module. This module then replies as to whether or not privacy was compromised for the particular email.

The privacy verification module[1] we developed is designed to accommodate the storage and processing of three layers of information. The first layer is the data whose privacy the system is trying to protect against privacy breaches. The data here, are the elements in the university domain described above. The second layer describes the additional knowledge needed to assist in the process of determining whether or not a recipient is granted access to the data in the email. This additional knowledge describes the ownership and the type of data being released in allowing the email to be delivered. The third and final layer describes the rules which restrict access to the data being controlled by the system. These rules define the access levels and recipient privileges for

---

[1] The prototype is implemented in Prolog, specifically in SWI-Prolog version 5.2.6 running on a WindowsXP Professional machine. The database, functions, and rules are implemented as Prolog facts, predicates and rules.

the data in the email based on its ownership and information types. Such access rules are extracted directly from the privacy policy adopted by the university.

In the following sections, we describe the structure of each of the three layers of the database system with an emphasis on the process of developing information access rules based on the privacy policy.

The Data Layer. The database contains several tables and entities that describe each of the following:

1. Personal Details (e.g., ids, names, addresses, etc. of all individuals involved in university activities, such as, students, faculty, and staff)
2. Employee Details (e.g., ids, rank, status etc., for employees of the university)
3. Course Details (e.g., codes and titles of courses offered at the university)
4. Program Details (e.g., program code and department offering the program)
5. Academic Details describes how the different database entities relate to each other. (e.g., what courses a particular student taking or a particular professor teaching)

This database can be implemented to reflect the complete structure of a university; however, our prototype system is designed as a proof of concept consisting of an implementation of the essential parts of the database system. The purpose is to demonstrate the effectiveness of our methods in preserving privacy. Given a comprehensive implementation of the database, the privacy protection methodology described here can be extended to a large scale database information system.

Information Types and Ownership Rules Layer. In order to define information access rules to a data entity D, we must introduce additional knowledge to assist in the decision of whether or not to make D accessible to the user. This additional knowledge must specify the ownership and information type of D.

A data entity D is defined as a primitive Prolog fact or item[2] (a Prolog term listed in the database). For instance, the arguments of the predicate personal_details are each considered as separate data entities. For each data entity we define Prolog rules to determine a type description and an owner identification number. For example, an identification number is a data entity of the type employee_id which identifies the person who owns this personal record. Similarly, the name argument is a data entity of type personal_name owned by the person identified by the identification number and so on for the remaining arguments.

Therefore, in addition to storing the data, the database also stores rules about the type descriptions for each of the data entities and their owners. The privacy policy description directly affects the definitions of the information types and ownership. Laws and regulations govern who owns what type of information. In our case, as mentioned previously, we use the information privacy policy in [2] to extract the following rules to determine data information type and ownership:

1. Identification numbers, personal names, home addresses, etc. are information types owned by the individuals who own the particular personal record.

---

[2] We are working to transfer the data to an SQL database.

2. Employee identification numbers, rank, and status are information types owned by individuals who are listed as being employed by the university.
3. Employee email addresses, office phone numbers, and names are information types owned by the university, which provides public access to the list.
4. Course codes and titles, program codes, degree titles, and departments are information types owned by the university.
5. Student registration information, listed by student names only, is also information owned by the university. This ownership setting allows for anyone to verify whether or not a student is registered at a university.
6. Student email addresses are information types owned by registered students.

Given the above information and ownership types, we can define information access rules to grant users access to the data based on privileges defined by the privacy policy.

Information Access Rules Layer. While they are extracted directly from the privacy policy, access rules must be expressed in a form suitable for representation in the database system. Our database system consists of tables and functions that provide users access to information stored in it. However, we assume that users may not access the general functions of the database directly but rather can only access functions designed to comply with our access rules. Therefore, given the privacy policy in [2], we implemented the following rules to control user access to the database:

1. Students registered in a program at the university are allowed access to public e-mail addresses, phone extensions, and names of employees in the university. In fact, such information is considered public information released by the university.
2. Active employees of the university who are teaching courses in a particular semester can be granted access to the identification numbers, names, and email addresses of only those students enrolled in a course they teach.
3. Student advisers and university staff members are permitted access to any information regarding any student (personal or academic).
4. Any information owned by the university is considered public information and can be released to the public. This rule may not be totally realistic, but given the scope of our prototype system, we felt it was reasonable. This includes any course or program related information, student confirmation of registration, and employee contact information.
5. Any individual has the right to access their own personal or non-personal data.

Please note that the above rules can be easily scripted in EPAL. Following is a translation of the first rule into EPAL. Similarly, all the other rules are represented and are not included in this paper due to space limitations.

```
<rule id = "r1" ruling= "allow">
- <user-category refid = "registered-students"/>
- <data-category refid = "non-personal-email-address"/>
- <data-category refid = "phone-extension"/>
- <data-category refid = "name"/>
- <purpose refid = "any-purpose"/>
- <action refid = "access"/>
```

Privacy Breach Detection in a Document. To complete the picture, the database now contains data entities, their ownership and information types, and rules to restrict their access. These access rules are consistent with the ownership properties as described in the privacy policy. Our system can now apply the following process to an email document in order to identify the existence of a privacy breach. The first two are provided by the entity extraction module and the third is performed by the privacy verification module.

1. Obtain the list IDs = [identification numbers of individuals receiving or sending the email document]
2. Obtain the list D = [data entities of interest appearing in the document]
3. For each tuple (id, d), where id is in IDs and d is in D, check for the existence of a privacy violation by applying all appropriate access rules to the tuple (id, d). If any such rule denies id access to d, then there exists a privacy breach.

Our system reports all privacy violations by indicating the identification of the individual attempting the access and by stating the data, the information type, and the identification of the owner of the data entity D.

A Complete Example. Consider the email example presented in Section 2. The email was sent from A to B and copied to C. The database stores information about A, B, and C. For instance, A is a program adviser at the university and has access to all information regarding the student B. C is a faculty member who teaches a course in which student B is enrolled. C is not permitted to view any personal information for student B. In this case, our system will build the two lists:

1. IDs = [idA, idB, idC] using a mapping between identifiers and email addresses of A, B, and C found in the database.
2. D = [email(A), email(B), email(C), name($nameA$), name($nameB$), name($name$-C), course($cis2520$), address($address$), phone($phoneNum$)] as extracted from the email text.

Then, the system will determine the privileges for each identifier in IDs and whether these privileges enable access to each of the data entities in the list D. Access privileges are determined once the system resolves the information and ownership types for each of the data entities in the list D.

Although, idB is enrolled in a course taught by idC, and idC is granted access to idB and name($nameB$), our information access rules identify two breaches of privacy by idC. He or she is accessing the address($address$) and the phone($phoneNum$) of idB. Therefore, the output for the first violation will be:

```
check_violation(idC,employee_id,phone(phoneNum),
personal_phone_number,idB)
```

where idC is the user's id of type employee_id. He or she is attempting to access phone($phoneNum$) which is of type personal_phone_number and is owned by idB.

Similarly, the output for the second violation is:

```
check_violation(idC,employee_id,address(address),
personal_home_address,idB)
```

where idC is the user's id of type employee_id. He or she is attempting to access address($address$) which is of type personal_home_address and is owned by idB.

4   Experimentation – Semi-automatic Processing

In this section, an evaluation of the system prototype is presented. First we describe the prescribed methodology and then present the results and analysis.

4.1   Experimental Setting

The following steps describe the experimental setup and methodology.

1. Obtain a set of actual email exchanges from one of the authors. This set is composed of 407 emails from the incoming mailbox, with 266 containing at least one of the information types of interest.
2. Extract the potentially private information.
3. Map this information to the non-sensitive elements in our hypothetical database.
4. Automatically generate a set of queries to pose to the system.
5. Report how many of the introduced violations were detected and how many non-violations were detected.
6. Introduce 20 privacy violations to non-violating emails. Craft these insertions such that a range of possible privacy violations are covered. Repeat steps 2-5.

4.2   Experimental Results

Here we present the results and analysis for the methodology described above. In the original 266 emails, 44 violations were detected. Of these, 34 were actual violations and 10 were wrongly identified as violations resulting in an overall precision of 34/44 or 77%. The reason for these 10 errors was due to the extraction process. It had identified a teaching assistant and a mass-mail list as external entities and was declaring, since student information was present, that a violation had occurred. Although these errors could be repaired by adding information to the database, the issue of data consistency was raised. In other words, by relying on the database to identify the entities present, we need to ensure that the database has accurate information. Also of note here is the number and type of violations detected. Although the number of violations was fairly significant ($\sim$13%), they were primarily of one type. The most common explanation for a violation was that a professor was allowed to see the student number of a student he or she was not teaching. This unintentional release of information is considered a breach of student privacy. Given that the task was performed using emails from a single individual, it was logical that we only saw one type of violation repeated several times. This fact led to a recall score of 100%. As more abstract types of privacy violations are introduced to the system this number is expected to fall. For future experiments, we will need to use emails from several people in order to increase the variety and number of violations.

As for the modified set of emails from step 6, all of the introduced violations were detected. For each, the correct reason for the privacy violation was identified. This result was expected as the inserted violations were all in the format expected by both the extraction module and the privacy verification module.

5   Conclusions and Future Work

The purpose of this paper was to present the prototype we constructed for privacy compliance enforcement in email. We described the intended functionality of our software, its overall organization, the details of its implementation and we evaluated its performance on a set of real and modified emails. The system was shown to perform admirably well in the real-world setting for which it was created, obtaining a precision of 77%.

Our experience, thus far, suggests several improvements to our design:

1. The information extraction step can be simplified by considering the rules more closely. Considering the scenarios where proper names should not be disclosed can reduce the need for this more difficult step. In other words, only do name recognition if other information types are present to warrant it.
2. The extraction step can be extended to allow for partial matches to be extrapolated in order for them to match elements in the database. A probabilistic approach is needed to resolve whether or not partial entity A is the same as entity B described in the database.
3. The privacy verification module needs to be less tied to the database. This greater separation will make it easier to augment the system to include items such as student grades. As only final grades would be stored in the database, the detection of these must be done independently of the database. The owner of the grade would also need to be specified "on the fly" so to speak. The system needs to be able to handle this situation and would require more sophisticated text processing techniques.

Although our current system was implemented in a university setting, our ultimate goal is to port the prototype system to a hospital environment. The system would help to protect the privacy of patients (and personnel) from potential disclosure. As email becomes a more and more ubiquitous means of communication, some form of protection against privacy leaks becomes necessary. Imagine for instance an email message specifying the treatment of a patient, sent from one physician to another, and copied to the hospital pharmacy so that specific drugs could be administered as part of the treatment plan. If, inadvertently, an external pharmacy is copied on this message, a potentially serious privacy breach will occur, by releasing patient's name, condition, and treatment to a commercial organization.

Acknowledgements

The authors acknowledge the support of the Natural Sciences and Engineering Council of Canada, the Research Partnership Program of the Communications and Information Technology Ontario, and the cooperation of The Ottawa Hospital.

References

1. Paul, A., Hada, S., Karjoth, G., Powers, C.: Enterprise Privacy Authorization Language v1.2. IBM (2003) http://www.w3.org/Submission/EPAL/.
2. University of Guelph: Departmental Policy on the Release of Student Information. (1996)
3. Ciravegna, F., Dingli, A., Petrelli, D., Wilks, Y.: User-system cooperation in document annotation based on information extraction. In Gomez-Perez, A., Benjamins, V.R., eds.: Proceedings of the 13th International Conference on Knowledge Engineering and Knowledge Management. Lecture Notes in Artificial Intelligence 2473, Springer Verlag (2002)
4. ICAIL-2001: Workshop on AI and Legal Reasoning. (2001) http://www.cs.uu.nl/people/henry/workshop2.html.
5. Hersh, W.R.: Information Retrieval: A Health and Biomedical Perspective. Springer Publishers (2003)
6. Cohen, W., Sarawagi, S.: Exploiting dictionaries in named entity extraction: Combining semi-markov extraction processes and data integration methods. In: KDD 2004. (2004)
7. Borkar, V.R., Deshmukh, K., Sarawagi, S.: Automatic segmentation of text into structured records. In: Proceedings of the ACM SIGMOD Conference. (2001)

Towards an Ontology-Based Spatial Clustering Framework

Xin Wang and Howard J. Hamilton

Department of Computer Science
University of Regina
Regina, SK, Canada S4S 0A2
{wangx, hamilton}@cs.uregina.ca

Abstract. Spatial clustering is an important topic in knowledge discovery research. However, most clustering methods do not consider semantic information during the clustering process. In this paper, we present ONTO_CLUST, a framework for ontology-based spatial clustering. Using the framework, spatial clustering can be conducted with the support of a spatial clustering ontology. As an illustration, the framework is applied to the problem of clustering Canadian population data.

1 Introduction

Spatial clustering is an important topic in knowledge discovery research. It can be used to find natural clusters (e.g., extracting the type of land use from the satellite imagery, merging regions with similar weather patterns), to identify hot spots (e.g., epidemics, crime, traffic accidents), and to partition an area based on utility (e.g., market area assignment by minimizing the distance to customers). In spite of the importance of spatial clustering, most existing clustering algorithms do not use semantic information during the clustering process. Typically, to create clusters, a user creates a flat file corresponding to a set of data objects and runs a clustering algorithm. A flat file is a sequence of lines, with each line containing values for all attributes for one data object, separated by tabs. The user specifies the parameters for the clustering algorithm, such as the number of clusters k for the k-Means method. Then the clustering algorithm partitions the data objects into clusters and outputs the results. Current clustering methods do not separate the semantics of the data from the clustering method. Thus, clustering occurs at the data level instead of the knowledge level, which prevent users from precisely identifying their targets and understanding the clustering results. Although some existing clustering methods consider constraints [1][4][16][17][19][21], they only consider very limited knowledge provided by users. A more sophisticated and systematic framework is needed to support semantics in clustering.

An *ontology* is a formal explicit specification of a shared conceptualization. It provides domain knowledge relevant to the conceptualization and axioms for reasoning with it.

B. Kégl and G. Lapalme (Eds.): AI 2005, LNAI 3501, pp. 205 – 216, 2005.

In this paper, we do not discuss how an ontology can be generated from the web or other resources. We assume that an ontology already exists and has been represented in an ontology language. Based on this assumption, we propose a framework ONTO_CLUST for ontology-based spatial clustering. The framework provides a template for performing spatial clustering using the following steps. First, the spatial clustering ontology is represented in a web ontology language. Secondly, the user's goal is translated into queries that perform reasoning on the ontology. Relevant algorithms and spatial data sets are selected and instantiated from the ontology with respect to the user's goal. Thirdly, the selected clustering algorithm performs clustering based on the results produced from queries. Finally, the results are explained through the ontology.

ONTO_CLUST is a framework to use an ontology to support spatial clustering. The purpose of the framework is to guide a user to an appropriate selection of a clustering algorithm and an appropriate interpretation of the results. At present, the ontology is not used by the selected clustering algorithm. The advantages of the framework are as follows. First, the user's goal is given at the semantic level. The user does not need to know details about the clustering algorithm. Secondly, the framework combines static knowledge (in the form of an ontology) with problem-solving methods (for spatial clustering). Incorporating domain ontologies and task ontologies in spatial clustering algorithms can enhance the quality of clusters produced for clustering tasks. Thirdly, the ontology is represented in OWL, the standard web ontology language, so the whole framework can be extended to find clusters in a variety of semantic web environments.

This paper emphasizes building the spatial clustering ontology and reasoning using the ontology based on the user's goal. The remainder of the paper is organized as follows. In Section 2, we briefly introduce some related work on spatial clustering and ontologies. Section 3 describes the framework for ontology-based spatial clustering. Section 4 describes the application of the framework to the problem of clustering Canadian population data. Conclusions and future work are given in Section 5.

2   Spatial Clustering and Ontologies

In this section, we briefly introduce spatial clustering methods and ontology research.

2.1   Spatial Clustering

In this subsection, we first give a broad categorization of clustering methods. Then we describe constraint-based clustering methods in more detail.

Based on the techniques adopted to define clusters, clustering algorithms have been categorized into four broad categories, hierarchical, partitional, density-based, and grid-based [14].

Hierarchical clustering methods can be either agglomerative or divisive. An *agglomerative method* starts with each point as a separate cluster, and successively performs merging until a stopping criterion is met. A *divisive method* begins with all points in a single cluster and performs splitting until a stopping criterion is met. The result of a hierarchical clustering method is a tree of clusters called a *dendogram*. An example of hierarchical clustering methods is BIRCH [24].

Partitional clustering methods determine a partition of the points into clusters, such that the points in a cluster are more similar to each other than to points in different clusters. They start with some arbitrary initial clusters and iteratively reallocate points to clusters until a stopping criterion is met. They tend to find clusters with hyperspherical shapes. Examples of partitional clustering algorithms include k-means, PAM [12], CLARA [12], CLARANS [13]and EM [22].

Density-based clustering methods try to find clusters based on the density of points in regions. Dense regions that are reachable from each other are merged to form clusters. Density-based clustering methods excel at finding clusters of arbitrary shapes. Examples of density-based clustering methods include DBSCAN [3]and DBRS [19].

Grid-based clustering methods quantize the clustering space into a finite number of cells and then perform the required operations on the quantized space. Cells containing more than a certain number of points are considered to be dense. Contiguous dense cells are connected to form clusters. Examples of grid-based clustering methods include CLIQUE [1] and STING [21].

Spatial clustering aims to group similar objects into the same group based on considering both spatial and non-spatial attributes of the object and a regular clustering algorithm can be modified to account for the special nature of spatial data to give a spatial clustering algorithm [14].

To discover interesting knowledge from huge amounts of data, we should support ad-hoc data mining, by which a user may provide various kinds of constraints to help the data mining tool search for desirable patterns [1]. The constraints for clustering can be classified into four categories [1]: constraints on individual objects, constraints specifying obstacles and facilitators, constraints specifying parameters for clustering algorithms, and constraints imposed on each individual cluster. However, we regard the constraints imposed on the clustering algorithm in terms of parameters as too specific (or too low-level) for appropriate semantics. A more appropriate way for clustering with semantics would take into account high-level semantics, such as user's goal, domain specific concepts, characteristics of data, and available methods.

2.2 Ontologies and the OWL Web Ontology Language

As mentioned, an ontology is an explicit representation of knowledge. It is a formal, explicit specification of shared conceptualizations, representing the concepts and their relations that are relevant for a given domain of discourse [5]. It consists of a representational vocabulary with precise definitions of the meanings of the terms of this vocabulary plus a set of axioms.

Hwang introduced a high-level conceptual framework for combining a formal ontology with spatial clustering [11]. This framework includes a user-interface, metadata, a domain ontology, a task ontology, and an algorithm builder. The usefulness of the framework is shown by two examples, one contrasting two task ontologies at different levels of scale, and the other contrasting two domain ontologies, one with an on-water constraint and the other without. Apparently no formal spatial ontology has been used in specifying the domain ontology.

Several ontology languages have been proposed to represent ontologies. They are based on various underlying paradigms such as description logic, first-order logic, frame-based representations, taxonomies, semantic nets, and thesauruses. OWL (Web Ontology Language) [10] is based on a description logic. It is designed for use by applications that need to process the content of web-based information instead of just presenting the information to humans. OWL facilitates greater machine interpretability of Web content than that supported by XML, RDF, and RDF Schema (RDF-S) by providing additional vocabulary along with a formal semantics [10]. Additionally, OWL is reasonably well supported by existing ontology construction tools. For example, the OWL Plugin [7] is an extension of Protégé-2000 with support for OWL.

3   Ontology-Based Spatial Clustering

The research process can be seen as aspects of three phases: understanding the problem, understanding the data, and performing data processing [15]. Right now, clustering can be regarded as occurring in the third phase, data processing, which purely operates on data. Arguably, the most appropriate clustering algorithm should be selected after taking into account factors such as the user's goal, relevant domain-specific knowledge, characteristics of the data, and available clustering algorithms. However, if queries were posed to the user about those factors in an arbitrary manner, it would be confusing. An ontology can provide a systematic way of organizing these factors such that they can contribute to the selection process and an orderly description of this process to the user.

Based on the above analysis, we propose a framework called ONTO_CLUST for ontology-based clustering, as shown in Figure 1. In ONTO_CLUST, the *spatial clustering ontology* component is used when identifying the clustering problem and the relevant data. Within this component, the *task ontology* specifies the potential methods that may be suitable for meeting the user's goals, and the *domain ontology* includes all classes, instances, and axioms in a spatial domain. A domain ontology could be built by users or domain experts, or derived from some existing ontologies.

With the framework, users first give their goals for clustering. The goals are initially represented in natural language. The goals are translated into the ontology query language (manually at present) and matched with task instances in the task ontology. The goals are also used to search the domain ontology. The results of these queries identify the proper clustering methods and the appropriate datasets. Based on these results, clustering is conducted. The clustering result can be used for statistical analysis or it can be interpreted using the task ontology and the domain ontology. The final result is returned to the user in an understandable format.

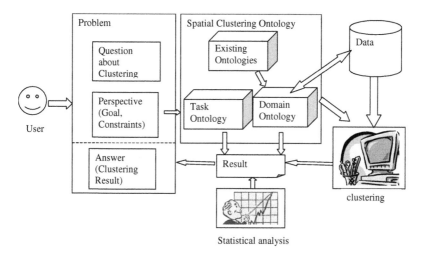

Fig. 1. The ONTO_CLUST framework of ontology-based clustering

Let us first describe our high-level spatial clustering ontology. The spatial clustering ontology includes five main classes:

1) `SpatialClusteringTask` is an abstract class. It is the superclass of all possible spatial clustering tasks that users may perform, including `FindHotSpotsTask` and `PartitionIntoClustersTask`. Each type of clustering task is connected to some classes of clustering algorithms. Based on the purpose of the clustering and the domain, domains, an appropriate clustering algorithm and dataset is selected. For example, two tasks are finding the best locations for shopping malls based on the population density and finding the best locations for shopping malls based on transportation convenience. According to our spatial clustering ontology, the former task should operate on population data with a density-based clustering method, and the latter task should operate on transportation data with a partitioning clustering method.

2) `SpatialThing` is an abstract class. As shown in Figure 2, its subclasses provide the basic classes of spatial-related concepts or entities. In our spatial clustering ontology, the `SpatialThing` class includes three subclasses, `GeometricThing`, `Place`, and `Border`.

Because in spatial clustering, all data are represented as geometric shapes for processing, the `GeometricThing` class includes all the kinds of shapes known to be relevant to spatial clustering. Under `GeometricThing`, two subclasses are included: `AbstractShape` and `Angle`.

Under the class `Place`, we have four subclasses, `ContactLocation`, `GeographicalRegion`, `EcologicalRegion` and `Planet`. Under `GeographicalRegion`, we have the `LandBody` and `BodyofWater` subclasses. `Continent`, `Country`, `Province/State`, and `City` belong to the `LandBody` class. `Sea`, `Gulf`, `Stream`, `Harbor`, and `Lake` are included under `BodyOfWater`.

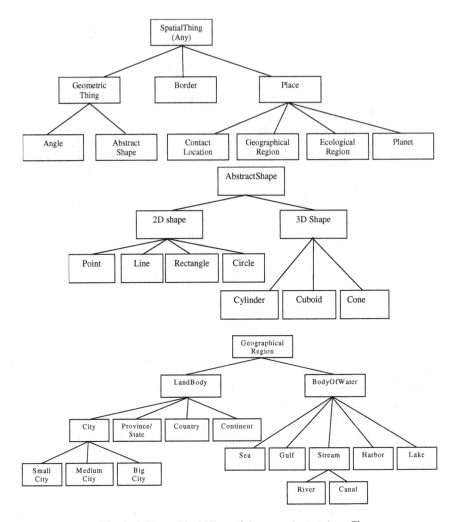

Fig. 2. A Hierarchical View of the SpatialThing Class

3) SpatialRelation represents a spatial relation among SpatialThings. The three kinds of spatial relations are direction relations, distance relations, and topological relations. Some examples of direction relations are north, south, up, down, behind, and front. Some examples of distance relations are far and close-to (near). Some examples of topological relations are contain, overlap, and meet.

4) SpatialData represents the properties of the spatial data that is registered for the web service. Basic properties of the class include the format of the data storage, the subject of the data, and the general location described by the data. Example formats are Access database, text file, and XML. Any datasets used in clustering is an instance of SpatialData.

5) `SpatialClusteringMethod` represents a list of all available clustering methods and their features. The methods are classified as described in Section 2.1. Every method is connected with some spatial clustering tasks. The attributes of the clustering methods, such as the parameters required for the method, and the shape of the clusters generated by the method.

4 Application to Canadian Population Data

In this section, we first describe how we materialized the above high-level spatial ontology to represent knowledge in the application to Canadian population data. Then we describe an example on how to reason on the ontology to facilitate spatial clustering for Canadian population data.

The data used in the application is the Canadian populations of geographic areas from the 1996 Census of Canada. The population and dwelling counts are provided by individual postal codes. The postal codes were transformed to longitude and latitude using GeoPinPoint [8].

Because OWL can formally represent the meaning of the domain terminology and it allows performing useful reasoning tasks on these documents, we used it as the language to represent the ontology. We use the OWL Plugin [7] of Protégé-2000 to construct the spatial clustering ontology.

The current ontology has 51 classes, including the high-level classes mentioned in Section 3 and some low-level classes to help building properties or relationships for high-level classes. For example, `SpatialData` is a high-level class with a property named `DataFormat`, which is used to describe potential formats for the data. Since the formats cannot be represented by any of the standard data types in OWL, we created a low-level class called `DataFormat` in the ontology.

Over one hundred instances exist in the ontology. It includes all Canadian provinces plus major cities, rivers, and lakes. For example, Saskatchewan is an instance of class `Province` and Regina is an instance of class `City`.

Suppose the user's goal is "to find the population clusters/groups of western Canada". Without geographic knowledge of Canada, the traditional clustering algorithm cannot proceed due to the lack of the definition of "western Canada". In the following discussion, we will use this example to explain how the knowledge is represented in the ontology and how the reasoning is being done to help find the proper databases and clustering methods.

Since in the spatial ontology, all provinces and major cities are represented as instances of the `Province` and `City` classes, respectively. Other geographical units, such as western Canada, are also defined. Figure 3 shows the OWL representation for "`Western Canada`", an instance of `GeographicalRegion`, produced by the OWL Plugin in Protégé-2000. It shows that 'Western Canada' is a geographical region inside 'Canada' (which is an instance of `Country`). It includes four provinces: Alberta, British Columbia, Manitoba, and Saskatchewan, each of which is an instance of `Province`.

In OWL, the relations among classes can be defined as properties. In this example, the properties can be classified into two kinds. The first kind of properties concerns pure spatial relations, such as eastOf, farAway, and inside. The "include" relationship in Figure 3 is defined as a property in OWL. The second kind of properties is used to describe the properties or attributes of a class. For example, hasName is used to define the names of instances of each class.

```
<GeographicalRegion rdf:ID="westerncanada">
<hasName>Western Canada</hasName>
<inside>
   <Country rdf:ID="canada">
      <hasName>Canada</hasName>
   </Country>
</inside>
<include>
   <Province rdf:ID="alberta">
      <hasName>Alberta</hasName>
   </Province>
</include>
<include>
   <Province rdf:ID="britishcolumbia">
      <hasName>British Columbia</hasName>
   </Province>
</include>
<include>
   <Province rdf:ID="manitoba">
      <hasName>Manitoba</hasName>
   </Province>
<include>
   <Province rdf:ID="saskatchewan">
      <hasName>Saskatchewan</hasName>
   </Province>
</include>
   </GeographicalRegion>
```

Fig. 3. OWL representation for Western Canada

After building the classes and instances in the spatial clustering ontology, the next question is how to reason about the OWL representation of the ontology. We use the above example ontology to illustrate how an ontology query could be processed. In the ontology, we have an instance of GeographicalRegion called 'Western Canada' as shown above. It includes four province instances: Alberta, British Columbia, Manitoba, and Saskatchewan. Each province instance is inside of Western Canada, as shown in Figure 4. The 'include' and 'inside' relations are defined as inverse properties. For example, as shown in Figure 5, Alberta is an instance of Province class. It is inside Western Canada and east of British Columbia. It is close to Saskatchewan and British Columbia, and it overlaps with the North Saskatchewan River. Two cities, Calgary and Edmonton, are inside the province.

Each instance of the SpatialData class connects to the instance of the GeographicalRegion through the property of 'aboutWhere' and to the instance of spatial format through property of 'format'. Figure 6 shows that a

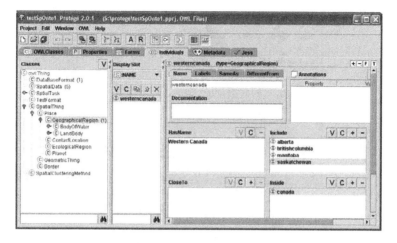

Fig. 4. Western Canada is an instance of GeograhicalRegion

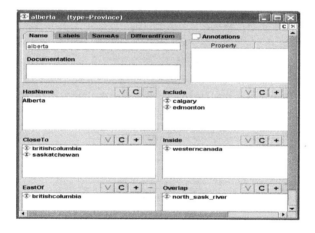

Fig. 5. Alberta is part of Western Canada

dataset called 'abpopdb' is available in Access database format. It contains population data for the province of 'Alberta'.

To reason in Protégé, we use a JessTab plug-in [9], which integrates Protégé with Jess, a fast rule engine and scripting environment. At present, the translation from the user's goal to the Jess query is performed manually. For the user's goal given above, we create a Jess query (or rule) as follows:

```
(defrule query1
  (object(is-a SpatialClusteringMethod)(hasName ?method_name)
         (forGeneralPurpose "Yes"))
  (object (is-a GeographicalRegion) (OBJECT ?gr1)
          (hasName "Western Canada") )
  (object (is-a Province) (OBJECT ?pr) (inside ?gr1))
  (object (is-a SpatialData) (hasName ?name)(
```

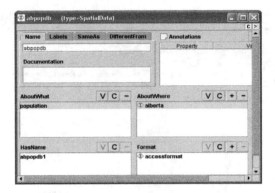

Fig. 6. abpopdb is an instance of SpatialData

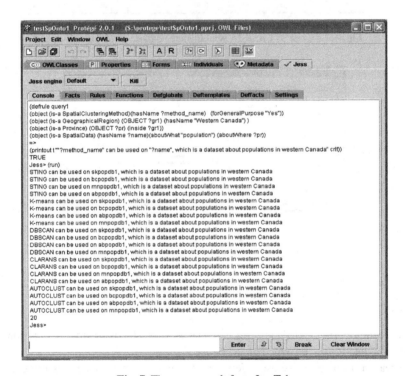

Fig. 7. The query result from JessTab

```
                    aboutWhat "population")(aboutWhere ?pr))
      => (printout t ""?method_name" can be used on "?name", which is a
dataset about populations in western Canada" crlf))
```

The result of running the Jess query is shown in Figure 7. The result indicates that four databases, i.e., abpopdb1, bcpopdb1, mnpopdb1, and skpopdb1, could be used as datasets for the clustering on the populations of western Canada. Five available clustering methods, including STING, K-means, DBSCAN, CLARANS, and AUTOCLUST, can be used to accomplish this general-purpose clustering task. Obtaining this type of result is a simple form of applying reasoning to the ontology. Thus for the task of finding the best locations for shopping malls based on the population density mentioned in Section 3, these are the appropriate datasets and methods.

Figure 8 shows the clustering result when we pick DBSCAN as the clustering method. The resulting clusters are matched with the locations of major cities or geographical area in the ontology, and then we can explain the clustering results. As shown in Figure 8, each cluster is represented by the cities or geographical areas and the number of points in the clustering.

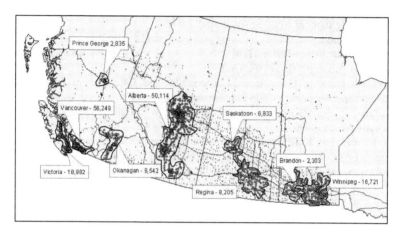

Fig. 8. Result of Clustering Population Counts of Western Canada

5   Conclusion

In this paper, we presented ONTO_CLUST, a framework for ontology-based spatial clustering. In the framework, spatial clustering can be conducted with the support of a spatial clustering ontology. The ontology can play an important role in organizing information related to the process of clustering. We presented an example showing how the framework could guide the choice of suitable data and clustering method for the task of locating shopping malls.

This paper focused on building the spatial clustering ontology and performing some simple reasoning on it. The existing framework needs to be extended with regard to its capabilities and its flexibility. For example, the ontology could be posted on the web. Currently, a GUI and a more sophisticated rule generator are under development.

References

[1] Agrawal, R., Gehrke, J., Gunopulos, D., and Raghavan, P.: Automatic Subspace Clustering of High Dimensional Data for Data Mining Applications, SIGMOD Record, 27(2) (1998) 94-105.

[2] Berners-Lee, T., Hendler, J., and Lassila, O.: The Semantic Web. Scientific American 284(5) (2001) 34-43

[3] Ester, M., Kriegel, H., Sander, J., and Xu, X.: A Density-Based Algorithm for Discovering Clusters in Large Spatial Databases with Noise, Proc. of 2nd KDD, Portland (1996) 226-23

[4] Estivill-Castro, V., and Lee, I. J.: AUTOCLUST+: Automatic Clustering of Point-Data Sets in the Presence of Obstacles. In: Proc. of Intl. Workshop on Temporal, Spatial and Spatio-Temporal Data Mining, Lyon, France (2000) 133-146

[5] Gruber, T. R.: A translation approach to portable ontologies. Knowledge Acquisition, 5(2) (1993) 199-220

[6] http://protege.stanford.edu/index.html

[7] http://protege.stanford.edu/plugins/owl/index.html

[8] http://www.dmtispatial.com/geocoding_software.html

[9] http://www.ida.liu.se/~her/JessTab/

[10] http://www.w3.org/2001/sw/WebOnt/

[11] Hwang, J.: Ontology-Based Spatial Clustering Method: Case Study of Traffic Accidents", Student Paper Sessions, UCGIS Summer Assembly (2003)

[12] Kaufman, L., and Rousseeuw, P.J.: Finding Groups in Data: An Introduction to Cluster Analysis, Wiley (1990)

[13] Ng, R., and Han, J.: Efficient and Effective Clustering Method for Spatial Data Mining, Proc. of Int'l Conf. on Very Large Data Bases, Santiago, Chile (1994) 144-155

[14] Shekhar, S. and Chawla, S.: Spatial Databases: A Tour, Prentice Hall, (2003)

[15] Sund, R.: Utilisation of administrative registers using scientific knowledge discovery. Intelligent Data Analysis, 7(6) (2003) 501-519

[16] Tung, A. K. H., Han, J., Lakshmanan, L. V. S., and Ng, R. T.: Constraint-Based Clustering in Large Databases. In Proc. 2001 Intl. Conf. on Database Theory, London, U.K. (2001) 405-419

[17] Tung, A.K.H., Hou, J., and Han, J.: Spatial Clustering in the Presence of Obstacles. In Proc. 2001 Intl. Conf. On Data Engineering, Heidelberg, Germany (2001) 359-367

[18] Wang, X., Hamilton, H.J.: Clustering Spatial Data in the Presence of Obstacles. In Proc. 2004 FLAIRS, Miami Beach, Florida (2004) 312-317

[19] Wang, X. and Hamilton, H. J.: DBRS: A Density-Based Spatial Clustering Method with Random Sampling. In: Proc. of the 7th PAKDD, Seoul, Korea (2003) 563-575

[20] Wang, X., Rostoker, C., and Hamilton, H. J.: Density-Based Spatial Clustering in the Presence of Obstacles and Facilitators. In Proc. of PKDD 2004, Pisa, Italy (2004) 446-458

[21] Wang, W., Yang, J., and Muntz, R.: STING: A Statistical Information Grid Approach to Spatial Data Mining, Proc. of 23rd VLDB, Athens, Greece, (1997) 186-195

[22] Witten, I.H., and Frank, E.: Data Mining: Practical Machine Learning Tools and Techniques with Java Implementations, Morgan Kaufmann (2000)

[23] Zaïane, O. R., and Lee, C. H.: Clustering Spatial Data When Facing Physical Constraints. In Proc. of the IEEE International Conf. on Data Mining, Maebashi City, Japan (2002) 737-740

[24] Zhang, T., Ramakrishna, R., and Livny, M.: BIRCH: An Efficient Data Clustering Method For Very Large Databases, SIGMOD Record, 25(2) (1996) 103-114

Moving Target Prediction Using Evolutionary Algorithms

Sung Baik[1], Jerzy Bala[2], Ali Hadjarian[3], Peter Pachowicz[3],
and Ran Baik[4]

[1] College of Electronics and Information Engineering,
Sejong University Seoul 143-747, Korea
sbaik@sejong.ac.kr
[2] School of Information Technology and Engineering,
George Mason University Fairfax, VA 22030, U.S.A.
jbala@gmu.edu
[3] Sigma Systems Research, Inc.
Fairfax, VA 22032, U.S.A.
{ahadjarian, ppach}@sigma-sys.com
[4] Department of Computer Engineering,
Honam University Gwangju 506-090, Korea
baik@honam.ac.kr

Abstract. This paper presents an approach for target movement prediction by using Genetic Algorithms to generate the population of movement generation operators. In this approach, we use objective functions, not derivatives or other auxiliary knowledge, and apply probabilistic transition rules, not deterministic rules, for target movement prediction. Its performance has been experimentally evaluated through several experiments.

1 Target Movement Prediction

Target movement prediction can be viewed as the search process for the optimal solution (probable moving target location). There are three basic movement prediction scenarios: 1) *Prediction from source* to search the movement space defined by a specific movement representation, in which movements are encoded and controlled by an objective function (e.g., formulated by a set of geographical constraints), 2) *Prediction from tracking* where the initial movement steps represent a tracked portion of the whole movement, which may be encoded in the movement representation, and 3) *Prediction from tracking with the use of domain knowledge* where the objective function (the search space evaluation function) is partially defined (constrained) by the background knowledge that incorporates motion and/or behavior patterns (acquired and induced from the tracked portion of the movement). These scenarios are depicted graphically in Fig. 1.

Fig. 2 illustrates the main concept behind the search process for prediction from tracking with the use of domain knowledge. The search space is defined by the set of

B. Kégl and G. Lapalme (Eds.): AI 2005, LNAI 3501, pp. 217–221, 2005.
© Springer-Verlag Berlin Heidelberg 2005

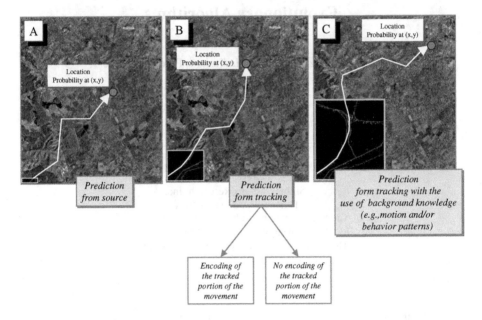

Fig. 1. Three basic movement prediction scenarios

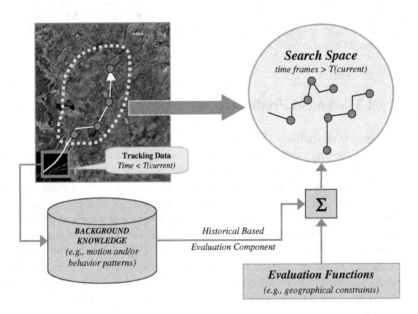

Fig. 2. Movement prediction as the search process

all parameters that describe movement properties (target state, behavior, identity, geographical and tactical constraints, etc). An evaluation measure is used to guide the search process towards optimal solutions. This measure is composed of two parts - the evaluation function and the background knowledge. An important property of most of the search techniques is that they suffer from combinatorial explosion. Various strategies for effective search have emerged from the fields of mathematics and computer science over the years. These range from totally uninformed search methods with no knowledge of the domain being searched to well-informed techniques in which knowledge of the domain is used effectively to speed the search.

2   Genetic Evolution of Movement

For movement prediction as a search process, we use Genetic Algorithms (GAs) [1,2] to generate the population of movement generation operators. GAs use objective functions whereas other search techniques require much auxiliary information in order to work properly. GAs also use random choice as the tool to guide a search towards regions of the search space with likely improvement (i.e., more probable movements) by using probabilistic transition rules. The genetic evolution approach for target movement prediction was described in a previous work [3]. The six steps in genetic evolution approach are 1) movements population seeding, 2) binary encoding, 3) application of genetic operators, 4) binary decoding, 5) evaluation, and 6) recombination. Step 5 evaluates movements in the population according to the evaluation function defined in Step 1. Each movement in the genetic population has to be evaluated according to an evaluation function. Fig. 3 explains the computation of values for this evaluation function.

3   Experimentation

We have experimentally evaluated the genetic evolution of movement according to its ability to converge the population of movements to the most probable movement in the lowest number of genetic cycles. Fig. 3 presents a view of the population of movements in the first cycle, where seven movements are displayed in the population of movements. After some evolutionary runs of the genetic engine, all movements and their corresponding significant points are mostly converged to one movement (Fig. 4). Table 1 summarizes the experimental results obtained by changing evaluation functions(Fig. 5). During experiments, a non-convergence result was observed in Exp. 4 when the evaluation function is formed for a highly multi-modal initial search space. The population of individual movements converged to two separate movements. Such results probably form a highly multi-modal initial search space (defined by the function in Eq. 4). In such case, the search process has to start from a larger set of initial movements (i.e., search from a larger number of points in the initial cycle of GAs). A higher mutation rate can also potentially alleviate this problem. In most cases, however, movement convergence results were observed. For an example, after eleven evolutionary runs of the genetic engine in Exp. 3, all movements and their corresponding significant points are converged to one movement.

Fig. 3. The view of the population of movements in the first cycle

Table 1. Experimental results obtained by changing evaluation functions

Exp	Eval. Function	Convergence	# of Genetic Cycles
1	Eq. 1	A five-step movement converged to a singular movement.	8
2	Eq. 2	A five-step movement converged to a singular movement.	8
3	Eq. 3	A five-step movement converged to a singular movement.	11
4	Eq. 4	F4 scenario did not converge to a five-step movement. It resulted in a two-movement final state.	12

$$A+B((x-2)(x-25)(x-50)(x-75)(x-98)+(y-3)(y-30)(y-60)(y-80)(y-99)) \quad \cdots (1)$$

$$A+B((x-2)(x-25)(x-50)(x-75)+(y-3)(y-30)(y-60)(y-80)) \quad \cdots\cdots (2)$$
(Simplified version of Eq. 1)

$$A+B((x-2)(x-25)(x-50)+(y-3)(y-30)(y-60)) \quad \cdots\cdots\cdots (3)$$
(Simplified version of Eq. 2)

$$A+B((x-2)(x-25)+(y-3)(y-30)) \quad \cdots\cdots\cdots\cdots (4)$$
(Simplified version of Eq. 3)

Fig. 4. The population is converged to a single optimal movement

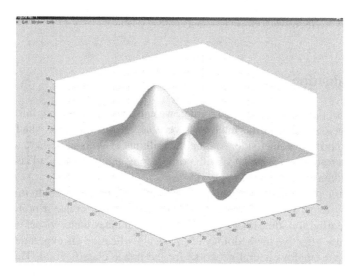

Fig. 5. Example of an evaluation function defined over 100*100 (x, y) coordinates plane

References

1. A. D. Bethke: Genetic algorithms as function optimizers, Ph.D. Thesis, Dept. Computer and Communication Sciences, Univ. of Michigan, 1981
2. A. Brindle: Genetic algorithms for function optimization, Ph.D. Thesis, Computer Science Dept., Univ. of Alberta, 1981
3. S. W. Baik, J. Bala, A. Hadjarian and P. Pachowicz: Genetic Evolution Approach for Target Movement Prediction, Lecture Notes in Computer Science, Vol. 3037, 2004

Multi Class Adult Image Classification
Using Neural Networks[*]

Wonil Kim[1], Han-Ku Lee[2,**], Jinman Park[1], and Kyoungro Yoon[3]

[1] College of Electronics and Information Engineering at Sejong University, Seoul, Korea
{wikim, jmpark}@sejong.ac.kr
[2] School of Internet and Multimedia Engineering at Konkuk University, Seoul, Korea
hlee@konkuk.ac.kr
[3] Dept of Computer Engineering at Konkuk University, Seoul, Korea
yoonk@konkuk.ac.kr

Abstract. As the Internet became popular, the volume of digital multimedia data is exponentially increased in all aspects of our life. This drastic increment in multimedia data causes unwelcome deliveries of adult image contents to the Internet. Consequently, a large number of children are wide-open to these harmful contents. In this paper, we propose an efficient classification system that can categorize the images into multiple classes such as swimming suit, topless, nude, sexual act, and normal. The experiment shows that this system achieved more than 80% of the success rate. Thus, the proposed system can be used as a framework for web contents rating systems.

1 Introduction

With the fast development of the Internet, we can access much more information than any time before. Though the Internet is very useful tool, without which we can not live, it also brings another side. Among the millions of Web sites, there are more than 500,000 web sites that are related with pornography and other X-rated issues that your young children should never see [1, 7].

The main purpose of this paper is to apply MPEG-7 to adult image filtering database systems. By analyzing MPEG-7 descriptors, we create a prototype system that can be used for adult image classification techniques under visual environments, and introduce effective methodology of image classification via experiments.

This paper employs neural networks for the image classification. The input value for the network is one or a combination of values of visual features extracted by MPEG-7 descriptors.

In the next section, we discuss several methods of the image classification. Then, we propose a Neural Network based adult image classification system in section 3. The simulation results are explained in section 4. Section 5 concludes.

---

[*] This paper was supported by the New Faculty Research Fund at Konkuk University in 2004
[**] Author for correspondence: +82-2-2049-6089

B. Kégl and G. Lapalme (Eds.): AI 2005, LNAI 3501, pp. 222–226, 2005.

2 Image Classification

Recently a number of adoptions of the image classification techniques that use statistical methods have been increased since database techniques have been advanced a lot. Especially the field of data mining has been much improved, and a new field of study has appeared; image mining. Thus, many research groups study and research the field of image classification via the image mining technique. The image classification can be categorized as the Neural Network, the Decision-Tree Model, and the Support Vector Machine.

One of the most common methods is the technique using Neural Networks. This method concentrates on study of decision-boundary surface distinguishing adult images from non-adult images via the computer-based classification rule, called perceptron [10, 11]. An Artificial Neural Network (ANN) is an information processing paradigm that is inspired by biological nervous systems, such as the brain process information. It is composed of a large number of highly interconnected processing elements (neurons) working in unison to solve specific problems.

The decision tree model recursively partitions an image data space, using variables that can divide image data to most identical numbers among a number of given variables. This technique can give incredible results when characteristics and features of image data are known in advance [9].

The support vector machine technique is a brand-new image classification method. The purpose of the method is to find decision lines or surfaces distinguishing data from others like the technique using neural networks. The technique using the neural networks is just to find decision surfaces classifying the training data. But, SVM is to find decision surfaces maximizing the distance of two sets. Jiao et al. experimented on adult image classifiers using SVM [5].

The nearest neighbor method is one of the simplest and the most effective methods. It selects an odd number of images similar to the source image. The class where most of the selected images are included is decided for the class of the source image. This method is similar to the technique used in [6].

In addition to classification techniques mentioned above, there could exist many other techniques adding heuristics [2, 3, 4]. Using hybrid methods by mixing many classification techniques might be much more effective than applying only one specific method [8]. The objective of this paper is to create a new, effective, and better algorithm for the multi class adult image classification using MPEG-7 descriptors. The standard MPEG-7 descriptors extract image features from a given image and use them as input values for the proposed neural network. We obtain over 80% of the successful classification rate for the adult image classification by combining values of the standard feature from MPEG-7 and employing the neural network approach. The detail of the proposed system is discussed in the next section.

3   The Proposed Adult Image Classification System

The proposed system consists of two modules; the Feature Extraction Module and the Neural Network Classifier Module. Features of a given image are extracted using MEPG-7 descriptors, and then used as inputs for the classifier module. The neural network classifier module can categorize a given images into one of the 5 classes such as swim suit images (aa), topless images (ab), nude images (ca), sex images (cb), and normal images (d).

Features of training images are extracted in XML format by executing the MPEG-7 XM program. This feature information in XML is parsed in the next step and is normalized into values between 0 and 1 with respect to values generated by each descriptor. These normalized values are used as inputs for the neural network classifier. After the process of extracting input data used in the neural network by MPEG-7 XM, each image is grouped as one of 5 classes.

The neural network classifier learns the relation of the feature values and the corresponding class by modifying the weight values between nodes. We use the backpropagation algorithm to train the network. The classifier consists of input layer, output layer, and multiple hidden layers. The number of input nodes depends on the dimension of each descriptor, whereas the number of output nodes is five. The class information of each class is (1,0,0,0,0) for swim suit images, (0,1,0,0,0) for topless images, (0,0,1,0,0) for nude images, (0,0,0,1,0) for sex images, and (0,0,0,0,1) for normal images. In the testing process, as in the training process, the system extracts features from query images using MPEG-7 descriptors, and classifies query images using the neural network that generated by the training process.

4   Simulation and Result

In the simulation, we use MPEG-7 reference software: the eXperimentation Model for feature extraction. The eXperimentation Model (XM) software is the simulation platform for the MPEG-7 Descriptors (Ds), Description Schemes (DSs), Coding Schemes (CSs), and Description Definition Language (DDL). Besides the normative components, the simulation platform needs some non-normative components, essentially to execute some procedural code to be executed on the data structures. The data structures and the procedural code together form the applications [12].

4.1   Environments

The simulation uses a total of 8510 images (1702 images for each class), and the experiment uses 5 descriptors; Color Layout (12), Color structure (256), Edge Histogram (80), Homogenous Texture (30), and Region Shape (35), where values in the parentheses indicate the input dimension. The inputs consist of MPEG-7 normalized descriptor values. The output layer consists of 5 nodes. The detailed class information is mentioned in the previous section. Also the combinations of descriptors, such as Color Layout and Homogeneous Texture (12+30), and Region Shape and Color Layout (35+12), are used for the image features. The classification module consists of 2 hidden layers, each with 50 nodes. The learning rate is 0.001 and the network is trained 100,000 iterations.

4.2 Results

Table 1 shows the test results of the proposed classifier with 1700 images that are not used in the training process. The Color Layout descriptor performs the best classification task, followed by the Homogeneous Texture and the Region Shape. Unlike classic adult image classification methods, which heavily depend on skin color, the proposed system has to learn not only the dominant skin color, but also

Table 1. Test Results of Neural Network (%)

descriptors		aa	ab	ca	cb	d	Total
Color Layout	aa	**69.71**	5.00	7.35	10.29	7.65	Total = 1700 Correct= 1330 Error = 370 Per(%)= 78.235
	ab	6.76	**68.24**	4.12	12.06	8.82	
	ca	3.24	2.65	**76.76**	9.71	7.65	
	cb	1.76	1.18	5.00	**87.06**	5.00	
	d	1.47	2.06	1.47	5.59	**89.41**	
Color Structure	aa	**41.18**	13.24	9.12	20.00	16.47	Total = 1700 Correct= 971 Error = 729 Per(%)= 57.118
	ab	20.00	**36.47**	12.35	13.24	17.94	
	ca	4.71	15.59	**67.94**	5.29	6.47	
	cb	12.94	11.18	6.76	**56.18**	12.94	
	d	2.65	2.65	1.47	9.41	**83.82**	
Edge Histogram	aa	**45.29**	18.82	14.12	12.65	9.12	Total = 1700 Correct= 981 Error = 719 Per(%)= 57.706
	ab	11.47	**45.29**	19.41	12.06	11.76	
	ca	7.35	15.59	**53.82**	12.06	11.18	
	cb	6.18	8.82	12.06	**61.18**	11.76	
	d	1.18	3.24	4.71	7.94	**82.94**	
Homogeneous Texture	aa	**67.94**	4.12	1.76	10.59	15.59	Total = 1700 Correct= 1204 Error = 496 Per(%)= 70.824
	ab	5.29	**63.24**	3.82	9.41	18.24	
	ca	0.29	2.65	**74.71**	7.06	15.29	
	cb	2.65	5.88	7.35	**72.94**	11.18	
	d	1.18	3.24	5.29	15.00	**75.29**	
Region Shape	aa	**68.24**	1.76	4.71	8.53	16.76	Total = 1700 Correct= 1197 Error = 503 Per(%)= 70.412
	ab	2.94	**69.71**	4.12	7.06	16.18	
	ca	0.59	1.76	**73.53**	6.76	17.35	
	cb	2.94	4.71	5.00	**68.53**	18.82	
	d	1.18	1.47	6.76	18.53	**72.06**	
Region Shape + Color Layout	aa	**79.41**	2.35	3.53	9.71	5.00	Total = 1700 Correct = 1367 Error = 333 Per(%)= 80.412
	ab	2.35	**72.06**	5.29	12.06	8.24	
	ca	3.24	3.24	**75.59**	10.00	7.94	
	cb	0.88	2.94	6.76	**85.00**	4.41	
	d	0.59	0.88	2.06	6.47	**90.00**	
Homogeneous Texture + Color Layout	aa	**74.71**	2.65	4.41	9.71	8.53	Total = 1700 Correct= 1404 Error= 296 Per(%)= 82.588
	ab	2.35	**80.00**	3.82	6.76	7.06	
	ca	1.76	3.82	**78.53**	6.76	9.12	
	cb	1.18	3.82	2.94	**87.65**	4.41	
	d	0.59	1.76	2.35	3.24	**92.06**	

other factors, such as texture and shape in the combination of descriptors. In order to investigate this factor, we test the performance of combined descriptors. The result of the combination of the Homogeneous Texture and the Color Layout is better than the combination of the Region Shape and the Color Layout.

5 Conclusion

This paper proposes an adult image classification system using neural networks. The selected MPEG-7 descriptors are used as inputs of the network. It classifies the images into multiple classes (5 classes) and the simulation shows that the system achieved 80% of the true positive rate for the hard tasks. When combined descriptors are used, the performance improves since, in case of multi classes, the effective feature values are different. The Color layout may be the best feature for adult-normal images whereas the Homogeneous Texture descriptor is more suitable for swim suit – topless image classification. The proposed system shows that the standard MPEG-7 descriptors can be used for well defined features and the framework can be effectively used as the kernel of web contents rating system.

References

1. Will Archer Arentz and Bjorn Olstad, "Classifying offensive sites based on image contents", Computer Vision and Image Understanding, Vol 94, pp293-310, 2004
2. Margaret Fleck, David Forsyth, and Chris Bregler. "Finding Naked People", 1996 European Conference on Computer Vision, Vol. II, pp592-602, 1996
3. Michael J. Jones and James M. Rehg, "Statistical color models with application to skin detection", Technical Report Series, Cambridge Research Laboratory, December 1998
4. Yuna Jung, E. Hwang, Wonil Kim, "Sports Image Classifier based on Bayesian Classification", Lecture Note in Artificial Intelligence 3040, 546-555, Springer, June 2004
5. Feng Jiao, Wen Giao, Lijuan Duan, and Guoqin Cui, "Detecting adult image using multiple features", IEEE conference, Nov. 2001, pp.378 - 383 vol.3.
6. Sung-joon Yoo, "Intelligent multimedia information retrieval for identifying and rating adult images", Lecture Note in Computer Science 3213, 165-170, Springer, June 2004
7. Mohamed Hammami, Youssef Chahir, and Liming Chen, "WebGuard: Web based adult content detection and filtering system", Proc. IEEE/WIC International Conference on Web Intelligence, pp 574-578, 2003
8. David Forsyth and Margaret Fleck, "Identifying nude pictures", IEEE Workshop on the Applications of Computer Vision 1996, pp103-108, 1996
9. David Hand, Heikki Mannila, and Padhraic Smyth, "Principles of Data Mining", MIT Press, pp343-347, 2001
10. F. Rosenblatt, "The Perceptron: A probabilistic model for information storage and organization in brain", Psychology Review 65, pp386-408
11. D.E. Rumelhart, G.E. Hinton, and R.J. Williams. "Learning representations by back-propagating errors", Nature (London), Vol. 323, pp533-536
12. http://www.chiariglione.org/mpeg/standards/mpeg-7/mpeg-7.htm

Probability and Equality: A Probabilistic Model of Identity Uncertainty

Rita Sharma and David Poole

Department of Computer Science, University of British Columbia,
Vancouver, BC V6T 1Z4, Canada
kegl@iro.umontreal.ca, poole@cs.ubc.ca

Abstract. Identity uncertainty is the task of deciding whether two descriptions correspond to the same object. In this paper we discuss the identity uncertainty problem in the context of the person identity uncertainty problem – the problem of deciding whether two descriptions refer to the same person. We model the inter-dependence of the attributes using a similarity network representation. We present results that show that our method outperforms the traditional approach for person identity uncertainty which considers the attributes as independent of each other.

1 Introduction

Identity uncertainty has been studied independently under various names by different user communities. Within the statistics community, this problem has been studied as record linkage [2]. The Fellegi-Sunter method [2] is the standard probabilistic method for solving this problem. In computer science literature the same problem has been studied under various names, duplicate detection [5], merge/purge problem [4], identity uncertainty [6], or unsupervised classification [7]. With the exception of [7], in all of the above approaches, an independence assumption is made: i.e., matching of one attribute doesn't depend on other attributes. However, this assumption is often faulty. For example, people living in the same household have the same address, phone number and often the same last name. In this situation, the independence assumption can cause a "false positive match". As an another example, when a person moves to a different city, his address, phone number, and postal code all change together. In this situation, the independence assumption can cause a "false negative match". In this paper we discuss the identity uncertainty problem in the context of person identity uncertainty. We model the dependence/independence between attributes using a similarity network representation [3]. To deal with data entry errors, we use different error models. To test the proposed approach, as real databases are confidential, we model a reasonably realistic distribution of attribute values by modelling the people in a set of households.

2 Probabilistic Modelling of Person Identity Uncertainty

X and Y are two records, which refer to the people to be compared and $Desc_X$ and $Desc_Y$ denote their corresponding descriptions. There are two hypotheses for records

B. Kégl and G. Lapalme (Eds.): AI 2005, LNAI 3501, pp. 227–231, 2005.

X and Y given their descriptions: X and Y refer to the same person ($X = Y$), or X and Y refer to different persons ($X \neq Y$). The odds, $Odds$, for hypotheses

$$Odds = \frac{P(X = Y)}{P(X \neq Y)} \times \frac{P(Desc_X \wedge Desc_Y | X = Y)}{P(Desc_X \wedge Desc_Y | X \neq Y)}$$

The ratio $\frac{P(Desc_X \wedge Desc_Y | X = Y)}{P(Desc_X \wedge Desc_Y | X \neq Y)}$ is a likelihood ratio (LR). The decision can be made using decision theory [1], given LR and the cost of false positive and negative matches.

To identify a person we consider the following seven attributes: *Social insurance number (SIN), first name (Fname), last name (Lname), date of birth (DOB), gender (Gen), phone number (PH),* and *postal code (PC).* We model the inter-dependence between the attributes using a similarity network representation [3].

2.1   The Model of Attribute Dependence for Hypothesis $X \neq Y$

The statistical dependence among the attributes that we assume is shown in Fig. 1 (a). Propositions *twins, relative, samehousehold,* and *samelastname* represent that X and Y are twins, relatives, living in the same household, or have the same last name. Attribute SIN doesn't depend on the other attributes. However, we cannot assume that the SIN of two different people is independent. Knowing a different person's SIN changes our belief in X's SIN, because, we expect that they shouldn't be the same; see [9] for details.

2.2   The Model of Attribute Dependence for Hypothesis $X = Y$

If records X and Y refer to the same person, we expect that the attributes values should be the same for both X and Y. However, there may be differences because of errors, for example: typing errors, nick names, and so on. We model the dependence among attributes using their actual values, the sloppiness of the data entry person (*SloppyX, SloppyY*), and the possibility of movement (*move*). The dependence between attributes is shown in Fig. 1 (b). The proposition *Afname* represents the actual first name. The proposition *EFx* represents the error in first name for record X. To make this paper more readable, we consider only the following errors[1] (values of *EFx*): *copy error (ce)*, an error where a person copies a correct name, but from the wrong row of a table, *single digit/letter error (sde)*, and the lack of any errors (*noerr*). The random variables $Fname_x$, $Fname_y$, and $Afname$ have, as domains, all possible first names. We assume that we have a procedural way for generating the prior probabilities of the variables that have very large domains (even unbounded); see [9] for details. For the probability $P(Afname|Sex)$, we use name lists available from the U.S. Census Bureau[2]. The conditional probability $P(Fname_x | Afname \wedge Sex \wedge EFx)$ cannot be represented in a tabular form because the domains of $Afname$ and $Fname_x$ are very large. To reason in an efficient manner we need a compact representation for the large CPTs.

---

[1] Although, we consider many more errors in the experiment.

[2] http://www.census.gov/genealogy/names/

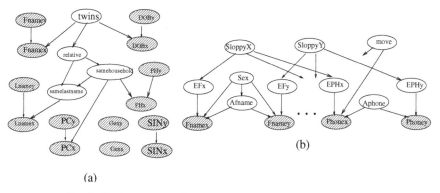

(a)

(b)

Fig. 1. Similarity network representation of attribute dependency

3   Representation of Large CPTs

We can represent the large CPTs in a compact form using both *intensional* and *extensional* representation. For example, the CPT $P(Fnamex|Afname \wedge Sex \wedge EFx)$ can be represented in a decision tree form by conditioning on the values of EFx as shown in Fig. 2. The predicate *equal* tests whether variables $Fnamex$ and $Afname$ have the

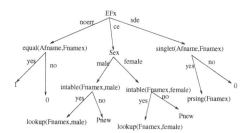

Fig. 2. A Decision Tree Representation of the CPT $P(Fnamex|Afname \wedge Sex \wedge EFx)$

same value or not, predicate *singlet* tests whether the values for variables $Fnamex$ and $Afname$ are a single letter apart or not, and predicate *intable* tests whether the value of $Fnamex$ exist is in the male (or female) name file or not. The function *prsing* is used to compute the probability when the data entry person makes the "single digit error" (sde). For example, if $EFx = sde$, $Fnamex = dave$ then $prsing(dave) = \frac{1}{100}$. The function $lookup(Fnamex, male)$ computes the probability of $Fnamex$ by looking in the male name file. We assume here that we have the procedures that can compute these predicates and functions in an efficient manner.

4   Inference

To compute the likelihood ratio we need to condition on the observations and marginalize over the unobserved variables in the Bayesian networks shown in Fig. 1. We can marginalize over the unobserved variables for Bayesian network shown in Fig. 1(a) using the Variable Elimination (VE) algorithm. We get the likelihood of the observed data given the hypothesis $X \neq Y$. The marginalization for the network shown in Fig. 1 (b) is complicated. The standard inference algorithms do not allow the intensional representation. To overcome this, we use the *Large Domain VE* algorithm [8] that allows us to make inference with intensional representation. The main challenges of applying the *Large Domain VE* algorithm to the "person identity uncertainty" problem are in the computation of *intensional functions* and predicates that arise in this problem. Due to space constraints, we omitted these details from this short paper; for details see the full version of the paper [9].

5   Experimental Evaluation

To test our approach for the person identity uncertainty (as real databases are confidential), we model a a small town of 1500 households. Persons living in the same household have the same address and phone number. The probability that a *single person* lives in a house is 0.4. The probability that a person is living with a *partner* is 0.6. For a *single person* there is a 30% chance of having one child[3]. The chances for a subsequent child is 10%. The probability that partners have the same last name is 0.5. For partners there is a 70% chance of having one child. The chances for a subsequent child is 30%. When both partners have different last names then the probability that the child will have any of the parent's last name is the same. Each record of the population contains seven fields as mentioned in Section 2. Personal first names and last names are chosen according to the distribution from U.S. census file[4].

After creating the true population, we made two datasets, D_A and D_B. To create D_A we randomly took 600 records from the true population and corrupt them using the database generator of Hernandez and Stolfo [4] using typographical errors and movement into the true record. We place these corrupted records in dataset D_A. Similarly, we made D_B but we took 1500 records from the true population. We compared each record of D_A with each record of D_B. In these comparisons there were 227 duplicate cases. We compute the likelihood ratio considering both attribute dependence and independence. After computing the likelihood ratio between all pairs of records, we set the deciding threshold equal to the maximum of maximum likelihood ratio from both cases. The pair of records with likelihood ratio greater than the deciding threshold were taken as duplicates. We compute the precision and recall. We reduce the deciding threshold with a step of 1 until the deciding threshold is equal to the minimum likelihood ratio from both cases. For each value of threshold we compute the precision and recall for both cases. Figure 3 shows the precision versus recall for both cases. The recall/precision curve shows that with attribute dependence the precision of the prediction is 95% with 100% recall, while with attribute independence precision is 70% for 100% recall. Also, with attribute dependence 100% accuracy is achieved with more coverage than attribute independence.

---

[3] For each birth there is a 3% chance that twins will be born.

[4] http://www.census.gov/genealogy/names/

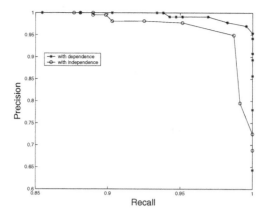

Fig. 3. Recall versus precision for both attribute dependence and attribute independence

6   Conclusion

We have presented a framework for reasoning about identity uncertainty in the context of "person identity uncertainty". The probabilistic modelling of identity uncertainty is difficult, since the domain of some of the variables is very large (even unbounded). For efficient inference in the Bayesian network we represent the big CPTs using the *intensional* and *extensional* representation. As Figure 3 shows, the proposed approach considering attribute dependence achieved a high level of accuracy over the standard approach considering the attribute independence.

References

1. R.O. Duda, P.E. Hart, and D.G. Stork. *Pattern Classification*. Wiley-Interscience Publication, John Willey and Sons Inc, second edition, 2000.
2. I.P. Fellegi and A.B. Sunter. A theory for record linkage. In *Journal of the American Statistical Association*, pages 1183–1210, 1969.
3. David Heckerman. *Probabilistic Similarity Networks*, 1990. Ph.D. thesis, Stanford University.
4. M.A. Hernandez and S.J. Stolfo. The merge/purge problem for large databases. In *Proceedings of the SIGMOD Conference, San Jose*, pages 127–138, 1995.
5. A. E. Monge and C. Elkan. An efficient domain-independent algorithm for detecting approximately duplicate database records. In *Research Issues on Data Mining and Knowledge Discovery*, 1997.
6. H. Pasula, B. Marthi, B. Milch, S. Russell, and I. Shpitser. Identity uncertainty and citation matching. In *Proceedings of the Neural Information Processing Systems (NIPS-02)*, 2002.
7. P. Ravikumar and W. Cohen. A hierarchical graphical model for record linkage. In *Proceeding of Twentieth Conf. on Uncertainity in Artificial Intelligence (UAI-04)*, 2004.
8. R. Sharma and D. Poole. Efficient inference in large discrete domains. In *Proceeding of Nineteenth Conf. on Uncertainity in Artificial Intelligence (UAI-03)*, 2003.
9. R. Sharma and D. Poole. *Probability and Equality: A Probabilistic Model of Identity Uncertainty*, February 2005. Technical Report TR-2005-02, Department of Computer Science, University of British Columbia.

A Logic of Inductive Implication or Artificial Intelligence Meets Philosophy of Science II[1]

Ricardo S. Silvestre[1] and Tarcísio H.C. Pequeno[2]

[1] Department of Philosophy, University of Montreal,
2910 Édouard-Montpetit, Montréal, QC, H3T 1J7, Canada
ricardo.silvestre@umontreal.ca
[2] Department of Computer Science, Federal University of Ceará,
Bloco 910, Campus do Pici, Fortaleza-Ceará, 60455-760, Brazil
thcp@ufc.br

Abstract. The general purpose of this paper is to demonstrate through a well defined example how philosophy of science and Artificial Intelligence (AI) can benefit from each other by sharing some of their ideas, methods and techniques developed to tackle similar problems. The problem we will focus is the expression of non-deductive inferences, which is performed in AI by the use of non-monotonic logics, and in philosophy of science by the attempt of constructing inductive logics. After analyzing to what extent one of the most wide spread nonmonotonic formalisms – default logic – can be taken as a logic of induction in the philosophical sense, and carefully considering the similarities and dissimilarities of the problems faced in these contexts, an expanded version of default logic, called by us a logic of logic of inductive implication, is introduced. It is then shown how this new framework can be used to represent different types of inductive calculi that may be of relevance to AI.

1 Introduction

In the introduction of a somewhat philosophical book of essays on Artificial Intelligence [4], the editors spouse the thesis that in the field of AI "traditional philosophical questions have received sharper formulations and surprising answers", adding that "… important problems that the philosophical tradition overlooked have been raised and solved [in AI]". They go as far as claiming that "Were they reborn into a modern university, Plato and Aristotle and Leibniz would most suitably take up appointments in the department of computer science." Even recognizing a certain amount of over enthusiasm and exaggeration in those affirmations, the fact is that there are evident similarities between some problems faced in AI practice and some classic ones dealt with within philosophical investigation. However, although there is some explicit contact between AI and philosophy in fields like philosophy of mind and philosophy of language, the effective contribution of ideas, methods and techniques from AI to

---

[1] This work is partially supported by CNPq trough the LOCIA (Logic, Science and Artificial Intelligence) Project.

B. Kégl and G. Lapalme (Eds.): AI 2005, LNAI 3501, pp. 232–243, 2005.
© Springer-Verlag Berlin Heidelberg 2005

philosophy is still something hard to be seen. In this paper we continue a project started in some previous works [14], [15] and present what we believe to be a bridge between these two knowledge fields that, in addition to its own interest, can also serve as an example and an illustration of a whole lot of connections we hope to come over in the near future.

In order to make that bridge concrete, let us start with the not so deep observation that the study of non-deductive inferences has played a fundamental role in both artificial intelligence and philosophy of science. While in the former it has given rise to the development of *nonmonotonic logics* [8], [10], [12], in the later it has attracted philosophers in the pursuit of a so-called *logic of induction* [3], [6]. Perhaps in virtue of the technical devices used in these two areas were *prima facie* quite different, the obvious fact that both AI researchers and philosophers were dealing with the same, or almost the same problem has remained virtually unnoticed. Of course, realizing this obvious connection is important because, at least in principle, computer scientists and philosophers can benefit from the results achieved by each other.

It is our purpose here to lay down what we believe to be an instance of (the fruitfulness of) such cooperation. From one hand, we pick one of the most wide spread nonmonotonic logics – default logic [12] – and try to find out to what extent it can be considered as a logic of induction in the philosophical sense as well as which sort of adjustments should we make to transform it into such a logic. This will be done in Sections 2 and 3. In Section 4 we make use of the conclusions laid down in the previous sections to introduce a modified version of default logic which, we believe, has interesting properties from the standpoint of AI. In Sections 5 and 6 we try to justify this last claim by showing why our logic might be relevant to AI research. Finally in Section 7 we present some conclusive remarks.

2 The Logic of Induction and Default Logic

Since the time of Rudolf Carnap [3], induction has been conceived (even though not uncontroversially) as *the class of rational non truth-preserving inferences*, being the task of inductive logic to represent such sort of inferences. The conception of non truth-preserving inference is straightforward, it means an inference whose conclusion may be false even when its premises are true. This contrasts with the second key term in the definition, "rational," which philosophers have shown to be a quite problematic term both in its characterization and in its operationality.

Considering single defaults as inferences rules, it is clear that default logic satisfies the negative, non truth-preservingness feature of induction: conclusion β of default $\alpha:\varphi/\beta$ may be false even in the case where its premise α is true. But how about the hard part in the concept of induction, its rationality? According to Carnap [3] and Carl Hempel [6], for example, the purpose of the logic of induction is basically one of confirmation, i.e., given a piece of evidence e and a hypothesis h, it should say whether (and possibility to what extent) e confirms or gives evidential support to h. In this way, the distinction between inductive inferences and fallacies will be achieved automatically: despite being non truth-preserving inferences, fallacies do not exhibit any sort of premises-conclusion confirmation relation.

Now, there is a strong parallel between default rules and the qualitative form of these confirmatory sentences. Since α: φ / β allows us to infer β only provisionally, we can say it means something like "α might be taken as an evidence for the hypothesis that β is the case with the proviso that $\neg \varphi$ is not the case." Taking a well-known example, the fact that Twenty is a bird confirms or gives evidential or inductive support to the hypothesis that it flies unless we know that it does not fly. In this way, we can read α: φ / β as "α confirms or inductively supports β, with the proviso that $\neg \varphi$ is not the case," or, equivalently, "α inductively supports β unless $\neg \varphi$."

From this perspective, it is clear why the positive side of inductive inferences is not taken into account by default logic. While a logic of induction is supposed to function as a black box having as input several pair of sentences *e-h* and as output a smaller number of sentences of the form "*e* inductively supports *h*," default logic deals only with the output of such box, functioning as a tool for representing such confirmatory sentences and detaching their hypotheses from the evidences. As a consequence of that, it is aloof from the problem of positively characterizing inductive inferences: such task is left to the knowledge engineer, who can use default logic to formalize rational non truth-preserving inferences but also any sort of nonsense. In order to really deal with both input and output, we would need to have a sort of meta-default logic able to automatically "generate" defaults from defaults or from something else than defaults as well as to reason about them. In other words, we would have to have a sort of calculus of defaults.

Now, how about if we had such calculus of defaults? What sort of new resources we would need to have in addition to the ones provided by default logic? And, which is more important, what kind of advantages this logic would give to us? Before answering these questions, let us take a look at another feature of the philosophical project of building a logic of induction which happens to be of fundamental importance for our comparative study.

3 Plausibility and Paraconsistency

If we have that evidence *e* confirms or supports hypothesis *h*, it is natural to wonder what we can conclude about *h* when *e* is true. Despite the diversity of approaches, all theorists agree on one basic point: given that *e* confirms *h* and that *e* is true, whatever we conclude about *h*, it should reflect the uncertainty inherent to inductive inferences. Almost invariably some *probability* notion has been chosen to do this job: even though from "e confirms h" and "e is true" we cannot conclude that *h* is true, we can conclude that it is probable. This notion of probability can be seen as an epistemic label we attach to inductive conclusions in order to make explicit their defeasible character. Carnap calls it pragmatical probability; we will use the less problematic term "*plausibility*."

It is important to note that characterizing inductive inferences in terms of pragmatical probability or plausibility implies changing our previous understanding of confirmation statements. Considering that the truth of evidence *e* warrants us to inductively conclude the plausibility of hypothesis *h* instead of its truth, what *e* confirms or evidentially supports is not the truth of *h*, but its plausibility. Therefore, rather than saying that *e* confirms or inductively supports *h*, we should say that *e* confirms or inductively supports the *plausibility* of *h*. And given that "*h* is plausible" will be possibly inferred, the whole thing might be read as "*e* inductively implies the plausibility of *h*." We call such statements *inductive implications*.

Turning back to AI, it is pretty clear that default logic embodies the mentioned detachment mechanism. After all, its whole purpose is exactly to find out which consequents of defaults can be concluded. So therefore reading $\alpha{:}\varphi/\beta$ as "α inductively implies β unless $\neg\varphi$" as well seems quite suitable. But here we arrive at a breakdown in our reading of defaults in terms of confirmation theory. Since original default logic provides no means to distinguish nonmonotonically obtained conclusions from deductively obtained ones, there is no way to represent "β is plausible" and consequently no way to represent the statement "α inductively implies 'β is plausible' unless $\neg\varphi$."

One might be wondering whether there is some harm in that. Well, it does harm from a philosophical point of view, by not representing the epistemological state of matters properly and consequently promoting the confusion between well-established conclusions and defeasible ones. From the point of view of formal reasoning, this lack of terminological precision does also have some problematic consequences, which will be centered around the question of whether or not nonmonotonic conclusions should be treated in further reasoning upon them in the same way as monotonic ones. At this point, precisely, our view departs from traditional nonmonotonic formulations [2], [10], even when we concern ourselves with just AI applications.

As it is well known, one of the most serious problems of default logic, and of most of nonmonotonic formalisms, is the so-called problem of *anomalous extensions*, which is due to the arising of contradictions among extensions (we could even say that the existence of several extensions is itself already a problem). According to some theorists, this phenomenon of appearance of inconsistencies is not simply an unfortunate feature of the available formalisms, but in fact an inevitable and essential characteristic of commonsense reasoning [10], [11]. By considering seriously that point, some AI scientists have tried to account for the inconsistencies that are sure to arise from the use of nonmonotonic inferences by embodying some sort of *paraconsistency*, i.e., mechanisms capable of reasoning non-trivially about inconsistent theories, in their nonmonotonic formalisms [2], [5], [10]. The logics conceived according to this view allow the tolerance to contradiction coming from a paraconsistent treatment only to nonmonotonic conclusions. There is no reason why we should tolerate every kind of contradiction: in opposition to ontological contradictions, only so-called epistemological contradictions arisen from the use of inductive inferences might be allowed [10]. Now, calling the conclusions of inductive implications plausible facts, we have an automatic way to distinguish monotonic from nonmonotonic or inductive conclusions and to know to which sort of formula the paraconsistency should be applied. In fact, paraconsistency looks like an essential feature of the notion of plausibility: holding two mutually contradictory propositions to be each one of them plausible seems to imply no sort of irrationality and consequently should not lead to logical trivialization.

4 A Logic of Inductive Implication

According to what we have discussed so far, any attempt to transform default logic into a logic of induction should encompass two things: (1) it must allow us to inferentially obtain defaults or inductive implications, or, which would be even better, to represent specific ways according to which defaults are inferred, and (2) mark the consequent of defaults with some plausibility symbol as to be able to express its special epistemic status and tolerate the contradictions that may arise from their use.

For the second task, we shall refer to some recent theoretical results pointing to the connections between paraconsistent logic and modal logic [1], [2] and use this latter as a sort of logic of plausibility. Taking $\Diamond \alpha$ as meaning "α is plausible," we shall force the consequents of all defaults to be of the form $\Diamond \alpha$. As result of that, the contradictions that might arise from the use of defaults will necessarily be of the form $\{\Diamond \alpha, \Diamond \neg \alpha\}$, being easily manageable by modal logic.

From a semantic point of view, the possible worlds of this plausibility interpretation of modal logic will be taken as *plausible worlds*. Now the interesting point about this kind of possible world is that since the consequent of our defaults will be $\Diamond$-marked, there will be a close parallel between plausible worlds and the extensions that would be generated by the corresponding $\Diamond$-less defaults. Given a particular ordinary default theory T, the contradictions that may eventually be inferred from it will be accommodated in different self-consistent extensions. If α belongs to all these extensions we say that it is a skeptical consequence of T; if it belongs to at least one we say it is a credulous consequence of T. Now, by marking the consequent of defaults with $\Diamond$ and using a modal logic as our underlying monotonic logic, contradictory conclusions will be accommodated in the same extension and the set of old extensions will correspond to a semantic interpretation to this new modal extension, being each extension an individual plausible world. In this way, $\Diamond$ will correspond to the credulous consequence relation, being thus called credulous plausibility, and $\Box$ ($\Box \alpha =_{\text{def}} \neg \Diamond \neg \alpha$) to the skeptical one, representing then a sort of skeptical plausibility notion [2].

For the first task, we shall consider an expansion of a specific modal calculus (interpreted as a calculus of plausibility) in such a way that inductive implications or defaults are added to the logical language and treated as atomic formulae by its axiomatic machinery. In this way we will be able to make defaults and ordinary formulae to interact with the help of standard logical connectives as well as have defaults appearing as the prerequisite, justification or consequent of another default. This logic will be used as the monotonic basis of our meta-default logic. In our representation of inductive implications, we shall change Reiter's notation in such a way as to better reflect our new interpretation. We also drop the explicit reference to the normal part of the default [2], automatically preventing the so-called abnormal defaults.

Definition 1. Let $\mathfrak{S}$ be a language. The *inductive language* $\mathfrak{S}_{\succ}$ built over $\mathfrak{S}$ is defined as follows: (i) If $\alpha \in \mathfrak{S}$ is such that it contains no one of $\mathfrak{S}$'s logical symbols, then $\alpha \in \mathfrak{S}_{\succ}$; (ii) If $\oplus$ is a monadic logical symbol of $\mathfrak{S}$ along with one of its non-logical complements, if there is any, and $\alpha \in \mathfrak{S}_{\succ}$, then $(\oplus \alpha) \in \mathfrak{S}_{\succ}$; (iii) If $\oplus$ is a dyadic logical symbol of $\Im$ and $\alpha,\beta\in\Im_{\gtrless}$, then $(\alpha\oplus\beta)\in\Im_{\succcurlyeq}$; (iv) If $\alpha,\beta,\varphi\in\Im_{\succcurlyeq}$, then $(\alpha\succcurlyeq\beta\lesssim\varphi)\in\Im_{\succcurlyeq}$; (v) Nothing else belongs to $\Im_{\succcurlyeq}$.

Item (iv) defines our version of Reiter's defaults, which we shall call from now on simply inductive implications. $\alpha\succcurlyeq\beta\lesssim\varphi$ means "α inductively implies β unless φ" and is equivalent to default $\alpha{:}\beta\wedge\neg\varphi/\beta$. Right away we see that given propositional language L, for example, $L_{\succcurlyeq}$ will contain formulae like $\alpha\succcurlyeq(\beta\succcurlyeq\varphi\lesssim\lambda)\lesssim\phi$, $(\beta\succcurlyeq\varphi\lesssim\lambda)\succcurlyeq\alpha\lesssim\phi$, $\alpha\wedge(\varphi\succcurlyeq\lambda\lesssim\beta)$ and $(\alpha\succcurlyeq\beta)\rightarrow((\beta\succcurlyeq\varphi)\rightarrow(\alpha\succcurlyeq\varphi))$. That is to say, besides allowing us to represent specific ways according to which defaults are inferred, by putting $\succcurlyeq$ and $\lesssim$ on the same level as the other logical connectives, $\Im_{\succcurlyeq}$ fully explores the representational potential of defaults. We call α the antecedent of the inductive implication, β its consequent and φ its exception. $\alpha\succcurlyeq\beta$ is an abbreviation of $\alpha\succcurlyeq\beta\lesssim\bot$ and $\beta\lesssim\varphi$ is an abbreviation of $\top\succcurlyeq\beta\lesssim\varphi$. We call any formula that is not an inductive implication an ordinary formula.

We represent a modal calculus M by a triple $<\Im,\Theta,\Lambda>$, where $\Im$ is its language, Θ its set of modal operators and Γ its set of axiom schemas and inference rule schemas. If we want to know the real set of axioms of M, for example, we have just to take the set of all formulae of $\Im$ satisfying one of the axiom schemas of Λ. We also say that $\Im$ is based on Θ. Classical logic could be represented in this notation, for example, by taking $\Im$ as propositional or first-order logic, $\Theta = \varnothing$ and Λ as one of its sets of axioms.

Definition 2. Let M = $<\Im,\Theta,\Lambda>$ be a modal calculus. The *pseudo-inductive modal logic* M' based on M is the modal calculus $<\Im_{\succcurlyeq},\Theta,\Lambda>$, where $\Im_{\succcurlyeq}$ is the inductive language built over $\Im$.

The set of axioms of M' is simply the set of all formulae of $\Im_{\succcurlyeq}$ which satisfies at least one of Λ's axiom schemas. The term "pseudo-inductive" indicates that the calculus in question is deductive rather than inductive but nevertheless contains and reasons (deductively) about inductive implications.

Definition 3. A *pseudo-inductive logic of plausibility* P is a pair $<M', \Theta'>$ where M' = $<\Im_{\succcurlyeq},\Theta,\Lambda>$ is a pseudo-inductive modal logic and $\Theta'\subseteq\Theta$ is a set of modal operators.

The difference between P and M' is that in P we have chosen a subset of Θ to be our plausibility modal operators. Because of that we call it a logic of plausibility. The definitions below show how Θ' shall play the role of a plausibility modality.

Definition 4. Let $\Im$ be a modal language based on a set of modal operators Θ and $\theta\in\Theta$ a modal operator. The notion of θ-*formula* is defined as follows: (i) If $\alpha\in\Im_{\succcurlyeq}$ is of the form $\theta\varphi$, then α is a θ-inductive formula; (ii) If $\alpha\in\Im_{\succcurlyeq}$ is a θ-inductive formula, then $\alpha\wedge\beta$, $\alpha\vee\beta$, $\alpha\rightarrow\beta$ and $\forall x\alpha$ are also θ-inductive formulae; (iii) If $\beta\in\Im_{\succcurlyeq}$ is a θ-inductive formula, then $\alpha\succcurlyeq\beta\lesssim\varphi$ is a θ-inductive formula; (iv) Nothing else is a θ-inductive formula.

Definition 5. Let $P = <M', \Theta'>$ be a pseudo-inductive logic of plausibility with $M' = <\mathfrak{I}_{\succcurlyeq},\Theta,\Lambda>$. The P-*inductive language* $\mathfrak{I}_p$ is defined as follows: (i) If $\alpha \in \mathfrak{I}_{\succcurlyeq}$ is an ordinary closed formulae, then $\alpha \in \mathfrak{I}_p$; (ii) If $\alpha \in \mathfrak{I}_{\succcurlyeq}$ is a closed θ-inductive formula such that $\theta \in \Theta'$, then $\alpha \in \mathfrak{I}_p$; (iii) Nothing else belongs to $\mathfrak{I}_p$. We call any set $A \subseteq \mathfrak{I}_p$ a P-*theory*.

Bellow we lay down the definitions which make clear how P-theories shall be used in order to generate what we have called P-extensions, which in its turn will be used to define the concepts of P-inductive consequence relation and inductive basis. The explanation of these notions and their use will be given in the following sections.

Definition 6. Let $P = <M', \theta>$ be a pseudo-inductive logic of plausibility with $M' = <\mathfrak{I}_{\succcurlyeq},\Theta,\Lambda>$, $A \subseteq \mathfrak{I}_{\succcurlyeq}$ a P-theory and $S \subseteq \mathfrak{I}_{\succcurlyeq}$ a set of closed formulae. $\Gamma(S) \subseteq \mathfrak{I}_{\succcurlyeq}$ is the smallest set satisfying the following conditions: (i) $W \subseteq \Gamma(S)$; (ii) If $\Gamma(S) \vdash_{M'} \alpha$ then $\alpha \in \Gamma(S)$; (iii) If $\alpha \succcurlyeq \beta \precsim \varphi \in A$, $\alpha \in \Gamma(S)$ and $\neg \beta \notin S$ and $\varphi \notin S$, then $\beta \in \Gamma(S)$. A set of formulae E is a P-*extension* of A iff $\Gamma(E) = E$, that is, E is a fixed point of operator Γ.

Definition 7. Let $P = <M', \Theta'>$ be a pseudo-inductive logic of plausibility with $M' = <\mathfrak{I}_{\succcurlyeq},\Theta,\Lambda>$, $A \subseteq \mathfrak{I}_{\succcurlyeq}$ a P-theory and $\alpha \in \mathfrak{I}_{\succcurlyeq}$ a formulae. α is a P-*inductive consequence* of A (in symbols: $A \vdash_p \alpha$) iff, for all P-inductive extensions E of A, $\alpha \in E$.

Definition 8. An *inductive basis* L is a pair $<P, \vdash_p>$ where P is a pseudo-inductive logic of plausibility and $\vdash_p$ is its relation of inductive consequence.

5 Default Logic, Universal Defaults and Anomalous Extensions

The first thing we observe about our default logic is its open character. Considering the familiar notion of underlying monotonic basis of a nonmonotonic logic, we take such logic (under the label of pseudo-inductive logic of plausibility) as a parameter rather than a fixed component. This makes the comparison with other default logics very straightforward. For instance, a skeptical version of default logic which *does not allow abnormal defaults* and is able to *reason about defaults* would correspond to an inductive basis built upon classical logic (represented as a modal calculus $<\mathfrak{I},\Theta,\Lambda>$ with $\Theta = \varnothing$) and $\varnothing$ as the set of plausibility modal operators Θ' of its corresponding pseudo-inductive logic of plausibility. With this "Reiter inductive basis" at hand, it is possible to answer the question as how our logic is related to other default logics.

Below we show how Reiter's normal and semi-normal defaults would be translated into our notation. Because the test of consistency of the consequent is made inside the very definition of extension (6.iii), at the same time that we do not need to write it on the exception, we automatically exclude abnormal defaults from the language.

Example 1. *Reiter's default* $\alpha:\beta/\beta$ $\alpha:\beta\wedge\varphi/\beta$

             Inductive Implication $\alpha \succcurlyeq \beta$ $\alpha \succcurlyeq \beta \precsim \neg\varphi$

Another representational feature of our framework concerns the representation of universal defaults. Due to our considering inductive implication as a logical component of the language, in order to represent default statements such as "typically birds fly" we can use $\forall$ along with an open formula, in this case an inductive implication and obtain formulae of the sort $\forall x(\text{bird}(x) \succ \text{flies}(x))$. If the pseudo-inductive modal logic in question has $\forall x P(x) \rightarrow P(x)$ as one of its theorems, then from $\forall x(\text{bird}(x) \succ \text{flies}(x))$ we will able to obtain all particular instances of "typically birds fly" which will be processed normally by definition 6. This, one should acknowledge, is much more effective than considering schemas of defaults and giving a sort of extra-logical account for this type of default statements, which are the very core of commonsensical default reasoning.

About the role of P-theories in our formulation and the use of a modal logic as the underlying monotonic basis, the main idea is of course to be able to syntactically distinguish between deductive and inductive facts. As we have observed, this approach, which is our counterpart to the philosopher's emphasis on distinguishing between certain and inductively probable statements, might be quite useful when dealing with the problem of anomalous extensions. In order to illustrate why this is so, let us define the inductive basis we shall use in the rest of the paper, which will be built upon modal logic S5 with $\diamond$ as its primitive modal operator.

Definition 9. Let S5' be the pseudo-inductive modal logic based on modal calculus S5. The pseudo-inductive logic of plausibility $P_\diamond$ is the pair $<S5', \{\diamond\}>$ and the inductive basis $L_\diamond$ is the pair $<P_\diamond, \vdash_{p\diamond}>$.

Now, the inductive implications allowed on the left-side of $\vdash_{p\diamond}$ have necessarily to be $\{\diamond\}$-inductive formulae, which means that they ultimately imply a plausible formula. Since then all inductive conclusions will be of the form $\diamond\alpha$, inductive contradictions will assume the form of pairs $<\diamond\alpha, \diamond\neg\alpha>$, which are consistently treatable inside S5'. Therefore, what in Reiter's logic would produce two extensions, in $L_\diamond$ there will be only one extension with the two plausible contradictory facts $\diamond\alpha$ and $\diamond\neg\alpha$. Bellow we show how this would work with Nixon diamond example [13].

Example 2. The $P_\diamond$-theory $A = \{(1),(2),(3)\}$ bellow has one and only one $P_\diamond$-extension: $\text{Th}_{p\diamond}(A \cup \{\diamond\text{Pacifist(Nixon)}, \diamond\neg \text{Pacifist (Nixon)}\})^2$.

1) $\forall x(\text{Republican}(x) \succ \diamond\neg\text{Pacifist}(x))$ *Typically republicans are not pacifists*

2) $\forall x(\text{Quaker}(x) \succ \diamond\text{Pacifist}(x))$ *Typically Quakers are pacifists*

3) $\text{Quaker(Nixon)} \wedge \text{Republican(Nixon)}$ *Nixon is a Quaker and republican*

Besides dealing with inconsistencies cases like the one above in which the information available does not allow us to decide in favor of one of the two contradictory conclusions, the taking into account of the logical asymmetry between deductively and inductively obtained formulae also helps in the proper representation of other

---

[2] $\text{Th}_{p\diamond}(A) = \{\alpha \mid A \vdash_{p\diamond} \alpha\}$.

cases classically taken as instances of the problem of anomalous instances. Take Twenty example [9], which might be formalized as follows:

Example 3. The $P_\diamond$-theory A = {(1),(2),(3),(4),(5)} bellow has one and only one $P_\diamond$-extension: $Th_{p\diamond}(A\cup\{\diamond Fly(Twenty)\})$.

1) $\forall x(Animal(x)\succ\diamond\neg Fly(x)\npreceq\diamond Winged(x))$	*Usually animals cannot fly*
2) $\forall x(Winged(x)\rightarrow Fly(x))$	*Winged animals are exceptions to this, they can fly*
3) $\forall x(Bird(x)\rightarrow Animal(x))$	*Birds are animals*
4) $\forall x(Bird(x)\succ\diamond Winged(x))$	*Birds normally have wings*
5) $Bird(Twenty)$	*Twenty is a bird*

Since we have here an effective way to distinguish between plausible and certain facts, we can, through the exception part of the inductive implication, set priorities between inductive implications. By telling in (1) that $\diamond Winged(x)$ is an exception to $Animal(x)$'s inductively supporting $\diamond\neg Fly(x)$, we set a priority of (4) over (1), for if through (4) we conclude $\diamond Winged(Twenty)$, we will not be able to conclude $\diamond\neg Fly(Twenty)$ through (1).

6 A Calculus of Defaults: Cumulativity, And, Or and Rationality

Perhaps the most singular feature of our approach is its ability to conclude, both monotonically and nonmonotonically, not just ordinary formulae but also inductive implications, which opens room for the possibility of building what we have called in Section 2 meta-default logic or calculus of defaults. What will follow in this section is an attempt to illustrate how such sort of calculus can be built inside our framework.

Since the middle of the eights, AI theorists have spent much of their efforts studying the metatheoretic properties of nonmonotonic logics [7]. Let $\vdash$ be the inference relation of an arbitrary nonmonotonic logic L. Among the properties of $\vdash$ usually taken as desirable we can list the following (A is a set of formulae, α, β and φ are formulae, and $\vdash_{CL}$ is classical logic's inference relation):

Supraclassicality	if $A\vdash_{CL}\alpha$, then $A\vdash\alpha$
Inclusion	$A,\alpha\vdash\alpha$
Cautious Monotony	if $A\vdash\beta$ and $A\vdash\alpha$, then $A,\beta\vdash\alpha$
Cut	if $A\vdash\beta$ and $A,\beta\vdash\alpha$, then $A\vdash\alpha$

Together, these properties characterize what is known as a *cumulative* inference relation[3]. Below we have some more of such metatheoretic properties which, contrary to the ones above-listed, make reference to the internal form of the formulas:

---

[3] Some authors do not include supraclassicality in their definitions of cumulative inference relation. Note that Inclusion follows from Supracl. and, below, And from Cut and Supracl.

And	if $A \vdash \alpha$ and $A \vdash \beta$, then $A \vdash \alpha \wedge \beta$
Or	if $A, \beta \vdash \alpha$ and $A, \varphi \vdash \alpha$, then $A, \beta \vee \varphi \vdash \alpha$
Rationality	if $A \vdash \alpha$ and $A \not\vdash \neg\beta$, then $A, \beta \vdash \alpha$

Thinking in terms of inductive implications instead of $\vdash$, the desirability of these properties can be automatically transferred to inductive implications themselves. After formally defining the notion calculus of inductive implication or logic of induction, we present two of such logics inspired in the just described meta-properties of defaults.

Definition 10. Let $P = <M', \Theta'>$ be a pseudo-inductive logic of plausibility with $M' = <\Im_\vDash, \Theta, \Lambda>$, $A \subseteq \Im_\vDash$ a P-theory, $T \subseteq \Im_\vDash$ a P-theory called the set of inductive axioms and $\alpha \in \Im_\vDash$ a formulae. α is a T-P-*inductive consequence* of A (in symbols: $A \vdash_{\text{T-P}} \alpha$) iff $T \cup A \vdash_P \alpha$.

Definition 11. A *logic of induction* or *calculus of inductive implication* C is a triple $<P, T, \vdash_{\text{T-P}}>$ where $P = <M', \Theta'>$ is a pseudo-inductive logic of plausibility with $M' = <\Im_\vDash, \Theta, \Lambda>$, $T \subseteq \Im_\vDash$ is a P-theory representing the set of inductive axioms and $\vdash_{\text{T-P}}$ is the T-P relation of inductive consequence. We also refer to $\vdash_{\text{T-P}}$ as $\vdash_C$.

Example 4. Let P be a pseudo-inductive logic of plausibility. The *Cumulative axioms* T_C in $\Im_\vDash$ is the set composed by all formulae of $\Im_p$ satisfying the following schemas of formula:

SCl:	$(\alpha \to \beta) \succcurlyeq (\alpha \succ \beta) \precsim ((\alpha \leftrightarrow \bot) \vee (\top \leftrightarrow \beta))$	*Supraclassicality*
In:	$\alpha \succ \alpha$	*Inclusion*
CM:	$(\alpha \succ \beta \precsim \varphi) \to ((\alpha \succ \phi \precsim \varphi') \to (\alpha \wedge \beta \succ \phi \precsim \varphi \vee \varphi'))$	*Cautious Monotony*
Cut:	$(\alpha \succ \beta \precsim \varphi) \to ((\alpha \wedge \beta \succ \phi \precsim \varphi') \to (\alpha \succ \phi \precsim \varphi \vee \varphi'))$	*Cut*

Let T be the cumulative axioms in $\Im_{P\diamond}$. The *Cumulative calculus of inductive implication* C_C is the triple $<P_\diamond, T, \vdash_{\text{T-P}\diamond}>$.

The reason for representing SCl through an inductive implication instead of a material implication formula is due to inability of $\to$ to capture the relevance aspect required by such property. If we represent SCl by $(\alpha \to \beta) \to (\alpha \succ \beta)$, we will have that for any sentence α and β, $\alpha \succ \diamond \top$ and $\bot \succ \diamond \beta$. Below we have the formalization of properties And, Or and Rationality.

Example 5. Let P be a pseudo-inductive logic of plausibility. The *And-Or-Rationality* or *AOR axioms* T_{AOR} in $\Im_p$ is the set composed by all formulae of $\Im_p$ satisfying the following schemas of formula:

And:	$(\alpha \succ \beta \precsim \varphi) \to ((\alpha \succ \beta' \succ \varphi') \to (\alpha \succ \beta \wedge \beta' \precsim \varphi \vee \varphi'))$	*And*
Or:	$(\alpha \succ \beta \precsim \varphi) \to ((\alpha' \succ \beta \precsim \varphi') \to (\alpha \vee \alpha' \succ \beta \precsim \varphi \vee \varphi'))$	*Or*
Rat:	$(\alpha \succ \beta \precsim \varphi) \succ (\alpha \wedge \phi \succ \beta \precsim \varphi) \precsim (\alpha \wedge \phi \leftrightarrow \bot)$	*Rationality*

Let T be the AOR axioms in $\mathfrak{I}_{p\diamond}$. The *AOR calculus of inductive implication* C_{AOR} is the triple $\langle P_\diamond, T, \vdash_{T\text{-}p\diamond}\rangle$.

Other interesting axioms we could mention are $\diamond\alpha \wedge \diamond\beta \succsim \diamond(\alpha \wedge \beta)$ (conjunction of plausible hypotheses, which S5 does not allow), $\diamond\alpha \succsim \Box\alpha \precsim \diamond\neg\alpha$ (inferring skeptically plausible hypotheses) and $\top \succsim \diamond(\neg\Box\alpha) \precsim \bot$ (autoepistemic axiom.)

7 Conclusion

In this work we have tried to establish some connections between the field of nonmonotonic logic in AI and the philosophical field of inductive logic. We tried to materialize our conclusions by proposing a logical system inspired in Reiter's default logic that fulfills the purpose of a logic of induction. We think our work represents a valuable contribution to both AI and philosophy in that it shows how AI tools can be useful in treating traditional philosophical problems such as the one of building a logic of induction, and on the other hand how ideas traditionally cultivated inside philosophical fields can throw some light upon AI problems, namely the problem of anomalous extensions and the problem of representation of defeasible reasoning.

About how much our logic departs from traditional default logics, the following points can be mentioned: (1) Defaults are represented through $\alpha \succsim \beta \precsim \varphi$, which is structurally equivalent to Reiter's semi-normal default $\alpha : \beta \wedge \neg\varphi / \beta$ and is read as "α inductively implies β unless φ." (2) Implicit in this notation is the taking into account of the consistency of the consequent in the definition of extension and the exclusion of abnormal defaults. (3) Rather than using classical logic as our underlying monotonic logic, we suggest that a traditional modal logic be used instead and all defaults have their consequents marked with $\diamond$, meaning "is plausible that." This has the advantage that now we are able to keep contradictions in the same extension and reason paraconsistently about them as well as to properly represent other cases of anomalous extensions. (4) Finally, defaults or, in our terminology, inductive implications are part of the logical language and treated by the axiomatic machinery more or less like atomic formulae. This has important representational consequences. First, we are able to represent universal defaults with the help of the logical symbol $\forall$ and, which is more important, represent, both monotonically and nonmonotonically, laws about defaults.

About this last point, we should mention that our work opens the door to something which has never been done before: the construction of a calculus of defaults or inductive implications akin to the calculus of material implication contained in classical logic. In the same way that MP detaches the consequence from the antecedent of material implication sentences and $\rightarrow$-axioms set the additional properties of $\rightarrow$, we can say that the definition of extension acts exactly like MP, being our responsibility to lay down the inductive axioms which will effectively set the properties we want inductive implications to possess. What we have done in Section 6 was an illustration of how this could be done. The proposal of a definitive calculus of inductive implication whose inference relation should, for instance, automatically satisfy all the properties we have shown in Section 6 is something we shall do in a future work.

References

1. Bèziau, J. Y.: S5 is a Paraconsistent Logic and so is First-Order Classical Logic. Logical Studies 9 (2002), http://www.logic.ru/LogStud/09/No9-01.html.
2. Buchsbaum, A. Pequeno, T., Pequeno, M.: The Logical Expression of Reasoning. To appear in: Béziau, J., Krause, D. (eds.): New Threats in Foundations of Science. Papers Dedicated to the Eightieth Birthday of Patrick Suppes. Kluver, Dordrecht (2005).
3. Carnap, R.: Logical Foundations of Probability. U. of Chicago Press, Chicago (1950)
4. Ford, M. , Glymour, C., Hayes, P. (eds.): Android Epistemology. The MIT Press (1995).
5. Gabbay, D., Hunter A.: Making Inconsistency Respectable. In: Jorrand, P., Kelemen, J. (eds.): Proc. of Fundamental of AI Research, Springer-Verlag (1991) 19-32.
6. Hempel, Carl G. (1945), Studies in the Logic of Confirmation, Mind 54: 1-26, 97-121.
7. Makinson, D.: General Patterns in Nonmonotonic Reasoning. In: Gabbay. D., Hogger, D., Robinson J. (eds.): Handbook of Logic in Artificial Intelligence and Logic Programming, Vol. 3, Oxford University Press, Oxford (1994).
8. McCarthy, J.: Applications of Circumscription to Formalizing Commonsense Knowledge. Artificial Intelligence 26 (1986) 89-116.
9. Morris, P. H.: The Anomalous Problem in Default Reasoning. Artificial Intelligence 35 (1988) 383-399.
10. Pequeno, T., Buchsbaum, A.: The Logic of Epistemic Inconsistency. In: Allen, J., Fikes, R., Sandewall, E. (eds.): Principles of Knowledge Representation and Reasoning: Proc. of Second International Conference. Morgan Kaufmann, San Mateo (1991) 453-460.
11. Perlis, D.: On the Consistency of Commonsense Reasoning. Computational Intelligence 2 (1987) 180-190.
12. Reiter, R.: A Logic for Default Reasoning. Artificial Intelligence 13 (1980) 81–132.
13. Reiter, R., G. Criscuolo: On Interacting Defaults. In: Proceedings of the 7th International Joint Conference on Artificial Intelligence, Morgan Kaufmann Publishers (1981) 270-276.
14. Silvestre, R., Pequeno, T: A Logical Treatment of Scientific Anomalies or AI Meets Philosophy of Science. In: Arabnia, H, Joshua, R., Mun, Y. (eds.): Proceedings of the 2003 Int. Conference on Artificial Intelligence, CSRA Press (2003) 669-675.
15. Silvestre, R., Pequeno, T: Is Plausible Reasoning a Sensible Alternative for Inductive-Statistical Reasoning? In: Bazzan, L.C, Labidi, S. (eds.): Advances in Artificial Intelligence – SBIA 2004 (LNAI 3171), Springer-Verlag (2004) 124-133.

Knowledge Distribution in Large Organizations Using Defeasible Logic Programming

Carlos I. Chesñevar[1], Ramón F. Brena[2], and Jose L. Aguirre[2]

[1] Artificial Intelligence Research Group – Departament of Computer Science,
Universitat de Lleida – E-25001 Lleida, SPAIN
cic@eps.udl.es

[2] Centro de Sistemas Inteligentes – Tecnológico de Monterrey,
64849 Monterrey, N.L., MÉXICO
{ramon.brena, jlaguirre}@itesm.mx

Abstract. Distributing pieces of knowledge in large, usually distributed organizations is a central problem in Knowledge and Organization Management. Policies for distributing knowledge and information are very often incomplete, or conflict with each other. As a consequence, decision processes for information distribution may be difficult to formalize on the basis of a rationally justified procedure.

This paper presents an argumentative approach to cope with the above problem based on Defeasible Logic Programming, a logic programming formalism for defeasible argumentation. Conflicts among policies are solved on the basis of a dialectical analysis whose outcome determines to which specific users different pieces of knowledge are to be delivered.

Keywords: knowledge management, defeasible argumentation, logic programming.

1 Introduction and Motivation

Nowadays in modern organizations information and knowledge (IK) have been identified as valuable assets [1, 2, 3] motivating the development of different Knowledge Management (KM) techniques. In the context of KM, distributing customized pieces of IK in large and distributed organizations is a central process. This process turns out to be a decision making problem as well, because IK to be distributed to different users is not the same, so you have to decide which IK item goes to each user. Organization policies for IK dissemination should be defined to deliver notifications to specific organization members, according to management criteria. Such policies, however, are frequently *defeasible*, as they may change in the light of new information (e.g. particular interests and/or information needs of users, exceptional situations, etc.), or even contradictory.

IK is characterized by *metadata* (such as a content classification in terms of technical disciplines, intended audience, etc.) and users are characterized by *profiles*, which give the user function or position in the organization, rights and

B. Kégl and G. Lapalme (Eds.): AI 2005, LNAI 3501, pp. 244–256, 2005.

duties, interests, etc. In this setting organizations typically have different criteria for establishing their information distribution *policies*, and in practice such policies are defeasible, compete with each other, and may include several exceptions. As a consequence, decision processes for IK distribution may be difficult to formalize on the basis of a rationally justified procedure.

Defeasible argumentation [4, 5] has evolved in the last decade as a successful approach to formalize commonsense reasoning and decision making problems as the ones discussed before. In the last few years particular attention has been given to several extensions of *logic programming*, which have turned out to be computationally manageable for formalizing knowledge representation and argumentative inference. Defeasible logic programming (DeLP) [6] is one of such extensions, which has proven to be successful for a number of real-world applications, such as web recommendation systems [7], clustering classification [8] and natural language processing [9], among others.

This paper presents an argument-based approach to solve the problem of knowledge distribution in large organization using DeLP. The proposed approach can efficiently deal with conflicting policies regarding IK distribution among specific users by applying a *dialectical analysis*. The rest of the paper is structured as follows. First, in Section 2 we present some relevant issues of IK distribution in large organizations. Section 3 outlines the basics of defeasible logic programming (DeLP). In Section 4 we describe how an argumentative approach for IK distribution can be defined on the basis of DeLP. We illustrate the proposed approach with a case study in Section 5. In Section 6 we discuss some implementation issues concerning DeLP, as well as related work. Finally Section 7 summarizes the conclusions we have obtained.

2   Characterizing Information and Knowledge Distribution in Large Organizations

As a basis for our analysis we will consider the organization structure and characteristics by means of *users profiles*. These profiles reflect information like *areas* or divisions to which they belong (e.g. marketing, finance department, etc.), as well as other attributes like rights and responsibilities. In large organizations we can also detect a number of common features which complicate knowledge dissemination, namely:

- Many different *hierarchies* of organization-related concepts: fields, roles, member interests, etc. These hierarchies can have *exceptions*, as sometimes they may come in conflict with organization policies.
- *Members* of the organization assigned to different areas or divisions and one or more roles within the organization structure (e.g. CEO, manager, supervisor), usually within a *personnel hierarchy*. Such hierarchies do not have exceptions, but they assign different decision power or "permissions" to their members, affecting the ultimate outcome of many decision making processes. Each member will also have his/her own *personal preferences* about IK delivery.

- There are different organization policies which prescribe how to proceed when IK items are to be distributed among different members or users. Many of such policies are *defeasible*, specially in the presence of potentially incomplete information concerning metadata and user profiles. As a result competing policies usually emerge, including exceptions and special cases at different levels within the organization structure.

In this context, given a set S of IK items to be distributed among the different members (or users) of the organization, the IK distribution problem could be summarized as sending every IK item $s \in S$ to the right user such that (a) he/she is supposed to receive s according to the policies from the organization management, and (b) he/she is supposed to receive s according to his/her user profile. As discussed above, the existence of multiple levels of exception (that is, exceptions even for the exceptions) cause that decision processes for information distribution are difficult to formalize on the basis of a *rationally justified procedure*. As we will see in the next Section, defeasible argumentation will provide us a sound framework for modeling this situation.

3   Defeasible Argumentation with DeLP

Defeasible argumentation [4, 5] has evolved in the last decade as a successful approach to formalize defeasible, commonsense reasoning. *Defeasible logic programming* (DeLP) [6] is a defeasible argumentation formalism based on logic programming. A defeasible logic program[3] is a set $K = (\Pi, \Delta)$ of Horn-like clauses, where Π and Δ stand for sets of strict and defeasible knowledge, respectively. The set Π of strict knowledge involves *strict rules* of the form $p \leftarrow q_1, \ldots, q_k$ and *facts* (strict rules with empty body), and it is assumed to be *non-contradictory*. The set Δ of defeasible knowledge involves *defeasible rules* of the form $p \relbar\mkern-9mu\prec q_1, \ldots, q_k$, which stands for "$q_1, \ldots q_k$ provide a *tentative reason* to believe p." The underlying logical language is that of extended logic programming, enriched with a special symbol "$\relbar\mkern-9mu\prec$" to denote defeasible rules. Both default and classical negation are allowed (denoted not and $\sim$, resp.). Syntactically, the symbol "$\relbar\mkern-9mu\prec$" is all that distinguishes a *defeasible* rule $p \relbar\mkern-9mu\prec q_1, \ldots q_k$ from a *strict* (non-defeasible) rule $p \leftarrow q_1, \ldots, q_k$. DeLP rules are thus Horn-like clauses to be thought of as *inference rules* rather than implications in the object language. Deriving literals in DeLP results in the construction of *arguments*.

Definition 1 (Argument). *Given a DeLP program $\mathcal{P}$, an argument $\mathcal{A}$ for a query q, denoted $\langle \mathcal{A}, q \rangle$, is a subset of ground instances of defeasible rules in $\mathcal{P}$ and a (possibly empty) set of default ground literals "not L", such that: 1) there exists a defeasible derivation for q from $\Pi \cup \mathcal{A}$; 2) $\Pi \cup \mathcal{A}$ is non-contradictory (i.e, $\Pi \cup \mathcal{A}$ does not entail two complementary literals p and $\sim p$ (or p and not p)), and 3) $\mathcal{A}$ is minimal with respect to set inclusion.*

---

[3] When it is clear from the context we will simply refer to a defeasible logic program as a "DeLP program" or just "program"

An argument $\langle \mathcal{A}_1, Q_1 \rangle$ is a sub-argument of another argument $\langle \mathcal{A}_2, Q_2 \rangle$ if $\mathcal{A}_1 \subseteq \mathcal{A}_2$. Given a DeLP program $\mathcal{P}$, $Args(\mathcal{P})$ denotes the set of all possible arguments that can be derived from $\mathcal{P}$.

The notion of defeasible derivation corresponds to the usual query-driven SLD derivation used in logic programming, performed by backward chaining on both strict and defeasible rules; in this context a negated literal $\sim p$ is treated just as a new predicate name no_p. Minimality imposes a kind of 'Occam's razor principle' on arguments. The non-contradiction requirement forbids the use of (ground instances of) defeasible rules in an argument $\mathcal{A}$ whenever $\Pi \cup \mathcal{A}$ entails two complementary literals.

Definition 2 (Counterargument – Defeat). *An argument $\langle \mathcal{A}_1, q_1 \rangle$ is a counterargument for an argument $\langle \mathcal{A}_2, q_2 \rangle$ iff (1) There is an subargument $\langle \mathcal{A}, q \rangle$ of $\langle \mathcal{A}_2, q_2 \rangle$ such that the set $\Pi \cup \{q_1, q\}$ is contradictory; (2) A literal* not *q_1 is present in some rule in $\mathcal{A}_1$.*
A partial order $\preceq \subseteq Args(\mathcal{P}) \times Args(\mathcal{P})$ will be used as a preference criterion[4] *among conflicting arguments. An argument $\langle \mathcal{A}_1, q_1 \rangle$ is a* defeater *for an argument $\langle \mathcal{A}_2, q_2 \rangle$ if $\langle \mathcal{A}_1, q_1 \rangle$ counterargues $\langle \mathcal{A}_2, q_2 \rangle$, and $\langle \mathcal{A}_1, q_1 \rangle$ is preferred over $\langle \mathcal{A}_2, q_2 \rangle$ wrt $\preceq$. For cases (1) and (2) above, we distinguish between* proper *and* blocking defeaters *as follows:*

- *In case (1) the argument $\langle \mathcal{A}_1, q_1 \rangle$ will be called a* proper defeater *for $\langle \mathcal{A}_2, q_2 \rangle$ iff $\langle \mathcal{A}_1, q_1 \rangle$ is strictly preferred over $\langle \mathcal{A}, q \rangle$ wrt $\preceq$.*
- *In case (1), if $\langle \mathcal{A}_1, q_1 \rangle$ and $\langle \mathcal{A}, q \rangle$ are unrelated to each other, or in case (2), $\langle \mathcal{A}_1, q_1 \rangle$ will be called a* blocking defeater *for $\langle \mathcal{A}_2, q_2 \rangle$.*

An *argumentation line* starting in an argument $\langle \mathcal{A}_0, Q_0 \rangle$ (denoted $\lambda^{\langle \mathcal{A}_0, q_0 \rangle}$) is a sequence $[\langle \mathcal{A}_0, Q_0 \rangle, \langle \mathcal{A}_1, Q_1 \rangle, \langle \mathcal{A}_2, Q_2 \rangle, \ldots, \langle \mathcal{A}_n, Q_n \rangle \ldots]$ that can be thought of as an exchange of arguments between two parties, a *proponent* (evenly-indexed arguments) and an *opponent* (oddly-indexed arguments). Each $\langle \mathcal{A}_i, Q_i \rangle$ is a defeater for the previous argument $\langle \mathcal{A}_{i-1}, Q_{i-1} \rangle$ in the sequence, $i > 0$. In order to avoid *fallacious* reasoning, dialectics imposes additional constraints (viz. disallowing circular argumentation, enforcing the use of proper defeaters to defeat blocking defeaters, etc.[5]) on such an argument exchange to be considered rationally acceptable. An argumentation line satisfying the above restrictions is called *acceptable*, and can be proven to be finite [6]. Given a DeLP program $\mathcal{P}$ and an initial argument $\langle \mathcal{A}_0, Q_0 \rangle$, the set of all acceptable argumentation lines starting in $\langle \mathcal{A}_0, Q_0 \rangle$ accounts for a whole dialectical analysis for $\langle \mathcal{A}_0, Q_0 \rangle$ (ie., all possible dialogues rooted in $\langle \mathcal{A}_0, Q_0 \rangle$), formalized as a *dialectical tree*.

Nodes in a dialectical tree $\mathcal{T}_{\langle \mathcal{A}_0, Q_0 \rangle}$ can be marked as *undefeated* and *defeated* nodes (U-nodes and D-nodes, resp.). A dialectical tree will be marked as an AND-OR tree: all leaves in $\mathcal{T}_{\langle \mathcal{A}_0, Q_0 \rangle}$ will be marked U-nodes (as they have no defeaters),

---

[4] Specificity [10] is used in DeLP as a syntax-based criterion among conflicting arguments, preferring those arguments which are *more informed* or *more direct* [10, 11]. However, other alternative partial orders could also be used.
[5] For an in-depth treatment of DeLP the reader is referred to [6].

and every inner node is to be marked as *D-node* iff it has at least one U-node as a child, and as *U-node* otherwise. An argument $\langle \mathcal{A}_0, Q_0 \rangle$ is ultimately accepted as valid (or *warranted*) wrt a DeLP program $\mathcal{P}$ iff the root of its associated dialectical tree $\mathcal{T}_{\langle \mathcal{A}_0, Q_0 \rangle}$ is labeled as *U-node*.

Given a DeLP program $\mathcal{P}$, solving a query q wrt $\mathcal{P}$ accounts for determining whether q is supported by a warranted argument. Different doxastic attitudes are distinguished when answering q according to the associated status of warrant, in particular: (1) Believe q (resp. $\sim q$) when there is a warranted argument for q (resp. $\sim q$) that follows from $\mathcal{P}$; (2) Believe q is *undecided* whenever neither q nor $\sim q$ are supported by warranted arguments in $\mathcal{P}$.[6]

4   Modelling Hierarchies and Policies with DeLP

In order to solve the problem of IK dissemination within a large organization, our proposal uses DeLP both for knowledge encoding and for performing a rationally justified procedure in cases of decision-making involving competing policies.

ALGORITHM DistributeKnowledgePieces
{*Executed by Organization Management to decide which knowledge pieces
   are to be sent to different specific users*}
INPUT: List $L = [k_1, \ldots, k_m]$ of knowledge pieces to be distributed
           Organization management knowledge $\mathcal{P}_{org}$
           User Profiles $\mathcal{P}_1, \ldots, \mathcal{P}_n$
OUTPUT: Distribution of L to Users according to $\mathcal{P}_{org}, \mathcal{P}_1, \ldots, \mathcal{P}_n$
BEGIN
  FOR every User Profile $\mathcal{P}_i$
     Check integrity for $\mathcal{P}_{org} \cup \mathcal{P}_i$
     $\mathcal{P}_L := \{ info(k_i), \ldots, info(k_m) \}$ {*encoding of k_i's as DeLP fact(s)*}
     FOR every user $User_i$ with User Profile $\mathcal{P}_i$
        FOR every $k_i \in L$ { *Select item k_i from L* }
          Let $\mathcal{P} = \mathcal{P}_{org} \cup \mathcal{P}_i \cup \mathcal{P}_L$
          IF query $send(k_i, User_i)$ is warranted
            THEN Send message k_i to user $User_i$
  END

Fig. 1. High-level Algorithm for Knowledge Distribution in Organization Management using DeLP

The organization knowledge concerning corporate rules defining hierarchies and (possibly conflicting) policies for knowledge distribution among users will be encoded as a DeLP program $\mathcal{P}_{org}$. Organization members will have their own *user profiles* mirroring their preferences, formalized as other DeLP programs

---

[6] It should be noted that that the computation of warrant cannot lead to contradiction [6]: if there exists a warranted argument $\langle A, h \rangle$ on the basis of a program $\mathcal{P}$, then there is no warranted argument $\langle B, \sim h \rangle$.

$\mathcal{P}_1$, $\mathcal{P}_2$, ..., $\mathcal{P}_n$. Given a list L of IK items to be distributed by the Organization among different users, a distinguished predicate $send(I, User)$ will allow him to determine whether a particular item $I \in L$ is intended to be delivered to a specific user $User$. The above query will be solved by the DeLP inference engine on the basis of a program $\mathcal{P}$ which will take into the organization management knowledge, the information corresponding to the incoming items to be distributed and the personal preferences $\mathcal{P}_i$ of the every one of the different users involved. This is made explicit in algorithm shown in Fig. 1.[7] Solving queries based on the $send$ predicate wrt the DeLP inference engine will automate the decision making process providing a rationally justified decision even for very complex cases, as we will see in the case study shown next.

5   A Case Study: Distributing Memos in ACME Inc.

We will show next how the proposed approach can be applied in a sample case involving a large organization in which pieces of IK (memos) have to be distributed to different specific users. We assume a typical corporate environment called ACME Inc., where people could have different rights and responsibilities (CEO, managers, supervisors, etc.). These people (users) will belong to different areas of the organization (production, marketing, etc.), and will have different personal interests and preferences represented as User Profiles. Periodically the company ACME Inc. generates a list of memos which have to be delivered to different users according to the organization policies, taking into account at the same time personal interests and preferences of the different users involved.

Within our organization, areas and topics are organized in *hierarchies*. Thus, for example, a hierarchy of topics of memos could be "computers – hardware – processors". It must be noted that managing such hierarchies involves performing inheritance reasoning to infer consequences related to subareas. Besides, organization policies could add *exceptions* to such hierarchies, e.g. by stipulating that a certain memo is mandatory, and should be delivered without regarding the user preferences. In our example, memos generated from ACME Inc. will be encoded with a predicate $info(Id, A, L, M, T, S)$, meaning that the memo with unique identifier Id is about area A can be accessed by users of at least level L. Other attributes associated with the memo are whether it is mandatory ($M = 1$) or optional ($M = 0$), top secret ($T = 1$) or not ($T = 0$) and source of origin S. Thus, the fact $info(id_3, computers, manager, 0, 0, marketing)$ indicates that the memo id_3 is about *computers*, it is intended at least for managers, it is not mandatory nor secret, and it has been produced by the department of marketing.

---

[7] When considering $\mathcal{P}_{org} \cup \mathcal{P}_i$ in the algorithm in Fig. 1, the integrity check performed amounts to detect that no contradictory literals follow from the strict knowledge in $\mathcal{P}_{org} \cup \mathcal{P}_i$. This can be easily enforced e.g. by avoiding clash of predicate names in heads of strict rules in $\mathcal{P}_{org}$ and $\mathcal{P}_i$. An in-depth analysis of such situations is outside the scope of this paper.

5.1 Characterizing Organization Knowledge

Figure 2 shows a sample DeLP code for our example.[8] Strict rules s_1 to s_9 characterize organization permissions and allow to extract specific information from memos. Rule s_1 defines that a user P is *allowed* access to item I if he/she has the required *permissions*. Granted permissions are given as facts (f_1, f_2 and f_3). Permissions are also propagated using the strict rules s_4, s_5 and s_6, where the binary predicate *depends* establishes the organization hierarchy, stating that the first argument person is (transitively) subordinated to the second one. This predicate is calculated as the transitive closure of a basic predicate

---

Organization Knowledge for Information Distribution

Strict rules

s_1) $allowed(I, U) \leftarrow info(I, A, L, M, T, S), permissions(U, L).$

s_2) $isAbout(I, A) \leftarrow info(I, A, L, M, T, S)$

s_3) $isAbout(I, A) \leftarrow subField(SuperA, A), isAbout(I, SuperA).$

s_4) $permissions(U, X) \leftarrow depends(X, Y), permissions(U, Y).$

s_5) $depends(X, Y) \leftarrow subordinate(X, Y).$

s_6) $depends(X, Z) \leftarrow subordinate(Y, Z), depends(X, Y).$

s_7) $source(I, S) \leftarrow info(I, \_, \_, \_, \_, S).$

s_8) $mandatory(I) \leftarrow info(I, \_, \_, 1, \_, \_).$

s_9) $topsecret(I) \leftarrow info(I, \_, \_, \_, 1, \_).$

Defeasible rules

d_1) $interest(I, U) \prec isAbout(I, A), intField(A, U).$

d_2) $send(I, U) \prec allowed(I, U), mandatory(I, U).$

d_3) $\sim mandatory(I, U) \prec permissions(U, manager), \sim interest(I, U),$
$\qquad\qquad\qquad\qquad\qquad$ not $topsecret(I).$

d_4) $send(I, U) \prec allowed(I, U), interest(I, U).$

Facts

Granted Permissions // People Hierarchy // Field Hierarchy

f_1) $permissions(joe, manager) \leftarrow$ f_5) $subordinate(manager, ceo) \leftarrow$

f_2) $permissions(peter, everybody) \leftarrow$ f_6) $subField(hardware, computers) \leftarrow$

f_3) $permissions(susan, ceo) \leftarrow$ f_7) $subField(processors, hardware) \leftarrow$

f_4) $subordinate(everybody, manager) \leftarrow$

Incoming Pieces of Knowledge – Information Items (facts)

f_8) $info(id_1, computers, everybody, 0, 0, external) \leftarrow$

f_9) $info(id_2, computers, everybody, 0, 0, techdept) \leftarrow$

f_{10}) $info(id_5, processors, manager, 1, 1, techdept) \leftarrow$

Fig. 2. A DeLP program modelling Organization Knowledge for Information Distribution. Facts f_8 to f_{10} correspond to temporarily available pieces of knowledge to be distributed

---

[8] Note that we distinguish strict rules, defeasible rules, and facts by using s_i, d_i and f_i as clause identifiers, respectively.

subordinate (defined by facts f_4 and f_5), which establishes subordinate relationships pairwise. Thus, having e.g. granted permissions as CEO allows the CEO to have access to every memo corresponding to lower level permissions. Note that the predicate *subordinate* uses generic *roles* as arguments, not specific person identifiers. Rule s_2 and s_3 define the predicate *isAbout(I, A)* as an information hierarchy among subfields. The basic case corresponds to a subfield for which specific information is available (rule s_2). Note that in our particular example facts f_6 and f_7 define the basic relationships in this hierarchy. Finally, rules s_7, s_8 and s_9 define auxiliary predicates *source*, *mandatory* (yes/no) and *topsecret* (yes/no) which allow to extract this particular attributes from the memos to be distributed that just extract information from *info*, facts, simplifying the subsequent analysis.

Defeasible rules characterize organization policies with possible exceptions. Rule d_1 defines when an item I is usually of interest for a specific user U, on the basis of the user's personal preferences. Rule d_2 and d_4 define a policy for memo distribution in our organization: a) an item (memo) I should be delivered to a user U if he is allowed to read this memo, and it is mandatory for him to read it; b) an item I should be delivered to a user U if he is allowed to read it, and it is interesting for him. Rule d_3 provides an exception for mandatory memos: users which have at least permission as managers are not obliged to read memos they are not interested in, *unless* they are top secret ones.[9]

5.2 Specifying User Profiles

For the sake of example, we will consider two user profiles, corresponding to *Joe* and *Susan*, who are organization members (see Fig. 3). A number of facts represent Joe's preferences: which are his interest fields, and his personal belief about other parts of the organization (e.g. reliability with respect to the source of incoming memo). Joe can provide also a number of defeasible rules associated with his preferences. Rule d'_1 establishes that Joe is not interested in a memo coming from an unreliable source. Rule d'_2 defines how to handle "negative inheritance" within the hierarchy of interests: Joe is not interested in any area A which is a subarea of another area *SuperA*, such that *SuperA* is not interesting for him. Similarly, we have some personal information concerning *Susan*: she is usually not interested in memos from the technical department, and she is interested in computers.

5.3 Solving Conflicts for Information Distribution as DeLP Queries

Let us assume that there is a list $L=[Memo_1, Memo_2, Memo_5]$ corresponding to three memos to be distributed to *Joe* and *Susan* by the organization management. Following the algorithm in Fig. 1 this list can be encoded as a

---

[9] Note how this last condition is expressed in terms of default negation not in rule d_3.

User Profiles for *Joe* and *Susan*

Defeasible rules

$d'_1) \sim interest(I, joe) \multimapdotinv isAbout(I, A), intField(A, joe).$
$\qquad\qquad\qquad\qquad source(I, S), \sim relies(joe, S).$

$d'_2) \sim interest(I, joe) \multimapdotinv isAbout(I, A), intField(A, joe),$
$\qquad\qquad\qquad\qquad isAbout(I, SuperA), \sim intField(SuperA, joe).$

Facts // User preferences

$f'_1)\quad intField(computers, joe) \leftarrow \qquad f'_3)\quad relies(joe, techdept) \leftarrow$
$f'_2) \sim intField(hardware, joe) \leftarrow \qquad f'_4) \sim relies(joe, external) \leftarrow$

Defeasible rules

$d''_1) \sim interest(I, susan) \multimapdotinv source(I, techdept).$

Facts // User Preferences

$f''_1)\ intField(computers, susan) \leftarrow$

Fig. 3. User profiles for *Joe* and *Susan* encoded as DeLP programs

number of DeLP facts P_L which will be temporarily added to the organization knowledge base, as shown in Fig. 2. Note that these facts have constant
names id_1, id_2 and id_5 which identify them univocally. *Joe* and *Susan* mirror
their preferences in terms of the DeLP programs $\mathcal{P}_{joe} = \{d'_1, d'_2, f'_1, f'_2, f'_3, f'_4\}$,
and $\mathcal{P}_{susan} = \{d''_1, f''_1\}$, resp. (Fig. 3). Following our algorithm first the in-
tegrity of $\mathcal{P}_{org} \cup \mathcal{P}_{joe}$ and $\mathcal{P}_{org} \cup \mathcal{P}_{susan}$ will be checked. Afterwards, queries
$send(id_1, joe)$, $send(id_2, joe)$ and $send(id_5, joe)$ will be solved wrt the DeLP pro-
gram $\mathcal{P}_{org} \cup \mathcal{P}_{joe} \cup \mathcal{P}_L$ in order to determine which memos are to be sent to Joe.
A similar procedure will be carried out for *Susan* with queries $send(id_1, susan)$,
$send(id_2, susan)$ and $send(id_5, susan)$ wrt $\mathcal{P}_{org} \cup \mathcal{P}_{susan} \cup \mathcal{P}_L$.

Example 1. Consider the query $send(id_1, joe)$. In this case the DeLP inference
engine will find the argument $\langle \mathcal{A}_1, send(id_1, joe) \rangle$, with:[10]

$\mathcal{A}_1 = \{send(id_1, joe) \multimapinv allowed(id_1, joe), interest(id_1, joe);$
$\qquad\quad interest(id_1, joe) \multimapinv isAbout(id_1, computers), intField(computers, joe)\}$

However, in this case, an argument $\langle \mathcal{A}_2, \sim interest(id_1, joe) \rangle$ which is a proper
defeater for $\langle \mathcal{A}_1, send(id_1, joe) \rangle$ will be found, with

$\mathcal{A}_2 = \{ \sim interest(id_1, joe) \multimapinv isAbout(id_1, computers), intField(computers, joe),$
$\qquad\qquad\qquad source(id_1, external), \sim relies(joe, external). \}$

Note that in this case, id_1 comes from an external source, and according to
joe's preference criteria, external sources are unreliable. Hence this information
should not be delivered to him. In this case, the dialectical tree $\mathcal{T}_{\langle \mathcal{A}_1, send(id_1, joe) \rangle}$
has two nodes in a single branch (see Figure 4-i). There are no other arguments
to consider, and $\langle \mathcal{A}_1, send(id_1, joe) \rangle$ is not warranted.

---

[10] For the sake of clarity, we use semicolons to separate elements in an argument $\mathcal{A} = \{e_1 ; e_2 ; \ldots; e_k \}$.

$\langle \mathcal{A}_1, send(id_1, joe)\rangle^D$	$\langle \mathcal{B}_1, send(id_2, joe)\rangle^U$
$\mid$	
$\langle \mathcal{A}_2, \sim interest(id_1, joe)\rangle^U$	
(i)	(ii)
$\langle \mathcal{C}_1, send(id_5, joe)\rangle^D$	$\langle \mathcal{D}_1, send(id_5, joe)\rangle^U$
$\mid$	$\mid$
$\langle \mathcal{C}_2, \sim interest(id_5, joe)\rangle^U$	$\langle \mathcal{D}_2, \sim mandatory(id_5, joe)\rangle^D$
	$\mid$
	$\langle \emptyset, topsecret(id_5)\rangle^U$
(iii)	(iv)

Fig. 4. Dialectical trees for queries $send(id_1, joe)$, $send(id_2, joe)$ and $send(id_5, joe)$ (examples 1, 2 and 3)

Example 2. Consider now the query $send(id_2, joe)$. In that case there is a single argument $\langle \mathcal{B}_1, send(id_1, joe)\rangle$, with

$$\mathcal{B}_2 = \{\quad send(id_2, joe) \multimap allowed(id_2, joe), interest(id_2, joe) ;$$
$$interest(id_2, joe) \multimap isAbout(id_2, computers),$$
$$intField(computers, joe) \}$$

This argument has no defeaters. Hence the corresponding dialectical tree $\mathcal{T}_{\langle \mathcal{B}_2, send(id_2, joe)\rangle}$ has a single node, marked as U-node (see Figure 4-ii). The original argument is therefore warranted.

Example 3. Finally consider the query $send(id_5, joe)$. There is an argument $\langle \mathcal{C}_1, send(id_1, joe)\rangle$, with

$$\mathcal{C}_1 = \{\quad send(id_5, joe) \multimap allowed(id_5, joe), interest(id_5, joe) ;$$
$$interest(id_5, joe) \multimap isAbout(id_5, computers), intField(computers, joe)\}$$

However, in this case, a defeater $\langle \mathcal{C}_2, \sim interest(id_5, joe)\rangle$ for $\langle \mathcal{C}_1, send(id_5, joe)\rangle$ can be found, with

$$\mathcal{C}_2 = \{\sim interest(id_5, joe) \multimap \quad isAbout(id_5, computers), intField(computers, joe),$$
$$isAbout(id_5, hardware), \sim intField(hardware, joe). \}$$

As in Example 1, the argument $\langle \mathcal{C}_1, send(id_1, joe)\rangle$ is not warranted (see Figure 4-iii). The DeLP inference engine searches then for alternative arguments for $send(id_5, joe)$. There is another one, namely $\langle \mathcal{D}_1, send(id_5, joe)\rangle$, with $\mathcal{D}_1 = \{send(id_2, joe) \multimap allowed(id_2, joe), mandatory(id_5, joe)\}$ which in this case is defeated by another argument $\langle \mathcal{D}_2, \sim mandatory(id_5, joe)\rangle$, with

$$\mathcal{D}_2 = \{ \sim mandatory(id_5, joe) \multimap permissions(joe, manager),$$
$$\sim interest(id_5, joe), \mathbf{not}\ topsecret(id_5)$$
$$\sim interest(id_5, joe) \multimap isAbout(id_5, computers), intField(computers, joe),$$
$$isAbout(id_5, hardware), \sim intField(hardware, joe) \}$$

which is defeated by a third, empty argument $\langle \mathcal{D}_3, topsecret(id_5)\rangle$, with $\mathcal{D}_3 = \emptyset$ (note that $topsecret(id_5)$ is logically entailed by the strict knowledge in $\mathcal{P}_{org}$, and hence no defeasible information is needed). Argument $\langle \mathcal{D}_3, topsecret(id_5)\rangle$ defeats

$\langle \mathcal{D}_2, \sim mandatory(id_5, joe)\rangle$, reinstating argument $\langle \mathcal{D}_1, send(id_5, joe)\rangle$. In this case, the argument $\langle \mathcal{D}_1, send(id_5, joe)\rangle$ is warranted (see Fig. 4-iv).

After solving the different queries as shown in the previous examples, memos id_2 and id_5 would be delivered to *Joe*, but not memo id_1. A similar analysis could be carried out for *Susan*. In her case, only memos id_1 and id_5 would be delivered to her, but not memo id_2 (as it comes from the technical department, and according to her personal preferences should be discarded).

6   Implementation Issues Related Work

Performing defeasible argumentation in the context of real-world applications is not an easy task, and demands an efficient computational implementation. To this end, a particular abstract machine called JAM (Justification Abstract Machine) has been developed for DeLP [6]. The JAM provides an argument-based extension of the traditional Warren abstract machine for PROLOG. On the basis of this abstract machine a Java-based integrated development environment was then implemented, which allows not only on-line compilation and query solving of DeLP code but also visualization of dialectical trees using a graphic interface [12]. [11] For applying DeLP specifically to IK distribution, we have used the JITIK [12] system [13, 14], which is intended for disseminating pieces of IK among the members of large distributed organizations. Before the use of DeLP, JITIK distribution decision methods were somewhat simple, dealing just with inheritance in hierarchies, but it was not able to consider conflicting policies, incomplete information, and in general all the kind of complexities that DeLP is able to handle. So, DeLP over JITIK gives a much more flexible system than JITIK alone.

To the best of our knowledge there are virtually no other works in the area of argumentation-based automated IK distribution. A somehow related research is reported in [15] about methods for helping in decision-making processes using argumentation. Besides the differences in the intended application of this system there is also a significative difference in the approach as they use static predefined argumentation schemas, whereas here we propose a general method for constructing arguments that is not restricted to a finite number of argument structures. Other works related to ours involve decision making and negotiation using argumentation among agents [16, 17]. In contrast, in our system the argumentation process itself is not distributed, taking always place in a central DeLP inference engine.

7   Conclusions

We have presented a novel argument-based approach for supporting IK-distribution processes in large organizations based on a defeasible argumentation

---

[11] See http://cs.uns.edu.ar/~ags/DLP/ for details.

[12] Just-In-Time Information and Knowledge, see http://lizt.mty.itesm.mx/jitik

formalism. As we have shown, the main advantage obtained by the use of an argumentation engine is an increased flexibility, as it is not necessary to explicitly encode actions for every possible situation. This is particularly important in corporate environments with potentially conflicting information distribution criteria.

Our approach is applicable in general to the distribution of IK that can be characterized by symbolic metadata expressed as ground terms in predicate logic. Currently, our experiments regarding this approach only account as a "proof of concept" prototype, as we have not been able yet to carry out thorough evaluations in the context of a real-world application, which we intend to do in the future. We stress that the sample problem presented in Section 5 was encoded and solved successfully using the methodology presented in this paper.

Acknowledgments

This work was supported by the Monterrey Tech CAT-011 research chair, by Projects TIC2001-1577-C03-01 and TIC2003-00950, by Ramón y Cajal Program (MCyT, Spain) and by CONICET (Argentina).

References

1. Atkinson, R., Court, R., Ward, J.:   The knowledge economy: Knowledge producers and knowledge users.   The New Economic Index (1998) http://www.neweconomyindex.org/
2. Carrillo, J.: Managing knowledge-based value systems. Journal of Knowledge Management **1** (1998)
3. Liebowitz, J., Beckman, T.: Knowledge Organizations. St. Lucie Press (1998)
4. Chesñevar, C., Maguitman, A., Loui, R.: Logical Models of Argument. ACM Computing Surveys **32** (2000) 337–383
5. Prakken, H., Vreeswijk, G.: Logical Systems for Defeasible Argumentation. In Gabbay, D., F.Guenther, eds.: Handbook of Phil. Logic. Kluwer (2002) 219–318
6. García, A., Simari, G.: Defeasible Logic Programming: An Argumentative Approach. Theory and Practice of Logic Programming **4** (2004) 95–138
7. Chesñevar, C., Maguitman, A.: ARGUENET: An Argument-Based Recommender System for Solving Web Search Queries. In: Proc. of the 2nd IEEE Intl. IS-2004 Conference. Varna, Bulgaria. (2004) 282–287
8. Gómez, S., Chesñevar, C.: A Hybrid Approach to Pattern Classification Using Neural Networks and Defeasible Argumentation. In: Proc. of 17th Intl. FLAIRS Conference. Miami, Florida, USA. (2004) 393–398
9. Chesñevar, C., Maguitman, A.: An Argumentative Approach to Assessing Natural Language Usage based on the Web Corpus. In: Proc. of the ECAI-2004 Conference. Valencia, Spain. (2004) 581–585
10. Simari, G., Loui, R.: A Mathematical Treatment of Defeasible Reasoning and its Implementation. Art. Intelligence **53** (1992) 125–157
11. Stolzenburg, F., García, A., Chesñevar, C., Simari, G.: Computing Generalized Specificity. J. of Non-Classical Logics **13** (2003) 87–113

12. Stankevicius, A., Garcia, A., Simari, G.: Compilation techniques for defeasible logic programs. In: Proc. of the 6th Intl. Congress on Informatics Engineering, Univ. de Buenos Aires, Argentina, Ed. Fiuba (2000) 1530–1541
13. Brena, R., Aguirre, J.L., Trevino, A.C.: Just-in-time information and knowledge: Agent technology for km bussiness process. In: Proc. 2001 IEEE Conference on Systems, Man and Cybernetics, Tucson, Arizona, IEEE Press (2001)
14. Aguirre, J., Brena, R., Cantu, F.: Multiagent-based knowledge networks. Expert Systems with Applications **20** (2001) 65–75
15. Lowrance, J.D., Harrison, I.W., Rodriguez, A.C.: Structured argumentation for analysis. In: Procs. of the 12th Intl. Conf. on Systems Research, Informatics, and Cybernetics, Baden-Baden, Germany (2000) 47–57
16. Parsons, S., Jennings, N.R.: Argumentation and multi-agent decision making. In: Proceedings of the AAAI Spring Symposium on Interactive and Mixed-Initiative Decision Making, Stanford, USA (1998) 89–91
17. Parsons, S., Sierra, C., Jennings, N.: Agents that Reason and Negotiate by Arguing. Journal of Logic and Computation **8** (1998) 261–292

On the Role of the Markov Condition in Causal Reasoning

Eric Neufeld and Sonje Kristtorn

Department of Computer Science, 110 Science Place, University of Saskatchewan,
Saskatoon, Sk., Canada S7K 5C9
eric@cs.usask.ca, wlf323@mail.usask.ca

Abstract. The Markov condition describes the conditional independence relations present in a causal graph. Cartwright argues that causal inference methods
have limited applicability because the Markov condition cannot always be applied to domains, and gives an example of its incorrect application. We question
two aspects of this argument. One, causal inference methods do not apply the
Markov condition to domains, but infer causal structures from actual independencies. Two, confused intuitions about conditional independence relationships
in certain complex domains can be explained as problems of measurement and
of proxy selection.

1 Introduction

According to certain authors, notably Spirtes, Glymour, and Scheines (SGS) (Spirtes
et al, 1993), it is a feature of causal graphs that a variable is conditionally independent
of its nondescendants given its parents. This 'Markov condition', they claim, is an
aspect of the overall relationship between probability distributions and causal graphs.
Against this, Nancy Cartwright (2003, 1999a, 1999b) argues that the Markov condition seldom obtains where causes are probabilistic; she contends, moreover, that in
the 'macroscopic world' (as opposed to the world of quantum physics) causality is, if
not probabilistic, at least for the most part best modeled probabilistically. The Markov
condition therefore cannot be assumed; it can be invoked only where there is good
evidence that it applies and she expects this to be rare. Since she regards the Markov
condition as essential to the causal inference methods of SGS, she concludes that
these methods are correspondingly limited in their applicability.

   In presenting this argument, Cartwright gives an illustration that, for some readers,
will confuse the use of the Markov condition as a convenient computational idealiza-
tion with its use as shorthand for describing sets of actual relationships. We show here
that it is possible for both the supposed actual and the hypothesized ideal relationships
to hold simultaneously, depending on how the problem domain are measured. Although one might say that directing an arc in a causal graph imposes a set of independence relationships on a subset of variables, the arc should only be added if the
said independence relationships exist in the data in the first place, at least
approximately.

B. Kégl and G. Lapalme (Eds.): AI 2005, LNAI 3501, pp. 257–267, 2005.

In the sequel, we introduce causal graphs, show the relevance of the Markov condition, show how causal graphs can be constructed from raw data in a few simple cases and then present Cartwright's criticism of the Markov condition. Her apparently paradoxical "factory" example can be resolved by considering the practicalities of proxy selection when measuring ill-defined variables. We show that different measurements acting as proxies for "factory activity", lead to different conclusions about the relationships of domain variables. Thus we see the Markov condition as a relationship that may or may not obtain, and its presence is an empirical problem that can not generally be settled by argument.

2 Causal Graphs

A causal graph (Pearl, 1988; 2000) consists of a directed acyclic graph $G=(V,E)$ and a set of conditional probability distributions $P(V_i \,|parents(V_i\,))$ for each V_i in V. Nodes in V represent random variables and edges in E define the *parent* relationship. The topology of the graph encodes the knowledge that the joint distribution of variables in V is the product of the conditional probability distributions stored at each node. This can be shown to be equivalent to the Markov Condition (Pearl, 1988). Although there are many examples of informal applications of causal graphs to problems where the independence relationships are imposed on the data for convenience, in fact, the structure of the graph is determined by independence relations actually in the data.

Causal graphs were originally proposed as a computationally useful way of compactly representing joint distributions of many variables, and of reasoning with them efficiently. The efficiencies are obtained by exploiting the independencies in the data. There is a significant literature on inference; (Pearl, 1988) is a good place to start.

However, AI practitioners noticed early on that typical independence assumptions in certain domains (e.g., in diagnosis, unconditional independence of diseases and conditional independence of symptoms) oriented the arcs in a causal direction. Pearl and Verma's (1991) following definition of *potential causality* provides philosophical justification for this.

Given variables A, B, C and a context S, Pearl and Verma say that A is a potential cause of C if

1. A and C are dependent in all contexts,
2. B and C are dependent, and
3. there is a context S such that A and B are independent.

To construct a graph from raw data, one begins by placing an undirected edge between each pair of variables that are dependent in all contexts. Now consider the collinear triple A—C—B, with nodes obeying the relationships in the preceding definition, plus B and C are dependent in all contexts. There is only one way to orient the arcs causally without creating logical errors, i.e., $A \rightarrow C \leftarrow B$. This is called a v-structure (Pearl, 2000). All other orientations contradict the third part of the definition. After all collinear triples have been considered, construction continues by orienting undirected arcs so that no new v-structures and no cycles are introduced. (It may not be possible to orient certain arcs unambiguously.) This definition is called potential cause, because the possibility remains that there is a hidden (unmeasured) variable L that may be a common cause of both A and C.

Note again that the causal arcs appear after the discovery of certain combinations of dependence and independence relations in the data: these relations are not imposed.

3 Cartwright's Criticism of the Markov Condition in Causal Graphs

Cartwright considers the Markov condition under two aspects: The first of these concerns temporal relationships between causes. Causes do not operate "across temporal gaps" (107), so conditioning on the parents of a variable makes it independent of the rest of its ancestor variables. The second aspect affirms the mutual independence, or 'screening off', of variables, given their common parents. Thus, conditioning on the parents 'screens' their shared effects from each other. It is this 'screening off' aspect of the Markov condition that is the subject of her argument

The SGS position, according to Cartwright, is that the Markov condition holds for "causal graphs of deterministic or pseudo-deterministic systems in which the exogenous variables are independently distributed." (SGS, 1993, p.57) She describes a pseudo-deterministic graph as a (correct) indeterministic subgraph of a more complete (and likewise correct) deterministic graph – bearing in mind that correctness, not completeness, is the achievable goal. Glymour describes a pseudo-indeterministic system more precisely as a system without feedback obtained from a larger system by "marginalizing out some exogenous causes" (Glymour, 1999, p.71). In any case, that the Markov condition holds for deterministic systems as well as for apparently indeterministic subsystems of deterministic systems is, she says, "trivially true".

When the relationship between cause and effect is deterministic, causes fix the values of their effects. So, for example, in the simple case of a single cause of two effects, if I know the value of the cause, I know the value of each effect. The effects are independent of each other, given the cause, since knowing the value of one effect tells me nothing about the value of the other that I do not already know, if I know the value of the cause. Formally, $p(E_1 \mid C, E_2) = P(E_1 \mid C)$, where C represents the cause and E_1 and E_2 represent the effects of C. This means that the joint probability of two effects, given the cause(s) of those effects, will factor: $p(E_1, E_2 \mid C) = p(E_1 \mid C) \, p(E_2 \mid C)$. However, according to Cartwright, deterministic causality is uncommon and the Markov condition does not (in general) hold where causality is probabilistic.

When a cause operates probabilistically the relationship between the value of the cause and the value of the effect is probabilistic: for a given value of the cause, there is a probability distribution over the possible values of the effects. (In the deterministic case, there is one possible value for each effect, given the cause, with probability 1.0; any other values have probability 0.0.) Cartwright argues that the value of one effect of a probabilistic cause will almost always provide some information about the value of a second effect, even if I know the value of the cause. In other words, there is no screening off here, no conditional independence. Likewise, the joint (conditional) probabilities will not factor.

Why should the fact that relationships between cause and effects are probabilistic lead us to draw this conclusion? Here Cartwright points to interactions between the operations of a cause to produce its different effects, something that is not directly represented in causal graphs. In the case of deterministic causality, these interactions need not be considered since a cause infallibly produces all of its effects. But in the case of probabilistic causality, we have to consider not only the probabilistic relationships between a cause and each of its effects but also the relationships, likewise probabilistic, between those causal relationships. When a cause can occur and yet not produce one or more of its effects, such interactions have to be taken into account when calculating the probability of one or another effect, given the cause. Cartwright apparently regards the screening-off aspect of the Markov condition as an attempt to evade or at least resolve this complexity by positing a "'split-brain' model of the common cause" (Cartwright, 1999, p. 108), according to which a cause operates independently to produce each of its effects. If the causal operations of a single cause are independent of each other, we need not consider the relationships between them. The heart of her objection seems to be an assertion that this simply is not so, or is very rarely so; usually it is a matter of 'joint operations', that is, there is a (probabilistic) relationship between the operations of a (probabilistic) cause to produce its various effects. So, even when we know the value of the cause, knowing the value of one effect is likely to tell us something about the value of the other.

Cartwright concedes the divorce-age-candy example of Blalock as an example that is consistent with the split-brain model. In that example, eating candy and divorce become conditionally independent, conditional on age; otherwise they have a negative association. The aging mechanism is complex and it seems intuitively agreeable that change in fondness for candy is governed by a mechanism independent of that which causes divorce—especially when compared to the smaller world of colds causing fevers and stuffy noses, where it seems almost impossible to imagine that the mechanism by which a cold causes one of these symptoms is independent of the other. However, given some reflection, it is not hard to imagine a few other variables that are comparable to age in complexity—for example, income, gender, nationality, personality type, height, etc. Each variable reflects an accumulation of inputs from a huge number of variables and to some extent hides a good deal of direct causal structure. As well, the outputs from the many variables become distilled into a single arc. Many features of age are highly correlated—perhaps Blalock's example is just one where many things balance out.

It is in this context that Cartwright presents her factory example. The main lines of this argument are as follows: There are two factories, D and P. Both produce a certain chemical, C, that is used immediately in a sewage plant. Factory D produces the chemical with probability 1.0, or deterministically. Factory P, on the other hand, produces the same chemical with probability 0.8, that is, probabilistically. Moreover, whenever P produces the chemical, it also produces a pollutant, B, as a byproduct. However, the owner of factory P maintains that the pollutant is produced when the chemical is used in the sewage treatment plant and, in support of this claim, advances an argument that assumes the Markov condition in its screening-off aspect, as follows: if the pollutant were a byproduct of factory P, then the probability of the pollutant would be independent of the probability of the chemical, given the factory that produced the chemical. Factory P argues that if it were responsible for the pollutant then $p(C,B \mid P) = p(C \mid P)p(B \mid P)$. But in fact $p(C,B \mid P)$ is 0.8 while the two factors are likewise each 0.8; therefore, argues factory P, it is not responsible for the noxious byproduct, since $0.8 \neq 0.8 \cdot 0.8$.

But factory P's argument is wrong, says Cartwright. Factory P *is* responsible for the byproduct. Factory P's error lies in its screening-off assumption. Because factory P produces both the chemical and the byproduct probabilistically, the probabilities of C and B are not independent given P and hence do not factor, that is, $p(C,B \mid P) \neq p(C \mid P)p(B \mid P)$; knowing something about the presence of the byproduct tells us something about the presence of the chemical. To pursue the 'split-brain' metaphor, the mechanisms whereby factory produces B and C are not independent.

In this example a cause, factory P, has two operations that produce two effects: one operation produces the chemical while the other produces the pollutant. The pollutant is a produced, apparently with probability 1.0, as a byproduct of the process that produces the chemical. Because of this relationship, the effects are conditionally dependent: even if we know the value for factory P, knowing the value of, for example, the chemical variable provides information about the value of the byproduct variable, B, that is not derivable solely from the value of their common cause, P. The value of the cause variable doesn't tell us whether the cause has been effective, whether it has, as Cartwright puts it, 'fired' and produced the chemical; it tells us only the probability that this is so. Knowing the value of the byproduct variable, B, provides this information and thereby provides information about the value of the chemical variable, C, that we would not know simply by knowing the value for P.

This example raises a few questions. First, there is a question about the consistency of the distribution as described. It would appear from the example that $p(C \mid D,P) = 1.0$, $p(C \mid \overline{D},P) = 0.8$, $p(C \mid D,\overline{P}) = 1.0$, and $p(C \mid \overline{D},\overline{P}) = 0.0$. Using Jeffrey's rule, and a little algebra,

$$p(C \mid P) = \frac{p(C,P)}{p(P)} \qquad \text{(Definition of Conditional Probability)}$$

$$= \frac{p(C,D,P) + p(C,\overline{D},P)}{p(P)} \qquad \text{(Jeffrey's Rule)}$$

$$= \frac{p(C \mid D,P)p(D \mid P)p(P)}{p(P)} + \frac{p(C \mid \overline{D},P)p(\overline{D} \mid P)p(P)}{p(P)}$$
$$\text{(Product Rule)}$$

$$= p(C \mid D,P)p(D \mid P) + p(C \mid \overline{D},P)p(\overline{D} \mid P)$$

$$= 1.0p(D \mid P) + 0.8p(\overline{D} \mid P)$$

$$= p(D \mid P) + 0.8(1.0 - p(D \mid P))$$

$$= p(D \mid P) + 0.8 - 0.8p(D \mid P)$$

$$= 0.8 + p(D \mid P)(1.0 - 0.8)$$

$$= 0.8 + 0.2p(D \mid P).$$

Hence, if $p(C \mid \overline{D}, P) = 0.8$ then $p(C \mid P)$ must have a value greater than the 0.8 given in the example. These are equivalent only if $p(D \mid P) = 0.0$; that, however, would mean that there was a dependency between D and P, which is contrary to the graph for the example (Cartwright, 1999, p.23). We could contrive the distribution so that $p(C \mid P)$ comes out to 0.8, using the above calculation. This would require that a value be assigned to $p(D \mid P)$ or, effectively, to $p(D)$ since, according to the graph, D and P are unconditionally independent. It would also require the assignment of an appropriate value (less than 0.8) to $p(C \mid \overline{D}, P)$. However, the same value would have to be assigned to $p(B \mid \overline{D}, P)$ and, equivalently in this case, to $p(B \mid P)$, contrary to the example. Although we consider this a flaw in the presentation of the problem, it is a relatively minor issue. The next two questions go deeper.

A second question is related to an objection raised by Glymour (1999) in a response to Cartwright. Glymour (1999, p 71) claims that it is very difficult if not impossible to find an example of a system that violates the Markov condition, *if all causes are considered*. We observed earlier that a pseudo-indeterministic system, where exogenous causes are 'marginalized out', does not violate the Markov condition. But apparent counter-examples, wherein the Markov condition does not hold, are possible if causes are left out in other ways. For example, common causes may have been overlooked. (Note that the SGS algorithm presupposes the inclusion of all common causes of measured variables.) Or there may be other problems. Thus, an apparent counter-example may overlook the fact that variable values have been collapsed into a reduced set or it may involve a mixture of different systems. Moreover, there are physical systems where state descriptions fail to screen off prior state descriptions but this violation of what Cartwright describes as the first aspect of the Markov condition is, according to Glymour, generally taken to indicate some incompleteness in the state descriptions. In fact, Glymour maintains that most, if not all, counter-examples derive from ignorance of one kind or another.

It would seem that examples like the factory example might be vulnerable to an objection of this sort. If, for example, a common cause of a parent cause and one of its effects is omitted from consideration, the effects will not be independent, given their common parent. But this is because a common cause has been omitted, not because the Markov condition does not hold for the causal system the example intends to describe. The Markov condition does hold – so this objection goes – if the incompleteness is remedied. If the common cause is included, the two effects will be independent, once we condition on all the parents.

We have two responses to the above. On the one hand, we can interpret Cartwright's claim about the inapplicability of the Markov condition as implying that the Markov condition is an impossible ideal, and Glymour's response as, in some sense, confirming this. One can strike a philosophical compromise by saying that the unachievable ideal is nonetheless a useful tool, analogous to propositional logic. Very little, if any, real world knowledge can be captured succinctly in propositional logic, yet it is widely used. The second response is to look seriously at the nature of what we call variables, and the ways we devise to measure them.

The philosophical compromise already exists in the way science is done, i.e., we use logic in the small and large roughly as follows: From experiences, we generalize to logical sentences, which we use until new experiences provide counterexamples. At that point, we have two choices. One, we can revise or reject the theory. Two, we can reject the evidence. Perhaps we have been fooled with false data or our eyes have been tricked, or we become convinced that the original evidence was a fluke. This is reasonably common in medical diagnosis – a physician may well order tests to be re-done before rejecting a reasonably strong diagnosis (Pople, 1982).

Alternatively, we can explain Cartwright's objection in terms of measurement. Measurement is that elusive idea of how we classify and measure the world (Kyburg, 1984). At the level of discrete measurement ('natural kinds'), a theory of measurement tells us how to decide when the proposition 'stone' is true, and when it is false, so that we can count how many stones we have. This information is not perfect: over the long run, we will make counting errors with some probability. We may decide to weigh the stones, to distinguish stones from rocks and pebbles, but then we have a new problem – defining an apparatus that weighs (or measures mass of) objects. The conceptualization and implementation of this apparatus is also a process that is subject to dispute.

The factory problem can be modeled as a measurement problem. How do we measure such events as P and D? A factory is not like a circuit with a switch, a battery and a light. Machines must·be warmed up, and cooled down. The consequences of certain effluents may take considerable time to obtain. The factory may operate at different levels of production during different seasons and measuring instruments may behave differently at different times. Achieving universal agreement on whether or not the factory is 'running' on any day is impossible. Of course, a set of reasonable observers will likely come up with *similar,* but not identical definitions. Any particular definition will provide an approximation, but none will agree exactly.

In applied statistics, researchers choose proxies for this type of variable. Suppose you wish to measure *Quality of Computer Science Graduate Program* for a set of Canadian universities. (A similar variable exists in a study by Rogers and Maranto (1989).) There is no way to measure this directly, but a possible proxy might be the number of Computer Science graduate students with NSERC scholarships, using the reasoning that NSERC scholarships are the most competitive and go to the brightest applicants, and the brightest applicants will chose the best graduate programs. However, some universities might reply that many students choose universities for geographical reasons, and moreover, NSERC scholarships are not awarded to international students. One could then consider counting the number of faculty with external research grants. Some universities argue that they have mostly junior members who are not well established and only a few senior members with large grants. This leads to the possibility of measuring the total value of all research grants. In the end, a combination of several variables – class size, perceived reputation – form a *figure of merit* that facilitates comparison. It is generally difficult to get consensus on any particular figure.

Although it is possible to model Cartwright's factories as light bulbs on a simple circuit, it is more realistic to imagine a more complex model that might make selection of measurement method difficult. So, for example, we can select a certain threshold value on a certain output valve, or we can analyze water supplies. Consider the model depicted below. M_1 is one possible measurement taken to determine whether the factory is running. M_2 is a different measurement. Moreover, M_2 is a common cause of both M_1 and B. Both M_1 and M_2 are proxies for whether the factory is running, and one is much better than the other. The conditional probability tables are as follows:

$p(M_2) = 0.1$

$p(M_1) = 0.15$

$p(M_1 | M_2) = 0.6$

$p(M_1 | \overline{M}_2) = 0.1$

$p(C | M_1) = 0.8$

$p(C | M_2) = 0.72$

$p(C | \overline{M}_1) = 0.6$

$p(B | M_1, M_2) = 0.8$

$p(B | M_1, \overline{M}_2) = 0.8$

$p(B | \overline{M}_1, M_2) = 0.6$

$p(B | M_1) = 0.8$

$p(B | M_2) = 0.72$

$p(C, B | M_2) = 0.528$

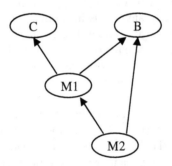

Fig. 1. A Causal Model for the Measurement Example

These probabilities were obtained using a simple brute force search, constrained to report only distributions where C and B are independent given M_1 and, dependent given M_2. We took care to select a distribution where M_1 and M_2 were otherwise as similar as possible. Both co-occur frequently, and both present C and B with approximately similar frequencies. We also took care to find distributions similar to the one in Cartwright's example.

From the topology of the graph, it is easy to show that if we condition on $M1$, the two factory outputs are independent, and if we condition on $M2$ they are dependent. The example further shows that there is no hidden independency buried in the conditional probability distributions. Assuming that both measurements would be acceptable to a human observer as reasonable proxies, one implies the conditional independence relationship associated with the Markov condition, and the other implies the dependence shown in Cartwright's example.

This gives us a different perspective on Cartwright's argument. Glymour's claim that the Markov condition always holds given all causes are represented is as difficult to defend as Cartwright's claim that it almost never holds. But given that the MC can hold, and the problem is one of choosing the correct metric, then the problem of finding a measurement consistent with the ideal we are trying to measure is a familiar one. Deciding the 'true' relationship between C and B may be difficult if disputes over methods of measurement cannot be resolved. However, this shows that whether the Markov condition holds or not in the ideal the proxy was intended to represent is an empirical, rather than a theoretical, question.

Such an argument may seem strange in the case of a fictional example. Someone who wants to dispute the example can perhaps claim that a crucial cause has been overlooked. But in the case of a fictional example, unless the alleged missing cause is implied in the example in the first place, it is difficult to see how such an argument can be sustained without begging the question. On the other hand, the one who puts forth the example can stipulate that no such cause has been overlooked. Thus, Cartwright's factory example specifically states that all causes of the chemical and the byproduct are included. Again, there seems to be an element of question-begging here. And therein lies another difficulty, also raised by Glymour: the factory example is entirely fictional yet it is intended to refute what Glymour calls a 'hypothesis about nature' (1999, p.72). Glymour argues that we can always imagine a counter-example to a hypothesis about nature but such imagined counter-examples cannot refute the hypothesis.

Glymour makes a similar rejoinder to another argument Cartwright advances. This argument, which might be considered a negative conceptual argument, is embedded in a kind of 'what are the odds?' argument: How likely is it, when we have a joint probability distribution over the effects of a common cause, that the distribution will be such that the effects are conditionally independent? The answer, she says, is "not very" and consequently screening off cannot be assumed; there must be good evidence for it in a particular case. This line of argument is buttressed by the claim that there is nothing in the concept of causality that implies 'screening off', that "nothing in the concept of causality, nor of probabilistic causality, constrains how nature must proceed" (*The Dappled World*, p.109). Glymour responds that something may be true in nature even though it is not a part of the relevant concepts. He also argues that it is entirely possible that the way human beings think about causes may indeed be inseparable from the Markov condition, whether this derives from hard-wiring or experience and whether this is explicit in our concept of causality or no. In fact, Glymour regards the Markov condition as a kind of 'rule of thumb', an empirical heuristic that is almost always valid and gives good results, rather than as a component of a well-established scientific theory on the one hand or an a priori principle on the other.

Thirdly, there is the question of the role Cartwright ascribes to the Markov condition. She argues that, given the situation described in her 'factory argument', B and C

must be conditionally independent, given P, if the Markov condition holds in this case. This intuition corresponds to a graph of the situation, depicted in the *Synthese* paper though not in *The Dappled World*, wherein P is the sole cause of both B and C. The Markov condition as applied to this graph implies the conditional independence of B and C, given P. She then points out that the expected conditional independence relationship does not hold, given the distribution in the example. Above, we suggested that whether or not this kind of intuition of conditional independence turns out to be valid can turn on measurement issues. However, measurement issues aside, an expectation of conditional independence can be falsified, as in this example, by the distribution. In the factory example, factory P's argument assumes not only the Markov condition but the graph to which it is applied. However, if B and C are not, according to the distribution, conditionally independent given P, the 'true graph' (as opposed to the intuitive model) will have an arc between B and C and therefore the Markov condition, in its 'screening off' aspect, will not, when applied to this graph, imply the conditional independence of B and C, given P. Any graph produced by the SGS algorithm will have an arc between B and C, if this conditional independence relationship does not apply. It is difficult to see, then, that the factory example casts doubt on 'screening off'. More broadly, it is difficult to see how what she has to say about probabilistic causality bears on this issue since a graph generated by the algorithm will show 'screening off' relationships only where the corresponding conditional independence exists.

The same kind of question arises in connection with the 'what are the odds' argument. It is difficult to see the significance of 'the odds' of conditional independence for the question of the validity of 'screening off' since a graph will display this kind of relationship only where the corresponding independence relationships are found in the distribution. The likelihood of such an occurrence does not seem to matter.

4 Conclusions

It is possible to interpret Cartwright's example as critical of causal reasoning formalisms because, to be effective, they require the imposition of the Markov condition prior to the determination of actual conditional independence relations and their depiction in a causal graph. We have raised three questions in response to this. The first question was minor, regarding the distribution as presented by Cartwright. Our second question showed that the presence or absence of the Markov condition is in theory arbitrary. Lack of clear intuitions about its presence or absence can easily arise as a consequence of different measurement criteria. Finally, we believe that independence is not a consequence of the depiction, but rather something inherent in the depicted relations.

Acknowledgements

This research was supported by an NSERC Discovery Grant.

References

Cartwright, N. (1999). Causal Diversity and the Markov Condition, *Synthese*, **121**:3–27 .

Cartwright, N. (1999). *The Dappled World: A Study of the Boundaries of Science*. Cambridge University Press, Cambridge.

Cartwright, N. (2003) What is wrong with Bayes Nets? In *Probability is the Very Guide of Life*, Henry E. Kyburg and Mariam Thalos eds., Open Court Publishing, Illinois, 253-276.

Glymour, C. (1999). Rabbit Hunting, *Synthese*, **121**: 55–78.

Kyburg, Henry E., Jr. (1984) *Theory and Measurement*. Cambridge University Press, Cambridge.

Pearl, J. (1988) *Probabilistic Reasoning in Intelligent Systems: Networks of Plausible Inference*. Morgan Kaufmann, San Francisco.

Pearl, J, and Verma, T. (1991) A Theory Of Inferred Causation. In *Proceedings of Second International Conference on Principles of Knowledge Representation and Reasoning*, 441–452.

Pearl, J. (2000*) Causality: Models, Reasoning, and Inference*. Cambridge University Press, Cambridge.

Pople, H.E. Jr. (1982). Heuristic Methods for Imposing Structure on Ill-Structured Problems: The Structuring of Medical Diagnostics. In *Artificial Intelligence and Medicine*, P. Szolovits, ed., Westview Press, Boulder, Colorado, 119–190.

Rodgers, R. and Maranto C. (1989) Causal models of publishing productivity in psychology. *Journal of Applied Psychology*, **66**: 688–701.

Spirtes, P., Glymour, C., and Scheines, R. (1993). *Causation, Prediction and Search*, Springer-Verlag, New York.

The Impact of Feature Extraction on the Performance of a Classifier: kNN, Naïve Bayes and C4.5

Mykola Pechenizkiy

Dept. of Computer Science and Information Systems, University of Jyväskylä,
Jyväskylä, Finland
mpechen@cs.jyu.fi

Abstract. "The curse of dimensionality" is pertinent to many learning algorithms, and it denotes the drastic raise of computational complexity and the classification error in high dimensions. In this paper, different feature extraction techniques as means of (1) dimensionality reduction, and (2) constructive induction are analyzed with respect to the performance of a classifier. Three commonly used classifiers are taken for the analysis: kNN, Naïve Bayes and C4.5 decision tree. One of the main goals of this paper is to show the importance of the use of class information in feature extraction for classification and (in)appropriateness of random projection or conventional PCA to feature extraction for classification for some data sets. Two eigenvector-based approaches that take into account the class information are analyzed. The first approach is parametric and optimizes the ratio of between-class variance to the within-class variance of the transformed data. The second approach is a nonparametric modification of the first one based on the local calculation of the between-class covariance matrix. In experiments on benchmark data sets these two approaches are compared with each other, with conventional PCA, with random projection and with plain classification without feature extraction for each classifier.

1 Introduction

Knowledge discovery in databases (KDD) is a combination of data warehousing, decision support, and data mining that indicates an innovative approach to information management. KDD is an emerging area that considers the process of finding previously unknown and potentially interesting patterns and relations in large databases [8]. Current electronic data repositories are growing quickly and contain huge amount of data from commercial, scientific, and other domain areas. The capabilities for collecting and storing all kinds of data totally exceed the abilities to analyze, summarize, and extract knowledge from this data. Numerous data mining techniques have recently been developed to extract knowledge from these large databases. Fayyad in [8] introduced KDD as "the nontrivial process of identifying valid, novel, potentially useful, and ultimately understandable patterns in data". The process comprises several steps, which involve data selection, data pre-processing, data transformation, application of machine learning techniques, and the interpretation and evaluation of patterns.

B. Kégl and G. Lapalme (Eds.): AI 2005, LNAI 3501, pp. 268–279, 2005.
© Springer-Verlag Berlin Heidelberg 2005

In this paper we analyze the problems related to data transformation, before applying certain machine learning techniques. In Section 2 the data transformation approaches are seen from two different perspectives. The first one is related to the so-called "curse of dimensionality" problem [5] and the necessity of dimensionality reduction [2]. The second perspective comes from the assumption that in many data sets to be processed some individual features, being irrelevant or indirectly relevant for the purpose of analysis, form poor problem representation space. Corresponding ideas of constructive induction that assume the improvement of problem representation before application of any learning technique are presented.

Feature extraction (FE) for classification is aimed at finding such a transformation of the original space in order to produce new features, which would preserve class separability as much as possible and to form a new lower-dimensional problem representation space. Thus, FE accounts for both the perspectives, and, therefore, we believe that FE, when applied either on data sets with high dimensionality or on data sets including indirectly relevant features, can improve the performance of a classifier.

We consider different types of feature extraction techniques for classification in Section 3, including Principal Component Analysis (PCA), Random Projection (RP) and two class-conditional approaches to FE. We conduct a number of experiments on 20 UCI datasets, analyzing the impact of these FE techniques on the classification performance of the nearest neighbour classification, Naïve Bayes, and C4.5 decision tree learning. The results of these experiments are reported in Section 4. And then, in Section 5 we briefly summarize with the main conclusions and further research directions.

2   Poor Representation Spaces: "The Curse of Dimensionality" and Indirectly Relevant Features

In this section the two main reasons are presented why data transformation might be an important step to be undertaken before a certain machine learning technique is applied. The first issue is related to the so-called "curse of dimensionality" and the necessity for dimensionality reduction. The second issue is related to the potentially poor representation of the problem in terms of some irrelevant or indirectly relevant features that represent the data and the corresponding necessity to improve the representation.

2.1 Dimensionality Reduction

In many real-world applications, numerous features are used in an attempt to ensure accurate classification. If all those features are used to build up classifiers, then they operate in high dimensions, and the learning process becomes computationally and analytically complicated, resulting often in the drastic rise of classification error. Hence, there is a need to reduce the dimensionality of the feature space before classification. According to the adopted strategy dimensionality reduction techniques are divided into feature selection and feature transformation (also called feature discovery). The key difference between feature selection and feature transformation is that during the first process a subset of original features only is selected while the second approach is based on the generation of completely new features [15]. Feature extraction is a dimensionality reduction technique that extracts a subset of new features from the original set of features by means of some functional mapping keeping as much information in the data as possible [10].

The essential drawback of all the methods that just assign weights to individual features is their insensitivity to interacting or correlated features. Also, in many cases some features are useful on one example set but useless or even misleading in another. That is why the transformation of the given representation before weighting the features in such cases can be preferable. However, feature extraction and subset selection are not, of course, totally independent processes and they can be considered as different ways of task representation. And the use of such techniques is determined by the purposes, and, moreover, sometimes feature extraction and selection methods are combined together in order to improve the solution.

2.2 Constructive Induction

Even, if the dimensionality of problem is relatively low, the problem is that most inductive learning approaches assume that the features used to represent instances are sufficiently relevant. However, it was shown experimentally that this assumption does not hold often for many learning problems. Some features may not be directly relevant, and some features may be redundant or irrelevant. Even those inductive learning approaches that apply feature selection techniques, and can eliminate irrelevant features and thus somehow account for the problem of high dimensionality, often fail to find good representation of data. This happens because of the fact that many features in their original representation are weakly or indirectly relevant to the problem. The existence of such features usually requires the generation of new, more relevant features that are some functions of the original ones. Such functions may vary from very simple as a product or a sum of a subset of the original features to very complex as a feature that reflects whether some geometrical primitive is present or absent in an instance. The discretization (quantization) of continuous features may serve for abstraction of some features when the reduction of the range of possible values is desirable. The original representation space can be improved for learning by removing less relevant features, adding more relevant features and abstracting features. We consider a constructive induction approach with respect to classification.

Constructive induction (CI) is a learning process that consists of two intertwined phases, one of which is responsible for the construction of the "best" representation space and the second concerns with generating hypotheses in the found space [16]. In Figure 1 we can see two problems – with a) high-quality, and b) low-quality representation spaces (RS). So, in a) points marked by "+" are easily separated from the points marked by "–" using a straight line or a rectangular border. But in b) "+" and "–" are highly intermixed that indicates the inadequateness of the original RS. A common approach is to search for complex boundaries to separate the classes. The constructive induction approach suggests searching for a better representation space where the groups are better separated, as in c).

However, in this paper the focus is on constructing new features from the original ones by means of some functional mapping that is known as feature extraction. We consider FE from both perspectives – as a constructive induction technique as a dimensionality reduction technique.

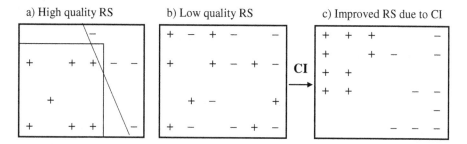

Fig. 1. High vs. low quality representation spaces (RS) for concept learning. Constructive induction (CI) aims to improve the quality of the low-quality RS [16]

3   Feature Extraction for Classification

Generally, feature extraction for classification can be seen as a search process among all possible transformations of the original feature set for the best one, which preserves class separability as much as possible in the space with the lowest possible dimensionality [10]. In other words we are interested in finding a projection $\mathbf{w}$:

$$y = \mathbf{w}^T \mathbf{x} \tag{1}$$

where y is a $k \times 1$ transformed data point (presented using k features), $\mathbf{w}$ is a $d \times k$ transformation matrix, and $\mathbf{x}$ is a $d \times 1$ original data point (presented using d features).

3.1 PCA

Principal Component Analysis (PCA) is a classical statistical method, which extracts a lower dimensional space by analyzing the covariance structure of multivariate statistical observations [12].

The main idea behind PCA is to determine the features that explain as much of the total variation in the data as possible with as few of these features as possible. The computation of the PCA transformation matrix is based on the eigenvalue decomposition of the covariance matrix $\mathbf{S}$ and therefore is computationally rather expensive.

$$\mathbf{w} \leftarrow eig\_decomposition \left(\mathbf{S} = \sum_{i=1}^{n} (\mathbf{x}_i - \mathbf{m})(\mathbf{x}_i - \mathbf{m})^T \right) \tag{2}$$

where n is the number of instances, $\mathbf{x}_i$ is the i-th instance, and $\mathbf{m}$ is the mean vector of the input data.

Computation of the principal components can be presented with the following algorithm:

1. Calculate the covariance matrix **S** from the input data.
2. Compute the eigenvalues and eigenvectors of **S** and sort them in a descending order with respect to the eigenvalues.
3. Form the actual transition matrix by taking the predefined number of components (eigenvectors).
4. Finally, multiply the original feature space with the obtained transition matrix, which yields a lower- dimensional representation.

The necessary cumulative percentage of variance explained by the principal axes is used commonly as a threshold, which defines the number of components to be chosen.

3.2 The Random Projection Approach

In many application areas like market basket analysis, text mining, image processing etc., dimensionality of data is so high that commonly used dimensionality reduction techniques like PCA are almost inapplicable because of extremely high computational time/cost.

Recent theoretical and experimental results on the use of random projection (RP) as a dimensionality reduction technique have attracted the DM community [6]. In RP a lower-dimensional projection is produced by means of transformation like in PCA but the transformation matrix is generated randomly (although often with certain constrains).

The theory behind RP is based on the Johnson and Lindenstrauss Theorem that says that any set of n points in a d-dimensional Euclidean space can be embedded into a k-dimensional Euclidean space – where k is logarithmic in n and independent of d – so that all pairwise distances are maintained within an arbitrarily small factor [1]. The basic idea is that the transformation matrix has to be orthogonal in order to protect data from significant distortions and try to preserve distances between the data points. Generally, orthogonalization of the transformation matrix is computationally expensive, however, Achlioptas showed a very easy way of defining (and also implementing and computing) the transformation matrix for RP [1]. So, according to [1] the transformation matrix **w** can be computed simply either as:

$$
w_{ij} = \sqrt{3} \cdot
\begin{cases}
+1 & \text{with probability } 1/6 \\
0 & \text{with probability } 2/3 \\
-1 & \text{with probability } 1/6
\end{cases}
\text{, or } \quad
w_{ij} =
\begin{cases}
+1 & \text{with probability } 1/2 \\
-1 & \text{with probability } 1/2
\end{cases}
\tag{3}
$$

RP as a dimensionality reduction technique was experimentally analyzed on image (noisy and noiseless) and text data (a newsgroup corpus) by Binghan and Mannila in [6]. Their results demonstrate that RP preserves the similarity of data vectors rather well (even when data is projected onto relatively small numbers of dimensions).

Fradkin and Madigan in [9] performed experiments (on 5 different data sets) with RP and PCA for inductive supervised learning. Their results show that although PCA predictively outperformed RP, RP is rather useful approach because of its computational advantages. Authors also indicated a trend in their results that the predictive performance of RP is improved with increasing the dimensionality when combining with the right learning algorithm. It was found that for those 5 data sets RP is suited better for nearest neighbour methods, where preserving distance between data points is more important than preserving the informativeness of individual features, in contrast to the decision tree approaches where the importance of these factors is reverse. However, further experimentation was encouraged.

3.3 Class-Conditional Eigenvector-Based FE

In [17] it was shown that although PCA is the most popular feature extraction technique, it has a serious drawback, namely the conventional PCA gives high weights to features with higher variabilities irrespective of whether they are useful for classification or not. This may give rise to the situation where the chosen principal component corresponds to the attribute with the highest variability but without any discriminating power.

A usual approach to overcome the above problem is to use some class separability criterion [3], e.g. the criteria defined in Fisher's linear discriminant analysis and based on the family of functions of scatter matrices:

$$J(\mathbf{w}) = \frac{\mathbf{w}^T \mathbf{S}_B \mathbf{w}}{\mathbf{w}^T \mathbf{S}_W \mathbf{w}} \qquad (4)$$

where $\mathbf{S}_B$ in the parametric case is the between-class covariance matrix that shows the scatter of the expected vectors around the mixture mean, and $\mathbf{S}_W$ is the within-class covariance, that shows the scatter of samples around their respective class expected vectors.

A number of other criteria were proposed in [10]. Both parametric and nonparametric approaches optimize criterion (4) by using the *simultaneous diagonalization algorithm* [10].

It should be noticed that there is a fundamental problem with the parametric nature of the covariance matrices. The rank of $\mathbf{S}_B$ is at most the *number of classes-1*, and hence no more than this number of new features can be obtained.

The nonparametric method overcomes this problem by trying to increase the number of degrees of freedom in the between-class covariance matrix, measuring the between-class covariances on a local basis. The k-nearest neighbor (kNN) technique is used for this purpose.

A two-class nonparametric feature extraction method was considered in [10], and it is extended in [20] to the multiclass case. The algorithm for nonparametric feature extraction is the same as for parametric extraction. Simultaneous diagonalization is used as well, and the only difference is in calculating the between-class covariance matrix $\mathbf{S}_B$. In the nonparametric case the between-class covariance matrix is calculated as the scatter of the samples around the expected vectors of other classes' instances in the neighborhood.

A number of experimental studies where parametric and nonparametric class-conditional FE have been applied for kNN [20], dynamic integration of classifiers [19] and data with small sample size and high number of feature [11] were considered.

4 Experiments and Results

The experiments were conducted on 20 data sets with different characteristics taken from the UCI machine learning repository [7]. The main characteristics of the data sets are presented in the first four columns of Table 1, which includes the names of the data sets, the numbers of instances included in the data sets, the numbers of different classes of instances, and the numbers of different kinds of features (binarized categorical plus numerical) included in the instances. Each categorical feature was replaced with a redundant set of binary features, each corresponding to a value of the original feature.

In the experiments, the accuracy of 3-nearest neighbor classification (3*NN*), Naïve-Bayes (NB) learning algorithm, and C4.5 decision tree (C4.5) [18] was calculated. All they are well known in the data mining and machine learning communities and represent three different approaches to learning from data. The main motivation to use 3 different kinds of classifiers is that we expect different impact of FE on the representation space not only with respect to different data sets but also with respect to different classifiers. In particular, for kNN it is expected that FE can produce better neigbourhood, for C4.5 – better (more informative) individual features, and for Naïve Bayes – uncorrelated features.

For each data set 30 test runs of Monte-Carlo cross validation were made to evaluate classification accuracy with the four feature extraction approaches and without feature extraction. In each run, the data set is first split into the training set and the test set by stratified random sampling to keep class distributions approximately same. Each time 30 percent of the instances of the data set are first randomly picked up to the test set. The remaining 70 percent of instances form the training set, which is used for finding the feature-extraction transformation matrix **w**. The test environment was implemented within the WEKA framework (the machine learning library in Java) [21]. The classifiers from this library were used with their default settings.

For PCA we used a 0.85 variance threshold, and for RP we took the number of projected features equal to 75% of original space. We took all the features extracted by parametric FE as it was always equal to *number of classes-1*.

Main results are presented in the last three columns of Table 1. Each cell contains the ordered list of 5 symbols from A to E, which code different FE techniques. A is RP, B - PCA, C - PAR (parametric FE), D - NPAR (nonparametric FE), E - Plain (case when no FE technique has been applied). At the first position is symbol that corresponds to the highest accuracy and the last one – to the lowest accuracy. A hyphen, when used instead of comma between the symbols, denotes the fact that the difference between the corresponding accuracies is less than 1%.

It can be seen from the table that for some data sets FE has no effect or deteriorates the classification accuracy compared to plain case E. In particular, for 3*NN* such situation is on 9 data sets from 20: Breast, Diabetes, Glass, Heart, Iris, Led, Monk-3, Thyroid, and Tic. For NB such situation is on 6 data sets from 20: Diabetes, Heart, Iris, Lymph, Monk-3, and Zoo. And for C4.5 such situation is on 11 data sets from 20: Car, Glass, Heart, Ionosphere, Led, Led17, Monk-1, Monk-3, Vehicle, Voting, and Zoo. It can be seen also that often different FE techniques are the best for different classifiers and for different data sets. Nevertheless, class-conditional FE approaches, especially the nonparametric approach are most often the best comparing to PCA or RP. On the other hand it is necessary to point out that the parametric FE was very often the worst, and for 3*NN* and C4.5 parametric FE was the worst technique more often than RP. Such results highlight the very unstable behavior of parametric FE.

Thus as it could be expected different FE techniques are often suited in different contexts not only for different data sets but also for different classifiers.

Table 1. – Datasets characteristics and relative accuracy results of 3*NN*, Naïve Bayes and C4.5 classifiers that were applied in different data spaces produced by corresponding FE techniques

Dataset	inst	class	feat	3*NN*	NB	C4.5
Balance	625	3	20	C,E,D,B,A	C,E,D,B,A	C,D,E,A,B
Breast	286	2	38	E,B,D,C,A	C,D,B-E,A	C,B,D-E,A
Car	1728	4	21	D,C,E,B,A	D-C,E,B,A	E,D,C,B,A
Diabetes	768	2	8	E,D,B,A,C	D-E,A,B,C	D,A-E,B,C
Glass	214	6	9	E,B-D,A,C	D,B,E,A,C	C-E,D-B-A
Heart	270	2	13	E,A,D,B,C	E,A,D,B,C	E,A,D,B,C
Ionosphere	351	2	33	D,B,E,A,C	D,B,A,E,C	A-B-D-E,C
Iris Plants	150	3	4	A-B-D-E,C	E-A,D-C,B	A,E,B-D,C
LED	300	10	7	E,B-C-D,A	B,C,D,E,A	B-C-D-E,A
LED17	300	10	24	C,E,B-D,A	C,E,D,B,A	E,C,D,B,A
Liver	345	2	6	D,E,B,A,C	D,B,C,E,A	B,E,C,D,A
Lymph	148	4	36	B,D-E,C,A	E,B,D,C,A	B,E,D,C,A
Monk-1	432	2	15	D,E,B,A,C	D,B,C-E,A	E,D,A,B,C
Monk-2	432	2	15	D,E,C,B,A	D,C,A-B,E	D,E,B,C,A
Monk-3	432	2	15	D-E,B,C,A	C-D-E,B,A	E,D,A-B,C
Thyroid	215	3	5	E,A-B,D,C	E,A,D-B,C	B,E,A,C-D
Tic	958	2	27	B-E,D,A,C	B,D,C,A-E	B,E,D,A,C
Vehicle	846	4	18	D,E,A,B,C	D,C,B,A-E	E,D,A,B,C
Voting	435	2	48	A,B-D-E,C	D,A-B-E,C	E,D,A-B,C
Zoo	101	7	16	C,D,B-E,A	D-E,C,A-B	E,B-A,D,C

Figure 2 summarizes ranking results of the FE techniques according to the classifiers performance on 20 UCI data sets. Each bar on the histograms shows how many times an FE technique was the 1st, the 2nd, the 3rd, the 4th, or the 5th among the 20 possible. The number of times certain techniques got 1st-5th place is not necessarily integer since there were draws between 2, 3, or 4 techniques. In such cases each technique gets the ½, 1/3 or 1/4 score correspondingly.

It can be seen from the figure that there are many common patterns in the behavior of techniques for 3 different classifiers, yet there are some differences too. So, according the ranking results RP behavior is very similar with every classifier, PCA works better for C4.5, parametric FE is suited better for NB. Nonparametric FE is also better suited for NB, it is also good with 3*NN*. However, it is less successful for C4.5.

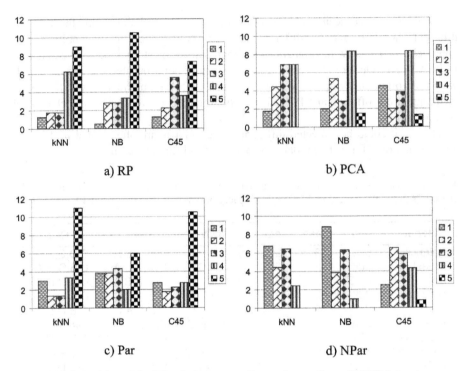

a) RP

b) PCA

c) Par

d) NPar

Fig. 2. Ranking of the FE techniques according to the results on 20 UCI data sets

In Table 2, averaged over 20 data sets, accuracy results are presented for each classifier. It can be seen from the table that among the FE techniques the nonparametric approach is always the best on average for each classifier, the second best is PCA, then parametric FE, and, finally, RP shows the worst results. Classification in the original space (*Plain*) was almost as good as in the space of extracted features produced by the nonparametric approach when kNN is used. However, when NB is used, *Plain* accuracy is significantly lower comparing to the situation when the nonparametric FE is applied. Still, this accuracy is as good as in situation when PCA is applied and significantly higher in situations when RP or the parametric FE is applied. For C4.5 the situation is also different. So, *Plain* classification is the best option on average. With respect to RP our results differ from the conclusions made in [9], where RP was found to be suited better for nearest neighbor methods and less satisfactory for decision trees (according to the results on 5 data sets). We can see from the two last columns of Table 2 that on average RP suits better for kNN than to C4.5 (*Plain-RP*) indeed (however the difference is only 0.5%). However, if we take into consideration PCA (*PCA-RP*), as in this context RP is often seen as an alternative for PCA, we can see that in fact RP produces new spaces that are better suited for C4.5 than to kNN (1.6%). It is interesting also to analyze these differences for NB. It can be seen that for *PCA-RP* the difference is the greatest while for *Plain-RP* the difference is the least. We believe that this is due to the poor performance of NB comparing to kNN and C4.5.

Table 2. Averaged over 20 data sets accuracy results

	RP	PCA	PAR	NPAR	Plain	PCA-RP(%)	Plain-RP(%)
kNN	.725	.774	.733	.808	.804	4.9	7.9
NB	.704	.767	.749	.799	.769	6.3	6.4
C4.5	.741	.775	.761	.806	.825	3.3	8.4

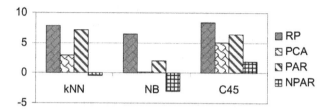

Fig. 3. The decrease/increase of accuracy due to the use of FE techniques, averaged over 20 data sets

In Figure 3 decrease/increase of accuracy due to the use of FE techniques is presented averaged over 20 data sets. It can be seen from the figure that on average, for 20 datasets analyzed FE has no effect on or deteriorates the classification accuracy. The only exception is combination of nonparametric FE and the NB classifier. In this situation averaged accuracy increases by 3%. In can be seen also that the nonparametric FE is the best among considered approaches from the accuracy perspective.

5   Conclusions

FE techniques are powerful tools that can significantly increase the classification accuracy producing better representation spaces or resolving the problem of "the curse of dimensionality". However, when applied blindly, FE may have no effect for the further classification or even deteriorate the classification accuracy. Moreover it is also possible that some data sets are so easy to learn that classification without any FE gains already the maximal possible accuracy and therefore it is hard to get any improvement due to FE.

In this paper, the experimental results show that for many data sets FE does increase classification accuracy.

We could see from the results that there is no best FE technique among the considered ones, and it is hard to say which one is the best for a certain classifier and/or for a certain problem, however according to the experimental results some major trends can be recognized.

Class-conditional approaches (and especially nonparametric approach) were often the best ones. This indicated the fact how important is to take into account class information and do not rely only on the distribution of variance in the data. At the same time it is important to notice that the parametric FE was very often the worst, and for 3NN and C4.5 the parametric FE was the worst more often than RP. Such results highlight the very unstable behavior of parametric FE.

One possibility to improve the parametric FE, we think, is to combine it with PCA or a feature selection approach in a way that a few principal components or the most useful for classification features are added to those extracted by the parametric approach.

Although it is logical to assume that RP should have more success in applications where the distances between the original data points are meaningful and/or for such learning algorithms that use distances between the data points, our results show that this is not necessarily true. However, data sets in our experiments have 48 features at most and RP is usually applied for problems with much higher dimensionality.

Time taken to build classification models with and without FE is not reported in this study, we also do not present here the analyses of number of features extracted by a certain FE technique. These important issues will be presented in our further study.

A volume of accumulated empirical (and theoretical) findings, some trends, and some dependencies with respect to data set characteristics and use of FE techniques have been discovered or can be discovered. In particular, it was shown that FE techniques are beneficial for data sets with highly correlated features [12]. The nonparametric FE was found to be successful especially for data sets with very limited sample sizes [11]. On the other hand, there are certain assumptions on the performance of classification algorithms under certain conditions.

Thus, potentially the adaptive selection of the most suitable data mining techniques for a data set at consideration (that is a really challenging problem) might be possible. We see our further research efforts in this direction.

We would like to emphasize also the possibility to conduct experiments on synthetically generated datasets that is beneficial from two perspectives. First, this allows generating, testing and validating hypothesis on data mining strategy selection with respect to a dataset at hand under controlled settings when some data characteristics are varied while the others are held unchangeable.

Acknowledgments. This research is partly supported by the COMAS Graduate School of the University of Jyväskylä, Finland. I would like to thank Dr. Alexey Tsymbal and Prof. Seppo Puuronen for their valuable comments and suggestions to the paper.

References

1. Achlioptas, D. Database-friendly random projections. Proceedings of the twentieth ACM SIGMOD-SIGACT-SIGART symposium on Principles of database systems, Santa Barbara, California, ACM Press (2001)
2. Aivazyan, S.A. Applied statistics: classification and dimension reduction. Finance and Statistics, Moscow (1989)

3. Aladjem, M. Multiclass discriminant mappings. Signal Processing, Vol .35, (1994) 1-18
4. Aladjem, M. Parametric and nonparametric linear mappings of multidimensional data. Pattern Recognition, Vol.24(6) (1991) 543-553
5. Bellman, R., Adaptive Control Processes: A Guided Tour, Princeton University Press, (1961)
6. Bingham, E., Mannila, H. Random projection in dimensionality reduction: applications to image and text data. Proceedings of the seventh ACM SIGKDD international conference on Knowledge discovery and data mining, ACM Press, San Francisco, California, (2001)
7. Blake, C.L., Merz, C.J. UCI Repository of Machine Learning Databases. Dept. of Information and Computer Science, University of California, Irvine CA, (1998)
8. Fayyad, U.M. Data Mining and Knowledge Discovery: Making Sense Out of Data, IEEE Expert, Vol. 11(5), (1996) 20-25
9. Fradkin, D., Madigan, D. Experiments with random projections for machine learning. Proceedings of the ninth ACM SIGKDD international conference on Knowledge discovery and data mining, ACM Press, Washington, D.C., (2003)
10. Fukunaga, K. Introduction to statistical pattern recognition. Academic Press, London (1990)
11. Jimenez, L., Landgrebe, D. High Dimensional Feature Reduction Via Projection Pursuit. PhD Thesis and School of Electrical & Computer Engineering Technical Report TR-ECE 96-5, (1995)
12. Jolliffe, I.T. Principal Component Analysis. Springer, New York, NY, (1986)
13. Kiang, M. A comparative assessment of classification methods, Decision Support Systems, Vol. 35, (2003) 441-454
14. Kohavi, R., Sommerfield, D., Dougherty, J. Data mining using MLC++: a machine learning library in C++. Tools with Artificial Intelligence, IEEE CS Press, (1996) 234-245
15. Liu, H. Feature Extraction, Construction and Selection: A Data Mining Perspective, ISBN 0-7923-8196-3, Kluwer Academic Publishers (1998)
16. Michalski, R.S.. Seeking Knowledge in the Deluge of Facts, Fundamenta Informaticae, Vol. 30, (1997) 283-297
17. Oza, N.C., Tumer, K. Dimensionality Reduction Through Classifier Ensembles. Technical Report NASA-ARC-IC-1999-124, Computational Sciences Division, NASA Ames Research Center, Moffett Field, CA, (1999)
18. Quinlan, J.R. C4.5 Programs for Machine Learning. San Mateo CA: Morgan Kaufmann, (1993)
19. Tsymbal A., Pechenizkiy M., Puuronen S., Patterson D.W. Dynamic integration of classifiers in the space of principal components, In: L.Kalinichenko, R.Manthey, B.Thalheim, U.Wloka (Eds.), Proc. Advances in Databases and Information Systems: 7th East-European Conf. ADBIS'03, Lecture Notes in Computer Science, Vol. 2798, Heidelberg: Springer-Verlag (2003) 278-292
20. Tsymbal A., Puuronen S., Pechenizkiy M., Baumgarten M., Patterson D. Eigenvector-based feature extraction for classification. In Proc. 15th Int. FLAIRS Conference on Artificial Intelligence, Pensacola, FL, USA, AAAI Press (2002) 354-358
21. Witten I. and Frank E. Data Mining: Practical machine learning tools with Java implementations, Morgan Kaufmann, San Francisco, (2000)

Instance Cloning Local Naive Bayes

Liangxiao Jiang[1,*], Harry Zhang[2], and Jiang Su[2]

[1] Faculty of Computer Science, China University of Geosciences,
Wuhan, China 430074
[2] Faculty of Computer Science, University of New Brunswick,
P.O. Box 4400, Fredericton, NB, Canada E3B 5A3

Abstract. The instance-based k-nearest neighbor algorithm (KNN)[1] is an effective classification model. Its classification is simply based on a vote within the neighborhood, consisting of k nearest neighbors of the test instance. Recently, researchers have been interested in deploying a more sophisticated local model, such as naive Bayes, within the neighborhood. It is expected that there are no strong dependences within the neighborhood of the test instance, thus alleviating the conditional independence assumption of naive Bayes. Generally, the smaller size of the neighborhood (the value of k), the less chance of encountering strong dependences. When k is small, however, the training data for the local naive Bayes is small and its classification would be inaccurate. In the currently existing models, such as LWNB [3], a relatively large k is chosen. The consequence is that strong dependences seem unavoidable.

In our opinion, a small k should be preferred in order to avoid strong dependences. We propose to deal with the problem of lack of local training data using sampling (cloning). Given a test instance, clones of each instance in the neighborhood is generated in terms of its similarity to the test instance and added to the local training data. Then, the local naive Bayes is trained from the expanded training data. Since a relatively small k is chosen, the chance of encountering strong dependences within the neighborhood is small. Thus the classification of the resulting local naive Bayes would be more accurate. We experimentally compare our new algorithm with KNN and its improved variants in terms of classification accuracy, using the 36 UCI datasets recommended by Weka [8], and the experimental results show that our algorithm outperforms all those algorithms significantly and consistently at various k values.

1 Introduction

Classification is a fundamental issue in machine learning. A typical problem setting for classification is that, given a set of training instances with class labels, a classifier is trained and used to predict the class of an unseen instance. An instance is represented by a vector of attributes. In this paper, an instance x

---

* This work was done when the author was a visiting scholar at University of New Brunswick.

B. Kégl and G. Lapalme (Eds.): AI 2005, LNAI 3501, pp. 280–291, 2005.
© Springer-Verlag Berlin Heidelberg 2005

is described by the attribute vector $< a_1(x), a_2(x), \ldots, a_n(x) >$, where $a_i(x)$ denotes the value of the ith attribute A_i of x.

Instance-based learning methods [1] are often used for classification. The most basic instance-based method is the instance-based k-nearest neighbor algorithm (KNN). In KNN, an instance of n attributes corresponds to a point in the n-dimensional Euclidean space $\Re^n$. The standard Euclidean distance is often used as the distance between two instances x and y, defined as follows.

$$d(x, y) = \sqrt{\sum_{i=1}^{n}(a_i(x) - a_i(y))^2}. \tag{1}$$

When all attributes are nominal, this function can be simplified as:

$$d(x, y) = \sum_{i=1}^{n}(1 - \delta(a_i(x), a_i(y))), \tag{2}$$

where δ is a function that $\delta(u, v) = 1$ if $u = v$.

KNN classifies an instance x by finding its k nearest neighbors $y_1, \cdots, y_k$, and then assigning the most common class of the k nearest neighbors to x, as shown below:

$$c(x) = \arg\max_{c \in C} \sum_{i=1}^{k} \delta(c, c(y_i)), \tag{3}$$

where $c(y_i)$ is the class of y_i. Essentially, the classification of KNN is based on a vote within the neighborhood that consists of the k nearest neighbors of the test instance.

An obvious approach to improving KNN is to weight the contribution of each of k neighbors according to their distance to the test instance x, by giving greater weight to closer neighbors. The resulting classifier is called instance-based k-nearest neighbor with distance weighted (KNNDW), defined as follows.

$$c(x) = \arg\max_{c \in C} \sum_{i=1}^{k} \frac{\delta(c, c(y_i))}{d(y_i, x)^2}. \tag{4}$$

KNN has been widely used for decades due to its simplicity, effectiveness and robustness. However, the classification of KNN based on voting is quite simple. It is believed that a more sophisticated local model within the neighborhood, instead of voting, would improve classification performance.

Naive Bayes is a simple, but effective classification model [5], in which all the attributes are assumed independent given the class (the conditional independence assumption). It has been observed that naive Bayes performs well when the training data is small [4]. Thus it is suitable to be a local model within another model, such as a decision tree.

In KNN, it is a natural thought to train a local naive Bayes for a test instance using only the k nearest neighbors. Recently, researchers have paid considerable attention to investigate the approach to combining KNN with naive Bayes [12, 11, 3]. Although the conditional independence assumption of naive Bayes is always violated on the training data as a whole, it is expected that the dependences within the neighborhood of the test instance is weaker than that on the whole data and thus naive Bayes classifies better. Generally, keeping the size of the neighborhood (the values of k) small will reduce the chance of encountering strong dependences. When k is small, however, the probability estimation in naive Bayes that is based on frequency in the training data, is not reliable. Thus, its classification would be inaccurate.

In this paper, we propose an method based on sampling to deal with this issue. For each neighbor, a number of clones are generated and added into the local training data in terms of its similarity to the test instance. Then, a naive Bayes is trained from the expanded training data. By that means, a small k value could be chosen and strong attribute dependences could be avoided. Thus a better classifier is expected. Our experimental results show that our new model outperforms KNN and its variants significantly.

The rest of the paper is organized as follows. In Section 2, we introduce the related work on combining KNN with naive Bayes. In Section 3, we present our model and the experimental results in detail. In Section 4, we make a conclusion and outline our main directions for future research.

2   Related Work

Naive Bayes is a simple but effective classifier. Although its conditional independence assumption is often violated, it performs surprisingly well in classification [2]. In addition, it performs well when the size of training data is small [4]. This feature makes it especially fit to be a local model embedded into another model, such as a decision tree, a KNN. Kohavi [4] proposes a model, NBTree, in which a local naive Bayes is deployed on each leaf of a traditional decision tree. An NBTree classifies an instance using the local naive Bayes on the leaf into which it falls.

KNN has attracted much attention from researchers for decades, due in part to its age and simplicity [1]. In recently years, researchers have done considerable work on combining KNN with naive Bayes [12, 11, 3]. The idea for combining KNN with naive Bayes is quite straightforward. Like all lazy learning methods, the training data is simply stored, and learning is deferred until classification time. Whenever a new (test) instance is classified, a local naive Bayes is trained using the k nearest neighbors of the test instance, with which the test instance is classified. The classification of the local naive Bayes is based on the following equation.

$$c(x) = \arg \max_{c \in C} p(c) \prod_{i=1}^{n} p(a_i(x)|c), \qquad (5)$$

where x is the test instance of n attributes. The parameters of the local naive Bayes are the probabilities $p(c)$ and $p(a_i(x)|c)$ in Equation 5 that are estimated from the local training data (the k nearest neighbors of x) based on frequency.

Frank et al. [3] present an model to combine KNN with naive Bayes, called locally weighted Naive Bayes(LWNB). In LWNB, each of nearest neighbors is weighted in terms of its distance to the test instance. Then a local naive Bayes is built from the weighted training instances. Their experiments show that LWNB outperforms naive Bayes significantly. Our work is inspired by this work.

Zheng and Webb [12] propose an approach, lazy Bayesian rule (LBR). LBR does not directly use the k nearest neighbors of the test instance as the training data for the local naive Bayes. Instead, before classifying a test instance, LBR generates a rule most appropriate to the test instance. The training instances that satisfy the antecedent of the rule are chosen as the training data for the local naive Bayes, and this local naive Bayes only uses those attributes that do not appear in the antecedent of the rule. In this paper, however, we are interested in learning the local model directly based on the k nearest neighbors of the test instance.

Xie et al. [11] propose a model, selective neighborhood naive Bayes (SNNB), in which multiple naive Bayes are learned by using different k values and a local naive Bayes is trained for each k value. The most accurate one is used to classify the test instance. In SNNB, a set of naive Bayes are trained. In this paper, we focus on training a single local model.

In this paper, we use KNNNB to denote the algorithm that directly uses the k nearest neighbors of the test instance to train a local naive Bayes.

3   Learning Local Naive Bayes Using Instance Sampling

3.1   Size of Neighborhood and Attribute Dependences

Most of the existing research works on combining KNN with naive Bayes are motivated by improving naive Bayes through relaxing the conditional independence assumption using lazy learning. It is expected that there are no strong dependences within the k nearest neighbors of the test instance, although the attribute dependences might be strong in the whole data. Essentially, they are looking for a sub-space of the instance space in which the conditional independence assumption is true or almost true. The size of the neighborhood, or the value of k, is critical. In general, small neighborhood helps to reduce the chance of encountering strong dependences [3]. Thus, a small k is preferred.

Frank et al. [3] presents a problem that predicts whether an instance belongs to a black or white square on a checker board given its x and y coordinates. In that problem, strong dependences between the two attributes exist. They show that KNN, KNNDW and LWNB performs well at $k \leq 5$, and degrade as k increases. That example shows that small k value is desirable when attribute dependences are strong. In addition, small neighborhood conforms closer to the data. In fact, KNN and KNNDW generally degrade in performance as k increases.

When k is small, such as 5 or 10, however, the training data is small. The parameters of naive Bayes cannot be accurately estimated from the training data. Thus, the classification of a local naive Bayes would be inaccurate. In NBTree[4], a threshold on the size of the training data on a decision node is set to avoid this problem. That is, there should be at least 30 training instances at a decision node. In LWNB, Laplace correction has been used to smooth probability estimation, and a relatively large k, such as $k = 30, 40, 50$, is chosen.

We believe that keeping the size of the neighborhood small would help reducing the chance of having strong dependences and thus improving classification accuracy. We propose to a novel approach to handling the issue of lack of training data by expanding the neighborhood. We "clone" each neighbor of the testing instance and add the clones to the training data. Thus, the parameters in naive Bayes can be estimated more accurately and reliably, and the classification of the local naive Bayes is more accurate.

There has been similar work on expanding or reducing training data by sampling to deal with the issue of class unbalance in machine learning [9]. When the class distribution of training data is highly unbalanced, instances in the majority class are eliminated (under-sampling), or instances are replicated in the minority class (over-sampling). Either way alters the class distribution of the training data. Our sampling is similar in the sense that copies of instances are added into the training data. The difference is that the sampling in dealing with class unbalance is typically based on a probability distribution, and our sampling is based on an explicit distance function and does not alter the class distribution.

3.2   A Learning Algorithm Based on Instance Cloning

At first, let us define a function to measure the similarity between two instances with nominal attributes. Let x and y are two instances, the similarity, denoted by $s(x, y)$, between them is defined as:

$$s(x, y) = \sum_{i=1}^{n} \delta(a_i(x), a_i(y)). \tag{6}$$

$s(x, y)$ is a function that simply counts the number of identical attributes of x and y.

Given a test instance x, we find its k nearest neighbors and put them into the local training data. For each neighbor y, we use Equation 6 to compute the similarity $s(x, y)$. Then, $s(x, y)$ clones of y are added to the local training data. A local naive Bayes is learned from the expanded training data with which x is classified. We call our method *instance cloning local naive Bayes*, or simply ICLNB. The ICLNB algorithm is depicted below.

Algorithm ICLNB(T, k, x)
Input : a set **T** of training instances, integer k, and a test instance x.
Output : the class of x
  1. Use the distance function in Equation 2 to find x's k nearest neighbors $y_1, \cdots, y_k$, from **T**.
  2. Local training set $\mathbf{L} = \{y_1, \cdots, y_k\}$
  3. For each neighbor y_i of x
     − Compute $s(x, y_i)$ using the similarity function in Equation 6.
     − Add $s(x, y_i)$ clones of y_i to **L**.

4. Create a local naive Bayes **NB** using **L** as the training data.
5. Classify x using **NB** and return the class label of x.

It is interesting to notice the similarity and difference between instance sampling (or cloning) and instance weighting [3]. In instance weighting, each training instance is assigned a different weight and thus plays a different role in classification. In instance sampling, each training instance is "cloned" different times. More clones generated, more important for that instance in classification. Thus, both change the importance of an instance. However, instance weighting generally does not aim at helping to improve probability estimation, while instance sampling does. "Cloning" expands the training data, and thus leads to more reliable probability estimation. Specifically, our instance sampling is simpler than the instance weighting in [3] in that our similarity function is very simple and there is no need to normalize the instance weights.

3.3   Experimental Methodology and Results

We ran our experiments on the 36 UCI data sets recommended by Weka [10], which are listed in Table 1. All these data sets come from the UCI repository [6]. We downloaded these data sets in format of *arff* from main web of Weka [8].

All the preprocessing stages of data sets were carried out by the Weka system. They mainly include the following three processes:

1. We used the filter of ReplaceMissingValues in Weka to replace the missing values of attributes.
2. We used the filter of Discretize in Weka to discretize numeric attributes. Thus, all the attributes are treated as nominal.
3. It is well-known that, if the number of values of an attribute is almost equal to the number of instances in a data set, this attribute does not contribute any information to classification. So we use the filter of Remove in Weka to delete these attributes. In the 36 data sets, there only exists three this type of attributes, namely Hospital Number in data set horse-colic.ORIG, Instance Name in data set Splice and Animal in data set zoo.

In our experiments, we use the Laplace estimation to avoid the zero-frequency problem. Assume that there are p instances of class c, N total instances, and C total classes in the training data. The frequency-based estimation calculates the estimated probability $p(c) = \frac{p}{N}$. The Laplace estimation calculates the estimated probability $p(c) = \frac{p+1}{N+C}$. In the Laplace estimation, $p(a_i(x)|c) = \frac{1+N_{ic}}{N_i+N_c}$, where N_{ic} is the number of instances in class c and with $A_i = a_i(x)$, N_c is the number of instances in class c, and N_i is the number of values for attribute A_i.

We conducted experiments to compare our algorithm ICLNB with KNN, KNNDW, KNNNB and LWNB in terms of classification accuracy. We implemented ICLNB, KNNDW, and KNNNB within the Weka framework [10], and used the implementation of KNN and LWNB (LWL with a base classifier being Naive Bayes) in Weka. In all experiments, the accuracy of each algorithm was based on the percentage of correct classifications on the test sets of each data set. The accuracy of each algorithm was measured via the ten-fold cross validation for all data sets. Runs with the various algorithms were carried out on the same training sets and evaluated on the same test sets. In particular, the cross-validation folds were the same for all the experiments on each data set. Finally, we conducted two-tailed t-test with significantly different probability of 0.95 to compare our algorithm with other algorithms. That is, we speak of two results for a data set as being "significantly different" only if the difference is statistically significant at the 0.05 level according to the corrected two-tailed t-test [7].

Table 1. Description of the data sets used in the experiments

dataset	Size	Number of Attribute	classes	missing value	Numeric
anneal	898	39	6	Y	Y
anneal.ORIG	898	39	6	Y	Y
audiology	226	70	24	Y	N
autos	205	26	7	Y	Y
balance	625	5	3	N	Y
breast	286	10	2	Y	N
breast-w	699	10	2	Y	N
colic	368	23	2	Y	Y
colic.ORIG	368	28	2	Y	Y
credit-a	690	16	2	Y	Y
credit-g	1000	21	2	N	Y
diabetes	768	9	2	N	Y
Glass	214	10	7	N	Y
heart-c	303	14	5	Y	Y
heart-h	294	14	5	Y	Y
heart-s	270	14	2	N	Y
hepatitis	155	20	2	Y	Y
hypoth.	3772	30	4	Y	Y
ionosphere	351	35	2	N	Y
iris	150	5	3	N	Y
kr-vs-kp	3196	37	2	N	N
labor	57	17	2	Y	Y
letter	20000	17	26	N	Y
lymph.	148	19	4	N	Y
mushroom	8124	23	2	Y	N
p.-tumor	339	18	21	Y	N
segment	2310	20	7	N	Y
sick	3772	30	2	Y	Y
sonar	208	61	2	N	Y
soybean	683	36	19	Y	N
splice	3190	62	3	N	N
vehicle	846	19	4	N	Y
vote	435	17	2	Y	N
vowel	990	14	11	N	Y
waveform	5000	41	3	N	Y
zoo	101	18	7	N	Y

Table 2. Experimental results for instance cloning local naive Bayes (ICLNB) versus instance-based k-nearest neighbor (KNN), instance-based k-nearest neighbor with distance weighted (KNNDW), instance-based k-nearest neighbor naive Bayes (KNNNB), locally weighted naive Bayes (LWNB) and naive Bayes (NB): percentage of correct classifications and standard deviation when $k = 5$

Datasets	ICLNB	KNN	KNNDW	KNNNB	LWNB	NB
anneal	98.66±1.26	96.88±2.15	98.55±1.05	97.33±2.24	98.78±1.11	94.32±2.38
anneal.O	91.2±3.08	87.31±3.35	90.09±2.93	88.09±2.96	91.53±3.04	87.53±4.69
audiology	77.81±9.23	60.57±7.87	75.57±8.92	68.58±6.77	77.37±9.21	71.23±7.03
autos	83.83±6.63	66.29±8.28	83.4±7.61	78.55±9.2	81.4±5.23	64.83±11.2
balance	83.84±4.41	83.84±4.71	83.84±4.71	84.16±4.03	83.99±4.22	91.36±1.38
breast	73.85±8.84	73.78±4.38	75.55±7.2	75.55±3.78	72.09±9.52	72.06±7.97
breast-w	96.85±2	94.99±2.81	95.28±2.79	96.57±2.54	95.99±2.52	97.28±1.84
colic	77.72±3.55	80.68±6.65	82.33±5.35	81.51±7.01	78.56±5.38	78.81±5.05
colic.O	76.09±4.91	70.63±5.06	73.35±5.64	73.08±6	75.81±5.5	75.26±5.26
credit-a	82.61±2.73	85.07±3.62	84.93±2.99	85.22±3.19	82.75±4.24	84.78±4.28
credit-g	73.5±3.03	71.5±2.42	72.6±3.41	73.3±3.33	70.9±5.17	76.30±4.76
diabetes	72.14±4.68	69.14±1.84	70.58±3.33	71.23±3.25	69.15±4.66	75.40±5.85
glass	65.41±8.64	58.92±7.8	62.23±6.79	64.52±7.69	61.21±7.77	60.32±9.69
heart-c	79.14±8.59	81.41±12.7	81.42±11.4	82.75±8.94	80.77±9.36	84.14±4.16
heart-h	82.7±6.35	81.36±6.65	81.34±6.27	81.34±6.3	81.31±5.99	84.05±6.69
heart-s	81.11±5.91	80.74±6	81.48±5.79	81.85±5.64	80.37±7.42	83.70±5.00
hepatitis	84.42±7.61	84.46±6.25	82.54±4.41	83.88±6.2	80.63±8.57	83.79±8.79
hypoth.	93.05±0.93	93.03±0.89	93.05±0.84	93.03±0.89	92.29±0.86	92.79±1.02
ionosphere	92.31±3.31	89.44±3.34	90.02±2.8	90.02±3.11	91.73±3.43	90.89±3.49
iris	95.33±5.49	93.33±6.29	93.33±7.03	94.67±5.26	94±5.84	94.67±8.20
kr-vs-kp	97.97±0.71	96.03±1.19	96.97±0.96	96.9±0.85	97.31±0.86	87.89±1.81
labor	86.33±13.3	91.67±11.8	91.67±11.8	91.67±11.8	90±11.65	93.33±11.7
letter	92.16±0.32	88.02±0.63	90.17±0.55	89.87±0.4	90.8±0.4	70.00±0.81
lymph.	81.67±9.18	82.33±9.81	82.29±10.9	83.62±9.52	82.9±11.18	85.67±9.55
mushroom	100±0	100±0	100±0	100±0	100±0	95.57±0.45
p.-tumor	43.65±3.26	41.26±8.05	42.44±4.98	44.22±5.71	40.38±5.71	46.89±4.32
segment	94.85±0.95	90.74±1.61	93.38±1.55	91.6±1.26	94.63±1.49	88.92±1.95
sick	98.2±0.48	97.51±0.59	97.72±0.49	97.72±0.49	98.01±0.53	96.74±0.53
sonar	80.81±7.38	80.79±10.06	80.79±8.72	81.74±6.72	82.24±10.3	77.50±12.0
soybean	93.11±2.42	90.76±3.76	91.79±3.36	91.94±3.22	92.38±3.02	92.08±2.34
splice	86.18±2.02	79.81±2.81	82.23±2.63	85.86±1.47	82.6±2.3	95.36±1.00
vehicle	72.45±3.78	70.57±3.02	71.27±4.46	72.46±3.41	70.57±5.64	61.82±3.54
vote	95.18±2.51	94.03±2.69	93.81±3.06	94.95±2.37	93.58±4.27	90.14±4.17
vowel	94.14±1.7	81.31±1.73	92.42±3.06	90.1±2.17	94.65±2.52	67.07±4.21
waveform	74.22±1.59	73.42±1.55	73.92±1.86	74.42±1.85	69.98±1.94	79.96±1.92
zoo	97.09±4.69	92.09±6.3	96.09±5.05	95.09±5.18	97.09±4.69	94.18±6.60
Mean	84.71±4.32	82.05±4.68	84.12±4.58	84.09±4.30	83.83±4.88	82.41±4.88

Table 2 and 3 show the accuracy and standard deviations of each algorithm on each data set, and the average accuracy and deviation over all the data sets are summarized at the bottom of the table. Table 4 and 5 shows the results of two-

Table 3. Experimental results for instance cloning local naive Bayes (ICLNB) versus instance-based k-nearest neighbor (KNN), instance-based k-nearest neighbor with distance weighted (KNNDW), instance-based k-nearest neighbor naive Bayes (KNNNB), locally weighted naive Bayes (LWNB) and naive Bayes (NB): percentage of correct classification and standard deviation when $k = 10$

Datasets	ICLNB	KNN	KNNDW	KNNNB	LWNB	NB
anneal	99±0.82	95.88±1.97	98.55±1.05	97.1±2.05	98.89±1.05	94.32±2.38
anneal.O	90.98±3.47	84.41±3.3	89.75±3.1	86.64±3.48	91.64±3.04	87.53±4.69
audiology	77.83±7.59	58.79±8.3	74.72±6.74	68.1±6.28	77.79±8.11	71.23±7.03
autos	80.38±6.8	62.52±8.03	82.88±6.63	76.57±8.47	81.88±5.84	64.83±11.2
balance	83.84±4.41	83.84±4.71	83.84±4.71	84.16±4.03	83.99±4.22	91.36±1.38
breast	73.15±8.78	73.09±4.25	75.22±5.58	74.85±4.09	72.8±8.74	72.06±7.97
breast-w	96.99±1.84	93.99±3.42	94.28±3.5	96.57±2.54	96.13±2.45	97.28±1.84
colic	77.98±5.65	83.13±6.29	84.23±5.09	83.13±5.75	80.98±3.82	78.81±5.05
colic.O	76.09±3.57	69.82±3.4	73.09±5.23	73.09±5.54	75.8±4.25	75.26±5.26
credit-a	83.77±2.54	86.09±4.39	85.51±3.74	86.52±4.21	83.33±4.11	84.78±4.28
credit-g	73.5±3.1	71.9±3.28	73.7±3.13	74.4±3.5	72.1±4.18	76.30±4.76
diabetes	72.01±5.47	69.02±2.19	69.27±4.12	72.01±4.5	69.4±4.23	75.40±5.85
glass	67.75±8.15	57.06±8.03	60.82±7.99	64.55±8.76	60.74±5.83	60.32±9.69
heart-c	78.85±7.28	81.09±9.77	81.42±9.55	83.1±7.37	80.11±8.99	84.14±4.16
heart-h	81.33±6.14	82.02±6.06	81.68±5.66	81.67±4.73	82.34±6.06	84.05±6.69
heart-s	80.74±6	82.22±7.37	82.96±6.1	82.59±5.53	80±7.45	83.70±5.00
hepatitis	84.38±7.13	84.5±6.22	83.25±5.35	83.92±6.93	82.54±6.17	83.79±8.79
hypothy.	93.21±0.66	93.08±0.64	93.16±0.58	93.21±0.62	92.37±0.87	92.79±1.02
ionosphere	90.9±4.58	89.74±2.78	89.74±3.37	90.31±3.62	91.44±3.03	90.89±3.49
iris	94.67±6.13	93.33±6.29	93.33±7.03	94±5.84	94±5.84	94.67±8.20
kr-vs-kp	97.59±0.81	95.06±1.34	96.84±0.95	96.46±0.78	97.56±0.76	87.89±1.81
labor	90±14.1	85.67±14.5	89.67±11.9	91.67±11.9	90±11.7	93.33±11.7
letter	92.83±0.33	86.56±0.67	89.68±0.64	89.73±0.55	91.25±0.43	70.00±0.81
lymph.	83±10.8	80.86±12.0	82.86±13.1	85±9.18	82.29±10.92	85.67±9.55
mushroom	100±0	99.91±0.08	100±0	100±0	100±0	95.57±0.45
p.-tumor	43.34±3.7	42.47±5.67	43.03±5.86	46±4.85	40.97±5.6	46.89±4.32
segment	95.45±0.82	89.65±1.84	92.68±1.59	91.6±1.54	94.81±1.43	88.92±1.95
sick	98.12±0.55	97.03±0.73	97.45±0.6	97.56±0.53	98.01±0.53	96.74±0.53
sonar	81.33±9.57	81.33±8.42	80.38±8.44	81.83±9.39	84.14±6.38	77.50±12.0
soybean	93.84±2.39	89.01±2.12	91.94±3.29	91.94±3.06	92.96±2.77	92.08±2.34
splice	91.76±1.45	83.26±2.42	85.2±2.11	90.5±1.25	86.65±1.69	95.36±1.00
vehicle	71.28±4.77	68.68±2.74	70.8±4.48	70.69±3.01	72.46±4.5	61.82±3.54
vote	96.1±2.64	92.9±3.61	93.36±3.28	94.95±2.81	93.57±3.86	90.14±4.17
vowel	93.54±1.73	67.68±4.04	91.62±3.63	89.49±3.02	94.24±2.02	67.07±4.21
waveform	76.76±1.33	76.36±1.15	76.34±1.15	77.2±1.35	72.7±1.86	79.96±1.92
zoo	98.09±4.03	89.18±9.78	96.09±5.05	95.09±5.18	97.09±4.69	94.18±6.60
Mean	85.01±4.42	81.14±4.77	84.15±4.56	84.34±4.35	84.36±4.37	82.41±4.88

tailed t-test between each pair of algorithms, and each entry $w/t/l$ means that the algorithm at the corresponding row wins in w data sets, ties in t data sets, and loses in l data sets, compared to the algorithm at the corresponding column.

The detailed results displayed in Table 2 and 3 show that our algorithm outperforms all the other algorithms significantly. Now, we summarize the highlights as follows:

1. ICLNB outperforms the traditional k-nearest algorithms KNN and KNNDW significantly. From our experiments, KNNDW is significantly better than KNN. Compared to KNNDW, ICLNB wins in 6 data sets, ties in 30 data sets and loses in 0 data set, when $k = 5$; and ICLNB wins in 5 data sets, ties in 31 data sets and loses in 0 data set, when $k = 10$.
2. ICLNB outperforms the existing algorithms of combining KNN with naive Bayes: KNNNB and LWNB significantly. Compared to KNNNB, ICLNB wins in 6 data sets, ties in 30 data sets and loses in 0 data set, when $k = 5$; and ICLNB wins in 7 data sets, ties in 28 data sets and loses in 1 data set, when $k = 10$. Compared to LWNB, ICLNB wins in 5 data sets, ties in 31 data sets and loses in 0 data set, when $k = 5$; and ICLNB wins in 6 data sets, ties in 30 data sets and loses in 0 data set, when $k = 10$.
3. In terms of the average classification accuracy, ICLNB is the best among all the algorithms compared. When $k = 5$, ICLNB's average classification accuracy is 84.71%, and the highest average classification accuracy of the other algorithms is 84.09% from KNNNB. When $k = 10$, ICLNB's average classification accuracy is 85.01%, and the highest average classification accuracy of the other algorithms is 84.36% from KNNDW.
4. ICLNB outperforms naive Bayes significantly, just as KNNNB and LWNB do. That verifies the idea that there are weaker attribute dependences within the neighborhood of the test instance.

From our experiments, we have other two interesting observations below, showing that the probability estimation in naive Bayes could not be improved by the instance weighting in KNNDW when k is small.

1. The difference between LWNB and KNNDW in classification accuracy is not significant. When $k = 5$, LWNB wins in 3 data sets and loses in 2 data sets. When $k = 10$, LWNB wins in 2 data sets, and loses in 2 data sets.
2. LWNB does not outperforms KNNNB significantly. When $k = 5$, LWNB wins in 4 data sets and loses in 3 data sets. When $k = 10$, LWNB wins in 6 data sets, and loses in 4 data sets.

In our experiments, we also tested some relatively large k values, and the experimental results are similar. For example, ICLNB outperforms LWNB in 5 data sets, ties in 30 data sets and loses in 1 data set, when $k = 50$. We have not presented the experimental results in this paper due to the limit of space. In fact, ICLNB consistently outperforms all other algorithms compared in this paper at all the various k values we tested.

Table 4. Summary of experimental results: classification accuracy comparisons when $k = 5$. An entry $w/t/l$ means that the algorithm at the corresponding row wins in w data sets, ties in t data sets, and loses in l data sets, compared to the algorithm at the corresponding column

	NB	KNN	KNNDW	KNNNB	LWNB
KNN	8/23/5				
KNNDW	10/22/4	8/28/0			
KNNNB	10/23/3	9/27/0	3/30/3		
LWNB	10/20/6	10/24/2	3/31/2	4/29/3	
ICLNB	10/23/3	12/24/0	6/30/0	6/30/0	5/31/0

Table 5. Summary of experimental results: classification accuracy comparisons when $k = 10$

	NB	KNN	KNNDW	KNNNB	LWNB
KNN	5/23/8				
KNNDW	9/22/5	11/25/0			
KNNNB	9/24/3	13/23/0	3/31/2		
LWNB	11/20/5	13/20/3	2/32/2	6/26/4	
ICLNB	10/21/5	15/21/0	5/31/0	7/28/1	6/30/0

4   Conclusions

In this paper, we have proposed a novel model ICLNB for learning local naive Bayes within KNN using instance sampling. Instance sampling leads to relatively large training data for the local naive Bayes, and results in a naive Bayes with more accurate parameters. Thus, the classification of the local naive Bayes is more accurate. Indeed, when the neighborhood size is small, ICLNB deals with the problem of lack of training data effectively. Moreover, ICLNB performs well for various sizes of the neighborhood.

Although considerable work has been done in combining k-nearest neighbor with naive Bayes, some questions still remain unknown. Firstly, the basic assumption in combining k-nearest neighbor with naive Bayes is that, within the small neighborhood, attributes have a less chance to have strong dependences. However, the underlying reason is not clear. Another interesting direction for future research is how to apply KNN and its variants to the problems beyond classification, such as the problems in which accurate probability estimates or an accurate probability-based ranking of instances are required.

References

1. Aha, David W., Dennis Kibler, Marc K. Albert. 1991. Instance-Based Learning Algorithms. Machine Learning, vol. 6, pp. 37-66.
2. Domingos, P., Pazzani M.: Beyond Independence: Conditions for the Optimality of the Simple Bayesian Classifier. Machine Learning **29** (1997) 103-130

3. Frank, E., Hall, M., Pfahringer, B.: Locally Weighted Naive Bayes. Proceedings of the Conference on Uncertainty in Artificial Intelligence (2003). Morgan Kaufmann(2003), 249-256.
4. Kohavi, R.: Scaling Up the Accuracy of Naive-Bayes Classifiers: A Decision-Tree Hybrid. Proceedings of the Second International Conference on Knowledge Discovery and Data Mining (KDD-96). AAAI Press (1996) 202-207
5. Langley, P., Iba, W., Thomas, K.: An Analysis of Bayesian Classifiers. Proceedings of the Tenth National Conference of Artificial Intelligence. AAAI Press (1992) 223-228
6. Merz, C., Murphy, P., Aha, D.: UCI repository of machine learning databases. Dept of ICS, University of California, Irvine (1997). http://www.ics.uci.edu/ mlearn/ MLRepository.html
7. Nadeau, C., Bengio, Y.: Inference for the generalization error. Advances in Neural Information Processing Systems 12 (1999) 307-313. MIT Press.
8. http://prdownloads.sourceforge.net/weka/datasets-UCI.jar
9. Weiss, G., M., Provost, F.: Learning when Training Data are Costly: The Effect of Class Distribution on Tree Induction. Journal of Artificial Intelligence Research, 19 (2003) 315-354.
10. Witten, I. H., Frank, E.: Data Mining –Practical Machine Learning Tools and Techniques with Java Implementation. Morgan Kaufmann (2000)
11. Xie, Z., Hsu, W., Liu, Z., Lee, M.: SNNB: A Selective Neighborhood Based Nave Bayes for Lazy Learning. Proceedings of the Sixth Pacific-Asia Conference on KDD. Springer (2002) 104-114
12. Zheng, Z., Webb, G. I.,: Lazy Learning of Bayesian Rules. Machine Learning, **41(1)** (2000) 53-84

Comparing Dimension Reduction Techniques for Document Clustering

Bin Tang, Michael Shepherd, Malcolm I. Heywood, and Xiao Luo

Faculty of Computer Science,
Dalhousie University, 6050 University Avenue,
Halifax, Nova Scotia, Canada, B3H 1W5
{btang, shepherd, mheywood, luo}@cs.dal.ca

Abstract. In this research, a systematic study is conducted of four dimension reduction techniques for the text clustering problem, using five benchmark data sets. Of the four methods -- Independent Component Analysis (ICA), Latent Semantic Indexing (LSI), Document Frequency (DF) and Random Projection (RP) -- ICA and LSI are clearly superior when the k-means clustering algorithm is applied, irrespective of the data sets. Random projection consistently returns the worst results, where this appears to be due to the noise distribution characterizing the document clustering task.

1 Introduction

Document clustering is a fundamental and enabling tool for efficient document organization, summarization, navigation and retrieval. The most critical problem for document clustering is the high dimensionality of the natural language text, often referred to as the "curse of dimensionality". While various dimension reduction techniques (DRTs) have been proposed [1, 2], there are two major types, feature transformation and feature selection [2]. Feature transformation methods project the original high dimensional space onto a lower dimensional space, while feature selection methods select a subset of "meaningful" dimensions from the original ones.

In this research, we compare DRTs in a systematic manner for the text clustering task. We investigate the relative effectiveness and robustness of four dimension reduction techniques; one feature selection method, Document Frequency (DF) [3], and three feature transformation methods, including Latent Semantic Indexing (LSI) [4], Random Projection (RP) [5] and Independent Component Analysis (ICA) [6].

This paper is organized as follows. Section 2 describes our data sets, Section 3 our experimental procedure and evaluation methods, Section 4 our results and Section 5 presents our conclusions and directions for future research.

2 Characteristics of the Data Sets

We used five data sets used widely in information retrieval and text mining research. The number of classes ranges from 4 to 50 and the number of documents ranges be-

B. Kégl and G. Lapalme (Eds.): AI 2005, LNAI 3501, pp. 292–296, 2005.
© Springer-Verlag Berlin Heidelberg 2005

tween 4 and 3807 per class. The WebKB4 data set consists of WWW-pages. Reuters-2 and Reuters-10 are derivatives of the Reuters-215781 newswire stories data set. Reuter-2 is a collection of documents, each with a single topic label. The version of Reuter-2 that we used eliminates categories with less than 4 documents, leaving only 50 categories. We derive Reuters-10 from Reuters-2, consisting only of the ten most frequent categories. 20NG-4 is a subset of the 20-Newsgroup data set, and only includes 4 categories. The fifth data set consists of technical reports (CSTR). Details of the datasets are found elsewhere [7]

The data sets were pre-processed to remove tags, non-textual data and stop words[1]. The remaining words were stemmed[2] and those stems with low document frequency were removed. For example, the cutoff for the Reuter-2 data set is 4. The stem-weighting scheme used is the most commonly used "*ltc*" variant of the *tfidf* function [8].The document vectors were then normalized to unit length.

3 Experimental Procedures and Evaluation

3.1 Experimental Procedures

All experiments were conducted in the Matlab 6.5.1 environment. Each data set was split into training and test sets in a ratio of 3:1. For each number of experimental dimensions, the reduced dimension version of the data was generated as per each of the DRTs. This data was renormalized to unit length for each document, and k-means clustering was applied, to generate the clusters using only the training set. The choice of k is *ad hoc*, larger than the number of classes in general. Each cluster was given a class label using majority voting (using training set) and the classification accuracy (only for test set) was determined as described below.

At each number of reduced dimensions, the seeds for the k-means clustering were generated for each data set by sampling the data set and finding the set of points around which the rest of the sample are tightly grouped (details in [7]).

3.2 Evaluation Methods

To judge the relative effectiveness of the DRTs, we apply them to text clustering tasks on different data sets. Based on the quality of their clustering results, we rank them accordingly. There are two perspectives to the ranking, the absolute clustering results and the robustness of the method. Here, good robustness implies that when using a certain DRT, reasonably good clustering results should be found across a relatively wide range of dimensions (reduced), i.e., the clustering results should degrade gracefully if non-optimal reduced dimensions are used.

To measure the quality of text clustering, we choose to use *Purity* as introduced in [9]. We modify the calculation of *Purity* as follows. Each cluster i is assigned a class label, T_i, based on a majority vote by its members using only the training set. Then, the purity of cluster i is defined as the proportion of points assigned as members of cluster i in the test set whose class labels agree with T_i. It is easy to establish that

---

[1] http://www.dcs.gla.ac.uk/idom/ir_resources/linguistic_utils/stop_words.
[2] http://www.tartarus.org/~martin/PorterStemmer/.

Purity is the clustering-version of the micro-average of classification accuracy. Hereafter, we refer to the cluster quality measure as *classification accuracy (CA)*.

To judge the relative robustness of DRTs, we combine a heuristic observation and student t test. We first plot the CA curves of the DRTs against the dimensionalities. Based on the CA values, it is visually possible to clearly establish the relative effectiveness of the DRTs based on these curves. For situations when more than one curve shares very similar CA values over "an interesting range of dimensions" (defined later), such that we cannot visually resolve performance levels, we perform a paired student t test. For each data set, the relative ranks of the DRTs are determined by the combination of visual observation and paired student t tests on the CA curves of the DRTs.

To ensure that the results are representative and systematic, many precautions have to be taken in the process of comparison. First, the choice of data sets has to be made in such way that a broad genre of text collections is covered in our test. The second issue concerns the usage of the clustering algorithm. We choose to use k-means, since k-means or its variants are the most commonly used clustering algorithms used in text clustering. A well-known problem for k-means is that poor choices of initialization often lead to poor convergence to sub optimal solutions. To ameliorate the negative impact of poor initialization, we devised a simple procedure, described in Section 3.1.

4   Experimental Results and Discussions

4.1   Comparisons of the Four DRTs

The DRT comparisons over each data set are conducted by the combination of visual inspection and paired student t tests. We are only interested in comparing their performance on the most "interesting" dimension range. By "interesting" dimension range, we refer to the dimension range within which the methods produced the best clustering results. Hereafter, we will use [a, b] to denote the "interesting" dimension range under investigation. To detect the "good range of reduced dimensions", we also plot the LSI performance against its singular values. Since ICA uses PCA as a preprocessing stage to "whiten" the raw data and determine the number of components (dimensions) to reduce to, we are also interested in the correlation between ICA performance and the number of eigenvectors (number of reduced dimensions) used in the PCA whitening step. This correlation may suggest how to determine the "good range of dimensions to reduce to" by ICA.

Due to space limitations, we cannot present all our results, which can be found elsewhere [21]. Since the DRTs show very similar performances over the 5 data sets, we only present the results on Reuter-2 in detail (Figure 1).

From our results we can make a number of observations. RP is inferior to DF for the whole range of dimensions being investigated. DF peaks around a dimension of 657 with CA of 0.85 and then settles around 0.8 with increasing dimensionality. ICA and LSI achieve their best results with lower dimensionalities ([30, 93]). The result of the t-test indicates superior performance of ICA over that of LSI. ICA also maintains very good performance over a much larger range of dimensions than LSI and, therefore, appears to be more robust.

The correlation between singular values and LSI performance (and eigenvalues and ICA performance) is not clear. We observe that, both the singular and eigen values decrease very rapidly within the first few to few tens of dimensions, after which there is general reduction. Hereafter, we refer to the part of the singular/eigen value curve that transits from very rapid reduction to slow reduction as the transition zone. This transition zone seems to correspond to the best performance of LSI/ICA. In all cases, it appears that over the transition zone, the CA curve of ICA reaches its peak and keeps at a constant level over a wider range of dimensions than that of LSI, indicating less feature sensitivity of ICA. For Reuter-2, considering all the factors, we rank the DRTs in the order of ICA > LSI > DF> RP, where ">" denotes better.

5 Conclusions and Future Work

In this research, we compared four well-known dimension reduction techniques, DF, RP, LSI and ICA, for the document clustering task using five benchmark data sets. In general, we can rank the four DRTs in the order of ICA >LSI >DF >RP. ICA demonstrates good performance and superior stability compared to LSI. Both ICA and LSI can effectively reduce the dimensionality from a few thousands to the range of 100 to 200 or even less. The best performances of ICA/LSI seem to correspond well with the transition zone of the eigen/singular value curve. The experiments with DF clearly indicate to us that most of the raw dimensions in the text data are very noisy and meaningless with respect to the document clustering task, which further explains the relatively poor performance of RP.

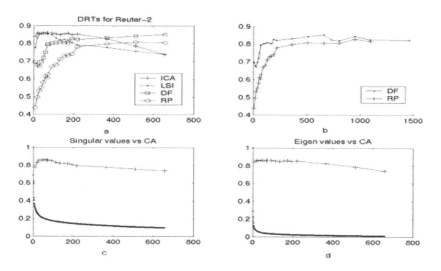

Fig. 1. DRT performance summary for Reuter-2.a. parallel comparison of four DRTs, x-axis: dimensionality, y-axis: CAs for DRTs. b. comparisons between DF and RP with extended dimensionality. c. correlation of classification accuracy and normalized singular value for LSI, '+' denotes the CA curve and '.' denotes the normalized singular value. d. correlation of classification accuracy of ICA and the normalized eigenvalues of its PCA step, '+' denotes the CA curve and '.' denotes the normalized eigenvalues

Our future research includes comparing the semantic meanings of the latent variables derived from ICA and LSI, and using DF to pre-screen the raw dimensions for LSI/ICA to further reduce the computational cost of LSI/ICA.

References

1. Fodor I.K.: A survey of Dimension Reduction Techniques. LLNL technical report, UCRL ID-148494, (2002) URL: http://www.llnl.gov/CASC/sapphire/pubs.html
2. Parsons L. et al.: Subspace Clustering for High Dimensional Data: a Review. ACM SIGKDD Explorations Newsletter. 6(1) (2004) 90 - 105
3. Yang Y. Pedersen J. O.: A Comparative Study on Feature Selection in Text Categorization. Proc. ICML (1997) 412-420
4. Berry M.W., Dumais S.T., and O'Brien G.W.: Using linear algebra for intelligent information retrieval. SIAM Review. 37(4) (1995) 573-595
5. Bingham E., Mannila H.: Random Projection in Dimensionality Reduction: Applications to Image and Text Data. Proc. SIGKDD (2001) 245-250
6. Hyvärinen A. Oja E.: Independent Component Analysis: Algorithms and Applications. Neural Networks. (4-5) (2000) 411-430. FastICA package: http://www.cis.hut.fi/~aapo/
7. Tang B. Luo X. Heywood M.I. Shepherd M.: A Comparative Study of Dimension Reduction Techniques for Document Clustering. TR # CS-2004-14, Faculty of Computer Science, Dalhousie University. (2004), http://www.cs.dal.ca/research/techreports/2004/CS-2004-14.shtml
8. Buckley C., Salton G., Allan J., Singhal A.: Automatic Query Expansion using SMART: TREC-3. Proc. TREC-3. (1995) 500-225.
9. Zhao Y. Karypis G.: Empirical and Theoretical Comparisons of Selected Criterion Functions for Document Clustering. Machine Learning.55 (3) (2004) 311 – 331.

Incorporating Evidence in Bayesian Networks
with the Select Operator

C.J. Butz and F. Fang

Department of Computer Science, University of Regina,
Regina, Saskatchewan, Canada SAS 0A2
{butz, fang11fa}@cs.uregina.ca

Abstract. In this paper, we propose that the select operator in relational databases be adopted for incorporating evidence in Bayesian networks. This approach does not involve the construction of new evidence potentials, nor the associated computational costs of multiplying the evidence potentials into the
knowledge base. The select operator also provides unified treatment of hard and
soft evidence in Bayesian networks. Finally, some query optimization rules, involving the select operator implemented in relational databases, can be directly
incorporated into probabilistic expert systems.

1 Introduction

Bayesian networks [3] are an established framework for uncertainty management and
have been successfully applied in practice in a variety of problem domains. Processing evidence is a fundamental task in Bayesian networks [2]. Evidence means that
some information about the values of a set E of variables is obtained. For instance, the
exact values $E = e$ are known or perhaps that E does not take specific values $E \neq e$.
Given evidence, say $E = e$, several techniques have been proposed for processing queries of the form $p(X \mid E = e)$, where X is a set of non-evidence variables. These techniques, however, have two disadvantages. First, the *construction* of a new probability
table, called an *evidence potential*, is required. Second, the evidence potential is *multiplied* with the probability tables stored in the knowledge.

Several researchers, including [4, 5], have pointed out the intrinsic relationship between Bayesian networks and relational databases [1]. More recently, Wong et al. [5]
established that the logical implication of probabilistic conditional independence exactly coincides with that of embedded multivalued dependency in relational databases
for the classes of Bayesian networks, Markov networks, and fixed-context.

In this paper, we propose that the *select operator* [1] in relational databases be
adopted for incorporating evidence in Bayesian networks. We first show that the select operator can be applied on probabilistic relations and not only traditional relations. As the name suggests, the select operator selects a subset of rows from a probabilistic relation that satisfy the select condition. Our main result is that incorporating
evidence with the select operator is equivalent to the approach with evidence potentials. Our approach does *not* involve the construction of new evidence potentials, nor

B. Kégl and G. Lapalme (Eds.): AI 2005, LNAI 3501, pp. 297–301, 2005.
© Springer-Verlag Berlin Heidelberg 2005

the associated computational costs of *multiplying* the evidence potentials into the knowledge base. The select operator also provides *unified* treatment of hard and soft evidence in Bayesian networks. Finally, some query *optimization rules*, involving the select operator implemented in relational databases, can be directly incorporated into probabilistic expert systems.

This paper is organized as follows. The select operator and query optimization rules are presented in Section 2. In Section 3, we discuss two methods for incorporating evidence in Bayesian networks. In Section 4, advantages of processing evidence with the select operator are provided. The conclusion is presented in Section 5.

2 The Select Operator

Wong et al. [4, 5] have shown how probability tables in Bayesian networks can be viewed as *probabilistic relations*, i.e., traditional relations in conventional databases [1] can be extended with a probability column. In this section, we incorporate the *select operator* [1] into this probabilistic setting.

Let $r(X)$ be a probabilistic relation on X. Let A be an attribute in X, $a \in dom(A)$, and *op* be an operator in $\{=, \neq, <, \leq, \geq, >\}$. Then

$$\sigma_{A \; op \; a}(r) = \{ t \mid t \in r \text{ and } t(A) \; op \; a \},\tag{1}$$

where $t(A)$ is the *restriction* of tuple t to attribute A.

Example 1. In Table 1, given the probabilistic relation r(z|h) on the left, $\sigma_{z=1}(r(z|h))$ and $\sigma_{z\neq0}(r(z|h))$ are shown in the middle and on the right, respectively.

Table 1. A probabilistic relation $r(z|h)$ (left). $\sigma_{z=1}(r(z|h))$ (middle). $\sigma_{z\neq0}(r(z|h))$ (right)

h	z	p(z|h)		h	z	p(z=1|h)		h	z	p(z≠0|h)
1	2	0.123		1	1	0.456		1	2	0.123
1	1	0.456		0	1	0.333		1	1	0.456
1	0	0.421						0	2	0.111
0	2	0.111						0	1	0.333
0	1	0.333								
0	0	0.556								

We now consider the relationship of the select operator with the multiplication and marginalization operators implemented in probabilistic expert systems. Here X and Y are sets of attributes and the select conditions do not involve probability columns. The soundness of these rules follows from the corresponding rules in databases [1].

1: The σ operator is commutative. Given select conditions c_1 and c_2,

$$\sigma_{c_1}(\sigma_{c_2}(r(X))) \;=\; \sigma_{c_2}(\sigma_{c_1}(r(X))).\tag{2}$$

2: Given a conjunction of select conditions $\{c_1, c_2, ..., c_m\}$ involving attributes in X:

$$\sigma_{c_1 \wedge c_2 \wedge ... \wedge c_m}(r(X)) \quad = \quad \sigma_{c_1}(\sigma_{c_2}...(\sigma_{c_m}(r(X)))). \tag{3}$$

3: If the select condition c only involves attributes in X, then

$$\Sigma_X(\sigma_c(r(XY))) \quad = \quad \sigma_c(\Sigma_X(r(XY))). \tag{4}$$

4: If the select condition c only involves attributes in X, then

$$\sigma_c(r(Y) \otimes r(X)) \quad = \quad r(Y) \otimes \sigma_c(r(X)), \tag{5}$$

where $\otimes$ is a multiplication join for probabilistic relations [4].

3 Incorporating Evidence in Bayesian Networks

Traditionally, evidence in incorporated into Bayesian networks [3] using *evidence potentials* [2]. We suggest using the select operator.

3.1 With Evidence Potentials

In the literature [2], there are two distinct kinds of evidence, namely, hard and soft.

Hard evidence is an instantiation of a set E of variables, i.e., it is observed that $E = e$. Hard evidence is incorporated into a Bayesian network as follows. First, a *finding potential* $F(E = e)$ is constructed. The probability column of $F(E = e)$ is set as follows: for the row with $E = e$, the probability value is one; for all other rows, the probability value is zero. Second, $F(E = e)$ is multiplied with the stored CPTs.

Soft evidence means $E \neq e$, i.e., it is known that the set E of variables does not take on value e. Soft evidence is incorporated into a Bayesian network as follows. First, a *likelihood potential* $L(E \neq e)$ is constructed. The probability column of $L(E \neq e)$ is set as follows: for the rows with $E \neq e$, the probability value is one; for all other rows, the probability value is zero. Second, $L(E \neq e)$ is multiplied with the stored CPTs.

Example 2. Suppose we observe hard evidence $z = 1$. The constructed finding potential $F(z = 1)$ is shown in Table 2 (left). The product $F(z = 1) \cdot p(z|h)$ is illustrated in Table 2, where $p(z|h)$ is the CPT from Table 1 (left). Similarly, given soft evidence $z \neq 0$, the CPT $p(z|h)$ is multiplied with the constructed likelihood potential $L(z \neq 0)$.

Table 2. Given hard evidence $z = 1$, the finding potential $F(z=1)$ is multiplied with the CPT $p(z|h)$ giving $p(z=1|h)$

z	F(z=1)		h	z	p(z|h)		h	z	p(z=1|h)
0	0	.	1	2	0.123	=	1	1	0.456
1	1		1	1	0.456		0	1	0.333
2	0		1	0	0.421				
			0	2	0.111				
			0	1	0.333				
			0	0	0.556				

3.2 With the Select Operator

Here, we incorporate evidence in Bayesian networks using the select operator.

Consider hard evidence $A_i = a_i$, where $a_i \in dom(A_i)$. The select condition c is the hard evidence $A_i = a_i$. Compute $\sigma_{A_i = a_i}(r(A_i|P_i))$, where $r(A_i|P_i)$ is the probabilistic relation for the CPT $p(A_i|P_i)$ of the hard evidence variable A_i.

Consider soft evidence $A_i \neq a_i$, where $a_i \in dom(A_i)$. The select condition c is the soft evidence $A_i \neq a_i$. Compute $\sigma_{A_i \neq a_i}(r(A_i|P_i))$, where $r(A_i|P_i)$ is the probabilistic relation for the CPT $p(A_i|P_i)$ of the hard evidence variable A_i.

Example 3. Recall the probabilistic relation r(z|h) in Table 1 (left). The hard evidence $z = 1$ is incorporated using the select operator as $\sigma_{z=1}(r(z|h))$, as shown in Table 1 (middle). Similarly, the soft evidence $z \neq 0$ is incorporated using the select operator as $\sigma_{z\neq0}(r(z|h))$, as shown in Table 1 (right).

Theorem 1. Given a Bayesian network, suppose hard evidence $A_i = a_i$ is observed. Incorporating $A_i = a_i$ with the select operator is equivalent to using a finding potential.

Proof: Consider the constructed finding potential $F(A_i = a_i)$. There is one row in table $F(A_i = a_i)$ for each value in $dom(A_i)$. The probability column in $F(A_i = a_i)$ is set as follows: one, for the row with $A_i = a_i$; zero, otherwise. Now consider the product of the finding potential $F(A_i = a_i)$ with the Bayesian network CPT $p(A_i|P_i)$ for variable A_i. By definition, rows of $F(A_i = a_i)$ will be multiplied with rows $p(A_i|P_i)$ provided they have the same value for A_i. Since the probability value in $F(A_i = a_i)$ is zero for all rows with $A_i \neq a_i$, the only rows appearing in the product $F(A_i = a_i) \cdot p(A_i|P_i)$ are those with $A_i = a_i$. Moreover, since the probability column of $F(A_i = a_i)$ is one when $A_i = a_i$, the probabilities of $p(A_i|P_i)$ with $A_i = a_i$ and $F(A_i = a_i) \cdot p(A_i|P_i)$ are equal. Hence, the result is the selection of those rows of $p(A_i|P_i)$ with $A_i = a_i$. This is the definition of $\sigma_{A_i = a_i}(r(A_i|P_i)) = \{ t \mid t \in r(A_i|P_i) \text{ and } t(A_i) = a_i \}$, where $r(A_i|P_i)$ is the probabilistic relation for the CPT $p(A_i|P_i)$ of the hard evidence variable A_i.

Corollary 1. Given a Bayesian network, suppose soft evidence $A_i \neq a_i$ is observed. Incorporating $A_i \neq a_i$ with the select operator is the same as using a likelihood potential.

For instance, the hard evidence $z = 1$ can be incorporated either using the select operator as in Table 1 (middle) or with a finding potential as in Table 2.

4 Advantages of Processing Evidence with the Select Operator

In this section, we give three advantages of using the select operator to incorporate evidence in Bayesian networks, namely, (i) there is no need to *construct* an evidence potential, (ii) we can *reduce* the number of multiplications, and (iii) the select operator *unifies* the notions of hard evidence and soft evidence.

The select operator does *not* require the construction of evidence potentials. On the contrary, the traditional approach [2] requires the construction of finding potentials for hard evidence, and likelihood potentials for soft evidence. See, for instance, $F(z = 1)$ in Table 2. It is well known that query optimization in Bayesian networks involves *reducing* the number of multiplications. While the traditional approach necessarily involves some multiplications to incorporate the evidence potentials into the knowledge base (i.e., Table 2), the select operator does not involve constructing evidence tables, nor their associated multiplicative costs (i.e., Table 1 (middle)). The last advantage concerns the *distinct* treatment of hard and soft evidence in the traditional approach. Here hard evidence is incorporated with *finding potentials*, while soft evidence involves *likelihood potentials*. On the contrary, the select operator readily handles both hard and soft evidence.

5 Conclusion

One objective in query optimization is to reduce the number of multiplications [2]. On the contrary, the traditional approach to incorporate evidence in Bayesian networks constructs new evidence tables simply to multiply them into the knowledge base (see Table 2). By adopting the select operator from relational databases, evidence can be incorporated without constructing evidence tables and without their associated multiplicative costs (see Table 1 (middle)). Moreover, the select operator provides unified treatment of both hard and soft evidence. We have also shown how select interacts with the multiplication and marginalization operators in probabilistic expert systems. Thus, the above analysis suggests that the select operator is a very convenient tool for incorporating evidence in Bayesian networks.

References

1. Abiteboul, S., Hull, R., and Vianu, V.: Foundations of Databases. Addison-Wesley Publishers, United States of America (1995)
2. Madsen, A.L. and Jensen, F.V.: Lazy Propagation: A Junction Tree Inference Algorithm Based on Lazy Evaluation. Artificial Intelligence 113 (1-2) (1999) 203-245
3. Pearl, J.: Probabilistic Reasoning in Intelligent Systems: Networks of Plausible Inference. Morgan Kaufmann Publishers, San Francisco, California (1988)
4. Wong, S.K.M., Butz, C.J. and Xiang, Y.: A Method for Implementing a Probabilistic Model as a Relational Database. 11th Conference on Uncertainty in Artificial Intelligence, Morgan Kaufmann Publishers, Montreal, Quebec (1995) 556-564
5. Wong, S.K.M., Butz, C.J. and Wu, D.: On the Implication Problem for Probabilistic Conditional Independency. IEEE Transactions on Systems, Man, and Cybernetics, Part A: Systems and Humans, Vol. 30, No. 6, (2000) 785-805

Quick Spatial Outliers Detecting
with Random Sampling

Tianqiang Huang[1], Xiaolin Qin[1], Qinmin Wang[2], and Chongcheng Chen[2]

[1] Department of Computer Science and Engineering,
Nanjing University of Aeronautics and Astronautics, Nanjing, 210016, China
Tianqianghuang@163.com
http://www.nuaa.edu.cn/
[2] Spatial Information Research Center in Fujian Province,
Fuzhou, 350002, China
http://www.sirc.gov.cn/

Abstract. Existing Density-based outlier detecting approaches must calculate neighborhood of every object, which operation is quite time-consuming. The grid-based approaches can detect clusters or outliers with high efficiency, but the approaches have their deficiencies. We proposed new spatial outliers detecting approach with random sampling. This method adsorbs the thought of grid-based approach and extends density-based approach to quickly remove clustering points, and then identify outliers. It is quicker than the approaches based on neighborhood queries and has higher precision. The experimental results show that our approach outperforms existing methods based on neighborhood query.

1 Introduction

The definition of spatial outlier varies with user needs and problem domain etc. Shekhar and Lu et al. [1,2] defined spatial outlier as spatially referenced object whose non-spatial attribute values are significantly different from those of other spatially referenced objects in their spatial neighborhoods. This definition emphasizes non-spatial deviation and ignores spatial deviation. In some application, domain specialist needs detecting the spatial objects, which have some non-spatial attributes, deviate from other in spatial dimension. For example, scientists researched the patients with a certain disease lived in different places. They would consider various kinds of situations which include abnormity of spatial attribute. We took into account of spatial and non-spatial attributes synthetically to define outlier. If the objects that have some non-spatial attributes are keep away from their neighbor in spatial relation. We defined them outliers.

There are many outlier-detecting algorithm. Existing approaches can be broadly classified into the following categories: Distribution-based approach [3], Depth-based approach [4], Clustering approach [5], Distance-based approach [6], Density-based approach [7] and Model-based approach [8,9]. There are many advantages in density-based algorithm but these approaches have poor efficiency. The grid-based approaches that are used to detect clusters of outliers calculate quickly but they have "dimension curse" and have poor precision. We absorb the thought of grid-based algorithm

B. Kégl and G. Lapalme (Eds.): AI 2005, LNAI 3501, pp. 302–306, 2005.
© Springer-Verlag Berlin Heidelberg 2005

to improve the density-based algorithm. The algorithm uses neighborhood expanding than divide spatial objects with spatial grid, which doesn't cause "dimension curse" and has high precision and can quickly identify outliers.

2 Spatial Outliers and Related Notions

In this paper we suppose the objects in dataset are in two dimensions space, which it is easy to extend to multidimensional space. Points in this paper are objects with spatial and non-spatial attributes, so the notion of point is equated with the object as following.

Given a dataset D, a symmetric distance function *dist*, parameters ε and *MinPts*.

Definition 1. The *square impact neighborhood* of a point $p(u, v)$, denoted by *SIN* (p), is defined as $SIN(p) = \{q \in D \mid |x - u| \leq \varepsilon, |y - v| \leq \varepsilon$ and spatial attributes satisfy $C\}$, u and v are point p's coordinates.

Definition 2. The *near square impact neighborhood* of p, denoted by *NSIN*, is the square impact neighborhoods near *SIN(p)*, i.e., the square impact neighborhoods have public point with *SIN(p)*. As Fig.1, *SIN(a)*, *SIN(b)*, *SIN(c)*, *SIN(d)*, *SIN(e)*, *SIN(f)*, *SIN(g)* and *SIN(h)* are *NSINs* of *SIN(p)*.

Definition 3. The *neighbor* of p is any point in square impact neighborhood of p except p. $|SIN(p)|$ represent the number of neighbors in square impact neighborhood of p.

Definition 4. If a point's square impact neighborhood has at least *MinPts* points, the square impact neighborhood is *dense*, and the point is *core point*.

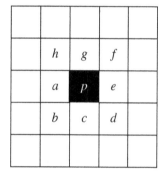

Fig. 1. Illumination of *NSIN*

Definition 5. If a point's square impact neighborhood has less than *MinPts* points, the square impact neighborhood is *sparse*. If a point is a neighbor of core point, but his neighborhood is sparse, the point is *border point*.

Definition 6. If a point is core point or border point, and it near a border point p, the point is *near-border point* of p.

Definition 7. The *local density* of p is defined as

$$LD(P) = |SIN(p)| \ / \sum_{o \in SIN(p)} Dist(p,o) \qquad (1)$$

$Dist(p, o)$ is a distance between p and o. $|SIN(p)|$ represents cardinality of Impact Neighborhood of p, i.e., the number of neighbors in square impact neighborhood of p. Intuitively, the Local Density of an object p is the inverse of the average distance based on the neighbors of p.

Definition 8. The *local deviation factor* is defined as

$$LDF(p) = |SIN(p)| \ / \sum_{o \in SIN(p)} (LD(p)/LD(o)) \qquad (2)$$

The Local Deviation Factor (*LDF*) of spatial object p represents the degree that outlier is deviating its neighbors. It is the average of the ratio of the local density of p and those of p's neighbors. It is easy to see that the lower p's local density is, and the higher the local densities of p's neighbors are, the higher is the *LDF* value of p.

Definition 9. *Outlier* p is the object that its *LDF* is higher than certain threshold value and it is in sparse square impact neighborhood.

3 *DBSODRS* Algorithm

The algorithms based on density have some advantages, but running efficiency is slow; grid-based algorithms are quick, but have "dimension curse" and lack precision. Our algorithm has absorbed their strong points. Existing density-based algorithm must examine the neighborhood of very object to guarantee finding density-based clustering or outliers, which operation is quit time-consuming. In our method, the algorithm discards these dense neighborhoods in first as grid-based algorithm, because these objects in it are impossibly outliers. Our algorithm didn't calculate the neighborhoods of all objects, so it is quicker than existing approaches based neighborhood query.

We present the **D**ensity-**B**ased **S**patial **O**utlier **D**etecting with **R**andom **S**ampling (*DBSODRS*) algorithm. *DBSODRS* is consisted of two segments: *selecting roughly* and *refining*.

The first segment (line 1~13) is *selecting roughly*. In first one point p randomly is selected as *start*, and algorithm calculate its *square impact neighborhood*. If the *SIN* is density, all points in it are not outliers; otherwise, all points in it are candidate outliers. Algorithm selects one *NSIN* of p and repeats it as far as algorithm can't find *NSIN* or all points in the *SIN* are visited, then algorithm randomly select another unvisited object in database as *start* and repeat above all until all points in database are visited. So, algorithm partitions all objects into two parts: clustering points and candidate outliers.

The second (line 14~18) is *refining segment*. *LDF*s of all candidate outlier are calculated. All objects that their *LDF* values are higher than threshold are spatial outliers.

```
Algorithm DBSODRS(DB, ε, MinPts)
1.While (!DB.IsAllVisited( ) )
2.    {p = SelectUnVisitedPoint(DB);
3.     PNB = DB.SquaImpactNeighbors(p, ε)
4.     NextP = PNB
5.     While ((!NextP.IsAllVisited)or(NextP = Empty))
6.          {if ( |NextP| > MinPts )
7.               DBNB[NextP]= ClusterLabel;
8.            else
9.               DBNB[NextP]= CandidateLabel;
10.          endif;
11.          NextP = NextSquaImpactNeighborhood(NextP)
12.          }
13.   };
14. For every CandidateLabeled point
15.       {q = Select_one_point();
16.        If (LDF(q) > h)
17.            OutlierSet = OutlierSet ∪ q;
18.       };
```

Line 1 is a repetition, which closes when all points in database are visited. Function *SelectUnVisitedPoint()* in line 2 selects an unvisited point as *start,* than algorithm begin one expanding process(lines 5~12), and algorithm detecting new square impact neighborhood while it can't find *NSIN* or all objects in all *SIN* are visited. Function *DB.SquaImpactNeighbors()* in line 3 is used to calculate square impact neighborhood of *p*. Lines 6~10 is used to judge whether the *SIN* is dense. All points in the *SIN* are clustering points if the *SIN* is dense; otherwise, they are candidate outliers. Function *NextSquaImpactNeighborhood()* in Line 11 is used to find the next square impact neighborhood, i.e., *NSIN*. Lines 14~18 are refining segment. Function *LDF()* is used to calculate the Local Deviation Factor of object *q*. the calculation are required in Definition 8 (Formulas (1)) and Definition 9 (Formulas (2)). If the *Local Deviation Factor* of object *q* is higher the threshold *h* that defined by user, the object *q* is spatial outlier.

4   Experimental Evaluation

We have done many experiments to examine the efficiency and effectiveness, but limiting to extension we only presented two. In first, we use synthetic data to explain effectiveness of our approach. Secondly, we use large database to verify the efficiency. Experiment results showed that our ideas can be used to successfully identify significant local outliers and performance outperforms the other approach based neighborhood query. All experiments were run on a 2.2 GHz PC with 256M memory.

GDBSCAN [10] is extension of *DBSCAN* [5]. To compare this algorithm with *GDBSCAN*, we use the synthetic sample databases that are used in [5]. In these dataset, the non-spatial property of the points is depicted by different colors. We add many points with different non-spatial attributes denoted with red color in the databases in [5]. Experiment focus on blue objects, and set *q.attrs* = blue. The result of the experiment shows *DBSODRS* can exactly identify all outliers.

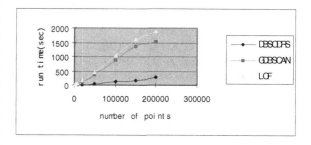

Fig. 2. Time efficiency comparisons between *GDBSCAN*, *LOF* and *DBSODRS*

For comparison computational efficiency of *DBSODRS* and *GDBSCAN* and *LOF*, we used synthetic datasets that are consisted of points from 2000 to 200,000. The *Eps* is 5, and *MinPts* is 10, when *DBSODRS* query the neighborhood. Parameters are the same when *GDBSCAN* run. We set *MinPts* = 30 and *LOF* > 1.5. Fig. 2 shows the running time for *DBSODRS* increases with the size of the datasets in an almost linear fashion, and the performance is obviously better than the other two.

5 Conclusion

We presented a spatial outlier detection approach in spatial databases. This algorithm absorbs the thought of the grid-based and the density-based approaches. It does not calculate neighborhood of very objects but expands the square impact neighborhood to remove clustering objects and then detect outliers quickly. Because the outliers are much few than clustering objects, this algorithm discards much region query of clusters and gained good efficiency.

Acknowledgements. This research supported by the National Nature Science Foundation of China (No. 49971063), the National Nature Science Foundation of Jiangsu Province (BK2001045) and the National High-Tech Research and Development Plan of China (No. 2001AA633010-04).

References

1. S. Shekhar, C.T. Lu, P. Zhang: A unified approach to detecting spatial outliers. GeoInformatica, 7, 2 (2003) 139-166
2. C.T. Lu, D. Chen, Y. Kou: Algorithms for spatial outlier detection. In Proceedings of the 3rd IEEE International Conference on Data Mining (ICDM 2003), 19-22 December 2003, Melbourne, Florida, USA, IEEE Computer Society (2003) 597-600
3. V. Barnett, T. Lewis: Outliers in Statistical Data. John Wiley (1994)
4. T. Johnson, I. Kwok, R.T. Ng: Fast computation of 2-dimensional depth contours. In Proc. KDD (1998) 224-228
5. M. Ester, H.P. Kriegel, J. Sander, X. Xu: A density-based algorithm for discovering clusters in large spatial databases. In: Proceedings of KDD'96, Portland OR, USA, (1996) 226-231
6. E. Knorr, R. Ng: Algorithms for Mining Distance-Based Outliers in Large Datasets. In Proc. 24th VLDB Conference (1998)
7. M.M. Breunig, H.P.Kriegel, R.T.Ng, J. Sander: LOF: Identifying density-based local outliers. In: Proceedings of SIGMOD'00, Dallas, Texas (2000) 427-438
8. T. Hu, S.Y. Sung: Detecting pattern-based outliers. Pattern Recognition Letters, 24 (2003) 3059-3068
9. Z. He, X. Xu, S. Deng: Discovering cluster-based local outliers. Pattern Recognition Letters, 24 (2003) 1642-1650
10. M. Ester, H.-P. Kriegel, J. Sander, and X. Xu: Density-Based Clustering in Spatial Databases: The Algorithm GDBSCAN and its Applications. Data Mining and Knowledge Discovery, 2, 2 (1998) 169-194

A Document Browsing Tool: Using Lexical Classes to Convey Information[1]

Lyne Da Sylva and Frédéric Doll

École de bibliothéconomie et des sciences de l'information
Université de Montréal
{Lyne.Da.Sylva, Frederic.Doll}@UMontreal.CA

Abstract. This research project is a contribution to the global field of information discovery in digital documents. We aim to provide the user with a tool for flexible access to the contents of digital documents: a text browsing facility inspired by traditional "back-of-the-book" style indexes. It gives at a glance the main topics discussed in the document, and presents certain kinds of relationships between these topics. These are captured automatically by exploiting certain lexical classes. Previous research on this and similar topics is reviewed, followed by the main characteristics of a research prototype, which relies on modeling of professionally produced indexes. Experimental results are presented, as well as remaining hurdles and potential applications.

1 Introduction

This research project is a contribution to the global field of information discovery in digital documents. We aim to provide the user with flexible access to the contents of large, potentially complex digital documents, with means other than a search function or a handful of metadata elements. The type of tool we develop is a text browsing facility, akin to traditional "back-of-the-book" style indexes; it suggests semantic information based on a fairly superficial linguistic analysis, and judicious use of different lexical classes in the data. The tool not only gives at a glance the main topics discussed in the document (with direct access via hyperlinks to specific passages), but also presents certain types of relationships between these topics. The relations are captured automatically by exploiting certain types of lexical classes. The methodology relies on modeling of similar hand-crafted indexes.

Figure 1 shows an example of the type of browsing tool produced by our system; underlined numbers signify hypertext links to corresponding numbered passages, paragraphs or sentences. The traditional tool which corresponds to this presentation is the 'back-of-the-book" style index (see [8] or [16]). It presents an inventory of the main concepts in the document, through structured the entries: under general main headings are grouped a number of subheadings which specify different aspects of the main headings discussed in a particular passage; all important discussions (or

---

[1] This research is funded by a grant from the Natural Science and Engineering Research Council of Canada.

B. Kégl and G. Lapalme (Eds.): AI 2005, LNAI 3501, pp. 307–318, 2005.

passages) are indexed, thus covering all material in the document. In a digital search environment, where a user's query may yield a number of long documents, building such a tool automatically would be quite helpful to browse a document's content quickly.

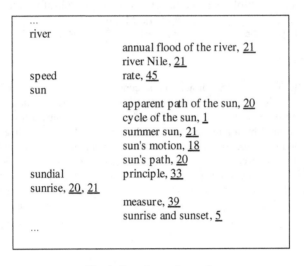

Fig. 1. Sample result sought

2 Related Work

Two types of research are relevant to our own: first, work on tools for browsing through collections of documents, and secondly work on automatic book indexing.

Recent advances in information retrieval produce systems which allow some type of document browsing. They typically extract useful phrases and construct a representation that allows the user to navigate among related terms or related documents (where relatedness is defined in a variety of ways). Among others: systems for "interactive information seeking" ([2]), "phrase browsing" ([17]), "text exploration" ([21]), "text structure presentation" ([10], etc.), "hierarchical summarization" ([13]) and "derivation of concept hierarchies for collections" ([14] and [19]). Although the products are useful for browsing the collection, they provide little help in accessing the content of a single document. Research in this direction can benefit from insights drawn from the information organization tradition.

Indeed, we believe there is much in the methodology of professional back-of-the-book indexing that can be usefully incorporated in an implementation for digital document indexing. Initial research in automatic book indexing (namely [3] and [7]) was met with limited success: extracting words or phrases from documents, counting occurrences and alphabetizing a list of high-frequency candidates, produced lists of phrases with little information on their relative importance nor their distribution throughout the text. One of the most important flaws is the inability to tease apart an important discussion of a concept from a mere mention of it. In fact, the top-frequency phrase in a document will appear in almost every passage; only a few will be useful for the index. Conversely, quite a few fairly rare phrases may constitute very interesting index entries. Hence, information derived from frequency is quite dubious, when used in this way. This shows an important difference between back-of-the-book indexing and indexing for information retrieval in databases (see [12] for a clear distinction between the two). (Note that our approach does use frequency data, but in conjunction with lexical information.)

Another difficulty lies in the grouping of phrases, to form coherent entries of significantly linked topics. Such semantically-based groupings prove very difficult to derive automatically. In addition, faced with a number of references on a given topic, it is quite difficult to automatically identify the ways in which the corresponding passages differ. Finally, the simple extraction of explicit phrases in the document will not provide much more than a search function would. Much of the "value-added" characteristics of a back-of-the-book style index lies in the semantic structure provided by the groupings and subdivisions of entries. The obvious difficulty of the task explains its absence in previous implementations.

3   A Browsing Tool Based on Professional Indexing Methodology

Our implemented approach hinges on a handful of observations from human indexer methodology; it presents interesting results and indicates a number of fruitful research directions. It is still however very much in the prototype stage and will benefit from many improvements. We sketch here the general approach (and note the independent work of [1], which is quite similar to our own).

3.1   Observing Human Indexers

This work has evolved out of teaching back-of-the-book indexing to future professional indexers (given our academic setting, in a school of library and information science). A comparison of indexing methodology with automatic book indexing procedures revealed striking differences between the two (in addition to revealing the scarceness of research on automatic book indexing). We aim to replicate a certain number of characteristics of professional back-of-the-book indexing. Indexing requires of course identifying the key concepts in the document. But it also involves identifying passages in the document – thematically coherent sections which form the basis of subsequent indexing. Indeed, indexers index passages, not words, labelling the passage with a limited number of appropriate specific topics; this is in sharp contrast with frequency-based automatic indexing which simply favours high-frequency words or phrases in the document. After this initial passage-tagging, human indexers then spot recurring themes in the document and group references to them in the index. The methodology described below explains how the modeling of this type of professional indexing is achieved in our prototype. In particular, the nature of words and phrases in the text is an important factor in devising the index.

3.2   Three Observations

Processing hinges on three observations on human indexing. The first regards text structure: a document is a collection of passages, which an indexer identifies and describes briefly. In other words, each passage (when delineated) can be treated as an independent "document" of a thematically-linked "corpus" (i.e. the whole document). Techniques used for indexing a collection, such as statistics regarding term frequency and dispersion in the "collection", can be applied to a collection of passages, to discriminate passages from each other. This yields the main topic(s) of the passage.

The second observation addresses the problem of grouping references into entries and distinguishing references to the same topic. Although semantic inference on a list of phrases is difficult, it is fairly easy to spot, in the source document, pairs of phrases in close proximity that are linked – by a semantic relation such as hypernymy or meronymy (part-whole relationship), for instance. They may be linked also because statistical analysis reveals an important correlation between the two. Hence we look for pairs of words or phrases that become candidates for two-level index terms (i.e. heading with subheading). This "two-level" approach has proven to be a simple development technique which actually produces much of the index's structure.

The third observation is a linguistic one: that, for indexing, not all words are created equal. Some expressions are extremely useful; namely, those belonging to the specialized vocabulary of the document. Some others are not very good indicators of the thematic content; words such as "theory", "introduction", "development", "example", etc. This in true independently of their frequency of occurrence (at least to a great extent). This linguistic observation will allow an interesting, yet easily-implementable type of main/subheading pairs.

Thus, (automatic) segmentation of the text is crucial to the methodology which we have implemented. But it will not be discussed here in great detail (simply put, we have our own implementation of a method based on lexical cohesion, similar to that of [9]). Rather, we will illustrate how exploiting different types of words, phrases, and pairs of these, can help to create index entries (or phrases for browsing) which are semantically suggestive – and thus very helpful for information discovery.

3.3 Relations in Indexes

A number of relation types are used by indexers in building book indexes. A quantitative analysis of some book indexes is presented in [6]. We retain the following relationships (corresponding examples are shown in Figure 2): (a)

a.	c.	e.
planet	globular clusters	telescope
Earth	see globular star clusters	Hubble telescope
Mars		Hubble space telescope
	d.	space telescope
b.	moonless Earth	
solar system	consequence	f.
sun		moonless Earth
stars		thinner atmosphere

Fig. 2. Sample main heading-subheading pairs illustrating types of relationships (page references omitted)

Hypernymy (general vs. specific term); (b) Meronymy (part-whole relationships); (c) Synonymy (i.e. semantic equivalence in the document); (d) Specialized vocabulary / basic scientific vocabulary – see explanations below; (e) Phrase factorization; and (f) Implicit coordination.

We review now these relationships by general type, with examples from the *Stargazers* text ([4]– exploring the possibility of life in space), used by [9] for testing text segmentation.

3.3.1 Thesaural Relationships

Some of the relationships above require external semantic or lexical resources. Namely, the first three (a. to c. above) are relations typically expressed in a thesaurus. Given a comprehensive thesaurus appropriate for the document's thematic content, one could hope to spot related pairs of phrases in the document and produce structured index entries (ex. planet, Mars). Even better, using the thesaurus, single specific terms could be spotted and paired with their hypernym or meronym (even if the latter is absent from the text), thus producing highly informative indexes which exhibit groupings that are impossible to do automatically otherwise. For synonyms, a thesaurus can yield two useful results. One is to allow the identification of variants of phrases in the document to be grouped in a single entry; the other is to provide cross-references, in the index, from one variant to the other. These are highly desirable characteristics of an automatically-derived index, but absent from our system, given the difficulty of acquiring a good domain-specific thesaurus, and the limited use of general-language thesauri. We concentrate mostly, for the time being, on other types of relations between a main heading and a subheading. Recall that candidate index entries will often present a two-level structure, with a heading and subheading (in some cases, three levels, as will be explained below).

3.3.3 Phrase Factorization

The structure of extracted phrases can be exploited to derive type e. above (see examples in Figure 3). Phrase factorization implies simply identifying recurring nouns within phrases and factoring them; an extremely simple technique for semantic grouping, it is yet not always implemented in indexing systems. In this case, two-level index entries are created, where the main heading is the noun, and the subheading is the phrase. All phrases using the same noun will be collapsed in the same entry.

system	galaxy
binary and trinary	stars in our galaxy
systems	
stars in our galaxy	star
single star systems	single star systems
solar system	
solar systems	
trinary systems	

Fig. 3. Phrase factorization

Note that a phrase containing more than one noun can be factored in as many ways. This multiplies index entries, adding not quite redundancy to the index, but additional "access points" to the information (especially useful when sifting through an alphabetical list). Thus phrase factorization achieves more than one purpose.

3.3.4 Specialized vs. Basic Scientific Terminology

As mentioned above, some very general words are poor candidates for index terms. They include words such as "theory", "introduction", "development", "example", etc., which would be discarded in most human indexing contexts. [20] refers to them as "basic scientific vocabulary" (BSV). When used as a subheading, however, and paired with a word or phrase belonging to the specialized vocabulary (SV) used in the document, they produce quite insightful descriptions of passages, as Figure 4a illustrates.

Our research on BSV suggests that it consists of a fairly stable list of words, used in all domains of scholarly writing, including pure and applied science, social sciences, humanities, arts, etc. The words are general and abstract in nature. BSV is different from Basic English ([18]) in that the latter includes verbs and adjectives as well as nouns, abstract or concrete, which describes an adult learner's basic vocabulary; in comparison, BSV corresponds roughly to the nouns of scholarly language formally learned in late adolescence. The BSV may be defined on linguistic grounds, by a semantic characterization, or it may be derived automatically by extraction from a suitably balanced corpus (we currently have other research underway on that topic). Our prototype uses a BSV list which has been manually constructed based on linguistic criteria, and produces output such as is presented here.

SV is simply identified in terms of high document frequency. For each passage, pairs of SV and BSV can be spotted and proposed as candidate two-level index entries.

Note that this pairing offers advantages over phrase extraction, as each member of the pair may not be adjacent in a sentence – indeed, they may occur in different sentences (the algorithm which determines which of the candidates end up in the index must of course take into account the distance between the SV and BSV terms, and favor pairs whose members are not overly distant). This is a first example of apparent semantic relationships captured by an association of candidates belonging to different lexical classes. It is done using very simple means; it would be quite difficult to produce something equivalent by a proper semantic analysis.

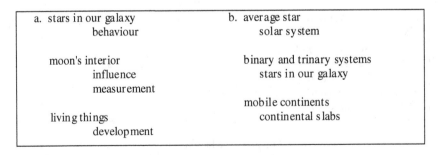

Fig. 4. Sample SV/BSV pairs (a) and phrase co-occurrence pairs (b)

3.3.4 Implicit Coordination

In typical indexes, a number of index entries are formed of two phrases, without explicit mention of the semantic relation between them in the text. Sometimes, the relationship is obvious (for example, *"Diabetes in children, dietary restrictions"*). In other cases, presumably, the reader must turn to the passage in question to discover it. In a system which automatically extracts phrases and calculates occurrence and co-occurrence statistics, it is fairly easy to identify whether the co-occurrence of two phrases is statistically significant (even with simple measures such as tf•idf). In that case, the pair may yield candidate pairs of phrases, such as those shown in Figure 4 b. In this fashion, the actual relation observed by statistical co-occurrence is never characterized. However, this is not necessary, as the main/subheading pair provides an evocative concept cluster.

3.4 Lexical Classes

Our system knows a number of lexical classes: first, single words, then phrases. Both words and phrases can potentially become index entries. However, among single words extracted from the document, a subset, those belonging to the BSV, will be excluded from the index as single one-level entries and reserved for subheadings of two-level index entries, such as the example below.

---

advanced civilisations existing at the same time
     possibility

As for phrases, they may undergo two types of processing. First, those considered salient for a passage will be identified and factored according to each noun in the phrase, thus yielding one or more two-level index entries (see example below).

---

tide
     enormous gravitational tides from a nearby moon
moon
     enormous gravitational tides from a nearby moon

Secondly, pairs of phrases whose co-occurrence in a passage is deemed statistically significant will produce two-level index entries, which will further be factored according to each noun in the top-level phrase, thus producing three-level entries.

---

life   space
    life in space   life in space
        images of Mars   images of Mars

More complete examples below will show how these locally constructed two- and three-level entries jointly produce a structured, semantically suggestive index.

4 The Prototype

4.1 Overview of Processing

The working prototype (in French and English) implements the three observations described above. Processing involves four main steps: identification and frequency counts of words and phrases (so-called "concept extraction"); automatic text segmentation; candidate term weighting; and index compilation. A brief description of some of these steps is outlined below; more details are given in [5].

Phrase extraction: lemmatization and part-of-speech (POS) tagging is performed, with the use of a dictionary; phrases are recognized by a simple algorithm which spots sequences of up to four non stop words (breaking on punctuation) and filters out impossible POS sequences. It gathers only noun phrases, as other types of phrases are generally not included in indexes. A frequency count is kept of all lemmatized words and phrases, which are used in subsequent processing.

Text segmentation: automatic segmentation is performed, based on lexical cohesion. The result is a complete segmentation into disjoint thematic units. Each thematic unit is assigned candidate index entries, of which only the most highly weighted ones will be retained in the final index.

Candidate term weighting: within each thematic unit, candidate terms receive a weight which is a function of their frequency and of their form (phrases are weighted more highly than single words, for instance). The distribution of words and phrases throughout the document is also a factor; the weighting thus uses a version of tf•idf, taken from [15], where tf = term frequency, N=number of text segments, d=term dispersion among segments and n=normalisation factor.

$$tf•idf = ((1 + \log(tf)) * \log(N / d)) / n$$

Index compilation: a limited number of candidates for each segment are transferred to the final index (the number is proportional to the size of the segment). This achieves keeping only the most salient or discriminative concepts for each segment, thus discarding non-salient (and probably uninformative) mentions of topics. Candidates are distributed unequally among candidate types: around 30% are drawn each from SV-BSV pairs, co-occurrence pairs and phrases, and 10% are single words (percentages were suggested on the analysis in [6]). Entries for all segments are placed in alphabetical order; entries with identical main headings are collapsed into a complex entry containing two or more subheadings.

4.2 Sample Results

We show below excerpts from an index for the *Stargazers* text. It illustrates how candidate terms of different types and different segments are brought together in the final index. Among the 20 most frequent words (see Figure 6), only a handful will make it to the final index. The others are either too rare (single occurrences) or too frequent (evenly spread out in the document) to be salient for any given passage. Or they belong to the BSV and are only included as subheadings. A last case is words appearing exclusively within a phrase: only the phrase is retained in the index.

earth	29	form	7	solar system	6	life in space	2
moon	28	crust	6	trinary systems	5	moon's interior	2
star	25	universe	6	solar systems	4	lunar surface	2
system	20	surface	6	single star	4	star cluster	2
life	19	year	6	binary and trinary		star systems	2
planet	15	time	6	systems	4	lava lakes	2
solar	12	scientist	6	advanced life	3	single star systems	2
astronomer	7	cluster	5	living things	3		
continent	7	telescope	5				
galaxy	7	material	5				

Fig. 6. Most frequent words and phrases extracted from the *Stargazers* text

Type of entry	Segment 1	Segment 7	Segment 8
Phrase co-occurrence	star, average star, solar system	system, star systems, single star solar system star, star systems, single star solar system	gas, giant balls of gas, solid surface ball, giant balls of gas, solid surface
Factored Phrase	space, life in space	system, trinary systems system, binary and trinary systems	system, trinary systems system, binary and trinary systems system, single star systems
SV / BSV	planet, average planet, assumption	system, planets in binary and trinary systems, data planet, planets in binary and trinary systems, data	galaxy, stars in our galaxy, behaviour star, stars in our galaxy, behaviour
Word	universe	astronomer	century

Fig. 7. Candidate index entries for segments 1, 7 and 8 of the sample text

astronomer, 7
ball,
  giant balls of gas,
    solid surface, 8
century, 8
life,
  life in space, 1
galaxy,
  stars in our galaxy,
    behaviour, 8
gas,
  giant balls of gas,
    solid surface, 8
planet,
  average planet,
    assumption, 1
  planets in binary and trinary systems,
    data, 7

space,
  life in space, 1
star,
  average star,
    solar system, 1
  stars in our galaxy,
    behaviour, 8
  star systems,
    single star solar system, 7
system,
  binary and trinary systems, 7, 8
  planets in binary and trinary systems,
    data, 7
  single star systems, 8
  star systems,
    single star solar system, 7
  trinary systems, 7, 8
universe, 1

Fig. 8. Result of collapsing entries from Figure 7

Similarly, some of the most frequent phrases are excluded from the index whereas some rare ones are included, based on statistically measured salience.

Figure 7 show, for three segments, index entries with the highest weight (above a specified threshold). During the index compilation phase, all these candidates are brought together (Figure 8). Following classic index presentation usage, entries from different segments that share the same main heading are collapsed under that shared heading; gathering two- and three-level entries thus performs some groupings as a side effect. Lemmatization increases the chance of such collapsing. Since phrases are factored under each noun they contain, topics which are similar but not identical can nonetheless be grouped in the index.

4.3 Advantages of a Browsing Tool

Each index entry is followed by a number, which is a hyperlink to the relevant document passage (the segment). The index thus provides an easy-to-use navigational tool to access specific passages dealing with a given topic. It differs from a summary in its non narrative format and hierarchical display of salient concepts. It should be clear that the resulting index is aimed at a human reader, as a reading-aid tool, and is not meant for further automatic processing.

This type of tool offers interesting advantages for information discovery over a classic search function. First, the fact that entries are structured allows the representation to suggest to the user concepts which are related to his or her search (other than actual keywords that may be submitted to a search function, but must be supplied by the user). Secondly, the structure of the index entries suggests some of the semantic relationships present among the concepts in the document, despite limited semantic knowledge in the system. In fact, the only linguistic knowledge stems from (i) the definition of the BSV list and (ii) the phrase extraction algorithm. The association of phrases with BSV, and of phrases amongst themselves, is performed by statistical analysis. Another key piece in the puzzle is the text segmentation, which relies on lexical cohesion, that is the degree to which adjacent sentences share vocabulary items. It is possible to add linguistic knowledge to the system (namely thesaural relationships). But even as it is, we consider this approach to have great potential for producing a useful browsing tool.

4.4 Current Limitations

The resulting index depends heavily on two crucial operations: term identification and text segmentation. Given the limitations of our part-of-speech tagger, our ad hoc limit of 4 content words and our lack of word sense disambiguation, inappropriate sequences are sometimes proposed as noun phrases. Since the term weighting which eliminates some candidate entries relies mainly on statistics, an ungrammatical sequence sometimes outweighs a better one, yielding a less than useful index. As for text segmentation, it has a great impact on the index, namely on the calculation of tf•idf of words or terms, which is determined the by the lexical content of each segment.

5   Conclusion and Future Prospects

Our approach to producing a tool for document browsing uses insights from professional indexing: automatic text segmentation produces a set of thematically-coherent passages, to each of which is attached a limited number of highly weighted index term candidates; the candidates may be isolated words and phrases, but preference is given to pairs of words or phrases, perceived to entertain semantic links within each segment. In this fashion, limited linguistic knowledge on lexical classes is used to produce an index structure which suggests semantic relationships. Relationships holding across segments are obtained by factoring, then joining, the entries. The resulting index is a structured list of concepts, which is more evocative than flat list of words or phrases.

We have yet to perform a proper quantitative evaluation. This presents important methodological difficulties (even humans have difficulty agreeing on index quality); but our future plans include an evaluation phase based on human judgements (similar to [11]). In any case, a number of significant improvements to the prototype are planned in the immediate future, including improved term extraction and use of XML mark-up to guide segmentation. Also, we note that no word sense disambiguation is attempted for polysemous BSV items such as "application". All occurrences of it will be considered either SV or BSV throughout (depending on its frequency) even though the two meanings can co-exist in a given text.

For this research, we foresee applications not only for indexing (such as a browsing tool for large documents found on the Web, including multiple-document indexing, computer-assisted book indexing, and a test-bed for theories on indexing), but also for producing abstracts, based on the segmentation and on the thematic description of each passage; however, more work needs to be done to transform the index entries into a coherent summary.

References

1. Aït El Mekki, T., Nazarenko, A.: Une mesure de pertinence pour le tri de l'information dans un index de "fin de livre". In: *TALN 2004*, Fès, April 19-21, (2004). http://www.lpl.univ-aix.fr/jep-taln04/proceed/actes/taln2004-Fez/AitElMekki-Nazarenko.pdf (accessed 2004/6/15).
2. Anick, P., Tipirneni, S.: The paraphrase search assistant: Terminological feedback for iterative information seeking. In: Hearst, M., Gey, F., Tong, R. (eds): *Proceedings on the 22nd annual international ACM SIGIR conference on Research and development in information retrieval*, (1999) 153-159.
3. Artandi, S.: *Book indexing by computer*. S.S. Artandi, New Brunswick, N.J. (1963).
4. Baker, D.: Stargazers look for life. *South Magazine*, Vol. 117, (1990) 76-77.
5. Da Sylva, L.: A Document Browsing Tool Based on Book Indexes. *Proceedings of Computational Linguistics in the North East (CLiNE'04)*, Concordia University, Montréal, (2004) 45-52.
6. Da Sylva, L.: Relations sémantiques pour l'indexation automatique. Définition d'objectifs pour la détection automatique. *Document numérique, Numéro spécial « Fouille de textes et organisation de documents »*, Vol. 8, no. 3, (2004) 135-155.

7. Earl, L.L.: Experiments in automatic extraction and indexing. In: *Information Storage and Retrieval*, Vol. 6, (1970) 313-334.

8. Fetters, L.K.: *Handbook of Indexing Techniques : a Guide for Beginning Indexers.* American Society of Indexers, Port Aransas, TX (1994).

9. Hearst, M.: TextTiling: Segmenting Text into Multi-Paragraph Subtopic Passages. In: *Computational Linguistics*, Vol. 23, no. 1, (1997) 33-64.

10. Hernandez, N., Grau, B.: What is this text about? Combining topic and meta descriptors for text structure presentation. In: *Proceedings of the 21st annual international conference on Documentation (ACM SIGDOC)*, San Francisco, 12-15 Oct. (2003), 117-124.

11. Jones, S., Paynter, G.W.: Human Evaluation of Kea, an Automatic Keyphrasing System. In: *Proceedings of the First ACM/IEEE-CS Joint Conference on Digital Libraries*, (2001) 148-156.

12. Klement, S.: Open-system versus closed-system indexing. *The Indexer*, Vol. 23, no. 1, (2002)23-31.

13. Lawrie, D., Croft, B.: Finding Topic Words for Hierarchical Summarization. In: *Proceedings of the 24th annual international ACM SIGIR conference on Research and development in information retrieval ()*, New Orleans, Louisiana (2001) 349--357.

14. Lawrie, D., Croft, B.: Discovering and Comparing Topic Hierarchies. In: *RIAO 2000*, (2000) 314--330.

15. Manning, C., Schütze, H.: *Foundations of Statistical Natural Language Processing.* MIT Press, Cambridge, Mass. (1999)

16. Mulvany, N.: *Indexing books.* University of Chicago Press, Chicago (1994).

17. Nevill-Manning, C.G., Witten, I.H., Paynter, G.W.: Lexically-generated subject hierarchies for browsing large collections. *International Journal of Digital Libraries*, Vol. 2 no. 2/3, (1999) 111--123.

18. Ogden, C.K.: *Basic English: A General Introduction with Rules and Grammar.* Paul Treber & Co., Ltd., London (1930, 1940).

19. Vinokourov A., Girolami M.: A Probabilistic Hierarchical Clustering Method for Organising Collections of Text Documents. In: *Proceedings of the 15th International Conference on Pattern Recognition (ICPR'2000)*, Barcelona, (2000) 182-185.

20. Waller, S.: *L'analyse documentaire. Une approche méthodologique*, ADBS Éditions, Paris (1999).

21. Yaari, Y.: *NLP-assisted exploration of texts.* http://citeseer.ist.psu.edu/412683.html (2000).

A Supervised Learning Approach to Acronym Identification*

David Nadeau and Peter D. Turney

Institute for Information Technology,
National Research Council Canada
Ottawa, Ontario, Canada
{david.nadeau, peter.turney}@nrc-cnrc.gc.ca

Abstract. This paper addresses the task of finding acronym-definition pairs in text. Most of the previous work on the topic is about systems that involve manually generated rules or regular expressions. In this paper, we present a supervised learning approach to the acronym identification task. Our approach reduces the search space of the supervised learning system by putting some weak constraints on the kinds of acronym-definition pairs that can be identified. We obtain results comparable to hand-crafted systems that use stronger constraints. We describe our method for reducing the search space, the features used by our supervised learning system, and our experiments with various learning schemes.

1 Introduction

Acronym identification is the task of processing text to extract pairs consisting of a word (the acronym) and an expansion (the definition), where the word is the short form of (or stands for) the expansion. For instance, in the sentence, "The two nucleic acids, deoxyribonucleic acid (DNA) and ribonucleic acid (RNA), are the informational molecules of all living organisms," there are two acronyms, "DNA" and "RNA", along with their respective definitions, "deoxyribonucleic acid" and "ribonucleic acid". In this work, we do not discriminate between acronyms (short forms of multiword expressions) and abbreviations (contractions of single words). We use the term *acronym* to include both cases.

The acronym identification task can be extended in many ways. It is possible to try to resolve acronyms even when there are no explicit definitions in the text. For instance, the familiar acronym "HIV" will often appear without being defined. Another extension to the task is to try to disambiguate polysemous acronyms (e.g., "CMU" means "Carnegie Mellon University" but also "Central Michigan University"). The task requires identifying the intended sense of the acronym even when its definition is absent. Ambiguous acronyms are particularly problematic for information retrieval.

B. Kégl and G. Lapalme (Eds.): AI 2005, LNAI 3501, pp. 319–329, 2005.

In this paper, we tackle the core task only. That is, given an input text, our algorithm will attempt to extract all explicit acronym-definition pairs. Our goal is to create a dictionary of acronym-definition pairs specific to a single text. An algorithm that addresses the core task can be used, for example, to enhance a list of author keyphrases by resolving acronyms. More importantly, such an algorithm is a key component in systems that handle the various extended tasks, such as co-reference resolution for named-entity recognition or automatic query expansion for information retrieval. The literature on automatic acronym identification presents many attempts to solve the core task, and our contribution is to present a supervised learning approach with weak constraints on the forms of acronyms and definitions that can be identified. Our results are comparable to what is achieved (on the same testing data) by human-engineered rule systems with stronger constraints.

The next section presents a detailed summary of related work. Section 3 presents our supervised learning approach to acronym identification and Section 4 discusses the training and testing corpus we used. At least three other papers use the same corpus for evaluating their systems (Pustejovsky *et al.*, 2001; Chang *et al.*, 2002; Schwartz and Hearst, 2003). The remaining sections discuss our experimental results and conclude the paper.

2 Related Work

In this section, we present previous work on the acronym identification task. We focus on the constraints that these systems use to extract valid acronym–definition pairs.

One of the earliest acronym identification systems (Taghva and Gilbreth, 1999) is AFP (Acronym Finding Program). The AFP system first identifies candidate acronyms, which the authors define as uppercase words of three to ten letters. It then tries to find a definition for each acronym by scanning a $2n$-word window, where n is the number of letters in the acronym. The algorithm tries to match acronym letters against initial letters in the definition words. Some types of words receive special treatment: stopwords can be skipped, hyphenated words can provide letters from each of their constituent words and, finally, acronyms themselves can be part of a definition. Given these special cases, the longest common sequence (LCS) between acronym letters and initial letters in definitions is computed.

Yeates (1999) proposes the automatic extraction of acronyms-definitions pairs in a program called TLA (Three Letter Acronyms). Although the name suggests that acronyms must have three letters, the system can find n-letter acronyms as well. The algorithm divides text into chunks using commas, periods, and parentheses as delimiters. It then checks whether adjacent chunks have acronym letters matching one or more of the initial three letters of the definition words. Further heuristics are then applied to each candidate, ensuring that the acronym is uppercase, is shorter than the definition, contains the initial letters of most of the definition words, and has a certain ratio of words to stopwords.

Larkey *et al.* (2000) developed Acrophile. They compared various strategies and found their Canonical/Contextual method to be the most accurate. First they force candidate acronyms to be in upper-case, allowing only embedded lower case letters (internal or final), periods (possibly followed by spaces), hyphens (or diagonal slashes) and digits (at most one, non-final digit). They allow a maximum of nine alphanumeric characters in acronyms. They search for expansions in a window of 20 words, adjacent to the given acronym. Stopwords can contribute to an inner letter, but only once for the entire acronym. Furthermore, an expansion is only valid if it fits a given pattern, such as being surrounded by parentheses or preceded by a cue phrase (e.g.,"also known as").

Recently the fields of Genetics and Medicine have become especially interested in acronym resolution (Pustejovsky *et al.*, 2001, Yu *et al.* 2002). Pustejovsky *et al.*, present an approach with weak constraints, designed to capture the wide range of acronyms that are abundant in medical literature. For example, "PMA" stands for "phorbol ester 12-myristade-13-acetate" and "E2" stands for "estradiol-17 beta". Pustejovsky *et al.*'s acronym resolution technique searches for definitions of acronyms within noun phrases. Acronym-definition candidate pairs must match a given set of regular expressions, designed to be very general, and the final decision about whether a pair is valid relies on counting the number of acronym characters and definition words that match.

Another strategy, also developed for the medical field, is from Schwartz and Hearst (2003).[1] Their approach is similar to Pustejovsky *et al.*'s (2001) strategy and the emphasis is again on complicated acronym-definition patterns for cases in which only a few letters match (e.g., "Gen-5 Related N-acetyltransferase" [GNAT]). They first identify candidate acronym-definition pairs by looking for patterns, particularly "*acronym (definition)*" and "*definition (acronym)*". They require the number of words in the definition to be at most $\min(|A|+5, |A| \times 2)$, where $|A|$ is the number of letters in the acronym.[2] They then count the number of overlapping letters in the acronym and its definition and compare the count to a given threshold. The first letter of the acronym must match with the first letter of a definition word. They also handle various cases where an acronym is entirely contained in a single definition word.

Byrd and Park (2001) combine mechanisms such as text-markers and linguistic cues with pattern-based recognition. The same combination was used by Larkey (2000). This removes some constraints on the acronyms that can be identified. The reason for these mechanisms is to cope with the growing popularity of acronyms that diverge from the tradition of using only the first letter of each word of the definition. They use cue expressions (e.g., "or", "short", "acronym", "stand") to reinforce the confidence in acronym-definition pairs. They also allow acronyms to include a digit at the beginning or the end; thus, "5GL (Fifth Generation Language)" would be a valid candidate.

Adar (2002) presents a technique that requires only four scoring rules for acronym-definition pair evaluation: (1) add one to the score if an acronym letter begins a definition word, (2) subtract one for each extra word that does not match acronym letters, (3) add one if the definition is next to a parenthesis and (4) the number of definition words should be less than or equal to the number of acronym letters; therefore, subtract one for each extra word.

Chang *et al.* (2002) present a supervised learning approach to acronym identification. In order to circumscribe the learning, they impose a strongly restrictive

---

[1] The Java source code for their system is available at http://biotext.berkeley.edu/software.html.

[2] This formula is borrowed from Byrd and Park (2001).

condition on candidate acronym-definition pairs, by searching only for *"definition (acronym)"* patterns. Interestingly, this pattern accounts for the majority of positive cases in their evaluation corpus. Chang *et al.*'s learning algorithm uses eight features describing the mapping between acronym letters and definition letters (e.g., percentage of letters aligned at the beginning of a word, number of definition words that are not aligned to the acronym, etc.). The learning algorithm they used is logistic regression.

Zahariev (2004) presents a complete review of the acronym identification literature in his thesis. He also extends the task to multi-lingual acronym identification and he offers an in-depth analysis of acronym phenomena. However, the proposed system uses the same strongly constraining patterns as Larkey *et al.* (2000).

Table 1 summarizes related work on acronym identification. In this table and in the forthcoming sections, "participation" means that a letter of the acronym is found in a word of the definition. Generally, either the constraints on the acronym are strong (e.g., "all acronym letters must be capitals" or "the number of letters must exceed some minimum") or the definition pattern is fixed (e.g., "the definition must be in parentheses"). Such strong constraints ensure reasonable precision but, in general (for heterogeneous text from unrestricted domains), they necessarily limit recall. In our work, we try to use only weak constraints on both the acronym and the definition.

Table 1. Summary of constraints on acronyms and definitions

Author (Year)	Strongest constraints on acronym candidate	Strongest constraints on definition candidate
Taghva and Gilbreth (1999)	• uppercase word of 3 to 10 characters	• must be adjacent • only first letters of definition words can participate
Yeates (1999)	• uppercase word	• must be adjacent • first three letters of definition words can participate
Larkey *et al.* (2000)	• need some uppercase letters • maximal size of 9 characters	• pattern "acronym (definition)" or "definition (acronym)" • cue (e.g., "also known as")
Pustejovsky *et al.* (2001)	• a word between parentheses or adjacent to parentheses	• pattern "acronym (definition)" or "definition (acronym)"
Schwartz and Hearst (2003)	• a word between parentheses or adjacent to parentheses	• pattern "acronym (definition)" or "definition (acronym)"
Byrd and Park (2001)	• at least 1 capital • from 2 to 10 characters	• parentheses pattern or linguistic cue (also known as, short for, etc.)
Adar (2002)	• one word between parentheses	• adjacent on the left of parenthesis
Chang *et al.* (2002)	• one word between parentheses	• adjacent on the left of parenthesis
Zahariev (2004)	• a word between parentheses or adjacent to parentheses	• pattern "acronym (definition)" or "definition (acronym)"

3 Supervised Learning Approach

The acronym identification task can be framed in terms of supervised learning. The concept we want to learn is a pair $\langle A, D \rangle$ made of an acronym A (a single token) and a definition D (a sequence of one or more consecutives tokens). Given a sequence T of n tokens, $T = \langle t_1, ..., t_n \rangle$, from which we wish to extract a pair $\langle A, D \rangle$, there are n possible choices for $A = t_i$. Each possible acronym ($A = t_i$) can be defined (D) by any combination of one or more consecutive tokens taken from the left context $\{t_1, ..., t_{i-1}\}$ or from the right context $\{t_{i+1}, ..., t_n\}$. The number of possible pairs is $O(n^3)$ (n choices for $A = t_i$ multiplied by n choices for the first token in D multiplied by n choices for the last token in D). Therefore, before applying supervised learning, we reduce the space of possible $\langle A, D \rangle$ pairs with some heuristics.

Section 3.1 describes our heuristics for reducing the search space for candidate acronyms and Section 3.2 discusses the constraints for candidate definitions. Together, these sections explain how we reduce the space of $\langle A, D \rangle$ pairs that must be considered by the supervised learning algorithm. After the space has been reduced, the remaining candidate pairs must be represented as feature vectors, in order to apply standard supervised learning algorithms (Witten and Frank, 2000). Section 3.3 outlines our set of seventeen features.

The constraints that follow (Sections 3.1 and 3.2) are relatively weak, compared to most past work on acronym identification, but they still exclude some possible acronym-definition pairs from consideration by the supervised learning algorithm. The resulting decrease in recall is discussed in Section 5.

3.1 Space-Reduction Heuristics for Candidate Acronyms

The acronym space (the set of choices for $A = t_i$) is reduced using syntactic constraints on the tokens, $T = \langle t_1, ..., t_n \rangle$, expressed by the conjunction of the following statements:

1. $A = t_i$, where $1 \le i \le n$.
2. $\text{Size}(t_i) \ge 2$, where $\text{Size}(t_i)$ is the number of characters in the token t_i (including numbers and internal punctuation).
3. $\text{NumLetter}(t_i) \ge 1$, where $\text{NumLetter}(t_i)$ is the number of alphabetic letters in the token t_i (excluding numbers and punctuation).
4. $(\text{Cap}(t_i) \wedge \text{UnknownPOS}(t_i)) \vee \text{Cue}(t_i)$, where $\text{Cap}(t_i)$ means that the token starts with a capital letter, $\text{UnknownPOS}(t_i)$ means that the part-of-speech of the token is neither conjunction, determiner, particle, preposition, pronoun nor verb, and $\text{Cue}(t_i)$ means that the token contains a digit, punctuation, or a capital letter.

The rationale behind $\text{Size}(t_i) \geq 2$ is that, in most cases, isolated letters such as "H" will not be acronyms (although "H" can stand for "Hydrogen"). Statement (4) says that the token t_i should have some capitalization or special characters, but in the former case, the token should not have a known part-of-speech. The calculation of $\text{UnknownPOS}(t_i)$ requires applying a part-of-speech tagger to the text. We used QTAG (Tufis and Mason, 1998) as our part-of-speech tagger.

The above heuristic constraints are less restrictive than previous approaches (compare with Table 1).

3.2 Space-Reduction Heuristics for Candidate Definitions

Once a candidate acronym $A = t_i$ is found in the text, we search for its definition D on both sides of t_i. First, we require that both acronym and definition must appear in the same sentence. This considerably reduces the search space for $\langle A, D \rangle$ by reducing the size n of T, although the space is still $O(n^3)$. We then need stronger criteria to define a reasonable set of candidate definitions. We impose the following additional constraints:

1. The first word of a definition must use the first letter of the acronym (Pustejovsky *et al.*, 2001).
2. A definition can skip one letter of the acronym, unless the acronym is only two letters long.
3. The definition can skip any number of digits and punctuation characters inside the acronym.
4. The maximum length for a definition is $\min(acronymlen + 5, acronymlen \times 2)$ (Byrd and Park, 2001). (Definition length is measured by number of words and acronym length is measured by number of characters.)
5. A definition cannot contain a bracket, colon, semi-colon, question mark, nor exclamation mark. (We found counter-examples for other punctuation. For instance, the acronym "MAM" expands to "meprin, A5, mu", where the comma is used.)

Typically, these constraints will dramatically reduce the number of candidate definitions (increasing precision) while including the vast majority of true positive cases (preserving recall).

To illustrate the remaining search space, consider the following sentence:

```
Microbial control of mosquitoes with special emphasis
on bacterial control (Citation).
```

The word "Citation" is not an acronym, but it fits our constraints, since it is a capitalized noun. Even with the above constraints, there are 92 candidate definitions in this example. Note that, according to the second rule above, the definition can skip one letter (except the leading 'C') of the acronym. Here is one of the candidate definitions (acronym letters are marked with square brackets):

```
[c]ontrol of mosqu[i]toes wi[t]h speci[a]l emphas[i]s
[o]n bacterial co[n]trol
```

3.3 Acronym-Definition Features for Supervised Learning

The above heuristics reduce the search space significantly, so that the number of ways to extract a pair $\langle A, D \rangle$ from a token sequence $T = \langle t_1, ..., t_n \rangle$ is now much less than $O(n^3)$. The next step is to apply supervised learning, to select the best $\langle A, D \rangle$ pairs from the remaining candidates. Standard supervised learning algorithms assume input in the form of feature vectors. We defined seventeen features to describe a candidate acronym-definition instance. The hand-crafted rules that are described in previous work inspired the design of many of the following features. Our features mainly describe the mapping of acronym letters to definition letters and syntactic properties of the definition.

1. the number of participating letters matching the first letter of a definition word;
2. (1) normalized by the acronym length;
3. the number of participating definition letters that are capitalized;
4. (3) normalized by the acronym length;
5. the length (in words) of the definition;
6. the distance (in words) between the acronym and the definition;
7. the number of definition words that do not participate;
8. (7) normalized by the definition length;
9. the mean size of words in the definition that do not participate;
10. whether the first definition word is a preposition, a conjunction or a determiner (inspired by Byrd and Park, 2001);
11. whether the last definition word is a preposition, a conjunction or a determiner (inspired by Byrd and Park, 2001);
12. number of prepositions, conjunctions and determiners in the definition;
13. maximum number of letters that participate in a single definition word;
14. number of acronym letters that do not participate;
15. number of acronym digits and punctuations that do not participate;
16. whether the acronym or the definition is between parentheses;
17. the number of verbs in the definition.

If the heuristics in Sections 3.1 and 3.2 propose a candidate acronym-definition pair $\langle A_1, D_1 \rangle$ then there are three possibilities:

1. In the manual annotation of the corpus, there is an officially correct acronym-definition pair $\langle A_2, D_2 \rangle$ such that $A_1 = A_2$ and $D_1 = D_2$. In this case, $\langle A_1, D_1 \rangle$ is labeled as positive for both training and testing the algorithm.
2. In the manual annotation of the corpus, there is an officially correct acronym-definition pair $\langle A_2, D_2 \rangle$ such that $A_1 = A_2$ but $D_1 \neq D_2$. In this case, $\langle A_1, D_1 \rangle$ is ignored during training but it is labeled as negative during testing (see Section 6.3 for details).
3. In the manual annotation of the corpus, there is no officially correct acronym-definition pair $\langle A_2, D_2 \rangle$ such that $A_1 = A_2$. In this case, $\langle A_1, D_1 \rangle$ is labeled as negative for both training and testing.

4 Evaluation Corpus

We use the Medstract Gold Standard Evaluation Corpus (Pustejovsky *et al.*, 2001) to train and test our algorithm.[3] The corpus is made of Medline abstracts in which each acronym-definition pair is annotated. The training set is composed of 126 pairs and the testing set is composed of 168 pairs. The main interest of this corpus is that it was annotated by a biologist using an informal definition of a valid pair. Therefore the corpus reflects human interpretation of acronym-definition pairs and acronym identification is challenging for an automated process.

Past results with this corpus are reported in Table 2. All of the results are based on modified versions of the Medstract Gold Standard Evaluation Corpus, and (unfortunately) they all use different modifications. Here are some remarks on each of the modifications:

1. Chang *et al.* (2002) do not describe their modifications.
2. Pustejovsky *et al.* (2001) note that they removed eleven elements that they judged were not acronyms.
3. Schwartz and Hearst (2003) mention that they made modifications, but do not describe what modifications they made.
4. We attempted to replicate the results of Schwartz and Hearst (2003), while making only minimal modifications to the original corpus. Our modifications were aimed at creating a valid XML file and a consistent set of tags. We had to remove embedded acronyms and remove or correct obvious errors.

Since Schwartz and Hearst's (2001) system is available online[4], we were able to repeat their experiment on our modified version of the corpus. This is the version of the corpus that we use in the following experiments, in Section 5.

Table 2. Performance reported by teams using their own version of the Medstract corpus

Team	Precision	Recall	F1	Corpus Modification
Chang *et al.*, 2002	80%	83%	81.5%	See (1)
Pustejovsky *et al.*, 2001	98%	72%	83.0%	See (2)
Schwartz and Hearst, 2003	96%	82%	88.4%	See (3)
Schwartz and Hearst (our replication)	89%	88%	88.4%	See (4)

5 Experimental Results

We use the Weka Machine Learning Toolkit to test various supervised learning algorithms (Witten and Frank, 2000). The results are reported in Table 3. We found that the performance varies greatly depending on the chosen algorithm. A good classifier was PART rules (rules obtained from a partially pruned decision tree) with

---

[3] http://medstract.org/gold-standards.html
[4] http://biotext.berkeley.edu/software.html

somewhat low recall but high precision. The Support Vector Machine (Weka's SMO) reaches F1 = 88.3%, a performance that rivals hand-craft systems. The Bayesian net also performs well. The OneR classifier (one rule) is shown as a baseline. Table 3 includes our replication of Schwartz and Hearst (2003) for comparison. Note that all results in this table are based on the same corpus.

Table 3. Performance of various classifiers on the Medstract corpus

Learning Algorithm	Precision	Recall	F1
OneR[5]	69.0%	33.1%	44.7%
Bayesian Net	89.6%	81.7%	85.5%
PART rules	95.3%	79.6%	86.7%
SVM (SMO kernel degree = 2)	92.5%	84.4%	88.3%
Schwartz and Hearst (our replication)	88.7%	88.1%	88.4%

We claim that our system has weaker hand-coded constraints than competing approaches. In support of this claim, it is worth mentioning that 1,134 candidate acronym-definition pairs satisfied the constraints in Sections 3.1 and 3.2, but only 141 candidates (12%) were classified as positive by the supervised learning algorithms. Therefore the hand-coded part of our system allowed more candidates than, for example, Schwartz and Hearst's system allows. In comparison, their system considered 220 patterns that involve parentheses and 148 (67%) are accepted by the rule-based system. In our system, the reduction from 1,134 candidates to 141 candidates is done by the supervised learning component, rather than by hand-coded constraints. The advantage of this approach is that the supervised learning component can easily be retrained for a new corpus. The hand-coded constraints are designed to be weak enough that they should not require modification for a new corpus.

6 Discussion

In this section, we discuss the interpretation of our experimental results.

6.1 The Parenthesis Feature

In our examination of previous work (Section 2), we criticized many authors for making use of overly constraining patterns. One of the problems is the use of parentheses. Many authors only accept acronym-definition pairs when one of the expressions is between parentheses. To avoid this kind of limitation, we did not impose this constraint in our model. However, the only way we were able to perform as well as hand-built systems was to use the feature "*whether the acronym or the definition is between parentheses*" (feature 16 in Section 3.3). The learner uses this feature, since it works well on the Medstract corpus. Our relatively weak constraints (Sections 3.1 and 3.2) allow 889 candidate acronym-definition pairs for which the

---

[5] The rule for OneR says that the pair is valid if 70.8% of acronym letters match the first letter of a definition word.

parenthesis feature is false (neither the candidate acronym nor the candidate definition is between parentheses). In the Medstract corpus, all of these 889 candidates are negative instances (none are true acronym-definition pairs). Thus this feature dramatically increases precision with no loss of recall. It is a very informative feature, but we do not wish to hard-code it into our constraints, since we believe it may not generalize well to other corpora. With a new corpus, our system can learn to use the feature if it is helpful or ignore it if it does not apply. This robustness is an advantage of using weak constraints combined with supervised learning.

6.2 The Best Features

When evaluating the contribution of the individual features (using the Chi Square Test), we found that three features significantly outperform others. Those features are, in order of predictive power, (1) the distance between the definition and the acronym (feature 6), (2) the number of acronym letters that match the first letters of definition words (feature 1), and (3) the parentheses feature (feature 16).

6.3 Effects of the Space-Reduction Heuristics

In Section 3, we presented heuristics for reducing the space of possible acronym-definition candidates. A particular case can be misleading for the supervised learning algorithm.

Consider a case in which our heuristics identify <PKA, protein kinase A> but the corpus annotation is <PKA, cAMP-dependent protein kinase A>. It is tempting to say that <PKA, protein kinase A> must count as a negative example for the supervised learner, but this could confuse the learner, since the match between PKA and protein kinase A is actually very credible and reasonable. Instead of counting <PKA, protein kinase A> as a negative example, we found that it is better to ignore this case during training. It would be incorrect to count this case as a positive example, but it would be misleading to count it as a negative example, so it is best to ignore it. During testing, however, such instances are added to the false negatives (thus reducing recall), because this is an error and the system must be penalized for it. (See Section 3.3.)

7 Conclusion

In this paper, we described a supervised learning approach to the acronym identification task. The approach consists in using weak hand-coded constraints to reduce the search space, and then using supervised learning to impose stronger constraints. The advantage of this approach is that the system can easily be retrained for a new corpus, when the previously learned constraints no longer apply. The hand-coded constraints reduce the set of candidate acronym-definition pairs that must be classified by the supervised learning system, yet they are weak enough that they should be portable to a new corpus with little or no change.

In our experiments, we tested various learning algorithms and found that a Support Vector Machine is comparable in performance to rigorously designed hand-crafted systems presented in the literature. We reproduced experiments by Schwartz and Hearst (2003) and showed that our test framework was comparable to their work.

Our future work will consist in applying the supervised learning approach to different corpora, especially corpora in which acronyms or definitions are not always indicated by parentheses.

References

Adar, E. (2002) S-RAD A Simple and Robust Abbreviation Dictionary, *HP Laboratories Technical Report*, September.

Chang, J.T., Schütze, H. and Altman R.B., (2002), Creating an Online Dictionary of Abbreviations from MEDLINE, *Journal of American Medical Informatics Association (JAMIA)*, 9(6), p.612-620.

Larkey, L., Ogilvie, P., Price, A. and Tamilio, B. (2000) Acrophile: An Automated Acronym Extractor and Server, *In Proceedings of the ACM Digital Libraries conference*, pp. 205-214.

Park, Y., and Byrd, R.J., (2001), Hybrid Text Mining for Finding Abbreviations and Their Definitions, *Proceedings of the 2001 Conference on Empirical Methods in Natural Language Processing*, Pittsburgh, PA.

Pustejovsky, J., Castao, J., Cochran, B., Kotecki, M., Morrell, M. and Rumshisky, A. (2001) "Extraction and Disambiguation of Acronym-Meaning Pairs in Medline", *unpublished manuscript*.

Schwartz, A. and Hearst, M. (2003), A simple algorithm for identifying abbreviation definitions in biomedical texts, *In Proceedings of the Pacific Symposium on Biocomputing* (PSB).

Taghva, K. and Gilbreth, J. (1999), Recognizing acronyms and their definitions, *International journal on Document Analysis and Recognition*, pages 191-198.

Tufis, D. and Mason, O. (1998). Tagging Romanian Texts: a Case Study for QTAG, a Language Independent Probabilistic Tagger, *Proceedings of the First International Conference on Language Resources and Evaluation (LREC)*, Spain, p.589-596.

Yeates, S. (1999), Automatic extraction of acronyms from text. *In Third New Zealand Computer Science Research Students' Conference*, pages 117-124.

Yu H, Hripcsak G, Friedman C. (2002) Mapping abbreviations to full forms in biomedical articles, *Journal of the American Medical Informatics Association* (9) 262-272.

Witten I, H, and Frank, E. (2000) *Data Mining: Practical machine learning tools with Java implementations,* Morgan Kaufmann, San Francisco.

Zahariev, M. (2004). *A (Acronyms)*, Ph.D. thesis, School of Computing Science, Simon Fraser University.

Adjectives: A Uniform Semantic Approach

Nabil Abdullah and Richard A. Frost[†]

School of Computer Science, University of Windsor,
Windsor, Ontario N9B 3P4, Canada
abdull2@uwindsor.ca, richard@cs.uwindsor.ca

Abstract. Despite their simple syntactic form, adjective-noun combinations seem to have no straightforward semantic method that parallels the simplicity of the syntax. This has led to the conventional belief that adjectives belong to a (semantically motivated) hierarchy. This has the consequence that a uniform treatment of adjectives is unattainable—without resorting to notions such as possible worlds, which are difficult to map into competent computer programs. Moreover, because of their seemingly "undisciplined" semantic behaviour, adjective-noun combinations have been used by some authors (e.g. [5]) to further the argument of non-compositionality of natural-language expressions. Contrary to such views, we believe that adjectives are more systematic in their behaviour than originally thought. In support of this claim and based on typed sets, we propose a uniform approach to the semantics of adjective-noun combinations. It hypothesizes that adjective-noun combinations can semantically be thought of as a set intersection involving the adjective(s) and the head noun of the compound.

1 Adjective Hierarchy: The Conventional View

It is a commonly-accepted view that adjectives have different underlying semantic rules (see [1,3,4,6,7,8,9,13,14,16,17]). This has led to the belief that adjectives assume a semantically-motivated hierarchy[1] . This hierarchy is listed below:

- Intersective e.g. 'red'.
- Subsective:
  o Pure, e.g. 'accomplished'.
  o Double, e.g. 'beautiful'.
- Non-subsective:
  o Non-privative or non-committal, e.g. 'alleged'.
  o Privative, e.g. 'fake'.

Intersective adjectives are the most restricted ones. The adjective *angry* in the sentence *That man is angry* is an example of an intersective adjective. The meaning of *angry man* then can be computed as the intersection of angry things and men.

[†] Acknowledgement: this work was supported by a discovery grant from the Natural Science and Engineering Council of Canada.
[1] A note concerning the terminology is in order. Authors use different terms to describe the different classes of adjectives. In some cases, syntactic and semantic terminologies overlap.

B. Kégl and G. Lapalme (Eds.): AI 2005, LNAI 3501, pp. 330–341, 2005.

The second class of adjectives is called subsective. They are so called because all that can be said about them is that the denotation of an adjective-noun combination is a subset of the denotation of the noun. The adjective 'accomplished' is an example of such adjectives. *Accomplished* in *Maria is an accomplished musician* does not mean that the denotation of Maria is accomplished and is a musician. All we can say is that Maria is in the set of musicians, i.e. accomplished musicians are musicians. Syntactically, adjectives similar to 'accomplished' are always in the attributive position. We term these adjectives "pure subsective" to distinguish them from the other kind of adjective in the same class—the double adjectives.

Double adjectives (or doublet as called by [16]) belong to the class of subsective adjectives. Syntactically, these adjectives can be in either position: the attributive or predicative. Semantically, they can have an intersective reading (i.e. referent-modifying) and a subsective reading (i.e. reference-modifying), regardless of their syntactic position. *Beautiful* in the sentence *That dancer is beautiful* is an example of a double adjective. Thus, *beautiful* can either be understood as attributing beauty to the dancing of the denotation of *that* or the physical beauty to the denotation of *that*. In the intersective, reading, the denotation of *that* belongs to the intersection of beautiful things and dancers. In the subsective reading the denotation of *that* belongs to a subset of the set of dancers, i.e. those who dance beautifully.

Finally, there are those adjectives that are neither intersective nor subsective, the so-called non-subsective adjectives. Within this class two sub-classes can be recognized—privative adjectives and non-privative. Adjectives such as 'former' and 'fake' are privative. They are called privative because the denotation of the privative-noun combination is not a subset of the denotation of the noun, e.g. *counterfeit money* is not money. The other member of the non-subsective class of adjectives is those adjectives that are non-subsective and non-privative. 'Potential' and 'possible' are examples of this class. A *potential winner* may or may not be a winner.

In some cases, the classification[2] is not clear-cut. For example, it is debatable, whether the adjective 'former' is privative. Also, the so called measure adjectives such as 'tall', 'small', etc. are considered intersective yet they fail the *consistency* test. For example, *tall* in *John is a tall surgeon* modifies the denotation (that is, the extension) of *surgeon* rather than meaning (that is, the intension) of *surgeon*. [3] and [16] argue that measure adjectives are in fact intersective. The failure of the substitutivity (i.e., consistency) test is due to the fact that measure adjectives are vague/context-dependent.

The assumption of the existence of the adjectival hierarchy has led to the conclusion that a uniform approach to the semantics of adjectives is possible only if they are treated as functions from properties to properties, i.e. functions from *intensions* to *intensions* [4]. This renders a set-theoretic approach to the semantics of adjectives unattainable from the conventional viewpoint.

---

[2] Semantically the most agreed upon classifying criterion is that of intension versus extension or, respectively, reference-modifying versus referent-modifying, as is used in [16]. Siegel uses the consistency test, as many authors do, to tell apart the intensional and extensional adjectives. This test roughly states that when an intersective adjective combines with co-extensive nouns, the resulting noun phrases remain co-extensive.

2 Fake Guns Are Guns

Language is inherently generative. With its, rather limited, stock of linguistic items it is capable of expressing novel concepts by means of combining existing linguistic items. In some cases, however, and because of the dynamic nature of concepts, new referents may fall under an already-existing concept. For example, in number theory, a number used to denote a natural number. With the conception of negative numbers, the concept "number" encompasses both negative and positive numbers. This process continued (and may continue) to include different kinds of numbers. This is because there is so much in common between the entities or mathematical objects we now call numbers.

In everyday language this process, we argue, is generally in use—consider, for instance the category "bird", as much studied and illustrated in *prototype theory* and *default logics* with regard to the property of "flying"—and specifically with regard to privative-noun combinations. A fake gun and a real gun have many properties in common—similarly, an artificial heart and a real heart. In some cases, the distinction between an instance of the denotation of a default-noun combination and that of a privative-noun combination is hard to tell, or requires domain knowledge, e.g. *artificial light* versus *natural light*, Table 1—if there is a difference, indeed. If it were for things denoted by a privative-noun combination not to fall under the extension denoted by the noun, there might have been a dedicated lexeme—interestingly, even the word *robot* (i.e. a single linguistic item) is originally chosen by the Czech playwright Karl Čopek (1890-1938) as a more suitable term for "artificial workers" in his play *Rossum's Universal Robots*[3] . Of course, this is not to claim that a concept must be denoted by a single lexeme. What is meant, however, is that the frequent use of a concept is usually reflected in language by being represented by a single linguistic symbol, as is the case with common nouns. Therefore, in answering the question of what is a fake gun, we argue that it is a gun, provided that fake and real guns are subsumed by the term 'gun'.

The notion of augmenting the concept, or equally the extension, denoted by the noun in an adjective-noun combination, is linguistically supported. In language, it is noticed that all privative adjectives have antonyms/contrasts, e.g. *intensifiers*. Privatives such as *fake*, *artificial*, and *false* have antonyms/contrast, respectively, *real/genuine*, *natural*, and *true*. It seems that there is a strong pairing between privatives and their (intensifier) counterparts to the extent that the use of the privative antonym is meaningless, if possible indeed, in isolation with its counterpart. The intensifier is usually implicit. Most of the time it is considered default or redundant when there is no ambiguity. The compound *real fur* is deemed necessary only when there is fake fur in the vicinity.

[12] reaches the conclusion that privative adjectives are subsective based on work done by other researchers (e.g., *see*, [11]) on the "Noun Phrase-split phenomena" in Polish, which reveals the absence of the privative adjective class in Polish. That is, the presence of the privative class of adjectives is an idiosyncrasy of some languages and English is one of them.

---

[3] See, http://capek.misto.cz/english/interesting.html for a translation of an article by the author of the play in the *Lidove Noviny*, 24.12.1933.

Table 1. Missing properties

Adjective Phrase	Property missing from the default set of features
Artificial heart	e.g. not flesh-and-blood
Artificial flower	e.g. doesn't grow
Artificial light	e.g. source
Former senator	e.g. temporal continuance
False teeth	e.g. not naturally grown
Cloned sheep	e.g. not naturally bred
Virtual reality	e.g. exists visually only
Imitation leather	e.g. genuineness
Wooden lion	e.g. "make-ness"—physical and non-living
Fake statue	e.g. originality
Fake perfume	e.g. substance/originality

In short, intensifier/privative seem to be (semantically) intimately related. If viewed as functions, they can be thought of as functions and their respective inverse functions. Alternatively, they can be viewed as set partitions of the set N, which represents the denotation of the noun an intensifier/privative pair combines with. The latter view is adopted in the approach proposed in this paper.

In our view, both "regular" adjectives such as 'red', 'angry', or 'skillful' and privative adjectives such as 'fake' or 'former' have one thing in common. They both pick out or further constrain the domain denoted by the noun of the compound. They differ in the means of doing it: regular adjectives by highlighting some property or properties of the noun, while privative adjectives by "masking" some property or properties of the noun.

Once the argument of augmenting the denotation of common nouns is accepted, expressions such as *that senator, that gun,* and *that heart* are considered elliptic forms, respectively, for that *current senator,* that *real gun,* and *that natural heart.* However, privative-common-noun combinations should be explicitly specified[4], i.e. *that former senator, that fake gun,* and *that artificial heart.*

The view that privative adjectives are subsective, results in the following adjective hierarchy:

- Intersective.
- Subsective:
  - o Pure.
  - o Double.
  - o Privative.

This analysis makes it possible that a generalized set-theoretic approach to adjectives is attainable.

---

[4] In some settings the opposite is true. For example, in a tòy store (i.e., a store that sells toys) the term *gun* would more plausibly mean a fake gun. Thus, *fake gun* is the default.

3 Our Approach

Some authors (e.g. Strawson, see [2], and Jespersen, see [15]) argue that common nouns and adjectives are ontologically different. We believe that representing common nouns on a par with adjectives is "forcing" a behaviour on adjectives that is not in their nature. This behaviour manifests itself in the intersection failure of sets representing adjectives and sets representing common nouns, which leads to the conclusion that adjectives must be of complex nature.

We argue that it is possible to represent all adjectives as sets, and yet capture their idiosyncrasies. This can be done by considering sets representing adjectives as having typed objects as their members. A schema for an adjective-representing set may look like the following:

$$\text{Set\_name} = \{\text{member: type1}\}: \text{type2}$$
$$\text{where type1 is a non-property type and type2 a property type} \tag{1}$$

For example, *clever pet*, *clever man*, and *clever police dog* in the sentences *John is a clever man*, *Fido is a clever pet*, and *Fido is a clever police dog* can be represented as follows:

$$\text{Clever} = \{\text{j: human, f: pet, f: policedog}\}: \text{clever}$$
$$\text{where j} = \| \text{John} \|^{5}, \text{ and } \| \text{ f} = \text{Fido} \|$$

This representation of the adjective 'clever' captures the intuition that although j and f are members of the set Clever, both are clever in their own way. John is clever as a man[6] while Fido is clever as a dog. What they have in common is "cleverness". This is reflected by ascribing the type "clever" to the set containing them.

This representation of adjectives makes it possible for an object to have more than one occurrence in adjective-representing sets, as done with "f: pet" and "f: policedog" in the set Clever.

Common nouns may have the following representation schema:

$$\text{Set\_name} = \{\text{member: type}\}: \text{type}$$
$$\text{where type is a non-property type} \tag{2}$$

The representation of (2) is different from that of (1) in that the members' type is the same as the set's type. The representation of (2) serves two purposes: 1) it makes the internal structure of common nouns similar to that of adjectives (i.e. "member: type" pattern); and, 2) it eliminates the co-extension problem. Regarding the latter point, if for example, as is the case in the actual world, the set of cordate contains the same elements as those in the set of renate (see, definition of set equality, below) the two sets are not equal. Hence, they do not mean the same thing.

3.1 Equality in Typed Sets

Since sets now contain typed elements, set operations must take the type of set members into consideration. This can easily be accommodated as follows:

---

[5] The symbols "‖ ‖" represent the interpretation function.
[6] The correct type for the intersective reading for 'clever' is "T", as explained in the next section.

The elements x1 and x2 are equal iff x1 and x2 are the one and the same and both of the same type.

We, also, require members of adjectives that are considered (by and large) independent or absolute, e.g. 'red', be given the most generic type "T". This type has the lowest precedence amongst types. It is the supertype of every type in the type hierarchy.

3.2 Examples Using the New Approach

This section contains examples (3-6) using the new approach. The examples cover different kinds of adjective-noun combinations.

> Maria is a vegetarian dancer
> Maria is a singer   (3)
> ---------------------
> Therefore, Maria is a vegetarian singer (valid)

Set representation:

```
Dancer=    {m: dancer    ,…} : dancer
Singer=    {m: singer,…} : singer
Vegetarian=   {m:T, …}: vegetarian   where   m = ||Maria||
```

Inference example:

$\vdash$ m ∈ (Vegetarian ∩ Singer) Expected answer: True

Reason: type "T" is a neutral type. It is overridden by all other types.

> Maria is a skillful dancer
> Maria is a singer   (4)
> ---------------------
> Therefore, Maria is a skillful singer (invalid)

(Here, we distinguish two senses of 'skillful', i.e. the reference-modifying and the referent-modifying. However, it is possible to use one set only)

Set representation:

```
Dancer= {m: dancer,…} : dancer
Singer= {m: singer,…} : singer
Skillful-1= {m: T,…} :skillful-1 i.e. the referent-modifying
Skillful-2= {m: dancer,…}:skillful-2 i.e. the reference-modifying
```

Inference example:

$\vdash$ m ∈ (Skillful-2 ∩ Singer)   Expected answer: False

Reason: the member "m: singer" is not in the intersection because of a type mismatch. That is, the element "m: dancer" of the set Skillful-2 does not match any member of the set Singer whose members are all of type singer.

> John is a guitarist
> John is a veteran musician   (5)
> -------------------------------
> Therefore, John is a veteran guitarist (invalid)

```
Guitarist  = {j: guitarist,…} : guitarist
Musician = {j: musician, …}: musician
Veteran  = {j: musician}: veteran
Where  j = ||John||
```

From this representation, it is clear that the statement *John is a veteran guitarist* cannot be affirmed. This is because j is not in the intersection of Veteran and Guitarist.

> Maria is a former teacher
> Maria is a programmer
> ---------------------------
> Therefore, Maria is a former programmer   (Invalid)

(6)

Set representation:

```
Human = {m: human,…} : human
Teacher= {m: teacher,…} : teacher
Former= {m: teacher,…} :former
Programmer={m: programmer,…} : programmer
```

Inference examples:

$\vdash$ m $\in$ (Former $\cap$ Programmer)   Expected answer: false
$\vdash$ m $\in$ (Former $\cap$ Human)   Expected answer: false

3.3 Multiple-Adjectives-One-Head-Noun Combinations

In the previous section, we presented an intersective treatment of adjective-noun combinations. In this section, we extend this treatment to include adjectival phrases with multiple adjectives and a head noun.

3.3.1 An Analysis

Providing an intersective account for expressions with multiple adjectives and a head noun is a more challenging task than single-adjective-noun combinations. This is because an adjective in a combination can have different scopes. To illustrate, consider examples (7).

> a) Oceania is a deep blue ocean
> b) Companies favour intelligent, aggressive people
> c) Jane is an attractive blond woman

(7)

In (7-a), *deep* may have wide scope, i.e. modifies *blue ocean*, or narrow-scope, i.e. modifies *blue*. (7-b) is not ambiguous, because of the comma. (7-c) is ambiguous, due to wide and narrow scope readings.

An at-face-value, set-theoretic representation for the examples in (7) is not possible, with the exception of example (7-b). This is due to the associative law of set theory, stated below:

$$\forall \text{ Sets A, B, and C}   A\cap (B \cap C) = (A \cap B) \cap C$$

Thus, for instance, mapping example (7) to set intersections would fail to capture the different possible readings. In particular, consider the wide-scope reading of *attractive* in (7-c). This reading can be expressed as follows:

$$\text{Jane is an [attractive [blond woman]]} \tag{8}$$

And, the set-theoretic representation of the adjectival phrase might look something like:

$$\text{Attractive} \cap (\text{Blond} \cap \text{Woman}) \tag{9}$$

However, this representation does not capture the intended meaning. That is, *attractive* in (8) modifies the expression *blond woman* as a whole. In other words, for someone who utters (8), *blond* is essential to the extent that if the denotation of *Jane* were not blond, the utterance (8) might not have taken place.

3.3.2 A Solution

In order to accommodate adjective phrases, we need to do two things. First, expand our ontology to include properties—assuming that adjectives denote properties. This will enable us to form new property types from the more basic ones. Second, we need a rigorous typing system, whereby every set has a type. The typing system we are proposing shortly will enable us to generate new types from the basic ones.

The type system must correspond to the grammar's production rules. Grammar rules for adjective phrases might look like the following:

$$\begin{aligned}
&\text{AP ::= AN} \\
&\text{N::= AN | man |woman |man |dancer| surgeon|} \ldots \\
&\text{A::= good | red |attractive| fragrant|} \ldots
\end{aligned} \tag{10}$$

The rules in (10) will recursively generate adjective phrases such as *good man*, *fragrant red roses*, etc. The grammar in (10) generates noun phrases by means of a string *concatenation* function. A typing system should parallel the grammar and be able to recursively define new types from existing ones. Such a system is inductively defined as follows:

a) The basic types are the nodes of the taxonomy of Figure 1, e.g. Nat(ural) Kind, Kind, Properties, Role, Implement, and $\top$.   (11)
b) If a is a property type and b is a basic type, then $a: b$ is a type, see the example regarding the wide-scope reading.
c) If a and b are property types then a-b is a property type, see the example regarding the narrow-scope reading.
d) If a is a type and b is a non-property type, then $a: b$ is a type.
e) Nothing else is a type.

(11-a) states the basic types assumed. In a full-fledged system, the set of admissible basic types must be larger than this. However, this set suffices to demonstrate our approach.

(11-b) states that the first basic type of a resulting set is a property type. This is because here we are only treating adjective-noun—not noun-noun—combinations, for example. (11-c) generates property types. This is necessary for dealing with narrow-scope readings, i.e. when an adjective modifies another adjective and both modify a noun or an adjective phrase. Both (11-b) and (11-d) ensure that the resulting type is that of the head noun.

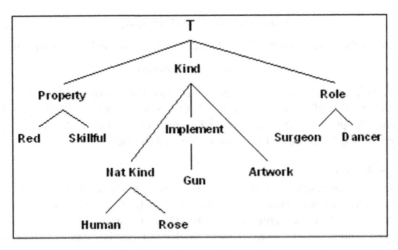

Fig. 1. A taxonomy with properties

With the typing rules of (11) in mind, the representation of the adjective phrase in (8) is as follows, ‖ Jane‖ = j:

```
Blond = {j: T,…}: blond
Woman = {j: woman,…}:woman
Blond ∩ Woman = {j: blond: woman, …}: blond: woman
Attractive = {j: blond: woman, …}: attractive
Attractive ∩(Blond∩Woman)={j:attractive:blond:woman}:
                                attractive:blond: woman
```

The syntactic-semantic steps that led to the above representation are shown below.

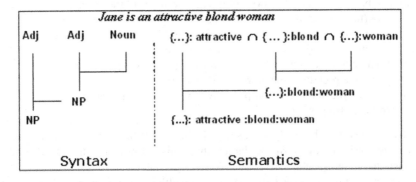

Fig. 2. Wide-scope reading of *Jane is an attractive blond woman*

It should be noticed that from reading (8) the following can be deduced:
> Jane is blond
> Jane is a woman

But not necessarily,
> Jane is attractive

This reflects the intuition that the sentence *Jane is an attractive (blond woman)* expresses a different proposition from that expressed by the sentence *Jane is an attractive, blond woman*. The latter reading would result in the inclusion of the element "w: woman" in the set Attractive.

Finally, narrow-scope readings are computed differently. The narrow scope-reading of *an (attractive blond) woman* is attributing "attractive-blond-ness" to the denotation of *Jane*. Such a reading is depicted in Fig 3.

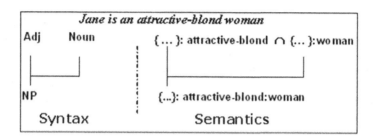

Fig. 3. Narrow-scope reading of *Jane is an attractive blond woman*

Notice that the set Attractive-blond is of type "attractive-blond". This results from applying the type formation rule of (11-c). The set representation of the narrow-scope reading is as follows:

```
Attractive-blond = {w:T}: attractive-blond
Woman = {w: woman}: woman
Attractive-blond ∩ Woman = {w:attractive-blond:woman}:
                           attractive-blond: woman
```

Thus, a semantic interpreter will have two or more different syntactic trees as input, each of which is treated differently semantically.

4 Consequences

- This work emphasizes the semantic unity of the category called "adjective", contrary to [16]. In this regards, this work agrees with [8]. However, it does so without "stretching" the ontology to contain events/states, as [8] does. Furthermore, using typed sets, we were able to account for the semantics of phrases with multiple adjectives.
- This approach is compositional. It is true, at least in the case of adjectives in English, that adjectives can syntactically appear exclusively predicative (e.g. 'asleep'), exclusively attributive (e.g. 'veteran'), or in on both positions (e.g. 'good'), but there is always a single semantic rule that computes the respective meaning of the adjective noun-combination, namely the intersection of the denotation of adjective(s) and the head noun.
- This approach is easily applied in a natural language processing system. This is because it is based on a well-defined mathematical system, i.e. set theory.

- Finally, this approach shows promising results in accommodating modal adjectives, e.g. 'possible', 'potential', 'alleged', etc. This type of adjectives has proved to be difficult to account for without resorting to approaches such as modal logics, which are not readily mapped into computer programs. For example, the sentence *John is an alleged criminal* can be represented as follows:

Criminal= {j: criminal :$\perp$}: criminal   where j = ||John||
Alleged= {j: criminal: $\perp$}:$\perp$.

The symbol "$\perp$" represents the absurd type, i.e. the subtype of every type. In the set Criminal, above, we want to indicate that *John* may or may not end up a member of it. Thus, by indicating that j is of type "$\perp$" we mean to capture john's partial membership in the set Criminal. Note that the above representation blocks all invalid inferences. For example, the answer to the query, "Is John a criminal?" would be negative. For, given the current state of affairs, j is not of type "criminal". In other words, John's membership in the set Criminal is partial or "pending".

References

1. Chierchia, G. and McConnell-Ginet, S.: Meaning and Grammar: An Introduction to Semantics. Cambridge, MA, The MIT Press. (1990)
2. Guarino, N., Carrara, M., and Giaretta, P.: An Ontology of Meta-Level Categories. In: Knowledge Representation: (1994) 270-280
3. Kamp H.: Two theories about adjectives. In: Keenan, E. L. (ed.): Formal   semantics for natural languages, Cambridge, UK (1975)
4. Kamp, H., and Partee, P.: Prototype theory and compositionality. Cognition 57, (1995) 129-191
5. Lahav, R.: Against compositionality: the case of adjectives. Philosophical Studies 57: (1989) 261–279
6. Larson, R.K.: The grammar of intensionality. In: Preyer, G. (ed.): On Logical Form, Oxford University Press (2002)
7. Larson, R.K.: Events and modification in nominals. In: Strolovitch, D, and Lawson, A. (eds.): Proceedings from Semantics and Linguistic Theory (SALT) VIII, Cornell University. Ithaca, NY (1998)
8. Larson, R.K.: Olga is a beautiful dancer. Winter Meetings of The Linguistic   Society of America, New Orleans, 5-8 de Janeiro (1995)
9. Levi, J. N.: The syntax and semantics of complex nominals. Academic Press New York (1978)
10. McConnell-Ginet, S.: Adverbs and Logical Form. In: Language 58: (1982) 144-84.
11. Nowak, A.: On split PPs in Polish. Ms. Amherst (unpublished General Paper,UMass.) (2000)
12. Partee, B. H.: Privative adjectives: subsective plus coe`rcion. To appear in Zimmermann, T.E. (ed.): Studies in Presupposition (2001)
13. Peters, I. and Peters, W.: The Treatment of Adjectives in SIMPLE: Theoretical Observations. The 2nd International Conference on Language Resources & Evaluation. (LREC'2000), Athens, Greece (2000)
14. Quirk, R., Greenbaum, S., Leech, G. and Svartvik, J.: A Comprehensive Grammar of the English Language. Longman (1985)

15. Raskin, V., and Nirenburg, S.: Lexical Semantics of Adjectives: A Microtheory of Adjectival Meaning, in: MCCS-95-288, Las cruces, N.M.: New Mexico State University (1995)
16. Siegel, M.: Capturing the adjective. PhD dissertation,. University of Massachusetts (1976)
17. Wheeler, S.C.: Attributives and their Modifiers. In: Nous, Vol. Vl, No. 4, (1972) 310-334

Automatic Acquisition of Gender Information for Anaphora Resolution

Shane Bergsma

Department of Computing Science,
University of Alberta,
Edmonton, Alberta, Canada T6G 2E8
bergsma@cs.ualberta.ca

Abstract. We present a novel approach to learning gender and number information for anaphora resolution. Noun-pronoun pair counts are collected from gender-indicating lexico-syntactic patterns in parsed corpora, and occurrences of noun-pronoun pairs are mined online from the web. Gender probabilities gathered from these templates provide features for machine learning. Both parsed corpus and web-based features allow for accurate prediction of the gender of a given noun phrase. Together they constructively combine for 96% accuracy when estimating gender on a list of noun tokens, better than any of our human participants achieved. We show that using this gender information in simple or knowledge-rich pronoun resolution systems significantly improves performance over traditional gender constraints. Our novel gender strategy would benefit any of the current top-performing coreference resolution systems.

1   Introduction

Anaphora resolution determines which previous entity (the antecedent) a given noun phrase (the anaphor) refers to. We focus on resolving third-person pronominal anaphora, including reflexives. Performing these resolutions has long been considered a challenging yet vital task for a number of Natural Language Processing applications. We present a new approach for determining the antecedents of pronouns using enhanced statistical gender and number information. Gender and number agreement provide one of the most important, intuitive, and widely-accepted constraints for resolving anaphora. In the following example, gender information allows us to select the correct antecedent:

1. John never saw the car. He arrived late. (resolve "he" to "John").
2. John never saw the car. It arrived late. (resolve "it" to "the car").

   How does one encode gender and number agreement when implementing an anaphora resolution system? Often, number information is available from the parsers used to pre-process the text. Number agreement can improve the performance of these technologies, while gender information is neglected [1]. We use

B. Kégl and G. Lapalme (Eds.): AI 2005, LNAI 3501, pp. 342–353, 2005.

Dekang Lin's parser Minipar to induce dependency trees and extract information on plurals [8]. There are also a number of so-called "surface clues" that give a textual indication to the gender[1] of a noun phrase. In English, pronouns are some of the few remaining overtly gender-indicating words. Gendered designators (such as Mr., Mrs., etc.) also provide gender information for a noun phrase, but gender-indicating suffixes such as those used in "actress" or "chairman" have fallen out of favour, and are hence unreliable [1].

In Section 2 we summarize related anaphora resolution systems and previous gender strategies. Most previous approaches treat gender as a hard constraint, a filter on candidate antecedents. If the gender is not known exactly, it is not used. Our approach treats gender as a probability – another factor that can be used in anaphora resolution. We seek to determine the probability that a given noun is masculine, feminine, neutral or plural. By counting occurrences of noun-pronoun patterns in parsed corpora and on the web, we automatically learn the probabilities that a name like "Alex" is used in a masculine (very common), feminine (less common), neutral or plural (zero probability) context. We automatically learn the neutral preference of company names and organizations, and which words, like "child" or "parent," are likely to be masculine or feminine, but not neutral or plural. Section 3 describes the gender-gathering templates and how gender probability is modelled from the resulting frequency counts.

The accuracy of our acquired data is tested in a novel gender classification task. A classifier uses the gender probabilities to guess the gender of noun tokens extracted from text. Section 4 describes how the within-context gender of these nouns is obtained. Section 5 shows that our classifier's results surpass those of human guessers, and that classifiers using the web-based probabilities, despite their noise, actually outperform those using the corpus information.

Finally, in Section 6, we demonstrate the superiority of using additional gender information by testing machine-learned anaphora resolution classifiers based on the gender statistics. When deciding whether a candidate antecedent co-refers with a pronoun, it makes sense to incorporate the probability this antecedent is of the pronoun's gender. When gender is used as a hard constraint, restricted to completely certain cases, significantly more antecedents are missed.

2   Related Work

Anaphora resolution systems typically employ some combination of constraints and preferences to select the correct antecedent. Constraints eliminate possible candidates by virtue of gender and number disagreement, binding theory violations, etc., while preferences encourage selection of antecedents which are more recent, more frequent, etc. These approaches are generally not based on machine

---

[1] There are four possibilities for gender and number of third-person pronouns: masculine, feminine, neutral and plural (e.g., *he, she, it, they*). Since our approach gathers information for all four, whenever we subsequently refer to the *gender* of a noun phrase, we implicitly include plural as one of the options.

learning from a corpus [7], [6]. Our approach follows a more recent trend toward using an annotated corpus to learn an anaphora resolution classifier [2], or coreference resolution classifier [12]. The first machine learning approach to anaphora resolution that uses the web is reportedly due to Modjeska, Markert and Nissim, who look at page counts of various patterns for other-anaphora resolution [10].

Current, top-performing coreference resolution systems selectively use surface clues and information derived from WordNet [12]. If a noun's most frequent sense in the WordNet synset is a subclass of a predefined gendered class (e.g., object, which is neutral), gender can be assigned. Despite the availability of surface clues and gender information in the lexicon, gender mismatch has been reported to account for over a third of all pronoun resolution errors [6].

Ge et al were the first to learn the gender of noun phrases from unlabelled text [2]. They applied simple, gender-unaware pronoun resolution algorithms (such as selecting the noun phrase at Hobbs distance one), and collected pronoun-antecedent pairs. Nouns were assigned the gender of whichever pronoun they most often pair with. Gender was correctly attributed in about 70% of the cases, using a group of proper names occurring with designators as the test set.

The majority of anaphora resolution approaches involve some form of manual involvement [9]. Ge et al use a manually-parsed corpus [2], while Lappin and Leass manually correct parser output [7]. We parse the text and perform noun-phrase identification fully automatically. Lappin and Leass have a module for automatic identification of pleonastic pronouns [7], such as the non-anaphoric "it" in "it is raining," while Kennedy and Boguraev manually identify and exclude these pronouns, as well as those that refer to verb phrases or propositions [6]. We also manually identify and exclude pleonastic pronouns, and those that do not refer to preceding noun phrases, including cataphoric pronouns (pronouns occurring *before* their antecedents). Of the 2779 total pronouns labelled, 144 are pleonastic, 59 do not refer to an explicit noun phrase, and 16 are cataphora. Results stated below do not include these excluded cases.

3   Pattern Matching for Noun-Pronoun Gender Pairs

Principle A of Government and Binding Theory states that a reflexive pronoun must be bound by an antecedent in its governing category [3]. For example, after seeing "John explained himself," we know that *John* binds *himself*, and hence is masculine. To determine the probability that a given word is masculine, feminine, neutral or plural, we might examine a large amount of text and count the number of times it binds with masculine, feminine, neutral or plural reflexives.

3.1   Parsed Corpus Frequencies

We need not restrict ourselves to the reflexive indicators. We can find other lexico-syntactic patterns in text that typically represent a bound noun and pronoun. On average, "John explained his..." would be more common than "John explained her," "John explained its" or "John explained their." In fact, if we let any verb occupy the place of "explained," then we have a generic pattern with which we can count the number of noun-pronoun occurrences for any noun in text. We collect gender information in corpora via five separate lexico-syntactic noun-pronoun patterns depicted below. In the following representation of dependency trees, the solid arrows indicate dependency relationships, while the broken arrows connect the noun-pronoun pair extracted by our system:

1. Reflexives (*himself, herself, itself, themselves*):

   E.g. *John* explained *himself...*

2. Possessives (*his, her, its, their*):

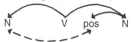   E.g. *John* bought *his* car...

3. Nominatives in *finite* sub-clauses (*he, she, it, they*):

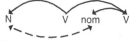   E.g. *John* thought *he* should...

4. Predicates: pronouns are subjects and nouns are in the predicate position:

   E.g. *He* is a *father*.

5. Designators: The noun is accompanied by a gendered designator:

     E.g. *Mr. Johnson*.

Some noise will be present in these pairs – parser errors, ungrammatical text and false bindings will pollute the results substantially. Thus a large amount of text is required for the correct gender probabilities to prevail.

3.2   Web Frequencies

No matter how large a corpus one has mined, there is always a strong probability one will encounter new words when looking at test data. A growing number of researchers address this problem by using the world wide web as a vast source of example data [5]. We use web page counts of various noun-pronoun patterns to get wide coverage for our gender learning strategy. The Google API and wildcard operator, "*", equal to a single word, are employed. Gender determination is based on the same ideas as were used in the corpus pair searching. Now, we count the number of *pages* returned for the following query patterns:

1. Reflexives: *himself, herself, itself*, and *themselves* in "*noun * reflexive*"
2. Possessives: *his, her, its*, and *their* in "*noun * possessive*"
3. Nominatives: *he, she, it*, and *they* in "*noun * nominative*"
4. Predicates: *he, she, it*, and *they* in "*nominative* is/are [a] *noun*"
5. Designators: *Mr.* and *Mrs.* in "*designator noun*"

A substantial amount of noise also afflicts the web approach. The Google queries do not restrict the wildcard to be a verb, nor the entire query string to be in the same sentence. Also, because our pairings tend to identify nouns in subject positions, we obtain limited data for nouns preferring object positions.

3.3   Modelling Gender Information

For each word, we seek to determine the probability that this word is masculine, feminine, neutral or plural, using the counts from each of the five parsed corpus templates and five web-mining templates. In this sense, the proportion of times a word is a given gender is a parameter we seek to learn from our frequency data. For a given word and gender, each of the ten templates can yield a probability value. The maximum likelihood formulation is to say that the probability the gender of a word is, for example, masculine, is equal to the number of times that word occurs with masculine pronouns in a given template, divided by the number of times it occurs with pronouns of all genders in that template. For example, we captured the parsed corpus pairs *doctor-himself* 224 times, *doctor-herself* 126 times, *doctor-itself* 0 times, and *doctor-themselves* 14 times. Thus our parsed-corpus reflexives indicate there is a 62% chance of doctor being masculine.

There are two issues with the above approach. First small counts will result in large probability swings. Second, we need a measure of how certain we should be in the resulting probabilities – e.g., a 60% chance of being masculine should be taken more seriously when we have five hundred pairs than when we have five. We address these issues by adopting a Bayesian approach. In Bayesian parameter learning, an hypothesis prior distribution is assumed for the parameter, and this distribution is updated as new information is available [11]. We initially assume any value for the gender probability is equally likely. Hence we begin with a uniform prior distribution for the parameter. Subsequently, we treat this prior distribution as the first prior in a family of *Beta* distributions. A *Beta* distribution models binomial proportions in Bayesian analysis. For a given gender, we treat the pair counts as binomial in that all pairs of that gender are treated as one event, while any pair not of that gender is considered a separate event. The *Beta* distribution depends on two hyperparameters, α and β, where $\alpha - 1$ and $\beta - 1$ are the number of times each type of event is observed.

An example will illustrate the procedure. Suppose we're determining whether the word "gretzky" can be replaced with a masculine pronoun. We build the *Beta* distribution for each of the ten gender sources. In our parsed corpus-possessive pairs, for example, we've seen the pair *gretzky-his* 4650 times, the pair *gretzky-her* 0 times, the pair *gretzky-its* 54 times and the pair *gretzky-their* 40 times. The *Beta* distribution that models masculine probability treats 4650 as the number of times masculine has been observed, and $0 + 54 + 40 = 94$ as the number of times non-masculine was seen. The *Beta* distribution is thus *Beta*[4651,95]. The mean, μ, of the *Beta* distribution is given as:

$$\mu = \frac{\alpha}{\alpha + \beta} \tag{1}$$

Here, the mean represents the probability that the word "gretzky," is masculine; it equals 98.0%. The variance of a *Beta* distribution is:

$$\sigma^2 = \frac{\alpha\beta}{(\alpha + \beta)^2(\alpha + \beta + 1)} \tag{2}$$

The variance quantifies how much the probability mass is converging around a single value in the parameter's distribution. Our "gretzky" example has negligible variance, approximately $4.1 * 10^{-6}$. Gender sources with little or no example counts have variance approaching $1/12$ – the variance of a uniform distribution.[2]

The above approach gives the determination of the gender probability and distribution variance for one gender of one of the ten templates. In practice, we need to simultaneously combine each of these sources of information into a single determination of gender (Section 5), or decide whether to exclude a candidate antecedent based on gender mismatch (Section 6). For these tasks, we assign the probability and variance values to dimensions in a gender *feature vector*, and use Support Vector Machine (SVM) learning to determine the optimum use of these values. Sections 5 and 6 describe the experiments and results.

4   The Data Sets

For the acquisition of the gender information, we collected noun-pronoun patterns from a number of corpora, including the AQUAINT corpus and the Reuters corpus. Together, the full set contains about 6 gigabytes of text. We extracted over 4 million reflexive pairs, 32 million possessives, 28 million nominatives, 5 million predicates, and 17 million words with gendered designators.

For the training data and separate testing data used by both the gender classifier described in Section 5 and the full anaphora resolution system described in Section 6, annotated data is required. We labelled third person pronoun-antecedent pairs in 118 documents from the slate section of the American National Corpus.[3] There are 1398 labelled pronouns in 79 documents in the training set and 1381 labelled pronouns in 41 documents in the test set (including non-anaphoric cases (Section 2)). Most of the slate documents are "gist" articles which provide factual background information for stories currently in the news.

Having a set of labelled pronouns also gives us a set of gender-marked nouns: the antecedents of each pronoun have the same gender, in that particular context, as the pronoun which refers to it. Filtering out pronouns which refer to other pronouns and the ignored cases mentioned above, and labelling each antecedent with the gender of its pronoun, we are left with 903 gendered noun phrases from the training section and 876 gendered noun phrases from the test section. These are extracted from the text; they form the lists of noun/gender pairs used for training and testing in Section 5. Roughly 24% of the nouns in the lists are masculine, 7.6% feminine, 33.8% neutral and 34.6% plural.

---

[2] Note that the information from the beta distributions is equivalent to using pure count statistics as features (the maximum likelihood estimation), except with add-one smoothing and the confidence measure from the variance. Neglecting smoothing or the confidence measure results in small but consistent decreases in performance.

[3] Instructions for obtaining the American National Corpus and our anaphora resolution labels are available at http://www.cs.ualberta.ca/~bergsma/CorefTags/

5   Testing Gender Classification

To test the accuracy of our gender statistics apart from their use in anaphora resolution, we built separate SVM classifiers for masculine, feminine, neutral and plural nouns using features derived from the parsed corpus and web-based data. Each classifier inspects a noun and decides whether it matches the classifier's gender. We used the SVM implementation SVM^{light} with a linear kernel, without normalization [4]. SVM is used because an efficient implementation is available, it easily incorporates the continuous-valued gender features, and it has been shown to provide good performance on various machine learning tasks [4]. For each of the parsed corpus and web-based *Beta* distributions, we include the mean (corresponding to the probability the word matches a given gender) and standard deviation (the certainty in the probability) of the distribution as features for the SVM. We trained the SVM on the pronoun-derived gendered nouns in the training list and tested it on the gendered nouns in the test list.

Note that the genders of the words in the noun lists do not represent the most likely genders or the "true" genders of the given nouns, but merely the genders of the nouns in this particular context. Contradictory instances are present: lawyer is masculine in one article, feminine in another. Nevertheless, the ability of our system to predict the gender of these nouns is a good indication of how adept our system would be in predicting gender for anaphora resolution.

Table 1. Gender Classification Performance Using All Features (%)

	Precision	Recall	F-Score
masculine	88.2	95.2	91.6
feminine	98.2	70.9	82.4
neutral	93.0	93.7	93.3
plural	98.6	89.8	94.0
micro-avg.	93.9	90.6	92.2

The entire set of words was classified once with each classifier, and resulting precision, recall and f-score were calculated (Table 1). Overall the classifiers performed quite well, correctly deciding gender match in 96% of the instances, with a micro-averaged f-score of 92%. Next we determined whether the web-mined or corpus-based sources contributed more to the overall performance. We trained and tested the classification using only the information from the corpus *Beta* distributions and then with only the web-based *Beta* distributions (Table 2). The web-based approach, with a micro-averaged f-score of 90.4%, outperforms the corpus-features, which score 85.4%. As expected, the corpus approach suffered mostly in recall, as many words have few or no instances in the corpus-derived gender pairs, leading to a number of false negatives. It also performs worse, perhaps surprisingly, in precision. We see that the larger coverage of web-based information extraction more than compensates for the greater noise in this task. It is also interesting to note how values from the web and parsed corpus templates work together in the combined classifier (Table 1). There is no need to

Table 2. Micro-averaged Performance for Various Classifiers (%)

	Precision	Recall	F-Score
Parsed-Corpus Features	90.9	80.6	85.4
Web-Mined Features	92.4	88.6	90.4
Average Human Performance	88.8	88.8	88.8

choose between web-based or corpus-based information, but instead one may combine the information from each to achieve superior performance.

To provide further perspective on our results, we asked three native English-speaking graduate students to classify gender on the same list of words. Like our classifier, the students made their decisions blindly without any context from the articles; they were simply asked to assign whatever gender they thought was most likely for each given noun from the noun list. To mitigate any systematic effects, the lists were randomized for the tests. The students achieved micro-averaged scores of 86.6, 88.5, and 91.3, respectively, with average results calculated and tabulated (Table 2). It is interesting that no human performed as well as our full-featured system. We must conclude that humans achieve their near-perfect performance on general pronoun resolution through contextual clues and other techniques, and not through explicit *a priori* noun gender knowledge.

All approaches had low recall with the female classifier. This is because many nouns are most often masculine, and thus appearances of these tokens in a female context is missed as female, providing a false positive to our masculine classifier (reducing precision) and a false negative to our feminine one (reducing recall).

6   Pronoun Resolution with Enhanced Gender

Although knowing the gender of a given word may have interesting applications on its own (e.g. for lexicon development), we are ultimately interested in whether our gender information improves the performance of an anaphora resolution system. We tested this by designing pronoun resolution classifiers of varying complexity and assessing the gain in performance when using gender statistics. The results are summarized in Table 3 and explained in the following subsections.

The general pronoun resolution approach is as follows: for each pronoun, we search backward in the text from this pronoun to previous noun phrases, rejecting ones judged not to match and stopping when we reach one judged to be the true antecedent. The system has correctly identified the antecedent if it eventually accepts a coreferent noun phrase. A correctly accepted noun phrase is not necessarily the most recent antecedent; more than one antecedent is possible in cases where multiple preceding noun phrases corefer with the pronoun.

Also, we search backwards for an antecedent only through the current and previous sentence in the text. If, by the beginning of the previous sentence we have not yet accepted an antecedent, we lower the threshold for classification in the SVM (i.e., decrease the signed distance from the hyperplane separating

Table 3. Pronoun Resolution Performance

Method: Set Antecedent to Most Recent NP...	Correct	Incorr.	Rate(%)
Baseline	336	954	26.0
Without Gen. Mismatch	397	893	30.8
Without Gen. Mismatch, Accepted by SVM Gen. Classifier	766	524	59.4
Accepted by SVM Classifier (minus new gender features)	815	475	63.2
Accepted by Full SVM Classifier (with new gender features)	946	344	73.3

positive (coreferent) and negative (non-coreferent) feature vectors), and begin our search again at the most recent noun phrase. We repeat the searching and threshold-lowering until some noun phrase has been accepted as antecedent. This modification is motivated by the observation that over 97% of anaphoric pronouns in our training set had an antecedent in the current or previous sentence.

6.1   Baseline Anaphora Resolution

The simplest baseline strategy is to always choose the previous noun phrase. This achieves an accuracy of 26.0% (Table 3). We added to this baseline system in two ways. First, we adopted the standard gender approach using only explicit surface clues, rejecting matches where the gender is known and it does not agree with the pronoun. This improved performance to 30.8% (Table 3). Our acquired gender information was then incorporated. Given the gender of a pronoun, we use the corresponding classifier built for the gender classification task in Section 5. We reject previous noun phrases that either mismatch in known gender (standard approach) or the corresponding gender classifier gender, until a match is obtained. This nearly doubles performance, to 59.4%, strikingly illustrating the immediate benefit of our new gender information.

6.2   Robust Anaphora Resolution

To further improve performance, we developed a machine-learned anaphora resolution system based on a number of syntactic and semantic features, including features based on the *Beta* distributions of our gender sources (Table 4). Features are collected after tokenizing, parsing, and linking nouns in the text. Linking nouns with matching strings enables us to count noun occurrences and send any gender information learned in one instance of the word to all other occurrences of that word in the chain. To create the training set, we adopt the procedure of Soon *et al* ([12]). Each pronoun and its closest preceding antecedent in our labelled set of training documents form a pairwise positive instance in the set of training vectors. All intervening noun phrases (between the antecedent and the pronoun) form pairwise negative instances with the pronoun. This forms a training set with 1251 positive examples and 2909 negative examples. We train the SVM on this training set, and apply it backward incrementally from each pronoun in the test set until a pronoun-antecedent match is accepted.

Table 4. Features for Pronoun Resolution

Type	Feature	Description
Pronoun Features	Masculine	1: pronoun masculine; else 0
	Feminine	1: pronoun feminine; else 0
	Neutral	1: pronoun neutral; else 0
	Plural	1: pronoun plural; else 0
Antecedent Features	Antecedent Frequency	Number of Occurrences / 10.0
	Subject	1: subject of clause; else 0
	Object	1: object of clause; else 0
	Predicate	1: predicate of clause; else 0
	Pronominal	1: pronoun; else 0
	Prepositional	1: prepositional complement; else 0
	Head-Word Emphasis	1: parent not noun; else 0
	Conjunction	1: *not* part of conjunction; else 0
	Prenominal modifier	1: noun is a prenominal modifier; else 0
	Org	1: an organization; else 0
	Person	1: a person; else 0
	Time	1: has time units; else 0
	Date	1: a date; else 0
	Money	1: a monetary denomination; else 0
	Price	1: a price; else 0
	Amount	1: ante has measurement units; else 0
	Number	1: number; else 0
	Definite	1: has definite article; else 0
	His/Her	1: ante first word of his/her pattern; else 0
	He/His	1: ante first word of he/his pattern; else 0
Gender Features	Std. Gender Match	1: gender known and matches; else 0
	Std. Gender Mismatch	0 if gender known and mismatches; else 1
	Pronoun Mismatch	0 if both pronouns and mismatch; else 1
	Web/Corpus Genders	mean/std. dev. of *Beta* distributions (20X)
Pronoun-Antecedent Features	Binding Theory	1: satisfies Principles B,C; else 0
	Reflexive Subj. Match	1: ante subj. of reflexive pron's GC; else 0
	Same Sentence	1: ante/pron in same sentence; else 0
	Intra-Sentence Diff.	Within-sentence difference/50.0
	In Previous Sentence	1: ante in previous sentence; else 0
	Inter-Sentence Diff.	Sentence distance/50.0
	Prepositional Parallel	1: ante/pron objs. of same preposition; else 0
	Relation-Match	1: ante/pron have same gramm. rel.; else 0
	Parent Relation Match	1: parents have same gramm. rel.; else 0
	Parent Cat. Match	1: parents have same gramm. category; else 0
	Parent Word Match	1: parents same word; else 0
	Quotation Situation	1: ante/pron both in/out of quotes; else 0
	Singular Match	1: both singular; else 0
	Plural Match	1: both plural; else 0
	MI Value	Mutual Information between ante and pron
	MI Available	1: MI value available; else 0

Using the full feature set, with all the gender information included, yields a performance of 73.3% on the test data (Table 3), much higher than any of the baseline approaches. We assessed the contribution of the new gender information to this performance by removing the modelled gender features (but including the features for the standard gender approach) and observed a performance of 63.2%. The 10% performance gain obtained by using the new sources of gender information again indicates the clear and immediate benefit of our work.

A pronoun resolution system performing at 73% on a set of challenging news articles provides a good base for future work. Comparison to other systems in the literature is difficult; different data sets are used and different kinds of manual intervention are performed. Kennedy and Boguraev achieved 75% performance on 306 anaphoric pronouns taken from a variety of texts, including news articles [6], while Mitkov *et al* reach 62% on 2263 anaphoric pronouns (excluding pleonastic pronouns) [9].

7   Conclusion

We have proposed a new approach to anaphora resolution using improved gender information. To the best of our knowledge, our system encompasses the broadest and most accurate gender information yet obtained for anaphora resolution and is the first to obtain gender information from web mining. The enhanced gender information is used in a classifier that outperforms humans at gender guessing tasks, and results in significant performance improvements when used as part of either simple or knowledge-rich anaphora resolution systems.

The quality of the obtained gender information depends on many factors. Parsing errors can lead to erroneous noun-pronoun pairings in the parsed corpus templates. Also, the size and variety of the corpora affect the available gender information. For the web-mined pairs, the more data on the web, the more accurate the resulting values. Thus with improved parsers, more data, and the continued growth of the world wide web, there is potential for improved performance using our method.

We will next focus on improving the anaphora resolution system itself. We will investigate new features for pronoun classification, and new approaches to employing the existing features. Modules to detect pleonastic pronouns and resolve cataphora are in development. Ultimately, we will incorporate anaphora resolution into a Question Answering system currently under development.

Acknowledgements

Thanks to Dekang Lin and all members of the Natural Language Processing Group at the University of Alberta. This work was supported by the Natural Sciences and Engineering Research Council of Canada.

References

1. Richard Evans and Constantin Orăsan. Improving anaphora resolution by identifying animate entities in texts. In *Proceedings of the Discourse Anaphora and Reference Resolution Conference*, pages 154–162, 2000.
2. Niyu Ge, John Hale, and Eugene Charniak. A statistical approach to anaphora resolution. In *Proceedings of the Sixth Workshop on Very Large Corpora*, 1998.
3. Liliane Haegeman. *Introduction to Government & Binding theory: Second Edition*. Basil Blackwell, Cambridge, UK, 1994.
4. Thorsten Joachims. Making large-scale SVM learning practical. In B. Schölkopf and C. Burges, editors, *Advances in Kernel Methods*. MIT-Press, 1999.
5. Frank Keller, Maria Lapata, and Olga Ourioupina. Using the web to overcome data sparseness. In *Proceedings of the Conference on Empirical Methods in Natural Language Processing*, pages 230–237, 2002.
6. Christopher Kennedy and Branimir Boguraev. Anaphora for everyone: Pronominal anaphora resolution without a parser. In *Proceedings of the 16th Conference on Computational Linguistics*, pages 113–118, 1996.
7. Shalom Lappin and Herbert J. Leass. An algorithm for pronominal anaphora resolution. *Computational Linguistics*, 20(4):535–561, 1994.
8. Dekang Lin. Dependency-based evaluation of MINIPAR. In *Proceedings of the Workshop on the Evaluation of Parsing Systems, First International Conference on Language Resources and Evaluation*, 1998.
9. Ruslan Mitkov, Richard Evans, and Constantin Orasan. A new, fully automatic version of Mitkov's knowledge-poor pronoun resolution method. In *Proceedings of the Third International Conference on Computational Linguistics and Intelligent Text Processing*, pages 168–186, 2002.
10. Natalia Modjeska, Katja Markert, and Malvina Nissim. Using the web in machine learning for other-anaphora resolution. In *Proceedings of the EACL Workshop on the Computational Treatment of anaphora*, pages 39–46, 2003.
11. Stuart J. Russell and Peter Norvig. *Artificial Intelligence: a modern approach*, chapter 20: Statistical Learning Methods, page 720. Prentice Hall, Upper Saddle River, N.J., 2nd edition edition, 2003.
12. Wee Meng Soon, Hwee Tou Ng, and Daniel Chung Yong Lim. A machine learning approach to coreference resolution of noun phrases. *Computational Linguistics*, 27(4):521–544, 2001.

Automatic Identification of Parallel Documents With Light or Without Linguistic Resources

Alexandre Patry and Philippe Langlais

Laboratoire de Recherche Appliquée en Linguistique Informatique,
Département d'Informatique et de Recherche Opérationnelle,
Université de Montréal,
C.P. 6128, succursale Centre-ville,
H3C 3J7, Montréal, Québec, Canada
http://rali.iro.umontreal.ca

Abstract. Parallel corpora are playing a crucial role in multilingual natural language processing. Unfortunately, the availability of such a resource is the bottleneck in most applications of interest. Mining the web for parallel corpora is a viable solution that comes at a price: it is not always easy to identify parallel documents among the crawled material. In this study we address the problem of automatically identifying the pairs of texts that are translation of each other in a set of documents. We show that it is possible to automatically build particularly efficient content-based methods that make use of very little lexical knowledge. We also evaluate our approach toward a front-end translation task and demonstrate that our parallel text classifier yields better performances than another approach based on a rich lexicon.

1   Introduction

Parallel corpora are currently playing a crucial role in multilingual natural language processing applications. Aligned at the sentence level, a task that has been shown to be fairly easy [1], a parallel corpus turns out to be already very useful for bilingual concordancers [2] and is the cornerstone of most of the commercial translation memory systems that have been and still are popular among professional translators.

Aligned at the word level, a task for which we have practical and now well understood techniques [3], a parallel corpus may be useful for many applications such as machine translation, word-sense disambiguation and cross-lingual information retrieval.

Few reasonably large, well organized *bitexts* (bilingual corpora where translation relations are explicitly marked) are in common use within the NLP community. The canonical example of such a resource is the so-called *Hansard*, that is, the Canadian parliament debates in both French and English. More and more bitexts of different quality and size are also available for various pairs of languages, among them the Chinese-English Hongkong Hansard, the proceedings of

B. Kégl and G. Lapalme (Eds.): AI 2005, LNAI 3501, pp. 354–365, 2005.

the European Parliament in twenty languages[1], as well as an English-Inuktitut Hansard[2] [4]. Other resources, such as the Bible, are translated in many different languages (but not necessarily organized into bitexts), and have shown some practical usefulness in recent machine translation tasks [5].

However, it is widely acknowledged that the availability of parallel corpora is the bottleneck in many applications of interest. The known available parallel corpora are of limited domain (*viz* legislative and newswire texts) and are mostly available for few well-represented language pairs. Several approaches have been proposed to overcome bitext sparseness, among them mining the web for parallel data [6, 7, 8], making use of *comparable corpora* (texts that are related without necessarily being translations) [9], as well as the challenging issue of using totally unrelated corpora in two different languages [10].

The present study is intended to be applied as a post-processing stage after a set of documents has been collected (for instance from the Internet). In section 2, we address the problem of automatically identifying parallel documents in a (likely noisy) set of texts. Doing so, we explore different approaches to the task that make use of few or no specific linguistic resources. In sections 3 and 4 we evaluate our approaches on two tasks: a controlled one on a part of the EUROPARL corpus, as well as a real task we faced when developing an English-Spanish concordancer. We then show that some of the approaches we investigated are very effective at identifying parallel texts and that their use for seeding a translation engine is also fruitful.

2   Methodology

Acquiring a bitext from the web requires several steps that have been carefully described in [6], the first of which consists in crawling Internet sites in order to download more or less any document that could be converted into a plain text file. We consider this step already done. We further assume that what comes out from the web crawling process is two sets of documents (a source set S and a target set T). The identification of the language of a document might be carried out automatically if not available.

For now on, we will assume that a text is simply an element of a set with no specific external information attached to it such as its name or its url. This precludes the use of name-based heuristics to pairing up the texts, such as the ones described in [7]. Our motivation for this does not lie in an aesthetic way of thinking, but corresponds to an attempt to evaluate as objectively as possible different linguistically poor content-based metrics. In any case, name-based filtering could be introduced as a preprocessing stage or could as well be considered a feature of the classifier we describe in section 2.2.

This being said, the identification of pairs of parallel texts is accomplished in two steps: the scoring of all the pairs of the Cartesian product $S \times T$ and the

---

[1] http://www.europarl.eu.int/home/default_fr.htm
[2] http://www.inuktitutcomputing.ca/NunavutHansards/

labelling of each pair as a parallel or not, on the basis of those scores. We now describe in section 2.1 the different content-based metrics we considered, and in section 2.2 the decision process we devised.

2.1   Content-Based Metrics

We considered three types of metrics to measure the similarity of two documents.

Cosine Measure. The cosine measure (COSINE) is a classical one in information retrieval and quantifies the similarity of two vectors. It is expressed by:

$$cos(v_1, v_2) = \frac{v_1 \cdot v_2}{||v_1|| \, ||v_2||} \tag{1}$$

where v_1 and v_2 are the two vectors to be compared. It takes values between zero and unity, where a greater value means a greater similarity. We followed the approach of Nadeau and Foster [11] and represented a document by a vector whose dimension expresses the number of different tokens in the corpus. One vector is built for each of the following feature families:

- Numbers (NUMBER): any sequence of digits.
- Selected punctuations (PUNCT): parenthesis, square brackets and double quote.
- Named entity (NAME): any capitalized word that is not the first in a sentence.

It has to be noted that this set of tokens is fairly language independent and would a priori apply well for many pairs of languages. A possible extension would be to add a feature family that contains all words that are entries in a bilingual lexicon.

Normalized Edit Distance. As mentioned by Nadeau and Foster [11], a bag of words representation is a rough approximation of a document. In order to improve on this hypothesis, they suggested to use the so-called *edit-distance* (EDIT) [12]. Each document is now treated as a sequence of features and the edit-distance between two sequences (that is, the minimal number of insertions, deletions and substitutions required to transform the first sequence into the second one) quantifies the similarity of the associated documents; the smaller the edit-distance is, the greater is the similarity of the documents. In order to work around the fact that the edit distance depends on the sequence length, we normalize it by the length of the longest of the two sequences.

We compute the normalized edit-distance on the same feature families as those used with the cosine measure. We show in Figure 1 an example of a feature vector and a sequence of named entities on a quotation from the EUROPARL corpus.

Alignment Scores. Another natural candidate to evaluate the parallelness of two documents is the output of a sentence aligner. A sentence aligner takes a pair of parallel documents as inputs and tries to pair sentences that are translations of each others. We used for that purpose the JAPA aligner which performs well

In conclusion, while key infrastructure projects have been supported by the $European_3$ $Regional_5$ $Development_2$ $Fund_4$ and the $Cohesion_1$ $Fund_4$, we should remember that the $European_3$ $Social_6$ $Fund_4$ has played a very important role in helping the less well-off in our society.

Named entities feature vector $(1, 1, 2, 3, 1, 1)$

Named entities sequence   "European", "Regional", "Development",
                               "Fund", "Cohesion", "Fund", "European",
                               "Social", "Fund"

Fig. 1. A feature vector and a sequence of named entities as used to compute the cosine measure and the edit-distance. The named entities are italicized and indexed with their position in the feature vector

and fast [1]. By default, JAPA produces a sequence of alignments whose patterns belong to the set *0-1*, *1-0*, *1-1*, *1-2*, *2-1* and *2-2* (a *1-2* pattern indicates that one source sentence is aligned with two target ones). Two documents that are parallel should present many one-to-one (*1-1*) patterns, while documents that are not should contain many insertion (*0-1*) or deletion (*1-0*) patterns. In addition, JAPA produces an alignment cost (ACOST) which measures the overall quality of the alignment.

Five scores are computed with the aligner output : the ratio of *0-1* and *1-0* alignments, the ratio of *1-1* alignments, the ratio of *1-2* and *2-1* alignments, the ratio of *2-2* alignments and ACOST. We named the group of the four ratios M-N.

2.2   Decision Process

Once a set of scores is associated with a pair of documents, all we need to do is decide whether or not they are translations of each other. We could set up a threshold based approach, but instead we trained an AdaBoost [13] classifier. The training process takes as input scored pairs of texts labelled as parallel or not. It then builds a function that will take a scored pair as input and output whether it is parallel or not.

AdaBoost is a learning algorithm that combines many weak classifiers[3] into a stronger one. It achieves this by training weak classifiers successively, each time focusing on examples that have been hard to classify correctly by the previous weak classifiers. In our experiments, we bounded the number of weak classifiers to 75 and used neural networks [14] with one hidden layer of five units as weak classifiers. Training and testing was done with the PLEARN software[4].

Because the classifier is trained on all the pairs of the Cartesian product $S \times T$, the ratio of parallel pairs is very low. To circumvent this imbalance, the examples are weighted to assign 50% of the probability mass to the parallel pairs. The training algorithm is described in Figure 2.

---

[3] The only constraint on a weak classifier is that it must be right more than half of the time.

[4] More informations on PLEARN can be found at http://plearn.sourceforge.net

Inputs : $\mathcal{D} = \{(x_1, y_1), (x_2, y_2), \ldots, (x_n, y_n)\}$ the training set of scored and labelled document pairs where $x_i \in \mathcal{R}^d$ is a vector containing the d observed scores for the ith document pair and $y_i \in \{parallel, not\text{-}parallel\}$ is the label of the ith pair.

1. Initialize the weight of each document pair for the training process such that non-parallel and parallel pairs have the same total weight

$$P_1(x_i, y_i) \leftarrow 0.5 \cdot \frac{1}{|\{(x, y) \in \mathcal{D} : y = y_i\}|}$$

2. For each round $t \leftarrow 1 \ldots T$
   (a) Train a small neural network $h_t : \mathcal{R}^d \rightarrow \{parallel, not\text{-}parallel\}$ that will take as input a scored document pair and classify it as parallel or not. The small neural network is trained on the data $\mathcal{D}$ and their weight P_t.
   (b) Compute the weighted ratio of the document pairs misclassified by $h_t(\cdot)$

$$\epsilon_t = \sum_{\{(x_i, y_i) \in \mathcal{D} : y_i \neq h_t(x_i)\}} P_t(x_i, y_i)$$

   (c) If $\epsilon_t \geq 0.5$ then $T \leftarrow t$ and goto 3
   (d) Compute the weight of the vote of $h_t(\cdot)$

$$\alpha_t = \frac{1}{2} \ln \left(\frac{1 - \epsilon_t}{\epsilon_t} \right)$$

   (e) Compute P_{t+1}, the weight of each document pairs for the next iteration, emphasizing on examples that have been misclassified by $h_t(\cdot)$

$$P_{t+1}(x_i, y_i) = \frac{P_t(x_i, y_i)}{Z_t} \times \begin{cases} e^{-\alpha_t} & \text{if } h_t(x_i) = y_i \\ e^{\alpha_t} & \text{if } h_t(x_i) \neq y_i \end{cases}$$

   where Z_t is a normalisation factor chosen such that $\sum_{(x_i, y_i) \in \mathcal{D}} P_{t+1}(x_i, y_i) = 1$
3. Return the strong classifier which performs a weighted vote on the small neural networks $(h_1(\cdot), h_2(\cdot), \ldots, h_T(\cdot))$

$$H(x) = \underset{type}{\operatorname{argmax}} \sum_{\{t \in [1,T] : h_t(x) = type\}} \alpha_t$$

where x is a scored document pair and $type \in \{parallel, not\text{-}parallel\}$.

Fig. 2. The AdaBoost algorithm used to train the parallel pair classifier. In our experiments, T was set to 75 and the $h_t(\cdot)$ were neural nets with one hidden layer of five units

3 Controlled Task

3.1 Corpus

EUROPARL is a large corpus of bitexts drawn from the European Parliament between April 1996 and September 2003 [15]. It includes versions of the documents in 11 languages, but we focus in this study on the English-Spanish bitext. Our test corpus contains 487 English documents (therefore 487 Spanish ones), thus summing to 237,169 potential pairs of documents. Each document contains an average of about 2,800 sentences.

3.2   Evaluation Protocol

The task was to identify the parallel documents in our corpus using the scores we discussed earlier. Since we had to train a classifier, we applied five fold cross-validation. The set of examples was partitioned into five subsets and five experiments were run, each time testing with a different subset and training with the remaining examples.

Since the EUROPARL corpus is already aligned at the document level, it is straightforward to determine *precision* and *recall*, as well as the *f-measure* (harmonic mean of both). Precision (resp. recall) is the ratio of pairs of documents correctly identified as parallel over the total number of pairs identified as such (resp. over the total number of parallel documents in the corpus).

3.3   Reference System

In order to assess the performance of the different classifiers we trained, we implemented a fair reference system which makes use of a *bilingual lexicon* (a set of pair of words that are translations of each other). This variant is named DICTIONARY hereafter. We downloaded the Spanish-English dictionary of the PYTHOÑOL project[5], a project devoted to helping English speakers learn Spanish. This dictionary contains more than 70 000 bilingual entries.

We represent a document by the set of its words that are less frequent than a given threshold (the value was set to 2 in this study). We explore the Cartesian product $S \times T$ following a greedy strategy. For each source document $s = \{s_i\}_{i \in [1,N]}$, we sort the target ones $t = \{t_j\}_{j \in [1,M]}$ according to the number of glosses found in the dictionary D between the words representing s and t (equation 2) and pick the best-ranked target document. Note that in the eventuality of two source documents paired to the same target one, we simply remove the two pairs from the bitext[6].

$$\frac{1}{N+M} \times \sum_{i \in [1,N]} \sum_{j \in [1,M]} \delta((s_i, t_j) \in D) \tag{2}$$

3.4   Results

We trained classifiers on various combinations of the scores we described in section 2.1. The performances of each classifier are reported in Table 1. The reference system did as well as our best configuration : a perfect score. The different configurations all performed almost equally on recall, but can be distinguished

---

[5] http://sourceforge.net/projects/pythonol/
[6] This did not happen in the EUROPARL experiment.

on their precision figure. The better performance of the classifiers which use the normalized edit-distance instead of the cosine measure leads us to believe that feature ordering is important when searching for parallel documents in a corpus like EUROPARL (long documents carefully translated).

The configurations using the alignment ratios did not perform well. They had an average f-measure 20% lower than the best metrics and were unstable across the five fold cross-validation process. While the f-measures of the four best configurations had a standard deviation lower than 3%, the configurations using alignment types had a standard deviation ranging from 15% to 18%.

We also observe that the normalized edit-distance on numbers alone (third line of Table 1) achieve a f-measure of 99%. This suggests that numbers are very good indicators of parallelism for this kind of corpus. Indeed, parliamentary proceedings contains many stable numbers like dates, law numbers and counts of votes. So our approach could be use with languages where named entities are not trivial to extract.

Last but not least, it is interesting to note that the best classifier we devised performs perfectly on this task, as did the dictionary variant, but without requiring any specific bilingual lexicon.

Table 1. Average precision, recall and f-measure (f_1) figures as a function of the scores the classifier has been trained on. Note that because these figures are averaged over a five folds cross-validation, the f_1 is not always coherent with the reported precision and recall. Ratios are expressed as percentages for more readability

Configuration							Performances		
COSINE	EDIT	NUMBER	PUNCT	NAME	ACOST	M-N	precision	recall	f_1
	√	√	√	√			100	100	100
√	√	√	√	√	√	√	99.8	99.8	99.8
		√	√				98.3	99.8	99.0
	√	√			√		96.6	99.8	98.1
					√		85.8	99.8	92.1
						√	65.6	99.4	77.1
					√	√	49.3	99.4	62.7
√		√	√	√			24.6	99.2	38.7
√			√				12.4	98.9	21.8

4   Real World Task

In response to frequent requests, we decided at RALI to extend TSRALI.COM[2], our bilingual concordancers, to the Spanish-English language pair. At that time, the RALI had an agreement with the Pan American Health Organization (PAHO) to create a *transbase* (a bitext searchable online via TSRALI.COM) out of the texts on their web site[7]. A priori, mining a web site in order to extract parallel texts is fairly easy, but in fact, it turned out to be a tricky task [16]. There was no clear hierarchy to rely on for pairing up the documents and the naming conventions were too inconsistent for identifying the language of each text: in short, a perfect test for our system!

4.1   Corpus

SILC[8] was run to discover the language of each file downloaded from the PAHO website, leaving us with 2,523 files identified as English and 4,355 ones as Spanish. Each document contains an average of about 180 sentences. Casual inspection of this material reveals that many files were duplicates (or close duplicates) and that some texts were bilingual. This is however the material we considered, which means that our classifier had to select parallel pairs among over 10 million candidates.

For testing purposes, we downloaded a bitext from the PAHO web site that was written one year after we collected the corpus mentioned above. This document was aligned at the sentence level by JAPA. Following a usual procedure, non *1-1* alignments were removed and the remaining pairs were manually checked for parallelness. A total of 520 pairs of sentences was thus obtained.

4.2   Evaluation Protocol

We devised an evaluation protocol different from the one we discussed in section 3.2. We now want to measure the usefulness of our approach for a real task, namely statistical machine translation (SMT). The reasons for this choice are twofold. First, the identification of parallel documents only makes sense when applied to a front-end (bilingual) application, and machine translation is the bilingual application par excellence. Furthermore, the building of a statistical translation engine is entirely automatic once a bitext is identified. The second reason for evaluating a front-end task lies in the fact that we do not have a clear gold standard bitext against which to evaluate our approach.

We applied the following protocol. We trained our classifiers on the EUROPARL corpus and used each of them to identify parallel document pairs in PAHO. Each set of parallel document pairs was then filtered to remove pairs sharing a document with another pair. This filtering step was introduced to remove uncertain pairs. Each filtered set of document pairs was then used to train a Spanish to English translation engine with which we translated the 520 test sentences (see section 4.1). The quality of the different configurations was evaluated by comparing the automatically translated Spanish sentences with the one we downloaded by applying automatic metrics that are commonly used within the machine translation community (see section 4.4).

In addition to the evaluation using a front end task, we manually checked the precision (see section 3.2) of each configuration.

---

[7] http://www.paho.org

[8] Information on SILC can be found at http://rali.iro.umontreal.ca

4.3   SMT

Our SMT engine follows the noisy channel paradigm introduced for machine translation by *Brown et al.* [3]. It can be characterized abstractly as follows:

$$\hat{e} = \underset{e \in \mathcal{E}}{\operatorname{argmax}}\, p(e|s) = \underset{e \in \mathcal{E}}{\operatorname{argmax}}\, p(s|e)p(e) \tag{3}$$

where $\hat{e}$ is the (English) translation we seek for a (Spanish) sentence s, and where $p(s|e)$ and $p(e)$ are the translation and language model respectively. The translation model tells us which words should be translation of each other, without necessarily knowing their final position in the translation, while the language model captures some knowledge on the fluency of a sequence of (English) words.

We followed the procedure described in [17] to train both models, and relied on the PHARAOH decoder [18] to perform the argmax operation.

4.4   Metrics

We used different metrics to evaluate the quality of the automatically produced translations. Each metric has its own strengths, the discussion of which is not the purpose of the present exposure. They all compare the candidate translations to a gold standard (in our case a human translation).

The two first metrics are error rates (the lower the better). SER (for Sentence-Error-Rate) is the percentage of sentences produced that are different from the gold standard. WER (for Word-Error-Rate) is the normalized edit-distance between a produced translation and its reference (a rate of 0 would express a perfect translation, a rate of 100, a maximally bad translation).

BLEU and NIST are precision metrics (the higher the better) that, roughly speaking, count the number of sequences that a translation shares with its reference, giving more credit to longer sequences. We used the script `mteval` available at the NIST web site[9] to compute those scores. The BLEU metric ranges between 0 and 1 (1 qualifying the reference itself), while the NIST score is not normalized and the reference itself would be rated 13.11.

4.5   Results

We compared the performance of our translation engine when trained on four different bitexts. The DICTIONARY one was obtained by the reference system described in section 3.3, EDIT is the bitext identified by the best-ranked classifier in the EUROPARL task (line 1 of Table 1), and COSINE is the classifier we trained on the cosine score on the same features (line 8 of Table 1).

Contrary to our former experiment, COSINE and EDIT performed similarly well. This could be explained by the shorter length of the documents and by the filtering step applied on the parallel pairs, which seems to eliminate untrusted pairs. Inspection of their bitexts showed that they shared only 229 document pairs, so we trained another translation engine on the union of those bitexts.

---

[9] `www.mteval.org`

Table 2. Evaluation of our parallel text identification procedure through a machine translation task where N is the number of document pairs identified as parallel. See the text for more

bitext	N	SER	WER	NIST	BLEU	precision
COSINE ∪ EDIT	494	99.42	60.02	5.3125	0.2435	99.0
DICTIONARY	529	99.42	61.67	5.1989	0.2304	89.2
EDIT	390	99.42	61.53	5.1342	0.2290	99.0
COSINE	333	99.23	62.23	5.1629	0.2256	99.7

The scores of all the translation engines are reported in Table 2. We observe that the performance of the engine trained on the bitexts identified by our COSINE ∪ EDIT classifiers is better than the performance of the engine trained on the DICTIONARY bitext. This is a very satisfactory result since no manual intervention was required, neither any special bilingual resource. Another encouraging result is that the precision of all our classifiers is very high (99% or greater).

5   Related Work

This study was inspired by the work of Nadeau and Foster [11] who suggested viewing a document as bags of features such as proper names, numbers, and the like. They have shown that coupled with a fairly tolerant filter on the date of issue of a news story, they could align with high accuracy the Canada Newswire news feed[10]. They also mention that considering word order in a document would be a better idea.

Our work, although independently developed, resembles that of Munteanu and al. [9]. In their study, the authors showed that a translation engine could benefit from parallel sentences automatically extracted from comparable corpora. The approach they propose is analogous to the one we described here, basically training a classifier (in their case via a maximum entropy approach) to identify pairs of sentences (while we look for pairs of documents). To do so, they relied on more extensive resources than what we considered here. For instance, they assumed the availability of a bitext in order to train a translation model that they used for aligning sentences at the word level. In fact, both approaches have their own merits and specificities of application. Our approach would be more suited for corpora where we know a priori that many documents are parallel.

6   Future Work and Conclusions

We have extended the approach of Nadeau and Foster [11] in three different ways. First, we tested this idea on different corpora that might not be as friendly as

---

[10] http://www.newswire.ca

news are. As a matter of fact, news inherently contain a lot of named entities and dates. Second, we experimented with whether maintaining the order of the features in the text would be beneficial. We showed that doing so can surpass or complement the bags of words representation. Third, we tested the impact of such methods on a real task: machine translation. We demonstrated that an approach using poor lexical metrics yields better results than a fair one relying on a rich lexicon.

The approach we propose is highly flexible because it relies on an automatic training procedure which allows us to easily integrate new features to describe a document. In this study, we decided to rely on features such as numbers and named entities; but we observed that the number of hits in a bilingual dictionary may also be a good feature for pairing documents. This could be added to our feature list.

In this study, we systematically considered the Cartesian product of the source and target document sets. This does not come without a computational load. We could also apply a risk-less pre-filtering stage following ad-hoc strategies, such as the length-based criterion proposed by [6].

Finally, we would like to investigate the impact of computing the features on only a part of the documents (for instance the first few sentences). This would speed up the edit-distance computation and therefore the overall process.

Acknowledgements

We would like to thank Marie Ouimet and Leïla Arras who provided us with the PAHO documents we used in this study. Elliott Macklovitch and Ol'ga Feiguina made some useful comments on the first draft of this document. This work has been subsidized by NSERC and FQRNT.

References

1. Langlais, P., Simard, M., Veronis, J.: Methods and practical issues in evaluating alignment techniques. In: Proceedings of the 36th Annual Meeting of the Association for Computational Linguistics (ACL), Montréal, Quebec, Canada (1998) 711–717
2. Macklovitch, E., Simard, M., Langlais, P.: Transsearch: A free translation memory on the world wide web. In: Second International Conference On Language Resources and Evaluation (LREC). Volume 3., Athens Greece (2000) 1201–1208
3. Brown, P.F., Pietra, S.A.D., Pietra, V.J.D., Mercer, R.L.: The mathematics of statistical machine translation: Parameter estimation. Computational Linguistics **19** (1993) 263–311
4. Martin, J., Johnson, H., Farley, B., Maclachlan, A.: Aligning and using an english-inuktitut parallel corpus. In: HLT-NAACL Workshop: Building and Using Parallel Texts - Data Driven Machine Translation and Beyond, Edmonton, Canada (2003) 115–118
5. Oard, D.W., Och, F.J.: Rapid-reponse machine translation for unexpected languages. In: Machine Translation Summit IX, New Orleans, Louisiana, USA (2003)

6. Kraaij, W., Nie, J.Y., Simard, M.: Embedding web-based statistical translation models in cross-language information retrieval. Computational Linguistics **29** (2003) 381–419

7. Resnik, P., Smith, N.A.: The web as a parallel corpus. Computational Linguistics **29** (2003) 349–380 Special Issue on the Web as a Corpus.

8. Ma, X., Liberman, M.: Bits: A method for bilingual text search over the web. In: Machine Translation Summit VII, Kent Ridge Digital Labs, National University of Singapore (1999)

9. Munteanu, D.S., Fraser, A., Marcu, D.: Improved machine translation performace via parallel sentence extraction from comparable corpora. In: Proceedings of the Human Language Technology and North American Association for Computational Linguistics Conference (HLT/NAACL 2004). (2004)

10. Rapp, R.: Automatic identification of word translations from unrelated english and german corpora. In: Proceedings of the 37th conference on Association for Computational Linguistics, Association for Computational Linguistics (1999) 519–526

11. Nadeau, D., Foster, G.: Real-time identification of parallel texts from bilingual news feed. In: CLINE 2004, Computational Linguistics in the North East (2004)

12. Levenshtein, V.I.: Binary codes capable of correcting deletions, insertions and reversals. Sov. Phys. Dokl. **6** (1966) 707–710

13. Y.Freund, Schapire, R.: A short introduction to boosting. Journal of Japanese Society for Artificial Intelligence **14** (1999) 771–780 Appearing in Japanese, translation by Naoki Abe.

14. Bishop, C.M.: Neural networks for pattern recognition. Oxford University Press (1996)

15. Koehn, P.: Europarl: A multilingual corpus for evaluation of machine translation. Draft (2002)

16. Ouimet, M.: Transsearch anglais-espagnol. `http://www.iro.umontreal.ca/~ouimema/ift3051/README.html` (2002)

17. Langlais, P., Carl, M., Streiter, O.: Experimenting with phrase-based statistical translation within the iwslt 2004 chinese-to-english shared translation task. In: International Workshop on Spoken Language Translation, Kytio, Japan (2004)

18. Koehn, P.: Pharaoh: a beam search decoder for phrase-based statistical machine translation models. In: Meeting of the American Association for Machine Translation (AMTA), Washington DC (2004)

Inductive Improvement of Part-of-Speech Tagging and Its Effect on a Terminology of Molecular Biology

Ahmed Amrani[1], Mathieu Roche[2], Yves Kodratoff[2],
and Oriane Matte-Tailliez[2]

[1] ESIEA Recherche, 9 rue Vésale, 75005 Paris, France
amrani@esiea.fr
[2] LRI, UMR CNRS 8623, Bât. 490, Université de Paris-Sud 11,
91405 Orsay, France
{roche, yk, oriane}@lri.fr

Abstract. In the context of Part-of-Speech (PoS)-tagging of specialized corpora, we proposed an inductive approach focusing on the most 'important' PoS-tags because mistaking them can lead to a total misunderstanding of the text. After a standard tagging of a biological corpus by Brill's tagger, we noted persistent errors that are very hard to deal with. As an application, we studied two cases of different nature: first, confusion between past participle, adjective and preterit for verbs that end with 'ed'; second, confusion between plural nouns and verbs, 3rd person singular present. With a friendly user interface, the expert corrected the examples. Then, from these well-annotated examples, we induced rules using a propositional rule induction algorithm. Experimental validation showed improvement in tagging precision. The relevance of the terminology of the considered field, here molecular biology, is greatly improved when the number of these tagging errors decreases.

1 Introduction

Knowledge extraction starting from 'raw' specialized texts is not yet really standard. In order to improve on this problem, several related steps must be carried out [1]: text gathering, text normalization, PoS-tagging, terminology extraction, corefence resolution, and detection of user-defined concepts.

In this paper, we focused on PoS-tagging. It associates to each word with a PoS-tag, according to word morphology and context. A prerequisite for building (automatically) a PoS-tagger is the availability of a (large) annotated corpus. Acquiring such a corpus is expensive and time consuming and it is often the bottleneck to build a tagger for a new application or domain. Another problem is that all the taggers, including human ones, make mistakes in the same difficult cases. These errors are due to the fact that words have different tags according to the context. The short-range contexts (i.e. bigrams and trigrams) are, in some cases, not differentiating enough to help inducing valid contextual rules.

We propose a methodology to solve the difficult problems that persist after the application of Brill's tagger [2] and ETIQ [3]. We were quite motivated by observing many particular contexts in which the proportion of errors was high.

B. Kégl and G. Lapalme (Eds.): AI 2005, LNAI 3501, pp. 366–376, 2005.
© Springer-Verlag Berlin Heidelberg 2005

These difficult cases occur for words having several tags in the lexicon. They can be further classified in two different kinds. The first kind happens when one word can have different functions in the sentence. For instance, the word 'transformed' can function as a past participle, a preterit, or a premodifier (then functioning as an adjective). The second kind happens when two different words are made of the same sequence of letters, such as in the case of 'functions' as the noun plural above "functions in the sentence" and the verb in "it functions in the sentence etc."

The procedure we follow is: We annotate the examples corresponding to these cases. We learn correction rules by using a propositional rule induction algorithm. The rules obtained are then inserted following the contextual rules of ETIQ and are applied in the same way. In this paper, we will show that a correct PoS-tagging improves quality of the terminology.

Section 2 recalls the state of the art on our topic, section 3 describes our tagging approach, and section 4 explains how we find the terms. Section 5 provides an experimental validation, and section 6 discusses our results.

2 State of the Art

2.1 Part-of-Speech Taggers

Several data-driven learning approaches have been applied to PoS-tagging. Among them, Inductive Logic Programming [4,5,6], Memory-Based Learning [7,8], Transformation-Based Learning [2], decision trees learning [9] and statistical approaches [10,11] can be cited. Other sophisticated techniques were used, based on the combination of several kinds of taggers [12,13]. These techniques are based on the fact that differently designed taggers produce different errors. Thus, the combined tagger shows a higher precision than each isolated ones [12,13]. Whatever the technology on which they are based, the current taggers obtain a very satisfactory level of precision. The published results are usually about 95% of correct tags, and even higher figures can be found. In these works, the test and training corpora are of similar nature, and that might explain these high performances. Obviously, some specific work has to be done in order to adapt these approaches to specialized, not-yet tagged corpora.

We use Brill's tagger [2] in order to obtain a first tagging. It is a rule-based supervised learning algorithm. The algorithm induces an ordered list of rules from an annotated corpus. These rules are of two kinds, lexical and contextual distributed in two independent modules.

2.2 Rule Induction Approaches

A variety of approaches to learn rules have been investigated. There are two major paradigms for rule induction: creating rules from decisions trees and direct rule learning techniques. The first one begins in generating a decision tree, then transforms it into a rule set, and finally simplifies the rules. The resulting rule set is usually about as accurate as a pruned tree, but more easily understood by people [14]. The other uses the direct strategy, as for instance the algorithm RIPPER [15]. In short, this strategy determines the most 'powerful' (several definitions of 'power' are possible) rule that covers the dataset, separates out the examples covered by this rule, and repeats the procedure on the remaining examples.

A propositional rule learning algorithm, named PART [16], combines the two major paradigms to induce rules. It adopts the direct strategy for building a rule, in removing the instances that it covers, and in continuing to recursively create rules for the remaining instances until the set of examples is empty. It differs from the standard approach in the way each rule is created. In order to generate each single rule, a partial decision tree is built for the current set of instances; the leaf with the largest coverage is made into a rule, and the tree is discarded.

PART constructs rules that accurately classify the training data. As usual for classifying rules, each rule is represented in the form of a conjunction of conditions:

```
if T₁ and T₂ and ... Tₙ then class Cx
```

"$if\ T_1\ and\ T_2\ and\ \ldots\ T_n$" is called the body of the rule. Cx is a target class to be learned. A condition T_i tests for a particular value of an attribute, and it takes the following form: $A_i = v$, where A_i is a nominal attribute and v is a legal value for A_i.

3 Part-of-Speech Tagging

3.1 Lexical and Contextual Tagging

The solution we propose is to adapt a tagger trained on a "general" corpus, to a corpus of specialty [3]. We thus basically preserve Brill's tagger as the base of our system. ETIQ, the tagger that we developed, displays for the expert the results of Brill's tagging and allows him/her to add specialized rules in a simple way. To add the Nth rule, the expert needs to observe the current state of the corpus after the execution of the (N-1) preceding rules. The overall strategy we use is as follows: We start with Brill's lexical rules. Observing their effect, the expert adds specialized lexical rules. The expert then observes the effect of Brill's contextual rules and specialized contextual rules can finally be added.

In the lexical module, the goal is finding specialized lexical rules to determine the most probable tags of the unknown words. To help the expert to detect the tagging errors, the system ETIQ gives him the possibility of visualizing groups of words of similar morphological features, and their tags. Reacting to the detected errors, the expert inserts adequate lexical rules to correct these errors. A lexical rule is, for example:

```
Assign the 'adjective' tag to the words having suffix
'al'.
```

Once the expert estimates that the tagging carried out during lexical stage brings no more improvement, contextual rules may be used. All the words that can receive several tags have to be treated by contextual rules: For instance, both the words 'functions' and 'complex' have two possible tags, respectively (NNS: *noun, common, plural* and VBZ: *verb present tense, 3rd person singular*), and (JJ: *adjective* and NN: *noun, common, singular*). The contextual rules change word tags according to the word in its context (*i.e.*, the word form, its tag, and neighboring words and their tags). Similarly to the lexical module, the expert can, in an interactive way, look for words, according to their forms, tags, and morphological criteria. This enables to visualize the contexts and to detect the errors. The expert can thus correct these errors by inserting specialized contextual rules.

All modules of ETIQ propose several solutions to the expert in order to build expressive rules by logical operators to combine simple conditions or predefined regular expressions. The writing, the modification, and the checking of each rule are done in a simple way by using a user-friendly interface.

3.2 Learning Rules to Correct Complex Tagging Errors

Which Errors Are Hard to Deal with?

By using ETIQ [3], we observed that PoS-tagging with standard Brill's tagger generates many tag confusions in some particular contexts. We observed that some tags can be easily confused (for instance, NNS-VBZ) or that some words bring confusion. (for instance, *complex*). The most frequent and most serious confusions occur in the following cases as shown in Table 1.

Table 1. Examples of words having various tags according to the context. The most frequent and serious confusions are: (1) JJ (adjective) and NN (noun, singular); (2) VBN (verb, past participle), JJ and VBD (verb, past tense); (3) VBZ (verb, 3rd person sing. present) and NNS (noun plural); (4) VBP (verb, non-3rd person sing. present) and NN. Note that in the example of 5th line, '*transformed*' is a VBD because '*constructs*' is a NNS

Tags	The left part of the sentence	Ambiguous words	The right part of the sentence
NN	... that is necessary and sufficient for association with the carboxyl terminus of Rap1p but not required for Sir	Complex	formation or histone binding.
JJ	Production of HC-toxin is under the control of a	Complex	formation or histone binding
JJ	... genes that are important for regulating normal and	Transformed	breast epithelial cell phenotypes
VBN	... DNA fragments fused to the N-terminal half of ubiquitin was constructed and	Transformed	into yeast strains...
VBD	PETARS constructs	Transformed	yeast at high frequencies and were maintained as minichromosomes consistent.
NNS	...enzymes may form direct protein-protein	Contacts	and we propose that...
VBZ	Mutational analysis reveals that HBx	Contacts	p127 via a region...

Methodology

Using a user-friendly interface ETIQ [2,17] (Figure 1), the expert can easily identify confusions (detailed in Table 1) produced by Brill's tagger at the contextual level. Once all mistakes are identified, we observe that it is sometimes very difficult to write down correction rules because the expert is unable to take into account all the possible exceptions. We thus adopted the following strategy: We annotate examples containing the ambiguous words (figure 1). The tagging process is made easier by sorting the examples according to the ambiguous target word and the words in its context. In that way, similar examples will be placed near to each other.

The expert will assign to the target word of each example (or group of examples) the corresponding PoS-tag. These annotated examples allow learning automatically correction rules. To determine the correct tag of the word concerned, the induced rules are based on the characteristics of this one, and the characteristics of the nearby words. In order to study the impact on performance of the representation of example, we varied the size of the context as well as the features used to learn the rules. The obtained rules correct the tag of the word according to its context. The rule learning is based on 'rather correct' contexts (*i.e.*, contexts containing as few as possible false tags). Indeed, it is practically impossible to learn efficient rules starting from a noisy context. The preliminary steps of ETIQ (lexical and contextual stages) make it possible to obtain contexts with a minimum error rate, and that will enable us to learn valid rules. The rule learning system we use is PART [16]. The obtained rules are then converted in the ETIQ format and are inserted at the end of the contextual rule list.

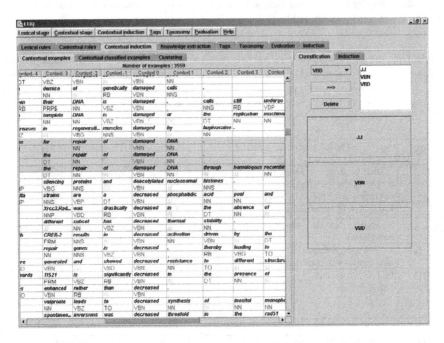

Fig. 1. A view of the software ETIQ: Example annotation task. Among the seven presented examples where the target word is *damaged*, the expert noted three similar examples all put in class *JJ* by clicking on the corresponding switch

4   Extraction of Terms

Following PoS-tagging, we are able to extract doublets or triplets of successive words, called collocations [18], showing specific PoS-tag series: Noun-Preposition-Noun, Noun-Noun, Adjective-Noun. The relevant collocations, *i.e.* collocations which are instances of a concept, are called "terms".

We use EXIT software that **EX**tracts **I**teratively complex **T**erms [19]. The EXIT system uses an iterative approach to extract complex terms (for example, *"DNA binding protein domain"*) with binary or ternary terms (for example, *"DNA binding"*).

The EXIT system is also based on statistical measures to order extracted collocations. Many statistical criteria exist to order collocations [20,21,22,23,24]. In this paper, we use a statistical measure called Occ_L which has the best behavior on different specialized corpora studied in [23]. Occ_L orders collocations according to their occurrence number (Occ) and collocations having the same number of occurrences are sorted by loglikelihood (L) [25].

Our approach to improve tagging and the consequences on quality of the terminology extracted by using this statistical measure was the subject of an application presented in the following section.

5 Experimental Validation

5.1 Part-of-Speech Tagging

To produce the rules of ETIQ, the expert used an English corpus, composed of 6000 MEDLINE abstracts in the field of Molecular Biology [3].

In order to validate our approach, we used a sub-corpus made of 600 abstracts. This sub-corpus was tagged with the lexical and contextual rules of Brill's tagger, following by the lexical and contextual rules of ETIQ. We then gave to an expert 4133 examples where the target word is tagged VBN (each example is constituted of a twenty words sentence extract, where the ambiguous target word is central). The expert annotated these examples. In a similar way, we gave to the expert another set of 3298 examples where the target word is NNS. The total number of NNS was 7708 of which 4410 were words with single tag. Then, from the annotated examples, we induced rules by using the propositional rule learner PART.

In order to obtain the best precision, we used the following representations. Let the precision be defined like the ratio of the correct examples on the whole set of examples.

VBN case: The target word is taken in a window of 10 words (5 words on the left and 5 words on the right) and each word is represented by: (i) Its PoS-tag, (ii) The group to which its tag (Verb, Noun or other) belongs and, (iii) Is the word an auxiliary verb or not.

NNS case: The target word is taken in a window of 4 words (2 words on the left and 2 words on the right) and each word is represented by: (i) Its PoS-tag, (ii) The group to which its tag (Verb, Noun or other) belongs, (iii) Is the word an auxiliary verb or not, (iv) the most frequent suffixes and prefixes of words.

According to the context, the annotator classified the target words in VBN, JJ or VBD (see figure 1) categories for the first set of examples and NNS or VBZ for the second set. For these examples, we calculated the precision of Brill's tagger, system ETIQ and system ETIQ plus induced rules. The precision of the induced rules was calculated by the method of ten-fold cross validation. The results obtained are presented in table 2.

We present below some examples of induced rules:

```
If the current word is tagged VBN and the precedent word is
tagged IN (Preposition or subordinating conjunction) and the
next word is tagged FRM (biological formula) then change the
current word tag to adjective.

If the current word is tagged VBN and the precedent (-4) word
tag does not belong to any of the groups Noun and Verb, and
the precedent word is tagged FRM then change the current word
tag to VBD.

If the current word is tagged NNS and the precedent word tag
does not belong to any of the groups Noun and Verb, and the
next word is tagged NN then change the current word tag to
VBZ.
```

Table 2. Precisions obtained on two sets of PoS confusion examples. (a) Brill's tagger provides a starting first tagging. (b) The expert writes rules using our Etiq system in order to improve the first tagging. (c) Etiq induces rules that are applied last

% of precision Confusion	(a) Brill	(b) Brill + expert's rules (ETIQ)	(c) Brill + ETIQ (expert's rules + induced rules)
VBN → VBN, VBD, JJ	54 %	76 %	94 %
NNS → NNS, VBZ	92 %	96 %	97 %

We also applied the obtained rules to another corpus composed of 123 MEDLINE abstracts of the same domain (biology), but of another specialty (ecology of *Photorhabdus luminescens*). In the VBN case, the precision on examples before application of rules was 75 %. After application of ETIQ rules (expert's rules and induced rules) the obtained precision was 91 %. We did not apply the induced rules for case of NNS-VBZ, considering the number of errors was unimportant on this corpus. We noted that the induced rules are also valid on corpora of the same genre.

5.2 Influence of PoS-Tagging on the Terminology

This section presents the consequences of using ETIQ and ETIQ plus induced rules on the quality of extracted collocations. The experiments consist in extracting collocations Adjective-Noun, Noun-Noun, Noun-Preposition-Noun starting from two tagged corpora. The first corpus is a corpus in Molecular Biology domain tagged by Brill's tagger. The second corpus used is the same corpus that was tagged by ETIQ with application of the rules presented in this paper. From one corpus to another, we note two types of errors: relevant collocations can be omitted and incorrect collocations can be extracted (see Table 3).

In our experiments, we were interested in the Noun-Noun relation that provides the more important number of collocations. As [26], we applied a pruning of value 3 consisting in taking only into account collocations having a number of occurrences more important or equal than three. This task makes it possible to preserve the collocations most representative of the field. Noun-Noun collocations extracted from each corpus are ordered by using Occ_L measure (see section 4).

Table 3. Tagging influence on the terminology: examples of collocations differently tagged by the systems and influences on their extraction

Brill's tagger	Brill + ETIQ (expert's rules + induced rules)
Relevant collocations with incorrect tags then omission	**Relevant collocations with correct tags then extraction**
DNA-binding/**VBG** ability/**NN** chain/**NN** complex/**JJ** membrane/**NN** spans/**VBZ**	DNA-binding/**JJ** ability/**NN** chain/**NN** complex/**NN** membrane/**NN** spans/**NNS**
Irrelevant collocations with incorrect tags then extraction	**Irrelevant collocations with correct tags then omission**
complex/**JJ** functions/**NNS** Tup1p/**NN** blocks/**NNS**	complex/**NN** functions/**VBZ** Tup1p/**NN** blocks/**VBZ**

The quality of the collocations extracted from the two corpora is evaluated according to precision. The definition of this measure is indicated below:

$$Precision = NRC / NC . \tag{1}$$

NRC is the number of relevant collocations extracted, and NC is the number of collocations extracted. Since we do not know what the total number of pertinent collocations is, recall is not computable.

As specified in [27], according to the use of terms (indexing, ontology, etc.), their relevance can differ. In our case, we judge that a collocation is relevant if it represents a linguistic instance of a concept. We calculated the precision with the 400 first Noun-Noun collocations extracted with the two studied corpora (corpus tagged with Brill's tagger and corpus tagged with Brill + ETIQ and application of induced rules). Our results show that using ETIQ and the induced rules improves precision (see Table 4). These results confirm the interest of using ETIQ and the induced rules to improve the quality of the extracted terminology.

Table 4. Precision with the 400 first Noun-Noun collocations extracted from the two corpora (tagged with Brill and Brill + ETIQ and induced rules) and ordering with Occ_L measure

Number of collocations	Brill's tagger	Brill + ETIQ	Number of collocations	Brill's tagger	Brill + ETIQ
50	94.0 %	96.0 %	250	88.4 %	89.6 %
100	93.0 %	95.0 %	300	87.3 %	88.3 %
150	91.3 %	93.3 %	350	86.6 %	87.4 %
200	88.5 %	90.5 %	400	86.5 %	86.0 %

6   General Discussion

The application of this methodology makes it possible to focus on the difficult and important PoS-tagging problems. The application of the rules is effective only after reduction of context errors by using the preceding stages of ETIQ. Indeed, in the lexical module, tagging of the unknown words was treated and in the contextual module the total precision was improved. The learned rules were applied after the set of lexical and contextual rules of ETIQ.

The obtained rules are expressive and easily understandable by the expert. The expert can thus refine them, improve them and adapt them. During the learning of rules, it is possible to vary the size of the context and the representation of the examples of a class of ambiguity to the other. This will make it possible to treat each ambiguity in an optimal way. In the cases of NNS-VBZ, the context necessary to the training is smaller than in the case of VBN-VBD-JJ. Obviously, confusions of different nature require a specific representation for each case.

For the confusion NNS-VBZ, the precision obtained by Brill's system (92%) is already correct owing to the fact that Brill's algorithm uses a reduced context and thus treats relatively well this ambiguity. However, in the case of ambiguity VBN-VBD-JJ requiring by nature a broader context to be taking into account, we note the very low precision obtained by Brill's algorithm. The good results obtained by ETIQ with induced rules compared to ETIQ with only expert's rules are explained by the fact that it is very difficult for an expert to create rules by taking into account of a broad context, which is possible by automatic induction. We also note that the rules learned on the examples picked up from the molecular biology corpus are also valid on a different corpus from the same genre.

We define generalized tags as 'VERB' (for any kind of verbal form) or 'NOUN' (for any kind of noun form), in order to decrease the total number of rules, and improve their understandability. Besides, some functional linguistic roles are particularly pertinent to decide of the proper tag they are a context of. For instance, knowing the nature of 'that' (subordinative, relative, or determinant) provides invaluable information on the nature (verb or noun) of the words that are just before and just after it. Inversely, some very important functional features, such as the distinction between an active and a passive form, rely on the determination of the auxiliaries, which in turn relies on knowing whether an -ed form is a preterit, a participle or an 'adjective'.

The reduction of errors in PoS-tagging will have a direct effect on the quality of the terminology that will be extracted directly after PoS-tagging. The important terms for descriptive biology are nominal (*i.e.*, collocations of nouns and adjectives and nouns). For example, if a noun is taken for a verb, the term that contains this noun will be omitted, and conversely, if a verb is taken for a noun, a term containing this verb will be extracted in an automatic way and will not be relevant. Due to the recursive nature of the tagging, since each word is the context of the other words, even seemingly non pertinent mistakes might have long range effects. For instance, we look for terms made of a noun-noun relationship as well as terms built from an adjective-noun one; it could then be believed that confusing a noun and an adjective is of little importance. This is not true because many rules use the fact that a determinant must be followed by a noun. If a noun is tagged as adjective, then the verb following the noun will be confused with a noun if the lexicon allows it.

7 Conclusion

Within the framework of a complete methodology for the PoS-tagging of specialized corpora, we supplemented our approach, developed in a previous work [3], by a method that deals with some of the difficult and specific problems of PoS-tagging. After finding of particularly ambiguous contexts, target ambiguous words were annotated in their contexts (examples). From these examples, we induced corrective tagging rules by using the algorithm PART. We applied our methodology to the classes of ambiguity VBN-JJ-VBD, and NNS-VBZ. A significant improvement in tagging precision was obtained. We also shown that improving the tagging improves in turn the relevance of the terminology we build from texts in molecular biology.

We will use our PoS-tagging approach to treat other classes of ambiguity such as VB (verb, base form)-NN (noun, singular). We will also test other methods of machine learning such as ILP by using LRI-developed PROPAL [28]. We also noted that rules learned by various algorithms such as PART and RIPPER could be complementary. The optimal combination of the rules obtained by various algorithms could improve the performances of tagging.

We are presently improving our system by including active learning techniques, in order to reduce the number of examples the expert has to consider.

References

1. Amrani, A., Azé, J., Heitz, T., Kodratoff, Y., Roche, M.: From the texts to the concepts they contain: a chain of linguistic treatments. In proceedings of TREC'04 (Text REtrieval Conference), National Institute of Standards and Technology, Gaithersburg Maryland USA, (2004) 712–722
2. Brill, E.: Some Advances in Transformation-Based Part of Speech Tagging, AAAI, (1994) Vol. 1, 722–727
3. Amrani, A., Kodratoff, Y., Matte-Tailliez, O.: A Semi-automatic System for Tagging Specialized Corpora, H. DAI, R. SRIKANT, C. ZHANG (eds.), Advances in Knowledge Discovery and Data Mining, PAKDD, May, Sydney, LNAI, (2004) Vol. 3056, 670–681
4. Cussens, J.: Part-of-speech tagging using Progol, S. Dzeroski et N. Lavrac, Eds., Proceedings of the 7th International Workshop on ILP, Vol.1297(1997)93–108
5. Eineborg, M., Lindberg, N.: ILP in Part-of-Speech Tagging - An Overview. J. Cussens et S. Dzeroski, Eds., Learning Language in Logic, LNAI, Vol. 1925 (2000)
6. Lindberg, N., Eineborg, M.: Learning Constraint Grammar-style Disambiguation Rules using Inductive Logic Programming. Proceedings of the 36th Annual Meeting of the Association for Computational Linguistics and 17th International Conference on Computational Linguistics (1998) 775–779
7. Daelemans, W., Zavrel, J., Berck, P., Gillis, S.: MBT: A Memory-Based Part of Speech Tagger-Generator, E. Ejerhed and I. Dagan Eds., Proceedings of the 4th Workshop on Very Large Corpora, Copenhagen (1996) 14–27
8. Zavrel, J., Daelemans, W.: Recent Advances in Memory-Based Part-of-Speech Tagging, Actas del VI Simposio Internacional de Comunicacion Social, Santiago de Cuba, (1999) 590–597
9. Marquez, L., Rodriguez, H.: Part-of-Speech Tagging Using Decision Trees, Proceedings of ECML (1998) 25–36
10. Brants, T.: TnT - A Statistical Part- of-Speech Tagger, Proceedings of the 6th Conference on Applied Natural Language Processing, Seattle (2000).
11. Cutting, D., Kupiec, J., Pedersen, J., Sibun, P.: A practical part-of-speech tagger, Proceedings of the 3rd Conference on Applied Natural Language Processing (1992)
12. Brill, E., Wu, J.: Classifier Combination for Improved Lexical Disambiguation. Proceedings of the 36th Annual Meeting of the Association for Computational Linguistics and 17th International Conference on Computational Linguistics (1998)

13. Halteren, V., Zavrel, J., Daelemans, W.: Improving Accuracy in Word Class Tagging through the Combination of Machine Learning Systems, Computational linguistics Vol. 27 (2001) 199–229
14. Quinlan, J.R: C4.5: Programs for Machine Learning, Morgan Kaufmann San Mateo, 1993.
15. Cohen, W.: Fast Effective Rule Induction, Proceedings of the 12th ICML (1995).
16. Frank, E., Witten, I.H.: Generating Accurate Rule Sets Without Global Optimization, Shavlik, J. Eds., Proceedings of the 15th International Conference on Machine Learning, Madison, Wisconsin (1998) 144–151
17. Amrani, A., Azé, J., Kodratoff, Y.: ETIQ: Logiciel d'aide à l'étiquetage morpho-syntaxique de textes de spécialité. Dans la revue RNTI, numéro spécial EGC'2005 (session démonstrations) Vol. E3 (2005) 673-678.
18. Halliday, M.A.K.: System and Function in Language, Oxford University Press., London, (1976)
19. Roche, M., Heitz, T., Matte-Tailliez, O., Kodratoff, Y.: EXIT: Un système itératif pour l'extraction de la terminologie du domaine à partir de corpus spécialisés, International Conference on Statistical Analysis of Textual Data (JADT'04) (2004) 946–956
20. Church, K.W., Hanks, P.: Word association norms, mutual information, and lexicography, Computational Linguistics Vol. 16 (1990) 22–29
21. Daille, B., Gaussier, E., Langé, J.: An evaluation of statistical scores for word association, The Tbilisi Symposium on Logic, Language and Computation, CSLI Publications (1998) 177–188
22. Nerima, L., Seretan, V., Wehrli, E.: Creating a multilingual collocations dictionary from large text corpora, Proceedings of Conference of the European Chapter of the Association for Computational Linguistics (EACL) (2003) 131–134
23. Roche, M.: Intégration de la construction de la terminologie de domaines spécialisés dans un processus global de fouille de textes. Thèse de Doctorat en Informatique (PhD thesis), Université Paris-Sud, France (2004)
24. Xu, F., Kurz, D., Piskorski, J., Schmeier, S.: A Domain Adaptive Approach to Automatic Acquisition of Domain Relevant Terms and their Relations with Bootstrapping, Proceedings of the 3rd International Conference on Language Resources and Evaluation (2002)
25. Dunning, T.,E.: Accurate Methods for the Statistics of Surprise and Coincidence, Computational Linguistics Vol. 19(1) (1993) 61–74
26. Thanopoulos, A., Fakotakis, N., Kokkianakis, G.: Comparative Evaluation of Collocation Extraction Metrics, Proceedings of 3rd International Conference on Language Resources and Evaluation (LREC'02), Vol. 2 (2002) 620–625
27. Aussenac-Gilles, N., Bourigault, D.: The Th(IC)2 Initiative: Corpus-Based Thesaurus Construction for Indexing WWW Documents, Proceedings of the EKAW'2000 Workshop on Ontologies and Texts, Vol. 51 (2000)
28. Alphonse, E., Rouveirol, C.: Lazy Propositionalisation for Relational Learning, Proceedings of the 14th European Conference on Artificial Intelligence (2000) 256-260

Vocabulary Completion Through Word Cooccurrence Analysis Using Unlabeled Documents for Text Categorization

Simon Réhel and Guy W. Mineau

Department of Computer Science, Université Laval, Québec, Canada
{Simon.Rehel, Guy.Mineau}@ift.ulaval.ca

Abstract. Automated text categorization consists of developing computer programs able to autonomously assign texts to predefined categories, on the basis of their content. Such applications are possible thanks to supervised learning, which implies a training on manually labeled documents. During this phase, the system discovers links between relevant terms (the vocabulary) and identified categories. However, the construction of a training set is long and expensive. This paper suggests a way to assist text classifiers in the gathering of the vocabulary when the number of examples is limited, in which case the success rate is not at its best. It proposes to analyze word cooccurrence within a collection of non-labeled documents in order to augment the vocabulary used by the classifier. The representation of new documents to classify would benefit from this augmented vocabulary. What is expected is an improvement of the classifier's success rate despite its limited training set.

1 Introduction

The continuous growth of the amount of information available to us brings an increasing need for efficient ways to manage it. Automated text categorization is one of these tools designed to facilitate information management, among others like information retrieval, databases, data mining, etc. While, at the beginning, knowledge engineering was the principal way to tackle this problem, since the end of the eighties, machine learning is considered a better solution for many types of application. Under this paradigm, a classifier is trained on a collection of texts already associated to category labels. It tries to associate words and specific categories so that this association is discriminating with regards to other categories. Such supervised learning implies the construction of a training set, i.e., the manually labeling of text documents. It is an expensive task and the perspective of having to undertake it can cause some projects to abort.

In this paper, we propose to consider the idea of word cooccurrence, which refers to the tendency of two words to appear in the same context [5], for instance in the same documents. Cooccurrence is appealing since it is easy to study it within unlabeled texts and, moreover, it refers to the semantic of words. Then it

B. Kégl and G. Lapalme (Eds.): AI 2005, LNAI 3501, pp. 377–388, 2005.

lets us believe that the text categorization process could benefit from this kind of knowledge, at a low cost since unlabeled data is involved.

The most popular way to represent texts submitted to a classifier is the vectorial model [8]. Each text is usually represented by a vector of n weighted terms, where each of the n features refers to a different word appearing in the text collection. The weight of each feature can be determined by different techniques, the most popular being the standard *tdidf* weighting function. The fact is that the vocabulary recognized by the classifier, i.e., the n features, is entirely determined by the training examples. Effectively, during the training phase, the labeled examples are transformed into vectors whose length is set by the number of different words appearing in the training collection (minus those rejected by the feature selection process). Later, when a new text is submitted to the classifier in order to be classified, it has to be transformed into a vector of the same length as the training vectors. The consequence of this phenomenon is that all the words unknown of the classifier are discarded and ignored by the categorization process. These words do not contribute to the determination of the document category. We can see an analogy with students learning a second language. When being asked a question in that language, they may deduce the meaning of the question with the only help of the words they already know, at that stage of their learning.

We can notice that a large training set will produce a large recognized vocabulary. Inversely, a small training set will involve a small recognized vocabulary. In this last situation, when new documents are submitted to the classifier, more words are ignored. These words are potentially useful to the categorization process, so we assume that the phenomenon we have just discussed is one of the reasons why a poor classification performance results from the use of a small training set.

The remainder of the paper is organized as follows. In Section 2, we discuss some literature related to our work. Section 3 describes the method we propose. Experimental settings chosen to evaluate our approach and results of our experimentations are presented in Section 4. Finally, conclusions and future work are discussed in Section 5.

2   Relevant Literature

The idea of exploiting unlabeled documents to assist text categorization has been explored a few times in the past, as it will be shown in this section. A fact supporting this proposition is that even if these documents do not contain information about category membership, they contain information about relations between words. Among others, [6] suggested to use an Expectation-Maximization (EM) algorithm in combination with a naive Bayes classifier. First, a model is learned with labeled examples. Then, several EM iterations allow the classification of unlabeled examples. After that process, the resulting collection of classified documents is used to estimate a new naive Bayes classifier. Iterations are performed until no more improvement is observed.

Another proposition about how to use unlabeled data was done by [11]. They suggested to take advantage of unlabeled data to perform latent semantic indexing (LSI). This technique consists of describing textual data in a new smaller semantic space. To achieve that, a singular value decomposition process is involved. Since this transformation does not need information about category membership, it can be done on both labeled and unlabeled documents. This additional knowledge enables a more accurate estimation of the new vectorial space, based on richer and more reliable patterns for data in the given domain.

Through [12], they also put in evidence that nearest-neighbor classification can use this background knowledge to assess the similarity of training and test examples. If an unlabeled document is close to both a training example and a test example, then these two texts can be considered close to each other, even if they do not share any words.

As for [1], they developed a co-training algorithm which applies to problems where the target concept can be described in different ways. Each view of the data is used to learn an hypothesis, and each hypothesis is used to classify unlabeled data. The data labeled by one classifier is then used to train the other learner.

Now, what we propose in this paper is another way of exploiting unlabeled documents in a text categorization context. But the originality of our work lies in the type of knowledge extracted from these documents: word cooccurrence. How we include this knowledge in the categorization process also distinguish our approach from those presented before: we modify the representation of the texts to classify before they are submitted to the classifier.

3   Using Word Cooccurrence in Unlabeled Documents

3.1   Proposed Method

To tackle the problem of the poor vocabulary resulting from a small training set, we propose to study word cooccurrence inside a collection of non-labeled documents and then to use this information to modify the representation of texts to classify. The idea is to simulate, in a given document, for each unknown word, the presence of a known word which appeared to be very cooccurrent with the unknown word, the cooccurrence being measured in the set of non-labeled documents. More precisely, on one side we take a subset of the words appearing in the documents to classify but not present in the vocabulary of the classifier. On the other side, we have a subset of this vocabulary. The cooccurrence of each pair of words is then computed inside a collection of non-labeled texts. This collection, larger than the training set, will probably contain a great part of the unknown words. So it becomes possible to study the relative behavior of these previously unseen words with those the classifier knows. The next step is, for each unknown word, to look at the known word with which it is the most cooccurrent. If their association score exceeds a certain threshold (determined empirically) then we assume that the presence of one of these words is a good indication of the presence of the other one. Then we simulate the presence of the known word in each text containing the unknown word. This will have an influence on the categorization process. These words being supposed to appear in the same context, they are supposed to appear in similar documents, and so in the same categories. This fact makes us believe that the impact of our method should be positive.

To reduce the computation time and to be sure that only significant words are processed, we chose to include in the cooccurrence study only a subset of the base vocabulary. For each category, we retain the word[1] which seems more related to it, on the basis of the chi-square (χ^2) test. As for the unknown words, we decided to only consider those which appear in a minimum number of documents. This way, the computation time is minimized and we avoid considering accidental words (noise) that do not have or should not have an impact on the results. Figure 1 illustrates the whole process proposed in this paper.

3.2 Cooccurrence Analysis

At this point, now that the overall process has been introduced, it is essential to bring some precision about the notion of cooccurrence that we use. As mentioned before, it is a form of association between words that are likely to appear in the same context [5]. Some examples are "doctor" and "nurse", "plane" and "airport", "teacher" and "student", etc. Many association measures exist to numerically assess the level of cooccurrence between two words. These measures are usually the same that are used to evaluate collocation, with the difference being the considered context. As for collocation, words have to appear close to each other. In the case of cooccurrence, we look for words appearing together in a larger context. We decided to consider as cooccurrent the words that are likely to appear in the same documents. Almost all of measures are based on the values filling Table 1:

Table 1. Contingency table used to compute an association score between two words

	Word 2 present	Word 2 absent
Word 1 present	a	b
Word 1 absent	c	d

Through our work, we studied in depth three principal measures: χ^2 test, mutual information and likelihood ratio, which are detailed in [5]. We retained the χ^2 test because it is a widely used measure and because it generated the best results in combination with our method, these results being presented in Section 4.2.

---

[1] We tried to keep more words for each category, but the best results were obtained when keeping only one of them, the most related to the category.

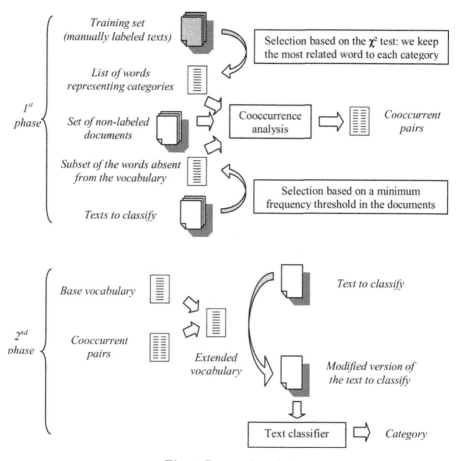

Fig. 1. Proposed method

3.3 Chi-Square Test Overview

The χ^2 test is a classic way of performing hypothesis testing. An independence hypothesis H_0 is formulated and then we compare the frequencies observed in a text collection with those expected if H_0 were true. If the difference is important, we can reject the independence hypothesis and assume there is dependence. This notion is reflected in this equation, based on Table 1:

$$\chi^2 = \sum_{i,j} \frac{(O_{ij} - E_{ij})^2}{E_{ij}} \,.$$

(1)

where i and j cover respectively the rows and the columns of Table 1, O_{ij} is the observed value for the cell (i, j) and E_{ij} is the expected value for the cell (i, j).

Observed values are extracted from a text collection, while expected values are computed from marginal probabilities. After some algebraic manipulations and simplifications[2] , we obtain the following expression from which we get the χ^2 value:

$$\chi^2 = \frac{N(ad - bc)^2}{(a + b)(a + c)(b + d)(c + d)} \; .$$ (2)

where N is the total number of documents.

When the sample size is sufficiently high, the χ^2 test follows a χ^2 distribution. We know the confidence level associated to the computed value by consulting a distribution table. For example, above the critical value $\chi^2 = 3.841$, we can reject the independence hypothesis with a 95% confidence level.

3.4   Implementation Considerations

In terms of implementation, the proposed method only requires a module computing the four values of Table 1, on the basis of the presence or not of words in documents. The implied manipulations consist of word tokenization and word search in a list. That seems to be simple, but some indexation and optimization considerations must be taken in account. An easy and effective way to achieve that is to use a search engine, to submit queries and to collect results. Besides the cooccurrence module, a procedure has to be added to a traditional text categorization application in order to modify the text representation according to the cooccurrence study. Again, this does not represent a great programming challenge.

3.5   Cooccurrence Threshold

The determination of the cooccurrence threshold which rules the addition of words into the documents is important. Its aim is to judge whether the cooccurrence between two words is strong enough to justify the simulation of one by the other in a text. With the χ^2 test that we chose, we can think of using distribution tables as mentioned above. This way, we can argue that a score larger than 3.841 confers a confidence of 95% to the dependence of the words. Though true, it does not indicate clearly if they are dependent enough to command an addition into the texts. Without any other theoretical background on which to base the threshold choice, the strategy that we were forced to adopt is the determination of an empirical threshold. We tried different values and the best results are presented in Section 4.2.

4   Experimentation and Results

4.1   Experimental Settings

Text Collections. To evaluate the benefits of the preceding approach, we chose three different collections available and easily accessible, used in past experiments and susceptible to be used in the future. These collections contain different

---

[2] See [5] for more details.

types of texts and involve different categorization tasks (number of categories, number of assignments for each document, etc.), since these factors influence significantly the results. Our goal was to make sure that our approach was useful in various contexts. For our results to be statistically significant, we also took care to choose test sets containing a sufficient number of documents.

First, we used Reuters Corpus Volume 1 (RCV1)[3], containing more than 800,000 short newswire stories, manually classified into more than 100 categories [7]. Training sets of different size (from 100 to 1000 documents) were formed, choosing the first documents of this collection. As for the test set, it stayed the same for each experiment: 10,000 consecutive documents beginning at the $400,000^{th}$ one. A third set was extracted from this collection, the non-labeled data where cooccurrence analysis was done: the last two months of the collection, July and August 1997, containing a little more than 100,000 texts.

A second collection was used, WebKB[4]. It included web pages from computer science departments of several American universities. Among the seven original categories, we retained only the four most populous except "Others": "Course", "Student", "Faculty" and "Project", like in [6] and [11]. The division between training and testing documents was done like in [6], as summarized in the next lines. Four test sets were formed, each containing the pages from one of the four computer science departments included entirely in the corpus (Cornell, Texas, Washington, Wisconsin). For each of them, ten training sets were formed by choosing randomly some texts among those not included in the given test set. Our results correspond to the average of the scores obtained for a given training set size on this corpus. To study the cooccurrence, we chose to use all the 8,007 documents of the collection, because this size was already quite small.

The third collection we chose is Ohsumed [2]. It is composed of 300,000 entries of a medical database, each containing a title and an abstract. In fact, they are references about medical literature managed by the National Library of Medicine. Labels correspond to valid MeSH[5] terms. Like in [4], we retained only the 49 sub-categories of "Heart Diseases" containing more than 75 documents. Traditionally, the training set contained 1988–1990 texts and the test set, 1991 texts. In our case, only the first 2,000 texts served for our training. Among them, we built sets of different sizes and again, our results correspond to the average of the scores obtained for a given training set size on this corpus. The last 10,445 documents of the training set were used for the cooccurrence analysis. But we used integrally the 3,632 texts of 1991 for the testing phase.

Classifiers. A second point to clarify about our evaluation methodology is the type of classifiers used. We chose two of the top-performing algorithms, kNN and SVM [9][10]. In either case, documents were represented according to the vectorial approach, each attribute representing a word in the vocabulary. No stemming and no stop words removing processes were used. As for the weighting

---

[3] http://about.reuters.com/researchandstandards/corpus/
[4] http://www-2.cs.cmu.edu/afs/cs.cmu.edu/project/theo-20/www/data/
[5] Acronym for "Medical Subject Headings".

technique, we chose the traditional *tfidf* function. We applied a feature selection process, which begins by removing all the words appearing in less than a fixed number of documents (empirically set to 4). Then, a second selection was done on the basis of the information gain criterion, a threshold being set to 0.01. The kNN classifier used in our experiments follows a standard configuration. The cosine similarity function is used to compare documents and 30 neighbors are considered. A threshold is learned on the training set for each category, a threshold ruling when to classify a text under a category. This threshold is chosen to minimize the number of classification errors on the training examples. As for the SVM classifier, the SVM^{light} package[6] was used [3].

Table 2. Evaluation of the proposed method on the RCV1 corpus

Training set size	Micro-F1 without cooccurrence analysis	Micro-F1 with cooccurrence analysis	Difference (absolute value)	Difference (percentage)
kNN classifier				
100	0.191	0.2142	+ 0.0232	+ 12.15
200	0.2152	0.2506	+ 0.0354	+ 16.45
300	0.2829	0.3065	+ 0.0236	+ 8.34
400	0.4015	0.4226	+ 0.0211	+ 5.26
500	0.4487	0.473	+ 0.0243	+ 5.42
1000	0.6143	0.6233	+ 0.0090	+ 1.47
SVM classifier				
100	0.2029	0.2077	+ 0.0048	+ 2.37
200	0.178	0.1709	− 0.0071	− 3.99
300	0.2633	0.266	+ 0.0027	+ 1.03
400	0.3828	0.3934	+ 0.0106	+ 2.77
500	0.415	0.4288	+ 0.0138	+ 3.33
1000	0.5674	0.5758	+ 0.0084	+ 1.48

4.2   Results

We performed several experiments to assess the validity of the technique that we propose. Here we present an overview of the results we obtained. Tables 2, 3 and 4 present respectively what was observed on the RCV1, WebKB and Ohsumed collections. We can compare micro-F1[7] scores obtained with and without cooccurrence analysis on different training set sizes, in the case of the two classifiers presented before. For each test, many cooccurrence threshold values were tried and the scores presented represent the best performance observed among these values.

---

[6] http://svmlight.joachims.org/
[7] Micro-F1 measure is clearly defined in [8].

A possible explanation for the slighter impact observed with the Ohsumed collection is that the vocabulary of these medical texts is probably more controlled and more specialized. Consequently, fewer synonyms would be encountered and fewer cooccurrence phenomena would occur.

Table 3. Evaluation of the proposed method on the WebKB corpus

Training set size	Micro-F1 without cooccurrence analysis	Micro-F1 with cooccurrence analysis	Difference (absolute value)	Difference (percentage)
kNN classifier				
20	0.5445	0.5591	+ 0.0146	+ 2.68
40	0.6033	0.6205	+ 0.0172	+ 2.85
80	0.6147	0.628	+ 0.0133	+ 2.16
SVM classifier				
20	0.4303	0.4736	+ 0.0433	+ 10.06
40	0.4775	0.5133	+ 0.0358	+ 7.50
80	0.5403	0.5743	+ 0.0340	+ 6.29

Table 4. Evaluation of the proposed method on the Ohsumed corpus

Training set size	Micro-F1 without cooccurrence analysis	Micro-F1 with cooccurrence analysis	Difference (absolute value)	Difference (percentage)
kNN classifier				
100	0.2409	0.2467	+ 0.0058	+ 2.41
500	0.4435	0.4529	+ 0.0095	+ 2.13
1000	0.5573	0.5592	+ 0.0019	+ 0.34
2000	0.586	0.5863	+ 0.0003	+ 0.05
SVM classifier				
100	0.1814	0.189	+ 0.0076	+ 4.19
500	0.4228	0.4367	+ 0.0139	+ 3.29
1000	0.5850	0.5888	+ 0.0038	+ 0.65
2000	0.635	0.6372	+ 0.0022	+ 0.35

[6] and [11] used respectively an EM algorithm and latent semantic indexing (LSI) to benefit from non-labeled documents. They tested their respective approach on the WebKB corpus, among others. In order to compare our results, we have run a naive Bayes classifier (because the EM algorithm is applied on

Table 5. Comparison of our approach with two others methods using non-labeled data

Training set size	Bayes only	Bayes + EM	LSI	Bayes only	Bayes + cooccurrence analysis
20	0.6031	0.6722	0.6477	0.6113	0.6176
40	0.6912	0.7458	0.6960	0.7116	0.7206
80	0.7599	0.7639	0.7255	0.7337	0.7374

this type of classifier) without and with cooccurrence analysis on the WebKB corpus. Table 5 shows published results about the EM algorithm and LSI, then results obtained from our experimentations about cooccurrence analysis. Training sets were formed in a similar way as in [6], but are not identical because the methodology involves a random factor. This explains the differences observed for the basic naive Bayes classifier.

We can see that the gains obtained with EM are superior than those obtained with our approach for very small training sets. But, for 80 training documents, the benefits are comparable. For larger training sets, EM even leads to a performance decrease. Cooccurrence analysis, even if it is less efficient for very small training sets, does not cause any decrease in performance with more training documents. Only the gains decrease gradually until they become negligible. Compared to the LSI approach, for 40 training documents, cooccurrence analysis makes the classifier reach a superior score. In a word, we cannot say that our approach is better than the other two, because they seem to perform differently depending on the conditions. However, we notice that on the WebKB corpus, their performances are at the same level. It would be interesting to perform a more exhaustive comparison.

5   Conclusion and Future Work

These results open an interesting discussion. We can notice that in all cases (except one), our cooccurrence approach generated some improvement in the success rate. In other words, modifying the representation of the documents to be classified according to the cooccurrence of new (unknown) words with words of the base vocabulary enabled a higher micro-F1 score.

As observed above, the improvement is slight. But, an important point in its favor is that its integration into a categorization application does not cost human work. The only required task is to collect additional non-labeled documents. It appears that it is a fast and easy activity which can be automated. When the precision of the classification task is important despite a small training set, it may be worth it to use our approach in any case.

It is also possible to notice that the proposed technique was profitable to both the kNN and the SVM classifiers. It is compatible with different types of learning algorithms and we can hope that it would be profitable to other classifiers as well (to be investigated).

One thing to keep in mind is that our results are based on small training sets. The reason is that the main interest of our approach is to soften the impact of a lack of training documents. When the training is done on a relatively large number of examples, the cooccurrence analysis process is not needed anymore, because there are fewer unknown words. Though not harmful, the approach becomes useless. This observation fits with the results of [6] and [11]. According to them, benefits of the use of non-labeled documents are smaller when the training set is larger. However, there should be enough training documents to allow a relevant cooccurrence study. It is why our experiments were focused on training sets relatively small, but containing enough examples so that the method can improve the categorization process.

Many variables play a role in the text categorization process. There are an almost infinite number of parameter configurations to test, but time is limited. It would have been interesting to observe the behavior of our approach on more than three text collections, though we chose very large collections typical of same applications. In a similar way, it would have been interesting to use more than two classifiers, though we chose those mainly used in text classification. Modifying some parameters of the classifier or the feature selection technique could have shown some other impact on the success rate. Also, our experiments did not take into consideration the nature of the non-labeled data: perhaps the fact that these documents are similar or not to the documents submitted to the classifier can influence the results. Also the size of this non-labeled collection has not been studied. Finally, another important thing to clarify is the determination of the cooccurrence threshold. It would be preferable to develop a precise way to choose it, instead of relying on empirical observations.

In conclusion, automated text categorization is a field where a lot has been accomplished, but which still offers a lot of challenges. This technology has the potential to support useful and interesting applications, but some problems are still to be solved. This paper aimed at one of these problems: the cost of building a training set. We have shown that studying word cooccurrence within a collection of non-labeled texts could help a classifier trained on a small number of documents by increasing its vocabulary and improving its capacity to classify new texts, at a low cost. Since it is inexpensive to implement and to run, and since it does not degrade the success rate, this approach can then be an alternative solution to the use of large training sets costly to build.

References

1. A. Blum & T. Mitchell. Combining Labeled and Unlabeled Data with Co-training. *Proc. of the 11th Annual Conference on Computational Learning Theory*, pp. 92–100, 1998.
2. W. Hersh, C. Buckley, T.J. Leone & D. Hickman. Ohsumed: an Interactive Retrieval Evaluation and New Large Text Collection for Research. *Proc. of SIGIR-94*, pp. 192–201, 1994.
3. T. Joachims. Text Categorization with Support Vector Machines: Learning with Many Relevant Features. *Proc. of the 10th European Conference on Machine Learning*, pp. 137–142, Springer Verlag, 1998.

4. D.D. Lewis, R.E. Schapire, J.P. Callan & R. Papka. Training Algorithms for Linear Text Classifiers. *Proc. of SIGIR-96*, pp. 298–306, 1996.
5. C.D. Manning & H. Schütze. *Foundations of Statistical Natural Language Processing*, MIT Press, 1999.
6. K. Nigam, A.K. McCallum, S. Thrun & T. Mitchell. Text Classification from Labeled and Unlabeled Documents using EM. *Machine Learning*, 39(2/3), pp. 103–134, 2000.
7. T.G. Rose, M. Stevenson & M. Whitehead. The Reuters Corpus Volume 1 - from Yesterday's News to Tomorrow's Language Resources. *Proc. of the 3rd International Conference on Language Resources and Evaluation*, pp. 827–832, 2002.
8. F. Sebastiani. A Tutorial on Automated Text Categorisation. *Proc. of the 1st Argentinian Symposium on Artificial Intelligence*, pp. 7–35, 1999.
9. Y. Yang. An Evaluation of Statistical Approaches to Text Categorization. *Information Retrieval*, 1(1/2), pp. 69–90, 1999.
10. Y. Yang & X. Liu. A Re-examination of Text Categorization Methods. *Proc. of SIGIR-99*, pp. 42–49, 1999.
11. S. Zelikovitz & H. Hirsh. Using LSI for Text Classification in the Presence of Background Text. *Proc. of the 10th ACM International Conference on Information and Knowledge Management*, pp. 113–118, ACM Press, 2001.
12. S. Zelikovitz & H. Hirsh. Integrating Background Knowledge into Nearest-Neighbor Text Classification. *Proc. of the 6th European Conference on Case-Based Reasoning*, pp. 1–5, Springer Verlag, 2002.

Voting Between Multiple Data Representations for Text Chunking*

Hong Shen and Anoop Sarkar

School of Computing Science,
Simon Fraser University,
Burnaby, BC V5A 1S6, Canada
{hshen, anoop}@cs.sfu.ca

Abstract. This paper considers the hypothesis that voting between *multiple data representations* can be more accurate than voting between *multiple learning models*. This hypothesis has been considered before (cf. [San00]) but the focus was on voting methods rather than the data representations. In this paper, we focus on choosing specific data representations combined with simple majority voting. On the community standard CoNLL-2000 data set, using no additional knowledge sources apart from the training data, we achieved 94.01 $F_{\beta=1}$ score for arbitrary phrase identification compared to the previous best $F_{\beta=1}$ 93.90. We also obtained 95.23 $F_{\beta=1}$ score for Base NP identification. Significance tests show that our Base NP identification score is significantly better than the previous comparable best $F_{\beta=1}$ score of 94.22. Our main contribution is that our model is a fast linear time approach and the previous best approach is significantly slower than our system.

1   Introduction

Text chunking or *shallow parsing* is the task of finding non-recursive phrases in a given sentence of natural language text. Due to the fact that the phrases are assumed to be non-overlapping, the phrase boundaries can be treated as labels, one per word in the input sentence, and *sequence learning* or *sequence prediction* techniques such as the source-channel approach over n-grams can be used to find the most likely sequence of such labels. This was the method introduced in [RM95] where noun phrase chunks were encoded as labels (or tags) on words: **I** for words that are inside a noun chunk, **O** for words outside a chunk, and **B** for a word on the boundary, i.e a word that immediately follows a word with an **I** tag. Chunking was defined as the prediction of a sequence of **I**, **B**, and **O** labels given a word sequence as input. Additional information such as part of speech tags are often used in this prediction. This paper concentrates on the text chunking task: both Base noun phrase (NP) chunking [RM95] and the CoNLL-2000 arbitrary phrase chunking task [SB00]. The CoNLL-2000 shared task considers other chunk types in addition to noun phrases (NPs), such as verb phrases (VPs), among others. The advantage in using these data sets is that they are freely available for experimental

---

* We would like to thank Fred Popowich and the anonymous reviewers for their comments.

B. Kégl and G. Lapalme (Eds.): AI 2005, LNAI 3501, pp. 389–400, 2005.

comparisons[1]. As a result, there are close to 30 publications that have reported results on these two data sets indicating that improvements on these tasks or even matching the best result is very unlikely to occur using obvious or simple methods.

In order to focus on the specific contribution of multiple data representations, we use a simple trigram model for tagging and chunking[2]. We show that a trigram model for chunking combined with voting between multiple data representations can obtain results equal to the best on the community standard CoNLL-2000 text chunking data set. Using no additional knowledge sources apart from the training data, we achieved 94.01 $F_{\beta=1}$ score for arbitrary phrase identification compared to the previous best $F_{\beta=1}$ 93.90 [KM01][3]. The highest score reported on the CoNLL-2000 data set is 94.17% by [ZDJ02] but this result used a full-fledged parser as an additional knowledge source. Without the parser, their score was 93.57%. We also obtained 95.23 $F_{\beta=1}$ score for Base NP identification. Significance tests show that our Base NP identification score is significantly better than the previous comparable state-of-the-art $F_{\beta=1}$ of 94.22 [KM01][4].

While voting is a commonly used method, it is commonly used as a means to combine the output of multiple machine learning systems. Like [San00] and [KM01] we examine voting between *multiple data representations*. However, we focus purely on the advantage of carefully chosen data representations. We use simple majority voting and a trigram chunking model to focus on the issue of the choice of data representation. Our results show that our approach outperforms most other voting approaches and is comparable to the previous best approach on the same dataset [KM01]. In addition, as we will show when we compare our approach to [KM01] our main contribution is that our model is a fast linear time approach. [KM01] uses multiple Support Vector Machine classifiers which is slower by a significant order of magnitude.

Based on our empirical results, we show that choosing the right representation (or the types of features used) can be a very powerful alternative in sequence prediction, even when used with relatively simple machine learning methods.

2   The Task: Text Chunking

The text chunking problem partitions input sentences into syntactically related non-overlapping groups or chunks. For example, the sentence:

---

[1] From `http://lcg-www.uia.ac.be/~erikt/research/np-chunking.html` and `http://cnts.uia.ac.be/conll2000/chunking/`

[2] Explained in many textbooks. See [Cha96], p.43-56.

[3] The score commonly quoted from [KM01] is 93.91% but this score was based on the IOE1 representation *on the test data* (see explanation in Section 3). In any case, their method provides almost identical accuracy across all representations, but comparable results can be shown only in the IOB2 representation.

[4] Some other approaches obtained their Base NP scores by first performing the arbitrary phrase chunking task and throwing away all other phrases except noun phrases. We do not compare against those scores here for simplicity, since it is technically a different task. Although we are competitive in this other comparison as well.

In early trading in Hong Kong Monday , gold was quoted at $ 366.50 an ounce .
can be segmented into the following noun phrase chunks:

In (early trading) in (Hong Kong) (Monday) , (gold) was quoted at ($ 366.50)
(an ounce).

The CoNLL-2000 shared task [SB00] was set up as a more general form of the text
chunking problem, with additional types in addition to noun phrase chunk types. The
CoNLL-2000 data has 11 different chunk types: $\mathcal{T} = \{$ ADJP, ADVP, CONJP, INTJ,
LST, NP, PP, PRT, SBAR, VP, UCP $\}$. However, it is important to note that despite the
large number of chunk types, the NP, VP and PP types account for 95% of all chunk
occurrences. The chunk tags in the data are represented the following three types of tags:

B-t first word of a chunk of type $t \in \mathcal{T}$
I-t non-initial word of a chunk of type $t \in \mathcal{T}$
O word outside of any chunk

The CoNLL-2000 data was based on the noun phrase chunk data extracted by [RM95]
from the Penn Treebank. It contains WSJ sections 15-18 of the Penn Treebank (211727
tokens) as training data and section 20 of the Treebank (47377 tokens) as test data. The
difference between the two is that Base NP chunking results are evaluated in IOB1 format,
while CoNLL-2000 shared task results are evaluated in IOB2 format (see Section 3 for
definitions of IOB1 and IOB2). The test data set is processed with a part of speech (POS)
tagger (for details, see [SB00]) in order to provide additional information. For example,
the above sentence would be assigned POS tags from the Penn Treebank POS tagset as
follows:

In_IN early_JJ trading_NN in_IN Hong_NNP Kong_NNP Monday_NNP ,_, gold_NN
was_VBD quoted_VBN at_IN $_$ 366.50_CD an_DT ounce_IN ._.

Given the high accuracy of POS tagging, only about 3% to 4% of the tokens are expected to be mistagged in the test data. Evaluation for this task is based on three figures:
precision (P) is the percentage of detected phrases that are correct, *recall* (R) is the
percentage of phrases in the data that were detected, and the $F_{\beta=1}$ score which is the
harmonic mean of precision and recall.[5] In this paper, these values are computed using
the standard evaluation script that is distributed along with the CoNLL-2000 data set.

3   Multiple Data Representations

We use the following different categories of data representations for the text chunking
task. In each case, we describe the non-overlapping chunks with one of the following
tag representations and then append the chunk type as a suffix, except for the **O** tag. An
example that shows all these representations is provided in Figure 1.

---

[5] $F_\beta = \frac{(\beta^2+1)pr}{\beta^2 p+r}$

word	IOB1	IOB2	IOE1	IOE2	O+C
In	O	O	O	O	O
early	I	B	I	I	B
trading	I	I	I	E	E
in	O	O	O	O	O
Hong	I	B	I	I	B
Kong	I	I	E	E	E
Monday	B	B	I	E	S
,	O	O	O	O	O
gold	I	B	I	E	S
was	O	O	O	O	O
quoted	O	O	O	O	O
at	O	O	O	O	O
$	I	B	I	I	B
366.50	I	I	E	E	E
an	B	B	I	I	B
ounce	I	I	I	E	E
.	O	O	O	O	O

Fig. 1. The noun chunk tag sequences for the example sentence, *In early trading in Hong Kong Monday , gold was quoted at $ 366.50 an ounce .* is shown represented in five different data representations. We only show noun phrase chunks in this example, all tags except **O** tags will include the type suffix for chunks of different types

3.1 The Inside/Outside Representation

This representation from [RM95] represents chunks with three tags as follows:

I Current token is inside chunk
B Current token is on the boundary, starting a new chunk with previous token tagged with **I**
O Current token is outside any chunk

[SV99] introduced some variants of this IOB representation: the above representation was now called IOB1. The new variants were called IOB2, IOE1 and IOE2. IOB2 differs from IOB1 in the assignment of tag **B** to every chunk-initial token regardless of whether the next token is inside a chunk. IOE1 differs from IOB1 in that instead of tag **B**, a tag **E** is used for the final token of a chunk that is immediately followed by a token with tag **I**. IOE2 is a variant of IOE1 in which each final word of a chunk is tagged with **E** regardless of whether is followed by a token inside a chunk. The representation used in the test data for CoNLL-2000 data set is the IOB2 representation. As a result, all figures reported using the CoNLL-2000 evaluation are based on this representation. Obviously, evaluation on different representations can be much higher but this kind of evaluation is not comparable with evaluations done using other representations and does not provide us with any insight about the methods we are evaluating. The objective in [SV99] was to see if the representation could improve accuracy for a single model. In contrast, in this paper we explore the question of whether these different representations can provide information that can be exploited using voting.

3.2   The Start/End Representation

This representation is often referred to as O+C and uses five tags. It was introduced in [UMM+00]. This representation was used as a single representation in [KM01] but was not used in the voting scheme in that paper.

B Current token begins a chunk consisting of more than one token (think of it as [)
E Current token ends a chunk consisting of more than one token (think of it as])
I Current token is inside a chunk consisting of more than one token
S Current token is a chunk with exactly one token (think of it as [])
O Current token is outside any chunk

[SV99] explored the use of open and close brackets as well, but as separate un-coordinated representations, and hence without the need for the **S** tag above.

4   The Model

We wanted to use a simple machine learning model in order to discover the power of voting when applied to multiple data representations. We chose a simple trigram-based model trained using the maximum likelihood estimates based on frequencies from training data where the output label sequences (state transitions, in this case) are fully observed. Decoding on the test data set is done using the Viterbi algorithm[6]. In our experiments, we used the TnT tagger [Bra00] which implements the model described above. The trigram model used in this paper deals with unseen events by using linear interpolation. The trigram probability is interpolated with bigram and unigram probabilities, and the interpolation weights are chosen based on n-gram frequencies in training data [Bra00].

4.1   Baseline

The baseline results of the CoNLL-2000 and Base NP chunking were obtained by selecting the chunk tag which was most frequently associated with the current part-of-speech tag. The trigram model described above when using only part of speech tags as input. The model produced an $F_{\beta=1}$ score of 84.33 in IOB2 representation on CoNLL-2000 and an $F_{\beta=1}$ score of 79.99 in IOB1 representation on Base NP chunking as the output respectively.

4.2   Specialized Data Representation

Having only part of speech tags as input to the chunking model leads to low accuracy (as seen in the previous section). We use the proposals made in [MP02] to lexicalize our model by manipulating the data representation: changing the input and output of the function being learned to improve the accuracy of each learner. The key is to add

---

[6] Since we evaluate based on per word accuracy, a search for the best tag for each word, rather than the Viterbi best tag sequence will provide slightly higher accuracy. However, we use Viterbi since it is expedient and we focus on the improvement due to data representation voting.

Input			Output $= f_s$(Input)	
w_i	p_i	y_i	p_i or $w_i \cdot p_i$	$p_i \cdot y_i$ or $w_i \cdot p_i \cdot y_i$
You	PRP	B-NP	PRP	PRP-B-NP
will	MD	B-VP	MD	MD-B-VP
start	VB	I-VP	VB	VB-I-VP
to	TO	I-VP	TO	TO-I-VP
see	VB	I-VP	VB	VB-I-VP
shows	NNS	B-NP	NNS	NNS-B-NP
where	WRB	B-ADVP	where-WRB	where-WRB-B-ADVP
viewers	NNS	B-NP	NNS	NNS-B-NP
program	VBP	B-VP	VBP	VBP-B-VP
the	DT	B-NP	the-DT	the-DT-B-NP
program	NN	I-NP	NN	NN-I-NP

Fig. 2. Example of specialization where the words *where* and *the* belong to the set W_s

lexicalization to the model, but to effectively deal with the sparse data problem. [MP02] propose the notion of *specialization* to deal with this issue. A *specialization function* converts the original input/output representation into a new representation which can then be used to train any model that could be trained on the original representation. The specialization function as defined by [MP02] closely fits into our framework of multiple data representations. The proposal is to produce a selective lexicalization of the original model by transforming the original data representation in the training data. The test data set is also transformed but we convert back to the original form before the evaluation step. Consider the original data which is a set of examples $L = \{\ldots, \langle w_i \cdot p_i , y_i \rangle, \ldots\}$ where w_i is the input word, p_i is the input part of speech tag and y_i is the output chunk label (which varies depending on the representation used). A specialization function f_s uses a set of so-called *relevant* words W_s to convert each labelled example in L into a new representation in the following manner:

$$f_s(\langle w_i \cdot p_i , y_i \rangle) =$$
$$\begin{cases} \langle w_i \cdot p_i , w_i \cdot p_i \cdot y_i \rangle & \text{if } w_i \in W_s \\ \langle p_i , p_i \cdot y_i \rangle & \text{otherwise} \end{cases}$$

An example of specialization applied to the training data set is shown in Figure 2.

We call the model **SP** if we only specialize the output using the part of speech tag (the *otherwise* case above). The selection of the set W_s produces various kinds of lexicalized models. Following [MP02] we use a development set consisting of a held-out or deleted set of 10% from the training set in order to pick elements for W_s. The held-out set consists of every 10th sentence. The remaining set is used as the training data. We used the following specialization representations. Each of these were defined in [MP02] and for each representation below also use the particular thresholds based on experiments with a held-out set or based on experiments on the training set:

SP+Lex-WHF W_s contains words whose frequency in the training set is higher than some threshold. The threshold is picked by testing on the held-out set. The threshold obtained in our experiments was 100.

Table 1. Arbitrary phrase identification results for each setting

Specialization criteria	P(%)	R(%)	$F_{\beta=1}$
Baseline	72.58	82.14	77.07
Trigram Model (no words)	84.31	84.35	84.33
SP	89.57	89.54	89.56
SP+Lex-WCH+WTE [MP02]	91.96	92.41	92.19
SP+Lex-WCH (5DR, Majority)	93.89	94.12	**94.01**
SP+Lex-WCH (3DR, Majority)	93.54	92.97	93.25
SP+Lex-WTE (3DR, Majority)	92.49	93.00	92.75

Table 2. Arbitrary phrase identification results of 5DR majority voting with SP+Lex-WCH in IOB2

Chunk type	P(%)	R(%)	$F_{\beta=1}$
ADJP	75.54	71.92	73.68
ADVP	80.80	79.21	80.00
CONJP	60.00	66.67	63.16
INTJ	50.00	50.00	50.00
NP	95.46	95.67	95.57
PP	97.69	96.61	97.15
PRT	66.02	64.15	65.07
SBAR	77.25	85.05	80.96
VP	92.69	94.16	93.42
all	93.89	94.12	**94.01**

SP+Lex-WCH W_s contains words that belong to certain chunk types *and* which are higher than some frequency threshold. In our experiments we pick chunk types NP, VP, PP and ADVP (the most frequent chunk types) with a threshold of 50.

SP+Lex-WTE W_s contains the words whose chunk tagging error rate was higher than some threshold on the held-out set. Based on the experiments in [MP02] we pick a threshold of 2.

The experiments in [MP02] show that specialization can improve performance considerably. By combining the **Lex-WCH** and **Lex-WTE** conditions, the output tag set increases from the original set of 22 to 1341, with 225 words being used as lexical material in the model and the accuracy on the CoNLL-2000 data increases to 92.19%[7] (see Table 1 for a comparison with our voting methods).

4.3 Voting Between Multiple Representations

The notion of specialization is a good example of how the data representation can lead to higher accuracy. We extend this idea further by voting between multiple specialized data representations. The model we evaluate in this paper is simple majority voting on the output of various specialized trigram models (described above). The trigram model is trained on different data representations, and the test data set is decoded by each model. The output on the test data set is converted into a single representation, and the final label on the test data set is produced by a majority vote. We experimented with various weighted voting schemes, including setting weights for different representations based on accuracy on the held-out set, but no weighting scheme provided us with an increase in accuracy over simple majority voting. To save space, we only discuss majority voting in this paper[8].

---

[7] We replicated these results using the same trigram model described earlier.

[8] In future work, we plan to explore more sophisticated weighted voting schemes that exploit loss functions, e.g. AdaBoost.

Table 3. Arbitrary phrase identification results of 3DR majority voting with SP+Lex-WCH in IOB2

Chunk type	P(%)	R(%)	$F_{\beta=1}$
ADJP	77.94	71.00	74.31
ADVP	80.12	78.18	79.14
CONJP	66.67	66.67	66.67
INTJ	50.00	50.00	50.00
NP	94.85	94.03	94.44
PP	97.52	96.47	96.99
PRT	64.29	59.43	61.76
SBAR	76.11	83.36	79.57
VP	92.65	93.39	93.02
all	93.54	92.97	93.25

Table 4. Arbitrary phrase identification accuracy for all DRs in five evaluation formats. Each column represents the evaluation format and each row represents the training and testing format

	IOB1	IOB2	IOE1	IOE2	O+C
IOB1	92.68	93.07	92.66	92.68	94.72
IOB2	92.82	92.63	92.82	92.82	94.47
IOE1	92.82	92.82	92.87	92.87	94.64
IOE2	92.53	92.53	92.53	92.53	94.43
O+C	92.45	92.45	92.49	92.35	94.28
3DR	93.03	93.25	92.82	93.07	94.92
5DR	93.92	93.76	93.90	94.01	95.05

5   Experimental Results

In order to obtain various data representations, we transform the corpus[9] into the other data representations: IOB1(or IOB2), IOE1, IOE2 and O+C. We then transform each data representation into the format defined by specialized trigram model. We obtain a held-out set by splitting the original training set into a new training set (90% of the original training set) and a held-out set (10% of the original training set) for each data representation. Once we have all five different data representation chunked, we start to use majority voting technique to combine them into one file. In order to evaluate the accuracy, we have to transform the results into the evaluation format. This is trivial since all we need to do is to remove the enriched POS tag and lexical information from the specialized output file. In the results shown in this section, SP represents the specialized trigram model without lexical information; SP+Lex-WCH represents the specialized trigram model with lexical information defined based on Lex-WCH; 5DR represents five data representations (DR), which are IOB1, IOB2, IOE1, IOE2, O+C and we pick O+C as the default DR; 3DR represents IOB1, IOB2, IOE1 and we pick IOB2 as the default DR; Majority represents majority voting.

5.1   Arbitrary Phrase Identification (CoNLL-2000)

Table 1 gives the results of our specialized trigram model without lexical information. Based on these experiments, we select SP+Lex-WCH as our specialization technique for the voting experiments[10]. Table 2 and 3 show the results of our specialized trigram model with lexical information defined by Lex-WCH, where *all* represents the results

---

[9] CoNLL-2000 data set is originally in IOB2 format and Base NP data set is originally in IOB1 format.

[10] As pointed out by an anonymous reviewer, the number of representations participating in voting can be increased by considering all the specialization techniques. Further experiments

obtained after 3DR or 5DR majority voting respectively. Table 6 compares the results with other major approaches. Tables 5 and 6 give the final results in IOB2 and IOE2 respectively. We achieved 94.01 on F-score for both formats, which is slightly higher than [KM01], but still lower than [ZDJ02] in Table 7. However, [ZDJ02] uses a full parser which we do not use in our experiments[11].

Table 5. Arbitrary phrase identification accuracy for all DRs and all DRs are evaluated in IOB2. The voting format is the format when conducting majority voting, all the DRs are converted into this format

Voting format	P(%)	R(%)	$F_{\beta=1}$
IOB1	93.89	93.95	93.92
IOB2	93.69	93.82	93.76
IOE1	93.79	93.77	93.78
IOE2	93.89	94.12	94.01
O+C	93.84	93.98	93.91

Table 6. Arbitrary phrase identification accuracy for all DRs evaluated in IOE1

Voting format	P(%)	R(%)	$F_{\beta=1}$
IOB1	93.81	93.79	93.80
IOB2	93.69	93.82	93.76
IOE1	93.87	93.93	93.90
IOE2	93.89	94.12	94.01
O+C	93.84	94.00	93.92

5.2   Base NP Identification

Table 9 shows the final results in IOB1 format after 5DR voting. Some published papers have picked IOB2 as their evaluation format. In our testing we have found no significant difference between IOB1 and IOB2 in terms of the results obtained, however, we will follow the IOB1 format since the original test data set is in IOB1 format.

Table 8 compares the Base NP chunking results with other major approaches. We achieved 95.23 on % $F_{\beta=1}$ score, which is the best state-of-the-art score so far. We also find the NP $F_{\beta=1}$ score obtained from an arbitrary phrase chunking process is slightly higher than that from a standard Base NP chunking process. This is to be expected since the arbitrary phrase chunking problem introduces additional constraints (since it is a multi-class model) when compared to the base NP chunker.

5.3   Runtime Performance

We compare our runtime performance against [KM01] since their accuracy is identical to ours in the CoNLL-2000 task (according to our significance tests). Our approach uses a simpler learner based on specialized trigram model, which runs in linear time, while [KM01] trains pairwise classifiers to reduce multi-class classification to binary classification, and they also apply weighted voting against multiple data representations.

---

are required, but these representations overlap substantially and so the gain is likely to be minimal.

[11] Our preliminary experiments along these lines using chunks obtained from a full parser have not yet produced an improvement in accuracy.

Table 7. Comparison of accuracy with major approaches for arbitrary phrase identification

Approach	$F_{\beta=1}$
Generalized Winnow [ZDJ02] (with full parser)	94.17
Specialized Trigram Model w/ voting	**94.01**
SVM w/ DR voting [KM01]	93.90
Generalized Winnow [ZDJ02] (without full parser)	93.57
Voting w/ system combination [vH00]	93.32
MBL w/ multiple DR and system combination [San02]	92.50
Specialized Trigram Model [MP02] (no voting)	92.19

Table 8. Comparison of Base NP identification accuracy with major approaches

Approach	$F_{\beta=1}$
Specialized Trigram Model w/ voting	**95.23**
SVM w/ voting [KM01]	94.22
MBL w/ system combination [SDD$^+$00]	93.86
MBL w/ system combination [San02]	93.26

Table 9. Base NP identification accuracy for all DRs evaluated in IOB1 format. In the best performing case, IOB1 is the representation used for voting *and* the evaluation is in the IOB1 format

Voting format	P(%)	R(%)	$F_{\beta=1}$
IOB1	95.11	95.35	**95.23**
IOB2	95.05	95.34	95.19
IOE1	94.96	95.11	95.04
IOE2	94.96	95.21	95.08
O+C	95.04	95.30	95.17

Table 10. McNemar's test between Specialized Trigram Model w/ voting and [KM01] on two chunking tasks

Task	P-Value
CoNLL-2000	0.0745
Base NP	< 0.001

Each SVM training step uses a quadratic programming step. Our simple voting system is considerably faster. Figure 3 compares the run time for training and decoding (testing) with a single data representation using our system compared with the time taken for the same task using the system of [KM01] (we downloaded their system and ran it on the same machine as our system).

5.4 Significance Testing

To examine the validity of the assumption that our approach is significantly different from that of [KM01] we applied the McNemar significance test (we assume the errors are made independently). The McNemar test showed that, for the CoNLL-2000 shared task of arbitrary phrase chunking, our score is not statistically significantly better than the results in [KM01]. However for the Base NP chunking task, our score is indeed better by a statistically significant margin from the results in [KM01].

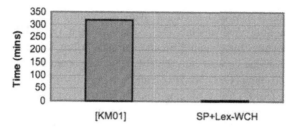

Fig. 3. Comparison of run times for training from the training data and decoding the test data between our system and that of [KM01] for a single data representation

6   Comparison with Other Voting Methods

We apply simple majority voting between five data representations (Inside/Outside and Start/End), while [KM01] only apply weighted voting between Inside/Outside representations, since their learner restricted them to vote between different data representation types. In our experiments, we find the Start/End representation usually catches more information than the Inside/Outside representations and in turn improves our performance. Previous approaches that use voting have all used voting as a means of system combination, i.e. taking multiple machine learning methods and taking a majority vote or weighted vote combining their output [SDD$^+$00]. This kind of system combination can be done using voting or stacking. Voting as system combination has been applied to the CoNLL-2000 data set as well: [vH00] obtains an $F_{\beta=1}$ of 93.32. [San02] combines the output of several systems but also does voting by exploiting different data representations. However, to our knowledge, there has not been a study of voting purely between multiple data representations using a single machine learning method ([San00] is a study of voting between multiple data representations but it combines this approach with multiple pass chunking in the same experimental study). Our results seem to indicate that even simple majority voting between multiple data representations does better than voting as a means for system combination.

7   Conclusion

The main contribution of this paper is that a single learning method, a simple trigram model can use voting between multiple data representations to obtain results equal to the best on the CoNLL-2000 text chunking data set. Using no additional knowledge sources, we achieved 94.01% $F_{\beta=1}$ score compared to the previous best comparable score of 93.90% and an $F_{\beta=1}$ score of 95.23% on the Base NP identification task compared to the previous best comparable score of 94.22%. Using the McNemar significance test, we show that our results is significantly better than the current comparable state-of-the-art approach on the Base NP chunking task. In addition, our text chunker is faster by several orders of magnitude than comparably accurate methods. We are faster both in time taken in training as well as decoding.

In our experiments, we use simple majority voting because we found weighted voting to be less accurate in our case: we use only five data representations (DRs) that were chosen carefully each with high accuracy. Weighted voting will be particularly useful if we scale up the number of distinct DRs, some which may not accurate overall but provide correct answers for certain difficult examples. Many DRs could potentially be created if we encode the context into the DR, e.g. a tag could be **IO** if the current tag is **I** and the previous tag is **O**. Other DRs could use tags that encode syntactic structure, e.g. SuperTagging [Sri97] uses a tagging model to provide a piece of syntactic structure to each word in the input and can be used as a DR that can participate in voting. In each case, an efficient mapping from the DR into a common voting format will be needed.

References

[Bra00]   T. Brants. TnT – a statistical part-of-speech tagger. In *Proceedings of the 6th Applied Natural Language Processing Conference: ANLP-2000*, Seattle, USA, 2000.

[Cha96]   E. Charniak. *Statistical Language Learning*. MIT Press, 1996.

[KM01]   T. Kudo and Y. Matsumoto. Chunking with support vector machines. In *Proceedings of the 2nd Meeting of the North American Association for Computational Linguistics: NAACL 2001*, 2001.

[MP02]   A. Molina and F. Pla. Shallow Parsing using Specialized HMMs. *Journal of Machine Learning Research*, 2:595–613, March 2002.

[RM95]   L. Ramshaw and M. Marcus. Text Chunking using Transformation-Based Learning. In *Proceedings of the 3rd Workshop on Very Large Corpora: WVLC-1995*, Cambridge, USA, 1995.

[San00]   E. F. Tjong Kim Sang. Text chunking by system combination. In *Proceedings of the Conference on Computational Natural Language Learning: CoNLL-2000*, pages 151–153, Lisbon, Portugal, 2000.

[San02]   E. F. Tjong Kim Sang. Memory-based shallow parsing. *Journal of Machine Learning Research*, 2:559–594, March 2002.

[SB00]   E. F. Tjong Kim Sang and S. Buchholz. Introduction to the CoNLL-2000 Shared Task: Chunking. In *Proceedings of the Conference on Computational Natural Language Learning: CoNLL-2000*, pages 151–153, Lisbon, Portugal, 2000.

[SDD+00] E. F. Tjong Kim Sang, Walter Daelemans, Hervé Déjean, Rob Koeling, Yuval Krymolowski, Vasin Punyakanok, and Dan Roth. Applying system combination to base noun phrase identification. In *Proceedings of COLING-2000*, pages 857–863, Saarbuecken, Germany, 2000.

[Sri97]   B. Srinivas. Performance evaluation of supertagging for partial parsing. In *Proc. of Fifth International Workshop on Parsing Technologies*, Boston, September 1997.

[SV99]   E. F. Tjong Kim Sang and J. Veenstra. Representing texting chunks. In *Proceedings of the 7th Conference of the European Association for Computational Linguistics: EACL-1999*, pages 173–179, Bergen, Norway, 1999.

[UMM+00] K. Uchimoto, Q. Ma, M. Murata, H. Ozaku, and H. Isahara. Named Entity Extraction based on a Maximum Entropy Model and Transformation Rules. In *Proceedings of the 38th Meeting of the ACL: ACL-2000*, 2000.

[vH00]   Hans van Halteren. Chunking with WPDV Models. In *Proceedings of the Conference on Computational Natural Language Learning: CoNLL-2000*, pages 154–156, Lisbon, Portugal, 2000.

[ZDJ02]   T. Zhang, F. Damerau, and D. Johnson. Text Chunking based on a Generalization of Winnow. *Journal of Machine Learning Research*, 2:615–637, March 2002.

A Novel Use of VXML to Construct a Speech Browser for a Public-Domain SpeechWeb

L. Su and R.A. Frost[1]

School of Computer Science, University of Windsor,
Windsor, Ontario, Canada N9B 3P4
{su5, Richard}@uwindsor.ca

Abstract. Despite the fact that interpreters for the voice-application markup language VXML have been available for around five years, there is very little evidence of the emergence of a public domain SpeechWeb. This is in contrast to the huge growth of the conventional web only a few years after the introduction of HTML. One reason for this is that architectures for distributed speech applications are not conducive to public involvement in the creation and deployment of speech applications. In earlier work, a new architecture for a public domain SpeechWeb has been proposed. In this paper, it is shown how a speech browser for this new architecture can be readily built through a novel use of VXML. A detailed description of the browser is given, together with a discussion of the advantages of this novel approach.

1 Introduction

A SpeechWeb is a collection of hyperlinked applications that are distributed over the Internet and which are accessible by spoken commands and queries that are input through remote end-user devices. Various architectures and technologies have been developed which are contributing to the development of SpeechWebs:

1. Speech interfaces to conventional web pages. These interfaces run on end-user devices and allow users to scan downloaded web pages and follow hyperlinks through spoken commands [e.g. Hemphill and Thrift 1995]. More sophisticated versions process the downloaded web pages and provide spoken summaries and allow some limited form of content querying.
2. The second architecture involves the use of networks of hyperlinked VXML Pages. VXML [Lucas 2000] is similar to HTML except that it is used to create hyperlinked speech applications. VXML pages, which are executed on VXML browsers, include commands for prompting user speech input, for invoking recognition grammars, for outputting synthesized voice, for iteration through blocks of code, for calling local Java scripts, and for hyperlinking to other remote VXML pages that are downloaded and executed in a manner similar to the linking of HTML pages in the conventional web. Speech recognition is carried out by the

---

[1] Both authors contributed equally to this paper.

B. Kégl and G. Lapalme (Eds.): AI 2005, LNAI 3501, pp. 401–405, 2005.

VXML browser running locally on an end-user device, or at a remote site which is accessed through the telephone.
3. The third architecture is the one used in call centers. End-users communicate with the call center using remote telephones. Speech recognition is carried out at the call center. Often VXML is used to code the call center application.

A comprehensive study of these architectures, and variations of them, can be found in EURESCOM [2000].

A public-domain SpeechWeb is one in which speech browsers run on end-user devices, and end users create speech applications and deploy them on their own web servers. It has been observed [Frost 2004] that the public-domain SpeechWeb is growing at a very slow pace despite the fact that VXML has been around for five years, and that the reason for this is that the three architectures above are not conducive to the involvement of a wide range of end-users. The first suffers from the fact that most conventional web pages are not designed for non-visual browsing, the second architecture requires applications to be written in VXML and also suffers from the fact that these applications have to execute on the end-user device which is not appropriate when large databases or sophisticated natural-language processing is involved. The third architecture requires expensive software to link between telephone access and the call-center application, and also requires end-user voice profiles to be stored at all call centers if high recognition-accuracy is needed.

A new architecture which is conducive to the development of a public-domain SpeechWeb has been proposed in Frost et al [2004]. That architecture is based on Local Recognition and Remote Processing (LRRP). The speech browsers run on local end-user devices, and the hyperlinked applications execute on remote servers. The LRRP architecture is described briefly in section 2 of this paper. The architecture assumes that the end-user speech browsers will be easy to create, easy to deploy, and will make use of the most-recent advances in grammar-based speech-recognition technology. In section 3 of this paper, we show how this can be done. Our approach involves a novel use of VXML. Section 4 contains the URL of a video demonstration of the SpeechWeb browser, and a discussion of current work to extend the capability of the browser to accommodate more advanced speech applications.

2   An Architecture for a Public-Domain SpeechWeb

The LRRP architecture is depicted in Figure 1. The architecture is simple and it is shown later how it can be implemented using readily-available software and commonly-used communications protocols. In the LRRP architecture, speech applications reside on conventional web servers. Each application consists of a recognition grammar and an interpreter. The grammar defines the application's input language. When a speech browser first contacts a remote application, the grammar is downloaded and used to tailor the browser for that application. This is necessary to achieve sufficient recognition-accuracy for non-trivial applications. It has been noted by Knight et al [2001] that grammar-based speech recognition is now the predominant technology used in commercial speech products.

When a user input is recognized by the local browser, it is sent as text to the remote application. The interpreter at the remote web site accepts the input, processes it, and returns the result as text to the browser on the end-user device. That result is then output as synthesized voice. If the user input is a request to follow a hyperlink to another application, then the interpreter return the URL of the new application as result. In this case the browser recognizes the result as such and contacts the new application for a new recognition grammar, and transfers all future input to the new application until the user requests transfer to another application. The question addressed in this paper is how to implement speech browsers for the LRRP architecture.

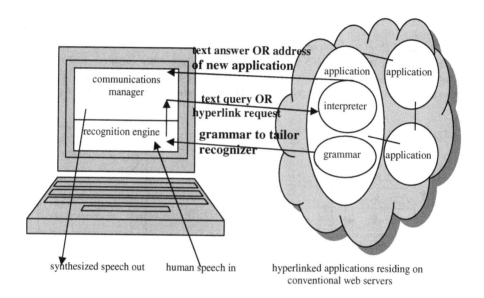

Fig. 1. The LRRP SpeechWeb Architecture

3 A Browser for a Public-Domain SpeechWeb

One approach that can be used to create an LRRP SpeechWeb browser is to use a commercial speech-recognition engine, such as IBM's ViaVoice technology, and to embed it in code which interfaces with the user and the Internet. Our initial browser, which was constructed in this way using JAVA, was satisfactory operationally but had several shortcomings as a vehicle for encouraging involvement in the development of a public-domain SpeechWeb: the code was complicated and consisted of several hundred lines associated with the end-user interface, low-level integration of the recognition engine API, communication with the remote applications, and all of the associated exception-handling. Secondly, the browser could not be deployed in its entirety as it used IBM's proprietary APIs.

Our solution to these shortcomings was to construct the speech browser as a single VXML page. The page can be executed by any VXML interpreter installed on an end-user device. Such interpreters are available from several venders and some can be downloaded for free in their beta versions. Our browser page begins by displaying a window which can be used to set a default start-up application and/or to direct the browser to a particular starting application for that session only. After that, the browser contacts the application, downloads the recognition grammar and waits for end-user input. When input is recognized it is sent to the application and the result, when received, is output in synthesized voice. The VXML code then loops back to process more user input. When a request to be transferred to another application is sent by the user, and the new URL received by the browser, it accesses the new grammar and begins over again. The only difficulty is that the current version of VXML does not provide a mechanism for a grammar identifier to have its value changed when looping through VXML code. Therefore it was necessary to include a Java object to deal with transfer to a hyperlinked application. The object intercepts the result returned from the remote application. If the result is a new URL, then the object makes a copy of the whole VXML page with a new grammar location, and replaces the original page with the new one. (The original page is maintained in a cache so that the user can "go back" if required). Fig. 2 shows the structure of the new browser.

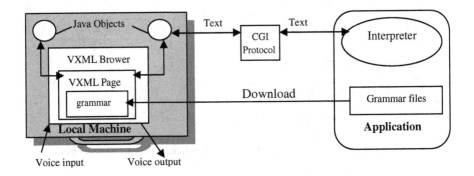

Fig. 2. A novel use of VXML to build a SpeechWeb browser

The following is an example session with a small SpeechWeb:

Application: Hi, I am solarman. I know about the planets and their moons.
User: Which moons orbit mars?
Application: Phobos and Deimos.
....
User: Can I talk to Monty?

The browser follows the hyperlink returned by Solarman to the new application Monty.
New Application: Hi, I am Monty. What can I do for you?

User: Tell me a joke.
....

This use of VXML is distinct from the intended use of VXML. Rather than create a SpeechWeb as a set of hyperlinked applications written as VXML pages, which are downloaded and executed on the end-user device when accessed, we have a single

VXML page which acts only as the speech interface to the remote hyperlinked applications which execute on the remote web servers. We claim several advantages for this approach. The browser consists of a few lines of easily-maintainable VXML code, together with two small Java objects. VXML handles exception handling, etc. at a high level. The full power of the available VXML interpreters can be taken advantage of. Our browser will benefit from all future improvements to VXML interpreters. It will be possible to tailor the browser to end-users when VXML interpreters become available that make use of voice profiles. Applications can be written in any language supported on the remote servers. All communication between the browser and the remote applications is through text. The applications can be deployed on regular web servers using any protocol (such as CGI) which supports http get and post operations.

4 Conclusion

The SpeechWeb browser has been successfully tested, and a demonstration of it can be viewed at the following, using QuickTime Player: http://davinci.newcs.uwindsor.ca/~speechweb/movie.mov

The browser has one significant shortcoming. It does not support dialogue. The CGI protocol which it uses accepts text from the browser, passes it through the standard input to the application on the web server, causes that application to execute, returns the standard output from the application as text to the browser, and then closes the application's execution. We are currently investigating various techniques to overcome this "single shot" limitation in order to support dialogue that is necessary for more complex and useful applications as discussed in [McTear 2002].

References

1. EURESCOM – The European Institute for Research and Strategic Studies in Telecommunications. Report EDIN 0010-0923 of Project P923-PF, MultiLingual WEB sites: Best practice, guidelines and architectures. (2000).
2. Frost, R. A., N. Abdullah, K. Bhatia, S. Chitte, F Hanna, M. Roy, Y. Shi and L. Su, LRRP SpeechWebs, IEEE CNSR Conference (2004) 91-98.
3. Frost, R. A. A Call for a Public-Domain SpeechWeb. Accepted in July 2004 for publication in the CACM.
4. Hemphill, C.T. and Thrift, P. R. Surfing the Web by Voice. Proceedings of the third ACM International Multimedia Conference (San Francisco 1995) 215 – 222
5. Knight, S. et al. Comparing Grammar-Based and Robust Approaches to Speech Understanding: A Case Study. In Eurospeech 2001, the 7th European Conference of Speech Communication and Technology (Aalborg Denmark 2001).
6. Lucas, B. VoiceXML for Web-based Distributed Conversational Applications. Communications of the ACM 43 (9) (2000) 53-57.
7. McTear, M. F. Spoken dialogue technology: enabling the conversational user interface. ACM Computing Surveys 34 (2002) 90-169.

Arabic Speech Synthesis Using a Concatenation of Polyphones: The Results

Tahar Saidane[1,2], Mounir Zrigui[2], and Mohamed Ben Ahmed[3]

[1] Centre de production de Sousse, Société Tunisienne d'Electricité et du Gaz, Tunisie
saidane.tahar@planet.tn
[2] Labaoratoire RIADI, Unité Monastir, Faculté des Sciences de Monastir, Tunisie
mounir.zrigui@fsm.rnu.tn
[3] Labaoratoire RIADI, Ecole Nationale des Sciences de l'informatique, Tunis, Tunisie
Mohamed.BenAhmed@riadi.rnu.tn

Abstract This research paper is within the project entitled "Oreillodule" : a real time embedded system of speech recognition, translation and synthesis. The core of our interest in this work is the presentation of the hybrid system of the Arabic speech synthesis and more precisely of the linguistic and the acoustic treatment. Indeed, we will focus on the grapheme-phoneme transcription, an integral stage for the development of this speech synthesis system with an acceptable quality. Then, we will present some of the rules used for the realization of the phonetic treatment system. These rules are stocked in a data base and browsed several times during the transcription. We will also present the module of syllabication in acoustic units of variable sizes (phoneme, diphone and triphone), as well as the corresponding polyphones dictionary. We will list the stages of the establishment of this dictionary and the difficulties faced during its development. Finally, we will present the results of the statistical survey of understanding, achieved on a corpus.

1 Introduction

This article will present the modules of this synthesis system such as the module of transcription, the module of syllabication, concatenation and the acoustic unit dictionary. We chose to establish our own strategy of selection of acoustic units following a deep study of the Arabic language and inspired by the recent methods of synthesis of variable size units. We are using three types of unit: the phoneme, the diphone and the triphone. The combination of the three units is governed by an optimization algorithm that presents the ideal combination to every situation. This choice allowed us to get a better quality of natural and to limit the number of units[4].

2 The Transcription

The linguistic analysis allowed us to establish a set of 133 rules [2]. We note that the order of application of these rules is important and influence on the final result.

B. Kégl and G. Lapalme (Eds.): AI 2005, LNAI 3501, pp. 406–411, 2005.

In what follows the description of some elaborate rules and incorporated in a data base including also all graphemes and their correspondents phonemes :

1.   [uu]={CS}+{}+{و}   [uu]={CL}+{}+{و}

When the و is preceded by the vowel´ and followed by a consonant, we get the phoneme of the long vowel [uu]. When the و is preceded by the vowel´ and that it is at the end of word, we get the phoneme of the long vowel [uu]. Example: حُوتٌ , دُونَ (fish, without) [1].

2.   {CS}+{أ}={CS}+{ال}+#   {CS}+{أ}+{V}+{C}={CS}+{ال}+{V}+{C}

When the ال is in beginning of sentence and is followed by a solar consonant, it is equivalent to the non presence of ال . When ال is between two lunar consonants, it is equivalent to the non presence of the أ. Example: ذَهَبَ الرَجُلُ , السَمِيعُ (the man went, the hearer).

3   The Syllabication

In this research, we have adopted a system of synthesis by concatenation whose acoustic units are of three types: the triphones, the diphones and the phonemes. We established a set of concatenation rules to transform the different occurrences of three phonemes to : a triphone, a diphone followed of one phoneme, one phoneme followed of a diphone, or possibly three phonemes. The dynamic selection of the units results in the research of the optimal sequence of representatives, in order to minimize discontinuities to the point of concatenation [8]. The figure 1 presents an example of syllabication for the expression «صَبَاحُ الخَيرُ » (sabaaðu. lxaj.ri[1] : Hello) [7]:

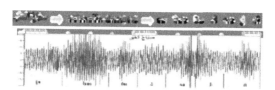

Fig. 1. Example of syllabication

The problematic of the selection of the units has been formalized using 6 rules, illustrated in the following list :

1.   [CVV] ={V}+{V}+{C} : When a consonant is followed by two vowels, the three graphemes constitute an acoustic unit of our system.
2.   [CV]={C}+{V}+{C} : When a consonant is followed by a vowel then by a consonant, the first two graphemes constitute an acoustic unit.
3.   [CC]={C}+{C}+{C} : When we have a succession of three consonants the first two graphemes constitute an acoustic unit.
4.   [C]={V}+ {C}+{C} : When we have two consonants followed by a vowel, only the first grapheme constitutes an acoustic unit of our system.

---

[1] Following the international phonetic alphabe IPA 96.

5.   [VV]={V}+{V} : When we have a succession of two vowels, both constitute an acoustic unit of our system.

6.   [V]={V} : An isolated vowel constitutes an acoustic unit of our system.

It is worth noting that the order of application of these rules is very important for a good syllabication and therefore a better resonant concatenation [3]. These elaborated six rules of syllabication are going to impose the types of acoustic units to use for the synthesis of the speech. The established dictionary contains 196 acoustic units (28 phonemes of C type, 84 diphones of type CV and 84 triphones of CVV type), which are enough for the realization of the different possible occurrences.

The module of concatenation requires the totality of the acoustic units under the shape of resonant registrations |9]. These registrations form the dictionary of our system. The established acoustic unit dictionary thus established has a size of 9 MØ (on average one phoneme takes 20 kØ, a diphone 40 kØ and a triphone 60 kØ). This is an example of segmentation :

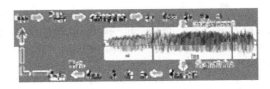

Fig. 2. An example of treatment for the obtaining of the triphone "haa" from the identification to the test

4 The Concatenation

For our system we wanted to start with a temporal smoothing treatment to measure the effect of a post treatment on the quality of the speech gotten. After the analysis of the different acoustic units of Arabic, it proves to be that these present an attenuation to the levels of their extremities. The retained idea consists then in proceeding, to an accentuation to the levels of a certain number of values of extremities before the concatenation. This treatment will touch also the end of the first unit and the beginning of the following.

A numeric signal of the speech is :

$$s(t) = \sum_{1}^{N} s_n \, \delta(t - nT) \tag{1}$$

s(t) : digital signal of the speech (sampled), sn = s(nT) : the value of the signal at instant nT et δ(t) : Dirac impulse. The concatenation of two units will be :

$$s(t) = s_1(t) + s_2(t) = \sum_{1}^{N} s_{1n} \, \delta(t - nT) + \sum_{1}^{M} s_{2n} \, \delta(t - nT) \tag{2}$$

The idea consists then in isolating X values of the first signal and Y values of the second. These values will undergo a proportional attenuation defined by :

$$s_i^{att\acute{e}nu\acute{e}} = s_i \frac{K - i}{K} \qquad i = 1 .. K \tag{3}$$

The result will be :

$$s(t) = \sum_1^{N-X} s_{1n} \delta(t - nT) + \sum_{N-X+1}^N s_{1n} \frac{N-n}{N} \delta(t - nT) + \sum_1^Y s_{2n} \frac{Y-n}{Y} \delta(t - nT) + \sum_{Y+1}^{M-Y} s_{2n} \delta(t - nT) \tag{4}$$

The function of attenuation so definite has been applied for a number of points representing 10% of the length of the signal of the acoustic unit. The gotten results are shown in what follows:

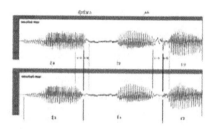

Fig. 3. Effect of the temporal smoothing on the shape of wave in the points of discontinuities

The previous curves show the effect of this temporal smoothing on an example of synthesis of the word «ظفر» (ḍafara : it won). Indeed, the first curve shows a simple concatenation and presents a flagrant discontinuity to the levels of the points of joints. The curve of the low introduces the result of a smoothed concatenation. The gotten result improved the quality of the voice synthesized. Nevertheless, we note an overlap between the units. To avoid such a problem we introduced a time of silence of 10 ms. The insertion of one pause between the units permitted to get a better intelligibility.

5   The Results of Tests

In order to evaluate our system, we have established a test procedure based on the monitoring and the identification of synthesized sentences. Therefore, we used a corpus of reference (Boudraa, 1993). This corpus is a set of twenty lists of ten Arabic sentences phonetically balanced. From this corpus we extracted 20 sentences of 53 words, 211 acoustic units of which 73 are different that makes 37.2% of the totality of the acoustic units. We made them listen to 8 people (4 women and 4 men) which permitted a statistical realistic assessment of the result. Every sentence is listened to three times. Each person must spell what he or she hears. The order of monitoring of the sentences is different from one person to another to achieve more realistic results. This is a summary of these results are shown in figure 4.

So, we can conclude to a percentage of identification of more than 80% since the first monitoring. This rate reaches more than 91% in the third phase. Otherwise, we have noticed that a phase of adaptation of 2 to 3 sentences was necessary to have a stabilization of the recognition rates. We also come to these results that the non current words are not easily identifiable (exp: لذعّة "irritated" sentence n° 4), and that some characters are more difficult than others for identification (exp:ذ sentence n° 3, 4 and 11). Their corresponding acoustic units need to be readjusted.

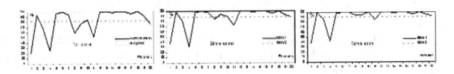

Fig. 4. The results of the tests

6 Conclusion

We presented in this article our system of synthesis of the speech, these different constituent, the different phases of its development and the technical choices kept for every module. The module of syllabication constitutes to our sense the starting point for another vision of the Arabic language, seen the total rupture with the methods used until today. We also exposed the operation of concatenation as well as the post treatment that we chose to remedy the problems of discontinuities.

Comparing these results to the existing ones remains difficult. The studies on the systems of synthesis of the Arabic speech are few and the results of assessment don't make the content of published articles. Nevertheless, we have reached that our system is based on a linguistic analysis that has permitted us to cut down only to 3 types of syllables (CVV, CV and C) contrary to the other studies recommending five to six different syllables (CV, CVV, CVC, CVVC and CVCC) [6] and that we have only used 196 acoustic units to synthesize any occurrence of standard Arabic whereas 310 units are the minimum till now [5].

References

1. Zrigui M., Mili A, Jemni M. 1991. Vers un système automatique de synthèse de la parole arabe, Maghrebin symposium on programming and system, Alger. p 180-197.
2. Saidane Tahar, Zrigui Mounir, Pr Ben Ahmed Mohamed. 2004. La Transcription Orthographique-Phonétique de la Langue Arabe. RÉCITAL 2004, Fès, Maroc.
3. Emerard Françoise. 1977. Les diphones et le traitement de la prosodie dans la synthèse de la parole. Bulletin de l'institut de phonétique de grenoble.
4. Dutoit Thierry. 1993. High quality text to speech synthesis of the french language. Thèse. Faculté polytechnique de Mons.
5. Elshafei M., Al-Muhtaseb, H., Al-Gamdi M. 2002. Techniques for high quality Arabic speech synthesis, Information sciences, Vol.140, 255-267.
6. Ben Sassi S., Braham R., Belgith A. 2001. Neural speech synthesis system for Arabic language using celp algorithm, Proc. Conference on Computer Systems and Applications.
7. Saidane Tahar, Haddad Ahmed, Zrigui Mounir, Pr Ben Ahmed Mohamed. 2004. Réalisation d'un système hybride de synthèse de la parole arabe utilisant un dictionnaire de polyphones. JEP-TALN 2004, Traitement Automatique de l'Arabe, Fès, Maroc.

8. Boula de Mareuil Philippe, Célérier Philippe, Cesses Thierry, Fabre Serge, Jobin Carine, Le Meur Pierre-Yves, Obadia David, Soulage Benoît, Toen Jacques. 2001. Elan text to speech : un système multilingue de synthèse de la parole à partir du texte. Elan TTS Toulouse.
9. Lemmety Sami. 2000. Review of speech synthesis technology. Thèse. Helsinki University of Technology.

English to Chinese Translation of Prepositions

Hui Li, Nathalie Japkowicz, and Caroline Barrière

School of Information Technology and Engineering,
University of Ottawa, Canada

Abstract. Machine translation of prepositions is a difficult task; little work has been done, to date, in this area. This article suggests addressing the problem using a semantic framework for the interpretation of the surrounding elements of a preposition in the source language. This framework, called Use Types, will reduce the set of possible prepositions in the target language, therefore helping the translation process. This approach is not language dependent, but we focus, here, on English and Chinese, and we also specifically look at three prepositions: in, on and at. The article describes machine learning experiments designed and conducted in which WordNet is employed to lead to an automatic discovery of the Use Types. Results are analyzed and discussed and a practical use of the system is suggested along with the preliminary results it obtains.

1 Translation of Prepositions: Looking into Use Types

Prepositions play a very important role in language. Without or with wrong prepositions, sentences are difficult to understand. Translation of prepositions is difficult and little research has been done on it compared to work done on other words. Furthermore, the issue received close to no attention in the context of English to Chinese. Although some automated translation systems, e.g. Worldling[1] are developed, prepositions are sometimes translated in a non-colloquial or non-understandable fashion. Among the 300 examples we collected from "The Bible" [8], 103 of them were meaningfully translated by Worldlingo, but 197 examples were translated in a non-understandable manner. The problem of translation of prepositions is twofold. First, high usage of prepositions unfortunately comes with a high degree of polysemy; and meanings in different languages do not necessarily match. Second, even for a single meaning, different prepositions are possible.

Our hypothesis turns toward work on conceptualization [2] which suggests an interpretation of a preposition based on the semantic interpretation of the nouns surrounding it. This hypothesis is grounded in earlier work by Japkowicz [4,5] in which differences between English and French locative prepositions were analyzed based on the observation that these two languages sometimes conceptualize objects in a different

---

[1] Worldlingo can be found at www.worldlingo.com.

B. Kégl and G. Lapalme (Eds.): AI 2005, LNAI 3501, pp. 412–416, 2005.
© Springer-Verlag Berlin Heidelberg 2005

way. As an example, consider the object *bus*. A *bus* has a roof and several sides, so it can be conceptualized as container as in French. However, a *bus* also has a platform which can be seen as playing a more important role than the roof or the sides, resulting in a conceptualization as a surface as in English. In our work, a similar idea of conceptualization of objects is explored but through the use of Use Types, as developed by Herskovits [3], which correspond to patterns of a set of sentences from the perspective of cognitive science. Herskovits summarized a list of Use Types for each preposition. In the present work, Use Types are adapted and their range extended outside of locations to include other situations, like time, state, and direction. Table 1 shows a sample of the Use Types for preposition in. The Use Types developed in this research are indicated by a "*". For the most part, we can see that a single Use Type corresponds to a single Chinese meaning, although in some cases, a few different Use Types may belong to the same Chinese meaning, as in the first four examples.

Table 1. A sample of the Use Types for preposition in

Use Types	Example of Sentence	Chinese meaning
Spatial entity in container	The preserves in the sealed jar	（指地点)在…中；在…内；在…上
Physical object "in the air"	The bird in the air	
Physical object in the roadway	The ruts in the road	
Person in institution	A man in a red hat	
Person in clothing	A man in a red hat	（指衣服等)穿着，戴着
* Physical object in situation, or state	They fell in love.	（表示情况或状态)在…状态中
* Physical object in environment	She is standing outside in the cold.	（表示环境或境遇等)在…环境下
* person in career, activity	He's in the army	（表示职业，活动）
* object in direction	He could number the fields in every direction	（指方向）在…方向
* Physical object in the time span it takes to finish the described action	I will be back in a short time	（指时间)过（若干时间），在（若干时间）内
* Physical object in shape, form, order	words in alphabetical order	（表示形式，形状，排列）
* Object in way, medium, tool, or material.	A message in code.	（表示表达的方法，媒介，工具，原料等）

The challenge then remains to automatically extract the Use Type from an English sentence, from which we will obtain the corresponding Chinese meaning (as found in a dictionary), thus leading to a reduced set of possible Chinese prepositions.

In the present work, we intend to use ML techniques to discover the Use Type directly from a preposition in context. Inspired by [5], we rendered some Use Types more specific, aiming at finding middle ground of generality/specificity that would make the Use Types useful as semantic interpretations for translation in different languages.

2 Experimentation and Results

To categorize an English sentence into a Use Type, the first step is to generalize the nouns surrounding the preposition to conceptual levels appropriate in Use Type definitions. For example, the noun *farmer*, present in a sentence should be generalized to its superclass person which could be part of a Use Type. Such relations can be found in a lexical knowledge base, such as WordNet [1,7], containing information organized as a lexical hierarchy. In more details, all of the nouns in WordNet are organized into synsets, which, in turn, are organized into hierarchies. We therefore design an experiment to make use of WordNet in the semi-automatic determination of the Use Type that will correspond to a preposition in context.

In order to translate prepositions from English to Chinese, we followed the following steps:

- Gather a corpus of English sentences with their Chinese translation
- Shallow-parse the sentences to extract the nouns around the prepositions: reference and located object
- Find the nouns' hypernyms using WordNet
- Use these hypernyms, together with the preposition, as features for ML training set.
- Label each training example with its class.
- Train some classifiers on the data gathered in the previous phases.

We used two labeling strategies to test whether Use Types are needed or not:

- Experiment 1 : Use the 62 Use Types as the classes to be learned
- Experiment 2 : Use the 74 Chinese prepositions directly without Use Types.

Table 2 show the result of learning by Use Type vs. by Chinese preposition. It displays error rates of classification and only shows the results of those classifiers that performed relatively better, where C4.5 is a decision tree learner, and PARTruleLearner is a learner that build rules from partial decision trees. Sentences used in the experimentation come from dictionaries [9, 10], Herskovits's book [3], the online corpus *The Little Prince* [11], Jane Austen's *Pride and Prejudice*, and HongKong Polytechnic University's online Magazine Articles. The total number of instances used is 2000, and we conducted a 10-fold Cross-validation testing policy. We also calculated and showed Baselines at the bottom of the table based on the following three ways. First, we randomly select a Use Type or a Chinese preposition (Baselines 1). Second, we choose the most frequent Use Type or Chinese preposition all the time (Baselines 2). Third, we randomly select a Use Type or Chinese preposition according to the probability that each Use Type or preposition is chosen (Baselines 3). Several other experiments are also reported in [6].

The best result we obtained is 30.6733% in the case of preposition *at* when learning by Use Type. The worst result is 66.2368% in the case of preposition *in* when learning by Chinese preposition directly. The baseline of the most frequent Use Type is as high as 96.95%, and the baseline of the most frequent Chinese preposition is 84.85%.

Furthermore, we found that, in general, the difference in performance of Usetypes versus Chinese prepositions directly can go as high as 20%. These results demonstrate the utility of using Use Types.

Table 2. Error rate of learning with each preposition separately

Classifier	At		In		On	
	Use Type	Cprep.	Use Type	Cprep.	Use Type	Cprep.
C4.5	30.6733	48.8778	42.0819	58.2206	55.814	62.4313
PARTruleLearner	30.9227	48.3791	41.2811	61.8683	56.4482	66.2368
Baseline 1	99.45	99.8	95.5	99.7	97.35	99.75
Baseline 2	95.05	84.85	90.15	95.25	96.5	92.4
Baseline 3	99.6	99.75	96.15	99.65	97.15	99.8

3 Practical Application of This Research

The practical purpose of our research was to build a post-processing unit that would correct the preposition output by the automated translator when necessary. To assess the accuracy of that unit, we use 300 examples from "the Bible", which were not used in previous experiments, and use these data only as test sets. We ran Worldlingo and our technique on these examples separately.

Our results are as follows: Among the 103 examples that Worldlingo translated understandably, 39 of them were wrongly translated by our system. However, among the 197 examples that were wrongly translated by Worldlingo, 108 of them were translated meaningfully by our system. This means that our post-processing unit allowed us to improve the output of Worldlingo on prepositions "in", "on" and "at" by 23%, bringing it from an accuracy of 34.33% to an accuracy of 57.33%. For example, the sentence *the man in red* was translated to 人在红色 in Chinese, which means *man at red* in English. While our approach will get the Use Type of *person in clothing,* which corresponds to the Chinese Meaning of （指衣服等）穿着，戴着, which means *wear* in English. The result suggests that our approach is a valuable addition to existing well-recognized translation system.

4 Conclusion and Future Work

The purpose of this paper was first to present Use Types as a possible semantic interpretation framework for prepositions in context, with a purpose of machine translation. We referred to previous related work by Herskovits, and Japkowicz, who focused on locative prepositions and broadened their work by expanding to Use Types for non-locative prepositions.

The experiments we conducted showed that introducing Use Types as an intermediate step can help improve the accuracy of translation. Furthermore, we found that Wordnet along with Machine Learning tools could be useful in the automatic assignation of a Use Type for a preposition. Our approach is also valuable practically as we showed that combined our approach to the output of WorldLingo lead to a non-negligible accuracy improvement of 23%.

For future work, we need to collect more data to better evaluate this approach. We also expect to apply this approach to other prepositions, and languages. Lexical resources other than Wordnet also need to be investigated.

References

1. Christiane Fellbaum, editor. 1998 *WordNet: An Electronic Lexical Database*. The MIT Press. 23-46
2. M. Grimaud. 1988 Toponyms, Prepositions, and Cognitive Maps in English and French. *Journal of the American Society of Geolinguistics*, vol. 14, pp. 5476.
3. A. Herskovits. 1986. *Language and spatial cognition: an interdisciplinary study of the prepositions in English*. Cambridge [Cambridgeshire]; New York: Cambridge University Press. 39-54, 86-94, 127-155
4. N. Japkowicz, J. M. Wiebe. 1991. A System for Translating Locative Prepositions from English into French. *29th Annual Meeting of the Association for Computational Linguistics* 29 (18-21 June):153-160.
5. Nathalie Japkowicz. 1990. *The Translation of Basic Topological Prepositions from English into French*. M.S. Thesis, published as Technical Report CSRI243, University of Toronto.
6. Hui Li, 2004. *Use Types for English to Chinese Translation of Prepositions*. M.S. Thesis, published as Technical Report, University of Ottawa.
7. Miller. 1990. WordNet: An On-line Lexical Database. In *International Journal of Lexicography*, 3(4)
8. *The Bible*. http://www.bible.org/page.asp?page_id=2485
9. *Oxford Advanced Learner's Dictionary of Current English With Chinese Translation*. The Commercial Press. Oxford University Press. 1994. 65-66, 573-574, 782-783
10. *The Advanced Learner's Dictionary of Current English With Chinese Translation*. Oxford University Press. 1978. 58, 536-538, 734-735
11. *The Little Prince*. The Hong Kong Polytechnic University. http://www.engl.polyu.edu.hk/tricorpus/

Generating Adaptive Multimedia Presentations Based on a Semiotic Framework

Osama El Demerdash[1], Sabine Bergler[1], Leila Kosseim[1], and PK Langshaw[2]

[1] Concordia University,
Department of Computer Science and Software Engineering
[2] Concordia University,
Department of Design and Computation Arts

Abstract. We describe a prototype for generating adaptive multimedia presentations through the dynamic selection of files from a large data repository. The presentation is generated based on a conceptual framework encompassing the technical (syntactic), semantic and relational textual annotation of the data as well as context-sensitive rules and patterns of selection discovered with the aid of the system during the preparation phase. The prototype was developed using Java, Flash-MX and XML.

1 A Semiotic Perspective of Multimedia

Multimedia is becoming increasingly accessible and diffusible. Much research in this area deals with content-based retrieval, the automatic recognition of the content of the medium [1]. However, modeling of the data and task is often biased toward information retrieval, incorporating temporal and spatial models, but ignoring other contextual and relational factors.

In this work, we use a repository of multimedia material consisting of approximately 2,000 files divided between images, video, animations, voice, sound and music excerpts to dynamically generate presentations through selecting and playing the most appropriate material based on the notion of the context of the performance.

2 Related Work

The MATN (Multimedia Augmented Transition Network) by Chen et al. [2] proposes a general model for live interactive RTSP (Real-Time Streaming Protocol) presentations, which models the semantics of interaction and presentation processes such as Rewind, Play, Pause, temporal relations and synchronization control (e.g. concurrent, optional, alternative), rather than the semantics of the content. In the HIPS project [3] and [4], a portable electronic museum guide transforms audio data into flexible coherent descriptions of artworks that could vary with the context. Kennedy et al. [5] developed a communicative act planner using techniques from Rhetorical Structure Theory (RST) [6]. These systems were not designed for changing context and are domain or task specific.

B. Kégl and G. Lapalme (Eds.): AI 2005, LNAI 3501, pp. 417–421, 2005.

3   An Adaptive Framework

We introduce here briefly the framework on which we based the prototype implementation. [7] and [8] provide a more detailed insight. The framework can be divided into static and dynamic components.

Static Components refer to elements not contributing directly to the adaptive potential of the framework. They include the following: **The Data Model** models multimedia objects as a general class with specialized classes for each medium. Meta-data describe semantic features of the media and are constant across media types. Each medium is also annotated according to its specific characteristics. Media include Text, Images, Moving Images and Audio. Relations between the data elements are represented using RST-style relations [6]. **Visual Effects** are techniques used to improve the visual quality of the presentation and to enhance the relation between two selections for example by associating a certain kind of relation with a transition. An **Information Retrieval Model** is necessary, since pre-arranging all possible combinations of media is not feasible in large repositories.

Dynamic Compnents are responsible for the adaptive aspect of the framework. We define it as follows: **The Context Model** includes several interdependent parameters: the *outline, time, space, presenter, audience, medium, rhetorical mode, mood,* and *history*. **Feature Relations** provide for overriding capabilities, and thus an additional interpretive layer. Feature Relations can also be used to express constraints, which can be considered as negative relations. **Heuristics** produce different interpretations of the performance, according to the context, and through the selection and ordering of data. **Generation Patterns** are recurring designs, behavior and conditions. Generation patterns are discovered while experimenting with the system during the preparation phase. Once identified and included in the interface, they can be retrieved explicitly during the presentation. Defining patterns also leads to more meaningful ways of describing the higher level goals of the presenter.

4   Implementation

A prototype was developed using a three-tier software architecture on Flash, Java and MYSQL platforms as illustrated in Table 1. The model tier consists of the data and annotations, relations and retrieval patterns. Business logic including operations on the database, heuristics and status information makes for the middle tier, while the presentation (view) tier has the user interface and interaction elements. Long-term experimental goals, the volatile nature of requirements and other practical considerations have influenced the three-layered, modularized architecture. Separating the presentation from the model and the business logic permits the substitution of any of these layers at minimum cost.

Figure 1 illustrates the interaction sequence for retrieving data, with the following scenario: The user indicates through the presentation graphical user

Table 1. Architecture of the System

	Client Tier	Application Tier	Model Tier
Application Specific	GUI	IR	Media Database
Application Generic	Techniques	XML Handler	MySQL
Middleware		java.xml	java.sql

interface (GUI) the features of the data to be retrieved. The presentation GUI reproduces the user's request in XML format and sends a message to the XML handler to process the request. XML sent by the presentation GUI to the XML handler includes elements for both <sound> (audio) requests and <content> (visual) requests. The XML handler forwards the request to the Query Processor. The Query Processor applies heuristics relevant to the required features. The Query Processor constructs a SQL statement according to the requested features and heuristics and runs it on the media database. The media database returns the result set to the Query Processor. The Query processor translates the result set into XML format and sends it to the XML Handler. The XML Handler forwards the XML result set to the Presentation GUI. The <Slides> element represents visual files while the <Sounds> element represents audio files. The presentation GUI displays the files specified in the result set.

The interface is used for informing the system of changes in the presentation/audience models and to control/override the system's suggestions using relevance feedback and possibly navigation of the knowledge base. The user controls the system through two types of menu buttons: media-centered for retrieval through direct manipulation of the technical (syntactic) features, and performance-centered buttons exploiting the content (semantic) features as annotated.

The user can select any of these features through the presentation GUI. They are linked internally to the context and data models to select files, or generate

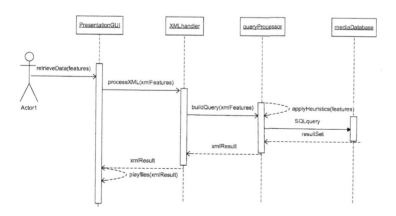

Fig. 1. Sequence Diagram for Retrieving Data

visual and audio effects. Using the relations and the user specifications, the most appropriate data files are retrieved from the multimedia database. Of the relevant data files, only a subset may be used in the final presentation. The final selection and ordering for the presentation is made by the selection heuristics and the generation patterns which ensure a coherent final presentation.

5   Evaluation

The prototype currently uses over 2,000 multimedia files and generates presentations of arbitrary length. The presented framework has to be evaluated over time on mostly qualitative reusability measures, such as applicability, scalability and ease of adoption. The TREC 2001 Proceedings [9], which included a video track for the first time, acknowledge the need for a different evaluation system for that track. [10] lists some of the performance criteria not captured by Precision and Recall such as speed of response, query formulation abilities and limitations, and the quality of the result. Schauble [11] introduces a notion of subjective relevance which hinges on the user and her information needs rather than on the query formulation. Thus we feel that the user's participation in determining the relevance of the result is an essential factor.

We propose here to use an alternative user oriented measure for the evaluation of the system. As reported by [12] Novelty Ratio is the ratio of relevant documents which were not expected by the user:

$$Novelty = \frac{\# \ of \ relevant \ documents \ retrieved \ previously \ unknown \ to \ the \ user}{total \ \# \ of \ relevant \ documents}$$

In order to apply this measure, a special evaluation environment needs to be set up to run the system in interrupted mode so that the user can evaluate the selections played without interfering with the system heuristics.

Finally, the users and audience could help evaluate the system through interviews and questionnaires for surveying their reaction.

6   Conclusion and Future Work

Multimedia presentations provide a powerful tool for communication. However, in order to exploit the full potential of multimedia presentations, it is essential to allow for a certain flexibility in the selection of the material for a more dynamic and less predictable presentation. We proposed a framework for adaptive multimedia presentations. As a proof of concept, we implemented a system that dynamically selects and plays the most appropriate selection of multimedia files according to the preferences and constraints indicated by the user within the framework. We borrowed concepts from text analysis to model the semantic dimension of the presentation. We also proposed adopting different methods of evaluation to reflect the subjective nature of the task.

References

1. Flickner, M., Sawhney, H., Nublack, W.: Query by Image and Video Content: The QBIC System. In: Intelligent Multimedia Information Retrieval. California:AAAI Press/ The MIT Press (1997)
2. Chen, S.C., Li, S.T., Shyu, M.L., Zhan, C., Zhang, C.: A multimedia semantic model for RTSP-based multimedia presentation systems. In: Proceedings of the IEEE Fourth International Symposium on Multimedia Software Engineering (MSE2002), Newport Beach, California, ACM (2002) 124–131
3. Not, E., Zancanaro, M.: The MacroNode approach: Mediating between adaptive and dynamic hypermedia. In: Proceedings of International Conference on Adaptive Hypermedia and Adaptive Web-based Systems. (2000)
4. Marti, P., Rizzo, A., Petroni, L., Diligenti, G.T..M.: Adapting the museum: a non-intrusive user modeling approach. In Kay, J., ed.: User Modeling: Proceedings of the Seventh International Conference, UM99, Banff, Canada, Springer Wien New York (1999) 311–313
5. Kennedy, K., Mercer, R.: Using communicative acts to plan the cinematographic structure of animations. In Cohen, R., et al., eds.: Advances in Artificial Intelligence: Proccedings of the 15th Conference of the Canadian Society for Computational Studies of Intelligence, AI2002, Calgary, May 27-29, Springer, Berlin (2002) 133–146
6. Mann, W., Matthiessen, C., Thompson, S.: Rhetorical Structure Theory and Text Analysis. In: Discourse Description: Diverse Linguistic Analyses of a Fund-raising text. John Benjamins Publishing Company, Amesterdam (1992) 39–78
7. El Demerdash, O., Langshaw, P., Kosseim, L.: Toward the production of adaptive multimedia presentations. In Thwaites, H., ed.: Ninth International Conference on Virtual Systems and Multimedia - Hybrid Reality: Art, Technology and the Human Factor, Montreal, International Society on Virtual Systems and Multimedia VSMM (2003) 428–436
8. El Demerdash, O.: A conceptual framework for adaptive multimedia presentations. Master's thesis, Concordia University, Montreal (2004)
9. Smeaton, A.: The TREC 2001 video track report. In Voorhees, E., Harman, D., eds.: The Tenth Text Retrieval Conference, TREC 2001. NIST Special Publication 500-250, NIST, Gaithersburg, Maryland (2001) 52–60
10. Narasimhalu, A.D., Kankanhalli, M.S., Wu, J.: Benchmarking Multimedia Databases. In: Multimedia Technologies and Applications for the 21st Century: Visions of World Experts. Kluwer Academic Publishers (1998) 127–148
11. Schäuble, P.: Multimedia Information Retrieval: Content-Based Information Retrieval from Large Text and Audio Databases. Kluwer Academic Publishers (1997)
12. Baeza-Yates, R., Ribeiro-Neto, B.: Modern Information Retrieval. ACM Press and Addison Wesley (1999)

Producing Headline Summaries for Newspaper Articles

Yllias Chali and Maheedhar Kolla

Department of Computer Science,
University of Lethbridge,
4401 University Drive,
Lethbridge, Alberta, Canada, T1K 3M4
{chali, kolla}@cs.uleth.ca

Abstract. In this paper we present a system that creates a headline summary for a newspaper article. We present an approach that constructs a headline by selecting the most important portion of the text, then reducing it using linguistic compression techniques. The compression is grammatical and retains the most important pieces of information, leaving it readable. In addition, we present experimental results that demonstrate the effectiveness of our approach.

1 Introduction

Current automatic summarizers usually rely on sentence extraction to produce summaries. However, rather simply extracting sentences and stringing them together, producing headlines automatically relies on shortening the summary and making it concise and coherent. For instance, sentence (1') is a shortened form of sentence (1):

(1) Dwight C. German, a professor of psychiatry at University of Texas Southwestern Medical Center in Dallas, said the study by Brzustowicz and colleagues, published in the April 28 issue of Science magazine, really may well be a landmark paper.

(1') Dwight C. German said the study by Brzustowicz and colleagues is a landmark paper.

We implemented an automatic headline generation system. Input to the system is the original document, the most important sentences are extracted from the original document. Output of the system is shortened forms of the extracted sentences as headline-like summaries. The production of headlines uses multiple sources of knowledge to make decisions, including syntactic knowledge, context and relevant information. Generating headlines improves the conciseness of automatically generated summaries, making it concise on target.

In the next section, we describe the headline generation algorithm in details. Then, we introduce the evaluation scheme used to assess the performance of the system and present evaluation results. Finally, we examine some possible future works.

B. Kégl and G. Lapalme (Eds.): AI 2005, LNAI 3501, pp. 422–426, 2005.

2   Headline Generation

Contrary to [1], the generation of headlines is a two-step process: (1) Extraction of relevant sentences, (2) Shortening the relevant sentences and making them concise. The algorithm for extracting the relevant sentences is as follows:

1. Split the original document into segments that address the same topic [2].
2. Tag the words in the segment with their respective Part of Speech tags [3].
3. Parse the tagged words into their syntactic structure using [4].
4. Extract the nouns and the compound nouns from the parsed segment.
5. Compute the lexical chains [5] for each segment.

$$LC = \{chainMember_1, \ldots, chainMember_n\}$$

   where $chainMember_i$s are word senses and there exists a semantic relation, such as identical, synonym, hypernym or hyponym, between all the *chain members* in a particular chain.
6. Rank the segments based on :

$$score(seg_j) = \sum_{i=1}^{m} \frac{score(chainMember_i, seg_j)}{s_i}$$

   where $score(chainMember_i, seg_j)$ is the number of occurrences of a *chain $Member_i$* in seg_j, m is their number, and s_i is the number of segments in which $chainMember_i$ occurs. The top segments - with the highest scores - are chosen for the process of sentence extraction.
7. Extract the relevant sentences (i.e., sentences with the highest scores) using a scoring process, which considers the number of words shared by the sentence and the chains that have been considered in the segment selection phase.

$$score(sen_j) = \sum_{i=1}^{m} \frac{score(chainMember_i, sen_j)}{s_i}$$

   where $score(chainMember_i, sen_j)$ is the number of occurrences of a *chain $Member_i$* in sen_j, m is their number, and s_i is the number of sentences in which $chainMember_i$ occurs. The top sentences - with the highest scores - are chosen for the process of sentence reduction.

The input to the sentence-shortening algorithm are parse-trees of the most important sentences of the original text selected as described above. In our case, we take the highest top two ranked sentences. The parse-tree then goes through several operations in order to trim it. We developed the following reduction operations for parse-tree trimming:

1. Eliminate the subordinate clauses.
   (2) **Schizophrenia patients** whose medication couldn't stop the imaginary voices in their heads **gained some relief after researchers repeatedly sent a magnetic field into a small area of their brains.**

(2') Schizophrenia patients gained some relief after researchers repeatedly sent magnetic field into a small area of their brains.

2. Eliminate the noun modifiers.

(3) **The V-chip will give the parents a** new and potentially revolutionary **device to block out programs they don't want their children to see.**

(3') The V-chip will give the parents a device to block out programs they don't want their children to see.

3. Eliminate the adverbial phrases.

(4) **Dwight C. German said the study by Brzustowicz and colleagues** really **may well be a landmark paper.**

(4') Dwight C. German said the study by Brzustowicz and colleagues may well be a landmark paper.

4. Eliminate the prepositional phrases.

(5) **India's foreign secretary flew to Bangladesh** on Sunday for high-level talks.

(5') India's foreign secretary flew to Bangladesh.

5. Shorten the noun phrases by eliminating the specifications

(6) **Schizophrenia patients gained** some **relief after researchers sent magnetic field into** a small area of **their brains.**

(6') Schizophrenia patients gained relief after researchers sent magnetic field into their brains.

6. Change the tense of the main verb into present tense.

(7) **Dwight C. German said the study by Brzustowicz and colleagues** may well be **a landmark paper.**

(7') Dwight C. German said the study by Brzustowicz and colleagues is a landmark paper.

The extracted sentences go iteratively through these reduction operations until the desired compression length is reached. If the desired length is not achieved even after completion of the above mentioned elimination steps, words like pronouns, prepositions, etc. are removed until the desired length is achieved.

3   Evaluation

Evaluation methods can be broadly classified into two categories [6]:*extrinsic* and *intrinsic*. Extrinsic evaluation methods determine the quality of the summaries based on its performance with respect to the completion of certain task, such as information retrieval. Intrinsic evaluation methods determine the quality of the system generated "peer" summaries based on the overlap with human generated "model" summaries.

We evaluated our headline generation techniques using the Document Understanding Conference (DUC) 2004 data [7], provided by NIST, and ROUGE evaluation package [8]. ROUGE is a collection of measures to automatically evaluate the quality of summaries, based on *n-gram* overlap (n=1,2,3,4) and word sequence similarity between the peer and model summaries. In our evaluation,

Table 1. ROUGE evaluation results (with stop words)

System	ROUGE-1	ROUGE-2	ROUGE-3	ROUGE-4	ROUGE-L	ROUGE-W
Our system	0.22485	0.04745	0.00993	0.00230	0.18822	0.10189
Best system	0.25302	0.06590	0.02204	0.00766	0.20288	0.12065
Avg. of human summarizers	0.29	0.08	0.03	0.01	0.24	0.13

Table 2. ROUGE evaluation results (without stop words)

System	ROUGE-1	ROUGE-2	ROUGE-3	ROUGE-4	ROUGE-L	ROUGE-W
Our system	0.26254	0.06489	0.01627	0.00321	0.22335	0.12826
Best system	0.29441	0.07500	0.02122	0.00489	0.23748	0.15241
Avg. of human summarizers	0.32	0.08	0.03	0.01	0.28	0.17

we used ROUGE-N (where N =1, 2, 3, 4), ROUGE-L (longest common subsequence), and ROUGE-W (weighted longest common subsequence) measures. Chin-Yew Lin [8] found that ROUGE-1, ROUGE-L and ROUGE-W correlates well with the human evaluation.

In 2004, NIST provided a collection of 500 documents and defined the task as to generate a very short summary (approximately 75 bytes) for each document. Apart from the test data, NIST also provides four human generated 'model' summaries for each document.

We compared the summaries of our system against the model summaries using ROUGE with the parameters set in the same way as in DUC 2004 evaluation. Table 1 shows the evaluation results of our system in comparison with the best system in DUC 2004 and the average of human summarizers. Our system is among the top ranked systems with respect to ROUGE-1, ROUGE-L and ROUGE-W measures.

We also performed another experiment to study the influence of "removal of stop words" in ROUGE evaluation (Table 2). We observed that there was a significant increase in almost all of the ROUGE measures.

In the Document Understanding Conference [9], that we participated using these sentence reduction techniques, we achieved the highest coverage-based headlines with score approximately 40%. This evaluation was carried out by human judges using the Summary Evaluation Environment (SEE) protocol [1].

4   Conclusion and Future Work

In this paper, we explained the process of generation of headline based on certain linguistically motivated principles. These linguistically motivated principles are based on the syntactic parse of the sentence and thus could be used in sev-

---

[1] http://www.isi.edu/~cyl/SEE

eral domains of texts. We evaluated the headlines generated by our system by comparing them with four "ideal" summaries and using ROUGE measures.

Though our system has a good performance when compared to many other systems, there is still a lot of scope for research into the techniques. We plan to investigate into methods to identify the relative importance of certain syntactic structures, based on their surrounding context words. We also plan to investigate the methods to identify the coherent portions, in order to present more readable content at a given compression rate.

References

1. Dorr, B., Schwartz, R., Zajic, D.: Hedge trimmer: A parse-and-trim approach to headline generation. In: Proceedings of the Document Understanding Conference, Edmonton, NIST (2003) 1-8
2. Choi, F.Y.Y.: Advances in domain independent linear text segmentation. In: Proceedings of the 1st North American Chapter of the Association for Computational Linguistics, Seattle, Washington (2000) 26 - 33
3. Ratnaparkhi, A.: A maximum entropy part-of-speech tagger. In: Proceedings of the Empirical Methods in Natural Language Processing Conference, University of Pennsylvania (1996)
4. Collins, M.: Three generative, lexicalized models for statistical parsing. In: Proceedings of the 35th Annual Meeting of the Association for Computational Linguistics and the 8th European Chapter Meeting of the Association for Computational Linguistics, Spain (1997)
5. Barzilay, R., Elhadad, M.: Using lexical chains for text summarization. In: Proceedings of the 35th Annual Meeting of the Association for Computational Linguistics and the 8th European Chapter Meeting of the Association for Computational Linguistics, Workshop on Intelligent Scalable Text Summarization, Madrid (1997) 10-17
6. Mani, I., Maybury, M.: Advances in Automatic Text Summarization. MIT Press (1999)
7. Over, P.: Introduction to DUC 2004: An intrinsic evaluation of generic news text summarization systems. In: Proceedings of the Document Understanding Conference, Boston, MA, NIST (2004)
8. Lin, C.Y.: ROUGE: A package for automatic evaluation of summaries. In: Proceedings of the Workshop on Text Summarization Branches Out, Barcelona, Spain (2004) 74 - 81
9. Proceedings of the Document Understanding Conference, NIST (2003)
10. Chali, Y., Kolla, M., Singh, N., Zhang, Z.: The university of lethbridge text summarizer at duc 2003. In: Proceedings of the Document Understanding Conference, Edmonton, NIST (2003) 148 - 152
11. Grefenstette, G.: Producing intelligent telegraphic text reduction to provide an audio scanning service for the blind. In: AAAI 98 Spring Symposium on Intelligent Text Summarization. (1998) 111-117

Regularized Classifiers for Information Retrieval

Abderrezak Brahmi and Ahmed Ech-Cherif

LAMOSI Laboratory - Department of Computer Science,
University of Sciences and Technology–USTO Mohamed Boudiaf,
BP: 1505 Oran El M'Naouer, Algeria
a_brahmi@hotmail.com, a.echerif@alum.rpi.edu

Abstract. We study a class of binary regularized least-squares classifiers (RLSC) for information retrieval tasks whose training involve the solution of a unique linear system of equations. Any implementation of RLSC algorithms face two major difficulties: the large size and the density of the Gram matrix. In this paper, we present a numerical investigation of an implementation based on the preconditioned conjugate gradient and introduce a novel reduced RBF kernel which is shown to improve the sparseness of the system.

Keywords: Kernel methods, regularized least squares, binary classification, preconditioned conjugate gradient, SVM, Reuters-21578, MNIST.

1 Introduction

Text (Web pages, news stories …etc.) categorization, document ranking with respect to a given query and information filtering (Spam or undesirable e-mails) are well known information retrieval tasks. A classifier based on a supervised learning model is represented by a decision function $f : X \rightarrow Y$ where X is the set of objects to be classified, Y is the set of categories. Any application $V : Y \times Y \rightarrow [0, \infty)$ such that $V(y, f(x)) = 0$ in case where $f(x) = y$, is called a loss function which intuitively measures the economic loss incurred by predicting $f(x)$) instead of y. In particular, support vector machines [10] use the hinge loss function:

$$V(y, f(x)) = \begin{cases} 0 & \text{if } yf(x) \geq 0, \\ 1 - yf(x) & \text{otherwise.} \end{cases} \tag{1}$$

The optimal separating hyperplane, which determines the weights of the classifier in feature space, can be obtained by the solution of a large convex quadratic programming problem (QP) whose size, m, is precisely the number of examples. In practice, state of the art implementations of SVM can only handle large corpora on powerful software and hardware platforms. In order to solve the large QP on moderate hardware (of the shelf computers for e.g.), chunking techniques which solve a sequence of smaller QPs have been introduced. The widely used sequential minimal optimization (SMO algorithm) solves QP sub-problems with only two variables [5] and has been used for text categorization [2].

B. Kégl and G. Lapalme (Eds.): AI 2005, LNAI 3501, pp. 427–431, 2005.

RLSC learning algorithms are based on a simple form of the loss function namely the square loss [1,7,8]:

$$V(y,f(x)) = (y-f(x))^2 \qquad (2)$$

In the next section, we give brief introduction to RLSC algorithms followed by numerical results of our RLSC/RBF implementation. In section 4, we present a new form of the RBF kernel, which is shown to improve sparsity of the Gram matrix without noticeable loss of precision, along with some preliminary results on the Reuters and MNIST Corpora. Finally, we comment our results and give some concluding remarks.

2 RLSC Theory

Regularized Least-Squares Classifiers (*RLSC*) solve binary classification problems in Reproducing Kernel Hilbert Space H: Given a set of labeled examples $S=(x_i, y_i)_{i=1..m} \subset R^N \times R$, a classifier $f \in H$: $X \rightarrow Y$ can be found by minimizing the empirical risk according to the ERM principle:

$$\min_{f \in H} \frac{1}{m} \sum_{i=1}^{m} (y_i - f(x_i))^2, \qquad (3)$$

which is an ill-posed problem in the sense of Hadamard (1801). In order to make (3) a well posed problem, one can use Tikhonov Regularization techniques which consist of minimizing -for a fixed positive parameter λ-, the regularized functional,

$$\min_{f \in H} \frac{1}{m} \sum_{i=1}^{m} (y_i - f(x_i))^2 + \lambda \|f\|_K^2, \qquad (4)$$

obtained by adding a regularization functional to the empirical risk in (3). The term. $\lambda \|f\|_K^2$ in (4) enhances smoothness and uniqueness of the solution ($\|f\|_K^2$ is the norm of f in H_K, the reproducing kernel Hilbert space defined by the kernel K). The coordinates (c_i) of the unique solution of problem (4) f_λ:

$$f_\lambda(x) = \sum_{i=1}^{m} c_i K_{xi}(x) \qquad (5)$$

in H_K, can be found by solving the linear system of equations:

$$(m\lambda I + K) \, c = y \qquad (6)$$

Where I is the identity matrix, $y=(y_1,\ldots, y_m)^T$ the vector of labels ($y_i=\pm1$) and K is the ($m \times m$) Gram matrix ($K_{ij}=K(x_i, x_j)$). The key algorithm of RLSC, described in [6] computes the decision function (5), by solving system (6) for a given kernel K. Several efficient approaches were proposed in numerical analysis to handle large sparse symmetric definite-positive linear systems[11], nevertheless algorithms capable of dealing with dense systems similar to (6), are limited to small size problems and are based on the preconditioned conjugate gradient algorithms (PCG). Motivated by the results obtained in [3], the incomplete Cholesky factorization PCG algorithm, considered as the state of the art in dense linear algebra, seems to be most appropriate for the solution of (6). ICF-PCG [3] was found to outperform the diagonal PCG on a variety of symmetric positive dense (SPD) test problems.

3 Experiments with RBF Kernel

Preliminary results of our RLSC implementation on Reuters-21578 corpus [13][1] show that ICF-PCG algorithms [3] converge in a single iteration with a small relative residual error. However, in terms of CPU time, the diagonal-PCG algorithms are much faster, for the same tolerance level, on subsets of sizes ranging between 1000 and 9000 examples. The following tables summarize the results obtained on the Reuters[2] corpus whose 9000 first examples were used for training and the last 1377 ones for testing.

Table 1. Performance results of an RLSC on Reuters-21578 corpus for the term «earn». *Gram* and *P_CG* columns indicate the CPU time for the Gram matrix generation and PCG algorithm

Training set		CPU time (sec.)			Classification (%)		
Size	Memory (byte)	Gram	P_CG	Total	Reco.	Pre.	Rec.
1 000	14 090 008	3.02	0.05	3.07	93.61	85.50	99.81
2 000	56 175 500	11.64	2.36	14.00	95.28	89.04	99.61
3 000	126 262 364	25.98	5.44	31.42	94.63	87.67	99.61
4 000	224 349 676	44.33	27.29	71.62	95.42	89.35	99.61
5 000	350 436 904	153.07	188.67	341.74	95.57	89.67	99.61
6 000	504 523 572	546.07	261.50	807.57	95.86	90.30	99.61
7 000	686 610 996	887.16	2 820.26	3 707.42	96.59	91.77	99.81
8 000	896 250 420	1 363.58	4 260.29	5 623.87	96.51	91.61	99.81
9 000	1 134 280 388	1 727.96	4 975.37	6 703.33	97.02	92.77	99.81

Table 2. Comparison of *RLSC* with *SVM-Light* for RBF Kernel (sigma=2). Training is performed on the first 4000 examples from Reuters for five terms having varying rates for positive labels (Pos. shown on the 2nd col.)

Reuters_4000		SVM		RLSC		
Term	Pos. (%)	CPU(s)	Reco.	Gram_CPU(s)	P_CG_CPU(s)	Reco.
"earn"	40.23	37	77.63	44.33	27.29	95.42
"acq"	20.65	36	77.56	48.33	26.97	89.98
"wheat"	2.93	41	98.33	44.92	21.53	98.18
"corn"	2.33	49	98.84	44.54	21.26	98.84
"cocoa"	0.50	55	99.56	44.87	25.11	99.64

---

[1] All the experiments were performed on an AMD850MHz/256Mb(RAM) PC.
[2] Contains 10377 documents represented by *tf* (*term frequency*) vectors of dimension 12113.

For the MNIST corpus of handwritten digits[3][12], the scanned images are represented by vectors of dimension (784=28x28) indicating the gray-levels of the pixels. Training on the first 4000 examples show similar performance results.

Table 3. Comparison of *RLSC* with *SVM-Light* on 2000 examples from MNIST Corpus. The RBF Kernel with sigma=250 is used

MNIST_2000		SVM		RLSC		
Digit	Pos. %	CPU(s)	Reco.	Gram_CPU(s)	P_CG_CPU(s)	Reco.(%)
_0	9.55%	23	90.20	31.96	1.38	99.15
_1	11.00%	22	88.65	26.97	1.32	98.67
_2	9.90%	20	89.68	32.19	1.98	98.29
_3	9.55%	22	89.90	32.08	1.43	97.93
_4	10.70%	22	90.18	32.19	1.37	98.08
_5	9.00%	21	91.08	26.86	1.15	97.84
_6	10.00%	23	90.42	32.07	2.25	98.93
_7	11.20%	21	89.72	26.75	1.15	97.99
_8	8.60%	22	90.26	31.53	1.65	97.63
_9	10.50%	22	89.91	26.75	1.20	97.02

4   Experiments with the Reduced RBF Kernel

We introduce a novel reduced RBF kernel (R-RBF), whose objective is to generate a sparse Gram matrix, obtained by trimming the Gaussian function to a given threshold (θ). R-RBF is defined by:

$$K_{\sigma,\theta}(x,y) = \begin{cases} \exp\left(-\dfrac{\|x-y\|^2}{2\sigma^2}\right) & \text{if } (\|x-y\|^2) \leq -2\sigma^2 \cdot \log(\theta) \\ 0 & \text{otherwise.} \end{cases} \tag{7}$$

For (θ=0), our R-RBF is identical to the classical RBF. In our experiments, the threshold θ was chosen to keep an acceptable prediction rate of the RLSC classifier and a minimal density of the Gram matrix.

Table 4. Comparison of RLSC using R-RBF(θ=0.01, σ=2), SVM(RBF σ=2) and RLSC with RBF (σ=2) for Reuters et MNIST corpora. (-) indicates that the algorithm failed

Training set		SVM (RBF)		RLSC (RBF)		RLSC (R-RBF)	
Corpus	Size	CPU(s)	Reco.	CPU(s)	Reco.	CPU(s)	Reco.
Reuters_earn	9 000	541	79.65	6 703.33	97.02	282.38	92.01
MNIST_0	30 000	19 361	90.20	-	-	7 325.25	90.27

---

[3] Contains 60.000 training examples and 10.000 test examples.

5   Conclusions

Numerical performance results show an improvement of the recognition rate of our RLSC implementation compared to that of SVM. However, RLSC is slower than SVM, in terms of CPU time, due to the time spent (more than 60%) in the generation of the full Gram matrix (Tables 1,3, col. Gram). The latter can be efficiently used in a *one-versus-all* (OVA) scheme[9] without extra computational effort for handling multiclass problems and may favor the use of RLSC for such tasks. The high density of the Gram matrix obtained by the RLSC formulation for large corpora severely limits the use of direct or iterative methods for the solution of the resulting linear system of equations. The latter task is much harder than supposed and declared in [6] using standard kernels.

The proposed reduced RBF kernel seems to be promising for handling the density problem. Preliminary results obtained by using the R-RBF kernel for training RLSC algorithm on large corpora favor its use in real world information retrieval learning tasks such as Web categorization.

References

1. A. E. Hoerl and R. W. Kennard. Ridge regression: biased estimation for nonorthogonal problems. Technometrics, 12(1):55–67, 1970.
2. T. Joachims. Text categorization with support vector machines : Learning with many relevant features. In Claire Nédellec and Céline Rouveiol, editors, Proceedings of the European Conference on Machine Learning, pages 137-142, Berlin, 1998. Springer.
3. Chih-Jen Lin and Romesh Saigal. An Incomplete Cholesky Factorization for Dense Matrices. BIT, 40:536–558, 2000.
4. S. Mukherjee, P. Niyogi, R. Rifkin and T. Poggio. Statistical Learning : CV_{loo} stability is sufficient for generalization and necessary and sufficient for consistency of Empirical Risk Minimization, AI memo, 2002.
5. J. C. Platt. Sequential minimal optimization : A fast algorithm for training support vector machines. Technical Report MSR-TR-98-14, Microsoft Research. 1998.
6. Tomaso Poggio and Steve Smale. The Mathematics of Learning: Dealing with Data. Notices of the AMS. May 2003.
7. Jason D. M. Rennie. Using Part-of-Speech Information for Transfer in Text Classification. December 2003.
8. Ryan Rifkin. Everything Old Is New Again: A Fresh Look at Historical Approaches in Machine Learning. PhD thesis, Massachusetts Institute of Technology, 2002.
9. Ryan Rifkin and Aldebaro Klautau. In Defense of One-Vs-All Classification. Journal of Machine Learning Research, 5 (2004) 101-141.
10. V. Vapnik. The Nature of Statistical Learning Theory. Springer Verlag, New York, 1995.
11. Lapack library http://www.csit.fsu.edu/~burkardt/f_src/lapack/lapack.html
12. MNIST-Yann LeCun, http://yann.lecun.com/exdb/mnist/index.html
13. Reuters-21578 Corpus, http://www.att.research.com/~lewis/reuters21578.html

Rethinking Language Models Within the Framework of Dynamic Bayesian Networks

Murat Deviren, Khalid Daoudi, and Kamel Smaïli

INRIA-LORIA, Parole team, 54602 Villers les Nancy, France
{daoudi, deviren, smaili}@loria.fr

Abstract. We present a new approach for language modeling based on dynamic Bayesian networks. The philosophy behind this architecture is to learn from data the appropriate relations of dependency between the linguistic variables used in language modeling process. It is an original and coherent framework that processes words and classes in the same model. This approach leads to new data-driven language models capable of outperforming classical ones, sometimes with lower computational complexity. We present experiments on a small and medium corpora. The results show that this new technique is very promising and deserves further investigations.

1   Introduction

A statistical speech recognition system estimates the most probable sequence of linguistic units (i.e. words, syllables, phonemes, etc.) given acoustic observations. The Bayesian formulation of the problem allows a factorization over the acoustic and linguistic components: $\hat{W} = \arg\max_W P(O|W)P(W)$, where O denotes acoustic observations and W denotes the underlying sequence of linguistic units. In this formulation, the language model, $P(W)$, encodes the a priori linguistic information, i.e. syntactic, lexical and/or morphologic properties of language. The specification of a language model involves the definition of implicit and/or explicit variables of language. For example n-gram models use *word* as the only variable in language whereas syntactic n-class models use both *word* and *syntactic classes* [1,2]. The dynamics of language is derived by these variables and their interactions through time. Each variable interacts with a certain number of factors that constitute its context. In probabilistic terms the context of a linguistic unit is defined with conditional independence properties. Given its context each linguistic unit is assumed to be independent of other linguistic events. For example classical n-gram models make the assumption that a word is independent of all preceding words given the most recent $n - 1$.

On the other hand, conditional independence is the core property of *dynamic Bayesian networks* (DBNs), it is indeed the exploitation of this property that leads to efficient and generic inference algorithms [3]. Moreover, as it will become clear in the following sections, n-gram and n-class models (and other language models) are very particular instances of DBNs. Thus, it is a natural idea to rethink language models within the general framework of DBNs and seek potential benefits from this rethinking.

It is our purpose in this paper to use the DBNs framework in order to achieve a better exploitation of each linguistic unit considered in modeling. We develop a unifying

B. Kégl and G. Lapalme (Eds.): AI 2005, LNAI 3501, pp. 432–437, 2005.

approach that processes each of these units in a unique model and construct new data-driven language models with improved performances. The principle of our approach is to construct DBNs in which a variable (word, class or any other linguistic unit) may depend on a set of context variables. These dependences between linguistic units can be determined automatically or manually. Of course our ultimate goal is to propose an automatic scheme to learn the optimal DBN structure from a training corpus. However, in order to investigate the feasibility of our approach, we start by analyzing DBN models for which the graphical structure is specified manually.

2   A Brief Overview of Dynamic Bayesian Networks

Dynamic Bayesian networks (DBNs) are generalization of (static) Bayesian networks (BNs) to dynamic processes. The Bayesian networks formalism consists of associating a directed acyclic graph to the joint probability distribution (JPD) $P(X)$ of a set of random variables $X = \{X_1, ..., X_n\}$. The nodes of this graph represent the random variables, while the arrows encode the conditional independences (CI) which (are supposed to) exist in the JPD. A DBN encodes the temporal dynamics of a time evolving set $X[t] = \{X_1[t], ..., X_n[t]\}$ of variables. The JPD of $\mathbf{X}_1^T = \{X[1], ..., X[T]\}$ is factorized as:

$$P(X[1], ..., X[T]) = \prod_{t=1}^{T} \prod_{i=1}^{n} P(X_i[t]|\Pi_{it}) \qquad (1)$$

where Π_{it} denotes the parents of $X_i[t]$. In the BNs literature, DBNs are defined using the assumption that $X[t]$ is Markovian [4]. In this paper, we relax this hypothesis to allow non-Markov processes (see [5] for details).

From this perspective, it is obvious that classical language models can be represented as DBNs. Indeed, n-gram models assume that the probability of a word sequence is factorized over the conditional probabilities of each word in the sequence given its recent history of $n - 1$ words. That is, if W is the word vocabulary and $w_1^T = w_1...w_T \in W^T$ is a word sequence, one assumes that: $P(w_1^T) = \prod_{t=1}^{T} P(w_t|w_{t-1}, ..., w_{t-n+1})$

Thus, if W_t is a discrete random variable taking its values in W for every t, n-grams can be represented as the DBN shown in Fig. 1-(a) (for $n = 3$, i.e., trigram) which is a Markov chain of order n. Class-based approaches represent the history on word classes rather than words. That is, if $C = \{l_1, ..., l_m\}$ is the set of class labels and $c_1^T = c_1...c_T \in C^T$ is an observed class sequence, one assumes that:

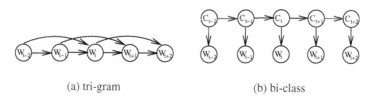

(a) tri-gram   (b) bi-class

Fig. 1. Tri-gram and bi-class models

$P(w_1^T, c_1^T) = \prod_{t=1}^{T} P(w_t|c_t)P(c_t|c_{t-1}, \ldots, c_{t-n+1})$. Thus, if C_t is a discrete random variable taking its values in C for every t, n-class models can be represented as the DBN shown in Fig. 1-(b) (for $n = 2$, i.e., bi-class).

3   Language Modeling with DBNs

n-gram and n-class models are the most commonly used language models in state-of-the-art speech recognition systems. In practice they are merged together either using linear combination or an integration of their respective characteristics in a single architecture using maximum entropy techniques [6]. This approach yields quite interesting results, however if we want to better exploit the lexical and syntactic information, a solution would be to consider them in a unique model that is trained within a single procedure.

The DBN formalism provides a theoretical and computational framework to achieve this goal. Our principle idea is to impose no *a priori* hypothesis on the way a language should be represented but to consider all available data (words, classes, ...) as observations of the dynamic system $\{W_t, C_t\}$. Our goal then is to find the model that has the best description (in terms of perplexity) of these observations. In this way, we let data dictate what influences the pronunciation of a word. In Bayesian networks terminology this is the *structure learning* problem: find the graph structure (and its numerical parameterization) that explains the data at "best".

In order to define a set of DBN structures plausible for language modeling, we need to specify conditional independence (CI) assertions that are linguistically informative and easy to interpret. We also want n-gram and n-class models to be included in this set in order to be able to exploit their linguistic properties. We define the following generalized CI assumptions:

Assumption 1. *Given the most recent $n - 1$ words and the classes of $m - 1$ previous and k future words, a word W_t is independent of all previous words and their classes $\{W_1, \ldots, W_{t-n}, C_1, \ldots, C_{t-m}\}$.*

Assumption 2. *Given the most recent $n - 1$ words and the class labels of previous $m - 1$ words $\{C_{t-1}, \ldots, C_{t-m+1}, W_{t-1}, \ldots, W_{t-n+1}\}$, the class C_t is independent of previous words and distant class history $\{W_1, \ldots, W_{t-n}, C_1, \ldots, C_{t-m}\}$.*

The first assumption specifies the context of a word from both word and class variables allowing also the incorporation of the classes of future words. Schematically the

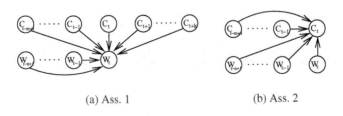

(a) Ass. 1   (b) Ass. 2

Fig. 2. Allowed dependencies due to assumption 1 and 2

allowed dependences are shown in Fig.2.a. The second assumption generalizes the class context to include word history. The schematic representation is shown in Fig.2.b.

The JPD for a specific model is: $P(W, C) = \prod_t P(W_t | \Pi_{W_t}) P(C_t | \Pi_{C_t})$, where Π_{W_t} and Π_{C_t} are the set of parents of W_t and C_t respectively.

4   Experiments

The first set of experiments is performed on the *Le monde* newspaper corpus. We use 22M words for training and a test corpus of 2M words. The vocabulary consists of the most frequent 5000 words. The training corpus has been labeled automatically by a set of 200 syntactic classes set by hand [7]. All models used in the experiments are smoothed using absolute discounting method [8].

Table 1 shows perplexity results of different Bayesian network language models. In order to achieve our objective to find the best model we set the bi-class model as baseline and extend it incrementally by incorporating additional lexical and/or syntactic context. We also introduce the concept of right context of a word. DBN6 is a typical example of this case that integrates not only the left class context of a word but also its right syntactic context. We obtain a 16.6% improvement with respect to DBN4 that proves the importance of right context. It is true that linguistically this is not a surprising result. DBN5, on the other hand, shows that left context is quite important. That is why its removal reduces the results by 7.8%. A significant perplexity reduction is observed if a word not only depends on its syntactic but also lexical context. Indeed, DBN7 yields an improvement of 24.6% with respect to DBN4. This results confirms that lexical history is indispensable and that syntactic history provides a significant improvement.

Pushing forward this strategy, we achieve a model that is not only much better than the bi-class but also better than the bi-gram. Indeed, the model DBN8 reduces the perplexity by 57.9% with respect to bi-class and 2.4% with respect to bi-gram.

The second set of experiments (SPORT) is performed on articles dedicated to sport news extracted from a French newspaper. The corpus consists of 8500 sentences, the tests are performed using an open vocabulary of 2000 words with different cluster sizes ($|C|$)and with or without $< UNK >$. Word classes are defined based on statistical criteria using the HTK toolkit.

Table 1. Perplexity results on "Le Monde 87" corpus

Model	$P(W)$	PP
2-gram	$\prod_t P(w_t | w_{t-1})$	65.24
2-class	$\prod_t P(w_t | c_t) P(c_t | c_{t-1})$	151.31
3-class	$\prod_t P(w_t | c_t) P(c_t | c_{t-1} c_{t-2})$	130.00
DBN4	$\prod_t P(w_t | c_t, c_{t-1}) P(c_t | c_{t-1})$	113.13
DBN5	$\prod_t P(w_t | c_t, c_{t+1}) P(c_t | c_{t-1})$	121.98
DBN6	$\prod_t P(w_t | c_{t-1}, c_t, c_{t+1}) P(c_t | c_{t-1})$	94.35
DBN7	$\prod_t P(w_t | w_{t-1}, c_t) P(c_t | c_{t-1})$	85.20
DBN8	$\prod_t P(w_t | w_{t-1}, c_{t-1}, c_{t-2}) P(c_t | w_t)$	**63.67**

Table 2. SPORT corpus perplexity results computed with/without $< UNK >$

Model	$P(W)$	$|C| = 1|$	$|C| = 15$	$|C| = 25$	$|C| = 45$
2-gram	$\prod_t P(w_t|w_{t-1})$	38.5/50.7			
3-gram	$\prod_t P(w_t|w_{t-1}, w_{t-2})$	30.9/39.3			
2-class	$\prod_t P(w_t|c_t)P(c_t|c_{t-1})$		94.1/139.2	84.2/122.7	77.5/111.9
3-class	$\prod_t P(w_t|c_t)P(c_t|c_{t-1}, c_{t-2})$		90.6/133.4	80.0/115.9	71.5/102.2
DBN9	$\prod_t P(w_t|w_{t-1}, c_{t-2})P(c_t|w_t)$		36.3/47.2	35.2/45.6	34.4/44.3

Table 2 shows different model performances for SPORT corpus. The first remark is that the use of a higher number of classes leads to a reduction of perplexity. The second one is that the use of a history which combines classes and words is beneficial to language models and yields better results. The best performance is obtained by DBN9 which yields an improvement of 12,6% in comparison to bigram. The other important point is that, even if the trigram computational complexity $(O(|W|^3))$ is higher than the one of DBN9 $(O(|W|^2|C| + |W||C|))$, there is only a difference of 5 points (in average) between their perplexities, which is relatively small. Thus we can hope that, with a larger vocabulary and with a classification containing more classes, we can build DBN models similar to DBN9 with equivalent performances as a trigram.

5   Conclusion

Using the framework of the dynamic Bayesian networks, we presented a new approach for language modeling that considers data (training corpora made up of words, classes, concepts...) as observations of a dynamical system with the goal to find the model that has the best description of these observations in terms of perplexity. Among the advantages of this approach, we can note that the linguistic units are not used separately as in classical models, but merged in a single process. We tested several DBNs on different corpora and hence on different applications. The results show for all corpora that the models are improved by introducing the left context of both words and classes. Some experiments showed that DBNs outperform the baseline models and in some cases they compete with the higher order baseline models. All these encouraging results illustrate the feasibility of our approach. The main direction of our future work is to investigate algorithms of structure learning problem in order to reach our final objective: find the graph structure and its numerical parametrization that explains the data at best.

References

1. Jelinek, F. In: Self-organized language modeling for speech recognition. Morgan Kaufmann (1989) 450–506
2. Brown, P., DellaPietra, V., deSouza, P., Lai, J., Mercer, R.: Class based n-gram models of natural language. Computational Linguistics **18** (1992) 467–478
3. Heckerman, D.: A tutorial on learning with bayesian networks. Technical Report MSR-TR-95-06, Microsoft Research, Advanced Technology Division (1995)

4. Friedman, N., Murphy, K., Russell, S.: Learning the structure of dynamic probabilistic networks. In: UAI'98, Madison, Wisconsin (1998)
5. Deviren, M., Daoudi, K.: Structural learning of dynamic Bayesian networks in speech recognition. In: Eurospeech 2001, Aalborg, Denmark (2001)
6. Rosenfeld, R.: Adaptive Statistical Language Modeling: A Maximum Entropy Approach. PhD thesis, Carnegie Mellon University, Pittsburgh, PA 15213 (1994)
7. Smaïli, K., Brun, A., Zitouni, I., Haton, J.: Automatic and manual clustering for large vocabulary speech re cognition: A comparative study. In: Eurospeech, Hungary (1999)
8. Ney, H., Essen, U., Kneser, R.: On structuring probabilistic dependences in stochastic language modelling. Computer Speech and Language **8** (1994) 1–38

Error Bounds in Reinforcement Learning Policy Evaluation

Fletcher Lu

University of Waterloo, 200 University Avenue West,
Waterloo, Ontario, Canada, N2L 3G1
f2lu@cs.uwaterloo.ca

Abstract. With the advent of Kearns & Singh's (2000) rigorous upper bound on the error of temporal difference estimators, we derive the first rigorous error bound for the maximum likelihood policy evaluation method as well as deriving a Monte Carlo matrix inversion policy evaluation error bound. We provide, the first direct comparison between the error bounds of the maximum likelihood (ML), Monte Carlo matrix inversion (MCMI) and temporal difference (TD) estimation methods for policy evaluation. We use these bounds to confirm generally held notions of the superior accuracy of the model-based estimation methods of ML and MCMI over the model-free method of TD. With our error bounds, we are also able to specify parameters and conditions that affect each method's estimation accuracy.

1   Introduction

The issue of policy evaluation deals with estimating the value of the future rewards in a Markov reward process for a fixed policy π. A variety of techniques for performing value estimation have been developed, the most common of which are the temporal differencing (TD) [1] and maximum likelihood (ML) [2] methods. The Monte Carlo matrix inversion (MCMI) method is an alternative model-based method for policy evaluation introduced by Barto and Duff [3]. The choice of estimation method has commonly been dictated by issues of storage requirements and runtime complexity. The model-free TD method has often been preferred due to its perceived faster execution time as well as minimal storage requirements [4]. However, recent work has shown that ML can be competitive with TD under a variety of circumstances in terms of execution time [5]. Also, the MCMI estimation approach is competitive with TD in terms of *both* execution and storage costs [6].

One criteria for choosing an estimation method that has often been only addressed empirically is the issue of value estimation *accuracy*. Model-based methods such as ML and MCMI have generally been perceived to be more accurate estimators compared to the TD model-free method [2] [3]. Much of this perception has been derived from intuitive arguments due in part to a lack, until recently, of rigorous error bounds for TD. Another reason for a lack of

B. Kégl and G. Lapalme (Eds.): AI 2005, LNAI 3501, pp. 438–449, 2005.

rigorous theoretical bounds for comparisons between estimation methods is that the direct ML approach uses a matrix factorization to derive a matrix inverse. Finding an error bounds for the ML estimation is complicated by the fact that there is no single factorization approach. Instead, there exists an entire family of factorization algorithms designed to handle different matrix properties.

In this paper, we provide error bounds for the ML and MCMI estimation methods and compare them to the Kearns and Singh TD error bounds introduced in 2000 [7]. With these theoretical error bounds, we are able to provide:

1. Conditions required for the ML method to produce accurate estimates;
2. Confirmation on the general perception of the superior accuracy of ML and MCMI estimation accuracy over TD due to TD's error bias;
3. Theoretical support that with decreasing discount factor (γ) size, estimation accuracy improves.

In addition to the theoretical analysis, we also provide some sample experimental data in support of our analysis.

2   Preliminaries

Consider a Markov reward process over a fixed policy π. This Markov reward process ranges over a finite set of N states with stationary transition probabilities $P(s_{i+1} = m | s_i = n)$, where s_i is the state entered into at time i. The rewards are given by a probability distribution $R(r_m | s_i = m)$, where r_m is the reward obtained for entering state m. The transition model can be represented by an $N \times N$ matrix P, where $P(n, m) = P(s_{i+1} = m | s_i = n)$. The reward model may be represented by an $N \times 1$ vector of expected rewards $\mathbf{r}$, where $\mathbf{r}(m) = E[r_m]$. The value function $\mathbf{v}(n)$ finds the expected sum of discounted future rewards for a state $s_0 = n$, that is $\mathbf{v} = \mathbf{r} + \gamma P \mathbf{r} + \gamma^2 P^2 \mathbf{r} + \dots$. If P and $\mathbf{r}$ are known, then $\mathbf{v}$ may be found by solving the matrix equation

$$(I - \gamma P)\mathbf{v} = \mathbf{r}, \tag{1}$$

where I is an identity matrix. The process of finding value estimates for states for a fixed policy in such a reinforcement learning problem is what is known as policy evaluation.

Policy evaluation methods may be divided into model-free methods such as TD and model-based methods such as ML and MCMI.

2.1   Background on TD

The model-free temporal difference method foregoes a model by estimating $\mathbf{v}$ with actual discounted rewards r_i obtained over sample trajectories and a bootstrapping method which uses old value estimates for states to avoid waiting until the end of a sample trajectory to update its estimates. The standard TD(λ) value estimation is given by

$$\hat{\mathbf{v}}(s_0 = n) \leftarrow \sum_{k=1}^{\infty} (1 - \lambda)\lambda^{k-1}[(1 - \alpha)\hat{\mathbf{v}}(s_0) + \alpha(R_k)], \tag{2}$$

where $R_k = r_0 + \gamma r_1 + \ldots + \gamma^{k-1} r_{k-1} + \gamma^k \hat{\mathbf{v}}(s_k)$, $0 \leq \alpha \leq 1$ and $0 \leq \lambda \leq 1$ [4]. Figure 3 of appendix A illustrates a sample TD algorithm.

In terms of storage and runtime costs, the TD method needs to only store each state's value estimates. Thus, it requires $O(N)$ space. For each of T sampling steps, TD may check up to N states to update a state value producing an $O(TN)$ runtime for the most efficient of TD algorithms.

2.2   Background on ML

The maximum likelihood method finds an estimate $\hat{\mathbf{v}}$ of the value function $\mathbf{v}$ from equation 1 by building an estimate $\hat{P}$ of matrix P and an estimate $\hat{\mathbf{r}}$ of the expected rewards $\mathbf{r}$ through sampling of the environment. We calculate $\hat{P}$ by $\hat{P}_{ij} = \frac{a_{ij}}{\sum_j a_{ij}}$ $\forall$ $1 \leq i,j \leq N$ where a_{ij} is the number of times during sampling we transitioned from state i to state j. Similarly, $\hat{r}(m) = \frac{\sum_{i=1}^k r_m(i)}{k}$, where $r_m(i)$ is the reward obtained for the i'th visit of state m and k is the total number of times state m was visited during sampling.

ML uses this model of matrix P to then solve for $\mathbf{v}$ by finding the inverse of matrix $(I - \gamma\hat{P})$ through matrix factorization and back substitution with $\hat{\mathbf{r}}$.

$(I - \gamma\hat{P})$ is an $N \times N$ matrix. Therefore in the worst-case, ML requires up to $O(N^2)$ space. In addition, the runtime for ML is dependent on the cost of factoring the matrix $(I - \gamma\hat{P})$ which is upper bound at $O(N^3)$ [5].

2.3   Background on MCMI

The Monte Carlo matrix inversion method finds an estimate $\hat{\mathbf{v}}$ of $\mathbf{v}$ by deriving an estimate $\widehat{(I - \gamma P)^{-1}}$ of matrix $(I - \gamma P)^{-1}$ directly using a statistical estimation approach and then producing the estimate $\hat{\mathbf{v}}$ by $\hat{\mathbf{v}} = \widehat{(I - \gamma P)^{-1}}\hat{\mathbf{r}}$.

This statistical estimation approach was first developed by Ulam & Von Neummann and published by Forsythe & Leibler [8] for the estimate of the inverse of a matrix $(I - M)$, where the eigenvalues of matrix M are less than one (ie. $\max_r |\lambda_r(M)| < 1$). Barto and Duff applied this approach to reinforcement learning [3]. One way to find $\mathbf{v}$ of equation 1 is to find the inverse of matrix $(I - \gamma P)$. As long as $\gamma < 1$, then the eigenvalue requirements to find the inverse of $(I - \gamma P)$ by the Monte Carlo matrix inversion method are satisfied.

In the MCMI policy evaluation method, we use a matrix $\hat{W}$, where

$$\hat{W}_{ij} = \frac{walk_{ij}}{(1-\gamma)(\sum_j walk_{ij})} \qquad \forall\ 1 \leq i,j \leq N, \tag{3}$$

and $walk_{ij}$ is a sampling walk, through our environment, which starts in a state i and ends in a state j. Lu and Schuurmans [6] showed that the expected value of $\hat{W}_{ij}$ is

$$E[\hat{W}_{ij}] = ([I - \gamma P]^{-1})_{ij}. \tag{4}$$

Figure 4 of appendix A illustrates a sample MCMI policy evaluation algorithm.

Due to various algorithmic efficiencies illustrated by Lu and Schuurmans [6], MCMI need only store space linear in N. Also, the MCMI algorithm has an upper bound time of $O(TN)$, where T is the number of sampling steps and N is the number of states.

3   Error Bounds

3.1   Error Bounds of TD

Kearns & Singh [7] formed an error bound on a modified form of TD(λ) called *phased* TD. Phased TD uses equal weighting of learning updates in order to avoid the moving average resulting from a fixed value of α in equation 2 of standard TD(λ). In phased TD(λ) we have

$$\mathbf{v}_t(s) \leftarrow \frac{1}{h}\sum_{i=1}^{n}\left(\sum_{k=1}^{\infty}(1-\lambda)\lambda^{k-1}(R_k^i)\right), \tag{5}$$

where $R_k^i = r_0^i + \gamma r_1^i + \ldots + \gamma^{k-1}r_{k-1}^i + \gamma^k \mathbf{v}_{t-1}(s_k^i)$ and r_k^i is the reward obtained at the k'th time step on the i'th trajectory and s_k^i is the state visited at the k'th time step on the i'th trajectory. There are a finite set of h trajectories where $1 \leq i \leq h$. Despite this modification, they showed that phased TD is analogous to standard TD with constant α [9].

Based on phased TD, Kearns & Singh [7] found a confidence interval error bound for temporal difference value estimate in a recursive format:

$$\triangle_t \leq \min_k \left[\frac{1-(\gamma\lambda)^k}{1-\gamma\lambda}\sqrt{\frac{3log(k/\nu)}{h}} + \frac{(\gamma\lambda)^k}{1-\gamma\lambda}\right] + \frac{(1-\lambda)\gamma}{1-\gamma\lambda}\triangle_{t-1}, \tag{6}$$

where $\triangle_t = \max_s[|\hat{\mathbf{v}}_t(s) - \mathbf{v}(s)|]$ with probability at least $1-\nu$, $0 \leq t \leq T$, $0 < \nu < 1$ and $1 \leq k \leq h$. We can modify equation 6 to form a relative residual error bound on the TD value estimate of $\hat{\mathbf{v}}$ by simply using equation 6 as a worst case upper bound for each of the N value estimate entries in $\hat{\mathbf{v}}$, to yield:

$$\frac{||\hat{\mathbf{v}}_t - \mathbf{v}||_1}{||\mathbf{v}||_1} \leq \frac{N}{||\mathbf{v}||_1}\min_k\left[\frac{1-(\gamma\lambda)^k}{1-\gamma\lambda}\sqrt{\frac{3\log(k/\nu)}{h}} + \frac{(\gamma\lambda)^k}{1-\gamma\lambda}\right] + N\frac{(1-\lambda)\gamma}{1-\gamma\lambda}\frac{||\hat{\mathbf{v}}_{t-1} - \mathbf{v}||_1}{||\mathbf{v}||_1}, \tag{7}$$

where $||\mathbf{a}||_1$ is defined as the 1-norm of vector $\mathbf{a}$.[1]

3.2   Error Bounds of ML

We now consider the superior accuracy issue of ML over TD by deriving an error bound on the value estimate produced by the maximum likelihood approach. In

---

[1] Equation 7 will hold for any norm. We use the 1-norm to facilitate comparison with the ML and MCMI error bounds which require the use of the 1-norm in their derivations in order to apply lemma 1 of appendix B.

order to handle the varying factorization approaches used to find a solution to a matrix equation of the form

$$Ax = b, \tag{8}$$

where A is an $N \times N$ matrix and b and x are $N \times 1$ vectors with x unknown, we use an approach known as *perturbation* theory to deal with any factorization differences. Let $A + \delta A$ represent an estimated matrix where A represents the true matrix and δA represents any *perturbed* deviation from A due to the random variate estimate. Similarly, let b and x represent the right-hand side and true solution, respectively, to the matrix equation with δb being any deviation from b and δx being any deviation from x due to the δA deviation and δb. The elegance of this approach is that δx may capture any deviation caused by method bias as well as numerical instability due to limits on machine precision [10]. We thus have $(A + \delta A)(x + \delta x) = b + \delta b$. Since $Ax = b$, this equation reduces to $A\delta x + \delta A(x + \delta x) = \delta b$. Multiplying by A^{-1} and rearranging, we get

$$\delta x = A^{-1}\delta b - A^{-1}\delta A(x + \delta x). \tag{9}$$

By taking the absolute value norm of both sides and using the triangle inequality, equation 9 becomes $||\delta x|| \leq ||A^{-1}|| \; ||\delta b|| + ||A^{-1}|| \; ||\delta A|| \; ||x|| + ||A^{-1}|| \; ||\delta A|| \; ||\delta x||$. Grouping the $||\delta x||$ terms, we get a bound of

$$||\delta x|| \leq \frac{||A^{-1}|| \; ||\delta b|| + ||A^{-1}|| \; ||\delta A|| \; ||x||}{1 - ||A^{-1}|| \; ||\delta A||}. \tag{10}$$

We can treat $||A^{-1}||$ and $||x||$ as constants because they represent the norm of the true inverse and norm of the true solution, respectively. If $||A^{-1}|| \; ||\delta A|| << 1$, then equation 10 can be reduced to

$$||\delta x|| \leq c_1(||\delta b|| + c_2||\delta A||), \tag{11}$$

where $c_1 = ||A^{-1}||$ and $c_2 = ||x||$. For our reinforcement learning problem $\delta b = \hat{r} - r$, $\delta x = \hat{v} - v$ and $\delta A = (I - \gamma\hat{P}) - (I - \gamma P) = \gamma(\hat{P} - P)$.

For our analysis, we will let the rewards be a deterministic function of states, $r(m) = r_m$. Therefore, $\hat{r} = r$. So equation 11 becomes

$$||\hat{v} - v|| \leq c_1 c_2 \gamma ||\hat{P} - P||. \tag{12}$$

Let us use the 1-norm for our analysis. Therefore, we have

$$||\hat{v} - v||_1 \leq ||(I - \gamma P)^{-1}||_1 \; ||v||_1 \gamma ||\hat{P} - P||_1, \tag{13}$$

where $c_1 = ||(I - \gamma P)^{-1}||$ and $c_2 = ||v||$. From lemma 1 of appendix B, we proved that by the Central Limit Theorem, there is a 95% probability that $||\hat{P} - P||_1 \leq \frac{\sqrt{N}}{\sqrt{T}}$. Substituting this result into equation 13 and rearranging we get

$$\frac{||\hat{v} - v||_1}{||v||_1} \leq \frac{||(I - \gamma P)^{-1}||_1 \gamma \sqrt{N}}{\sqrt{T}}, \tag{14}$$

under the assumption that $||(I - \gamma P)^{-1}|| \; ||\hat{P} - P|| << 1$, which should hold with a large enough sampling size of T.

If we now compare equation 14 with the error bound equation of TD, equation 7, we see that TD has a biasing term, TD Bias $= \frac{1-(\gamma\lambda)^k}{1-\gamma\lambda}\sqrt{\frac{3\log(k/\nu)}{h}} + \frac{(\gamma\lambda)^k}{1-\gamma\lambda}$. This bias is the result of TD tending to use old value estimates. In contrast, ML's error bound has no such bias, converging to zero as the number of sampling steps grows. This analytically explains past empirical evidence for ML tending to produce more accurate value estimates than TD.

3.3 Error Bounds of MCMI

As specified in equation 4, $\hat{W}_{ij}$ has an expected value of $([I - \gamma P]^{-1})_{ij}$. From equation 3, we can see that the N^2 random variates, $\hat{W}_{ij}$, that are estimating the N^2 elements of matrix $[I - \gamma P]^{-1}$, have the property that $\sum_{j=1}^{n} \hat{W}_{ij} = \frac{1}{1-\gamma}$ $\forall$ $1 \leq i \leq N$. Let $\hat{P}$ be an $N \times N$ matrix such that, $\hat{P}_{ij} = (1 - \gamma)\hat{W}_{ij}$, for all $1 \leq i, j \leq N$. Then

$$[I - \widehat{\gamma P}]^{-1} = \frac{1}{1-\gamma}\hat{P}, \tag{15}$$

and $\hat{P}$ is a probability matrix with rows summing to 1.[2] Since the sum of the entries in a given row of $\hat{P}$ must equal 1, then $\hat{P}_{ij}$ is stochastically dependent on $\hat{P}_{ik}$. However, entries in different rows have no such restrictions. Therefore, $\hat{P}_{ij}$ is stochastically independent of $\hat{P}_{kl}$, where $k \neq i$. Let $E[\hat{P}] = P$. Then combining equations 15 and 4, we get

$$P = E[\hat{P}] = E[(1 - \gamma)[I - \widehat{\gamma P}]^{-1}] \tag{16}$$

$$= (1 - \gamma)[I - \gamma P]^{-1} \tag{17}$$

As in the ML error analysis, we will let the rewards be a deterministic function of states. Therefore, $\hat{r} = r$. Since $v = [I - \gamma P]^{-1}r$ then,

$$\hat{v} - v = [I - \widehat{\gamma P}]^{-1}r - [I - \gamma P]^{-1}r. \tag{18}$$

From equations 15, 17 and 18, we get $\hat{v} - v = \frac{1}{1-\gamma}(\hat{P} - P)r$

Also as in the ML error analysis, let us take the norms of this equation to get

$$||\hat{v} - v|| \leq \frac{1}{1-\gamma}||\hat{P} - P|| \; ||r||. \tag{19}$$

Since $\hat{P}$ is a probability matrix then from lemma 1 of appendix B, the Central Limit Theorem states that there is a 95% probability that $||\hat{P} - P||_1 \leq \frac{\sqrt{N}}{\sqrt{T}}$.[3] Using this result and taking the 1-norms of equation 19, we have a 95% probability that

$$||\hat{v} - v||_1 \leq \frac{1}{1-\gamma}||\hat{P} - P||_1 \; ||r||_1 = \frac{\sqrt{N}||r||_1}{(1-\gamma)\sqrt{T}} \tag{20}$$

---

[2] Note: $\hat{P}$ is not generally equal to P (where P is the probability matrix of equation 1). The relationship being that P_{ij} is the probability of moving from state i immediately to next state j, while $\hat{P}_{ij}$ is related to a path of states that start in state i and eventually reach a state j.

[3] A comment on sample points: One efficiency that [8] noted was that we can use every sampling step in a sample run as the start of a new sample walk. Therefore, with T sampling steps you can have T sample walks. So the number of sample points, T, can be the same in both ML and MCMI.

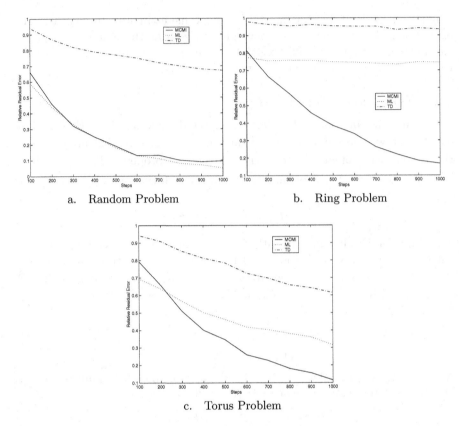

a.   Random Problem   b.   Ring Problem

c.   Torus Problem

Fig. 1. Error Reduction vs. # of Sampling Steps (T) for differing state transition environments, N = 300, $\lambda = .9$, $\gamma = .8$, $\alpha = .5$

Dividing by $||\mathbf{v}||_1$ on both sides of equation 20 gives us a relative residual error. We therefore have a 95% probability that for N states and T sampling steps,

$$\frac{||\hat{\mathbf{v}} - \mathbf{v}||_1}{||\mathbf{v}||_1} \leq \frac{\sqrt{N}||\mathbf{r}||_1}{(1-\gamma)\sqrt{T}||\mathbf{v}||_1}, \tag{21}$$

Looking closely at equation 21 and comparing it with equation 7, we can see that, similar to ML, the error bound on MCMI value estimates have no biasing term as TD's does. Therefore, MCMI can be expected to produce superior value estimates to those of TD.

4   Experiments: Comparing Estimation Accuracy

In our first set of experiments of figure 1, we compare the residual error of MCMI, ML and TD on three different state transition networks: a Random network, a

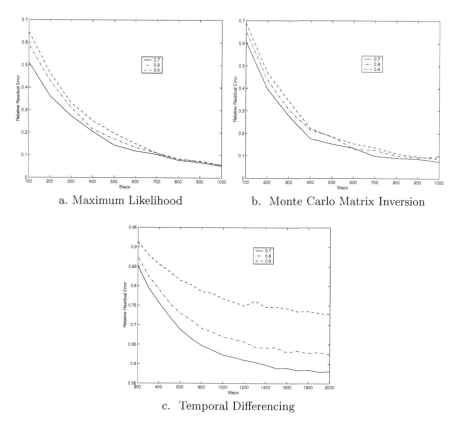

a. Maximum Likelihood   b. Monte Carlo Matrix Inversion

c. Temporal Differencing

Fig. 2. Error Reduction vs. # of Sampling Steps (T) for differing solvers on a randomly generated matrix, N = 300 with $\lambda = .9$, $\alpha = .5$ and γ values ranging from 0.7 to 0.9

Ring network and a Torus network as the number of sampling steps grow.[4] In all three graphs the TD method produces the largest error followed by ML with MCMI having the least residual error. Figure 1.b & 1.c illustrates that at times ML can be significantly worse than MCMI due to a poorly conditioned matrix.[5] In this regard MCMI can be considered more fault-tolerant than the ML method. Figure 1.a illustrates the effect of the biasing term of TD [7] and the unbiasedness of the ML and MCMI with TD asymptoting at about 0.68, while both the ML and MCMI methods converge to under 0.1.

---

[4] In our experiments, the relative residual error is calculated as $\frac{||\hat{\mathbf{v}}-\mathbf{v}||_1}{||\mathbf{v}||_1}$, normalizing over all N states. The composition of the Ring and Torus state transition environments are illustrated in Lu et al. 2002[5]. The Random state transition environment was generated from a uniform distribution.

[5] From equation 14 we can see that the ML method is heavily dependent on the size of the true inverse of $I - \gamma P$. If $||(I - \gamma P)^{-1}||$ is very large then the condition number of the matrix is large and a very accurate $\hat{P}$ estimate of P is needed for ML to be able to produce any estimate of $\mathbf{v}$. Condition number of A = $||A|| \; ||A^{-1}||$.

Another notable property of our theoretical error bounds is that, from equation 14, 21 and 7 of the ML, MCMI and TD bounds (respectively), we may predict that as the parameter γ decreases, our error bounds get tighter and thus our estimations should become more accurate. Figure 2 illustrates this effect for varying γ values. Figure 2.c also illustrates that with decreasing γ, TD's error asymptotes to a decreasing error bound [7]. One interesting result of this analysis is that with a small enough γ TD and MCMI may become equally accurate and since both TD and MCMI have similar storage and runtimes then one may choose TD for its faster updates due to its bootstrapping. However with larger γ values MCMI may be favourable.

5   Conclusions

In this paper we have provided the first rigorous error bounds for policy evaluation for the maximum likelihood method and a new error bound for the Monte Carlo matrix inversion method for policy evaluation. In doing so, we have been able to also provide the first analytical comparison between these two methods and the temporal differencing error bound. We have used these bounds to verify intuitive beliefs, based on past empirical evidence, about their comparable accuracies; specifically that ML and MCMI tend to be more accurate than TD and that MCMI is the most fault-tolerate of all three methods. We have also used these theoretical bounds to demonstrate how changes in a parameter (such as γ) would affect a method's estimates. In general, as the value of the discount factor (γ) decreases, all three methods improve in accuracy.

In terms of future work, we may use these bounds to illustrate precise numerical tradeoffs between accuracy, storage and runtime efficiency among the various evaluation methods.

References

1. R. S. Sutton. Learning to predict by the method of Temporal Differences. In *Machine Learning*, volume 3, pages 9–44, 1988.
2. S.P. Singh and R.S. Sutton. Reinforcement Learning with Replacing Eligibility Traces. In *Machine Learning*, volume 22, pages 123–158, 1996.
3. A. G. Barto and M. Duff. Monte Carlo matrix inversion and reinforcement learning. In *NIPS: Proceedings of the 1994 Conference*, pages 687–694, San Francisco, 1994. Morgan Kaufmann.
4. R. S. Sutton and A. G. Barto. *Reinforcement Learning: An Introduction*. MIT Press, Cambridge, Massachusetts, 1998.
5. F. Lu, R. Patrascu, and D. Schuurmans. Investigating the Maximum Likelihood alternative to TD(λ). In *Proceedings of the 19th ICML*, pages 403–410, San Francisco, 2002. Morgan Kaufmann.
6. F. Lu and D. Schuurmans. Monte Carlo Matrix Inversion Policy Evaluation. In *UAI: Proceedings of the 19th Conference*, pages 386–393, San Francisco, 2003. Morgan Kaufmann.

7. M. Kearns and S. Singh. Bias-variance error bounds for temporal difference updates. In *Proceedings of the 13th Annual Conference on Computational Learning Theory*, pages 142–147, 2000.

8. G. E. Forsythe and R. A. Leibler. Matrix inversion by a Monte Carlo Method. In *MTAC*, volume 4, pages 127–129, 1950.

9. M. Kearns and S. Singh. Finite-sample convergence rates for q-learning and indirect algorithms. In *NIPS: Proceedings of the 1998 Conference*, pages 996–1002, 1998.

10. G. H. Golub and C. F. Van Loan. *Matrix Computations*. Johns Hopkins University Press, Baltimore, MD, 1989.

11. S.P. Singh and P. Dayan. Analytical Mean Squared Error Curves for Temporal Difference Learning. In *Machine Learning*, volume 32, pages 5–40, 1998.

A   Algorithms

We implemented temporal differencing using eligibility traces, as shown in figure 3 [4]. Subtle variants of this procedure are obtained by changing the way the eligibilities are updated. For example, if n is the current state and $\ell \neq n$, then all procedures use the update $\mathbf{e}(\ell) \leftarrow \gamma\lambda\mathbf{e}(\ell)$, however for state n "accumulate trace" uses the update $\mathbf{e}(n) \leftarrow \gamma\lambda\mathbf{e}(n) + 1$ whereas "replace trace" uses the update $\mathbf{e}(n) \leftarrow 1$ [11]. TD(λ) is also perceived to be computationally efficient, as it runs in $O(TN)$ time, in the worst case, while requiring $O(N)$ space.

Initialize $\hat{\mathbf{v}}_{td}(n) =$ arbitrary value, $\mathbf{e}(n) = 0, \forall\ 1 \leq n \leq N$
Repeat for each trajectory:
    Draw an initial state n according to $\mathbf{p_0}$
    Repeat for each step of trajectory:
        Observe next state m and reward r
        $\delta \leftarrow r + \gamma\,\hat{\mathbf{v}}_{td}(m) - \hat{\mathbf{v}}_{td}(n)$
        For all states ℓ:
            $\hat{\mathbf{v}}_{td}(\ell) \leftarrow \hat{\mathbf{v}}_{td}(\ell) + \alpha\,\delta\,\mathbf{e}(\ell)$
            $\mathbf{e}(\ell) \leftarrow \gamma\,\lambda\,\mathbf{e}(\ell)$
            $\mathbf{e}(\ell) \leftarrow$ update-eligibility(ℓ)
        $n \leftarrow m$
    Until state n is terminal

Fig. 3. On-line TD(λ) with eligibility traces

B   Bounding $\hat{P}$

Lemma 1. *Given P is an $N \times N$ probability matrix and $\hat{P}$ is an estimate of P using T sampling data points, then by the Central Limit Theorem, with probability of 95%, $||\hat{P} - P||_1 \leq \frac{\sqrt{N}}{\sqrt{T}}$, where $||A||_1$ is the 1-norm of a matrix A.*

Initialize column vectors $\mathbf{t} = \mathbf{0}$, $\mathbf{s} = \mathbf{0}$, $\mathbf{v} = \mathbf{0}$,
set γ, fix policy π
and U is a uniform probability distribution $\{0,1\}$
Repeat for each trajectory:
    Draw an initial state n
    Repeat for each step of trajectory:
        $\mathbf{t}(n) \leftarrow \mathbf{t}(n) + 1$
        Choose $x \in U$
        While $x \leq \gamma$ and n is not an absorbing
        state repeat:
            Draw next state n
            $\mathbf{t}(n) \leftarrow \mathbf{t}(n) + 1$
            Choose $x \in U$
    $\mathbf{s} \leftarrow \mathbf{s} + \mathbf{t}$
    $\mathbf{v} \leftarrow \mathbf{v} + \mathbf{r}(n)\mathbf{t}$
For each state n:
    $\mathbf{v}(n) \leftarrow \frac{\mathbf{v}(n)}{(1-\gamma)\mathbf{s}(n)}$
where $\mathbf{r}$ are rewards observed during trajectory
sampling

Fig. 4. Monte Carlo Matrix Inversion Policy Evaluation

Proof

The matrix $\hat{P} - P$ is a matrix of N^2 random variates, $\hat{P}_{ij}$ where $1 \leq i, j \leq N$. Recall from section 2 that our probability transition matrix, by construction, is a set of *conditional* probabilities where $P_{ij} = Prob(nextstate = i | currentstate = j)$. Therefore, $\sum_{j=1}^{N} \hat{P}_{ij} = 1 \; \forall \; 1 \leq i \leq N$, then the random variates within a row are correlated with each other since they must sum to 1. However, the random variates between rows have no such correlation and can be considered independent of each other (ie. P_{ij} is independent of P_{kl} where $i \neq k$). Now consider an arbitrary column j of the matrix $\hat{P} - P$. Let us define a function $\mathcal{P}_{*j}$ of this matrix, such that

$$\mathcal{P}_{*j} = |\hat{P}_{1j} - P_{1j}| + |\hat{P}_{2j} - P_{2j}| + \ldots + |\hat{P}_{Nj} - P_{Nj}|. \tag{22}$$

In other words, $\mathcal{P}_{*j}$ is the sum of the absolute values of the j'th column of matrix $\hat{P} - P$. $\mathcal{P}_{*j}$ is a function of N random variates. We can find the variance of the function, defined as $\sigma^2_{\mathcal{P}_{*j}}$. Recall that only variates within a row of $\hat{P}$ are correlated. Two variates in different rows of $\hat{P}$ are stochastically independent of each other. Therefore, all random variates, $\hat{P}_{ij}$ of $\mathcal{P}_{*j}$ for any column j, are independent of each other. P is the true probability matrix and is therefore a constant. Therefore,

$$\sigma^2_{\mathcal{P}_{*j}} = \sigma^2_{|\hat{P}_{1j} - P_{1j}|} + \sigma^2_{|\hat{P}_{2j} - P_{2j}|} + \ldots + \sigma^2_{|\hat{P}_{Nj} - P_{Nj}|}. \tag{23}$$

Note, each random variate $\hat{P}_{ij}$ can be considered a binomial function, with $E[\hat{P}_{ij}] = P_{ij}$ and variance $\sigma^2_{\hat{P}_{ij}} = P_{ij}(1 - P_{ij})$. Since $0 \le P_{ij} \le 1$ for all $1 \le i,j \le N$, then by taking the derivative of $\sigma^2_{\hat{P}_{ij}}$ as a function of P_{ij} we can show that

$$\sigma^2_{\hat{P}_{ij}} \le \frac{1}{4}. \tag{24}$$

Also note that,

$$\sigma^2_{|\hat{P}_{ij} - P_{ij}|} = E[(|\hat{P}_{ij} - P_{ij}| - |P_{ij} - P_{ij}|)^2] = E[(\hat{P}_{ij} - P_{ij})^2] = \sigma^2_{\hat{P}_{ij}} \tag{25}$$

Therefore, from equations 24 and 25, $\sigma^2_{|\hat{P}_{ij} - P_{ij}|} \le \frac{1}{4}$. Therefore, from this bound on each of the variances of equation 23, we get, $\sigma^2_{\mathcal{P}_{*j}} \le \frac{N}{4}$. Recall that the 1-norm of a matrix A is defined as $||A||_1 = \max_j \left\{ \sum_{i=1}^{N} |A_{ij}| \right\}$. Therefore, $||\hat{P} - P||_1 = \max_j \mathcal{P}_{*j}$. Since the variance $\sigma^2_{\mathcal{P}_{*j}} \le \frac{N}{4}$ for all $1 \le j \le N$, then the variance of $||\hat{P} - P||_1$, which is equal to the variance of the largest $\mathcal{P}_{*j}$, is also bound by $\frac{N}{4}$, ie.

$$\sigma^2_{||\hat{P} - P||_1} = \sigma^2_{\max_j \mathcal{P}_{*j}} \le \frac{N}{4} \tag{26}$$

Assuming the function $||\hat{P} - P||_1$ is found using T sampled data points, then by the Central Limit Theorem (CLT), $Pr\left[\frac{||\hat{P} - P||_1 - ||P - P||_1}{\sigma_{||\hat{P} - P||_1}/\sqrt{T}} \le 2 \right] \le 0.95$. Rearranging and simplifying this equation, we get $Pr\left[||\hat{P} - P||_1 \le \frac{2\sigma_{||\hat{P} - P||_1}}{\sqrt{T}} \right] \le 0.95$. Substituting equation 26 into this CLT equation, we get

$$Pr\left[||\hat{P} - P||_1 \le \frac{\sqrt{N}}{\sqrt{T}} \right] \le 0.95. \tag{27}$$

∎

Real-Time Decision Making for Large POMDPs

Sébastien Paquet, Ludovic Tobin, and Brahim Chaib-draa

DAMAS Laboratory,
Department of Computer Science and Software Engineering,
Laval University
{spaquet, tobin, chaib}@damas.ift.ulaval.ca

Abstract. In this paper, we introduce an approach called RTBSS (Real-Time Belief Space Search) for real-time decision making in large POMDPs. The approach is based on a look-ahead search that is applied online each time the agent has to make a decision. RTBSS is particularly interesting for large real-time environments where offline solutions are not applicable because of their complexity.

1 Introduction

Partially Observable Markov Decision Processes (POMDPs) provide a very general model for sequential decision problems in partially observable environments. The main problem with POMDPs is that their complexity makes them applicable only on small environments.

In this paper, we introduce a novel idea for POMDPs that, to our knowledge, has not received a lot of attention. The idea is to use an online approach based on a look-ahead search to find the best action to execute at each cycle in the environment. By doing so, we avoid the overwhelming complexity of computing a policy for every possible situation the agent could encounter. Since there is no computation offline, the algorithm is immediately applicable to previously unseen environments, if the environments' dynamics are known. Also, since we need a fast online algorithm, we opted for a factored POMDP representation and a branch and bound strategy based on a limited depth first search instead of classical dynamic programming. The tradeoff obtained between the solution quality and the computing time is very interesting.

2 Belief State Value Approximation

The main idea of our online approach is to estimate the value of a belief state by constructing a tree where the nodes are belief states and where the branches are a combination of actions and observations (see Figure 1). To do so, we have defined a new function $\delta : B \times \mathbb{N} \rightarrow \mathbb{R}$ which is based on a depth-first search. The function takes as parameters a belief state b and a remaining depth d and

B. Kégl and G. Lapalme (Eds.): AI 2005, LNAI 3501, pp. 450–455, 2005.
© Springer-Verlag Berlin Heidelberg 2005

returns an estimation of the value of b by performing a search of depth d. For the first call, d is initialized at D, the maximum depth allowed for the search.

$$\delta(b,d) = \begin{cases} U(b) & , \text{ if } d = 0 \\ R(b) + \gamma\max_{a} \sum_{o\in\Omega} \left(P(o \mid b, a) \times \delta(\tau(b, a, o), d - 1)\right) & , \text{ if } d > 0 \end{cases} \quad (1)$$

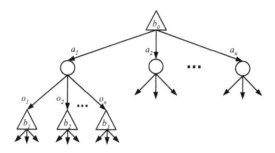

Fig. 1. A search tree

When $d = 0$, we are at the bottom of the search tree. In this situation, we need a utility function $U(b)$, that gives an estimation of the real value of this belief state. If it is not possible to find a better utility function, we can use $U(b) = R(b)$. When $d > 0$, the value of a belief state at a depth of $D - d$ is the immediate reward for being in this belief state added to the maximum discounted reward of the subtrees underneath this belief state.

Finally, the agent's policy which returns the action the agent should do in a certain belief state is defined as:

$$\pi(b, D) = \arg\max_{a} \sum_{o\in\Omega} P(o \mid b, a)\delta(\tau(b, a, o), D - 1) \quad (2)$$

3   RTBSS Algorithm

We have elaborated an algorithm, called RTBSS (see Algorithm 1), that is used to construct the search tree and to find the best action. Since it is an online algorithm, it must be applied each time the agent has to make a decision.

To speed up the search, our algorithm uses a "Branch and Bound" strategy to cut some sub-trees. The algorithm first explores a path in the tree up to the desired depth D and then computes the value for this path. This value then becomes a lower bound on the maximal expected value. Afterwards, for each node of the tree visited, the algorithm can evaluate with an heuristic function if it is possible to improve the lower bound by pursuing the search (PRUNE function at line 10). The heuristic function must be defined for each problem and it must always overestimate the true value. Moreover, the purpose of sorting the actions at line 13 is to try the actions that are the most promising first because it generates more pruning early in the search tree.

1: **Function** RTBSS(b, d , $rAcc$)

Inputs: b: The current belief state.
   d: The current depth.
   $rAcc$: Accumulated rewards.
Statics: D: The maximal depth.
   $bestValue$: The best value found up to now.
   $action$: The best action.

2: **if** $d = 0$ **then**
3:    $finalValue \leftarrow rAcc + \gamma^D \times U(b)$
4:    **if** $finalValue > bestValue$ **then**
5:       $bestValue \leftarrow finalValue$
6:    **end if**
7:    **return** $finalValue$
8: **end if**
9: $rAcc \leftarrow rAcc + \gamma^{D-d} \times R(b)$
10: **if** PRUNE($rAcc, d$) **then**
11:    **return** $-\infty$
12: **end if**
13: $actionList \leftarrow$ SORT(b, A)
14: $max \leftarrow -\infty$
15: **for all** $a \in actionList$ **do**
16:    $expReward \leftarrow 0$
17:    **for all** $o \in \Omega$ **do**
18:       $b' \leftarrow \tau(b, a, o)$
19:       $expReward \leftarrow expReward + \gamma^{D-d} \times P(o|a, b) \times$ RTBSS($b', d - 1, rAcc$)
20:    **end for**
21:    **if** ($d = D \wedge expReward > max$) **then**
22:       $max \leftarrow expReward$
23:       $action \leftarrow a$
24:    **end if**
25: **end for**
26: **return** max

Algorithm 1: The RTBSS algorithm

With RTBSS the agent finds at each turn the action that has the maximal expected value up to a certain horizon of D. As a matter of fact, the performance the algorithm strongly depends on the maximal depth D of the search.

4   Experiments and Results

In this section we present the results we have obtained on two problems: *Tag* [1] and *RockSample* [2]. If we compare RTBSS with different existing approaches (see Table 1), we see that our algorithm can be executed much faster than all the other approaches. RTBSS does not require any time offline and takes only a few tenths of a second at each turn. On small problems the performance is not as good as the best algorithms but the difference is not too important. However, on the biggest problem, RTBSS is much better than HSVI.

Another advantage of RTBSS is its adaptability to environment changes, which enable agents using RTBSS to be deployed immediately and obtain good results even if the environment configuration has never been seen before. Offline

Table 1. Comparison of our approach

Problem	Reward	Time (s)
Tag (870s,5a,30o)		
Q_{MDP}	-16.75	11.8
RTBSS	-10.56	0.23[1]
PBVI [1]	-9.18	180880
BBSLS [3]	⌒ -8.3	⌒100000
BPI [4]	-6.65	250
HSVI [2]	-6.37	10113
Perséus [5]	-6.17	1670
RockSample[4,4] (257s,9a,2o)		
RTBSS	16.2	0.1[1]
PBVI [2][2]	17.1	∼ 2000
HSVI [2]	18.0	577
RockSample[5,5] (801s,10a,2o)		
RTBSS	18.7	0.1[1]
HSVI [2]	19.0	10208
RockSample[5,7] (3201s,12a,2o)		
RTBSS	22.6	0.1[1]
HSVI [2]	23.1	10263
RockSample[7,8] (12545s,13a,2o)		
RTBSS	20.1	0.2[1]
HSVI [2]	15.1	10266

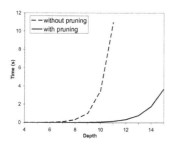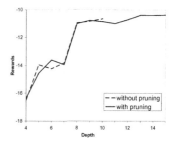

Fig. 2. Average deliberation time and reward on *Tag*

algorithms require recomputing a new policy for each new configuration while our algorithm could be applied right away.

---

[1] It corresponds to the average time taken by the algorithm at each time it is called in a simulation.

[0] PBVI was presented in [1], but the result on *RockSample* was published in [2].

Figure 2 compares our RTBSS algorithm with a version without pruning. On the first graphic, we see that the heuristic can greatly improve the performance of the search. The complexity is still exponential but it grows slower than the brute force version. The second graphic presents the performance of our algorithm in function of the depth of the search used. The rewards obtained are the same whether we use the pruning or not; the slight variation comes from randomness in the tests. We see that our algorithm does not require an heuristic to work properly. However, if we are able to find a good heuristic for a problem, it greatly improves the algorithm's speed.

The two graphics on Figure 2 are also used to choose the maximal depth D allowed. The depth is chosen experimentally depending on the problem and the amount of time available to make a decision, considering that at a certain depth, it might not be worth exploring much deeper. For example, on Figure 2, we can see that the agent does not get much better after depth 8 and the time needed is really small until depth 10, thus a depth of 10 would be a good maximal depth for this problem.

5   Related Work and Conclusion

For POMDPs, very few researchers have explored the possibilities of online algorithms. [6] used a real-time dynamic programming approach to learn a belief state estimation by successive trials in the environment. The main differences are that they do not search in the belief state tree and they need offline time to calculate their starting heuristic based on the Q_{MDP} approach.

To summarize, this paper introduces RTBSS, an online POMDP algorithm useful for large, dynamic and uncertain environments. The main advantage of such a method is that it can be applied to problems with huge state spaces where other algorithms would take way too much time to find a solution. Our results show that RTBSS becomes better as the environment becomes bigger, compared to state of the art POMDP approximation algorithms. Also, because of its adaptability, RTBSS is more suited for environments in which the initial configurations can change and when the agent has to be deployed rapidly, compared to existing offline approaches.

References

1. Pineau, J., Gordon, G., Thrun, S.: Point-based value iteration: An anytime algorithm for pomdps. In: Proceedings of the International Joint Conference on Artificial Intelligence (IJCAI-03), Acapulco, Mexico (2003) 1025–1032
2. Smith, T., Simmons, R.: Heuristic search value iteration for pomdps. In: Proceedings of the 20th Conference on Uncertainty in Artificial Intelligence(UAI-04), Banff, Canada (2004)
3. Braziunas, D., Boutilier, C.: Stochastic local search for pomdp controllers. In: The Nineteenth National Conference on Artificial Intelligence (AAAI-04). (2004)

4. Poupart, P.: Exploiting Structure to Efficiently Solve Large Scale Partially Observable Markov Decision Processes. PhD thesis, University of Toronto (2005) (to appear).
5. Spaan, M.T.J., Vlassis, N.: A point-based pomdp algorithm for robot planning. In: In Proceedings of the IEEE International Conference on Robotics and Automation, New Orleans, Louisiana (2004) 2399–2404
6. Geffner, H., Bonet, B.: Solving large pomdps using real time dynamic programming (1998)

Author Index

Lecture Notes in Artificial Intelligence (LNAI)

Vol. 3229: J.J. Alferes, J. Leite (Eds.), Logics in Artificial Intelligence. XIV, 744 pages. 2004.

Vol. 3228: M.G. Hinchey, J.L. Rash, W.F. Truszkowski, C.A. Rouff (Eds.), Formal Approaches to Agent-Based Systems. VIII, 290 pages. 2004.

Vol. 3215: M.G.. Negoita, R.J. Howlett, L.C. Jain (Eds.), Knowledge-Based Intelligent Information and Engineering Systems, Part III. LVII, 906 pages. 2004.

Vol. 3214: M.G.. Negoita, R.J. Howlett, L.C. Jain (Eds.), Knowledge-Based Intelligent Information and Engineering Systems, Part II. LVIII, 1302 pages. 2004.

Vol. 3213: M.G.. Negoita, R.J. Howlett, L.C. Jain (Eds.), Knowledge-Based Intelligent Information and Engineering Systems, Part I. LVIII, 1280 pages. 2004.

Vol. 3209: B. Berendt, A. Hotho, D. Mladenic, M. van Someren, M. Spiliopoulou, G. Stumme (Eds.), Web Mining: From Web to Semantic Web. IX, 201 pages. 2004.

Vol. 3206: P. Sojka, I. Kopecek, K. Pala (Eds.), Text, Speech and Dialogue. XIII, 667 pages. 2004.

Vol. 3202: J.-F. Boulicaut, F. Esposito, F. Giannotti, D. Pedreschi (Eds.), Knowledge Discovery in Databases: PKDD 2004. XIX, 560 pages. 2004.

Vol. 3201: J.-F. Boulicaut, F. Esposito, F. Giannotti, D. Pedreschi (Eds.), Machine Learning: ECML 2004. XVIII, 580 pages. 2004.

Vol. 3194: R. Camacho, R. King, A. Srinivasan (Eds.), Inductive Logic Programming. XI, 361 pages. 2004.

Vol. 3192: C. Bussler, D. Fensel (Eds.), Artificial Intelligence: Methodology, Systems, and Applications. XIII, 522 pages. 2004.

Vol. 3191: M. Klusch, S. Ossowski, V. Kashyap, R. Unland (Eds.), Cooperative Information Agents VIII. XI, 303 pages. 2004.

Vol. 3187: G. Lindemann, J. Denzinger, I.J. Timm, R. Unland (Eds.), Multiagent System Technologies. XIII, 341 pages. 2004.

Vol. 3176: O. Bousquet, U. von Luxburg, G. Rätsch (Eds.), Advanced Lectures on Machine Learning. IX, 241 pages. 2004.

Vol. 3171: A.L.C. Bazzan, S. Labidi (Eds.), Advances in Artificial Intelligence – SBIA 2004. XVII, 548 pages. 2004.

Vol. 3159: U. Visser, Intelligent Information Integration for the Semantic Web. XIV, 150 pages. 2004.

Vol. 3157: C. Zhang, H. W. Guesgen, W.K. Yeap (Eds.), PRICAI 2004: Trends in Artificial Intelligence. XX, 1023 pages. 2004.

Vol. 3155: P. Funk, P.A. González Calero (Eds.), Advances in Case-Based Reasoning. XIII, 822 pages. 2004.

Vol. 3139: F. Iida, R. Pfeifer, L. Steels, Y. Kuniyoshi (Eds.), Embodied Artificial Intelligence. IX, 331 pages. 2004.

Vol. 3131: V. Torra, Y. Narukawa (Eds.), Modeling Decisions for Artificial Intelligence. XI, 327 pages. 2004.

Vol. 3127: K.E. Wolff, H.D. Pfeiffer, H.S. Delugach (Eds.), Conceptual Structures at Work. XI, 403 pages. 2004.

Vol. 3123: A. Belz, R. Evans, P. Piwek (Eds.), Natural Language Generation. X, 219 pages. 2004.

Vol. 3120: J. Shawe-Taylor, Y. Singer (Eds.), Learning Theory. X, 648 pages. 2004.

Vol. 3097: D. Basin, M. Rusinowitch (Eds.), Automated Reasoning. XII, 493 pages. 2004.

Vol. 3071: A. Omicini, P. Petta, J. Pitt (Eds.), Engineering Societies in the Agents World. XIII, 409 pages. 2004.

Vol. 3070: L. Rutkowski, J. Siekmann, R. Tadeusiewicz, L.A. Zadeh (Eds.), Artificial Intelligence and Soft Computing - ICAISC 2004. XXV, 1208 pages. 2004.

Vol. 3068: E. André, L. Dybkjær, W. Minker, P. Heisterkamp (Eds.), Affective Dialogue Systems. XII, 324 pages. 2004.

Vol. 3067: M. Dastani, J. Dix, A. El Fallah-Seghrouchni (Eds.), Programming Multi-Agent Systems. X, 221 pages. 2004.

Vol. 3066: S. Tsumoto, R. Słowiński, J. Komorowski, J.W. Grzymała-Busse (Eds.), Rough Sets and Current Trends in Computing. XX, 853 pages. 2004.

Vol. 3065: A. Lomuscio, D. Nute (Eds.), Deontic Logic in Computer Science. X, 275 pages. 2004.

Vol. 3060: A.Y. Tawfik, S.D. Goodwin (Eds.), Advances in Artificial Intelligence. XIII, 582 pages. 2004.

Vol. 3056: H. Dai, R. Srikant, C. Zhang (Eds.), Advances in Knowledge Discovery and Data Mining. XIX, 713 pages. 2004.

Vol. 3055: H. Christiansen, M.-S. Hacid, T. Andreasen, H.L. Larsen (Eds.), Flexible Query Answering Systems. X, 500 pages. 2004.

Vol. 3048: P. Faratin, D.C. Parkes, J.A. Rodríguez-Aguilar, W.E. Walsh (Eds.), Agent-Mediated Electronic Commerce V. XI, 155 pages. 2004.

Vol. 3040: R. Conejo, M. Urretavizcaya, J.-L. Pérez-de-la-Cruz (Eds.), Current Topics in Artificial Intelligence. XIV, 689 pages. 2004.

Vol. 3035: M.A. Wimmer (Ed.), Knowledge Management in Electronic Government. XII, 326 pages. 2004.

Vol. 3034: J. Favela, E. Menasalvas, E. Chávez (Eds.), Advances in Web Intelligence. XIII, 227 pages. 2004.

Vol. 3030: P. Giorgini, B. Henderson-Sellers, M. Winikoff (Eds.), Agent-Oriented Information Systems. XIV, 207 pages. 2004.

Vol. 3029: B. Orchard, C. Yang, M. Ali (Eds.), Innovations in Applied Artificial Intelligence. XXI, 1272 pages. 2004.

Vol. 3025: G.A. Vouros, T. Panayiotopoulos (Eds.), Methods and Applications of Artificial Intelligence. XV, 546 pages. 2004.

Vol. 3020: D. Polani, B. Browning, A. Bonarini, K. Yoshida (Eds.), RoboCup 2003: Robot Soccer World Cup VII. XVI, 767 pages. 2004.

Vol. 3012: K. Kurumatani, S.-H. Chen, A. Ohuchi (Eds.), Multi-Agents for Mass User Support. X, 217 pages. 2004.

Vol. 3010: K.R. Apt, F. Fages, F. Rossi, P. Szeredi, J. Váncza (Eds.), Recent Advances in Constraints. VIII, 285 pages. 2004.

Vol. 2990: J. Leite, A. Omicini, L. Sterling, P. Torroni (Eds.), Declarative Agent Languages and Technologies. XII, 281 pages. 2004.

Vol. 2980: A. Blackwell, K. Marriott, A. Shimojima (Eds.), Diagrammatic Representation and Inference. XV, 448 pages. 2004.